All Things Austen

All Things Austen

A Concise Encyclopedia
of Austen's World

Kirstin Olsen

Greenwood World Publishing
Oxford / Westport, Connecticut
2008

All Things Austen in two volumes first published in 2005 by
Greenwood Press
This edition first published in 2008 by Greenwood World Publishing

1 2 3 4 5 6 7 8 9 10

Greenwood World Publishing
Wilkinson House
Jordan Hill
Oxford OX2 8EJ
An imprint of Greenwood Publishing Group, Inc
www.greenwood.com

British Library Cataloguing-in-Publication Data: a catalogue record
for this book is available from the British Library

Library of Congress Cataloging-in-Publication Data

All things Austen : an encyclopaedia of Austen's world / Kirstin
Olsen.
       p. cm.
  Includes bibliographical references and index.
  ISBN 0-313-33032-8 (set : alk. paper) – ISBN 0-313-33033-6 (vol. 1 :
alk. paper) – ISBN 0-313-33034-4 (vol. 2 : alk. paper) 1.   Austen,
Jane, 1775–1817 – Encyclopaedias. 2.   Novelists, English –
19th century – Biography – Encyclopaedias. 3.   Women and
literature – England – History – 19th century – Encyclopaedias.
I.   Title.

  PR4036.A275 2005
  823'. 7B – dc22

                                        2004028664

Library of Congress Catalog Card Number:
ISBN: 978-1-84645-052-5 (pbk.)
An expanded hardcover edition of *All Things Austen: An
Encyclopedia of Austen's World* is available at Greenwood Press,
an imprint of Greenwood Publishing Group, Inc.

ISBN: 978-1-84645-052-5

Designed by Fraser Muggeridge studio
Typeset by TexTech International
Printed and bound in China by South China Printing Company

Contents

For Eric

Acknowledgements

I would like to thank the staff at the Lewis Walpole Library, particularly Sue Walker and Brian Parker, for their invaluable assistance with many of the illustrations for this book. They truly went above and beyond the call of duty, and I am extremely grateful. I am also thankful to the many people who shared their enthusiasm and expertise, including Eunice and Ron Shanahan, who graciously provided photographs of franked and crossed letters and advised me about the history of postmarks; Eliot Jordan, tea buyer for Peet's Coffee and Tea, who helped me track down information about historical tea varieties; David Lisot of Heritagecoin.com, who granted permission for the use of photos from his company's website; and Neil Handley of London's College of Optometrists, who patiently explained turnpin-temple spectacles to me. Any errors in these departments are not theirs but my own. I am indebted to my family for their constant support and their patient pretence of interest when I come to the dinner table overflowing with newly acquired information about tea urns, court plaster or chamber pots.

Alphabetical List of Entries

Guide to Related Topics

Behaviour

Etiquette
Gentry
Titles
Visiting

Business, Work and Finance

Debt
Inns
Lodgings
Money
Servants
Shops

Clothing and Accessories

Clocks and Watches
Clothing
Complexion
Cosmetics
Fan
Gloves
Hair
Hats
Jewellery
Pocketbooks and Reticules
Shoes
Spectacles
Stockings
Umbrellas and Parasols

Education and Intellectual Life

Education
French
Newspaper
Picturesque
Reading
Titles

Entertainment

Bathing
Cards
Dance
Entertainment
Games
Hunting
Masquerade

Music
Sewing
Theatre

Food and Drink

Beverages
Food
Tea

The Household

Architecture
Clocks and Watches
Dishes
Fire
Furniture
Gardens and Landscape
Gothic
Housework
Lodgings
Servants
Sewing

Military Life

Marines
Navy

People

Death
Debt
Marriage
Widow

Reading and Writing

Gothic
Newspaper
Pen
Pencil
Picturesque
Reading
Writing
Religion
Clergy
Parish

Riding and Hunting

Horses
Hunting

Science, Medicine and Technology

Bathing
Insanity
Medicine
Spectacles
Teeth

Time and Places

Bath
Gardens and Landscape
Holidays
London
Places
Public Places
Time

Transportation and Travel

Barouche
Carriages and Coaches
Carts and Wagons
Chair
Chaise
Gig
Inns
Landau
Lodgings
Phaeton
Places
Public Places
Travel
Walking

Index of Austen's Works

For readers wanting background information on a specific play or poem, the principal articles relating to each of Austen's works are arranged below.

A Collection of Letters
Primary entries
Dance, Food, Reading
Secondary entries
Places, Servants, Time, Titles, Visiting

The Adventures of Mr Harley
Primary entries
Navy
Secondary entries
Clergy, Hair

Amelia Webster
Primary entries
Marriage, Reading, Titles, Travel

The Beautiful Cassandra
Primary entries
Hats, London, Places, Servants, Titles
Secondary entries
Architecture, Bath, Carriages and Coaches, Etiquette, Food, Widow

Catharine or the Bower
Primary entries
Clergy, Clothing, Dance, Education, London, Places
Secondary entries
Chaise, Cosmetic, Etiquette, Gardens, Hats, Horses, Medicine, Reading, Servants

Edgar & Emma
Primary entries
Architecture, Carriages and Coaches, Clothing, Medicine, Titles
Secondary entries
Education, Fire, Food, Furniture, Places, Servants, Travel, Visiting

Emma
Primary entries
Architecture, Cards, Carriages and Coaches, Clothing, Dance, Food, Games
Secondary entries
Bath, Clergy, Education, Furniture, Gardens and Landscape, Gentry, Holidays, Medicine

Evelyn
Primary entries
Architecture, Food, Garden and Landscapes
Secondary entries
Etiquette, Furniture, Marriage, Places, Servants, Travel

The First Act of a Comedy
Primary entries
Inns

Frederic & Elfrida
Primary entries
Clothing, Food, Marriage
Secondary entries
Carriages and Coaches, Clergy, Complexion, Cosmetics, Gardens and Landscapes

The Generous Curate
Primary entries
Clergy, Education
Secondary entries
Navy

Henry & Eliza
Primary entries
Inns, Places, Titles
Secondary entries
Carriages and Coaches, Food, Marriage, Money, Travel, Widow, Writing

The History of England
Primary entries
Games, Places, Reading
Secondary entries
Education, French, Pens, Theatre

Jack & Alice
Primary entries
Education, Marriage
Secondary entries
Bath, Beverages, London, Navy, Places, Reading, Titles

Lady Susan
Primary entries
Architecture, Education, London
Secondary entries
Food, Horses, Medicine, Music, Places

Lesley Castle
Primary entries
Education, Food, Music, Places, Reading, Title
Secondary entries
Architecture, Clothing, Dance, Etiquette

Love and Friendship
Primary entries
Architecture, Carriages and Coaches, London, Places, Theatre

Secondary entries
Clothing, Debt, Marriage, Reading,
Servants, Travel

Mansfield Park
Primary entries
Food, Gardens and Landscapes, Navy,
Places, Reading, Servants
Secondary entries
Carriages, Clergy, Clothing, Dance,
Education, Marriage, Music, Theatre,
Travel

Memoirs of Mr Clifford
Primary entries
Carriages and Coaches, Gig, Places
Secondary entries
Landau, London, Medicine, Phaeton, Travel

The Mystery: An Unfinished Comedy
Primary entries
Architecture, Clergy, Furniture, Reading

Northanger Abbey
Primary entries
Architecture, Bath, Clothing, Food, Places
Secondary entries
Dance, Education, Furniture, Gardens and
Landscapes, Horses, Marriage, Time,
Travel, Writing

Ode to Pity
Primary entries
Architecture, Gardens and Landscape,
Reading, Travel

On a Headache
Primary entries
Food

**On Sir Home Popham's Sentence,
April 1807**
Primary entry
Navy

Persuasion
Primary entries
Architecture, Bath, Food, Navy, Reading
Secondary entries
Carriages and Coaches, Clothing,
Education, Furniture, Inns, Medicine,
Titles

Plan of a Novel
Primary entries
Clergy, Education
Secondary entries
Music, Navy, Places, Reading

Pride & Prejudice
Primary entries
Architecture, Clergy, Dance, Food, Places,
Servants

Secondary entries
Carriages and Coaches, Etiquette,
Furniture, Gardens and Landscapes,
London, Marriage, Walking, Writing

Sanditon
Primary entries
Architecture, Bathing, Food, Gardens and
Landscape, Medicine, Reading
Secondary entries
Carriages and Coaches, Dishes, Furniture,
Gig, Hat, Lodgings, Shoes, Travel

Scraps
Primary entries
Places, Shoes
Secondary entries
Architecture, Etiquette, Food, Furniture,
Money, Visiting

Sense & Sensibility
Primary entries
Architecture, Clergy, Food, London,
Servants
Secondary entries
Carriages and Coaches, Clothing, Gardens
and Landscapes, Music, Reading, Visiting,
Walking

Sir William Mountague
Primary entries
Hunting, Places
Secondary entries
Lodgings, Reading, Titles, Widow

The Three Sisters
Primary entries
Carriages and Coaches, Marriage, Reading
Secondary entries
Dance

The Visit: A Comedy in 2 Acts
Primary entries
Architecture, Food
Secondary entries
Etiquette, Furniture, Servants, Title

The Watsons Novels
Primary entries
Cards, Carriages and Coaches, Dance, Food,
Servants
Secondary entries
Architecture, Etiquette, Fire, Furniture,
Hunting, Inns, Marriage, Places, Shoes,
Titles

List of Works and Abbreviations

Minor Works (abbreviation followed by MW)

Amelia	Amelia Webster
Beaut Desc	A Beautiful Description of the Different Effects of Sensibility on Different Minds
Cass	The Beautiful Cassandra: A Novel in Twelve Chapters
Cath	Catharine or the Bower
Clifford	Memoirs of Mr Clifford
Col Let	A Collection of Letters
Curate	The Generous Curate
E&E	Edgar & Emma
Evelyn	Evelyn
F&E	Frederic & Elfrida
First Act	The First Act of a Comedy
H&E	Henry & Eliza
Harley	The Adventures of Mr Harley
Headache	On a Headache
History	The History of England
J&A	Jack & Alice
L&F	Love and Friendship
Lesley	Lesley Castle
LS	Lady Susan
Mount	Sir William Mountague
Mystery	The Mystery: An Unfinished Comedy
Ode	Ode to Pity
Plan	Plan of a Novel
Popham	On Sir Home Popham's Sentence, April 1807
Sand	Sanditon
Scraps	Scraps
3S	The Three Sisters
Visit	The Visit: A Comedy in 2 Acts
Watsons	The Watsons Novels
E	Emma
MP	Mansfield Park
NA	Northanger Abbey
P	Persuasion
P&P	Pride and Prejudice
S&S	Sense and Sensibility

References to the Kotzebue play Lovers' Vows, included by R. W. Chapman in his edition of Mansfield Park, are indicated by the abbreviation MP, LV.

Introduction

Jane Austen is normally thought of as avoiding richly detailed settings and confining herself almost entirely to the development and interactions of her characters. Certainly, she is a restrained author, eschewing unnecessary details and emphasising the revelation of character through dialogue, but this is not to say that historical detail does not occur in her works and does not require explanation. If anything, the details she uses require more explanation rather than less, for she chose them with great care and with an expectation that her readers would understand their full significance.

Astute modern readers can grasp the basics of many of her references through context. It becomes evident, for example, that barouches, phaetons, curricles and post-chaises were all carriages of some kind. For Austen's contemporary audience, however, these vehicles were as different from each other in form, purpose and connotation as sports cars, minivans and rental cars today. One misses a great deal of what she says about character and fails to appreciate the truly elegant economy of her language without a full comprehension of the objects and ideas to which she refers.

This book, therefore, attempts to provide the background material that makes her work more fully comprehensible. It discusses types of carriages and the associations they elicited, the value and size of certain coins, the difference between a pelisse and a spencer, and hundreds of other areas in which obsolete or unfamiliar terms distance us from Austen's original intentions. The result is a compilation of the available scholarship on everything from the history of food to the composition of medicinal remedies and takes us through the dawn of tourism, the discovery of chemical elements, the bathing rituals and the rules of etiquette.

There are six principal components of this book, other than the index, to help readers of Austen navigate through her world. One is the alphabetised series of more than seventy articles, ranging from a few sentences to chapter length, depending on the complexity of the subject and its relevance to Austen's work. The second, embedded in the articles, is a system of abbreviations guiding readers to passages in Austen's writings that pertain to the articles' subject matter. These abbreviations refer to the page numbers of the *Oxford Illustrated Jane Austen* (third edition), edited by R. W. Chapman, which is the standard text for Austen scholarship. Most scholars, however, have tended to abbreviate all of Austen's *Juvenilia* and fragmentary novels with the simple notation 'MW' for the 'Minor Works' volume in the series. I have chosen to be somewhat more specific, and readers will find a prefix such as *Visit* or *L&F* before citations from the Minor Works volume (see the List of Works and Abbreviations). Thus, a parenthetical notation such as (*L&F*, *MW* 105) means the juvenile fragment *Love and Freindship* [*sic*], Minor Works volume, p.105. In some cases, including all references to a particular subject (such as instances of the word 'servant') would have been unwieldy; therefore, unless otherwise stated, the references are representative and not exhaustive.

The third source of information is the illustrations, most of them from the Lewis Walpole Library. They are richly informative in their present state, but the Lewis Walpole Library also has an excellent website where the pictures can be viewed in colour and in greater detail. Each caption has the LWL call number, which can be entered into a search engine on the website for easy access to a specific image.

The fourth guide for readers is the Guide to Related Topics, which separates the articles in this encyclopedia by broad topic. For example, the category 'Business, Work and Finance' contains the articles on Debt, Inns, Lodgings, Money, Servants and Shops. This listing can serve as a study guide for readers interested in a particular aspect of Austen's works.

Under the articles 'Places', 'Bath' and 'London', readers will find maps of most of the locations mentioned by Austen (with the exceptions, noted in the text, of a few far-flung places easy to locate without help, such as Europe).

Readers will learn the origin of the term 'reticule' and will investigate the mystery of exactly what sort of spectacles Frank Churchill was fixing at the Bateses'. They will discover why William Price could not get promoted from midshipman to lieutenant without help, what a calling card looked like and how the games of casino, whist and loo were played. Crucially, they will learn how terms still used today, such as 'public place' and 'pocketbook', differ in their usage from the same terms in Austen's day.

A

Architecture

From the beginning of the eighteenth century until Jane Austen's birth in 1775, English architecture was dominated by a classical revival. New construction tended to be in Greek or Roman styles, with symmetrical façades, pedimented windows and, sometimes, porticoes and columns reminiscent of ancient temples. Lines were simple, and floors were constructed according to a mathematical formula, with the tallest rooms on the ground floor. Sometimes a line of stone or brick indicated the change in floors from outside, and this might be accentuated by a slight change in window style.

During the last quarter of the century, however, several new fashions took root. One of these was the Gothic style (*NA* 177), an imitation of medieval architecture that featured turrets, buttresses, crenellated parapets, mock moats and, most commonly, pointed-arched windows. Uvedale Price, a leading proponent of the Picturesque style in art and landscape, found Gothic windows charming, a 'triumph of the picturesque', full of 'extreme richness and intricacy'. It is chiefly the windows of Northanger Abbey that Catherine Morland notices (*NA* 161, 162), as they are almost the only remnant, from the outside, of the genuine medieval abbey that forms the basis of General Tilney's massive country house.

Where original Gothic ruins (*NA* 141–142) did not exist, it was necessary to invent them. Landowners invited architects to design faux-Gothic ruins for their gardens, complete with rubble and artfully planted moss; Gothic guesthouses, lodges, pavilions and gatehouses; and, eventually, entire Gothic mansions. Adlestrop Park, a magnificent house owned by Mrs Austen's rich cousins, had been demolished in the 1750s and replaced with a grand Gothic mansion with a renowned southwest façade, ashlar buttresses and fretted balustrades. Newly built parsonages were sometimes designed in the Gothic style, as there seemed to be a pleasing harmony between a clergyman's house and an architectural style reminiscent of churches and cathedrals. Sometimes, a Gothic look was achieved on the cheap by remodelling and installing pointed-arched windows, while leaving the rest of the building untouched. Gothic wallpapers were also available from about the 1760s.

The rage for what Uvedale Price called the 'splendid confusion and irregularity' of the Gothic led to a general willingness to make houses asymmetrical (*E* 358). Even houses in other styles could now adopt a lopsided, patched-together profile and remain fashionable in their informality. Accordingly, owners added all sorts of wings and special-purpose rooms, without concerning themselves about balancing the additions on the other side of the house. Conservatories, greenhouses, servants' halls (*MP* 141), wings that contained suites of bedrooms for the family and other useful or ornamental structures sprouted on the sides of country manors.

At the same time, drawing rooms, dining rooms and other public areas of the house were drifting down to the ground floor (*Evelyn, MW* 189; *E* 476). Historically, they had been located on the next storey up (called the first floor in Britain, the second floor in America). Now they were relocated downstairs, closer to the gardens, which could be seen through large windows or even accessed directly through French doors (*Sand, MW* 395).* To compensate, the bedrooms moved upstairs.

A relaxation of symmetry and of the boundary between interior and exterior space was reflected in a sudden interest in cottages (*Ode, MW* 75; *L&F, MW* 79; *S&S* 29, 72, 75, 251–252, 260; *MP* 57, 195, 375). It became desirable to have a picturesque cottage somewhere in view (*NA* 214), either occupied by an actual labourer (*Sand, MW* 366; *MP* 82; *E* 83, 86) or vacant and preserved for its rustic appearance. Conscientious landlords might also build 'model cottages' for their labourers or tenants, and these were fairly simple dwellings for which pattern books were available. They resembled the older cottages of farms and villages (*L&F, MW* 100; *Sand, MW* 383; *NA* 212) but were newer and usually cleaner. The ideal model cottage, according to a 1797 report by the Board of Agriculture, had a main downstairs room about 12 feet by 12 feet, used as the multipurpose living room, workshop and kitchen. A second room might have served as a bedroom, while smaller areas provided storage space for food, linen and tools. A second storey above contained one or two bedrooms, one of them heated by a fireplace. The windows, one per room, would be casement windows, which were less fashionable than double-hung sash windows; the relative lack of windows was not an attempt to deprive the poor of light but a realistic recognition of the fact that windows were not only expensive in themselves (*P&P* 161) but also taxed (*MP* 85) and therefore that every window implied an ongoing expense. Walls could be made of any cheap and readily available local material: mud, wood, brick and so on. No plumbing was included; the closest pump or well was the water source, and a privy in back of the house was the only toilet.

However, not all cottages belonged to people of the working class. Some people who could afford to live in any sort of home they liked chose to live not in massive stone mansions (*L&F, MW* 79; *P&P* 265; *MP* 243; *P* 36, 123) but in 'cottages' (*NA* 120, 141). These, however, were not dingy workers' shacks but carefully designed *cottages ornées* (*Sand, MW* 377; *S&S* 376), the plans for which could be selected from a pattern book. These were built to look rustic from the outside but were often quite comfortable and

---

*Older mansions, with formal balconies and terraces (*MP* 103) overlooking the gardens and joining the two areas with large, imposing flights of stone steps, now came to seem stodgy and old-fashioned.

extensive, with modern conveniences and modern furnishings inside. The Musgroves' 'cottage' at Uppercross (*P* 83, 123), 'with its viranda, French windows, and other prettinesses' (*P* 36), is one of these modern houses in disguise, described by historian Mark Girouard as fostering 'the simple life, lived in simple luxury in a simple cottage with – quite often – fifteen simple bedrooms, all hung with French wallpapers'. Lady Elliott's cottage in *Sense and Sensibility* contains a dining parlour, a drawing room, a library and a saloon (252), while Barton Cottage has a sitting room (*S&S* 342) and four bedrooms. Austen's description of it gives a good sense of its size while mocking the demands of picturesque rusticity placed on cottages by genteel enthusiasts:

> A small green court was the whole of its demesne in front; and a neat wicket gate admitted them into it.

> As a house, Barton Cottage, though small, was comfortable and compact; but as a cottage it was defective, for the building was regular, the roof was tiled, the window shutters were not painted green, nor were the walls covered with honeysuckles. A narrow passage led directly through the house into the garden behind. On each side of the entrance was a sitting room, about sixteen feet square; and beyond them were the offices and the stairs. Four bedrooms and two garrets formed the rest of the house. (*S&S* 28)

The references to tile and honeysuckle reflect a popular prejudice in favour of deeply thatched cottages drowning in climbing vines, a prejudice so strong that Humphry Repton was obliged to remind his clients not to add so much ivy that it blocked off the chimneys. Non-fictional cottages had the same sorts of amenities as some of Austen's creations: numerous bedrooms, halls, parlours, withdrawing rooms, music rooms, billiard rooms, boudoirs, conservatories, studies, dining rooms and even, in some cases, baths and water closets.

A villa (*NA* 120) was another type of relatively informal country house, but it tended to be much grander in scale and design than a cottage. There was little effort expended to make the house seem rustic and tumbledown, and rooms for large parties were standard, as were conservatories, balconies, breakfast parlours, dressing rooms and so on. Whereas a cottage might contain some or all of these rooms, in a villa they were considered positively necessary. In short, they were the richer and more elegant cousins of cottages.

In towns, the architectural trends were somewhat different. Here, it was difficult to create a crenellated ruin; though the marquis of Lansdowne, the Austens' landlord in Southampton, had built a short-lived castle in that town, he was very much in the minority. In towns, uniform blocks of townhouses, united to form one gigantic façade, were the norm. London spread out to the west in blocks and circles, with mansion-like rows of townhouses (*S&S* 160; *MP* 416) planting themselves in neat geometric arrangements, looking like the building blocks of some enormous child. They often employed the pedimented windows and demarcated floors of the classical style, with the central and most imposing townhouse being distinguishable from the others in some way, often by a large pediment at the roof line. In Bath, this formula was imitated, with terraces (*Sand, MW* 384) climbing one above the other, each occupied by a wall of homes joined together to make a uniform front. The crowning achievement of Bath was its Royal Crescent, a gracefully curving structure that inspired imitators in other towns (*Sand, MW* 380).

Types of Rooms

The number of rooms and their specificity of purpose depended on the wealth of the owner. The houses of the Herefordshire yeomanry, according to a letter in the *Gentleman's Magazine* in 1819, had 'a large culinary sitting-room, through which the visitor passes to a parlour'. The 'culinary sitting-room' had the sound of a multipurpose room, and in many smaller houses one room was made to serve various needs. It might be a parlour for receiving visitors, a sitting room for the women of the family, a breakfast room and a supper room. In larger houses, different roles were assigned to various rooms, and one person might have several rooms dedicated to his or her use.

The public rooms, in the sorts of houses Jane Austen visited, usually included a dining room (*Visit, MW* 53; *Evelyn, MW* 189; *NA* 165–166, 213; *S&S* 143, 252; *P&P* 65, 158, 168, 246, 289, 317, 340, 351, 352–353; *MP* 52, 226; *E* 116, 207, 220, 298, 364, 424; *P* 7) in which dinner was eaten. In smaller houses, breakfast would also be served here. In larger houses, there was a separate breakfast room (*Evelyn, MW* 189; *LS, MW* 283, 284; *NA* 173, 175, 228; *S&S* 96; *P&P* 32, 41, 75, 113, 301, 304, 315, 317, 346; *MP* 74, 127, 298, 357, 362; *P* 128), which might double as a morning sitting room (*E* 272); there was very seldom a room dedicated to supper (*NA* 222), even in the largest houses; supper, if it was eaten at all, was generally served wherever the family happened to be congregated, as was also the case with evening tea and coffee.

Most of the day was passed by women in sitting rooms (*Sand, MW* 427; *S&S* 28, 30, 69, 292, 342; *P&P* 168, 250, 352; *MP* 41, 151–152, 168; *E* 69, 240, 453), drawing rooms and parlours (*E&E, MW* 32; *Visit, MW* 50; *Mystery, MW* 56; *L&F, MW* 84, 107; *Col Let, MW* 151; *Cath, MW* 197, 214; *LS, MW* 291; *Watsons, MW* 323, 327, 344, 351, 355; *NA* 116, 240; *S&S* 29, 60, 73, 75, 77, 96, 106, 107, 348; *P&P* 73; *MP* 377–378, 381, 444; *E* 27, 28, 247; *P* 40, 114, 154), all of which are names given to rooms for engaging in leisure activities and receiving guests for grand dinners or parties.

The drawing room (*Visit, MW* 51; *Watsons, MW* 350, 357, 358; *Sand, MW* 394, 395, 413; *NA* 34, 91, 102, 118, 161, 180, 187, 203; *S&S* 29, 110, 114, 143, 175, 203, 252, 257, 274, 294, 311, 316, 334; *P&P* 37, 47, 75, 152, 168, 310, 341, 345, 352–353; *MP* 14, 15, 18, 52, 69, 71, 84, 125, 176–177, 180, 183–184, 205, 206, 223, 224, 272, 273, 336, 387, 447; *E* 27, 117, 124, 213, 215, 219, 302;

P 7, 10, 37) was where the evening began and ended. Guests for dinner were shown into this room as they arrived (*NA* 165), and from the drawing room the entire company paraded to the dining room to eat. In large homes, the drawing room and dining room would be separated by a few rooms (*MP* 84) to give the assembled company the feeling of being in a grand procession. After dinner, the men remained in the dining room to smoke, drink and talk (*MP* 334–335), while the women paraded back to the drawing room to chat (*P&P* 37, 54, 163, 341). When the gentlemen joined them, tea, coffee, cards, music and dancing ensued. Some homes had multiple drawing rooms (*P* 138, 216, 219, 220, 242, 245) for different times of the day, different levels of formality or different sizes of parties; others had to make do with only one. During the day, the drawing room was primarily the province of women, and the gentleman of the house received his guests in his study, if he had one.

Bedrooms (*Evelyn, MW* 186; *Cath, MW* 193; *LS, MW* 286; *Watsons, MW* 351, 353; *Sand, MW* 401; *NA* 163, 181, 192, 193; *S&S* 28, 29, 39, 155, 294; *P&P* 250; *MP* 125, 182, 312, 387; *E* 57, 243, 412; *P* 114, 154) were scattered throughout the house, mostly upstairs (*P&P* 352). Bedrooms for servants might be located in a separate wing of the house, in the basement, in the attic (*P&P* 310; *MP* 9–10, 15, 387) or garret (*S&S* 28, 29) or in a combination of these places. Ladies' maids sometimes had rooms adjacent to, or at least near, the apartments of their mistresses. Other upper servants, such as butlers and housekeepers, also sometimes had special rooms of their own (*E* 204).

In large households, the wife and husband would either share a bedroom or have separate bedrooms, with a study (*P&P* 168) and dressing room (*S&S* 259; *MP* 218; *P* 57, 127) for the husband and a dressing room (*F&E, MW* 6; *E&E, MW* 31; *Col Let, MW* 151; *Evelyn, MW* 181–182; *Cath, MW* 214; *LS, MW* 276, 281, 287; *NA* 194; *S&S* 340; *P&P* 333, 345, 358, 377; *MP* 370–371) or sitting room for the wife. The dressing room, which at various times had been a semipublic space in which certain visitors might be received (*Evelyn, MW* 189), was developing into a place to sit and sew, read or draw; Austen wrote in December 1798 that she and her mother 'live entirely in the dressing-room now, which I like very much; I always feel so much more elegant in it than in the parlour'. Many houses also had a state bedroom for important guests, though this bedroom, like almost all bedrooms, was moved upstairs from its traditional place on the ground floor. Another specialised type of bedroom was the nursery (*LS, MW* 275; *MP* 9; *P* 122), reserved for small children and the servants who cared for them.

The more important bedrooms in large homes might also have water closets, still a relative novelty and quite a luxury. The water closet was patented in 1778 by Joseph Bramah, who claimed to have sold 6,000 of them by 1797. This convenient device, where it occurred, was reserved for the family; the servants still had to use chamber pots and privies. The early water closets were operated by piped or pumped water or by cistern-stored rainwater and were not, by modern standards, reliable. Bathtubs were somewhat more common than water closets, but they were usually cold-water plunge baths. Preheated piped water was still only a wistful fantasy, and water for hot baths had to be heated over the fire; most people only took warm or hot baths when visiting a spa such as Bath. Instead of a bathroom sink with piped water, most people used a basin, filled from a pitcher, both of which stood on a nightstand in the bedroom.

Some houses had special rooms for certain kinds of activities. Libraries (*L&F*, *MW* 95; *Cath*, *MW* 232; *S&S* 252, 304; *P&P* 9, 37, 55, 71, 111, 112, 305, 344, 349, 361), often containing thousands of books, could be found in larger homes, while smaller houses resorted to scattered bookcases in bedrooms and studies. Saloons (*S&S* 252; *P&P* 267, 270) were large downstairs rooms, either in a line with the wide entrance hall (which was a room in itself) or elsewhere on the ground floor; the saloon could be used as an art gallery (*Lesley*, *MW* 127; *NA* 85, 162, 171, 185–186, 191, 194; *P&P* 250) or a ballroom (*MP* 275), but unlike most rooms designated 'galleries', it tended to be more square than rectangular. Another downstairs room was the conservatory (*E* 306), found in large homes; this was a room with enormous windows, sometimes with nothing but windows on at least two sides, giving it the look of a greenhouse. It did not feature the damp atmosphere of many greenhouses, but it did include specimens of plants that could be enjoyed and examined by family and guests alike. Older mansions sometimes had chapels (*MP* 86) that had been designed for the private worship of the family and staff.

Some homes had a special music room, but most placed the instruments in the drawing room, where they would be handy for after-dinner concerts. (Mary Bennet's appears to be placed upstairs, perhaps in a dressing room – see *P&P* 344–345.) A billiard room (*MP* 125, 127, 182) was an increasingly common luxury, but not every house with a billiard table placed it in its own room. It might occupy a portion of a hall, library or gallery or be ensconced in a bow-windowed alcove of a parlour. Two competing trends battled each other: on the one hand, people liked the status value of being able to say they could afford to have a music room, several drawing rooms, a billiard room and so on; on the other hand, there was that yearning for informality that made hosts want to break their crowds of guests into little groups, together in the same room, yet occupied with different forms of amusement.

In some cases, there would be a secondary house, known as a lodge (*P&P* 210; *P* 123). The lodge might be rented out to tenants or allotted to guests. Lodges arose from the habit of building small homes on large estates, usually at some distance from the main house, to be used as a base for hunting parties. Many lodges in Austen's days, however, were quite close to the main house and were sometimes the medium by which landowners experimented with new architectural trends.

Some rooms, the 'offices' (*NA* 195; *S&S* 28, 393), were used chiefly by the servants. They included the kitchen (*Watsons*, *MW* 354, 360; *S&S* 72; *P&P* 65; *MP* 379, 385, 392; *E* 236); the butler's pantry (*E* 204; *P* 127); other sorts of pantries (*Lesley, MW* 114) and storerooms (*Lesley, MW* 113; *MP* 31) for food, beer, linen and other supplies; cellars; laundries; and so on. The family noticed the size, proportion and decoration of drawing rooms, while the servants cared about the efficiency and cleanliness of the offices and made their objections known if these rooms were inadequate.

One room that might be found in almost any part of the house was the 'closet' (*Visit, MW* 54; *Scraps, MW* 176–177; *S&S* 274, 316; *E* 239). This was not, as it is now, a storage cabinet crammed full of clothes, sports equipment, shoes, umbrellas and so on but a small room that could be used for a variety of purposes. There were closets for getting dressed in the morning, adorned with pictures and mirrors. There were closets that were essentially pantries. There were closets full of collections of artwork and scientific specimens. There were Bramah water closets, some of them quite ornately decorated and hidden behind mirrored panels.

Austen was acquainted with houses of all sizes, from those with rooms doing double and triple duty to those with a room for everything, and several rooms left over, just in case. Steventon Parsonage, the house in which Austen was raised, was neither a mansion nor a cottage. It had a square front and was symmetrically designed, with a door in the middle, two windows to the right of the door looking into the kitchen and two on the left (*Watsons, MW* 322) looking into the better of the two parlours, which also doubled as the dining room (*P&P* 168). The entryway was actually the second-best parlour (*MP* 377–378) rather than a wide hall (*Cath, MW* 220; *NA* 161; *S&S* 334; *P&P* 65, 251, 317, 352, 371; *MP* 172, 194, 233, 357; *E* 189, 346–347, 411) or a narrower vestibule (*Cath, MW* 220; *S&S* 316; *P&P* 112, 315; *MP* 206, 215; *P* 79). Also downstairs were Mr Austen's study, which had a south-facing bow window overlooking the garden, and pantries of various sorts. On the floor above were seven bedrooms, including the one shared by Jane and Cassandra and the one they converted into a dressing room in 1798; the latter held Jane's piano and books. In the garret were three more bedrooms, which were at times used by the pupils whom Mr Austen boarded and tutored. There was no separate servants' hall.

Chawton Cottage, where Jane lived from 1809 until just before her death in 1817 and where she wrote or revised most of her novels, was smaller than Steventon and more closely resembles *Sense and Sensibility*'s Barton Cottage. An L-shaped house, it had an entrance hall, to the right of which was a dining room where Jane did her writing and to the left of which was a drawing room. The offices were also downstairs; six bedrooms and two garret rooms lay upstairs, one of them reserved as a 'state' or 'best' bedroom and the others in use by the family and the three servants. The cottage was small, with walls that were sometimes damp, and must have presented the occupants with few options for hosting guests. Even Steventon had been so small that guests had had to wait until the school holidays, when Mr Austen's pupils went home. Other members of the lower gentry had similar difficulties finding room for visitors (*Watsons, MW* 351; *MP* 28;

E 126; *P* 113); Parson Woodforde, when his friends Mr and Mrs Jeanes slept over, was forced to displace his niece Nancy in order to find them a suitable bed. When 'Mrs. Jeans, two Daughters and Nurse' slept there again in 1792, 'Mrs. Jeans slept with Nancy in the best Chamber, with Miss Jeans on a Mattress on the floor of the same Room, and the youngest about 7 months old with her Nurse, Susan Harrison in the Attic Story.'

By contrast, Stoneleigh, a house in Mrs Austen's family, was a quadrangular mansion based on the remains of a twelfth-century Cistercian abbey. A symmetrical baroque wing with forty-five windows was added to the west side of the house in the early eighteenth century, making the house look entirely modern when approached from that side. The offices were in the old abbey, while the newer portions held a dining room, breakfast parlour and multiple drawing rooms decorated in 'rather gloomy brown wainscot and dark crimson furniture', according to Mrs Austen. There were also two galleries for pictures and prints, two small parlours, a billiard room and twenty-six bedrooms in the new wing alone, including a state bedroom, Mrs Austen added, 'with a high dark crimson bed, an *alarming* apartment just fit for a heroine'.

Interiors

The appearance of rooms, like their use, was evolving. The dark wainscot (wall panelling – see *E* 187) of earlier centuries was removed or painted in light colours; open-beamed ceilings were stuccoed or plastered to hide the beams and given delicate texture by slightly raised plaster ornaments in the shapes of vines, urns, medallions and leaves (*S&S* 108; *MP* 183; *E* 81). Lighter colours – white, pale blue and gold – gained favour, while the 'dark crimson' Mrs Austen noted at Stoneleigh was considered very old-fashioned (*NA* 158). Huge fireplaces built of dark brick were contracted to small coal fire-grates surrounded by elegant mantelpieces (*Sand*, *MW* 413; *NA* 162; *S&S* 75, 160, 332; *P&P* 75, 144, 190, 247; *E* 46, 69) in wood or marble, carved in simple, classically influenced styles.

An increasing emphasis on light and an effort to create the feeling of greater space focused attention on windows (*Cass*, *MW* 46; *Watsons*, *MW* 322; *Sand*, *MW* 413; *NA* 34, 82, 91, 122, 162, 163, 167, 172; *S&S* 121, 190, 203, 281, 360; *P&P* 9, 73, 121, 162, 333; *MP* 212, 243; *E* 90; *P* 79). Leaded casement windows (*S&S* 105; *E* 437), with their small panes, were replaced with large double-hung sash windows (*Evelyn*, *MW* 180; *E* 252, 437). French doors or windows, as noted above, were installed in rooms that overlooked the gardens, admitting more light and allowing easy access to the outdoors (*P* 36). Among the windows that did not open as doors, there were tall, multipaned windows that stretched almost the full height of the tall downstairs rooms and reached all the way down to the ground (*NA* 213; *MP* 65, 69); 'bow' windows that had two short sides extending outwards from the house at an angle and joined by a long wall of glass divided into panes (*NA* 213); and Venetian windows, which had a large centre panel with a narrower panel to either side (*Sand*, *MW* 384).

Window seats (*NA* 167) allowed people to lounge in the natural light, talking, reading or taking in the view.

One of the ways of introducing colour into a room was changing old velvet hangings (*NA* 158, 159, 163, 214) in dark, sombre colours for new bed draperies, valances and curtains (*NA* 167; *E* 83, 252; *P* 179) in lighter shades. Another technique was installing a floor carpet in a fashionable colour and pattern.

Another strategy was to hang wallpaper (*NA* 163, 214; *S&S* 374; *E* 253), which increasingly replaced old tapestries (*NA* 158, 163) and wainscot. Wallpaper, one of the many commodities that was taxed by the government, could be decorated with stamps or stencils on white or coloured backgrounds. Some papers were flocked by making shapes with varnish and then allowing coloured lint to stick to the varnished areas. English-made wallpapers tended to be fairly drab, and it was the French wallpapers, with their beautiful colours and floral designs, that were truly fashionable. Papers that were decorated with birds, non-flowering plants and classical motifs were also popular. Wallpaper manufacturers, also called 'paperstainers', were sometimes consulted on the choice of other furnishings, so that upholstery and drapery would harmonise with the paper.

See also Furniture; Gardens and Landscapes; Gothic; Picturesque.

B

Barouche

The barouche was the supremely desirable vehicle for summer or for fair-weather travel around town. Two seats, one facing backwards, one facing forward, accommodated a total of four persons comfortably (*P* 174, 176), and the box (*MP* 75, 91, 105) held two more – usually a driver and a footman, for unlike a coach, the barouche had no rear step on which a footman could ride. This made a total of six people, and six, of course, is the exact number carried on the outing to Sotherton in *Mansfield Park* (*MP* 74), although the 'coachman' is Henry Crawford himself, and the footman's place is occupied by Julia Bertram (*MP* 80). Austen also makes a point of selecting a barouche for the outing rather than a chaise, which was enclosed and did not have a retractable top:

> 'But why is it necessary', said Edmund, 'that Crawford's carriage, or his *only* should be employed? Why is no use to be made of my mother's chaise?'

Barouche

'What!' cried Julia: 'go box'd up three in a post-chaise in this weather, when we may have seats in a barouche! No, my dear Edmund, that will not quite do'.

'And my dear Edmund', added Mrs. Norris, 'taking out *two* carriages when *one* will do, would be trouble for nothing' (*MP* 74).

Mrs Norris makes a valid point; a chaise seated passengers facing forward only, while a barouche seated them facing both ways. Therefore, a barouche can hold the entire party all by itself.

The barouche had a long, shallow, curved body with a single hood that could be raised to cover the back passenger seat only – hence its unsuitability for rainy weather. A cover could also be unfolded to shield the rear passengers' legs from the rain, but this was an expedient for emergencies only. Typically, it was drawn by two horses only, although in processions, four or even six horses might be used for aesthetic reasons, and in this event a postilion would be seated on one of the horses to help guide the carriage. The body rested on springs that determined not only how smooth the carriage's ride was but also how high above the wheels the body sat. The higher the body, the better the view, but high-bodied carriages were top-heavy and thus more likely to overturn.

See also Carriages and Coaches.

Bath

Visiting Bath (*J&A*, *MW* 24; *Clifford*, *MW* 43; *Cass*, *MW* 48, 49; *L&F*, *MW* 78–79; *Lesley*, *MW* 112; *NA* 56, 70–71, 155–156, 226, 238; *MP* 192, 193, 435; *E* 140, 189; *P* 13, 28, 33, 35, 42, 105, 107, 138, 188) in August 1791, novelist Fanny Burney wrote that the city was 'beautiful and wonderful through-out'. She remarked, as many later visitors would, on the terraces of buildings marching up the town's steep hills:

> The Hills are built up and down, and the vales so stocked with streets and Houses, that in some places, from the Ground floor on one side a street, you cross over to the attic of your opposite neighbour. The White stone, where clean, has a beautiful effect, and even where worn, a grand one. ... in truth, – It looks a City of Palaces – a Town of Hills, and a Hill of Towns.

She was an enthusiast where Bath was concerned, writing in 1815 that every time she visited she saw some new marvel to enchant her. It was, even then on her fourth visit, 'in a state of luxurious beauty that would baffle description, and almost surpass even the ideal perfection of a Painter's fancy'. She liked it even with all of its construction, noise and chaos, and she was not alone. French visitor Louis Simond, viewing the town in 1810, found it 'very beautiful' and admired the vast fronts of the mansion-like townhouses, all carved from the same local limestone. 'This town looks as if it had been cast in a mould all at once', he wrote; 'so new, so fresh, so regular'. Hester Thrale Piozzi, a close friend of Samuel Johnson's, called Bath 'the head Quarters of Pleasure and Gayety'.

Thousands of visitors every year agreed with Burney, Simond and Piozzi, but the verdict on Bath was not unanimous. Charles Dibdin, writing in 1787, declared that the place was 'like a Frenchman's shirt – the ruffle is very fine, but the body very coarse. ... In short, all is either splendidly dull or dirtily vulgar'. Four years later, James Beattie remarked on Bath's situation in a valley, which deprived it of fresh breezes and made 'the air much more close and stifling than that of London'. (Even Hester Piozzi admitted that Bath could be a 'stewpot' at times.) Beattie gave the architecture of Bath his lukewarm approval but complained of the chalk soil, which generated huge amounts of dust in dry weather and similar amounts of mud when it rained (*NA* 84). Overall, he concluded, 'it is an irregular and very inconvenient town'.

Jane Austen seems to have been in Dibdin's and Beattie's camp on the subject of Bath. She visited the town in 1797 and 1799 and possibly at other times as well, eventually coming to dislike it so heartily that, upon being informed that her family was moving there in 1801, she reportedly fainted from the shock. Much like Anne Elliot, 'She disliked Bath, and did not think it agreed with her – and Bath was to be her home' (*P* 14). She found it rainy (*NA* 83; *P* 135), gloomy and, after the decline of the public assemblies, dull. The doctors, she thought, were too quick to write prescriptions, and the price of certain commodities was too high. Any pleasant associations that might have remained vanished when, in 1805, her father died and was buried in Bath, and she moved away from the city the following year with feelings of joy and relief.

Bath's development was directed by two natural phenomena – the hills that surrounded it and the mineral springs that had made it a spa since Roman times. The older parts of the city were located in the valley, while newer houses crept up the hillsides and across the River Avon. About 5,000 houses were built there from the 1720s to 1800, with especially frenetic periods of construction in the 1760s and from 1788 to 1793; about 1,000 houses were built in the second period alone. The building of the Circus was followed by that of the Royal Crescent, a huge curved row of thirty houses, completed in 1775.

The second boom ended abruptly with the outbreak of war with France in 1793; many people failed to travel at all because of the war, while others shifted their allegiance to different spas. As late as 1801, unfinished houses still lined the London road. Building eventually began again but with less frantic enthusiasm.

Aristocrats had once flocked to Bath in order to drink or bathe in its waters, but by Austen's day, the aristocrats had gone elsewhere. Bath was instead a haven for the gentry, professionals and tradesmen. It continued to draw large numbers of visitors from these classes, however – an estimated 10,000 people came every year, staying for weeks or even months at a time – and the town prospered. West Indian planters came with dozens of relatives and servants straggling behind them; adventurous men and professional gamblers came to play for high stakes, until most games of chance were banned in 1749. Prostitutes came to ply their trade, and speculators came to start new mineral wells or sell patent medicines. Increasing number of people came not as visitors but as new residents, and by 1815, Bath was one of the nation's dozen most populous towns.

Bath as a Medical Centre

The ostensible reason for Bath's existence was its waters, which were piped into pump rooms or into an assortment of hot, cold and warm baths. People in ill health (*J&A*, *MW* 26; *Scraps*, *MW* 170; *S&S* 208–209; *E* 275, 307) went to take the waters, either internally or externally, as recommended by their doctors. In the Pump Rooms, people paid to drink glasses of the warm water (*NA* 71; *P* 146). Rates were posted from 1804 onwards; there was a charge of 7*s.* for the first week's water, followed by a guinea a month for the invalid and 10*s.* a month for the rest of his family. Pumpers of water could not ask for tips, but they could receive them if offered. Many patrons would begin the day with a bath between 6:00 and 9:00 a.m., and then proceed to the Pump Room for a glass of mineral water.

In the baths (*P* 152), people of both sexes immersed themselves with the help of an attendant. In order to preserve everyone's modesty, men had to wear drawers or a waistcoat while bathing, women had to wear a shift and male attendants had to wear a special cap to identify themselves. Suitable attire could be rented for 6*d.* if the bather did not wish to get his own clothes wet. The baths were supposedly of great help to people with joint or limb pain; they were recommended, for example, in cases of arthritic complaints or gout (*LS*, *MW* 295–296, 298; *Sand*, *MW* 374; *NA* 17; *MP* 425; *P* 163–164). Mrs Austen's brother, James Leigh-Perrot, for example, spent half of every year in Bath for the treatment of a gouty foot, and the reason Jane went to Bath in 1799 was that her brother Edward was travelling there to relieve his own gouty symptoms. For those too crippled to come to the baths, the baths, in a sense, came to them. Tubs in which to soak one's feet could be filled with the hot bathwater and brought to one's lodgings for a fee.

Bath as a Social Centre

Not everyone who came to Bath, however, was ill. Even the people seeking medical treatment, unwilling to leave their families for weeks at a time, brought wives, husbands, children, servants and family friends in tow. These friends and family quite naturally wanted something to occupy their time other than watching invalids soak in hot water, so businesses of all kinds evolved to entertain the hangers-on. There was always something to do in Bath (*NA* 78–79).

There were bookstores and circulating libraries for those who liked to read (*P* 146).

By the time of Jane Austen's first visit to Bath in the 1790s, the town had nine circulating libraries. Subscribers paid a fee for the year or the quarter and could then borrow as many books as they liked. This fee changed over time, but in 1789 six of the libraries agreed on rates of 15*s.* per year and 5*s.* per quarter.

Those who preferred newspapers to books could subscribe to reading rooms that took in a number of papers, including the local Bath paper (*NA* 206). They could also go to one of Bath's coffeehouses and read the paper there. The newspapers were considered important not only for their coverage of political and financial events but for their advertisements and their lists of new and notable visitors lately arrived in town.

Music lovers had plenty of options. Amateurs could join the Bath Catch Club, which from 1784 held weekly meetings to sing all sorts of songs, or the Harmonic Society, which was giving occasional Friday-evening concerts in the Lower Rooms by 1812. There was music at the Pump Room and at the assembly rooms, paid for by the patrons of the various rooms; as the musicians were crucial for balls, there was always much anxiety over whether they were being paid enough. The Pump Room band, which played music from 1:00 to 3:30,* was paid £50 8*s.* per season in 1795. This was considered adequate payment at that time, but by 1801, a total of £130 8*s.* for the bands at the Upper and Lower Rooms was thought so little that the number of performances had to be scaled back.

There were also weekly concerts (held on Wednesdays at the Upper Rooms in 1812–1813), special benefit concerts for distinguished performers (*P* 180) and musical evenings at private homes.

Those who preferred the outdoors could walk (*NA* 35, 68, 80, 97) or ride. There were several good walks around Bath, including that to the summit of Beechen Cliff (*NA* 106, 111) on the south side of the Avon. Jane, an avid walker, recorded, shortly after her family had moved to Bath, taking a brisk walk with a similarly determined lady named Mrs Chamberlayne. The two ladies walked so fast, she informed Cassandra, that they would have been entirely alone 'after the first two yards, had half the inhabitants of Bath set off us'. Equestrians (*NA* 35) and carriage drivers (*P* 168) could ride or drive up any of the numerous nearby hills, such as Claverton Down (*NA* 61), near the burial place of Bath notable Ralph Allen, or Lansdown Hill (*NA* 47), a hill just north of town where a Civil War battle had been fought in 1643. The route to Claverton Down afforded good views of the Royal Crescent, and the Down itself, 400 feet above the town, boasted extensive views in all directions and, according to Pierce Egan, a 'beautiful extensive level of velvet turf'. If one travelled north past

---

*In 1819 (P. Egan, *Walks through Bath*).

Lansdown, one arrived at Wick Rocks, an area of rugged scenery and cliffs up to 200 feet tall.

Other Bath visitors simply enjoyed spending time with friends. Some people came year after year to Bath, meeting friends and family who lived in other parts of the country (*P* 170, 178). They dined at each other's houses or met in the evenings to play cards (*MP* 203).

Bath was also known for its theatre (*NA* 195, 217), which became the first Theatre Royal in the provinces when it was constructed in 1768. This Orchard Street theatre attracted top performers from London, making Bath, for many years, the second-best theatre city in the kingdom. The theatre building itself, however, was small and inconveniently located in the older part of town that still featured narrow medieval streets. In 1805, it closed and was replaced by a newer, larger theatre located in Beaufort Square, midway between the Upper and Lower portions of Bath. Elaborately decorated in red and gold, it cost £20,000 to build and contained twenty-six private boxes, beautiful ceiling paintings and magnificent chandeliers. Austen is known to have attended a performance at the Orchard Street theatre, and it seems likely that she saw others there. It is also possible that she saw plays at the new theatre, although she moved away from Bath only a few months after its completion.

Some visitors wanted a little bit of everything, and this they found at Bath's pleasure gardens. These included Spring Gardens (1735–1796), which hosted public breakfasts, teas and music, in addition to pleasant walks on garden pathways. Villa Gardens (1782–1790) had a more working-class appeal and may have failed for that reason; almost everyone in Bath wanted to believe that they might be rubbing elbows with peers. The queen of Bath's gardens was Sydney Gardens, referred to as 'the Vauxhall of Bath'. Sydney Gardens, which opened in May 1795, featured elegant landscaping, cast-iron bridges, a faux castle and outdoor public entertainment such as concerts and breakfasts. Four or five times a year, there were especially large night-time events lit by as many as 5,000 oil lamps. Austen's first home in Bath was located near the gardens, and she attended events there. In 1799, she made a reference in one of her letters to the public breakfasts, but it is not known if she attended them.

Assembly Rooms

The quintessential Bath diversions, however, were the balls (*NA* 33; *E* 156) held at the town's various assembly rooms (*NA* 130, 195, 201; *E* 156). The oldest of these (*Watsons, MW* 325) in Austen's days was the Lower Rooms (*NA* 89), a cluster of assembly rooms located in the lower, older part of the town. The proprietors hired a master of ceremonies (MC – see *E* 156), who welcomed new visitors to the town and gave those who needed it a little discreet advice on the standards of behaviour expected at assemblies. Those who opted to partake of the balls paid a subscription fee admitting them for the season.

The expansion of the town uphill, however, made travelling down to the Lower Rooms and back an annoyance for those living on the heights. Accordingly, in 1771 another set of rooms was built closer to the newly constructed homes. This collection of assembly rooms, known as the New Rooms or Upper Rooms (*NA* 20, 21), drew fashionable customers away from the Lower Rooms, eventually eclipsing them altogether. Much of its success was due to its convenient location, but part was also due to its amenities. Its ballroom, lined with forty Corinthian columns, was 105 feet long, just over 42 feet wide and a few inches over 42 feet high. It also boasted a tearoom (*NA* 22) with a raised gallery for musicians and a 48-foot-wide octagonal card room (*NA* 20, 51) through which the concertgoers pass in *Persuasion* (181, 190).

Attempts were made to keep the two sets of assembly rooms from competing too aggressively with each other. The MCs tended to work out a schedule that allowed each set of rooms to reign supreme on chosen nights. On Mondays, the Upper Rooms held their formal dress ball. On Tuesdays, the Lower Rooms hosted a cotillion. The Upper Rooms held its cotillion on Thursdays, and the Lower Rooms held its formal dress ball on Fridays. The schedule was somewhat different by the season of 1812–1813; by that time, there were balls at the Upper and Lower Rooms, respectively, on Mondays and Tuesdays; concerts on Wednesdays at the Upper Rooms; another ball at the Upper Rooms on Thursdays; and theatre performances on most other nights, except for Sundays.

A third important site, the Guildhall, hosted balls as well, but it does not feature in Austen's writing. This is because its dramatic usefulness would have been limited by the fact that only residents of Bath could attend balls there. As the purpose of assemblies, for the participants as well as for Austen, was to bring together potential marriage partners from different parts of England (*E* 275), balls restricted to local residents did not hold much appeal.

The assemblies, like almost everything else in Bath, were seasonal. For a resort town, Bath had an unusually long season, or rather, two seasons. The first lasted from the end of the hunting season until the combined heat of Bath and desire to visit one's country estate drove visitors away – that is, from February to June. After the 'stewpot' had cooled a little, people came back for a second season from September until late December; as the Christmas holidays approached, many visitors returned home to be with family. As time went on, however, many people began staying for part or all of the winter (*Sand, MW* 374; *E* 183; *P* 14, 42, 206), making a third Bath season.

Amenities

Bath's leaders realised very early in the eighteenth century that the tourist trade was its chief hope of worldly glory, and they made efforts to make the city as comfortable for visitors as possible. Standard rates for lodgings were set to avoid gouging renters, and lists of available lodgings made it easy for new arrivals to find a place to live. Little could be done about the streets in the old part of town, which still bore its medieval footprint, but the streets in the upper town were broad and attractive, with sidewalks (*P* 178–179) to help ladies keep their dresses clean. Drainpipes were mandatory from 1757 to keep rainwater from sheeting off the roofs onto pedestrians below, and reservoirs to meet seasonal water demand were built at Beechen Cliff and two other locations in 1765, 1790 and 1799. From 1801, the streets were lit at night by 960 lamps.

On Sundays, visitors could choose to worship in one of the many proprietary chapels built specifically to accommodate visitors and funded, like everything else, by subscription. These included the Octagon Chapel (1767) in Milsom Street, at which Austen is believed to have worshiped, the Kensington Chapel (1795) in Walcot, Laura Chapel (1796) in Bath-wick and All Saints Chapel (1794) in Lansdown Place. The proprietary chapels were a necessity, as the Church of England was very slow to build new churches (and, in the process, split existing clergymen's livings) under any circumstances. Building new churches for temporary residents was quite out of the question. There were, however, traditional churches for local residents, including Walcot Church (*NA* 46), where Jane's father married her mother in 1764 and was buried in 1805.

The most prized amenity in a hilly town was the presence of licensed 'chairmen', pairs of men who would carry an individual in a sedan chair. These chairmen were especially necessary at the Orchard Street theatre, as the crowded streets in that part of town would not admit hordes of carriages. By regulation, thirty pairs of chairmen had to be in place outside the theatre by 9:00 p.m., but this was never really adequate, and patrons often had a long wait for a chair. Public concerts also had to have at least thirty sedan chairs ready, and public balls had to have fifty. By 1801, there were 340 pairs of chairmen licensed in Bath; they charged 6*d.* inside the old city, 6*d.* for trips up to 500 yards within the 'liberties' (adjacent areas), 6*d.* for trips of up to 300 yards in seven especially steep areas and 1*s.* for all other journeys, up to a maximum of one mile.

Shops

For many visitors, the chief attraction of Bath was its assortment of shops (*NA* 25, 29, 217; *P* 141), generally agreed to be second only to that found in London.

There was, for example, plenty of good food. In 1799, 31 percent of Bath's retailers were involved in some way with the provision of food, from the eighty-five grocers and tea merchants and the thirty-seven bakers to the thirty-three butchers and sixteen fruiterers. Many of them were concentrated in the Walcot area in the northeast part of the city. They brought in famously good mutton from Lansdown, freshly made local butter or cheap Welsh butter shipped by the barge-load, a wide assortment of fish, fresh vegetables and excellent North Wiltshire cheese. Poulterers supplied all the normal types of domestic poultry, plus game of all kinds, including woodcock, snipe, goose, duck and even larks. Cooks and housekeepers revelled in the marketplace next to the Guildhall, which Robert Southey praised for its 'order and abundance'. The main market was held on Wednesdays and Saturdays, the fish market on Mondays, Wednesdays and Fridays. The discerning bought their poultry from a dealer in Wade's Passage and their fish from the fishmongers in High Street or Bath Street.

Sweets sold especially well. Bath got its first ice cream shop in 1774, and the city was renowned for its confectioners. Loiterers of both sexes could step into a pastry shop, such as Mrs Molland's at 2 Milsom Street (*P* 174), and eat ices, jellies and cakes. Another famous pastry shop was Gill's, located in Wade's Passage between two buttresses of the Abbey Church.

Another important set of businesses dealt in transportation, enabling visitors to get to Bath quickly and easily. The town had five horse dealers in 1800 and numerous commercial stables (*MP* 193). In 1799, there were four coach makers, nine saddlers and six farriers, plus drivers of coaches and wagons who hauled people and goods up and down the new turnpike roads. By 1800, 147 vehicles had regular service at least once a week from Bath to London or from London to Bath, and by 1812, this number had risen to 265. Coaches also ran to Exeter, Bristol, Birmingham, Gloucester and Cheltenham.

Retailers of cloth and clothing (*P* 221) included drapers, milliners, hosiers, mercers and glovers. In 1800, there were twenty-two milliners and dressmakers, eight shoemakers, fifty-three tailors and habit makers, forty-four hairdressers and perfumers and nineteen mantua makers. About 21 percent of retailers in 1799 were engaged in the clothing trades. The drapers and mercers sold fabric by the yard, while the mantua makers and so forth made the clothes to patterns specified by the customer. Hosiers sold stockings; glovers, obviously, sold gloves; and milliners sold hats (*NA* 39) and trimmings like lace and ribbons. One such shop was Smith's at Bath and Stall Streets, run by a Mrs Gregory; it was here that Jane's aunt Mrs Leigh-Perrot was accused of shoplifting some lace in 1799.

Another large segment of the retail trade was devoted to household goods such as glass and china. Josiah Wedgwood had a showroom in Bath, initially in Westgate Buildings but later in Milsom Street. There were cabinetmakers, ironmongers and dealers in earthenware. Toy shops sometimes sold toys for children, but most were devoted to trinkets, knickknacks and clothing accessories such as fans, pocketbooks, decorative souvenir boxes, jewellery, combs, knives, scissors and cosmetics.

Toy shops were primarily interested in attracting female customers, but men as well as women patronised Bath's wig makers, print shops (*P* 168–169), bookshops, music shops and goldsmiths.

Bath

Notable Sites in Bath

Austen mentions a number of sites in Bath that would have been familiar to any of her readers who had visited there. There are fewer of these references in *Persuasion*, where most of the action has moved into private homes, but even *Persuasion* mentions a few landmarks. One of these is Molland's, cited above; another is the White Hart Inn (*P* 216), a well-known coaching inn that stood opposite the Pump Room and would thus have been seen almost daily by most tourists in Bath. People often stayed there when they meant to stay only a few days in Bath, or they slept there for a night or two while they searched for appropriate lodgings.

The inn, sometimes styling itself a 'hotel' (a more fashionable term), was considered one of the best in Bath.

Northanger Abbey is richer in references to public spaces, as Catherine Morland is far more interested in the traditional entertainments of Bath than Anne Elliot. One of the most commonly mentioned sites is the Pump Room (*NA* 35, 39, 83, 84, 91, 143, 149, 217), where pumpers served glasses of mineral water from a fountain (*NA* 71). The Pump Room was, in some sense, the headquarters of social Bath. New arrivals signed the guest book (*NA* 35, 43) to announce their presence in town to their friends. Visitors walked up and down the room (*NA* 25, 34, 35, 147) in the morning, looking for acquaintances (*NA* 31), studying the latest fashions worn by their fellow walkers (*NA* 71) and getting some indoor exercise on cold winter days. The curious, if they wished to do so, could look out the windows onto the baths below, watching the invalids bob and tiptoe in the water. In the afternoon there was music played by a twelve-member band.

The Pump Room had already been renovated and enlarged once in the 1760s, but by the 1780s, the city fathers felt that more changes were necessary. Accordingly, the building was remodelled again in the late eighteenth century, a process that seemed to take forever and that disrupted its business. Even before it emerged from this cocoon as the Great Pump Room, it was a splendid place.

Nearby was the abbey churchyard, which Austen calls the pump-yard (*NA* 43, 44, 91; *P* 228). This was a paved courtyard, one of the official places where sedan chairmen could wait for customers, and had a view of the abbey; the south front of the Pump Room, with its Greek inscription (translated as, 'Water Is Best'); and the low colonnade (*P* 222), to the right as one faced the Pump Room.

Farther away from the city centre, one finds the residential districts in which Austen and her fictional characters resided. Some streets were considered far more genteel than others (*P* 165). To the west of the old city, and unfashionably close to it, lay Westgate Buildings (*P* 152–153, 157–158, 192), one of the places that the Austens considered living when they moved to Bath. Jane wrote to Cassandra in January 1801 that 'Westgate Buildings, tho' quite in the lower part of the Town are not badly situated themselves; the street is broad, & has rather a good appearance.'

1. Map of Bath, 1804.

Bath Map Key

1. Abbey churchyard (pump yard)
2. Argyle Buildings
3. Avon
4. Baths
5. Beaufort Square theater
6. Beechen Cliff
7. Belmont
8. Bond Street

9. Broad Street
10. Brock Street
11. Camden Place
12. Cheap Street
13. Circus
14. Claverton Down
15. Edgar's Buildings
16. Gay Street

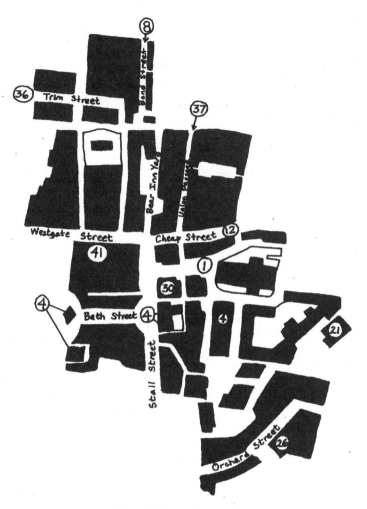

2. Map of the Lower Town, 1804.

17. Gravel Walk
18. Green Park Buildings
19. Lansdown Hill
20. Laura Place
21. Lower Rooms
22. Marlborough Buildings
23. Milsom Street
24. Octagon Chapel
25. Old Bridge
26. Orchard Street theater
27. The Paragon
28. Pulteney Bridge
29. [Great] Pulteney Street
30. Pump Room

31. Queen Square
32. Rivers Street
33. Royal Crescent
34. Sydney Gardens
35. Sydney Place (Sydney Place ran to both the north and south sides of Sydney Gardens)
36. Trim Street
37. Union Passage (Replaced, along with the Bear Inn Yard to the west, by Union Street)
38. Upper Rooms
39. Walcot Church
40. Westgate Buildings
41. White Hart Inn
42. Wick Rocks

Little housing was built to the south, but there had been a bridge across the Avon in that direction for many years. In *Persuasion*, Lady Russell's carriage takes Anne 'through the long course of streets from the Old Bridge to Camden-place' (135), and indeed this would have been a long, busy and noisy route. The old southern bridge was about as far south as one could go and existed mostly to bring out-of-town traffic into the city. Camden Place was very far to the north along some of the busiest roads in Bath.

To the northeast, the Avon was spanned by Pulteney Bridge, a lovely arched stone bridge built by Robert Adam in 1770 to 1774 and lined with shops. It led past Argyle Buildings (*NA* 87, 94) to the diamond-shaped Laura Place (*NA* 86; *P* 149, 157), named for Henrietta Laura Pulteney, daughter of one of Bath's landlords and developers. This area was rejected by the house-hunting Austens in 1801; as Jane put it, 'The Houses in the Streets near Laura Place I should expect to be above our price.' On the other side of Laura Place, Great Pulteney Street (*NA* 19, 51, 80, 86, 149; *P* 178) extended northeast to Sydney Gardens. It was in this neighbourhood, at 4 Sydney Place, that the Austens finally settled in 1801. (The neighbourhood was to prove too expensive for them, however, and they would be forced to move in 1804 to Green Park Buildings, a rather plain-looking row of three-storey houses in the southwest quadrant of the city.)

The northern or 'upper' portion of the town contained the Paragon, where the Leigh-Perrots lived at No. 1; Jane disliked this street, which was narrow, busy and dark. Not too far away lay Queen Square (*P* 42), where she stayed in June 1799.

Between Queen Square and the Circus lay 25 Gay Street (*P* 240), where the Austens moved after Mr Austen's death. By 1806, they had shifted again, to tiny Trim Street just southeast of Queen Square. Milsom Street (*NA* 39, 47, 91, 102, 129, 154, 155, 170, 174, 238) was also very near Queen Square, lying just a few streets to the east. It was originally designed as a residential street, but in later years became famous as a site for fashionable shops. At its northern end stood Edgar's Buildings (*NA* 43, 47, 92, 115, 149), approached by a steep flight of steps.

Just west of the Circus, along Brock Street (*NA* 101), was the Royal Crescent (*NA* 68, 97, 101), where on pleasant Sundays most of Bath liked to walk. A gravel walk (*P* 241) connected the Circus with the Crescent. On the other side of the Crescent were Marlborough Buildings (*P* 139, 156, 197). A few blocks north of both the Royal Crescent and the Circus was Rivers Street (*P* 136, 215), and still farther north was Camden Place (now Camden Crescent). Camden Place's (*P* 124, 136, 137, 192, 240) construction woes have been mentioned already, but despite its lopsided appearance, its houses offered splendid views. To reach Camden Place, one walked or rode up Broad Street, then turned to the right near the place where Broad Street continued north as the Lansdown Road (*NA* 85).

The upper and lower towns met near the abbey churchyard. Cheap Street (*NA* 44) ran north of the churchyard and eventually became

Bath

Westgate Street, while York Street ran along the south side and became Bath Street (*P* 217, 228) as it ran westwards. To cross from Cheap Street to the upper part of town, one had to walk either through the yards of the Bear Inn or through Union Passage (*NA* 44), a narrow alley that inevitably became choked with traffic at busy times of the day. In the first decade of the new century, the newly constructed Union Street (*P* 175, 239), made possible by the demolition of several buildings, made it much easier to get from one part of town to the other.

Towards its northern end, Union Street was crossed by New Bond Street, a fairly recent development. A wine merchant, Thomas Emery, had begun building houses on the north side in 1805, and a few years later, a carpenter, Joseph Cave, began building on the south side. Soon shops, such as that of a London hairdresser, began opening in the street. The old Bond Street (*P* 141) was one of the southern continuations of Milsom Street. Streets in Bath had a tendency to change names every block or two. For example, High Street ran northwards from Cheap Street, then became Northgate Street. It split into two arms, the more westerly of which was Broad Street (*NA* 85). Broad Street then forked again as it ran northwards. The eastern branch became Bladuds Buildings, then the Paragon and then Ax-ford Buildings, leading past Walcot Church. The western branch became Oxford Row and Belmont, then Belvidere, then Lansdown Street and finally left town as the road to Lansdown and Wick Rocks (*NA* 85–86).

See also Places; Public Places.

Bathing

Health and entertainment had long been linked in the British mind. For centuries, people had been travelling to spots whose waters were supposed to have healthful properties, and as drinking from, or bathing in, mineral springs took time, they generally brought their families along. By the late eighteenth century, leisure activities had been found not only for the patients but for those who accompanied them.

However, in the early nineteenth century, a significant shift occurred in the type and location of water cures and their attendant diversions. An interest in the seaside, nurtured by the romantic interest in nature and encouraged by the wealth of coastline available in an island nation, shifted public interest from the inland spas to coastal towns. People began travelling to the ocean to witness its beauty and to bathe, tentatively at first, in its waters. Physicians lauded the restorative properties of ocean bathing (*Sand, MW* 367; *P&P* 229; *E* 101, 102), and a few brave souls actually drank seawater, trusting that its purgative properties were cleansing them of what ailed them. Those too ill or too frightened to enter the water (*Sand, MW* 424) could at least benefit, it was thought, from breathing the salt air (*Sand, MW* 367; *E* 101, 105–106).

The change in preference from spas to seaside happened gradually, but by the last years of Austen's life, the shift was well underway. David

Selwyn sees in *Persuasion* the official passing of the torch from one type of 'public place' to another, with the pallid joys of Bath being superseded by the romantic power of the coastline. Certainly, Austen found much to observe, enjoy, analyse and criticise in the vogue for sea-bathing, as she followed *Persuasion* with the incomplete *Sanditon*, which is set primarily in a nascent Sussex resort.

The season in seaside towns was short, confined to the late summer and autumn (*E* 91, 105) months; few people were as bold as Jane's cousin Eliza de Feuillide, who bathed with her chronically ill son at Margate in January and February 1791. Novelist Fanny Burney bathed in November in 1782, and the Austens also bathed in November on one occasion, but they preferred September and October. At Margate, Kent's principal seaside resort, lodging house proprietor William Stone charged 2 guineas a week during May and June, 2½ in July, 3 in August and 3½ in September and early October. Prices then diminished for the less popular late-autumn, winter and spring months.

However, there were compensations for the short season. Walks on the beach were pleasant exercise, and children and adults alike enjoyed collecting seashells and even seaweed. Those with an artistic bent enjoyed the visual effects of light, cloud and waves (*Sand*, *MW* 396), and those who, like Austen, were put off by the stuffiness of the spa towns could relax in the generally less formal seaside resorts. The seaside was also cheaper than a spa (*Sand*, *MW* 369); lodgings and fees usually cost less, which must have also appealed to the Austens.

Bathing itself was conducted extremely carefully and never alone. The days of splashing, swimming and frolicking in the waves lay ahead; in Austen's time, one first 'bespoke' or hired a 'bathing-woman' as Fanny Burney did in Brighton in November 1782. She rose before dawn and found the water 'cold but pleasant. I have bathed so often as to lose my dread of the operation'. In order to preserve her modesty, she would have gone out not on foot or by swimming but in a bathing 'machine', essentially a small wagon that could be pulled by a horse into the water. She would have disrobed down to her shift inside the machine and exited out the back so that no one from the shore could observe her. Then her 'bathing-woman' would have helped her to duck completely under the water several times. The use of bathing machines (*Sand*, *MW* 424; *P* 96) had at least one effect on the development of likely resorts – the underwater area adjacent to the beach had to have a suitable slope, preferably gradual and predictable, so that the machines could proceed easily into the water.

Other desirable characteristics for a seaside resort were cliffs to block the wind, picturesque scenery nearby to be pursued on walks or rides and a firm, flat beach. To these natural amenities developers added promenades for afternoon and Sunday strolls, circulating libraries (*Sand*, *MW* 389; *P* 130), assembly rooms, indoor seawater baths, public gardens, theatres, card rooms and billiard rooms (*Sand*, *MW* 384). The building of extensive rows of uniform townhouses, which had become a prominent feature of many spa towns, most notably in Bath, was not yet a feature of most of the seaside resorts. Development of extensive crescents and terraces (*Sand, MW* 384) was in its infancy there, and most such towns did not begin speculative building (*Sand, MW* 371) until the 1790s. Even then, it was a risky proposition; Southend's Royal Terrace bankrupted its builders shortly after completion. In many places, lodgers were simply accommodated in existing homes for the short duration of the fashionable season.

Austen would have had a chance to sample many of the facilities of coastal towns, as she lived in Southampton from 1806 to 1809, visited Ramsgate in 1803 and went with her family on seaside holidays to Sidmouth in 1801, to Dawlish and possibly Teignmouth in 1802 and to Lyme in 1803 and again in 1804. However, it was the bathing and scenery rather than the assembly rooms that really interested her; in Lyme, on September 14, 1804, she wrote

> The bathing was so delightful this morning and Molly so pressing with me to enjoy myself that I believe I staid in rather too long, as since the middle of the day I have felt unreasonably tired. I shall be more careful another time, and shall not bathe tomorrow as I had before intended.

She was suspicious of resorts that had become too fashionable and too extensively developed; Margate, for example, fares badly in her works. Like many 'public places', it is full of superficial acquaintances and moral temptations. In 1804, remaining in Lyme while Cassandra went on to Weymouth, she wrote that 'Weymouth is altogether a shocking place, without recommendation of any kind,' and though she was exaggerating in this instance for humorous effect, she appears genuinely not to have had much affection for the place.

As stated above, Margate was the most popular seaside town in Kent, with Ramsgate and Worthing as lesser attractions, but Kent was not the premier county for sea-bathing. Devon, Dorset and especially Sussex (*Sand, MW* 368) were more amply supplied with resorts. Devonshire had Dawlish, Teignmouth and Sidmouth; Dorset had Austen's beloved Lyme, with its often-rebuilt medieval jetty, the Cobb (*P* 96), on which walks could be taken. Sussex, during the last decade of Austen's life, was being heavily promoted and developed as a tourist destination and as a cheap retirement location for military officers on half-pay after the French Wars. Austen's fictional Mr Heywood found the pace of development disturbing:

> Every five years, one hears of some new place or other starting up by the Sea, & growing the fashion. How they can half of them be filled, is the wonder! *Where* People can be found with money or Time to go to them! Bad things for a Country – sure to raise the price of Provisions & make the Poor good for nothing (*Sand, MW* 368).

The principal prospects for development were chiefly in southern and western England, with the notable exception of Scarborough in Yorkshire.

Scarborough, however, was a special case, as it had begun its life as a spa and had only recently turned to sea-bathing to supplement its amenities.
See also Medicine; Places; Public Places.

Beverages

The beverages drunk by Jane Austen's contemporaries fell into several categories, including milk, hot drinks, wines, beer and hard liqueur. On occasion, these categories overlapped, as in the case of the syllabub, a mixture of wine and milk, or as in the case of chocolate, which was a hot drink made with milk. Water is seldom mentioned as a drink on its own, though it was mixed with wine and heated to make tea and coffee. Water delivery to towns was improving after 1800, as entrepreneurs built piping systems, but prices were high and pipe maintenance erratic. Pollution of water by human, animal and industrial waste made it often unsafe to drink from the local lake or river. There were places in the country where wells and streams could be trusted, but for the most part, when we hear of people in this era drinking water on its own, they are drinking mineral water in a spa as part of a medical cure.

Milk was drunk on its own and was very much appreciated when it came fresh from one's own farm's dairy. Town milk was far more suspect. Sometimes diluted with water, almost always thin, blue and dirty, it was made even more unpalatable in places such as Bath by the methods of its production. The cows that yielded the local milk were kept in barn stalls rather than in grassy fields, and their inferior fodder yielded inferior milk. Still, for many people, it was the only option. It was sold in the streets by milk-women, who carried two pails suspended from a pole across the shoulders, or directly from cows or asses who were milked at the door of each house.

The problem was that good milk was simply too expensive.

The poor often had milk only in their tea, but at the other end of the social spectrum, it was enjoyed in a variety of forms. For wealthy invalids, especially those with tuberculosis, there was asses' milk (*Sand, MW* 393, 401), which had fewer nutrients than cows' or goats' milk but also had less protein and fat and was thus more easily digested. Mixed with cocoa, milk became 'chocolate', a luxurious breakfast drink enjoyed at the homes of the wealthy and on special occasions. Chocolate was heated in special pots, similar to coffeepots, but with an aperture at the top for a stirring rod or mill, which acted like a whisk.

Other Hot Drinks

Like chocolate, other hot drinks were associated with specific purposes or times of day. For example, 'caudle' was a warm drink composed of oatmeal, mild spices, water and wine or ale; it was considered especially appropriate for invalids and for postpartum women. Negus, on the other hand, was associated with late-night parties, particularly balls held during the winter, when dancers might need a warming beverage between periods of activity.* It was made with white wine, red wine or port mixed with lemon juice and spices. Maggie Lane states that it was also made without sugar but with calf's-foot jelly and mixed about twenty minutes before serving to allow the jelly to melt; other recipes, such as Mrs Beeton's from a half century later, leave out the jelly and add the sugar.

Wine

Since wine grapes grew poorly in the English climate, almost all of the nation's grape-derived wine (*S&S* 185; *E* 130, 213, 329) was imported from the Continent. From France came Burgundies, claret (light red wines, specifically those of Bordeaux – see *J&A*, *MW* 18, 23; *MP* 47), champagne[†] and Frontignac (a sweet wine from southern France). Port (*P&P* 76) came from Portugal (hence its name), sherry and alicant from Spain and Chian from the Greek island of Chios. The sweet, expensive Muscat known as Constantia (*S&S* 197) came from South Africa, while Canary sack and Madeira (*MP* 74; *E* 365) were named for the islands that produced them. 'Mountain' was a sweet white wine from Malaga, while 'Rhenis' hailed from the Rhine region. Many of the favourite wines were fortified with brandy for increased alcohol content. Port, for instance, had just undergone a revolution in the 1770s; new bottling technology allowed it to mature for ten to fifteen years, instead of the previous three or four, and the richer wines that resulted were extremely popular. Marsala, too, a sweet Sicilian wine, was fortified with brandy.[‡]

However, though the English had to import their best grape wines, they themselves produced wines from other fruit, including gooseberries, currants, apricots, orange, elderberries and quince; the Austens made gooseberry, orange and currant wines, sometimes from home-grown, sometimes from purchased fruit. Their friend Alethea Bigg was well-known for her orange wine, the recipe for which Jane requested in January 1817. Orange wine was typically made in the winter, when Seville oranges were in season, and shifted into casks in the summer. The English also created faux versions of Continental wines – a useful skill when enemy blockades disrupted supply. Contemporary cookbooks feature recipes for mountain wine, Cyprus wine, Frontignac, sack and champagne, most of which involve steeping imported raisins for several days, then fermenting the strained liquid. Another home-brewed drink,

*Although Parson Woodforde drank white wine negus at an inn in Sherborne at 11 a.m. on August 3, 1789.

[†]Champagne, at this date, might be either red or white and was likely to be bubble-free.

[‡]Frederick Accum, in 1820, printed statistics on the alcohol content of various alcoholic beverages. Madeira, he said, averaged 22.27 percent alcohol by volume; port, 22.96; white Constantia, 19.75; red Constantia, 18.92; red Madeira, 20.35; Cape Madeira, 20.51; claret, 15.1; Malmsey Madeira, 16.4; gooseberry wine, 11.84; elder wine, 9.87; mead, 7.82; and brandy, 53.39.

mead, was made by fermenting honey. The Austens kept bees at both
Steventon and Chawton, and they were fond of mead, despite the fact
that it was losing favour in the nation as a whole. Recipes for mead varied
widely; some included the sorts of spices we associate with mulled wine
or cider, such as nutmeg, mace and cloves, while others used green herbs
such as marjoram, thyme or rosemary.

Wine was most often served during dinner, especially during the dessert
course (*Watsons*, *MW* 325; *S&S* 355). Neighbours sitting near each other
drank toasts together, and the men tended to pour the wine for the ladies.
These ladies kept their consumption to a minimum, then retired and
allowed the men to get down to the serious drinking, which concluded
when they joined the women in the drawing room for tea and coffee.
Austen also records in her letters drinking wine at parties and, mixed
with water (*MP* 66; *E* 25, 365), after returning home from the theatre.

Austen was well aware of the bibulousness of her age. On November 20,
1800, she called her own overindulgence in wine at Hurstborne a 'venial
error' and mentioned it only because the after effects – was she hungover? –
seemed to be affecting her handwriting. She also frequently comments
in her novels and letters on the drunkenness of others. The most sustained
example of drunkenness in her works is *Jack & Alice*, a humorous early
work in which the main characters are nearly always three sheets to the
wind. They are variously 'Dead Drunk' (*MW* 14), 'a little addicted to the
Bottle' (13), 'heated by wine (no uncommon case)' (15), 'dead drunk' again
(19), overly fond of claret (18, 23) or overly fond of liqueur in general (23).
Alice's brother Jack dies of drink (25), while her father is 'a drunken old
Dog to be sure' (25). Most of the humour of *Jack & Alice* comes from the
ridiculousness of a family resorting quite so freely to the bottle – no one
in Austen's own family could have supposed this a realistic portrait – but
imagine a young woman in 1860 or 1880 drawing a light, comic portrayal
of alcoholism and its fatal consequences. Such levity would not have been
acceptable in Queen Victoria's day, and Austen's casual jocularity says a
great deal about how much heavy drinking was tolerated in her own time.
Indeed, even as a product of the rowdy Georgian age, she often voices
disapproval of drinking (*MP* 426). Fanny Price's father comes in for some
of her strongest condemnation; Fanny is 'sadly pained by his language
and his smell of spirits' (*MP* 380), and the narrator, not pained but simply
disgusted, concludes, 'he swore and he drank, he was dirty and gross'
(*MP* 389).

Wine was sometimes bought in bottles (which were occasionally
disguised with a false crust around the neck to simulate age), but it was
also bought in large quantities and bottled at home. Parson Woodforde,
for example, would buy a quarter of a pipe of port at a time from his wine
merchant (*Col Let*, *MW* 158), Mr Priest. (A pipe equalled 105 imperial
gallons or 131.25 US gallons, so Woodforde was buying enough port to fill
a sizable fish tank.) Then it was decanted into a decorative container, and
a label made of silver, enamel or ceramic was hung around the neck of the

decanter to identify its contents. This method of labelling wine would last until the late nineteenth century and the advent of printed paper labels that identified the wine and its vintage. If there were a butler in the home, it would be his job to bottle, store and serve the wine, as well as to care for the decanters and glasses.

Wine was used as an ingredient in food and in mixed drinks such as the caudle described above. Another mixed drink containing wine was the syllabub, a mixture of milk or cream and wine. Traditionally made with milk fresh from the cow and served on the spot, it was by Austen's time a drink prepared beforehand. The frothed milk or cream was separated and allowed to stand and drain, then replaced over the 'thin'. The contrast between the translucent mixture at the bottom of the glass and the stiff, long-lasting foam at the top was the chief attraction of a syllabub.

Beer

Beer and ale are less present in Austen's works than wine, although beer was, along with tea, one of England's most popular drinks. Historically, it had been brewed at home, supplying much the same place at the table that water would now; servants typically drank at least a quart a day. Mrs Austen brewed beer at Steventon in the last years of the eighteenth century and at Chawton cottage many years later, but home brewing was slowly being overtaken by commercial brewing. In 1788, a total of nearly 5 million barrels were produced by common brewers and brewing victuallers such as innkeepers and publicans, and 9 million barrels were produced at home. By 1800, commercial and domestic brewers were producing roughly equal volumes, and by 1815, home brewing had fallen behind.

Several types of beer and ale were made. Ale and beer were divided into 'strong', 'table' and 'small' varieties, differentiated from each other by alcohol content*; an 1806 letter written by Jane's mother at Stoneleigh describes the mansion's 'strong beer' and 'small beer' cellars. Pubs might offer a cheap brown ale, a more heavily hopped brown ale and an expensive, high-quality pale ale; when the three types were mixed together in one glass, the resulting concoction was known as 'three threads'. A very dark, heavily hopped, bitter, high-alcohol beer was introduced in 1722; soon thereafter, it became known as 'porter' because of its popularity with London porters. It was popular with brewers, too, because the dark colour and strong taste hid impurities. They built enormous production vats; the Meux brewery, in 1795, had a vat that could hold 20,000 barrels (almost 750,000 gallons). Much to the brewers' chagrin, in the late eighteenth century, pale ales came back into fashion.

*Frederick Accum, writing in 1820, estimated the alcohol content of various beers and ales: Burton ale, 8.88 percent alcohol; Edinburgh ale, 6.2 percent; Dorchester ale, 5.5 percent; brown stout, 6.8 percent; London porter, 4.2 percent; London small beer, 1.28 percent. Beer brewed in the countryside tended to be less alcoholic than beer brewed in London.

Spirits

Gin, brandy and rum were the most widely drunk types of hard liqueur (*MP* 4); each, according to Frederick Accum in 1820, was more than 50 percent alcohol by volume. Gin, also known as 'Hollands' or 'Geneva', was made domestically and had acquired a fairly nasty reputation earlier in the century, when its low price and wide availability occasioned Britain's first major urban drug crisis. Dram shops had advertised that a person could get drunk for a penny and dead drunk for 2 pence; rooms with straw on the floor were provided for those who wanted to pay a little extra to have a place to sleep off their liqueur. The crisis was eventually controlled by the imposition of taxes that raised the price of gin. Taxation made it harder to acquire cheap gin, but not impossible, as illegal distilleries were happy to supply their customers 'by moonshine'. Parson Woodforde was an avid customer; in 1781 he drank 'some smuggled gin which I liked'.

Brandy came from abroad, principally from France, and was also a popular item with smugglers.

Rum came from even farther away. It was a by-product of the West Indian sugar industry, and since Britain had quite a number of sugar colonies, rum was fairly cheap. The liqueur fermented from leftover molasses formed the basis of grog, the sailor's typical drink afloat, a mixture of rum, water and lime juice. Ashore, rum was mixed up as punch, a popular drink at all festive occasions, but especially when men got together for club events.

See also Dishes; Food; Tea.

C

Cards

Card playing (*Col Let*, *MW* 160; *Watsons*, *MW* 343; *S&S* 143; *P&P* 35, 38, 54, 346; *MP* 248; *E* 100, 311, 382) was one of the few forms of entertainment that cut across all classes and both genders. Men of all classes enjoyed blood sports such as cockfighting, but such sports were frequently considered inappropriate for women, either as spectators or as participants. Music was enjoyed by all classes, but not every family could afford a musical instrument for after-dinner amateur concerts. Cards, however, were cheap, widely available and considered entirely acceptable (except by the most radical religious enthusiasts) for everyone. Contemporary prints show people of all ranks playing cards, and even if the purpose is sometimes to make fun of the pretensions of servants who imitated the card parties of their employers, it also becomes clear that card games had broad popular appeal.

The equipment for card games was mostly the same as today. Decks of cards were not identical throughout Europe, but as the English deck corresponded to the modern deck, with its clubs, diamonds, hearts and spades, running from ace through king, nothing need be said about alternate decks elsewhere. One distinct difference from modern decks, however, was the lack of numbers or letters in the corners of the cards. This was not much of problem with the face cards, which were fairly easily identifiable, but it must have occasioned some confusion with some of the eights, nines, tens and so on. A certain amount of ongoing pip counting would have been necessary. Another difference between the decks of Austen's time and those of today was that there was no design on the backs of the cards; they were simply white. The obvious disadvantage of the undecorated back was that it was easy for gamblers to make small marks on the backs of the cards that could be easily detected by alert eyes. Even unintentional smudges could give an advantage to those who wished to cheat. Therefore, a conscientious host or hostess would provide new packs of cards (*E* 290), sealed with a government stamp, to ensure the cleanest possible backs. The cards would be acquired and passed around to the various tables by a servant, who would then receive 'card money', or tips, for his trouble. The relatively impoverished Watsons, in Austen's unfinished novel of the same name, cannot afford a new deck for every evening and must rely instead on finding a used but 'tolerably clean pack' (*Watsons, MW* 357).

All card games involved a certain amount of gambling, and players often kept track of their winnings not with actual money but with 'fish' (*Watsons, MW* 357; *P&P* 84, 166), the eighteenth-century version of the poker chip. Fish were small pieces of ivory that were, indeed, vaguely fish-shaped; if it was necessary to have items marking two different monetary values, then 'counters', a marker with a different shape, were added to the fish. They were kept in piles in front of the players on the card table (*Watsons, MW* 332, 357, 359; *S&S* 144, 145, 151; *P&P* 47, 54, 76, 166, 169; *MP* 203, 249), which appears, to judge from contemporary illustrations, to have been covered with a green mat similar to that used on poker tables today. Most card tables were square, but a few tables, earlier in the eighteenth century, had been designed with three-player games in mind and were triangular. Since card games were usually played in the evening, candles were a necessity on the table (*E* 290), and they were ideally placed at the corners of the table so that each player's hand was illuminated without the need to lean forward and possibly expose one's hand.

The usual time for card playing was between tea (*S&S* 144, 200; *P&P* 342) and supper (*P&P* 84), that is, in the evening (*S&S* 54), when people amused themselves in various ways. Those fond of music would play or listen; if there were enough people interested in dancing, they might form a set in the drawing room. The majority of the family and their guests, however, would probably not be interested in dancing or in playing music. They needed an alternative form of entertainment, which was usually a card game of some sort. For the servants, relaxing after the efforts of preparing, serving and washing up after the meal, playing cards was a way of passing the time with fellow servants from other households until the guests were ready to leave. At balls, a special card room (*Cath*, *MW* 221; *Watsons*, *MW* 327, 328; *NA* 20, 52; *E* 254), adjacent to the ballroom, was set up for people who had no interest in dancing. In 'public places', such as balls and seaside resorts, the card room was a chief attraction for the older members of a family.

Some people did more than settle on cards as an alternate activity, however. They were enthusiasts who made special efforts to secure fellow players. For women, this meant hosting or attending card parties (*Watsons*, *MW* 350; *E* 20, 156, 290; *P* 245), where no effort was made to provide music or dancing at all. The whole purpose was to play cards and to gamble on the outcome, for higher or lower stakes depending on the participants' income. Men also attended such card parties, but they had another outlet for their interest in the form of card clubs. Clubs of all kinds were popular during the eighteenth and nineteenth centuries – scientific clubs, musical clubs, book clubs, sporting clubs and card clubs. Card clubs, which were predominantly formed for the purpose of playing the intellectually demanding game of whist, tended to be established and populated by men (*Watsons*, *MW* 324–325; *E* 68, 197).

Card games fluctuated in popularity, even within a single family. In or before 1809, for example, Jane appears to have introduced the game of speculation to her brother Edward's family, and she pretended to be dismayed at its ouster in 1809 by a new game, brag. Parson James Woodforde, an avid card player, went through periods of playing only or mostly quadrille, punctuated by brief flirtations with cribbage and loo. Later, he developed a fondness for whist and commerce, both of which began to appear frequently in his accounts of games played.

Whist

Whist (*Watsons*, *MW* 324–325; *S&S* 166; *P&P* 76, 82, 84, 342; *MP* 119, 227, 239, 246; *E* 96, 325) is the game most commonly associated with the eighteenth and nineteenth centuries, and it was indeed popular. It was similar to bridge, in that it was a game for four players, with tricks taken by partners who remained partners for the duration of the game. Partners were chosen by cutting the cards, with the two highest and the two lowest forming the teams.

The ranking of cards was according to the system used in most modern games, with ace high and deuce low, and players were required to follow suit. Trump was determined by the last card dealt, which was dealt face up and remained there until all but the dealer had played a card on the first trick, whereupon the trump card was added to the dealer's hand. Complex rules of etiquette, mostly involving the unintentional revelation of information about a player's hand, could result in players compelling the offender to play in a certain manner or to reveal information in a formal way; these rules were so numerous and specific that it would be tedious to relate them here.

A 'rubber' (*MP* 240, 246; *E* 81, 326) of whist consisted of three games, the winner of each game being the partnership that first scored 5 points.* 'Book' was six of the thirteen tricks, and each trick (*MP* 245) above book counted for one point; a team that collectively held ace through jack of the trump suit ('honours') scored 4 points; a team that held three of the honours scored 3 points. A game might take more than one hand to win. If this were the case and the leading partnership had 4 points at the beginning of a new hand, honours were not counted towards winning points.

Once 5 points were reached and the game won, the actual score became meaningless, except as it determined the value of the victory. A game's value was determined by comparing the score of the victorious team with that of the losing team. A shut-out or 'treble' gained the winning team 3 points; a score of five or more to two or fewer was a 'double', worth 2 points; a score of five or more to the other team's 3 or 4 points was a 'single', worth 1 point. Two points were awarded to the winners of the rubber, who, if they won the first two games, did not need to play the third to establish their victory. The losers' winning game points, if there were any, were subtracted from the winners' games to establish the final score.

It is tempting to read every reference to a rubber (*Watsons*, *MW* 336; *S&S* 145, 151, 178) in Jane Austen's works as a reference to whist, primarily because the term 'rubber' is now so strongly associated with bridge, but this assumption would be incorrect. A rubber was a grouped series of rounds in a number of types of card games, including casino. It was one of many specialised terms that had to be learned by new card players, and the novelist Frances Burney congratulated herself on having added it to her vocabulary, writing in April 1780, 'I returned to finish the Rubber; – don't I begin to talk in a good old Cattish manner of Cards?'

Quadrille

Austen mentions a number of card games by name. Quadrille (*P&P* 88, 105, 166; *E* 21), one of Parson Woodforde's favourites, makes several appearances. Though whist, a forerunner of bridge with very similar rules, was thought of as the quintessential thinker's game, quadrille required every bit as much concentration. Its rules seemed deliberately designed to foil the beginner. Descended from a three-player game, ombre, it was a game for four players and was played with an ordinary pack from which

---

*Until about 1804 or shortly thereafter, the game was to 10 points, with only 2 points being awarded for three honours.

the eights, nines and tens had been removed. The ranking of cards differed from the modern order in most games and also varied within the game depending on whether the suit was red or black, trump or not.

Face cards had the same relative value as in most games today, while the number cards varied, valued either from highest to lowest or lowest to highest depending on the colour of the suit. Some cards were always trump, while others took on a special value only if their suit was named trump.

The cards were dealt counterclockwise, beginning with the player to the dealer's right, in three rounds: three cards to each player, another three cards to each player, and four cards to each. Each player began, according to James Beaufort in 1775, with seven *mils* worth of markers – a *mil* being equal to ten fish, and a fish being equal to ten counters. The value of each token was agreed on beforehand. The players also agreed on the number of 'tours' to be played, a tour equalling four hands, or one turn for each player to be dealer. Ten tours, or forty hands, were typical.

Before the deal, each player placed a counter into the pool as an opening bet. The dealer also offered a fish, making the total pool equal in value to fourteen counters. Beginning with the eldest hand (the player to the dealer's right), the players each had a chance to bid for the right to name trump. The easiest bid to make was 'asking leave', in which the bidder proposed to take six of the ten tricks in partnership with another player. This player was chosen by 'calling a king', that is, naming a specific king not held by the bidder and enlisting the holder of that king as a temporary partner.* The partner, however, did not immediately identify herself; the partnership became evident only during the course of play. If no one bid higher, the successful bidder named trump, called her king, and played the hand, following suits and trumping as in most modern trick-taking games, with the exception of the special privileges of matadors and, of course, the unconventional ranking of the cards.

A player with a stronger hand could bid *sans prendre*,[†] offering to take six tricks[‡] without an ally. This bid ranked higher than asking leave, but an earlier bidder also ranked higher than a later bidder and was given a chance, if she liked, to up her bid to *sans prendre* and regain control of the hand.

If she declined, the contract went to the new bidder, and play proceeded. At any time between the bidding and the taking of the first six tricks,

---

*If the bidder held all the kings, she could call a queen instead. Rarely, for strategic reasons, a player might 'call' a king that she held in her own hand, which was perfectly legal but made her, in secret, a player *sans prendre*. The exception to calling a king was the king of trump, which could not be called. Likewise, if the player opted to call a queen, the queen of trump could not be called.

[†]Without drawing new cards.

[‡]Trick-taking games are card games with a common structure: Each round of play is divided into units called tricks, during which each player selects one card from his or her hand. For each trick, one player will have the lead, the right and obligation to play the first card of the trick.

a player could 'declare the vole', announcing that she would attempt to take all ten tricks. If an especially confident bidder chose to bid the vole from the outset, this overruled a bid *sans prendre*. The vole was normally declared, if at all, after the first six tricks were taken, but on occasion the cards justified more confidence.

A player who did not choose to declare the vole, after taking the first six tricks, could simply claim her winnings and stop the hand. If she continued to play, however, she was assumed to be declaring the vole, and each player, including the player trying for the vole, had to ante three more counters to a separate pool. A player who had a partner and was considering trying for the vole had to ask, after winning the first six tricks, 'May I?' and wait for her partner to respond yes, or no. A further condition was that, if a king had been called, the king in question had to be played before a vole could be declared.

If no player was willing to bid, the bid became 'forced *spadille*'. The holder of the ace of spades was obliged to play the hand, calling a king (or a queen if she held all the kings) and naming a trump suit. Play continued in the same manner as for other bids, except that a player playing forced *spadille* was not permitted to declare the vole.

At the end of the hand, the distribution of winnings was nearly as complicated as the ranking of the cards. A player *sans prendre* won the pool, plus the pool for the vole if applicable, plus additional chips from each player.

If the bidder had called a partner, the partner split these winnings equally and could also contribute to the collection of *matadores* and *punto*.*

The bidder could lose in two ways: by *remise* or by *codille*. *Remise* meant taking only four or five tricks; *codille* meant taking three or fewer. Taking no tricks at all was called *devole* but appears to have borne no special penalties. A player who lost by *remise* doubled the size of the pool – alone if she had played *sans prendre* or with her partner if she had had one. She (or they) then paid to each player the appropriate consolation, plus the amount that the bidder(s) could have claimed for holding *matadores*,

---

*There were cards that had specific names, based on what suit was trump:

Name	Is This Card	When This Suit Is Trump
Spadille	Ace of Spades	Any suit
Manille	Deuce of Spades	Spades
	Deuce of Clubs	Clubs
	Seven of Hearts	Hearts
	Seven of Diamonds	Diamonds
Basto	Ace of Clubs	Any suit
Punto	Ace of Hearts	Hearts
	Ace of Diamonds	Diamonds

The first three of these, *Spadille, Manille* and *Basto*, were collectively called *matadores* and had a privilege in play; when a lower trump card was led, the holder of one of these three cards did not have to follow suit. He or she could play any card he or she liked. However, if a higher *matadore* was led as the first card in a trick, and the player held a lower *matadore* and no other trump, he or she was obliged to play it.

had she (or they) won. A player who lost by *codille* paid the same sums, but her partner (if she had called one) did not have to contribute to the losses, and the opposing players, in addition to being paid by the loser, divided the pool between them. If partners lost by *remise* and the original bidder had failed to take at least three tricks on her own, the called partner was likewise exempted from losses, and the original bidder paid the entire sum. The exception to this rule – there was always an exception in quadrille – was in the case of forced *spadille*, where losing partners split the losses regardless of how many tricks the nominal player of the hand took.

Voles complicated matters still further, as they had the side pool and could be announced at different points in the game. A vole that was bid at the outset, where the bidder took at least six tricks, lost nothing but the side-stake for the vole, which was divided among the opposing players. No one was 'beasted' or 'basted' (forced to double the size of the pool). A vole declared after the first six tricks were taken, however, was subject to substantial penalties; the player had to pay each opponent what she would have won had she succeeded in her attempt.

Loo

Loo (*P&P* 37, 47), like quadrille, involved the taking of tricks, but, unlike quadrille, was designed for five or more players. It was thus a 'round game' (*Watsons*, *MW* 354, 359; *MP* 239) – a game for a variable number of players, as opposed to games like whist or quadrille, which had a fixed number required. Round games were socially useful, as they accommodated odd numbers of players; Austen's characters with an affinity for whist or quadrille are frequently found scrambling to find a fourth for a game (*S&S* 144, 166; *P&P* 342) or to find occupation for superfluous players (*MP* 239).

Loo arrived in England through France in the mid-seventeenth century and had a three-card and a five-card version. In both versions, players anted a specified number of counters. In each hand, players opted to remain in the game (and pay an additional sum into the pool) or bow out at no charge. Players who remained in had to take at least one trick or add to the pool. There were two schools of thought about how to make this addition. In limited loo, the sort preferred by Parson Woodforde, the penalty was a small, fixed sum. In unlimited loo, the amount was equal to that already in the pool, which meant that if there were successive hands where many players opted to compete, the pool could grow geometrically.*
It is probably unlimited loo, then, that was being played at Netherfield, when Elizabeth Bennet declined to play for fear the stakes were too 'high' (*P&P* 37).

---

*A game in which the pool grows in a similar manner is the poker variant known as 'Guts'. In college in the 1980s, I saw a penny-ante game of guts grow until the pot stood at over $160.00. Small wonder, then, that Elizabeth Bennet shrinks from playing a game where small bets can reach disastrous heights.

Cards

Casino

Casino (*Watsons*, *MW* 332; *S&S* 144, 175), sometimes spelled 'Cassino', could be played by two to four players. The ace was worth 1 point, numbered cards were worth their face value, and the jack, queen and king were worth 11, 12 and 13, respectively. Each player received four cards, and four were dealt face up in the middle of the table, while the remaining cards were set to one side. Unlike games such as whist, quadrille and loo, it was not a game that involved taking tricks. The point of the game was to score points by capturing cards from the centre section.

Captures were accomplished by equalling the value of one or more cards with cards from one's own hand. For example, if the four face-up cards were a five, a two, a seven and a jack, player A could use a seven from their own hand to capture *either* the seven *or* the five and the two together. Then the captured card(s) and the card used to capture them are placed face down in front of the player. If the player managed a 'sweep', however – a capture of all the face-up cards – the capturing card remained face up next to the player's captured cards; this enabled players to keep track of sweeps for scoring purposes. A player who ran out of cards drew four more from the leftovers; if all the face-up cards were removed in a sweep, or if a player could not make a capture, she had to 'trail', that is, leave one of her own cards among the face-up cards in the centre.

When all the cards had been dealt and captured, players calculated their totals, using the following formula:

most cards captured	3 points
tie for most cards captured	0 points
Great Cassino (ten of diamonds)	2 points
Little Cassino (two of spades)	1 point
most spades captured	1 point
each ace	1 point
each sweep	1 point

The game, or rubber, was usually to 11 points. Later versions of casino introduced the concept of 'building', which allowed players to group cards prior to making a capture in a later turn, but this did not become a uniform part of the game until the twentieth century, and it is not known whether Austen could have been familiar with this variation.

Speculation and Brag

Speculation (*Watsons*, *MW* 354, 358; *MP* 239–242) was a round game with a conventional deck and conventional ranking, that is, ace high to deuce low. A mid-nineteenth-century description indicates that the object was to acquire the highest trump card. The dealer anted six fish, the other players anted four fish each and each player was dealt three cards, one at a time, but did not look at them (*MP* 240). After the cards were dealt, the next card was turned face up. The suit of this card was 'trump', though no tricks were taken. Only trump cards counted towards the resolution of the game, and the others were useless except as decoys.

If the revealed trump card was an ace, the dealer immediately won the pool; if not, he could auction it off to the highest bidder or keep it himself. The player to the dealer's left then turned his top card face up and, if it was a better trump than the dealer's, could keep it or sell it as he chose (*MP* 241, 242–243, 244). If it was not a superior trump card, the next person in clockwise rotation revealed his top card, and so on. If a trump card was revealed and purchased, the player to the purchaser's left was the next to expose a card. The holder of the highest visible trump card was not obliged to turn any cards face up until all the rest had been uncovered. When all cards had been uncovered, the holder of the highest trump card got the pool (*MP* 243). The players anted again, and the next hand was apparently dealt without shuffling the used cards back into the deck, as the 1847 description advises,

> To play this game well, little more is requisite than recollecting what superior cards of the trump suit appeared in the preceding deals, and calculating thereby the probability of the trump offered for sale proving the highest in the deal.

If no trump were dealt to any player (other than, obviously, the first card turned up at the end of the deal), the fish remained in the pool, everyone anted again, and a new dealer dealt another round of cards. Anyone turning over the ace of trump, of course, won automatically.

Jane Austen was fond of speculation, having introduced it to Edward's family at Godmersham, and several of her letters chart the rise and fall of this game in his home. In December 1808, she writes that 'I hope Speculation is generally liked.' On 10 January 1809, she responds to a letter that evidently reported the eclipse of speculation by brag, another card game:

> The preference of Brag over Speculation does not greatly surprise me I beleive [*sic*], because I feel the same myself; but it mortifies me deeply, because Speculation was under my patronage; – & after all, what is there so delightful in a pair-royal of Braggers? it is but three nines, or three Knaves, or a mixture of them. – When one come to reason upon it, it cannot stand its ground against Speculation – of which I hope Edward is now convinced. – Give my Love to him, if he is.

A week later, she must have heard that brag, in its turn, had been momentarily ousted by some other game, for she sent a nephew the following verse:

> 'Alas! poor Brag, thou boastful Game! What now avails thine empty name? – Where now thy more distinguished fame? – My day is o'er, & Thine the same. – For thou like me art thrown aside, At Godmersham, this Christmas Tide; And now across the Table wide, Each Game save

Brag or Spec: is tried.' – 'Such is the mild Ejaculation, Of tender hearted Speculation.'

Brag was a three-card descendant of the fifteenth-century game of 'post and pair'. Three cards were dealt, the last face up, and players competed for three stakes. The first stake was awarded for the highest face-up card, the second for the best combination of three cards, and the third for the player whose cards were closest to 31 points without going over. As the game evolved from the early-eighteenth century to the mid-nineteenth, it acquired wild cards or 'braggers': jack of clubs, ace of diamonds and nine of diamonds. The second stake was awarded to the holder of the highest pair, or, better yet, the highest pair royal (a set of three, also called a *prial*). By the mid-nineteenth century, additional winning hands had been added, so that, from lowest to highest, hands were ranked as follows:

Pair

Flush (all one suit)

Run (three cards in numerical sequence)

Running flush (all one suit and all in sequence) Prial

Brag fell out of favour not merely in Edward (Austen) Knight's household but in the nation as a whole. It was in decline already by the first decade of the nineteenth century and was decidedly out of favour by mid-century. It was to acquire new life in the late-nineteenth century as a single-stake game related to poker.

Commerce

Commerce was a popular game among the Austens' circle of friends. In November 1800 she wrote to Cassandra, 'The three Digweeds all came on tuesday, & we played a pool at Commerce.' In October 1808, she informed Cassandra that she had played the game again, for particularly high stakes given her limited income:

We found ourselves tricked into a thorough party at Mrs Maitlands, a quadrille & a Commerce Table, & Music in the other room. There were two pools at Commerce, but I would not play more than one, for the Stake was three shillings, & I cannot afford to lose that, twice in an event –

Novelist Frances (Fanny) Burney also played commerce and, though she rarely gave details about card games, offered a portrait in 1779 of a particularly silly, flirtatious fellow player that reads like an episode in one of Austen's own novels. The offender in this case was Peggy Pitches, the nineteen-year-old daughter of a wealthy merchant:

When it came to her turn to deal, she mixed the cards, let them drop, tittered, and flung herself into sundry attitudes, and then begged the Captain to shuffle and deal for her.

Captain Fuller, to Ridicule, I believe, her affectation, took the contrary extreme; he put on an awkward, clownish Countenance, shuffled the Cards with a ludicrous clumsiness, and making various vulgar grimaces, *licked his Thumb* in order to deal!

This failing, her next attempt was more spirited; she looked over his Hand, and, declaring all cheating was allowable at Commerce, snatched one of his Cards to make her own Hand better.

The Captain, however, had so little gallantry, that instead of regarding this theft as a favour, and offering her choice of what she pleased, he insisted upon having his Card returned! – and when she resisted, recovered it, in an easy manner, by exposing all her Hand, and then, very composedly, proceeded with the Game without comment.

Commerce was played with a standard fifty-two-card deck, with conventional ranking and with aces either high or low. Players anted a set amount to the pool, and each was dealt three cards. A ghost hand, the widow, was dealt three cards as well. The dealer could exchange his hand for the widow's, and after he had decided whether to exchange or not, players in clockwise rotation opted to exchange a card with one from the widow's hand or not. Exchanges continued until two players had knocked on the table to indicate that they were satisfied with their hands. All hands were then revealed, and the best won the pool.

The ranking of hands was as follows, from lowest to highest:

Point: Highest total face value of the three cards, with aces equalling 11 points, face cards 10 points, all others their number of pips; ties broken by highest number of cards in a single suit or, if these are equal, proximity to dealer's left.

Sequence: A three-card 'straight flush' – cards of the same suit and in numerical sequence; aces can be low or high for this purpose, but sequences cannot wrap around; that is, A-K-Q is legal, as is A-2-3, but 2-A-K is not.

Tricon: A set of three cards of the same rank, e.g. three 3s or three kings.

There were variations on the method of exchanging cards. In one version, also known as 'trade and barter', new cards could be bought from the dealer or exchanged, blind, for cards from the next player's hand; in this version there was no widow.

Vingt-et-un

The name Vingt-et-un is French for '21', and it is the game known in modern times either as twenty-one or blackjack. Known either as vingt-et-un or vingt-un (*Watsons*, *MW* 358), it was played by the Austens on at least two occasions in January 1801. On Wednesday, 21 January,

Cards

Jane wrote to Cassandra that she dined at Deane and 'played at Vingtun'; five days later, she reported, 'We met nobody but ourselves, played at *vingt-un* again, and were very cross.'

In vingt-un, the dealer (*Watsons, MW* 358) dealt two cards face down to each player, including himself. Beginning with the player to his left, the dealer offered to deal each player more cards face up. Each player could refuse to take cards or stop accepting cards at any time. The goal was for all the cards, both face up and face down, to total 21 points, or as near as possible to 21 without going over. Face cards counted for 10 points each, numbered cards counted as their number of pips and aces could be worth either 1 or 11 depending on the player's preference. An ace and a ten or face card, a natural 21, repaid the player double the normal winnings. If he went over 21, he lost his stake immediately.

When all players had ceased to take new cards, the dealer turned over his own cards and attempted to take cards himself until he had the best possible hand. At that point, he won the stakes of all who had equal or lesser hands, and paid out stakes to players with better hands. In some cases, the dealer received a double stake from all players if he himself had a natural 21; some played with the rule that a non-dealer with a natural 21 received a forfeit from all players and the right to be the next dealer. Modern blackjack permits a player to 'split' identical cards, at the outset, into two different hands, matching the original stake for the second hand. Perhaps this is what Tom Musgrove means when he refers to Lord Osborne 'overdraw[ing] himself on both his own cards' (*Watsons, MW* 358). Perhaps Lord Osborne has split a pair of fours, or some other pair, into two hands, and gone over 21 on both.

See also Games.

Carriages and Coaches

To modern readers, eighteenth- and nineteenth-century carriages (*Cath, MW* 213, 219–220, 240; *L&F, MW* 85, 90, 107; *H&E, MW* 38; *LS, MW* 275, 291; *Col Let, MW* 151; *Scraps, MW* 177; *Watsons, MW* 327, 335, 354, 357; *NA* 44, 60, 161, 210, 222; *S&S* 77, 106, 109, 160, 175, 197, 222, 249, 286, 312, 333, 341; *MP* 74, 104, 251, 273, 375; *P&P* 30–32, 84, 102, 194, 219, 257, 281, 286, 315, 353, 358; *P* 50, 123, 135, 163, 176; *E* 19, 110, 112, 187, 213, 217, 230, 323, 374, 451) are something of a mystery. What on earth is the difference between a barouche and a landau or, for that matter, between a landau and a landaulette? What makes a vehicle a chair or a chariot, a chaise or a coach, a stagecoach or a post-coach? Why does Austen refer to the same vehicle by different names, calling it here a carriage and there a coach, a chaise or a curricle (*E&E, MW* 31; *P&P* 166, 293; *NA* 229, 233; *P* 105, 117; *S&S* 67; *MP* 203)?

Interpreting all these terms requires both an understanding of the concrete features that distinguished one type of carriage from another and also a comprehension of the use of, and attitudes towards, the different vehicles. Carriages, though a minority of the population owned them, served the same purpose for that population that cars do for today's drivers. Not all cars are the same in shape, use or emotional subtext, and we have no difficulty recognising the difference between a little red convertible, a pickup truck, a postal delivery truck, a public bus and a family sedan. Likewise, Jane Austen's contemporary audience knew what sort of person would drive or ride in a curricle, a dogcart, a mail coach, a stagecoach and a post-chaise.

'Carriage', though it technically meant the lower structure of the vehicle, the part that attached to the wheels, in general usage it meant any type of wheeled passenger vehicle. (It was analogous, in other words, to the word 'car' today.) Several features then distinguished one type of carriage from another. These included how many wheels it had (two or four), whether it had a roof and whether that roof was retractable, how the lower part was 'sprung' (attached to the wheels with springs), how the upper part was shaped, how many horses drew it and whether they were harnessed singly or in pairs, whether there was a 'box' or coachman's seat and whether that seat was attached to the main body, how many people could fit on a seat, what sort of cargo room was available and whether it had passengers seats facing forward and backward or only forward.

Coaches: The Stagecoach

A coach, for example, was a large, four-wheeled vehicle with a non-retractable roof, and seats facing both forward and backward. The roof made it a 'close carriage' (*Watsons, MW* 315), suitable for driving in all types of weather. It served multiple purposes, though it was unfashionable for private family use. It was more commonly found as a public conveyance: as the stagecoach, running along a specified route with scheduled stops, much like a long-distance bus today; and as the mail coach, carrying mail and a limited number of passengers at high speeds for high prices, much like an express intercity train.

The stagecoach was a decidedly unfashionable way to travel (Austen's brother Frank once prevented her from travelling by stagecoach), though the foreign traveller Parson Moritz found stagecoaches 'quite elegant, lined in the inside with two seats, large enough to accommodate six persons; though it must be owned when the carriage is full the company are rather crowded'. Part of the stigma attached to stagecoach travel was the lack of freedom. Whereas, in a post-chaise, one had control over destination, companions and pace, the stage one was subject to external schedules and to the crowding, snoring, dreary conversation and offensive personal hygiene of one's fellow travellers. These travellers could be quite numerous. In addition to the six who were crammed rather tightly inside, four were legally allowed to ride on the roof of the coach. The limit of four, however, was routinely exceeded; Moritz saw one stagecoach with at least twelve people riding on top. (Private coaches run by the gentry would hardly have had riders on the roof, which is why Austen's youthful description of a visit by a family of eleven, all crammed into the same coach [*E&E, MW* 31], would have been humorous to the small audience who read it.) Passengers also sometimes rode with the luggage in the rear basket (*L&F, MW* 103, 106) or rumble-tumble, but Moritz found this inconvenient; when the coach went downhill, he was buried in luggage. Outside passengers, who included women as well as men, paid half fare.

1. *The Union Coach*, Isaac Cruikshank, 1799.

The advantage of the stagecoach was its price. It cost only 2*d.* or 3*d.* a mile plus tips to the coachman (who expected 2*s.* to half-a-crown) and the guard who looked out for highwaymen, as opposed to a post-chaise, which cost 1*s.* 6*d.* per mile, plus a 3*d.*-per-mile tip to the post-boys who rode and directed the horses, plus 6*d.* to each inn's ostler for tending to the horses (*Watsons, MW* 349).

Night-coaches were thought to be the worst of the worst; even the 'Stage Waggon' (*F&E, MW* 10) in which passengers thumped along in a springless, fabric-roofed, glorified farm cart, permitted its passengers to alight for the night at inns. Night-coaches had the worst of everything – the worst coachmen at the worst pay, coaches with rotting harnesses and moth-eaten cushions and horses half in the grave.

Austen seems to have little animosity for stagecoaches, as long as they are ridden by people of the right sort. Robert Martin, for example, appears to take a stagecoach without any censure from the author, indeed with hardly any comment at all. The vehicle is not specifically identified as such, but Mr Knightley indicates that Mr Martin 'came down [from London] by yesterday's coach' (*E* 472); the use of 'yesterday's' implies a schedule, which in turn implies the stagecoach. Mr Martin's taking a stagecoach, however, elicits no shock or surprise; he is not, technically, a gentleman, and therefore not used to having the world bend its timetables to suit him.

Those who took the stage had to adjust to a particularly inconvenient timetable, for, in addition to all its other woes, the stagecoach was slow. Because it was large and heavy, and because it might be carrying a large number of passengers and their baggage, it tended to be drawn by four or even six horses (*L&F*, *MW* 90–91), but this expedient did not make it speedy. It was slower still when pulled by the 'unicorn' arrangement, with a pair of horses near the wheels (one ridden by a post-boy) and a single horse in front. The 'flying' coaches, which changed horses frequently, were faster, but the regular coaches simply stopped for hours to 'bait', or rest, the same horses.

Still, despite its inconveniences, the stagecoach was an important part of English life. It enabled people of limited means to make long journeys for either business or pleasure, fostering communication between different parts of the nation and stimulating Britain's nascent tourist industry. On festive occasions, the coaches shared in the revelry. Coachmen decorated their vehicles with holly during Christmas, with garlands of flowers on May Day and with wreaths of laurel after important military victories. While the stagecoach was not an everyday sight in small towns – there were only 400 stagecoaches in 1775, the year of Austen's birth – it was common enough in the large towns. Steventon, where Austen grew up, had no stagecoach stop, but Deane, a nearby town, had departures twice a day to London.

The Hackney Coach

A hack or hackney coach (*Cass*, *MW* 45) was simply a rented vehicle, which might or might not come with its own coachman. The Parkers, in *Sanditon*, rent a coach but bring their coachman from home (*MW* 364). The hack coach was a step above the stagecoach, but it was still disdained by people who could afford to keep their own carriages. Those with their own coaches typically used their own horses for the first stage; these horses would rest and be sent back to their home stable, while the family travelled on with horses rented at an inn, called hack horses or post-horses (*Sand*, *MW* 406; *P&P* 351). At the next inn, they would exchange horses again, and so on.

The procedure was the same for hackney coaches, except that all the horses were 'hack' or rented (*Cath*, *MW* 214). There is always something vaguely tacky about hack vehicles in Austen. When she wants to convey a sense of comfortable, sophisticated travel, she uses the phrase 'post-chaise' or something similar. Hackney coaches are associated with poverty, disgrace, anonymity and disappointment. Lydia Bennet's transfer from a chaise to a hackney coach indicates the beginning of her fall into scandal (*P&P* 274–275, 282), and it is two 'Hack-Chaises' that bring the laughably small population of the eagerly expected vacationing seminary to Sanditon (*Sand*, *MW* 414, 420). Likewise, Catherine Morland's return to her home after being expelled from *Northanger Abbey* takes place not in a string of fashionable phaetons with 'three waiting-maids in a travelling chaise-and-four', but in a 'hack post-chaise', which 'is such a blow upon sentiment, as no attempt at grandeur or pathos can withstand' (*NA* 232).

Like sedan chairs or like taxis today, hackney coaches could be found by chance as they returned from carrying passengers, or they could be found reliably at stands where they waited for customers. Like stagecoaches, they bore painted marks of identification – in this case not nicknames but numbers (*P&P* 293) – and like stagecoaches, they had four wheels. Two-wheeled hackney coaches would come into use in London later in the nineteenth century, becoming a standard symbol of urban life, but Austen would have been familiar with the four-wheeled variety.

The Mail Coach

If one had to travel in a public vehicle with a regular schedule, the mail coach (*MP* 266, 443) was the superior alternative. Invented by John Palmer of Bath in 1784 to take advantage of improving road conditions and to replace post-boys on horseback, the mail coaches delivered the nation's mail with comparative speed and safety. The safety came in part from the presence of a guard on every coach, armed with a cutlass and a blunderbuss with a folding bayonet. Paid only 10*s*. 6*d*. a week, the guards nevertheless made a fairly good living by collecting tips and also by surreptitiously carrying parcels in the coach-box for less than the going rate. The latter practice was tolerated by the Post Office except in egregious cases, such as one guard's attempt to privately deliver 150 pounds of meat and ice.

The guards, who between their various sources of income might make a few hundred pounds a year on good routes, became confident, sometimes arrogant, fellows. They had reason to be cocky, for they ruled the mail coach and all in it. Even the coachman was subject to the guard's authority, and the guard could report him for drunkenness, rudeness or incompetence. The guard determined when the mail would leave each stop, kept an official watch in a locked case inside a pouch (for verifying that the schedules were kept) and turned the watch in to postmasters at intervals for inspection, winding and repair.

They were responsible for the integrity of the mail, which they kept at the rear of the coach in a locked box; in practice, however, they seem to have been lax about this part of the duty, for guards were regularly reprimanded and fined for leaving their mail boxes open. (The typical fine in 1792 amounted to a week's pay.) If the carriage broke down, the guard had final say over what to do – try to effect repairs, hire a post-chaise or go on ahead himself with the mail on one of the lead horses. If necessary, he was to walk; the mail had to proceed one way or another to its destination. Furthermore, guards had to jump on and off the coach on downhill slopes to set the iron shoe skids that served as brakes and then to replace them on their hook. They helped in some cases to change horses, often in the dark, if the local ostlers were absent or asleep. All of these tasks were performed night and day, in good weather and bad, over 40- to 60-mile stretches before a quick sleep and a journey of equal length in the opposite direction.

The guard was a little king on the road, chief officer of a vehicle invested with unique prestige. He got to blow a horn that signalled the toll gates to open, and all other coach traffic had to give way before the mail and, of course, there were the pay, the tips and the illicit extra money to be made from carrying private letters and packages.

For passengers, the mail coach was nearly as exciting. Author Thomas De Quincey gushed about the virtues of this mode of travel. Chief among its attractions were speed and, more important to De Quincey, the sensation of speed. Some passengers found the speed and the springiness of the mail coach nauseating, with the result that once they arrived at an inn, they were unable to eat anything, but De Quincey seems not to have suffered from motion sickness. He was intrigued by everything, from the comic sight of a cart of apples or eggs overturning as it struggled to get out of the mail coach's way to the exact amount of time it took to change horses at each stop. In 1804 or 1805, on the Bath road, he estimated that it took just under 7 minutes to make the exchange; a decade later he thought it took 80 seconds.

One unique feature of the mail coach was its paintwork. Carriages in general could be any colour, though private carriages tended to be painted in sober dark colours – black, brown or green, for example. The silly fiancée of Austen's youthful work *The Three Sisters* wants her husband's new carriage to be 'blue spotted with silver' but he insists on 'a plain Chocolate' with unfashionably low springs (*3S, MW* 58). Public conveyances such as stagecoaches tended to advertise themselves by means of bright colours, lots of text and memorable nicknames: the Flying Machine, the Telegraph and so on. The mail, by contrast, had a set and undeviating colour scheme: red wheels, maroon doors and lower body and black upper body. Each door bore the royal arms, and on each of the four upper panels (one to each side of the door, on both sides of the coach) appeared one of the stars of the principal orders of knighthood: Garter, Bath, Thistle and St. Patrick. The fore boot bore a symbolic reference to the current king, and the hind boot displayed the particular coach's number. As opposed to the stagecoaches, which were heavy with wording, the mail coaches simply bore the names of the terminal cities of its route and the words 'Royal Mail'.

Carriages and Coaches

Private Coaches

However, not all coaches were operated as public vehicles. Many families had their own coaches (*Cath*, *MW* 197, 225; *S&S* 274), thinking of them in much the same way that people today might think of a van or a minivan: as a serviceable, practicable, but not especially speedy or flashy way to get a large number of passengers from point A to point B. Private coaches could be distinguished from public ones chiefly by their paint-work. No labels indicating destinations were present, nor were the ubiquitous symbols of the Royal Mail. Instead, a simple colour scheme was usually chosen, with a coat of arms or symbols of nobility if the owner was entitled to them. These arms were generally painted on the door of the coach, below a window or 'glass' that could be opened; Mr Elliot's arms are thus accidentally covered by a greatcoat hung out the window (*P* 106). One presumes that Sir Walter Elliot's carriage had arms painted on it, though no mention is made of it; Lady Russell's certainly does (*P* 158). In the Juvenilia, we encounter a lord's carriage decorated with a coronet (*L&F*, *MW* 91), a kind of heraldic crown depicted in slightly different ways according to rank. Princes, dukes, earls, viscounts and barons were all entitled to use coronets above their arms, with the ranks being indicated by varying numbers of leaves or pearls; see the illustration *The Pacific Entrance of Earl-Wolf, into Blackhaven* (Landau) for a carriage decorated with an earl's coronet. Given that only a minority of people could afford to keep a carriage, that of these only some would choose to keep a coach (e.g. rather than a chaise or a gig) and that each coach was custom-made and decorated, it is not surprising that people could often recognise private coaches and make a guess as to the identity of the occupants (*L&F*, *MW* 108).

2. *A Trip to Brighton*, Dent, 1786.

The occupants, or at least the owners, were seldom likely to be dashing young men eager to make a good impression. Coaches were stolid family vehicles, a fact reflected in Austen's works. Her fictional coach owners are substantial and often middle-aged: Lady Greville (*Col Let, MW* 158–159), Lady Russell (*P* 157), the Edwardses (*Watsons, MW* 314), the elder Musgroves (*P* 50), the Middletons (*S&S* 119) and the decidedly frugal and unfashionable Heywoods (*Sand, MW* 373). The Bennets, too, need a coach for its seating capacity; after all, they have five daughters to transport (*P&P* 75, 298). A notable exception, not meant to be taken seriously since he apparently owns one of every type of carriage ever invented, is Mr Clifford of *The Memoirs of Mr. Clifford*. He travels in his coach-and-four but also has the choice of 'a Chariot, a Chaise, a Landeau, a Landeaulet, a Phaeton, a Gig, a Whisky, an Italian Chair, a Buggy, a Curricle & a wheelbarrow' (*Clifford, MW* 43). As will become clear later in this article, Mr Clifford would have had to be the king of England to afford so many carriages.

The Body of a Carriage

The body of a carriage, for the most part, distinguished it from other types of vehicle. Though wheels and springs mattered – gigs, for example, had only two wheels and often a special type of spring called a grasshopper or horizontal spring – it was the body that was most often the defining element. The coach, for example, as has already been described, had a rigid body, a fixed roof and seats facing backward and forward. The seats were 4-feet wide inside, on occasion a couple of inches wider, allowing room for three people to sit on each. The chariot was identical to the coach except that it had only a forward-facing seat and thus accommodated three people instead of six. The elder Mrs Rushworth, Mrs Jennings and John and Fanny Dashwood all own chariots (*MP* 202; *S&S* 184, 275), and so does Mr Clifford of the Juvenilia – but then the redoubtable Mr Clifford owns one of everything (*Clifford, MW* 43). The post-chaise was very similar to a chariot, but it had no coachman's box – in lieu of a coachman, a postilion rode one of the horses – and had a 3-feet 5-inches seat (*NA* 163) that accommodated only two passengers.

Carriages with retractable roofs had different names: a landau was essentially a coach with a roof that folded in two sections, while a barouche was a coach with a roof that unfolded to protect only one side. A phaeton had no roof at all. Neither did a dogcart, which was distinguished from other types of carriages by having a louvered compartment under the seat for transporting hunting dogs. Gigs and chairs, too, had no roofs; it is a gig that is referred to in *Northanger Abbey* as an 'open carriage' (*NA* 47, 61, 84, 104). Austen is not specific about the 'open carriages … to be employed' for the proposed outing in *Sense and Sensibility* (62), but one presumes they were gigs, phaetons or the like.

A carriage body began with drawings of the sides and top. Then the coach maker built wooden pattern pieces and built the frame out of ash, the panelling of mahogany or cedar and the floor, lining and roof interior of deal. The roof exterior, if there was one, was made of leather stretched over the frame while wet. Windows were made of glass (*E* 114), and some could be opened; the number of windows varied depending on the type of carriage. Stagecoaches, for example, had only two windows – one on each side, over the door (*P&P* 217; *MP* 376). Private coaches, however, might have three 'side glasses' (*P&P* 316) on each side – the one over the door, plus one in each side panel. A 1786 print of the Prince of Wales' coach shows a rectangular window over the door and two curved windows in the side panels, one of which is covered with a shade or blind (*P&P* 222). A carriage that had only forward-facing seats, such as a chariot or a post-chaise, would have had a 'front glass', a forward-facing window, as well; such a window is mentioned in *Love and Freindship* (*MW* 89).

From start to finish, a fine carriage, also sometimes called an 'equipage' (*Watsons*, *MW* 338; *Sand*, *MW* 382; *NA* 64, 65; *P* 158), would require the skills of wheelwrights for the wheels, carriage makers for the mechanism, body makers for the coach body, blacksmiths for the manufacture of springs and iron hardware, a woodcarver for decorative trim, upholsterers and embroiderers for the interior, curriers for the leather components, painters for the colours and arms, more painters for the many coats of varnish (*MP* 74), lamp makers for the lamps or 'moons' that provided a feeble illumination (*S&S* 316), glaziers for the glass windows (*E* 357), perhaps a locksmith for door locks and a gilder for additional decorative touches. The carriage was a master work of art and was recognised as such; coach maker William Felton bragged that, by 1790, 'the art of Coach-building had been in a gradual state of improvement for half a century past, and had now arrived at a very high degree of perfection, with respect to both the beauty, strength and elegance of our English carriages'. So exceptional was English work, he claimed, that the export of carriages 'to foreign nations is become a profitable and considerable branch of British commerce'.

Felton, in 1796, provided a detailed diagram and description of the internal conveniences of a carriage. These included handholds (a real necessity in a jolting vehicle travelling over bad roads without seatbelts), decorative trim, pockets (*NA* 235) and nets to hold personal belongings, a box under the seat for additional storage, and curtains, blinds or shutters for the windows. He noted that closed carriages were generally lined with light-coloured cloth, that open carriages usually had dark linings and that scarlet or crimson lining made 'an addition of exactly one-third in the price of the cloth'. Exterior trimmings included the hammer-cloth, handgrips for the footmen, different types of steps for getting into and out of the carriage and lamps. Of these last he wrote,

Lamps were originally used as necessary conveniences to a carriage, but are now principally used for ornament. ... There have been some few lamps used of the patent principle for burning oil, but the smoke they create renders their use objectionable; the hard spermaceti candle is the best to burn. The lamps are frequently smothered, or the lights go out, for want of sufficient openings at the bottom and top to receive the air, and to discharge the smoke.

The material used for the lamps was most frequently tin. Again and again, he notes that there is a wide difference in the price of a carriage based on the elegance and expense of the trimmings. Just as, today, a car can be made more expensive by adding options such as leather seats or entertainment systems, the carriage could be furnished in a very basic style or in a profusion of lace and fancy paintwork that proclaimed the individual owner's wealth.

Not all carriages, however, were purchased by individuals. Some were retained by the coach maker and used as rental vehicles. John Thorpe and James Morland visit a coach maker before they go out driving with Catherine and Isabella (*NA* 61). Inns also purchased vehicles with the intention of renting them; artist Thomas Rowlandson drew a sketch of himself hiring the first post-chaise for a long journey in a busy inn yard. A sign hanging from the inn's balcony advertises 'Post Chaises Saddle Horses ... Phaetons Whiskeys Gigs to lett'.

Staff: The Coachman

The care of all this English excellence required specialised servants. A coachman (*F&E*, *MW* 6; *MP* 375) was an absolute necessity, and postilions or post-boys might be required as well. A large household would also have one or more under coachmen, stable boys to help groom the horses and tend to their feed and bedding, and footmen to ride at the back of the carriage to look splendid in their matched livery and to assist the passengers upon arrival.

Of all these servants, the most important was the coachman. He was in many ways the public face of the household and therefore was expected to exhibit 'sobriety, steady conduct and respectable appearance', according to an 1825 manual for servants written by Samuel and Sarah Adams. The ideal coachman, in the Adamses' opinion, was a careful driver and scrupulous in his dealings with coach makers, farriers and horse dealers. He was to inspect the carriage frequently, buy fodder for the horses, supervise the other stable workers, make basic repairs, consult with a blacksmith or a coach maker if he thought more extensive repairs were warranted, clean and grease the carriage mechanism and clean and polish the harness. He must drive expertly and in all weather, day and night, perched on a high box as the carriage rocked and jolted (*MP* 189; *E* 126).

On an ordinary day, the coachman would rise early and spend the morning supervising the care of the horses. By breakfast, or shortly after, he would turn to the inspection and cleaning of the harness, brushing it 'with a dry hard brush' and polishing the brass or silver bits. Then he washed the carriage (*Sand*, *MW* 386) and wheels with mop and brush, blackened the leather parts, polished the decorative metal, greased the works and checked the security of the linchpins on the wheels. Then he turned to the inside of the carriage, brushing the upholstery, wiping the windows, cleaning the lamps and trimming the lamp wicks. If the family owned more than one carriage, there would be a separate coachman for each, with each performing these tasks on the carriage assigned to him.

If the carriage were to be used that day, the master or mistress would probably already have delivered orders to that effect. People certainly called for their carriages with little notice, but this was the exception rather than the rule. Much had to be set in motion to bring out a coach-and-four. The horses had to be physically ready, the coach itself washed, the harness dry and clean and the coachman dressed in his uniform and wig (*MP* 189). Once all was ready, the coachman made a final inspection, took his whip in his left hand, mounted the box and drove around to the house. It was a complicated business.

For this reason, carriages in Austen are 'ordered' (*Watsons*, *MW* 341; *L&F*, *MW* 89; *E* 127, 392; *P&P* 307) or 'spoken for' (*E* 128) hours or even days in advance (*Cath*, *MW* 236; *NA* 224; *E* 210; *MP* 221); it is rare indeed for a spontaneous demand to be made. Even when a character is on a visit (*Watsons*, *MW* 359; *P&P* 45), and the order is expected, it takes time to bring the carriage around to the front door (*Evelyn*, *MW* 183; *P&P* 220–221; *E* 362; *S&S* 178). On long visits, the horses would have been removed from their harness and fed in the host's stable (*E* 8); they would then have to be 'put to' again at departure time, which could cause a few minutes' delay. Then the coachman must make himself ready again, perhaps breaking off in the middle of a friendly meeting with servants from other houses.

If the party were especially large – the ball in Fanny's honour at Mansfield Park comes to mind – it would take extra time simply to match up the proper coachmen with the proper horses, and each must get in line and wait his turn to gather his passengers (*P&P* 342). Delays in bringing the carriage were so customary that Austen uses the phrase 'till the Carriage is at the door' to mean 'until the very last minute' (*Sand*, *MW* 367). For the coachman, waiting around for departure time could be pleasant enough, as long as he had a comfortable place to sit and other servants with whom to socialise. When he was in a city, however, waiting for his employers was less amusing. There was sometimes nowhere to wait but in the street, and this could lead to crowding and ill temper. In the *Bath Herald* of 15 June 1799, for example, merchants complained that their shops were being obstructed by the carriages of doctors and brewers and that when they requested that the offending carriages be moved, they were subjected to 'unwarrantable insolence' from the servants holding the horses.

When the coachman finally got his employers safely home, he returned the carriage to the stable or coach house, unhitched the horses and saw to their care, washed and sponged the harness and hung it up to dry, put his whip away and did as much of the next morning's cleaning as he could.

If he had been out late on his duties, for example while taking his employers to and from a ball, he was allowed to sleep in late the next morning; it is partly because of this customary privilege that Emma Watson is told that she cannot expect to be taken home in the morning by the Edwardses' carriage, which took her to a ball on the previous night (*Watsons*, *MW* 340). However, the prejudice against use of the horses on the day after the ball was based on more than the coachman's convenience; it was difficult, though not impossible, to put everything in readiness again so quickly.

Staff: Postilions, Post-Boys and Ostlers

Some carriages could not be driven by a coachman. Some were intended to be driven by the owner, while post-chaises had no box for a coachman, and other carriages required both a coachman and additional attendants. In the last two instances, the near horse or horses were ridden by a man who was usually called a postilion (*L&F*, *MW* 85, 90; *F&E*, *MW* 8; *H&E*, *MW* 38; *P&P* 293) when he was employed by the passenger's household and might be called either a postilion or a post-boy (*Watsons*, *MW* 349; *NA* 232; *S&S* 354) when he was hired along with a post-chaise. In *Mansfield Park*, Mrs Norris reveals the name of a postilion, Charles, when she reassures the ailing coachman that 'Charles has been upon the leaders so often now, that I am sure there is no fear' (*MP* 189). Presumably, Charles has been accustomed to ride the near lead horse, in which capacity he would help to control the horses as they pulled the carriage and serve as a groom when they stopped or were stabled.

Readers seldom fail to assume that postilions were adult men, but they often misinterpret the term 'post-boy'. A post-boy was usually not a boy at all but a grown man, indeed often a middle-aged man. He was based at an inn (*S&S* 354; *E* 383), from which he was hired by passing travellers. He made 3*d.* a mile to ride in all weathers, wrestling recalcitrant horses, negotiating roads in fatally bad repair and deferring to often spoiled or unreasonable customers. Some post-boys became so disenchanted with their occupation that they conspired with local highwaymen to rob their passengers; others simply drank to excess.

The ostler was the public equivalent of the stable boy. An employee of the local inn, he tended to the horses, whether hired or owned, that were brought in by travellers. In theory, he was supposed to feed, water and tend to the hot and weary animals; in practice, or at least in the published complaints of the day, he was all too often dishonest or lazy. Ostlers, it was claimed, gave the horses inferior fodder and pocketed the difference. Or, some claimed, they were asleep on the job, forcing the post-boys, coachmen or guards to do their work instead. Austen steers clear of these controversies. Her token ostler is 'old John Abdy's son ... head man at the Crown' (*E* 383) and struggling to make ends meet and maintain his invalid father. We know little about him, except that he seems to fill a variety of posts at the inn and that he appears to have one post-chaise available for rent (*E* 383). An ostler who, unlike Abdy, was hired by the publican would make most of his money from tips or 'vails'. Good ostlers were very much in demand and might move from one inn to another if they were offered better wages.

Carriage Costs

Though carriages seem to be everywhere in Austen's writing, they were actually rather uncommon in the England she inhabited. They were simply too expensive for most people to keep. It was not merely the expense of buying a carriage, though this was significant; a chariot for use in town cost about £91 in 1801. Nor was it the upkeep, though this, too, added up: there was the coachman's salary; fodder, shoeing and doctoring for the horses; maintenance of the coach; and perhaps additional wages for a groom or two. All these costs would have been daunting in themselves, but to them was added a burdensome and entirely new level of taxation. England's wars with France came at a cost, and one of the expedients to which the government resorted was a tax on private carriages.

Again and again in Austen's works, the keeping of one or more carriages is a measure of wealth. Mrs Bennet assesses the value of her daughters' marriages according to the sorts of jewels, clothes and carriages they will be able to afford (*P&P* 376, 378), while the sensible Elinor Dashwood laughs at Marianne's plans of keeping two carriages (*S&S* 91) and motivates their mother to sell their carriage because it will be too expensive to keep (*S&S* 12, 26). The Edwardses, in the incomplete novel *The Watsons*, are introduced as 'people of fortune who lived in the Town & kept their coach' (*Watsons*, *MW* 314), and Anne Steele assures Elinor Dashwood that her friends the Richardsons 'are very genteel people. He makes a monstrous deal of money, and they keep their own coach' (*S&S* 275). In *Emma*, the Jane Fairfax subplot turns at one point on a reference to the town's apothecary, Mr Perry, planning 'to set up his carriage'. The genial Mr Weston, hearing of it, remarks, 'I am glad he can afford it' (*E* 345), though, as it turns out, Mr Perry *cannot* afford it and abandons the plan. In such circumstances, when one of the leading citizens of Highbury has to dismiss keeping a carriage as too expensive, it is no wonder that the town is agog at Mrs Elton's brother-in-law, who keeps 'two carriages!' (*E* 183).

See also Barouche; Carts and Wagons; Chair; Chaise; Gig; Landau; Phaeton; Travel.

Carts and Wagons

Carriages and coaches were the glamorous vehicles of the Regency, but carts and wagons did the practical work of the nation. Along with canal barges and ocean-going ships, they hauled goods from one place to another, carried the heavy luggage that lumbered behind swiftly travelling upper-class tourists (*E* 186), brought in the harvest (*MP* 58), and made commercial deliveries within towns (*NA* 44; *P* 135). They were much more common than fine carriages, a fact that Mary Crawford notices without managing to grasp its significance (*MP* 58). Edmund Bertram understands; moving a harp is not necessary to the life of the nation, but getting in the harvest is, and for that the humble wagon trumps a phaeton or a barouche. For the English, nervous about revolution and dictatorship across the Channel, 'the heavy rumble of carts and drays' (*P* 135), noisy as it no doubt was, was the music of commerce.

Drays were exclusively commercial vehicles; they were two-wheeled vehicles without sides and often carried large barrels, for example, the barrels of brewers. Carts and wagons, however, might also carry passengers. Some small passenger vehicles were called carts, and there were larger, two-wheeled carts that were designed to carry people. Wagons had four wheels. When they carried hay or other produce, they were typically uncovered, but when they carried baggage or passengers, they were covered with arched, tubular cloth covering, making them look like the Conestoga wagons of the Old West. The passenger wagon, or 'Stage Waggon' (*F&E*, *MW* 10), was the humblest of public conveyances – crowded, slow, but cheap and less likely to be targeted by highwaymen. Its patrons were tolerated rather than welcomed when they stopped at an inn for the night, and contemporary engravings show passengers who look rather the worse for their long, bumpy trip.

See also Carriages and Coaches.

Chair

'Chair' is a problematic term in Austen's works because it means two different conveyances. One of these usages occurs only in the Juvenilia, the other in the novels, but readers unfamiliar with either meaning can find the use of the term confusing. In the Juvenilia, the word refers to a kind of simple, two-wheeled, springless carriage, similar to a gig.

By an 'italian Chair', Austen may mean specifically a kind of Italian gig or chair that had a seat for only one person; a seventeenth-century example of such a chair is in the collections of the Museums at Stony Brook, Long Island, New York. A 'chair' is also found in a more serious context in *The Watsons*. Here, a family so impoverished that it just barely manages the appearance of gentility keeps a chair as its only carriage. This 'convenient but very un-smart Family Equipage' (*Watsons*, *MW* 338) is driven either by a servant or by one of the Watson sisters and carries the girls to the nearest town to do their shopping and to go to balls. The most genteel of the Watsons, Emma, who has had an education superior to that of her sisters, is taken aback by the idea of travelling in such

Chair

a basic vehicle at night to a ball (*Watsons, MW* 319), and, to be sure, a low open carriage would have exposed its riders not only to possible bad weather but also to dirt flying up from the horse's hooves – not a very attractive prospect to a girl with a limited number of good ball gowns.

Despite its disadvantages, however, the chair was a popular vehicle in provincial towns. One variation, the 'rib chair', had a semicircular wooden seat connected to a semicircular upper rail by a row of small wooden rods. It was simple to make, cost only £12 to purchase, and, if the words 'taxed cart' were painted upon it, had only a 12s. annual tax levied on it, versus the £3, 17s. annual tax for fancier two-wheeled carriages. For a gentry family that simply wanted a quick, practical way to get from point A to point B, the attractions of the rib chair were obvious. Jane Austen's brother Edward, who as the wealthy owner of Godmersham could certainly afford any sort of carriage he wanted, owned a chair for just such purposes; on visits to Godmersham, Jane wrote of Edward taking another gentleman 'to Canterbury in the chair' and of going herself 'in the chair' to tour the Canterbury Gaol.

The other type of chair, the sedan chair (*NA* 24, 81, 96), was found in towns such as London and Bath and was both wheel-less and horseless. A descendant of the ancient and medieval litter, it was a vertical, enclosed, windowed box with a seat inside. The box was suspended from two poles that extended before and behind and were held by two 'chairmen'. These chairmen picked up the box and carried the passenger to her destination. Eighteenth-century Londoners, dismayed by the increasing size of the city, bemoaned the lot of the poor chairmen who had to convey heavy passengers through the ever-lengthening streets, and no doubt it was hard work. Austen's examples come not from London but from Bath, where, due to the town's steep hills, chairmen were also probably very weary by the end of their labours. Chairmen also worked in the rain, while their passengers sat in the closed box and stayed dry; in both *Persuasion* and *Northanger Abbey* there are references to keeping dry in a sedan chair (*P* 177; *NA* 83), though there would have been no protection for the chairmen in such cases.

In Bath, the chairmen, who wore blue coats, congregated mostly in the abbey churchyard, which Austen calls the pump-yard. However, it would have been possible on certain occasions to find a chair headed back to the centre of town after dropping off a passenger. In special circumstances, such as when concerts or plays let out, chairs would be waiting for fares outside the building, though there were fewer sedan chairs than theatregoers, and people had to wait their turn (*NA* 95). If one was on the street on one's own, it was perfectly acceptable to go in search of a chair (*P* 177), but at home, or anywhere else where servants were present, a servant would be sent on this errand (*P* 238).

See also Carriages and Coaches; Gig; Travel. For indoor chairs, *see* Furniture.

Chaise

The chaise* (*Clifford*, *MW* 43; *Lesley*, *MW* 110; *Cath*, *MW* 225; *NA* 163, 229, 233, 235; *S&S* 318, 354–355; *P&P* 152, 286; *E* 383; *P* 121) was a closed (*MP* 74), four-wheeled carriage that could be thought of as a half-coach. Whereas a coach had seats facing both front and back, each holding up to three passengers (*NA* 232), the chaise had only the forward-facing seat and thus accommodated only three (*P* 116). Admittedly, it was more comfortable for two; Parson James Woodforde remarked in his diary in 1785, after two people called for his niece in a post-chaise, that he 'did not like that Nancy should crowd into the Chaise with them and for no Purpose whatever'. However, because it did seat three, the chaise offers Austen a final chance to highlight the selfishness of Lucy Steele; Lucy could easily have taken her sister Anne away from London on her way to her honeymoon with Robert Ferrars, but instead she borrows or steals all of Anne's money, leaving the elder Miss Steele no way to hire a post-chaise of her own (*S&S* 370–371).

In most respects, including the number of passengers, the chaise was identical to a chariot, the chief difference being the location of the driver. In a chariot, the driver sat on a box, while a chaise had no box. A driver would ride one of the horses if there were two horses in harness, and postilions would ride the near wheeler and the near leader if there were four horses (*NA* 131, 212, 232; *Cath*, *MW* 213, 214; *P&P* 3; *P* 7). (The wheelers were the horses adjacent to the carriage wheels, while the leaders were the horses in front. The near horses were those on the left side if one were seated in the carriage facing forward, and the off horses were those on the right.) Four horses were not strictly necessary; however, four were preferable if either speed or show were desired (*P* 115). Thus, Elizabeth Elliot and Sir Walter are loath to part with two of their four carriage horses, not because they cannot do without them, but because they are used to going faster and looking richer (*P* 13, 35).

An extension in the back of the carriage held luggage (*P&P* 216) and additional servants. The disadvantage of the chaise versus the coach was the loss of passenger and baggage room. The advantage was additional speed, as the weight of passengers, baggage and the carriage itself was less. For this reason, it was the predominant choice of fashionable travellers, who either bought their own chaises (a typical model cost £93 in 1801) or hired them (as did Rowlandson). All in all, the chaise was a practical, yet not stodgy, vehicle; it seems appropriate that it is what the jovial, earthy, sensible Mrs Jennings uses (*S&S* 153, 341). It also seems to be the right vehicle for Mr Rushworth – straightforward, fashionable enough not to make him ashamed of it, yet not fashionable enough to

---

*Chaise was also, somewhat confusingly, a term applied to a large, one-horse, two-wheeled carriage with whip springs at the rear and elbow springs in front.

rival Henry Crawford's elegant barouche (*MP* 84, 203). Mr Bingley, too, a man of good nature and few pretensions, owns a chaise (*P&P* 30, 34).

There was some overlap in how the terms 'post' and 'chaise' were used. The hired or 'hack' chaise (*Sand, MW* 414, 420; *P&P* 19; *MP* 377), which came with its own staff to drive and manage the horses, was usually called a post-chaise (*F&E, MW* 8; *NA* 232; *S&S* 218; *Watsons, MW* 355). This kind of conveyance could frequently be hired at an inn (*P* 114). 'Post' (*S&S* 65) or 'travelling post' (*MP* 266, 372) was a somewhat more general term; it meant travelling with control over the route and stops, rather than in a public stagecoach or hackney coach, and stopping as necessary to exchange horses; this could take place in any kind of carriage, attended by one's own servants or by rented ones (*L&F, MW* 90). Thus, a privately owned chaise could also be called a post-chaise (*MP* 74) if it were used for posting. Henry Crawford, for example, travels post in his own carriage (*MP* 266).

Whether the servants were one's own or hired for the journey, a driver of some kind was a necessity. The chaise was not the sort of fashionable carriage driven by the gentry for fun. Therefore, in Austen's youthful work *Catharine or the Bower*, we are meant to find it funny that 'a Gentleman [arrives] in a Chaise & 4', but 'he has not a single servant with him, and came with hack [i.e. rented] horses' (*Cath, MW* 214). The superiority of the private post-chaise to the hackney coach, a cheaper public vehicle, also provides the alert reader with another clue to Lydia Bennet's imminent ruin, for in Clapham Wickham removes her 'into a hackney-coach and dismisse[s] the chaise that brought them from Epsom' (*P&P* 274, 282).

See also Carriages and Coaches; Travel.

Clergy

The Church of England was governed, in name at least, by the king. Below him stood the two archbishops, the archbishop of Canterbury and the archbishop of York and twenty-seven English and Welsh bishops (*Cath, MW* 203, 206). Then came archdeacons and deacons and then, finally, the numerous parish clergy (*Curate, MW* 73–74; *Cath, MW* 193; *Watsons, MW* 329; *Sand, MW* 401; *NA* 30; *S&S* 102, 296; *P&P* 101, 200–201; *MP* 21, 30, 91–92, 93, 145, 289), called parsons or priests, with whom Austen mostly concerns herself. These were divided into three classes: rectors, vicars and curates. The difference between them was not their duties but their source of income.

Income
Tithes (*Plan, MW* 429, 430; *S&S* 293, 368; *P&P* 101) were a percentage of produce, typically 10 percent, paid in specified instalments by the local farmers to the parson. The great tithe included grain, and the small tithe

included livestock and vegetables. The difference between rectors and vicars was that rectors (*F&E, MW* 5; *P&P* 101, 364; *P* 78) received both the great and small tithes, while vicars (*E* 21, 66) were entitled to the small tithe only (*E* 35). A curate (*Visit, MW* 49; *Curate, MW* 73–74; *Cath, MW* 203; *Plan, MW* 428; *NA* 221; *S&S* 61, 273, 275; *MP* 110; *P* 23, 73, 76, 78, 103) received no tithe at all. He was paid either by the legitimate holder of the 'living' (the job of caring for a particular parish – see *Cath, MW* 203; *NA* 135; *P&P* 328; *MP* 3, 109, 241) or else by a layman whose ancestors had managed to secure the right to the tithes for themselves. These 'lay impropriators' were far from being a majority, but by one estimate, in 1836 they held 20 percent of the tithes collected. They tended to favour the more lucrative great tithes, holding these in perhaps as many as 50 percent of parishes and making them, technically, the rectors of the affected parishes. Some impropriators were clergymen and did the duties of the parish; most, however, hired a vicar or curate to do the duties for them.

So far, this seems fairly straightforward, yet nothing was perfectly simple or uniform in Georgian England. Agreements made decades or even centuries before could complicate the payment of tithes in a particular parish. Some farmers or parishes had made arrangements to pay a fixed sum, called a modus, instead of a tithe, which kept the accounting somewhat simpler. In many cases, however, it merely shifted the complexity of tithe collection by forcing the parson to tally hens instead of eggs or pennies instead of pigeons.

A modus was a source of grief to the parson in prosperous years and to the farmer in lean years. Some farmers chose to make a composition instead of a tithe; this was similar to a modus and had the same advantages and disadvantages but was calculated by the acre. In some parishes, the clergy had agreed to accept 'commutation', a gift in exchange for tithes, often presented either as a sum of cash or as a plot of land to be farmed by the parson himself. Even in areas where the 10 percent tithe was the norm, certain types of land were exempted from tithes.*

Tithes could be collected either as cash or as a percentage of the actual produce of each farm. The latter method was referred to as 'tithing in kind' and served as the subject matter for a popular print, occasionally dusted off and reissued during Jane Austen's lifetime. Entitled *Tithing in Kind*, or a variation on that title, it showed a fat parson running from a grinning farmer who was making his tithe payment with exactly one-tenth of an angry swarm of bees. Tithing in kind had been replaced in many places by tithes in cash, but it was still common in many English counties in the 1790s, including Cheshire, Lancashire, Durham, Shropshire, Berkshire,

---

*Exempt lands included barren land; crown forests; land tithe-free since 'time immemorial' (which, in legal terms, meant since 1189); land owned before 1215 by Cistercians, Templars or Hospitallers; land owned tithe-free at the Dissolution of Catholic institutions by Henry VIII; and the parson's own glebe.

Clergy

Buckinghamshire, Kent, Surrey, Wiltshire, Somerset, Cumberland, Westmorland and Austen's own Hampshire.

A large amount of time was spent by parsons in calculating tithes, collecting them and storing the produce in the case of tithes in kind. Farmers did not necessarily make the process any easier. They were not especially eager to offer the fruits of their labours, and some went out of their way to make collection more difficult, specifying inconvenient times for pickup or requiring that the parson collect ridiculously small amounts at frequent intervals. Others simply lied about how many animals they had or how good the harvest had been; a parson needed to be vigilant, and the more vigilance he exercised, the greater the local resentment grew (*Cath*, *MW* 195). Farmers who invested in improvements to their land felt cheated as well, because it seemed to them that they were working hard to enrich the parson. Constant negotiation and a careful assessment of how many years each composition agreement should last were necessary to make the system run smoothly.

Commutation was extremely popular with the clergy, as it accelerated their rise among the gentry. It was also a common solution to the tithe problem in Austen's time, because many communities opted for the enclosure of common land. Since parsons typically had a stake in the use of common land, their consent was usually required for the passage of an enclosure act. Their support was therefore purchased by a gift of land, written into the enclosure act. Commutation, however, did not solve all the problems of tithe collection, for enclosure did not always affect the whole parish.

A particular clergyman's income (*Curate*, *MW* 73) was affected by tithe arrangements, by the number of arable acres in his parish, and by the fertility of the local soil (*S&S* 368). Income could also depend on the number of parishioners he served. In many cases he received a small payment per parishioner, and he could also augment his income by means of 'surplice fees', fees paid for his services at marriages, christenings and funerals.

Total incomes varied widely, with many clergymen falling below what most gentry families would have thought of as the poverty line. Elinor Dashwood rejected out of hand the idea of living on a mere £350 a year, but in 1802, an estimated 1,000 livings (out of a total of about 12,000) earned their incumbents less than £100 a year, while another 3,000 brought incomes of £100 to £150. Curates, in some regions, could earn as much as £75 per year, but most scraped by on about £35 to £50 in the 1790s. Austen's brother Henry, after a free-spending life as a militia officer and banker, was reduced to a curacy in his later life and in 1818 had an income of only £54 12s. William Jones, a curate with nine children, never made more than £60 a year from his curacy at Broxbourne. Some parsons who hired curates allowed these poor fellows to keep the Easter offerings or the surplice fees, but this never amounted to very much. Many curates, along with the rectors and vicars of inconsequential parishes, were forced to teach school in order to make ends meet; Austen's father, though his income was quite respectable, took in pupils (at £35 to £65 per year each) to pay for the upbringing of his eight children.

Clergymen faced a unique set of social and financial pressures as they neared retirement. Unless they had managed to save a substantial sum over the years, they could not hope for any sort of retirement in the conventional sense. Curates could not hope to retire at all, and rectors and vicars could retire only by subcontracting their jobs to others (*P* 78, 103). Parson Woodforde, for example, when he became too infirm to perform his duties, hired a curate for £30 plus surplice fees, a fraction of the amount of the parish tithes. Austen's father (*Mystery, MW* 55) did the same, hiring his eldest son, James, as a curate for Steventon and retiring for a few years on the difference between the income of his living and the £50 he paid James. For any elderly cleric, there was always an uncomfortable awareness that someone – the patron of the living, a young and ambitious divinity student, perhaps even his own son or nephew – was calculating, consciously or subconsciously, how much longer it would be until the living was vacant, in other words, until the current incumbent died (*MP* 473). A shortage of available livings, especially good livings, meant that the sharks were always circling. Once a clergyman died, his widow and children had to leave the parsonage and yield it to the next incumbent, which often meant real hardship (*Cath, MW* 194–195, 203).

Efforts were made from time to time to improve this situation. Queen Anne had, early in the eighteenth century, introduced a program to purchase land to augment the poorest livings. It was a successful initiative, but it was able to assist only a portion of those clergymen who needed help. The gap between the bottom of the scale, represented by men making less than the average member of Parliament's upper servants, and the top of the scale, represented by the archbishop of Canterbury's £7,000 a year, was huge.

Parsonage and Glebe

The value and comfort of a living depended to a great extent on the property that came with it. This property, which was held only for the lifetime of the incumbent and could not be willed to his heirs, consisted of the parsonage and the glebe. The parsonage* (*F&E, MW* 5; *S&S* 296; *P&P* 88, 155, 172; *MP* 8, 23, 82, 205, 222, 241) was provided by the parish, but there was no guarantee as to the quality of the building or the attractiveness of its furnishings. Its upkeep, moreover, was the responsibility of the incumbent (*P&P* 101), and if he allowed it to fall into disrepair, his heirs could be sued by the next tenant for 'dilapidations' (*MP* 55).

---

*A parsonage occupied by a rector was a rectory (*S&S* 282; *P&P* 63); if inhabited by a vicar, it was known as a vicarage (*E* 113, 280, 305, 455).

However, if he did not live in the parsonage to begin with, an incumbent was extremely unlikely to spend money to repair it, and this perfectly understandable reluctance led to the worst parsonages falling deeper and deeper into disrepair. Worse still, as late as the nineteenth century, an estimated 3,000 parishes had no parsonage at all.

Austen was certainly acquainted with parsonages at all points in the spectrum (*MP* 242–243). The parsonage at Deane, her father's first parish, had uneven floors and ceilings so low that they prevented tall people from standing up straight (*S&S* 292). Henry Austen's Chawton parsonage was considered 'exceedingly bad' in 1796. Steventon parsonage, in which Jane was brought up, was somewhat better, with an attractive, if simple, façade, two parlours, a study, seven ordinary bedrooms and three attic bedrooms. Yet James Edward Austen-Leigh, Jane's nephew, thought the kitchen and the servants' quarters entirely inadequate and the walls and ceilings unfashionably bare. The building was eventually demolished, some years after Jane's death, when her brother Edward built a better parsonage with the hope of installing one of his sons there. Other friends and relatives of the Austens had better parsonages (*NA* 175–176; *P&P* 328; *E* 204); the rectory at Wrotham and the parsonage at Ashe, for example, were elegant houses.

Some parsons remodelled their houses to suit their own tastes (*S&S* 372, 374; *MP* 241–242), putting up wallpaper, planting extensive gardens and even building bowling greens. Others moved into quarters they liked better and let the parsonage remain empty. Most clergymen liked to live near the local squire or lord of the manor (*S&S* 197, 290; *MP* 82), and, in cases where the magnates had moved away from the village or town, a parsonage was sometimes built near the large country houses rather than near the church.

The glebe (*S&S* 368), like the parsonage, was an important aspect of any living. The glebe was land affiliated with the living that could be farmed by the parson. The Steventon glebe was fairly small, only three acres, but George Austen also rented 200 acres at Cheesedown and was able to add as much as 50 percent to the value of his living by farming this land. Many parsons were forced to do likewise, as the glebe was often too small to be very useful; others simply gave up and rented the glebe to someone else with adjacent lands. Legislative efforts were made to improve the situation. A 1776 Act of Parliament allowed parsons to take out government loans to add to the glebe, and an 1802 act struck down a centuries-old statute that barred clergy from renting the glebe to others, the latter law a ratification of a practice already widely adopted. Enclosure also enabled many to add to the glebe.

Church and Vestry

Though the parsonage and the glebe were the clergyman's responsibility, the upkeep of the church (*Watsons*, *MW* 321, 350; *S&S* 273, 374; *P&P* 319; *MP* 82, 86, 203, 241; *E* 204) and churchyard (*NA* 178) was the duty of the parish, as represented by the vestry, or governing body (*E* 455). An annual meeting of the vestry was held anytime within a month of Easter and, with a greater or lesser degree of contentiousness, depending on the mood of the parish, elected overseers of the poor, made a report to the local magistrates, and levied taxes as necessary to maintain the church. Membership in the vestry and thus the right to attend this meeting were typically extended to all landowners and to the incumbent priest or his delegate, who presided over the parish meeting.

In theory, the vestry was responsible for all parts of the church except the chancel. This included the pews (*E* 175, 270), roof, font, pulpit (*MP* 93, 341), altar (*P&P* 107) and such basic supplies as Bible, prayer book and communion vessels. In practice, there were complaints that churches and their property were in poor repair. William Cowper complained that too many churches had 'scarce any other roof than the ivy'. A number of churches, including the little church at Steventon, were quite old, with plain windows, no heating and perhaps some rushes on the floors. The walls and floors of some churches were decorated with carved plaques in honour of deceased local dignitaries; a monument of this type would eventually be placed in Winchester Cathedral in memory of Jane Austen herself and can still be seen there today.

Education and Job Placement

In order to join the clergy, it was necessary for a young man to complete a course of study at one of the universities (*P&P* 79, 200). This automatically eliminated most poor boys, though the majority of candidates appear not to have come from the gentry and aristocracy. Over the course of the eighteenth century, the number of upper-class clergy increased, but it was still only perhaps 20 percent by Austen's time. Austen's writings tend to leave the impression that all clergymen were born gentlemen, but this was not in fact the case, and for many families, putting a son into the clergy was a way of rising in social status.

There were general trends in university matriculation. Southern parishes tended to favour Oxford graduates, for example. Patrons with an Evangelical bent might choose a candidate from Cambridge, where the Evangelical movement was especially strong. Austen's family were of the Oxford camp; Mr Austen, James and Henry all attended St. John's College, Oxford, which one of the family forebears had founded. As 'founder's kin' they all received scholarships. The university education might begin at quite an early age – James Austen enrolled at age fourteen – although ordination (*L&F*, *MW* 82) could not take place until the age of twenty-three. The studies were not especially arduous, nor was the process of ordination (*S&S* 274, 275, 291; *P&P* 62, 200; *MP* 89, 255, 341), which in many cases was a mere formality. The requirements for ordination were a university degree, a testimonial from the candidate's college and a brief examination by a bishop. Ben Lefroy, who married one of Jane's nieces and was ordained in 1817, was asked no questions about Scripture or the liturgy, but only whether he knew Jane's father, whom the bishop in question remembered from years past.

The ordination over, newly minted clergymen began the really difficult work of finding a living. In some cases, this was no more work than Ben Lefroy's ordination had been. Wealthy family members might save a living for a worthy relative, installing a curate in the post until the prospective candidate was of age (*P&P* 79; *P* 217). This appears to be the plan followed by Sir Thomas Bertram in *Mansfield Park* (23, 109), but financial pressures force him to yield one of the two livings being saved for his son Edmund. He gives up the living of Mansfield to an incumbent in exchange for a cash payment; this was a common practice, and landowners and clergymen alike were well aware of the going rates for a living (*S&S* 294–295; *MP* 23). The owners of advowsons (rights to employ clergy for particular benefices) based the price on both the value of the living and the life expectancy of the current incumbent. Sir Thomas, like Colonel Brandon in *Sense and Sensibility*, need not worry about a current incumbent and can sell the occupancy of the living at a good price.*

Those who could not get a living right away tried to settle for a curacy, but there was a glut of applicants for these posts as well. Those with relatives or friends among the senior clergy might apply for curacies in their parishes (*S&S* 275); those with indirect influence exerted it (*S&S* 149; *MP* 109; *P* 76); the rest advertised for posts in magazines and newspapers. Those who failed to find anything resorted to teaching school or to poorly paid naval chaplaincies (*Harley, MW* 40; *MP* 111). Everyone, even those already gifted with a living, scrambled to ingratiate themselves with the people who could provide a benefice, a second benefice or a better benefice (*P&P* 169). These patrons were of various types.

There were, in the middle and later years of Jane Austen's life, about 11,600 livings available, spread through 10,500 parishes and staffed by as many as 15,000 clergymen of all ranks. About 2,500 of these livings were in the gift of church patrons, such as bishops (*Cath, MW* 206; *P* 76). Another 600 or so could be distributed by the universities and the prominent public schools; these went primarily to masters and fellows of the various institutions and were generally awarded by election after a competitive debate between rival candidates. The crown owned about 1,100 livings, which were given out to political supporters and their relatives by the prime minister. Most of the remaining livings, about 5,500, were in the gift of private landowners (*S&S* 149, 282–283, 289; *P&P* 79) who either sold the posts or gave them away to friends and relatives. On occasion, a landowner who was himself ordained might

---

*The right to hire the next incumbents of both Deane and Ashe were purchased by Mr Austen's uncle Francis Austen in 1770; Deane was awarded to Jane's father, George Austen, and Francis resold the presentation of Ashe to another, who installed George Lefroy in the post.

take the post himself, keeping the tithes and hiring a curate to perform the day-to-day duties. More rarely, the landed occupant performed the duty himself (*NA* 135).

There was constant pressure to please one's patron (*P&P* 383), both because parson and patron often lived in the same village and because there was always the hope of something better. Tom Fowle, a former pupil of George Austen's, became engaged to Jane's sister Cassandra while holding a small living at Allington, Wiltshire. He had hopes of a better living from his patron, Lord Craven, and to please his lordship, signed on as chaplain on a naval expedition that Craven was sending to the West Indies. While on his mission, Fowle died of yellow fever, a casualty of the race for a better post. Few paid so high a price, but all sought rich livings and prestigious appointments, such as cathedral 'stalls' (positions as canons, who cared for the cathedral and elected its bishop – see *MP* 469).

Austen's Clerical Connections

Austen's familiarity with the clergy was not limited to Tom Fowle, her father and her brothers. She had too many relatives and acquaintances in the profession to name, but they included Mr Lloyd of Ibthorpe, two of whose daughters married Austen sons; Samuel Blackall, who showed matrimonial interest in Jane; Jane's godfather Samuel Cooke, the husband of one of her mother's cousins; Thomas Leigh, another of her mother's cousins; George Moore, eldest son of the archbishop of Canterbury and a relative of Edward Austen's by marriage; and John Rawstone Papillon, vicar of Chawton, whom Jane joked about marrying when she moved into the neighbourhood:

> I am very much obliged to Mrs Knight [Edward's mother-in-law] for such a proof of the interest she takes in me – & she may depend upon it, that I will marry Mr Papillon, whatever may be his reluctance or my own.

There were Ben Lefroy, the neighbour whom Anna Austen, James' daughter, married, and Michael Terry, another clergyman to whom Anna was briefly engaged. Jane's friend Catherine Bigg married a clergyman, Herbert Hill of Streatham. She had ample opportunity, in other words, to observe the habits and foibles of a number of clergymen, which is undoubtedly why so many of them appear in her works and why she takes such an unsentimental view of their habits.

She found many of them to be exceedingly dreary. Her cousin Edward Cooper had too much of an Evangelical bent, in her opinion, and she was much amused, or provoked, or both, by the pretensions of James Stanier Clarke, a naval chaplain who was patronised by the Prince of Wales and, on the prince's behalf, escorted Jane on a tour of the Carlton House library. Thereafter, he pestered her to write a book according to his own suggestions; suggestions that made it clear that the book he had in mind was a fictionalised biography of himself:

> Do let us have an English Clergyman after *your* fancy – much novelty may be introduced – shew dear Madam what good would be done if Tythes were taken away entirely, and describe him burying his own mother – as I did – because the High Priest of the Parish in which she died – did not pay her remains the respect he ought to do. I have never recovered the Shock. Carry your Clergyman to Sea as the Friend of some distinguished Naval Character about a Court – you can then bring foreward ... many interesting Scenes of Character & Interest.

Austen demurred, whereupon he urged her to write a 'historical Romance illustrative of the History of the august house of Cobourg', and she again politely refused. Afterwards, she mocked him privately in her *Plan of a Novel, according to Hints from Various Quarters*, in which the virtuous father describes his life in a long aside to his daughter, detailing his adventures in an almost word-for-word repetition of Clarke's ridiculous outline (*Plan, MW* 429). Clarke's flattery of her, combined with his absolute failure to understand the nature of her work, is the sort of unwittingly revealing juxtaposition so often used to illuminate Austen's fictional clergymen.

Clerical Duties

Austen offers allusions to, rather than detailed descriptions of, the professional duties (*MP* 248–249, 394) of clergymen, but her readers should not therefore assume that a parson's time was entirely taken up in hunting, riding and eating large dinners. True, parsons enjoyed a good deal of leisure in comparison to artisans or day labourers, and their enthusiasm for good food was considered axiomatic (*MP* 110, 111, 469), but they were not idle. Bishops – not all of them as lax as the one who interrogated Ben Lefroy – conducted ordinations (*S&S* 275), sat in Parliament, and were nominally responsible for the parochial 'visitations' that were supposed to ensure compliance with church rules. Archdeacons took on most of the actual duties of these visitations, and deacons, just coming into a period of great activity in the second decade of the nineteenth century, made inspections of church repairs, schools, charities and so on, reporting on their findings to the bishops.

Parish priests were supposed to offer both a morning (*P&P* 60) and an evening service (*NA* 190) each Sunday, though this schedule was routinely adhered to in only about half of all parishes. This, however, was not necessarily the fault of the clergy. There is some evidence that the clergy were merely acceding to the wish of the people, many of whom appear to have been content with one service. In some cases, it was a matter of necessity; pluralists with closely spaced parishes often tried to do the duty in both, which meant a morning service in one parish and an evening service in the other. Communion was offered once a month by a few scrupulous parsons, usually in the north and west, but most parsons offered it only the required minimum of three times a year: at Easter, at Christmas and once more at their discretion, usually with at least a week's notice.

The parson's most important duty, if public enthusiasm is to be believed, was his Sunday sermon (*P&P* 66, 328; *MP* 226, 227, 249, 341; *E* 75). Parishioners loved to hear good preaching (*MP* 93, 340–341), and they were disappointed if the parson failed to preach on a particular Sunday, or if he preached badly. They would at times travel to a different parish to hear an especially good speaker or to hear any preaching at all if they knew in advance that there would be no sermon that day at their own parish church. Parsons were given extra credit in the public mind if they wrote their own sermons (*P&P* 101; *MP* 92); it was not exactly considered cheating to use one of the many books of prewritten sermons, such as those written by Scottish rhetoric professor Hugh Blair (*MP* 92) or Jane's own cousin Edward Cooper, but neither was it considered laudable. The rabble-rousing enthusiasm of later preachers was viewed with suspicion in Austen's time; instead, formality, audibility and sincerity of expression were prized (*Watsons*, *MW* 343–344).

Clergymen were also expected to officiate at the rites of passage of the community. They baptised newborn children (*P&P* 64), sometimes publicly, sometimes privately in the parents' home. This was done right away in the case of sickly infants but was sometimes delayed for healthier children, to allow far-flung godparents (*NA* 63; *P&P* 79, 199; *MP* 387; *P* 6) time to arrive for the ceremony. Austen herself, who was born in December, was not christened (*E* 79) until the following April, as the guests were not expected to travel in the unusually harsh winter of 1775–1776. Shortly after the baptism, the mother was 'churched', which meant she was symbolically reintroduced to the full community as she gave thanks for her safe deliverance from the potential dangers of childbearing. Churchings and most christenings, along with weddings (*S&S* 296; *P&P* 64; *MP* 89; *E* 482–483), could be scheduled in advance, but deaths might occur at any time, and funerals (*P&P* 64) and emergency baptisms required clergymen to be flexible about their schedules. A clergyman may be seen officiating at a wedding in the illustration *The Wedding* (Marriage).

When they were not composing sermons, conducting services or performing ceremonial duties, clergymen taught children the catechism and visited the sick (*P* 20). Once a year, often at Shrovetide, they administered communion to those too sick to leave their beds. Some parsons also held weekday services and officiated at special occasions, such as services of thanksgiving on patriotic holidays. Increasingly, parsons were also serving as justices of the peace, though they were a minority on the bench. They might be consulted on questions of religion or on issues of public importance, and they were often

Clergy

asked to lend credibility to some new venture by their presence
or participation.

Clergymen sometimes assisted each other in their duties. They took
turns, for example, helping each other to perform sick communion, and
they might step in for a neighbouring priest in an emergency (*P&P* 63).
James Woodforde noted on 25 March 1785, that Mr Mattishall, a nearby
parson, was 'very ill' and that he had accordingly agreed to handle
Mattishall's Easter Sunday evening service. Parsons who intended
to preach a sermon on a particular Sunday also consulted with the
clergy in neighbouring parishes, trying to make sure that no one's
sermon conflicted with anyone else's, so that the populace could
attend more than one sermon in a single day.

See also Parish.

Clocks and Watches

Clocks (*Cath*, *MW* 218; *Watsons*, *MW* 322, 359; *NA* 83, 189, 193; *P&P* 33;
E 189) took many forms. There were longcase clocks of mahogany or oak,
the kinds of pendulum clocks often called grandfather clocks today. On
these clocks, as on most clocks and watches of the time, the hours were
marked in Roman numerals, with 'IIII' replacing the correct 'IV' because
it seemed more aesthetically harmonious with the 'VIII' on the opposite
side. Minutes were typically marked in Arabic numerals and might
appear on a concentric circle with the hours, or as a completely separate
ring. From the mid-eighteenth century, the trend was towards minute and
hour hands of matching style. Seconds, which had not been of any concern
in previous centuries, were now considered important enough to merit a
dial or ring of their own. The roughly triangular areas between the round
dial and the square edges of the case were the 'spandrels', and they were
usually made of sand-cast brass and gilded. Typical designs included
cherubs' faces, flowers or depictions of the four seasons.

Minutes, hours and seconds were not the only features tracked on
elaborate longcase clocks. Some of these clocks had dials that told the
calendar date or the phases of the moon. Others indicated the state of tides
or the position of the sun in the zodiac.

Some clocks were designed to stand on tables or fireplace mantels
(*P* 144); originally built with square dials, they might have round dials
instead from about the mid-eighteenth century. The dial was protected
by a hinged glass door that could be opened to reset the clock by manually
adjusting the position of the hands. Wall clocks were out of favour for
much of the eighteenth century but became fashionable again, in round
or octagonal forms, at the beginning of the nineteenth. One especially
characteristic type of wall clock was the tavern clock, which appears in
many prints and paintings of the day. It had an exceptionally large dial,

sometimes as much as 2 or 3 feet in diameter, and had a minute hand, an hour hand and a pendulum to mark the seconds. Tavern clocks came into their own from 1797 to 1798, when Prime Minster Pitt imposed a tax of 5s. a year on watches and clocks – 10s. for gold watches – that induced some people to relinquish their watches and keep time by occasional peeks into the local tavern. A device that increased foot traffic so effectively was naturally popular with tavern keepers, who prized their 'Act of Parliament' clocks and competed to have the handsomest and most accurate clock in town.

Watches (*NA* 45, 67, 155, 162, 165, 171; *MP* 95, 218, 279; *E* 246) were 'pocket' watches, although they were not always kept in the little watch pockets that formed a feature of many waistcoats. Many were worn suspended from belts or sashes, so that their beautifully ornamented covers could be admired by acquaintances and passers-by. Like clocks, they might well have separate dials for minutes, hours and seconds. Inside the cover, the owner might place a 'watch paper' – a decorative cloth or paper lining.

Clothing

The clothing (*E&E*, *MW* 30; *L&F*, *MW* 107; *Cath*, *MW* 198; *Sand*, *MW* 421; *NA* 20, 33, 216; *S&S* 119; *P&P* 160–161, 222, 376; *MP* 14, 282–283, 444; *E* 321; *P* 43, 142–143) of Jane Austen's childhood was much as it had been throughout the eighteenth century. For women, this meant voluminous silk dresses, open at the front to reveal ornate matching petticoats; tall, powdered clouds of hair; low bodices with the exposed flesh covered by lightweight bits of fabric called handkerchiefs, fichus or modesty pieces. For men, this meant heeled shoes and white stockings; powdered wigs in a bewildering assortment of styles; and a three-piece suit of knee breeches, knee-length, full-skirted frock coat and waistcoat (vest), with all three pieces often made of the same fabric. By the time she began publishing her novels in 1813, fashion was entirely different, and only the most old-fashioned people, usually elderly men, wore anything like the styles they had worn thirty years before.

Men's Clothing

Men's clothing began to evolve in the 1790s in response to three enthusiasms. One of these was vogue for classical literature, art and architecture, which led men to adopt Roman-style short haircuts and fashions that echoed the lines of Greek statuary. A second was sympathy for the egalitarian sentiments of the French Revolution – not a common sentiment in England but quite common in France, which developed simpler Republican styles of dress designed to bridge the differences between the classes; these fashions then crossed the Channel and influenced English costume. The third was an interest in hunting and equestrian sports, which in some men bordered on obsession. These gentlemen had taken to wearing their informal shooting jackets (*S&S* 43; *MP* 138–139) and high-top boots almost everywhere, and their example was imitated by men who longed, even indoors, for the comfort of hunting attire.

In response to these influences, both the colour and cut of men's clothes changed. Parsons still continued, for the most part, to wear black, and some men persisted in wearing old-fashioned bright colours (*F&E*, *MW* 8; *J&A*, *MW* 13), but most men shifted their allegiance from suits all of one colour (or from those where the breeches and coat, at least, matched) to a coat (*Cath*, *MW* 222; *Watsons*, *MW* 353, 445; *S&S* 86; *P* 49) of one colour, breeches (*NA* 172) of another and waistcoat (*L&F*, *MW* 98, 445; *NA* 172; *S&S* 38, 378) of still another. The frock coat was usually blue (*F&E*, *MW* 8; *P&P* 9, 319) or black, double-breasted, with large buttons, only the bottom few of which were fastened. The remainder were left undone so that an increasingly large expanse of white could be seen at the throat: white shirt, white waistcoat and white cravat. Then buff or black breeches and boots or shoes and stockings completed the picture. The breeches were replete with buttons. They fastened in front with a vertical row of buttons, with a small horizontal flap at the bottom of this fly fixed in place by two or three more buttons. Then there were buttons at each knee, on the outside of the leg.

As the new style evolved, both the coat and the breeches underwent additional refinements. Knee breeches and boots, for example, were a poor match; there was always just a little bit of boot stocking showing between the two. One solution, adopted around 1800, was to add short gaiters to the tops of the boots, allowing them to be buttoned above the knee. A more common solution was to extend the breeches well below the knee so that their bottoms were entirely hidden by the boots. From this move it was just a short step to pantaloons, tight-fitting trousers that were made of stockinette (a knitted fabric) or doeskin. Some of these pantaloons were so tight-fitting, in fact, that they had to be worn with a lining in their upper part to prevent young ladies from getting a premature education in male anatomy. A fashion for somewhat lower boots lengthened the line of the leg, and the buff colour enhanced the illusion of classical nudity. Later in Austen's lifetime, black pantaloons became increasingly popular, a trend that was to lead to the sober three-piece suits of the Victorian era.

The frock coat lost its voluminous skirts and, like the pants, hugged the body. It was cut either straight across or with a curve, frequently exposing the bottom of the waistcoat, and cut away sharply to the side and back. A little coattail was left on the sides of the body, but not much. The lapels and collar off the coat gradually expanded, focusing attention on the cascades of white linen at the throat and chest, and the collar was stood up a bit in back.

There were, of course, exceptions to this pattern of dress. Old men stuck to the comfortable, roomy coats they had known in their youth. Some younger men favoured buff waistcoats rather than white, or single-breasted coats rather than double-breasted. Evening dress, worn from dinner on, was always different and far more formal (*Watsons*, *MW* 327, 357; *E* 114; *P* 55, 99).

The standard outer garment for men was the greatcoat (*Watsons*, *MW* 356; *Sand*, *MW* 407; *NA* 83, 131, 155, 210; *E* 58; *P* 106). This, unlike the frock coat, did not shrink appreciably in size. It remained a large, comparatively shapeless garment and was worn at any time when an additional layer was deemed necessary for warmth or protection from rain. Coachmen favoured a style that had multi-layered capes below the lapels, and for a time in the late 1790s this was adopted by fashionable men as well (*NA* 157). The court, however, and the prince regent's arbiter of sartorial taste, George Bryan 'Beau' Brummell, rejected the coachman's greatcoat.

Shirts (*NA* 172) were relatively plain around the turn of the century, reacquiring ruffles in about 1806 for evening wear. Daytime shirts remained plain, and more and more of the shirt began to show in the gap between cravat and coat. The other principal item of underwear was drawers, long and sometimes footed when worn with pantaloons, knee-length or just above when worn with breeches. They buttoned down the front and sometimes had tapes or strings in the back to perfect the fit. The pantaloons themselves were held up with leather braces (suspenders), which came into common use around 1800. The cravat (*NA* 28, 172, 240) or neckcloth was a square of clean white linen, at least 40 to 45 inches square. It was folded in half diagonally. The folded edge was placed around the throat, near the chin or sometimes, to judge from some illustrations, up around the ears. This left a deep triangle to be tucked into the shirt and two loose ends, which were wrapped around the back of the neck and brought to the front again, where they were tied together in a variety of patterns. Some had discreet little knots, while others produced waterfalls of puffs and folds. The tying and arranging of the ends were the tricky part. The cravat was often stiffly starched, making it rub uncomfortably against the throat and jowls, and a man in a properly tied cravat was almost incapable of moving his head. To look around, he had to swivel his whole upper body.

At night men wore long, baggy linen nightshirts and sometimes caps as well. When they lounged around indoors, they might wear a dressing gown – a loose, long, comfortable garment with a shawl collar – in place of the frock coat. This could serve as a general-purpose indoor garment and could also be worn to protect the clothes during the powdering of hair (*P&P* 300).

Women's Clothing

Women's clothing (*P* 215), like men's, underwent a process of streamlining and simplification. The 1780s and early 1790s had featured full, round

Clothing

skirts, slightly puffed out at the back, though not sporting the wide panniers that had spread the skirt far to the sides in the middle of the eighteenth century. As if to compensate for the bulge behind, generously sized fichus had covered the bosom, puffing out in front. As France's Republican and classical styles spread across the Channel, however, the bulk of the skirt gradually diminished; it took ten yards to make a dress in 1796, but only seven yards in 1801, when Jane asked Cassandra to buy 'Seven yards for my mother, seven yards and a half for me' to make dresses. The number of supporting petticoats (*E* 225) diminished, too, until some women were wearing only one, or even none at all (to the scandal and shock of moralists and the secret delight of lascivious men). In the fashions of earlier decades, the petticoat had been a prominent part of the dress, highly decorative and so visible between the folds of an 'open robe' – a dress that parted in the front – that it often appeared to be part of the dress itself. Now the petticoat retreated under the gown (*P&P* 36), and even gowns that still opened in the front wrapped completely and fastened in place. Now the petticoat, if it showed at all, showed only as an ornamental band at the bottom of the dress.

In addition to the petticoat, many women now took to wearing drawers. These were quite long – long enough that Lady de Clifford pointed out

3. *Progress of the Toilet – The Stays*, James Gillray, 1810.

to Princess Charlotte that hers were visible every time she got into or out of a carriage. Unimpressed, the princess replied, 'the Duchess of Bedford's are much longer, and they are bordered with Brussels lace.' There was, as the princess implied, little effort taken to hide the drawers, which came into fashion around 1806.

Above the petticoat, a chemise was worn. This was a knee-length linen or cotton shirt, often with a frill of some kind at the neckline and short sleeves. It was usually, but not always, worn beneath a dress. If it were worn, part of it, for example, the decorative neckline, often peeked from underneath the dress.

As the silhouette slimmed, the waistline rose, until it ended just under the breasts. The dress itself was rather loose and was pulled into classical folds of drapery, often by tightening drawstrings at the neckline and artificial waistline. Beneath this apparent ease and lightness, many women retained the stays they had worn for centuries. These were corsets made of heavy cotton fabric or silk and stiffened with whalebone. They were sometimes assisted in front with a 'divorce', a triangular piece of padded metal that separated the breasts. Their height fluctuated from short to long in about 1800, then back to short again in about 1811, but they generally came either to the top of the hips or to just below them. An 1807 advertisement for a staymaker (*L&F*, *MW* 106) promised that his stays would 'give the wearer the true Grecian form'. Stays could cost about three or four guineas. Necklines were very low and revealed a great deal of the bosom, so many women retained the modesty pieces of earlier decades, tucking a gauzy piece of fabric around the back of the neck and into the top of the gown, sometimes crossing the ends of the fabric in front. During the day, women wore what was known as 'morning' or 'walking' dress (*Cath*, *MW* 211), which covered almost all of the skin. They wore long sleeves and, if they went outside, gloves and bonnets. The fichu covered the chest, and often a jacket of some sort was worn. Indoors, before a woman went out, she might wear a dressing gown (*P&P* 344), not the voluminous and decorative indoor coat of the same name worn by men but a loose and comfortable gown appropriate for wearing while the rest of her toilette was completed. Morning gowns were often white, a difficult colour to keep clean and thus a silent advertisement for the leisure that women of Austen's class enjoyed. (Thus, Mrs Norris is pleased that the Sotherton housekeeper has fired maids for their pretensions in wearing impractical white gowns – *MP* 105–106.) Walking dresses, which were meant to be worn outdoors, were similar to morning gowns but were more frequently coloured in order to hide dirt. Jane Austen, at various times, owned pink, brown and yellow-and-white dresses.

At dinnertime, women changed into evening dress (*NA* 162–165, 195; *S&S* 193; *MP* 141), a process that could take anywhere from half an hour to upwards of two hours. They traded their coloured walking dresses for evening gowns in white (*NA* 91; *MP* 222; *E* 178) or very pale colours.

Clothing

The evening gowns were exclusively short-sleeved until about 1814. In March of that year, Jane wrote to Cassandra from London with the radical intention of adopting the new fashion of wearing long sleeves at night (*P&P* 140): 'I wear my gauze gown today', she explained, 'long sleeves & all; I shall see how they succeed, but as yet I have no reason to suppose long sleeves are allowable.' In the end, it was all right; a family friend, Mrs Frances Tilson, informed her that they were indeed 'allowable'. 'Mrs Tilson had long sleeves too', Jane reported, '& she assured me that they are worn in the evening by many. I was glad to hear this.' Later that same year, again in London, she confirmed that 'long sleeves appear universal, even as *Dress*'.

Fichus were set aside in the evening, and women displayed their low necklines to full advantage. Gloves that reached above the elbow were kept handy; they would be taken off for dinner and replaced for the evening, especially if dancing was planned. Evening gowns had trains for the first few years of the century, losing them by the time Austen began publishing. Those who planned to dance would gather up the train (*NA* 37) before lining up in the set; those who preferred to play cards could leave their trains to sweep grandly along the floor. No doubt this is part of Mrs Allen's concern in the assembly rooms at Bath. She is extremely glad to walk through the crowded ballroom without 'injury' (*NA* 22).* Dresses for balls were especially grand (*Col Let*, *MW* 156; *Cath*, *MW* 216; *MP* 254, 257); women brought out their best and most flattering attire on such occasions.

One example of a ball gown, from an 1801 issue of the *Gallery of Fashion*, is a 'robe' (*NA* 26). A robe was a descendant of the open-fronted gown that exposed the petticoat, and this particular example still belongs very much to the eighteenth century. The skirt of the white muslin petticoat is full and plain, with a narrow band of trim near the hem. The black velvet robe, trimmed with gold braid, is actually quite small in comparison to the rest of the dress. Trimmed with gold lace, it drops very low at the neckline and is cut quite high at the front of the skirt, leaving only a tiny horizontal band that is laced like a medieval bodice. There are no sleeves to the robe, only shoulder straps; the sleeves are instead part of the under-dress or part of the chemise. From the sides, the back of the robe falls away rapidly from the front, leaving at least half the circumference of the petticoat exposed, and trails away into a train.

Just as a 'robe' meant a very specific kind of dress, so did 'frock' and 'gown' (*Watsons*, *MW* 323, 327, 353; *NA* 28, 52, 70, 73, 74, 91, 93, 104, 118, 165, 238; *S&S* 249; *P&P* 13, 36, 214, 238, 292; *MP* 99–100, 146, 222, 272; *E* 178, 271, 302, 324; *P* 142). From the front, these two kinds of dresses looked very similar. They presented the appearance of a single tube of fabric, gathered at the waist if necessary and given sleeves (*NA* 70) as appropriate. The

*As *Northanger Abbey* was written in 1790s and only minimally revised, it retained the anachronistic train when it was finally published after Austen's death. The other example of a train comes from (*The Watsons*, *MW* 327), presumed to have been written in 1804, when trains were still common on evening wear.

difference between them was in the back, where the gown was still uninterrupted, while the frock was open at the back, at least nominally, and gathered together with pins or other fastenings. Austen uses the term 'gown' almost universally, referring to 'frock' only in relation to children's clothing (*Lesley*, *MW* 111; *MP* 13), so it may be that the people she knew used the term in a general, rather than specific, sense.

4. *Progress of the Toilet – Dress Completed*, James Gillray, 1810.

She may also have used the term 'gown' to refer to dresses that opened in front, not in the manner of a robe, but in the manner of a 'stomacher' (*E* 86). The stomacher had a front flap made either of part of the skirt or part of the skirt and the front panel of the bodice. The wearer got into the gown and, in the case of stomachers that incorporated part of the bodice, pinned or buttoned this portion at the shoulders. Then a drawstring in the waist of the flap was pulled to cinch in the waist and tied in a bow in back. In the case of stomachers where the flap was only part of the skirt, the flap was tied around the waist using a string that was part of the flap. Then the bodice was closed by wrapping, lacing (with a shirt underneath to cover the gap under the crossed laces) or buttoning down the middle.

Like the robe, the frock or gown could be adapted with equal ease to morning or evening wear.

Clothing

As with men, there were exceptions to every rule for dress. Older women tended to be better than older men at keeping up with the latest fashions, but they were expected to modify their dress to reflect their more advanced years. Accordingly, they retained the fichus and tuckers that partially covered the bosom, kept to more old-fashioned hairstyles that relied on powder, frizzing and sausage curls and wore long sleeves more frequently than younger women, even at night. Court dress, as always, was behind the times and retained old-fashioned fitted bodices, hoop petticoats and powdered hair.

Outer Garments

The thinness of the classical garments worn in the first years of the nineteenth century left women in a somewhat uncomfortable position, as the English climate was rather different from that of Greece or Rome. Therefore, women needed a variety of garments to keep them warm. One of the most popular of these accessories, used as a decorative quasi-classical drapery as well as serving as a warm wrap, was the shawl.

The shawl (*MP* 212, 251; *E* 48, 322, 346, 349; *P* 117) was a large rectangle of fabric, initially of cashmere from Tibetan mountain goats and made in India. It often came in bright or deep colours and featured decorative borders with repeated patterns such as spades, so-called pinecones (actually bunches of flowers) or paisley swirls. Other shawls featured borders with Greek motifs. The shawl was typically allowed to drape over both shoulders, with its loose ends hanging in some cases almost down to the ground.

Shawls quickly became popular in England, so popular that several unsuccessful attempts were made to introduce Kashmir goats to the British Isles. Despite the repeated failures, British manufacturers in Norwich, Edinburgh and Paisley began making machine-woven shawls in the 1780s and 1790s, but these remained inferior to the Indian originals (*MP* 305), which were handwoven, slowly crafted and often sewn back-to-back to make them equally soft on both sides. Un-patterned, solid-colour Indian shawls were so fine and light that they could be passed through a ring and were known as 'ring shawls'. Nonetheless, British manufacturers eventually produced shawls that were interesting in their own right. A silk example from about 1810 to 1820 reproduces the outline of the 'pinecone', but instead of fanciful eastern flowers, it fills the space with roses, acorns, ears of wheat and other British flora.

The shawl remained primarily decorative in nature, but other garments were more practical. The spencer (*E* 173) was a jacket with long sleeves, cut very short to end at the false waist of the dress. Jane Austen had one in 1808, which she wore for walks on June evenings.

The pelisse (*LS*, *MW* 27; *Cath*, *MW* 211; *Watsons*, *MW* 341; *NA* 32; *MP* 395; *P* 142) was a warmer garment, almost a dress in itself. It wrapped with one side over the other or met in the middle and frequently covered the dress almost entirely. Like the spencer, it had long sleeves.

A relative of the shawl was the tippet (*NA* 51; *E* 328), a small scarf with the ends worn loose in front. It was almost too small to qualify as an outdoor garment, being more of an accessory, but it kept the neck and chest warm. The cloak (*NA* 28, 40) was a relatively shapeless wrap with slits for the arms. Styles popular in 1801 included Hungarian silk cloaks of scarlet trimmed in black; varieties from 1810 included triangular mantles with hoods that could be tied under the chin. On the latter type of cloak, the arm slits could be buttoned closed. Short cloaks came into fashion in 1812, and in Austen's last years mantles with capes appeared. In her youth, Austen owned a muslin cloak, or so it would appear from her dedication of *Frederic and Elfrida* to Martha Lloyd 'for your late generosity to me in finishing my muslin Cloak'.

Accessories

Streamlined clothing did not give women many places to carry extra belongings, but they might store a fan, a handkerchief or a bottle of scented water in a reticule. Handkerchiefs could be pocket handkerchiefs, used for blowing noses and wiping eyes (*NA* 28, 98, 229; *S&S* 75, 121, 133, 182), or they could be somewhat larger and used to tie a hat to the head. Jane is known to have made cambric pocket handkerchiefs for her friend Catherine Bigg, sending a poem along with the gift (*MW* 446). In Austen's childhood, 'handkerchief' had also meant a large muslin scarf whose ends were crossed in front and tucked into the skirt or sash (*S&S* 120; *P&P* 344; *MP* 14); in other words, it was yet another variation on the fichu. It is probably in this more old-fashioned sense that Jane refers to a handkerchief in a letter of November 1800, where she reports that she 'wore my aunt's gown and handkerchief'. The sash into which handkerchiefs were often tucked was worn tied around the waist like a belt; it had been an important element in defining the rising waistline from the 1780s on.

Ribbons (*Sand, MW* 426; *NA* 114; *E* 235, 237; *P* 8, 221) were used to trim almost everything. They were folded into rosettes and added to shoes and hats or braided and used as trim at necklines and hems (*NA* 26). In March 1814, Jane wrote to Cassandra from London,

> I have determined to trim my lilac sarsenet with black sattin ribbon just as my China Crape is, 6^d width at bottom, 3^d or 4^d at top. – Ribbon trimmings are all the fashion at Bath, & I dare say the fashions of the two places are alike enough in that point, to content *me*. – With this addition it will be a very useful gown, happy to go anywhere.

A few days later she confessed, 'I have been ruining myself in black sattin ribbon with a proper perl edge; & now I am trying to draw it up into kind of Roses, instead of putting it in plain double plaits.' Ribbons were also used, especially at the turn of the century, to pull women's hair into Greek-style curls bound close to the head. They appeared as straps on sandals and ties for bonnets. Their versatility made them a near necessity for female attire.

Clothing

Aprons (*MP* 146), reinvented as gauzy, decorative swatches of expensive fabric, had been a fashionable accessory for much of the eighteenth century. By Austen's time, however, they were usually purely practical items, worn by working-class women and servants.

In cold weather, even the gloves habitually worn by women outdoors were not enough to keep their hands warm. For this purpose, they often carried fur muffs (*S&S* 168), which could be quite enormous – a foot or more in diameter. Usually they were all of one colour of fur, but at least one fashion plate from the period shows alternating diamonds of tan and black fur.

Fabrics

All fabrics used during the period were weaves or knits of four natural fibres: linen, cotton, wool and silk. Up until the time of Austen's birth, linen, wool and silk had reigned supreme – linen for sheets (*E* 306), tablecloths and napkins (*Lesley, MW* 113; *Watsons, MW* 347; *S&S* 13, 26, 225, 355; *E* 24), shirts, chemises and similar items; wool for anything that needed to be warm or especially durable; and silk, in the form of satin (*MP* 180; *P* 40), velvet or brocade, for the most expensive and stylish clothes. However, during Austen's lifetime, all three of these fabrics were ousted by cotton (*F&E, MW* 6), imported from India or America and manufactured by an increasingly mechanised and efficient process. By the early-nineteenth century, British cotton fabrics were considered so superior that even Empress Josephine and her daughter wore English cotton, lying to Napoleon when he questioned them about the fabric's origin and claiming that it was French linen. Wool, linen and silk were still in use, but their share of the market diminished steadily. Even bedclothes such as sheets and counterpanes (*NA* 164) were, by Austen's time, often being made of cotton.

The principal cotton fabric in use for women's clothing was muslin (*NA* 22; *P&P* 72, 292, 307, 310; *E* 233, 235), a lightweight and semitransparent woven fabric. Indian muslin (*F&E, MW* 6; *NA* 28) was especially soft and opaque, while mull (*NA* 74) was similar to Indian muslin, but not quite as silky in texture. Some muslins were 'figured' (*E* 235); that is, they bore a pattern of some kind. Sprigged muslin (*NA* 26, 105) was decorated with tiny sprigs of leaves or flowers. Spotted muslin (*NA* 68, 73, 74; *S&S* 276) was decorated with dots rather than with sprigs. Tamboured muslins (*NA* 73) were those decorated with embroidery; the tambour was a kind of rectangular embroidery frame. Muslins varied widely in price according to their quality.

Austen usually refers to muslin as a fabric for dresses, but it could be put to other purposes as well. As Henry Tilney points out, it was used in the making of caps and cloaks (*NA* 28–29). It was also used for fichus, aprons, shawls and veils.

Other cotton fabrics differed from muslin chiefly in their weight. Cambric was very light and lawn lighter still to the point of being almost

entirely transparent.* Jaconet (*NA* 74) was a lightweight cotton fabric,
lighter than many muslins but a little heavier than the cambric used for
handkerchiefs. Calico (*P&P* 307) – whose name, like the name jaconet,
was a corruption of the name of a town in India – was originally imported
from India and later made in England. Calicoes, heavier than muslins,
were usually printed with some sort of design. Dimity (*NA* 194) was
a kind of cotton with a raised pattern, often tiny dots.

Silks remained important for evening dresses, particularly in the winter.
Both satins and velvets were worn in the winter. Sarsenet (*NA* 118) was
a lighter silk appropriate for summer wear. Linen, too, was still in use for
underclothes and bed and table linens, but it was being rapidly displaced
by cotton. Wool and wool blends were comfortable in the winter, but they
were not usually fashionable. Baize, for example, was a cheap, coarse
wool fabric with a nap; it is no doubt chosen as the curtain fabric for the
Mansfield Park play because of its low cost and quality (*MP* 195). If well
made, however, wool fabrics were perfectly acceptable. Poplin (*E* 302),
a wool and silk blend with a fine corded texture, had a respectable
reputation. Women wore a good many other fabrics; bombazine
(a silk-worsted blend) and China crape (a thick silk) are only two
of those mentioned in Austen's letters.

Buying and Making Clothes

Clothes might be made at home or by a person hired to do the job.
Relatively few items were sold ready-made, even at the end of the period
in question. A few things, such as caps, cloaks, aprons, skirts and jackets,
most of them designed for middle- and working-class consumers, could
be bought in the 'warehouses' (*NA* 68; *S&S* 215; *P&P* 288) of large cities,
which often sold fabric by the yard as well, but coats, dresses and other
substantial items of clothing could be bought ready-made only if they
were bought second-hand. Most women of Austen's class selected fabrics
personally from a linen-draper (who sold linen and cotton fabrics – *E* 56),
a mercer (who sold silks) or a woollen-draper (who sold wool). They took
the fabric they had bought to a dressmaker (*E* 178), sometimes called
a mantua-maker, and specified how they wanted the garment to be made.
If they had skilled housemaids (*MP* 130, 254), they might also hand the
fabric over to them to be turned into a gown, a pelisse or some similar
garment. Rarely did they make an entire garment from start to finish.
They confined almost all of their needlework to simple clothes for the
poor and to decorative embroidery on small pieces such as handkerchiefs
and workbags.

It was not possible, therefore, to purchase a dress on short notice
(*NA* 73). The selection of the fabric alone could take quite a while. If
a woman lived far from good shops, for example, as the Austen women

---

*Parson Woodforde bought some cambric for handkerchiefs in 1794 for 6*s.* a yard. They must
have been enormous handkerchiefs. He claimed that the 4 yards he bought would 'make me
five good handkerchiefs, and a small one for Nancy besides'.

did for most of their lives, she would have to wait until she or a friend or relative travelled to someplace with a wider selection, such as London or Bath (*P* 217, 221). London visits were especially useful, as not only did they afford the largest selection, but the streets and houses of the city presented the alert consumer with walking models of the latest fashions.

Patterns (*Cath*, *MW* 207; *S&S* 120; *E* 86) were devised either from a paper pattern or, more commonly, from studying existing garments. Friends and even shops were usually willing to lend a pattern garment (*E* 235) so that it might be examined and copied. For example, Mary Austen, James' wife, borrowed such patterns for children's clothes from Edward Austen's family at Godmersham. Innovations to the existing design might then be made after a careful consultation of fashion magazines, of clothes worn by acquaintances and of opinions from those who were considered especially tasteful or well informed about current trends.

Some items were bought not from shops but from travelling salesmen.

Men had their coats, waistcoats and breeches made by tailors or specialist breeches makers. Their linen, however – shirts, cravats and so on – was often made by female relatives.

See also Clocks and Watches; Cosmetics; Fan; Gloves; Hair; Hats; Jewellery; Pocketbooks and Reticules; Servants; Shoes; Spectacles; Stockings; Umbrellas and Parasols.

Complexion

There were generally understood to be four types of complexion (*F&E*, *MW* 4; *MP* 198; *E* 39, 199, 478; *P* 104): sallow, ruddy, brown and fair. The sallow skin (*F&E*, *MW* 8; *NA* 42) had a yellowish cast. The ruddy skin (*J&A*, *MW* 17; *Col Let*, *MW* 159; *P* 48) was inclined to redness and was generally attributed to overexposure to sun and wind (*P* 19, 22). Brown skins (*Watsons*, *MW* 337–338, 357; *NA* 42; *S&S* 46; *P&P* 270; *MP* 44) are what today we might call olive, or approaching olive; the term is also used simply to indicate that a person has dark hair and eyes and a skin colouration consistent with the hair and eye colour. Fair skins (*Watsons*, *MW* 357; *NA* 42; *E* 478) were pale, at times almost translucent, with just a faint blush to the cheeks; this skin tone was most often associated with blondes.

To Austen's contemporaries, the important thing was that the skin be even in tone, without blotches or blemishes, and that the skin be expressive. An expressive skin was clear enough of make-up that blushes and the glow of exertion could be clearly detected by observers; it was supposed to reveal thoughts and emotions, portraying its occupant in a true and natural state. This was a novel concept, for during most of the eighteenth century fashionable women had buried their faces under layers of white make-up, adorned these white canvases with tiny black fabric patches, drawn artificial blue veins to simulate the translucency of a very fair skin and otherwise taken great pains to disguise their natural complexions.

Yet the period associated with Regency style – though it is not really contiguous with the actual, political Regency – was characterised by an interest in what was 'natural' in behaviour, dress, education and personal appearance. Some found the thin, flowing gowns that women adopted in this period scandalous, a mere step away from nudity, but the Regency woman was naked in a way that her mother and grandmother had not been. She exposed far more flesh to public view, not only on her face but on her arms, neck and chest. Daytime costume was still fairly modest, with the arms and throat covered, but evening dresses were often short-sleeved and low-necked, and women began to worry about how their skin looked all over.

Women were suddenly being inspected and judged in ways that were unfamiliar to them, and they naturally felt insecure. Books such as *The Toilet of Flora* offered recipes to remove freckles (*P&P* 22; *P* 34, 146), wrinkles and warts. Pastes and creams to improve the complexion could be homemade or bought in well-stocked shops. With a little assistance, women were promised, they could withstand the scrutiny to which their 'natural' selves were subjected.

See also Cosmetics.

Cosmetics

During Jane Austen's lifetime, the English attitude towards cosmetics shifted dramatically. At her birth, heavily powdered white faces were the norm; by the time of her death, the appearance of artificiality in the skin was abhorrent, a sign of bad taste and poor judgement. Throughout most of the eighteenth century, women achieved a pale complexion through the use of face paint and powder (*F&E*, *MW* 7; *Cath*, *MW* 218), whose chief ingredient was poisonous white lead. Then they enhanced this pallid mask with rouge (*Lesley*, *MW* 119, 127, 137) and tiny velvet patches (*F&E*, *MW* 7) pasted on the face to draw attention to particularly attractive features. The effect was completed by a towering hairstyle, plastered into place with pomade (*F&E*, *MW* 7; *Cath*, *MW* 218) and sprayed with white or grey powder.

This toilette (*Sand*, *MW* 390; *P&P* 289; *MP* 34) was time-consuming and uncomfortable to achieve and maintain, and it was therefore natural that, when an alternative was offered, women would seize it eagerly. The alternative arose in 1789, when the French Revolution caused Europeans to question every assumption they had hitherto held. Everything from political systems to hairstyles came under reasoned appraisal, and the gigantic headdresses, the pallid face and the stiff women's clothing with its voluminous skirts all fell victim to the Revolution. There was a vogue for seeking what was natural in human behaviour and dress, and simpler styles of clothing and cosmetics followed. The white face-paint was an early casualty, not merely because it had come to seem ridiculous but also because it was discovered to be poisonous.

However, rouge (*P* 215) survived, but it must never appear to be artificial colour, nor must it cover the whole cheek, nor must it lose translucency, so that a natural blush may be noticed by observers.

It took more than one substance to achieve the appearance of unadorned natural beauty, and many contemporary manuals for housewives and servants give instructions for compounding a wide variety of cosmetics. There are perfumes, lotions, creams, washes for the face, potions for the hair, tooth powders, lip salves, wart removers, depilatories, breath fresheners, wrinkle creams, hair dyes and preventives against fleas and lice. Oils, ointments and soaps abound.

Many of these concoctions had multiple purposes. Lavender water (*NA* 77) and orange-flower water, for example, could be used on their own as perfumes (*P* 192) or in concert with other ingredients for a variety of purposes. *The Toilet of Flora*, for example, includes a remedy for toothache that consists of rinsing the mouth daily with a teaspoon of lavender water mixed with a teaspoon of warm or cold water.

Other perfumes were used to add fragrance to gloves or to soap.

Books that included cosmetic recipes often offered several types of creams for the skin. Hannah Glasse's *The Art of Cookery Made Plain and Easy* described a '*Nun's Cream*' made of 'One ounce of pearl-powder, twenty drops of oil of Rhodium, and two ounces of fine pomatum' and a '*Cold Cream*' compounded of 'one pint of trotter-oil, a quarter of a pound of hog's-lard, one ounce of spermaceti, [and] a bit of virgin-wax' warmed with rose water. *The Toilet of Flora* included '*An excellent Cosmetic for the Face*' made of hartshorn, rice powder, ceruse, 'Powder of dried Bones', frankincense, gum mastic, gum Arabic and rose water. The author of *The Mirror of the Graces* no doubt disapproved of this compound, as she specifically prohibited cosmetics made with ceruse (another name for white lead). *The Toilet of Flora* also contained a recipe for whitening the skin, made from a distillation of 'the Roots of Centaury and the White Vine, a pint of Cows Milk, and the crumb of a White Loaf'.

She or he also advises rinsing the face with 'Virgins Milk', a ubiquitous lotion whose creation is described in almost every book that touches on the subject of cosmetics. So standard was this item on the dressing table that the author of *The Mirror of the Graces* acknowledges that a book about beauty 'would certainly be looked upon as an imperfect performance, if we omitted to say a few words upon this famous cosmetic'. The miraculous 'milk' was also said to remove spots, freckles and pimples.

In addition to face and skin creams, women used soap, often scented soap, to wash their faces, arms and hands. Full immersion in a bathtub was extremely rare, but Englishwomen liked to keep their visible parts clean. Accordingly, books of the time are replete with recipes for 'wash-balls' or soaps. There are tinted wash-balls, almond wash-balls, 'Windsor soap' scented with caraway oil, white soap and honey soap. *The Toilet of Flora*'s white soap 'is made with one part of the Lees of Spanish Potash and Quick-lime, to two parts of Oil of Olives or Oil of Almonds'. Its honey soap, like many similar concoctions, is promised to whiten the skin; a fair skin was almost always considered desirable.

For the reddening of the cheeks, several methods were advised. One was the carmine powder mentioned above. Other rouges used alkanet root, red wine, sandalwood or Brazil wood to achieve the desired shade; one particularly unusual technique involves wetting a red ribbon and rubbing it against the face.

One wonders, however, whether the average woman hovered over a still, with an alchemist's array of potions and wood shavings and loaves of white bread. It seems likely that most women left the mixing and decocting to others and simply bought such products ready-made. Most cosmetics were available in well-stocked stores, to judge from a 1786 tax imposed on beauty aids. The act listed, under the category of taxable goods, hair powder, tooth powders, perfumes and perfumed goods, pomatums and ointments for the hair, rouge, white paint, creams and pastes. Several brand names were listed specifically, including Pomade de Nerole, Duchess pomatum, Powder of Pearl of India and a wash called Venetian Bloom. Sir Walter Elliot's Gowland's Lotion (*P* 145–146), though not listed in 1786, was by 1814 at least an actual product available for sale, not an invention of Austen's. Like most of the face and skin lotions of its day, it optimistically promised to heal all problems of the skin and sold for 8*s*. 6*d*. a quart.

Many of these beauty products and their exotic ingredients, far from being made at home, were imported from as far away as the East Indies and the Levant. Indeed, it seems likely, from the sheer number of products available for sale, that most women did not manufacture their own cosmetics unless they lived far away from a reliable supplier.

See also Complexion.

D

Dance

Dance (*Lesley, MW* 111; *Col Let, MW* 158; *Watsons, MW* 330; *NA* 37, 103, 130, 134; *S&S* 44–45, 47, 171; *P&P* 13, 25, 92; *MP* 250, 252; *E* 229, 245, 247, 258, 328, 333; *P* 43, 72) was an important element of society and courtship, allowing young people to mingle with the opposite sex in a controlled

environment, displaying their charms to potential marriage partners
(*MP* 39). It was also, for those who enjoyed it, a tremendous amount of fun.
The music, the challenge of learning new steps and figures, the subdued
competition, the necessary cooperation with the other dancers and the
physical exercise could all be exhilarating. There were few things that
people enjoyed as much as a ball (*3S*, *MW* 58; *Lesley*, *MW* 133; *Cath*, *MW*
193; *Watsons*, *MW* 315, 321, 323, 444; *NA* 79, 89; *P&P* 6, 300, 317, 349; *MP* 35,
250, 251, 270; *E* 191, 276), and both men and women looked forward to such
events. Austen herself was an avid dancer; so was her brother Charles.
Jane was always proud of herself when she could dance all evening
without running out of partners and without getting tired. She lost her
relish for balls only in the last few years of her life, when it seemed to
be more trouble than it was worth. However, many older people who no
longer danced (*E* 327) enjoyed a ball, for it was a chance to meet friends,
talk and play cards. A separate room was usually provided for those who
played cards, so that they could talk and concentrate on their whist hands
without too much interference from the music.

The Ball

There were two types of balls: public and private. Public balls were given
by subscription, which meant that anyone who could afford the fee could
attend all the balls in a given season. The peak season was winter, when
outdoor activities were harder to engage in and when people felt trapped
indoors. Rural areas and small towns tended to hold their balls once
a month at the full moon, a time chosen to make night-time travelling
easier. In small towns, public balls (also called 'assemblies' – *Watsons*,
MW 314; *P&P* 6; *MP* 249) were often held in inns (*E* 197–198, 250–251),
which usually kept a ballroom for this very purpose. The assemblies at
Basingstoke, which Jane attended when she lived at Steventon, were held
in the Town Hall, with smaller gatherings using the ballroom at the Angel
Inn and semiannual 'club balls' sponsored by a local gentleman's club
using either the Maidenhead Inn or the Crown Inn; the public balls in
Southampton were held at either the Dolphin Assembly Rooms in High
Street or the Long Rooms near the West Quay.

In Bath and other resort towns, there were one or more assembly
rooms in which balls were given, and there might very well be a master
of ceremonies. His job kept him extremely busy. He had to greet new
arrivals to town and instruct them, if necessary, on the conduct expected
of them at the assemblies. During the balls, he was to maintain the proper
atmosphere, enforce rules of behaviour and dress, introduce suitable
partners to each other and arrange the dancers for each dance. A couple,
having agreed to dance together, would approach the master of ceremonies
and ask him for permission to join the next dance. Once he knew the
identities of the dancers, he could establish which couples belonged at
the top and which at the bottom of the set, arranging them according to
social class and precedence. Just before the dance began, he would consult

with the top couple and confirm their choice of dance, ascertain to the best of his ability whether they could call it successfully and ensure that it was not a dance that had been chosen already that evening. Then he would instruct each set, if necessary, about how to perform the dance.

Private balls were usually much less formal. The guests tended to know one another and their relative precedence already, so there was no need for help in arranging themselves (*Cath, MW* 223–224; *P&P* 90; *MP* 275; *P* 7). Repetition of the same dance in a given evening was still frowned upon, but among close friends it would have been overlooked. The number of couples dancing was also usually smaller, not only resulting in less initial confusion and instruction but also making each dance shorter in duration, as we will see. An advantage of the private ball (*P&P* 91) was that the guest list could be carefully controlled (*Watsons, MW* 350), ensuring a congenial gathering; a disadvantage was that one tended to see the same people at all such occasions, and this could grow tiresome.

The hostess of a private ball (*Col Let, MW* 155; *Cath, MW* 202, 203, 207, 219; *NA* 209; *S&S* 33, 53, 99, 152, 171; *P&P* 45, 46; *MP* 210, 252–254) would first establish that she had a room large enough for dancing (*S&S* 252; *P&P* 91; *MP* 253). There needed to be room not only for the couples to line

A MASTER of the Ceremonies Introducing a PARTNER.

5. *A Master of the Ceremonies Introducing a Partner,* Thomas Rowlandson, 1795.

up but also for them to make the set wider, as some figures required. They also needed room to move forward and back. Once a proper room had been chosen, the hostess compiled a suitable guest list and sent out invitations (*P&P* 55, 86), either handing them out in person or, more commonly, sending a servant around to all the houses in question.

Dance

The guests arrived at, or a little after, the starting time (*Watsons*, *MW* 319, 327, 328); some people liked to arrive late in order to make an entrance. Only girls who were 'out', that is, who were officially on the marriage market, could attend (*Col Let*, *MW* 150; *Cath*, *MW* 226; *MP* 51, 275; *P&P* 122, 165), and the first attendance of a girl at a ball probably generated some interest (*MP* 267), especially if she were an heiress or considered to be particularly beautiful. The dancing began and went on for two or three hours, and then refreshments were served. Dancers tended to become overheated and needed plenty of liquids. At public balls, participants took tea (*Watsons*, *MW* 329, 332; *NA* 25–29); at a private ball, there would be a full supper (*MP* 278, 282; *E* 248), with soup (*Watsons*, *MW* 315; *P&P* 55), several other dishes and a variety of beverages, including wine, negus and orgeat. It was customary for the gentlemen to sit at tea or supper with the woman they had just been dancing with (*Watsons*, *MW* 332; *NA* 59); hence, Henry Crawford tries to arrange to dance with Fanny just before supper, so that he will have an excuse to be near her through the meal (*MP* 278). Likewise, Mr Elton's snub of Harriet is all the more cruel and pointed because it occurs just before supper is due to begin (*E* 326). The entertainment then continued until late at night (*Col Let*, *MW* 157) or rather, early the next morning. Fanny's debut ball at Mansfield Park is still going on at 3:00 a.m., when she goes up to bed (*MP* 279), and Austen herself attended a ball in 1800 at which the dancing began at 10:00 p.m., the supper began at 1:00 a.m., and she was not back until 5:00 a.m.*

Of course, not all balls were this elaborate. Sometimes impromptu dancing occurred after dinner (*S&S* 54; *MP* 117; *E* 208, 229–230; *P* 47, 71), when guests or family members felt like dancing and some member of the company was willing to play some music. Parson James Woodforde recorded such an occasion in July 1785, when he had had some company for dinner. 'After Tea the Ladies and Gentlemen got to dancing and danced and sang till Supper Time,' he wrote in his diary. 'About 12 o'clock this night we all got to dancing again.'

The Dance

In all balls, however, public or private, planned or proposed on a whim, it was the men who sought partners and the women who could merely accept or refuse. If they refused, it was incumbent on them to avoid looking as if they refused that particular gentleman. Even if a woman found the gentleman who asked her to dance repulsive or clumsy, she had to spare his feelings by refusing to dance with anyone, usually for the rest of the evening (*P&P* 102). Austen herself resorted to this tactic at a private ball at Kempshott Park, where, she told Cassandra, 'One of my gayest actions was sitting down two Dances in preference to having

---

*Some public balls ended earlier; those in Bath ended at 11:00 p.m., even in the middle of a dance, but a public ball at Tunbridge Wells in 1787 went on until at least 2:00 a.m.

Lord Bolton's eldest son for my Partner, who danced too ill to be endured.' A woman who wished to avoid dancing could claim fatigue or disinclination, the two most common excuses, but under no circumstances could she refuse one man and then stand up immediately with another. Most women who liked to dance, therefore, manoeuvred around the room in the hope of avoiding unsavoury partners, while positioning themselves conveniently close to men with whom they wished to dance. They also frequently chose to dance with bad dancers in order to keep themselves available for dancing for the rest of the evening. All too often, women had the opposite problem: too few partners (*Watsons*, *MW* 315; *MP* 267).

Fewer men than women generally wished to dance, and so it was considered a kind of civic obligation for eligible young men to make themselves available as partners as often as possible (*P&P* 10–11, 175). Jane wrote to Cassandra after a ball in November 1800, 'There were only twelve dances, of which I danced nine, & was merely prevented from dancing the rest by want of a partner.' At some balls, the host solved the problem of partners and choices by simply drawing lots and assigning partners at random. At times, women might dance with each other if there were simply not enough men to go around.

In earlier years, a woman had been committed to one partner for the entire evening, and this made it all the more important to be asked by the right person (*NA* 131). By Austen's day, the rules had relaxed somewhat. Dances were grouped in pairs, and when a gentleman asked a lady to dance, he did so for two dances (*Watsons*, *MW* 335, 336; *MP* 278–279; *E* 250, 326). He could 'engage' her before the ball even started, requesting that she save two dances for him, and she was obliged to accept or not dance at all (*Cath*, *MW* 214; *Watsons*, *MW* 328, 330; *NA* 50; *P&P* 292; *MP* 256, 268, 272, 274; *E* 250). However, dancing more than twice with the same partner in the same evening was frowned upon (*Watsons*, *MW* 334; *S&S* 54), except in the case of engaged or married couples (*MP* 117). Even dancing twice with the same partner (*Cath*, *MW* 224; *Watsons*, *MW* 320; *P&P* 12–13; *MP* 278) indicated a marked romantic preference, so a woman could legitimately refuse to dance a second pair of dances with a given gentleman on the grounds of decorum; in this case, she could still accept other partners and keep dancing (*NA* 57, 76). The most serious offence of all was to agree to dance with two men for the same pair of dances; earlier in the eighteenth century, this sort of gaffe could ruin a woman's reputation and even lead to a duel. The fact that Miss Osborne, in *The Watsons*, offers this insult to young Charles Blake is a sign not only of her own selfishness but also of her inability to see the boy as a human being with rights and feelings (*Watsons*, *MW* 330).

The dancers, who had removed their gloves to eat dinner, now put them on again (*Col Let*, *MW* 157; *Watsons*, *MW* 331) and, in the case of a country dance, lined up 'longways', two by two, with the line of men facing the line of women, each gentleman across from his partner. If there were a great many dancers, this arrangement, called a 'set' (*Watsons*, *MW* 331, 340;

NA 52, 80; *E* 328), would be divided into smaller sets (*NA* 55) within the line that would interact with each other as well as with the larger group. Alternatively, as in large assemblies, there might be completely separate sets dancing at the same time. The couple at the top (*MP* 118) – which was usually the end of the line closer to the musicians – selected the dance and called the figures in the proper order. Ideally, the dance was chosen with reference to the level of skill of all the dancers and the nature of the tune, but as dancing teachers were fond of pointing out, this could be a tricky task, and without doubt many a young man or woman stood nervously hoping that he or she could complete the dance without making any serious mistakes. It was customary for the musicians to play the tune once through before the dancers began, to give the dancers a chance to refamiliarise themselves with the tune, run through the figures in their heads and accustom themselves to the tempo. Dancers who joined the set after the dance began, regardless of their social standing, had to enter at the bottom of the set (*NA* 80). When the next dance began, the second couple (or the first couple in the second set, if there was one) called the dance.

The dancers moved through a variety of figures, including the hey (a figure in which the dancers wove in and out of their respective lines) and hands across (*NA* 133). Hands across was a figure for four dancers, two men and two women; each person held out his or her right hand and took the hand of the person diagonally across the set, forming a little circle with four right arms extended into the centre. All four then walked or danced around the circle halfway, so that they stood where their diagonal opposites had stood a moment before. The right hands were released, and the dancers did the same movement in the other direction, joining left hands and dancing back to place. Some figures called for the dancers to move sideways along their own line, while others called for partners to move together, either down the middle of the set or in parallel along the outside. Not all of the figures utilised all of the dancers, and couples at the end of the line might be standing idle for a few minutes while they waited for their opportunity to move again. This was a perfect time to talk, flirt and look around the room (*P&P* 91; *MP* 278).

As the dance progressed, the top couple gradually moved down the set, taking the place of the second couple, then the third, while the displaced couples moved up towards the top. The second couple would follow them, and then the third and so on (*E* 327), so that the relative arrangement of the dancers was constantly shifting. One could suddenly come into proximity to a person who had been very far away at the beginning of the dance. When all the dancers had had a turn at the top, the dance was over. A small set, therefore, meant a short dance (*NA* 131), while a large set meant that each dance took a good while to complete. Elizabeth Bennet mentions 'half an hour' (*P&P* 91) as a typical length for a dance, and this seems to have been average, though as Thomas Wilson pointed out, a dance could last anywhere from five minutes to an hour, depending on the size of the set. Many ballgoers, Jane Austen included, measured the success of a ball by the number of 'couple' who stood up to dance (*Watsons, MW* 340; *S&S* 171; *P&P* 91; *MP* 117, 253; *E* 230, 248, 325); more dancers was almost always considered better. Austen considered a ball with seven couples 'a very small one indeed' and one with eight 'a very poor one'. She considered 'seventeen couple' a respectable number. Her cousin Eliza de Feuillide considered a large set fairly challenging; at a ball in Cheltenham, she bragged that she 'danced every dance, which was taking a tolerable degree of exercise considering there were above thirty couple'.

The music for impromptu dancing might be provided by a single pianoforte played by the hostess, one of her daughters or a female guest (*P* 47, 72). In the case of Fanny Price's first 'ball', the music is played by a violinist from the servants' hall (*MP* 117); the ability of a servant to play music for such occasions was a valuable skill and often contributed to finding a good place. At public assemblies, there was a full band (*Watsons, MW* 328), which might consist of anything up to about twelve musicians. Sometimes the musicians were placed on a dais; at other times, they were housed in a balconied gallery above the ballroom floor. As opposed to dances at home, where the keyboard was the dominant instrument, music at larger balls tended to be heavy on the stringed instruments, especially violins (*Watsons, MW* 327; *S&S* 171; *MP* 275). The nature of the music varied. Minuets were slow and sedate, while 'Scotch and Irish airs' (*P&P* 25, 511) were lively. Most English country dances fell somewhere in between.

Good dancing (*NA* 72), like good behaviour, was prized wherever it was found. It was not always easy to come by (*P&P* 90), as different types of dance required very different movements and styles; cotillions and quadrilles, for example, could be safely embellished with balletic postures, while the country dance was to be performed easily and gracefully without any quasi-professional airs or attitudes.

Learning to dance was considered an essential part of the education of any young lady or gentleman (*Lesley, MW* 119–120; *P&P* 39; *MP* 276), and responsible parents hired dancing masters to teach their children to move elegantly. To judge from the number of satirical prints whose titles turn on the phrase, 'Hold up your head' seems to have been the most common advice offered by these dancing masters. When the dancing teachers were not present, families practised the steps (*Cath, MW* 212; *MP* 273) of old dances to keep them well memorised and learned new ones together. The quadrille, a complicated dance, appears to have been one of the dances that required copious drawing-room rehearsal. Dancers also kept themselves up to date by buying books that came out annually and featured the dances that were currently most popular. Dancing also formed part of the curriculum in many boarding schools. Charles Austen was taught to dance at the Naval Academy at Portsmouth. His report for February 1792 noted, 'Dances tolerably', but he must have improved, because by 1793–1794 the assessment had changed to 'Dances very well'.

Types of Dances

The most formal and old-fashioned of the dances that was still performed with any frequency was the minuet. It had different variations, one of which was the minuet de la cour mentioned in *Love and Freindship* (*MW* 78). It was a demanding dance with small steps in which posture, timing and graceful positioning of the limbs were essential, and it was usually performed by only two people at a time. It was rarely danced in private balls or in impromptu dances at home, but it was still danced at the major assembly halls, such as Almack's in London and the Upper and Lower Rooms at Bath. Balls at Bath were divided into two types, 'dressed' and 'undressed' (or 'cotillion' or 'fancy') balls (*NA* 35, 73); the references to clothing were because the minuet had a stricter dress code than other dances. Dressed balls began with minuets and then proceeded to other types of dances, chiefly country dances, after tea. The minuet lost favour fairly steadily over Austen's lifetime; by 1811, *The Mirror of the Graces* could state that the '*minuet* is now almost out of fashion'.

The cotillion's (*NA* 74) name derived from the French word for 'petticoat', and as a French-derived dance, it, too, was more formal than country dancing. A contemporary manual for performing sixteen cotillions describes the dance as being for four couples, sometimes with minuet steps, sometimes with hand clapping and with a set that sometimes arranged itself longways and sometimes reshaped itself as a circle. It did not require nearly as much skill as the minuet and replaced the minuet at the beginning of cotillion balls. By the early nineteenth century, it had become a five- or six-figure dance known as the 'quadrille', first introduced in public by Lady Jersey, who danced it at Almack's in 1815. The quadrille does not appear in the novels but appears in the letters, when in February 1817 she thanked her niece Fanny Knight for sending her some quadrille music. However, she reserved the time-honoured right of the older generation to disapprove of innovation. She was 'Much obliged' for them, she wrote; they were 'pretty enough, though of course they are very inferior to the Cotillions of my own day'.

The most popular type of dance for most of Austen's lifetime was the country dance (*Lesley*, *MW* 129; *NA* 74, 76–77; *E* 229, 245; *P* 47), an undemanding form of dance that chiefly required that the dancers be able to carry themselves gracefully. Thomas Wilson, who approved strongly of country dancing when it was done properly, wrote that the 'general character of this style of Dancing is simplicity, ease, freedom, and liveliness, rather inclining to the mirthful than the graceful, and to cheerfulness than elegance'. The steps were simple, consisting mostly of a step-hop forwards or backwards.

Scottish dances (*Cath*, *MW* 212), such as reels (*MW* 448; *P&P* 52), were even more informal than country dances and used considerably more energy. Scottish and Irish reels, jigs and country dances became extremely popular beginning in the 1790s, with examples such as 'New Tartan Pladdies', 'Ranting Highlanders' and 'Limerick Jig' appearing in books of music and manuals of dance steps.

Other popular dances included contredanse, a square dance for four or eight dancers, and the Boulangere (Baker's Wife – *P&P* 13), a dance in which the dancer turned first one partner and then another. On 5 September 1796, Jane reported from Goodnestone (her brother Edward's first house, before he moved to Godmersham) that 'We dined … & in the Evening danced two Country Dances & the Boulangeries.'

Many dances were imported from the Continent, but while imports such as the cotillion and quadrille met with favour, others were deemed too immodest for young British women to perform. The fandango, because it was a solo dance, was thought to attract too much attention to the individual. The author of *The Mirror of the Graces* found it shocking:

> Imagine what must be the assurance of the young woman, who, unaccustomed by the habits of her country to such singular exhibitions of herself, could get up in a room full of company, and, with an unblushing face, go through all the evolutions, postures, and vaultings of the Spanish fandango?

The same author also disapproved of the bolero, a partner dance that an unscrupulous male partner could shift 'from gaiety into licentiousness'.

The dance that was destined to oust most of these forms, however, was the waltz (*MW* 448). It had just been introduced in the last years of Austen's life, arriving in England in about 1812, but bits and pieces of the dance had been trickling in for years and adopted as figures in other dances, while the music for waltzes was often played, not as accompaniment to the waltz but as the background to country dancing (*E* 229, 242). What was so shocking about the waltz was the degree of physical contact it permitted, even mandated, between the couple, and the first illustrations of the full-fledged dance emphasised its sensuality.

It was not until 1814, when it was performed at Almack's, that the waltz began to gain in popularity. Still, it was the arms entwined around partners' waists that truly shocked English observers of this dance. Nor can it have helped that the waltz was associated in many minds with German romanticism, and German sentimental novels and plays had been identified with many of the emotional excesses mocked by Austen.

Another type of dance is mentioned by Austen, but this was not a social dance. It was the 'figure-dance' (*MP* 124), a showy sort of dance often performed between dramatic pieces at the theatre. Each dance had several parts, and each part might be symbolic in some way. Joseph Strutt, in *The Sports and Pastimes of the People of England* (1801), described the dance as 'pantomimical representations of historical and poetical subjects, expressed by fantastic gestures'.

See also Bath; Music.

Death

There were relatively few hospitals in the late eighteenth and early
nineteenth centuries, and most people died (*Lesley, MW* 114, 442; *P* 96)
at home. If time permitted, those at the deathbed would gather their
relatives (and sometimes their servants as well) (*S&S* 54), issue final
words of advice, perhaps revise or write a will and make their wishes
known about disposal of certain items of sentimental value.* The doctor
might come; frequently, the only time a family hired a physician, whose
rates tended to be exorbitant, was when death was already unavoidable.
The local parson would show up as well and offer prayers and possibly
communion. There was a set formula for prayers at a sickbed, concluding
with a prayer whose nature was based on the likelihood of recovery; the
prayer for 'a sick person at the point of departure' went as follows:

> O ALMIGHTY God, with whom do live the spirits of just men made
> perfect, after they are delivered from their earthly prisons: We humbly
> commend the soul of this thy servant, our dear brother, into thy hands,
> as into the hands of a faithful Creator, and most merciful Saviour; most
> humbly beseeching thee, that it may be precious in thy sight. Wash
> it, we pray thee, in the blood of that immaculate Lamb, that was slain
> to take away the sins of the world; that whatsoever defilements it
> may have contracted in the midst of this miserable and naughty world,
> through the lusts of the flesh, or the wiles of Satan, being purged and
> done away, it may be presented pure and without spot before thee.
> And teach us who survive, in this and other like daily spectacles of
> mortality, to see how frail and uncertain our own condition is; and so
> to number our days, that we may seriously apply our hearts to that holy
> and heavenly wisdom, whilst we live here, which may in the end bring
> us to life everlasting, through the merits of Jesus Christ thine only Son
> our Lord. Amen.

We are told that on her own deathbed, Austen purposely received
religious rites while still conscious enough to comprehend the words, so
one assumes the above prayer was read for her. When death was sudden,
none of this was possible (*E* 387).

Death was a regular visitor in the households of Austen's era. Birth
rates were high, and so was infant mortality. Diseases caused by poor
hygiene, poor nutrition and crowding routinely thinned the population
of London, which continued to rise only because immigration to the city
outpaced the death rate. While some people lived to be genuinely elderly,
most died young by modern standards (*S&S* 10–11). It was quite common,
particularly given the fact that many women continued to give birth until

---

*Some property was 'entailed' (*LS, MW* 256; *P&P* 28, 164, 308) – that is, its inheritance was
limited by earlier family wills and had to pass to heirs designated by the entail. This legal
device was often used to keep property in the male line of descent within a family.

they reached menopause, for a child to grow up without one or both parents (*J&A*, *MW* 16; *NA* 180; *E* 96, 163). Jane's father, George Austen, lost his own father when he was only nine years old, and Jane's cousin Jane Cooper lost her mother to an epidemic when she, too, was just a child.

After the death, the body was cleaned, often dressed in clothing, and then wrapped in a shroud, the material of which was regulated by the government. Wool shrouds had been required by law for centuries in order to support England's wool industry, and until the law was repealed in 1814–1815, those wishing the deceased to be buried in a linen shroud had to pay a fine. The family, or servants hired for the purpose, sat with the body until the time of burial came, a period known as the 'wake' (*MW* 444).

The funeral (*Evelyn*, *MW* 189; *S&S* 5; *E* 388) procession walked to the church, the mourners dressed in black robes, the coffin (*NA* 191) covered by a cloth called a 'pall' (hence the term 'pallbearers') and the procession ·led by a man called a 'mute' who carried a staff topped with a gathered bundle of black crape. Sometimes a tray of black ostrich plumes, called a 'lid of feathers', was carried by a 'featherman'. The pall was usually black with a white cross, sometimes red with heraldic decorations for the rich and always white for girls in honour of their virginity. Girls' coffins were also decorated with garlands of flowers. The flowers might be real or artificial and if the latter, might be made of paper, wire, silk, wood, dyed horn or painted eggshells. A woman's coffin was often borne by female pallbearers; if the deceased were a spinster, these pallbearers would usually wear white. White was also worn at the burials of children.

At the churchyard, the church bell tolled (*MW* 448) to inform the community that someone had died. Three peals were rung for the death of a child, six for a woman and nine for a man. (An unbaptised child could not be buried in the churchyard, and no bell was rung to mark its passing.) The procession then entered the churchyard, and here the paths diverged based on class. Paupers were buried in communal graves, while most people were buried in single graves with headstones (*F&E*, *MW* 9) of varying size according to their wealth. The upper classes might be buried in the churchyard, but they preferred to be buried in a tomb (*MW* 442) under the church itself or in a family vault (*E* 398), a small building that might be located either on the church grounds or on the family estate. If buried in the church, as Jane Austen was buried in Winchester Cathedral, a plaque or other monument (*NA* 190) inside the church would replace the traditional headstone.

Bodies were not usually carried very far by the pallbearers. They travelled most of the way in a hearse, a black carriage drawn by two or four horses. Refreshments were typical of funerals at the time; cakes, wine, ale, chocolate and so forth were often served to the mourners either before or after the funeral. Largesse was also sometimes distributed to the poor or to members of the household staff; ladies' maids, for example, could expect to receive some of their mistress' clothes upon her death.

After the funeral, a fee was paid to the officiating clergyman. Parson Woodforde recorded receiving £1 1s. for his services at the burial of a young man in 1790. In 1785, he was given £5 5s. for burying the squire's sixteen-week-old daughter. Gifts, frequently hatbands (*P* 147), rings, black ribbons or gloves, were distributed to the mourners; at the 1790 funeral, Woodforde received 'a black silk Hatband and a pair of Beaver Gloves'. If the deceased were a woman, some or all of these 'tokens' might be white, as were the gloves Woodforde received at the funeral of Mrs Howes.

Funeral expenses could be kept down by renting the trappings of mourning. Parishes sometimes had a communal pall that could be rented, and mourning scarves, hoods and cloaks could be rented from undertakers for the procession. Members of trade guilds and associations often clubbed together to pay for each other's funerals, and this was of great help.

Money could also be saved by dyeing one's garments to make mourning clothes rather than buying new ones. Relatives and servants of a deceased person were expected to wear mourning for a period of time that varied depending on the closeness of the relationship (*Lesley*, *MW* 130–131). In May 1799, on a journey to Bath, Jane wrote to Cassandra that she had 'met a Gentleman in a Buggy, who on a minute examination turned out to be Dr Hall – & Dr Hall in such very deep mourning that either his Mother, his Wife, or himself must be dead'.

Mourning clothes would be distributed to the servants (*P* 105, 106), and garments might be dyed black or ordered newly made in dark and sombre colours. First mourning was all black (*P* 8), from hat to shoes. Women could wear black silk crape (*P* 147) or bombazine, materials universally approved because they were not shiny, with small touches of white here and there. A sample mourning outfit from a 1799 fashion magazine shows a full-skirted, high-waisted black robe and petticoat with white half-diamond edging along the edges of the robe and the sleeve hems, black gloves, simple black jewellery, a white ruffle at the neck, black ostrich plumes in the headdress and a white fur muff. Female servants were dressed in black bombazine or in bombazet, a cheaper fabric than bombazine. Men, too, dressed in black for first mourning (*P* 104). Shoes were 'shammy' – chamois leather, which like crape had little gloss. People in first mourning were not expected to retreat entirely from society, but they were expected to refrain from riotous or noticeably joyous activity (*MP* 121–123).

After a period of time (usually a few months – *E* 460) had elapsed, the deceased's family began to wear second mourning. Men wore grey at this time, while women wore black, white and touches of colour, especially shades of purple. After a few months of second mourning, life and dress were expected to return to normal (*P* 159). Many people also wore mourning on the death of the king or a member of the royal family, and those at court also wore mourning on the death of foreign monarchs. The duration of mourning in these cases typically depended on the rank of the deceased.

Debt

Debt (*P* 12, 209), never a pleasant thing in any society, is especially in the sink-or-swim commercial atmosphere of Austen's Britain. Generous bankruptcy (*Col Let*, *MW* 158) laws with forgiveness of debt were unheard of; a debtor had to pay every cent he owed, no matter what, or reach a private agreement with every creditor. Creditors who lost their patience could pay to have the local bailiffs arrest the debtor, seize his goods (*L&F*, *MW* 88–89) and throw him into debtors' prison (*S&S* 207). A less serious take on the subject was a satirical print that parodied traditional images of the hunt; in this case, however, the hunters are the bailiffs, and the quarry is a debtor on whom they seek to execute a warrant. The 'Execution in the House' in *Love and Freindship* is along these lines: not an execution in the sense of putting someone to death, but the execution of a warrant for the arrest of a debtor (*L&F*, *MW* 88). As unpleasant as it was to go to jail for debt, at least it did not carry the death penalty, despite Sophia's concern that her debtor husband has been 'hung' (*L&F*, *MW* 97).

A debtor in jail could not carry on his trade, making it much less likely that the debt could ever be repaid. Furthermore, while in prison, the debtor had to pay for his own sustenance, a situation that led to the pathetic sight of debtors pleading through the windows of the jails for largesse from passers-by. The spectre of debt haunted anyone at financial risk – families with a son or husband who had a penchant for dice or drink (*S&S* 70; *P&P* 297–298; *MP* 23–24), merchants with cargo-laden ships at sea, a wife whose husband, by law, had complete control of all the couple's finances, no matter how foolish or unscrupulous he might be (*P* 152–153). Often debt was simply a matter of poor spending habits. Gentlemen ran up bills with numerous tradespeople (*P&P* 294; *P* 9), such as tailors and china merchants, relying on generous credit terms, until they found that they could not pay the bills (*LS*, *MW* 246). Meanwhile, their creditors, unable to collect, frequently found themselves dragged down into debt along with their genteel customers.

There were few ways out once a person was deeply in debt. Landowners who had incoming rents could economise and hope to squeak by until the debts were paid off (*S&S* 194; *P* 13). This was the tack taken by the Austens' friend John Harwood, who inherited nearby Deane House along with massive debts from his father. He sacrificed a great deal to maintain control of the family estate, including marriage to a woman whom he loved but whose dowry was inadequate to rescue him. When a newly widowed woman gave birth unexpectedly in his house, however, he gave up some of the last of his stores of wine to make caudle for her.

Inheritance hurt rather than helped John Harwood, but sometimes inheritance could rescue a profligate son – at least for a time. Marriage to a wealthy woman could also effect a repair of one's fortune (*S&S* 194), as wives brought dowries with them in the form of cash, jewels, land or goods. On occasion, friends might offer some help in paying creditors (*P&P* 265, 313, 324, 387), but usually only if they could be sure that they themselves would be repaid, or at least that the descent into debt would not be repeated.

Dishes

Until about the seventeenth century, dishes had been fairly limited in both type and composition. The poor ate off wood or cheap earthenware; the 'pitcher' owned by the poor family in *Emma* is no doubt a rough earthenware pitcher, for instance (*E* 88). The rich ate off silver plate, and the middling sort might have something in between – pewter, perhaps. The seventeenth and eighteenth centuries, however, saw a revolution in both the materials used for dishes and the number of kinds of dishes considered necessary for a well-equipped house. The impetus in both cases was trade with the East Indies, which brought regular shipments of tea and of Chinese porcelain (hence the name 'china' for porcelain – *NA* 162; *P&P* 75). Drinking tea required 'tea things' to drink it out of, and porcelain was such a fascinating new material, so strong, so impervious to heat, that the rich found they *had* to have it.

The catch was that no one quite knew the chemistry behind porcelain's strength and lightweight beauty. They knew that it had something to do with the kind of clay used and with very high heat in the kiln, but it was many years before people discovered European deposits of the special clay – kaolin – and acquired enough skill to exploit it properly. Nonetheless, recapturing some of the money spent on millions of pieces of imported porcelain was a profound incentive. At first, Europeans created fake porcelains that contained no kaolin. These included soft-paste porcelains, such as the early products of Vincennes and Sèvres (the 'Sève' of *NA* 175), the so-called porcelain of Chelsea and faience, a tin-glazed earthenware.

The Germans mastered the new technology first, in a manufactory at Meissen, near Dresden (*NA* 175). This facility flourished due to an influx of royal commissions, a wide range of products and high artistic quality, but war interrupted its trade somewhat, and manufactories in Vienna, Sèvres, Höchst and elsewhere were able to capture more of the business. All of these facilities were mixing kaolin, feldspar, water, quartz and varying additives into a paste, storing it for a while to improve its quality and then shaping it into dishes or figurines. The shaped pieces were then baked at about 900°C, leaving them dry and porous. They were then dipped in a glaze, also of porcelain, and fired again at a much higher temperature – 1350°C to 1460°C – which fused the kaolin and feldspar. Then they could be painted and fired a third time, or even a fourth, depending on the number of colours added and whether there was gilding. In the early years of porcelain manufacture, all these designs were hand painted, by artists who specialised in a certain type of subject, such as flowers, landscapes or portraits. The reason they painted on top of the glaze was that the extreme heat of the second firing meant that few colours could be added before glazing, as the kiln would simply burn them away. A handful of colours, however, could survive this process, including cobalt blue, which is why much of the Chinese ware that arrived in Europe was blue and white and why so many European manufacturers created blue-and-white dishes.

The royal manufactory at Sèvres was merely the most successful and influential of many French porcelain workshops. French porcelains were much admired, and their artistic decorations were widely copied elsewhere in Europe. In England, the principal workshops were at Chelsea, Bow, Derby and Worcester – all of which produced soft-paste porcelain – and at Plymouth and Bristol, which made hard porcelain from Cornwall kaolin, the only source in all of England. Most of the items made in Europe were relatively small in size – small boxes, oil and vinegar cruets, needle cases, snuffboxes, thimbles, jugs, ewers, basins (sizable bowls – see *Watsons*, *MW* 359; *MP* 180), vases, candlesticks, inkstands, clocks, dish covers and wine coolers.

Then, of course, there were the breakfast (*NA* 175; *S&S* 13) and tea services – teapots (*Sand*, *MW* 416), coffeepots, chocolate pots, sugar bowls or boxes, creamers, teacups (initially without handles, hence the colloquial phrase 'a dish of tea' – see *MP* 378), saucers and tea caddies. Twelve teacups was a standard number. Sometimes a service would have separate teacups and coffee cups (*P&P* 341), and some sets had a slop basin and a plate for it to rest on, a spoon tray, and plates (*MP* 413) for bread and butter or cakes. When Austen refers to 'tea things' (*Watsons*, *MW* 357; *Sand*, *MW* 416; *S&S* 144, 200; *P&P* 342; *MP* 335, 378), she means this sort of set of dishes, plus a board (*MP* 344) or tray (*Sand*, *MW* 416) on which to carry them; either an urn (*MP* 344) or, in humbler homes, a kettle (*MP* 383), in which to heat the water for the tea; and tongs for the cubes of sugar, all three of which would have been made wholly or partially of some kind of metal. A breakfast service would also have one or two special pieces, such as, perhaps, a toast rack.

Soup tureens, often shaped like animals or vegetables in England and Germany, but rarely in France, were a popular item to be made from porcelain; since the glaze and the core of the item were both made of porcelain, they expanded at the same rate when exposed to heat and thus suffered no cracking in the glaze. They were not the only items to be given whimsical shapes. Sauceboats, too, might be shaped like ducks or like foxes' heads; dram bottles might be shaped like pistols or fish; and mugs might look like a seated man or like a man's head. Dinner plates (*MP* 171) and bowls, much more sober in their design than these fanciful vessels, were often made from porcelain for those who could afford this still-expensive material. Huge platters, however, still had to be imported from China, as no one in Europe as yet could quite figure out how to make such large pieces.

Earthenware and Bone China

For those who could not afford porcelain, there were increasing numbers of attractive, inexpensive alternatives. Two important potteries arose in Staffordshire (*NA* 175) in the second half of the eighteenth century, and these two firms – Spode and Wedgwood – along with many others were responsible for a sort of small revolution on the tabletop. Josiah Wedgwood (1730–1795), an avid experimenter and a marketing genius, saw that people wanted to imitate the classes above them. He therefore aggressively courted royal and noble favour for his products and then used the information to make his products fashionable. His creamware, for example, earthenware with a warm, pale-yellow glaze, was purchased in the 1760s by Queen Charlotte, and he promptly renamed the style 'Queen's Ware'.

He opened a London showroom, streamlined production, made use of the recent improvements in turnpikes and canals to transport his goods with less chance of breakage and, though he created elaborate art pieces, such as vases, for the rich, always kept some of his ceramics within the reach of the status-conscious middle class. They answered his call by discarding their old, rough mugs and dishes and replacing them with delicate, beautifully painted creamware.

Meanwhile, he continued to experiment. He embraced the interest in classical design in the 1760s and 1770s, producing vases in imitation of Attic red-figure originals and introducing classical motifs such as laurel leaves and Greek key borders into many of his pieces. He invented, or at least popularised, a clay 'body' (a specific mixture of components) called 'Black Basalt'. This had a deep black, satiny finish and was used both for art pieces and for ordinary, useful items such as teapots; Parson James Woodforde bought 'a black Tea Pot' in October 1783, probably either Wedgwood's or an imitator's.

Wedgwood had a fascination with reproducing the colours and textures of non-ceramic materials, principally types of stone. Some of his pieces look as if they are made of agate or granite, but he is best known for his Jasper ware, which has the appearance of a cameo, with the background and figures being of two distinct colours. He had a great deal of difficulty developing this technique. Pieces kept shattering in the kilns, some lots showing failure rates of as high as 75 percent, and the cobalt used to colour the background was extremely expensive. In 1782, however, he invented a 'pyrometer' for measuring kiln temperature, composed of a series of ceramic rods that could be inserted into a kiln for a specific length of time, after which they were drawn out and compared to the width of a standard tube. Their degree of shrinkage indicated temperature. He also constructed a special kiln just for firing Jasper ware and reduced the amount of cobalt required by making the bulk of the piece of white clay and then dipping it in a thin coating of the blue. By the late 1770s, he was making all sorts of dishes out of Jasper ware, not only in 'Wedgwood blue', but in two other shades of blue as well, plus lilac, with grey, yellow and dark brown used as backgrounds for decorative pieces such as portrait medallions. Another of his inventions was caneware, a yellow ceramic that resembled bamboo; he had difficulty with it as late as 1779, but it was being marketed in his catalogues by 1787. The various clay bodies were used to make all the standard dinnerware and tea items listed above, plus the large plates, bowls and platters that could not yet be manufactured in porcelain.

Most items corresponded to the sorts of dinnerware we would expect to see on a table today, with a few additions, such as 'salts' (small salt dishes), tall pie dishes shaped like the elaborate standing crusts of poultry pies and custard and ice cups (dessert cups, rather like tea or coffee cups, but with a lid to cover the chilled confection inside). Customers might also buy a pap boat (a sort of cross between a baby bottle and cereal bowl) or a cheese plate, not really a plate at all, but a tall round stand and cover that looked like a small, fancy soup pot. Even simple dinner plates were sometimes much more elaborate than those widely available today. Some of the plates had scalloped rims, pierced rims (with lozenge-shaped sections cut out at regular intervals) or a shell-like edging of tapering grooves.

Josiah Spode Sr (1733–1797) and his namesake son were also busy innovating. At their pottery in Stoke-on-Trent, which comprised several groups of buildings punctuated by bottle-shaped brick ovens three or four storeys tall, they, too, were making punch bowls, tea and coffee sets, plates, mugs and vases. The younger Spode, in 1798, perfected a recipe for bone china (S&S 26), a type of hard porcelain made of ox bones that had been boiled, dried, burned and powdered; china clay; and Cornish stone.

The process of making earthenware began with amassing the ingredients and allowing the clay to sit outside for several months, exposed to the elements, to remove salts that could injure the finished pieces. Though the Spode works was located in Staffordshire, its clay did not usually come from the immediate area, which was noted for its coarse red clay, but from such places as Dorset, Devon and Cornwall. The finely ground ingredients were mixed with water into a wet mixture called 'slip', which was sieved to remove lumps and passed over a magnet to remove iron. After evaporating much of the moisture from the slip, workers cut it with bronze spades into workable pieces from which they kneaded all the air. A thrower used a potter's wheel, operated by a child apprentice, to shape the pieces, which were now called 'green ware'. This green ware was dried and arranged in 'saggars', large round clay containers that protected the pieces from the kiln's most severe heat. After a thorough baking in a biscuit kiln that could hold 500 to 600 pieces at once and that was heated to a temperature of 1100°C to 1250°C, the dishes or statuettes emerged as 'biscuit ware', fired but undecorated and unglazed. At this point, until the mid-eighteenth century, the ware would have been glazed, fired, hand painted and fired again at a lower temperature, but at mid-century, a new technique drastically expanded the variety of decoration available and simultaneously lowered the cost of production.

This was underglaze printing, which was accomplished by one of two methods: paper transfer or bat printing. In paper transfer, the biscuit piece – let us assume it was a plate – was heated to make it more porous. Meanwhile, a copper-plate engraving, with grooves carved into its face where the lines were meant to be, was also heated. Colouring, called 'oil', was applied to the plate, and the excess was wiped away, leaving the oil only in the grooves. A piece of tissue paper, moistened with soap and water to increase its flexibility and decrease its absorbency, was placed over the plate and pressed down with a felt pad. Then it was carefully lifted off and handed to an apprentice – usually a little girl – who cut away the excess paper and cut the parts of the design into separate pieces. These were then rearranged, face down, on the warm plate, by a worker who pressed the paper against the plate to make the colour adhere. The plate was then handed to another worker, who rinsed the plate in water to dissolve the tissue, leaving the colour on the surface of the plate.

Bat printing was similar, in that it transferred the design from an engraved copper plate, but this method used not tissue paper but a 'bat', a sheet of flexible, dried glue, and the copper plate was impregnated not with colouring but with linseed oil. The oil pattern was transferred to the biscuit plate, and powdered colours were sprinkled over the plate, adhering to the places where oil was present. At the end of the day, the used bats were collected by a worker who reboiled the glue and spread it out to dry on plates; in the morning these recycled bats would be ready for use.

In both cases, bat and paper transfer alike, the coloured plate was then taken to a 'dipper', who dipped the piece into a solution containing materials that would harden into a glassy coating when heated.* Underglaze printing was adapted with great success to Spode's Chinese-style plates, including two of its earliest and most popular patterns, Mandarin and Willow. (Willow, probably the most famous blue-and-white ware, featured a bridge with three figures on it, a willow tree, a boat, a house, two birds at the centre top and a fence in front of the house and its garden; Mandarin was very similar, but omitted the fence, birds and bridge.) Spode was, however, not the only pottery to use the underglaze method; it was widely used throughout the industry, as

---

*This glaze was often made with lead, and dippers were known to suffer from the effects of lead poisoning.

the method drastically reduced costs and allowed potters to decorate their dishes with a wide variety of landscapes, figures and other motifs, often copied from popular prints.

Not all pottery was decorated with underglaze prints. Some was still hand painted, and Spode, Wedgwood and others were always anxious to find good painters for their wares. The painting might involve several steps, each followed by a firing. For example, a teapot with a floral design might be painted with a 'resist', a liquid that resisted the application of colour, everywhere that flowers were intended to be painted. Then a background colour would be painted on and the teapot fired. After firing, the resist was removed, the teapot was glazed and fired again, and the first colours of the flowers were hand painted by a floral specialist. More enamel colours would be applied, and the teapot would be fired as many times as necessary in between applications, this time at a lower temperature of 600°C to 900°C to avoid destroying the more delicate enamel colours. Finally, gold mixed with mercury and oil would be added as a detail, and the pot would be fired at a still lower temperature to avoid damaging the gold.

Though any of the large potteries would seem quaintly unmechanised to a modern factory worker, they were adopting many new methods to make and sell their wares. Spode, for example, invested in an early steam engine for grinding flint and the ingredients in enamel colours, supplementing it in 1810 with a more powerful engine that could also turn the potting wheels. Both Spode and Wedgwood built beautiful London showrooms to whet customers' appetites for their products and sent out salesmen with samples – either on paper in books or in the form of sections of glazed plate rim – that showed the selection of hand-painted designs available. Moulds were used whenever possible to speed up production, and lathes were employed to create patterns of ridges.

Metal

Certainly, some of Jane Austen's acquaintance had great stores of family 'plate' (S&S 13, 26; P&P 162) – dishes made of silver that gleamed in the candlelight and made a beautiful display at dinner, but even those who did not own much silver might own a few pieces that would make the best possible show for company, such as teaspoons and ladles. It was this kind of acquisitions that the genteelly poor Austens made in 1808. 'My Mother has been lately adding to her possessions in plate', Jane wrote in December, '– a whole Tablespoon & a whole dessert-spoon, & six whole Teaspoons, which makes our sideboard border on the Magnificent. ... A silver Tea-Ladle is also added.' An individual item of silverware was also considered a welcome gift, and accordingly, in July 1808, Jane wonders in a letter whether to buy Frank's wife 'a silver knife – or ... a Broche', planning to spend about half a guinea on the present. A silver knife, spoon or pap boat was also often given as a christening gift (MP 386–387, 396–397).

Dishes

People like the Austen women had to limit themselves to a few pieces, for silver was quite expensive, not only because it was intrinsically valuable but because there were high taxes on its manufacture. By the late 1780s, silversmiths were being charged 6*d*. per ounce for the silver they used; in 1797, the tax was raised to a shilling an ounce, and by 1815 it had risen again to 1*s*. 6*d*. Parson Woodforde considered it 'a great Bargain' when, in 1789, he managed to buy twelve tablespoons and six dessert spoons for £10; this was no small outlay of cash for a man whose annual income was in the low three figures. Many people, daunted by the cost of solid silver, resorted to cheaper alternatives, such as pewter or Sheffield plate. The former was an alloy of tin and lead or other metals, while the latter was a copper core plated with silver. In the case of hollowware items such as urns and teapots, both outside and inside might be plated with silver, or the inside might be plated with tin instead, to save money. Items made of Sheffield plate included urns; tea, coffee and chocolate pots; tea caddies; salt cellars (which would be lined with either gold or blue glass to protect the silver from the corrosive effects of the salt); mustard pots, also lined with blue glass; cream and sugar containers; punch bowls; toast racks; serving trays (*MP* 65); and various serving utensils, such as fish servers, soup ladles, punch ladles and cheese scoops. All these items, of course, could be made with solid silver as well.

Another type of metal dish was the entrée dish, which kept food warm – an important consideration when several dishes were served on the table simultaneously – by having a reservoir beneath it, which could be kept hot either with a piece of hot iron or, after 1810, by hot water. Deeper breakfast dishes could be heated from below by a spirit lamp. Supper dishes, soup tureens and a wide variety of forks (*MP* 413, 446; *P* 64), knives (*MP* 413; *P* 64) and spoons were also made of various types of metal. Table knives had blunt tips but were nevertheless often used to pick up food and bring it to the mouth; forks, then as now, were held in the left hand both for cutting food and for conveying it to the mouth. The forks might be all of metal or have handles of a different material, such as mother-of-pearl. The largest forks were the toasting forks, which sometimes had wooden handles to protect the toaster's hand from the conducted heat of the fire. Another type of specialised utensil was the egg scissors, which had spiked blades that neatly cut off the top of a boiled egg.

Silverware would have been kept in the sideboard, which was an all-purpose piece of furniture for the convenience of the servants. Food could be placed here either in preparation for serving or as a supplement to the dishes on a crowded table. The butler could open and pour wine here, and in some cases, basins of water were incorporated for washing the silverware. Atop the sideboard might be a knife box for holding the table knives, while inside were drawers for holding corkscrews, napkins and flatware, and a chamber pot for the relief of the gentlemen after the ladies had departed for the drawing room.

Wood and Glass

Wood was no longer an acceptable material for dishes in fashionable homes, though it could be found occasionally in the homes of the poor. It was used, however, for a few specific items. Tea caddies could be of wood, especially if they were elaborately inlaid or equipped with decorative metal fittings. Implements for serving salad, likewise, could be made of wood without shame; Parson Woodforde mentioned an instance in February 1793, when the local squire's wife gave Woodforde's niece 'a large wooden Spoon and a four-pronged wooden Fork for dressing up a Sallad, quite fashion'.

Glass was used primarily for the serving of beverages. Wine glasses (*S&S* 197), for example, were an absolutely essential part of any well-equipped household; these were smaller than the average wine glass today and would have been the responsibility of the butler, if the household had a butler. Only in the homes of the wealthy would the table have had the 'finger glasses' for washing the fingertips, which filled Susan Price with such anxious anticipation (*MP* 446), but most homes of middle class or above would have had a decanter in which to serve wine. The decanter, then as now, had a narrow neck and a wide base, and in order to identify its contents, the butler or, in less well staffed homes, a lesser manservant would place a decorative tag around the decanter's neck. These tags might be made of silver or ceramic.

See also Beverages; Food.

E

Education

Education (*Cath, MW* 193, 203; *Sand, MW* 376; *S&S* 127; *P&P* 139; *MP* 276; *E* 15, 62, 164, 169; *P* 74, 89, 150, 202) was undergoing a revolution in the second half of the eighteenth century. Even after the changes the educational system was still pervasively flawed, the new theories had a good deal of merit. The most influential thinkers about education were John Locke, whose *Some Thoughts Concerning Education* (1693) exerted influence throughout the eighteenth century and beyond, and Jean-Jacques Rousseau, whose *Émile* (1762) encouraged parents to think of their children as naturally innocent and infinitely mouldable. Severe corporal punishment and rote learning were to be discouraged, while good nutrition, healthful exercise and lessons that made learning pleasant were to be embraced. The number of rules should be reduced, and children given more liberty and playtime.

The rise of Locke and Rousseau, however, did not mean the development of an educational system that we would find comfortingly familiar. Almost all aspects of the educational system differed from their modern counterparts, not least the fact that there was no 'system' as such. The government did not concern itself with education, and there was no interest in universal education or in using education as a tool to help people rise through the social and economic system. Education was privately purchased or distributed as charity to poor children in the form of Sunday schools.

The Sunday schools made no claim to a full education, nor did they aspire to one. All they strove for was basic literacy, mostly to fit children to become better servants and better Christians. The fact that Sunday schools kept children inside on their one true holiday a week – for most children worked to help feed their families – was an added bonus. If the children were not idle, they would not get into trouble. The parish school mentioned in *Emma* (456) is probably a Sunday school, as it is described as being 'under the patronage' of two genteel ladies and as being linked in size with its parish – a religious as well as a civil district. Sponsoring of Sunday schools was a relatively common charitable endeavour for upper-class men and women, while support of a mere day school was not.

Working-class children worked themselves, but those in the next tier up might attend a day school in their village or town, run either by a poorly paid clergyman seeking to increase his income or by a woman, depicted in most descriptions as elderly. Such a school run by a woman, called a 'dame school' (*Gen Cur, MW* 73–74), was considered notoriously inadequate, and popular prints depicted the students as often possessing more knowledge than their supposed instructor. Such schools do not fare well in Austen's works either. The idea of sending a child to such a school is played for laughs in *The Generous Curate*, and it is clear that the uncouth and impoverished Price boys attend a similar school, as they are released every afternoon (and early on Saturdays – *MP* 381, 388, 391). Children in such schools stayed few years, as a rule, and were lucky to master the hornbook – a wooden and vellum or paper paddle printed with the alphabet, the Roman numerals and the Lord's Prayer. These rudiments of learning, sometimes supplemented by a didactic verse, were sealed, as Cowper's *Tirocinium* explained, 'Beneath a pane of thin translucent horn' (l.120). The dame schools charged 2*d*. or 3*d*. a week and cared for some children who were almost too young to walk; these were tied to table legs or to the teacher's skirts. There was no pretence of teaching these toddlers; they were sent to school merely to get them out from underfoot at home. Slightly superior schools might charge 6*d*. a week and have real books instead of hornbooks. They taught not only reading and spelling but also, perhaps, a little Latin. Neighbourhood schools such as these often accepted female pupils as well as male.

Austen barely touches on these schools except to point out their isolation from the world she inhabited. The school in *The Generous Curate* is resorted to only because of the comic poverty of the curate; the Sunday school in *Emma* is a charitable venture to which the female patrons would never send their own children; and the school to which the Price boys are sent is merely a foil to the lavish education that Fanny Price has received at Mansfield Park. Boys and girls of Austen's class were tutored at home or sent to boarding schools or there was a combination of the two. Austen herself was taught at home by her mother and father for most of her life and had tutors for subjects that required specialised knowledge. Not only did she have a music teacher and a drawing teacher, for example, but she also went to two different boarding schools for short periods of time: Mrs Cawley's school in Oxford (later Southampton), where she fell ill in an epidemic and nearly died, and then the Abbey School in Reading, where the head teacher was Mrs La Tournelle, an Englishwoman with a French name, a cork leg, a wardrobe that never changed from one day to the next and a passionate devotion to the theatre. In all, the years of Austen's boarding-school education totalled only about three years, and the rest of the time she was taught at home.

Tutors and Governesses

The information about tutors and governesses accords fairly well with what we know about the education of most girls. At home, they learned from their mothers needlework, the rudiments of running a household and basic literacy (*NA* 15, 110; *P&P* 164). If they were lucky and had parents like the Austens, they were also exposed to good books and important ideas. If not, they grew up silly and empty-headed, concerned only with handling a husband and dressing in the latest fashions. Austen must have known plenty of such girls, for she is merciless towards parents who neglect their children's education and towards those of her characters who are incapable of discussing any subject seriously and intelligently. Catherine Morland's haphazard education – a little reading and recitation, some dabbling in music, an incompetent and self-taught bout of drawing and a smattering of French, writing and arithmetic (*NA* 14) – was probably more common than most gentry families would have liked to admit. In some cases, this superficial education was actually the intended result.

In wealthy families, a special full-time tutor called a 'governess' (*J&A*, *MW* 16; *LS*, *MW* 244, 251; *Sand*, *MW* 393; *P&P* 67, 82, 164, 165, 322; *MP* 9, 10, 14, 19–20, 22, 51, 134, 150, 169; *E* 5–6, 37, 164, 278, 299–301, 380, 382; *P* 152) was hired to live in the household and instruct all the young children; in the case of girls who did not go away until boarding school, their duties could last until the girls were in their teens (*J&A*, *MW* 17). The governess occupied an anomalous position in the home, a status to be explored far more fully after Austen's death in Charlotte Brontë's *Jane Eyre*. The governess was not a member of the family, but neither was she a servant in the traditional sense. She was, after all, hired for her education and her accomplishments – achievements that were often superior to those of the people who paid her salary (*E* 301). She could not therefore be automatically dismissed from consideration the way other servants could or relegated to another class of humanity. This special status often earned her the resentment of the rest of the staff, but it did not buy her full membership in the life of the family.

In addition to the governess, 'masters' (*J&A*, *MW* 3; *Cath*, *MW* 198; *Sand*, *MW* 420–421; *P&P* 164; *MP* 20), or specialised tutors, might be hired to teach such subjects as music, drawing and dancing.

Education solely by tutors (*Watsons*, *MW* 329, 331; *S&S* 130, 250–251) and governesses was more common for girls than for boys, though boys, too, experienced the system. Admiral Lord Thomas Cochrane recalled of his tutor that 'my most vivid recollection is a stinging box on the ear, in reply to a query as to the difference between an interjection and a conjunction; this solution of the difficulty effectually repressing further philological inquiry on my part'. Cochrane went to sea late and thus missed out on the education doled out to the 'young gentlemen' aboard ship by a naval schoolmaster (*P* 52).

Boarding Schools

After a little preliminary education at home, many boys and girls were sent to boarding schools (*J&A*, *MW* 16; *Lesley*, *MW* 112; *Cath*, *MW* 203; *Sand*, *MW* 393, 420–421; *NA* 31, 68; *S&S* 208; *P&P* 199–200, 201; *E* 21–22, 23; *P* 14, 31, 40, 152). These might be quite small establishments. Mr Austen, for example, kept a little school in his house, teaching his own sons and taking in a handful of boarding pupils at a time. At the other extreme, they might be England's renowned 'public schools' – a term that often confuses American readers, as public schools in England are what are called private schools in the United States. These included Westminster (*S&S* 251; *MP* 61); Tonbridge School, which Mr Austen had attended as a boy; Rugby; and Eton College (*E&E*, *MW* 32; *MP* 21), founded in the fifteenth century and already one of the most prestigious of the public schools.

Boys destined for the military might attend a specialised boarding school. For future naval officers, this was the Royal Academy in Portsmouth (*Gen Cur*, *MW* 73); for aspiring army officers, it was the Royal Military Academy, which was eventually located at Sandhurst. Austen's brothers Frank and Charles both attended the Portsmouth academy. These schools, however, were in the minority; most boys simply went to sea at about eleven to thirteen years old and picked up a good deal of practical knowledge plus whatever they acquired from the ship's schoolmaster.

Girls could not attend the public schools, but they were on occasion sent to boarding schools for a polite education. These, like boys' schools, varied widely in size and in reputation. The best schools were considered to be in London (*L&F*, *MW* 78; *LS*, *MW* 244, 245–246, 247, 252–253, 266;

S&S 160), where a young lady could pick up a metropolitan accent
and study with the best tutors. Girls' schools in other parts of the
country also brought in male tutors for some subjects (*Sand, MW* 412),
but they often had to be less selective in their choice of masters. Catholic
families sometimes sent their daughters to the Continent to be educated
at convents, a strategy used by Austen only in comic circumstances
(*L&F, MW* 77).

Children at boarding schools spent most of the year there, coming home
only at specified holidays (*MP* 127; *P* 129, 133, 163). At some schools, there
was only one annual holiday at Christmas, and children were in school
the rest of the time. Many students were deeply homesick, including the
schoolboy in Cowper's *Tirocinium*, of which Fanny Price keeps thinking
while she is isolated in Portsmouth (*MP* 431).

Not all public schools separated boys from their families; a handful
were day schools, including Merchant Taylors' (*NA* 32), a school founded
in London in the sixteenth century by the Worshipful Guild of Merchant
Taylors and given a second campus in Crosby in the seventeenth century.
Cowper favoured private tuition at home over a boarding-school
education. He asserts in *Tirocinium* that boarding schools teach boys to
drink, solicit prostitutes, revere the disorderly older boys and gamble.
While acknowledging that fathers felt nostalgia and quite naturally
wanted to send their sons to the places where they themselves had been
happy, he condemned fathers who would take personal charge of the
training of a horse or a dog but not of their own sons. Public schools,
he felt, were sure to confirm faults already present and create new ones,
resulting in 'The pert made perter, and the tame made wild' (l. 346). (He
noted the unruly behaviour of the students, which was legendary at some
schools, but he glosses over the savage corporal punishments.) Austen
seems to share Cowper's dim view of public schools, at least judging by
her side-by-side portrayals of the conscientious Edward Ferrars (privately
tutored, though not at home) and his superficial, immoral brother Robert
(sent to a boarding school). She has Robert make the contrast explicit,
blaming Edward's 'extreme gaucherie' on his private education, while he,
Robert, 'merely from the advantage of a public school, was as well fitted
to mix in the world as any other man' (*S&S* 250–251). The quietly noble
Edmund Bertram attends a public school and does not seem ruined
by the experience, but perhaps his being sent there is another of the
means by which Austen indicts Sir Thomas Bertram's hands-off style
of parenting.

Universities

After surviving the boarding school, many boys proceeded on to one of
England's two universities: Oxford (*MW* 447; *NA* 64, 107) and Cambridge
(*MW* 447).* Their academic reputation for most of the eighteenth century

*Scotland had highly regarded universities of its own (*Lesley, MW* 118).

was not stellar, and, like the boarding schools, they were renowned chiefly for their ability to place ambitious boys in close proximity to future peers who could be of use in furthering their careers later in life (*P&P* 70). The two universities had a long-standing rivalry and a slightly different emphasis in curriculum and theology. The rivalry may help to explain why almost all of Austen's 'good' university students attend Oxford (*S&S* 362; *MP* 21, 88, 94, 376) while the disreputable ones tend to attend Cambridge (*P&P* 200; *MP* 61); her father was an Oxford man, a distant ancestor had founded St. John's College at Oxford, and her brothers James and Henry were both students there. Oxford graduates predominated in the southern clergy familiar to Austen, which would also perhaps have endeared the university to her, while Cambridge was the home of the Evangelical movement, of which she was suspicious.

Students at university entered a college (*NA* 33; *MP* 376), a collection of buildings where the students dined, studied and lived. The colleges had been founded over the centuries, often by royal patrons, and had individual histories of which they were proud. Oxford's many colleges included St. John's, with which the Austen family was affiliated; Christ Church (*NA* 46); Balliol, where Mrs Austen's relative Theophilus Leigh was master; All Souls, where Mrs Austen's father had been a fellow; New College; and Oriel (*NA* 47).

Boys often entered universities at a much younger age than today. They went whenever their studies had rendered them ready to attend. James Austen, for example, matriculated at the age of fourteen. Most boys attending went into the church, though a small percentage entered law and medicine. Some went to learn a little, to form friendships and to have a frolic or two before heading off to the Continent for the Grand Tour (*Cath*, *MW* 196) and the really *serious* partying. Examinations at the universities were regularly scheduled but not difficult to pass, especially as the subjects rarely changed and could be studied in advance. A final oral examination, based both on college-specified texts and on three authors of the student's choice, was brief and virtually impossible to fail. It was said that one could get a BA at Cambridge by reading only two authors: Euclid and William Paley. Those students who were guaranteed of a comfortable income and an easy life studied very little, leaving the academic drudgery to those who needed to adopt a profession after graduation.

Women were not permitted to attend the universities, though Austen appears not to have pined after a university education. A letter to her brother James' Oxford magazine, *The Loiterer*, which may have been written by Jane under the pseudonym Sophia Sentiment, pokes fun at many of the same literary excesses that Austen lampooned in her Juvenilia. It also claims that the author 'never, but once, was at Oxford in my life' and was not impressed by it. It was nothing, she claimed, but 'so many dismal chapels, dusty libraries, and greasy halls, that it gave me the vapours for two days afterwards'.

Curriculum

The subjects studied differed somewhat for boys and girls. Both sexes
were expected to be able to read (*Lesley, MW* 129; *Cath, MW* 197; *LS,
MW* 273) and write English with fluency, to possess a decent grasp of
English grammar (*NA* 120; *S&S* 150; *E* 50–51), to have neat handwriting
(*NA* 14) and to be able to perform simple arithmetic (*NA* 14). Recitation
formed part of the traditional education (*NA* 14), though not, in Edmund
Bertram's opinion, enough of it (*MP* 340–341). A good education also
included a solid foundation in religious doctrine, history (*Hist
Eng, MW*; *Cath, MW* 230–231; *NA* 108–109; *MP* 18, 22, 419) and
geography.

Geography (*MP* 18), in an age of wars and expanding empire, was
considered quite important. Students were expected to be knowledgeable
in 'the use of the globes', as it was called, meaning not only the traditional
terrestrial globe but also a celestial globe that showed the positions of the
constellations in the night sky.

Here the paths for boys and girls diverged. Girls were channelled into
the acquisition of 'accomplishments' (*Plan, MW* 428; *P&P* 12, 39; *MP* 42;
E 21–22, 104; *P* 40), a set of mostly artistic skills that were designed to
keep them busy in their life of leisure and to enhance the pleasure of those
around them. In an age without recorded music, it was considered of first
importance that girls be musical (*J&A, MW* 20; *Lesley, MW* 124; *Cath,
MW* 198, 229, 232; *LS, MW* 253; *Plan, MW* 428; *NA* 14, 56; *P&P* 164; *E* 301),
so that they could play and sing in the evenings to entertain parents,
siblings, husbands, children and guests. An accomplished woman should
also be able to speak French and perhaps Italian as well (*J&A, MW* 20;
Cath, MW 198; *LS, MW* 253; *Plan, MW* 428; *NA* 14; *MP* 22, 312). She should
be able to paint in watercolours and sketch in pencil (*J&A, MW* 20; *Lesley,
MW* 124; *Scraps, MW* 176; *Cath, MW* 197, 198, 206, 232; *LS, MW* 253; *NA* 14,
56, 110–111), although prowess in oils was unladylike. She should be adept
with a needle (*Cath, MW* 197; *S&S* 160; *MP* 18), not merely for the purpose
of sewing and mending clothes, but for the sort of ornamental embroidery
that adorned walls, pillows, footstools, slippers and reticules. Finally, she
should be able to dance gracefully (*J&A, MW* 20), so that she could engage
in one of the central acts of courtship – the country dance.

The authors to whom parents turned for advice in raising their
daughters agreed in the importance of good manners and morals for girls.
Hester Chapone thought that academics and accomplishments could be
added to these essentials, as long as care was taken not to become too
masculine:

Politeness of behavior, and the attainment of such branches of
knowledge, and such arts and accomplishments, as are proper to your
sex, capacity, and station, will prove so valuable to yourself through
life, and will make you so desirable a companion, that the neglect
of them may reasonably be deemed a neglect of duty.

Education

John Gregory, an earlier writer, but one whose *Father's Legacy to His Daughters* was still widely read, stressed modesty and religion far more than academic excellence and in fact cautioned his daughters to avoid wit, which could 'create you many enemies', humour, which was relatively innocent but 'will never procure you respect', and even the appearance of erudition:

> Be even cautious of displaying your good sense. It will be thought you assume a superiority over the rest of the company. But if you happen to have any learning, keep it a profound secret, especially from the men, who generally look with a jealous and malignant eye on a woman of great parts, and a cultivated understanding.

A man of real genius and candour is far superior to this meanness. But such a one will seldom fall in your way.

His advice seems to confirm Austen's dour appraisal of what attracts men:

> The advantages of natural folly in a beautiful girl have been already set forth by the capital pen of a sister author; – and to her treatment of the subject I will only add in justice to men, that though to the larger and more trifling part of the sex, imbecility in females is a great enhancement of their personal charms, there is a portion of them too reasonable and too well informed themselves to desire any thing more in woman than ignorance. (*NA* 111)

Girls who acquired too much learning and were too eager to show it off risked being stigmatised as 'bluestockings' – women so eager to invade masculine realms of study that they neglected the feminine spheres of dress and personal grooming. They became, in short, unmarriageable.

Boys, meanwhile, were expected to grapple with the higher forms of mathematics, such as algebra (*MP* 119) and geometry. They, too, were expected to be able to dance (*E* 328), but the ability to play music or sing was desirable but unnecessary. The main focus of their education was Greek and Latin, with the emphasis on Latin. The curriculum at Eton consisted of writing, arithmetic, Euclidean geometry, algebra, Greek and Roman history, a handful of English literary classics, such as the works of Pope and Milton, and Latin and Greek grammar. Other schools added geography, navigation and modern languages. At the Naval Academy in Portsmouth, which two of Jane's brothers attended, the curriculum included geometry, arithmetic, logarithms, French, fencing, writing, drawing and dancing. Oxford's curriculum was made up of about two-thirds classics and one-third 'sciences', where sciences were defined as logic, rhetoric, geometry, morals and politics. Cambridge stressed classics less and mathematics and moral philosophy more.

See also Music; Reading; Sewing.

Entertainment

While the working class had less leisure than they do today, routinely working Saturdays and often working long hours on weekdays, they had many ways of spending their few free hours. The gentry and aristocracy, with many more leisure hours to fill, found even more ways of passing the time pleasantly. One of their most common recreations was giving and attending parties of one kind or another (*E* 276, 290). They ate dinner at each other's houses and after dinner played cards, played and listened to music or, on occasion, danced. Other parties were formed specifically for dancing, while others featured hired musicians and focused on the quality of the music (*S&S* 248). In 1811, for example, Austen's brother Henry and his wife, Eliza, threw such a party at their house on Sloane Street in London; 'above 80 people are invited for next tuesday Even^g', wrote Jane, '& there is to be some very good Music, 5 professionals, 3 of them Glee-singers, besides Amateurs.... One of the Hirelings, is a Capital on the Harp, from which I expect great pleasure.' On such occasions, it was essential to be (or at least to *pretend* to be) an educated listener and a devout music lover. Private parties (*P* 180, 220, 223, 227) began to predominate among the gentry and aristocracy in the later years of Austen's life, partly because many 'public places' admitted people of any class with the ability to pay the entrance fee. In order to maintain exclusivity (*E* 116), it was necessary to hide in one's home rather than attending public balls.

Outdoor parties (*S&S* 33, 62; *E* 274, 352, 354), which became increasingly popular between 1790 and 1820, took people by boat or carriage to scenic sites, where they might stroll, take in picturesque views or eat picnic food. The Austens, when they lived in Southampton, appear to have taken excursions over the water (*E* 160) to nearby places of interest, including Netley Abbey and the Isle of Wight. One suspects that these outings were rather informal, if only because of the Austens' fairly limited income, but some picnics and 'exploring parties' could be quite lavish, with fully set tables loaded with dishes by liveried footmen.

A 'rout' (*Lesley*, *MW* 136) was an altogether different kind of party, a fashionable evening party that appears, from contemporary prints, to have been designed chiefly to pack as many people into a house as possible. Guests were crammed into hot, crowded rooms (*S&S* 175), where they attempted to talk, play cards or dance without being jostled, groped, tripped or otherwise manhandled. Some people no doubt enjoyed the close quarters and the consequent compression of personal space; satirical prints show jokesters playing pranks on their neighbours at such events, while dirty old men lift skirts, look down dresses or squeeze just a little too close to attractive young women. For others, including, perhaps, the attractive young women, the rout must have been a foretaste of hell.

6. *A Rout*, 1790.

People of all classes liked to go to exhibitions, many of which were priced to admit a wide cross section of the population. Parades and processions on public occasions were free of charge, and even servants and apprentices, if given permission, could afford to go.

Some pleasure gardens, too, charged reasonable admission rates for illuminations, concerts and fireworks. London had a few museums of curiosities that had low prices or were free and existed to draw in customers to some other sort of business. Many shows and displays travelled from town to town. Unusual people or animals – dwarfs, giants, accomplished blind men, performing pigs and bears and so on – were always a hit, particularly in the provinces. James Woodforde recorded in his diary the arrival of such shows with much enthusiasm. In 1784, he paid 6*d*. to see 'the Dwarf Man that is at Norwich'. In 1785, also in Norwich, he saw the 'learned Pigg', wearing a supposedly magical collar, which could spell words by indicating letters on tiles spread before it. This pig was quite famous, was drawn by Rowlandson, and appeared in the writings of James Boswell and Robert Southey. The pig's show cost 1*s*., and afterwards Woodforde paid another 2*s*. 6*d*. to hear a lecture on astronomy and see an 'Eidouranion or transparent Orrery' (evidently some sort of illuminated representation of the movement of the planets).

When Woodforde was in London, he had a wider range of entertainment options. He visited the Shakespeare Gallery, a collection of waxworks in the Strand and an exhibition of 'some very curious wild Beasts'. However, Norwich was not without variety. In addition to travelling dwarfs and pigs, there were 'Bunns Rural Gardens' and, in 1790, an iron foundry that could be toured by visitors. There were occasional concerts – one in September 1790 featured the renowned opera singer Nancy Storace – and, on the king's birthday, fireworks. In Woodforde's own small parish, more rural entertainment was offered. Usually, it consisted of competitions between working-class people: 'smock races' (races run by women, often in various stages of undress, with a smock as the prize), races between men for a shirt and ploughing contests.

Country towns might also be the sites of fairs. Fairs were sometimes primarily intended for business, with stock breeders, farmers or manufacturers coming together to trade livestock or other commodities. In this case, entertainment was provided, but it was somewhat incidental to the business at hand. Other fairs, however, had lost almost all their utilitarian core and were exclusively places to have fun. Puppet shows and pantomimes took the stage; children feasted on gilded gingerbread loaves pressed into fanciful shapes; showmen displayed 'raree-shows', boxes with elaborate scenes constructed inside, which could be viewed for a small fee, usually a penny. Lovers bought each other souvenir trinkets such as bowls, cups and ribbons. Learned animals, animals with extra limbs and other oddities were on display as well.

Jane Austen, sadly, never takes her readers to the fair. (One yearns to know what she would have thought of the learned pig.) She does, however, take us, if only indirectly, to Astley's (*E* 471–472, 481), one of London's most popular showplaces. Sergeant Major Philip Astley (1742–1814), who had begun his career as a horse-breaker for the fifteenth Dragoons, had in 1768 established a riding school that featured periodic performances by himself, the versatile Mrs Astley and 'the Little Military Learned Horse', who could play dead, set a tea table, jump through hoops, heat a kettle and make tea, play hide-and-seek, do mathematical calculations and fire a pistol. By 1776, the emphasis was entirely on the performances, which included not only trick riding but also tumbling, rope-vaulting, 'The Grand Temple of Minerva' and 'le force d'Hercule, or the Egyptian pyramids, an entertainment never seen in England'. Admission prices were 1*s*. or 2*s*., depending on seating. Astley's performance ring acquired a roof in 1779, along with the title 'The Amphitheatre Riding-House, Westminster Bridge'. A rival establishment, Charles Hughes' Royal Circus, flourished from the 1770s until its destruction by fire in 1805; it flourished thanks to such acts as an eight-year-old girl who could ride two horses simultaneously at a full gallop.

Astley kept trying to circumvent the law limiting the number of London theatres by staging pantomimes and other theatrical shows within his walls, but his main focus remained stunts: feats of equestrian skill, animal training or athletic prowess. A 1788 programme featured a broadsword combat between performers dressed as 'a British sailor' and 'a Savage Chief', tumbling, music, dancing, displays of horsemanship, a transparent painting (illuminated, most likely, from behind) and horses dancing a minuet. It was not only the horses who could dance; Astley's son, according to the enthusiastic spectator Horace Walpole, could dance a minuet himself – while riding three galloping horses.

Astley's first amphitheatre burned down in the early 1790s and was rebuilt; a second fire in September 1803 claimed not only the theatre but Astley's mother-in-law and fifty of his horses. The theatre was rebuilt yet again and reopened in 1804, drawing large crowds. This theatre was probably the second theatre that Austen visited in 1796, when she was sightseeing in London. She wrote in August, 'We are to be at Astley's to night, which I am glad of,' but if she described her evening in a later letter, it has not survived.

See also Dance; Games; Music; Public Places; Theatre.

Etiquette

Etiquette was barely a subject of discussion in the Regency, mostly because a strong distinction was still maintained between the trading middle class and the upper class, containing the gentry and the aristocracy. People of Austen's class were 'brought up to the trade' of politeness; they had been reared from birth inside the system and educated year after year by parents, tutors and peers. Any mistakes they made were swiftly corrected (Watsons, MW 332), either by their parents and governesses or by the disapproval of those outside the family. They needed no conduct books or manuals to explain the use of forks or the proper way to make a bow. Their conduct manuals were more concerned with morals and life's major choices: how to think about religion, how to choose a wife or a husband with discretion and wisdom, what books to read and how to converse intelligently and politely. In the Victorian era, a middle class that had chosen to ally itself with the upper class would devour books about the minutiae of daily life, seeking to ape the behaviour of those above them in the hopes of joining their ranks, or at least feeling more like them and simultaneously distancing themselves from the ragged poor. This makes it easier for the historian to determine both what the ideal was and in what ways people were failing to live up to it.

For the Regency, it is harder to determine the specifics of polite behaviour. There are only hints here and there in novels and diaries of the period, and these hints are often maddeningly vague or refer only to the incorrect performance of some point of etiquette, not the ideal being sought. There are detailed accounts of court etiquette available, but the court was a world unto itself, with fashions and modes of behaviour that applied nowhere else in the kingdom. One can search early-Victorian conduct manuals and extrapolate backwards, but this is risky. While some standards of behaviour no doubt remained consistent across both periods, others may have evolved. Certainly, the moral and religious climate of the Victorian era was entirely different from that of the Regency, and it is entirely possible that small points of etiquette added themselves over time, like coral accretions that slowly amassed a mammoth structure.

The chief emphasis, when behaviour was discussed in the early nineteenth century, was on doing things gracefully (Lesley, MW 136; Sand, MW 394–395; NA 45; P&P 39; E 99, 278; P 143). Movements should be smooth, fluid and apparently unstudied. Indeed, by the time men and women reached adulthood, these movements were unstudied, as they had been practised for a whole lifetime. Only when there was a shift in fashion – as, for example, when sofas and upholstered chairs became fashionable, and people needed to learn to lounge, rather than to sit stiffly upright in unpadded wooden chairs – did people of the gentry and aristocracy need to study their posture or gestures.

Bowing (*L&F*, *MW* 94; *Lesley*, *MW* 136; *Watsons*, *MW* 333, 335; *NA* 243; *S&S* 108, 110; *P&P* 73, 92, 166, 195; *MP* 51, 193; *E* 82, 192, 195, 206; *P* 36, 59, 181, 188) was to be done elegantly and gracefully, with no extravagant show of humility (*P&P* 162). A 'scrape' (*NA* 45), which was a backward sliding of one leg while making the bow, was to be avoided, as it looked clumsy and rustic. The depth and duration of the bow depended on the circumstances, as a short, curt bow, more like a nod, could indicate displeasure or mere formal acknowledgment (*NA* 93), while a long bow could be ridiculous in some situations and lend emphasis to one's words or departure in others. Gentlemen were expected to bow upon taking leave of a lady, rather than simply turning tail and walking away. Bows or tips of the hat were also offered as greetings to women, to social superiors and to acquaintances seen at a distance. (Labourers without hats, confronted with a member of the gentry, would bob head or upper body in a bow and pull on the hair at the front of their heads to indicate that they would have removed their hats if they had had them.) Certainly there was some relaxation of these rules among close friends and relatives, who would not expect to be constantly acknowledging each other's presence and departure and who would adopt more informal ways of greeting each other (*E* 99–100, 424).

What applied to the bow also generally applied to the curtsey (*F&E*, *MW* 6; *Cass*, *MW* 45, 46; *Lesley*, *MW* 136; *Cath*, *MW* 215; *Watsons*, *MW* 333, 336; *Sand*, *MW* 394–395; *S&S* 175; *P&P* 214, 267, 335; *P* 59, 181). Women used it as a way of formal greeting and farewell, and it had lost the deep knee bend of earlier centuries to become a quick placement of one foot behind the other and a short bend of the knees, along with a brief inclination of the head. For more informal greetings, women could choose to shake hands (*NA* 34; *S&S* 176; *P&P* 214; *E* 99, 261, 444), even with a man, though conduct books indicated that this was a favour to be distributed with care.

Still less should they allow people to kiss them hello, a custom that had been nearly universal in Shakespeare's day. The author of *The Mirror of the Graces* was sent into paroxysms of disapproval by the mere thought:

> As to the salute, the pressure of the lips: that is an interchange of affectionate greeting or tender farewell, sacred to the dearest connections alone. Our parent; our brothers; our near kindred; our husband; our lover, ready to become our husband; our bosom's inmate, the friend of *our heart's care*; to them are exclusively consecrated the lips of delicacy, and woe be to her who yields them to the stain of profanation!

Among men, the handshake (*Scraps*, *MW* 171; *Evelyn*, *MW* 190; *Watsons*, *MW* 335) was exchanged only between those of roughly equal social class.

Etiquette

Speech was fairly strictly regulated. Conversation (*Col Let, MW* 167; *Scraps, MW* 171; *Cath, MW* 201, 229, 230–231; *Watsons, MW* 323; *NA* 25, 56; *S&S* 233; *P&P* 54, 72, 172; *MP* 47–48; *P* 58, 97) should be on subjects considered appropriate for one's age, sex and class. It would be considered inappropriate, for example, for women of Austen's class to debate fiscal or military policy (*Cath, MW* 212), though they could comment on the price of veal or the welfare of their cousins in the army. They should do so, moreover, in quiet and appealing tones of voice (*P&P* 39). Shouting (*MP* 392), arguing (*MP* 379) and even whistling were forbidden. Men, of course, could do all three of these things, but gentlemen did them out of the hearing of ladies. Conversation was to be adapted not only to one's own class but to the class of those with whom one spoke. One's manner to social inferiors was to be polite and considerate but not overly familiar. When speaking to social superiors, it was critical to remember the proper forms of address and to be neither obsequious nor offensively informal. Bragging (*L&F, MW* 77–78), mannered or affected speech patterns and habitual exaggeration were to be avoided, as were monopolising the conversation (*P&P* 163), indiscretion about family matters, wit at the expense of others or detailed discussions of any part of the body. These specifics were all aspects of the principal rule, which was to think about the feelings of others.

Introductions, one assumes, were made much in the same manner as in the Victorian era, when it was customary for the person of lesser social standing to be introduced to the other, as in, 'Lady Whateverington, may I present Miss Taylor?' In the case of a lady being introduced to a gentleman, the lady was usually treated as the superior by virtue of her sex. The lady would curtsey and the gentleman would bow. Of course, not all introductions would have been this formal, but a degree of formality was considered necessary, especially when people of very different social standing were to be introduced to each other. Furthermore, it was essential that a third party known to both make the introduction (*Evelyn, MW* 187; *NA* 25; *P&P* 6, 256, 351; *P* 141); one did not simply introduce oneself, especially to a social superior (*P&P* 97). Genteel people who had not been introduced simply did not speak to one another (*NA* 22).

An introduction was a matter of some importance, as once two people were introduced, they had to 'know' each other for good (*MP* 183; *P* 176), acknowledging each other's presence every time they met and accepting visits back and forth. The only way out of perpetual acquaintance was for one of the two to do something so horrific and unforgivable that the other could 'cut' him. A cut was a deliberate failure to refuse to acknowledge an acquaintance. For example, two men are walking in different directions on a sidewalk, gradually approaching each other. Their eyes meet. One tips his hat and nods his head towards the other, wordlessly indicating that he has seen him, knows him and wishes him well (or at least pretends to). The other, seeing this, walks past without making any sign of greeting. Or, even more directly and publicly, at a social gathering that included both men, one could refuse to shake the other's hand or to speak to him.

The cut was a serious breach and either required serious provocation or a complete lack of manners on the part of the person delivering it. This is the reason that Marianne reacts so dramatically to Willoughby's cold reception of her at a London party (*S&S* 177). It is also one reason that Elizabeth Bennet is disposed to think Mr Darcy proud and contemptuous; as she has seen nothing in Wickham's manner that would make her think him less than a gentleman, she can only conclude that Mr Darcy's near-cut of him in Meryton (*P&P* 73) reflects a fault in Mr Darcy. The cut, in one form or another, appears repeatedly in Austen's novels, because in her social world it was almost as dramatic an incident as could possibly happen. Sometimes it is the fault of the party who is cut – as it is in Wickham's case. Sometimes it is intended to reflect poorly on the one delivering the cut, as it is in Willoughby's case, Sir Walter Elliot's extremely minimal acknowledgment of Frederick Wentworth (*P* 181) and Miss Bingley's return visit to Jane Bennet (*P&P* 148), which in its form and manner is as close as it could come to being a cut without actually being one.

Dinner etiquette was a little simpler than it would be in later years. The guests often walked into the dining room in couples (*Visit*, *MW* 53), with the rank of the ladies determining the order in which they entered.

7. *The Honor of Precedence*, 1804.

Where rank was equal, married women went before single women, and older ladies took precedence over their juniors (*P&P* 317; *E* 298; *P* 7, 129, 250). Where rank, age and marital status overlapped, there could be confusion and hurt feelings about who went first (*P* 45–46). Once inside the dining room, the hostess sat at the top of the table (*Visit, MW* 52; *Lesley, MW* 121; *P&P* 310), the host at the bottom (*Visit, MW* 52). The pre-eminent male guest was seated on the hostess' right hand, the chief female guest (*MP* 223) at the host's right (*MP* 52). Otherwise, people sat where they liked. They were encouraged to make conversation with their neighbours, and men helped women to the various dishes before them on the table. After dinner, the ladies would drink a glass or two of wine with the men, then retire to the drawing room, again in order of precedence. The men would remain a while in the dining room; in the early part of the period, they had all returned to the drawing room together in a group, but later they were permitted to depart individually.

All then took tea and coffee, signalling by leaving a spoon in the cup or across it when they were done drinking. A cup, once poured, had to be drunk. A contemporary print makes fun of a Frenchman who, not knowing the spoon rule, has his cup refilled over a dozen times before he realises his mistake.

See also Dance; Gentry; Titles.

F

Fan

Fans (*NA* 75, 77) might have sticks of bone, horn, ivory, wood, tortoise shell, mother-of-pearl or metal. The leaf, or covering, of the fan was usually elaborately decorated on both front and back, and the variety of this decoration was quite surprising. There were, as one might expect, scenes of gardens or lovers courting and of episodes and characters from classical mythology. However, there were also fans that showed architects consulting with clients, royal weddings, scenes from popular works of literature and elements of Chinese or Japanese art. Chapel or church fans were printed with verses from the Bible and commonly used prayers and psalms. Some bore riddles, puns, puzzles or games. Businesses issued fans as a form of advertising, using them as a medium to promote plays, spas and coach routes. Vendors in cities such as Rome and Venice made fans painted with pictures of popular tourist sites; these were sold as souvenirs to travellers. A few fans, intended perhaps as the ballroom equivalent of a cheat sheet, included the steps for tricky dances. The designs might be hand painted or printed; in some cases, the design was purely ornamental rather than pictorial and was worked into the ivory or metal sticks in delicate, lacelike patterns.

The construction of a fan involved several steps. The leaf was made first out of lace, cloth, vellum or paper. If made of paper, it would be stuck to another sheet with pliable glue and stretched tightly on a circular frame to dry. Then it would be decorated. Meanwhile, a different craftsman began carving the sticks to the proper size, making them thickest at the bottom, where a rivet would fasten all the sticks together. If the sticks bore decorations of some kind, the stick maker would consult with the leaf decorator to make sure the designs were harmonious. The sticks might be gilded or studded with gems. Then the leaf was placed on a special mould, and a craftsman ensured that the pleats of the fan would fall in an aesthetically pleasing way – for example, never bisecting an important figure. Then folds were marked on the mould and flattened with the fingers. The layers of the leaf were carefully separated at the proper places and the sticks inserted. The sticks were joined with a rivet, and the entire fan was stored either in a small, roughly triangular case, usually of bright green shagreen, or a bag made of silk, satin or brocade.

See also Clothing.

Fire

When twenty-first-century readers imagine an eighteenth-century fireside (*L&F*, *MW* 79; *MP* 188; *E* 22, 113, 303, 461), they usually surmise that the author means a *wood* fire. This is an entirely understandable assumption, since most fireplaces today use either wood or gas for fuel, and gas was not available for this purpose in Jane Austen's day. Furthermore, pictures of stately old houses often show large, open kitchen fireplaces, clearly meant to hold sizable logs. Therefore, it is eminently sensible to assume that when Austen speaks of a fire (*E&E*, *MW* 32; *L&F*, *MW* 100; *Col Let*, *MW* 167; *Watsons*, *MW* 319, 343; *S&S* 90, 193, 307; *P&P* 54, 71; *MP* 139, 151, 178, 249, 340, 398, 446; *E* 24, 53, 115, 320, 322, 323, 340, 372; *P* 134), she means a wood fire. However, it is an incorrect assumption. Wood fires were so rare in Austen's time that she makes a special point of mentioning wood as fuel on the rare instances when it appears (*NA* 167).

The reason her fires are not fuelled by logs has to do with the rate at which the English were consuming their natural resources. England had once been thickly forested in many places, but a rapacious desire for timber for building houses and ships, coupled with a need for fuel, decimated the forests. Timber was so valuable that *plantations* of trees were one of the most prized assets on large estates. Austen's wealthiest brother, Edward Austen (later Edward Knight), had multiple plantations designed for periodic harvesting. Trees were simply too expensive to burn, and when they were burned, it was usually to create charcoal for industrial purposes.

Most people burned a more plentiful natural resource: coal (*MP* 379). Coal was stored near the fireplace in a large box and shovelled into a grate (*S&S* 39; *MP* 168) of horizontal bars that kept it from spilling out. The top bar of the grate could, in many houses, move to the level of the second bar, forming a little shelf for pots and pans. Side flaps inside the grate could be moved in or out to expand or contract the size of the fire. An assortment of devices and tools surrounded the fireplace, depending on its location and use; fireplaces in drawing rooms, for instance, might have decorative brass holders for wood or coal, while such adornments would not be found in the kitchen or in a single-fire home. Many fireplaces also had fenders (*NA* 167), or screens (*P&P* 162; *E* 208), which helped to deflect sparks and excessive heat. A chimney board (*S&S* 274) covered the fireplace in the summer months.

The kitchen usually had the largest fireplace, and here one would find the standard assortment of tools for maintaining the fire – shovel, bellows, poker and so forth – as well as racks, hooks, cranes, spits, pots and pans for cooking. The fire also needed a curfew (a metal cover for banking the fire at night), a tinderbox for lighting the fuel and, in the rare instances when wood was used, irons (*Sand*, *MW* 387) for moving the logs. Towards the end of the eighteenth century, tin reflector ovens were introduced. These stood in front of the fire and partially surrounded roasting meat, making it easier to salvage drippings and harder for the sizzling fat to land on the floor. Toasting or grilling forks would also be present, and some homes had plate warmers, trivets, gridirons for grilling steaks and salamanders (irons that were heated and passed over food to brown it).

Fireplaces in other parts of the house (*Watsons*, *MW* 327; *MP* 308), such as the parlour (*Watsons*, *MW* 355, 356), drawing room (*S&S* 175; *MP* 125, 273) or sitting room (*MP* 312, 322; *E* 240), had fewer associated tools and might well be smaller, as they were for heat only, not for cooking large meals. However, even here, some cooking might be done. Toast or cocoa might be heated here during tea (*Sand*, *MW* 416–417), and some contemporary prints show people cooking more substantial food over a small fireplace in what appears to be a room other than the kitchen. Bedroom fireplaces (*NA* 167; *S&S* 190; *MP* 312) were used for heat throughout the night, and a few coals could be removed slightly before bedtime and placed in a warming pan, a device somewhat like a flat-lidded skillet with a very long handle. The coal-filled warming pan was placed between the chilly layers of bedding to raise them to a comfortable temperature.

The household fire was much appreciated for its usefulness in cooking and for the comfort it offered on cold days. Invalids and the aged, in particular, were thought to benefit from a seat close to the fire (*Sand*, *MW* 413, 415; *E* 10, 217, 351, 357), though it was not only the old and sick who delighted in 'a good seat by the fire' (*Watsons*, *MW* 327; *S&S* 247). Austen herself wrote in 1813, after a party at someone else's house, 'I find many *douceurs* in being a sort of chaperon, for I am put on the sofa near the fire and can drink as much wine as I like.' It is easy to forget in an era of central heating that the internal temperature of a house could easily drop into the forties (on Fahrenheit scale) on winter nights. It is also easy to forget that it was not the master or mistress of the house, typically, who would rise before dawn on frigid mornings to light the family's fires. This task would, in many cases, be performed by a servant (*S&S* 180), who would sweep out the previous day's ashes (*E* 236) and clean the fireplace. According to Eliza Haywood's *A New Present for a Servant-Maid* (1771), this was no simple matter. First, the housemaid had 'to rub the stove and fire-irons with scouring-paper, and to clean the hearth'. Iron and brass fittings could be cleaned with vinegar and ashes, 'then with an oily rag, and after that with scouring paper, rotten-stone, or white-brick' or, alternatively, with goose fat. Steel irons had to be oiled, rubbed with emery and then scoured. The maid then had to fill the grates with coal hauled from a storage area, light the fire with a tinderbox, fan it with a bellows, wash the hearth with hot water and soap, dry it and then move on to the next fireplace.

Fireplaces were troublesome not only to the servants who tended them. They were, on the whole, extremely inefficient. They tended to heat only a small part of the room and to create a draft in other parts, as air was heated and funnelled upwards through the chimney. Air circulation was not always sufficient, and in these cases, smoke poured back into the room (*P* 128). The fireplace linings were often cast of iron, which absorbed heat rather than reflecting it into the room. In short, the English fireplace was a great deal less useful than it appeared. However, English consumers repeatedly rejected attempts to woo them away from open hearths towards efficient, enclosed stoves.

Some attempts at reforming the design of fireplaces were made by the American Benjamin Thompson, later Count von Rumford (1753–1814), whose hearths were considered the state of the art in warmth and efficiency (*NA* 162). He changed the size of the fireplace opening and tinkered with the height and shape of the flue, moved the fire farther forward, recommended firestone or plastered bricks for the fireplace lining and introduced a movable tile for easier sweeping. He sought, as much as possible, to send heat into the room rather than up the chimney and to lengthen the time that it took to consume the fuel, so as to generate more heat for less money.

See also Food; Housework.

Food

Food in Austen's lifetime differed greatly from food consumed in industrialised countries today. From the methods by which it was brought into the household and prepared, to the timing, elements and presentation of the meals, the food was – though containing many of the same components as modern food – alien enough that it would surprise a modern diner in many ways. The quality, quantity and variety of the food depended, like so much else, on economic and social class, and it could be said that in these respects the fare enjoyed by the poor differed as much from that of the rich as both did from modern food. However, some generalisations can be made, especially if we confine ourselves to the sorts of meals likely to have been consumed by Austen's characters.

Acquisition

Food was acquired from various sources, none of them as consistent or as amply supplied as a modern supermarket. Some items were produced on the family farm. There might be livestock that could be slaughtered as needed, a kitchen garden, orchards, fishponds, and fields in which grain was grown. A farm's livestock offered a potential source of fresh meat. In 1798, for example, Jane writes from Steventon of being able 'to kill a pig soon', and Mr Austen also kept sheep, which were sometimes butchered as well.

Some types of meat, particularly among the gentry and aristocracy, would come from the hunting or fishing activities of the family's men. Other items were acquired by purchase from neighbours or by exchanges with family and friends. Those who lived near the sea might send fish to inland relatives and receive, in exchange, a return gift of apples or game birds.

Not all such exchanges were purely friendly. Some were rather more mercenary. Woodforde, for instance, sometimes sold his surplus animals to neighbours or to the local butcher (*Sand, MW* 392; *MP* 58; *E* 186; *P* 202). On 22 December 1788, he reported paying his yearly butcher's bill (£39 11s.) and receiving from the butcher, Harry Baker, a refund of £1 15s. 8d. for a calf. It seems likely that most farmers would have engaged in similar deals with tradesmen, offering whatever they had in surplus as partial payment for their purchases.

In all these types of exchange, buyers, sellers and donors alike were at the mercy of the seasons. Increasingly, throughout the eighteenth century, livestock were able to survive the winter as improved agricultural methods improved the supply of winter fodder; previously, there had been a mass slaughter in late fall or early winter of animals that would otherwise starve. However, even if meat was more continuously available to those who could afford it, fruits and vegetables were restricted to their own particular seasons. Preserving and pickling could extend their life span, but it was not the same thing as having the fresh items at hand all year long.

Some foods were imported, but these were rarely brought in to extend the season of domestically raised produce. Instead, they were foods that did not grow successfully in England or that were deemed better when processed elsewhere. These items included citrus fruits, spices, tea, sugar and Woodforde's fine piece of Parmesan. Such foods tended to be expensive, their prices reflecting the additional costs of importation, and their consumption indicated relative affluence and, in some cases, genuine wealth. Their presence was certainly not taken for granted.

Still other foods were available year round, or nearly so, but were subject to spoilage in an age before refrigeration. Eggs fell into this category, as did milk and some of its by-products. Milk had to be processed immediately: skimmed, strained, preserved as cheese, or the cream churned into butter. Meat, fish and poultry, too, suffered from storage difficulties. Dr. Grant's green goose (*MP* 212) is Austen's most notable example of the failure of meat to keep as long as one might wish.

One way of avoiding some of the thorniest issues of supply and demand was to purchase one's food from specialist shops: a butcher (*Sand*, *MW* 392; *P&P* 331; *MP* 379) who dealt in meat, in large cities perhaps a poulterer (*MP* 212–213) who specialised in birds, a confectioner for sweets and jellies, a baker (*Sand*, *MW* 392; *E* 233) for bread, a grocer for imported items such as chocolate or tea, a fruiterer for fruit and so on. Sometimes there was a significant distance between these sorts of specialist retailers and one's home. When the Austen women lived at Chawton, there was a market in nearby Alton, but it was not especially impressive, and most of the marketing was done in Winchester or Farnham. Some items, such as tea, were ordered from as far away as London. In earlier years, at Steventon rectory, the marketing took place mainly in Basingstoke. The principal grocer in Basingstoke, the nearest town to Steventon, advertised in 1794 that his wares included 'Old Raisin Wine, Confectionery, Perfumery, Stationery, & c. Oils, fine Westmoreland Hams, Burgess's Essence of Anchovies, Mushroom and India Soy, Sauce Royal, Devonshire Sauce, Lemon Ketchup, Olives, Capers, Vinegar & c'. As suggested by this list, shopkeepers could offer a wider variety than farm and friends afforded, and they could offer a more consistent, and sometimes fresher, supply. In some cases, patronising shops was not a matter of choice; residents of towns, such as Mr and Mrs Austen, Jane and Cassandra, during the years they lived in Bath, often had no other options. Without a farm or a kitchen garden, they were naturally dependent on shops.

Food in Austen's day was distributed into different areas by type. This could happen in one of several ways: the food might be available, as described above, in discrete shops – permanent, fully interior spaces, such as a grocer's shop. These shops, with attractive bow windows filled with goods on display, were increasingly replacing the old-fashioned stalls, which were shops open to the street, with the wares arranged on a counter or hanging from hooks. Then there were markets, which might be permanent or temporary and which were set up in sizable 'market towns' (*E&E*, *MW* 29; *H&E*, *MW* 34; *Watsons*, *MW* 322; *P* 10). At a market (*NA* 68), one or more days of the week were set aside for the display and sale of all kinds of goods. As in the case of shops, the vendors remained specialists. One went to a butcher for meat, to a fishmonger for fish, to a grocer or chandler for tea and sugar, and to yet another vendor, usually a farm woman, for eggs or butter or local cheese. Of course, in many cases these multiple errands were simplified by familiarity; the merchant might simply make a notation in his books rather than demanding cash for every purchase. A merchant might also come to recognise the level of quality demanded by a particular client and make no attempt to deceive or haggle, and customers learned to avoid merchants whose wares did not suit them.

The Austens were fortunate in at least one respect. In the years they resided in Bath, the town was blessed with a number of particularly well-stocked shops. Aside from the markets, held on Wednesdays and Saturdays (and on Mondays, Wednesdays and Fridays for fish), there were respected dealers in meat, fruit, vegetables, fish, milk products and even imported wines. Pastry cooks sold confections, ice, jellies and savoury snacks that could be eaten in the shop or taken home. Two of the more prominent Bath pastry shops were Molland's in Milsom Street, mentioned in *Persuasion* (174), and Gill's, built between two buttresses of the Abbey Church.

Shops charged a premium for the variety and convenience they offered; bakers in particular were singled out by public opinion as price gougers. Furthermore, many shops were guilty, intentionally or accidentally, of diluting or adulterating the products they sold. Meat was hard to adulterate, but tainted meat might, by various stratagems, be disguised as fresh. A cask of stale butter might be passed off as fresh by hiding a lump of fresh butter within the cask and offering tastes from this small lump to prospective shoppers. Bread was whitened with chalk or alum, and many foods, from pickles to milk, ranged from substandard to poisonous in quality. Pickled items were sometimes made in copper vats, which not only lent colour to the food but also made it poisonous. Vinegar was sharpened by the addition of sulphuric acid. Pastry cooks used cherry laurel leaves to lend a bitter-almond flavour to desserts, not knowing, or not caring, that the pleasant almond flavour came from cyanide. Prepared anchovy sauce was coloured with a lead compound called 'Venetian red', while olive oil was often processed abroad using lead press plates or lead cisterns, and then imported by unsuspecting consumers. Clearly, customers had to be cautious.

Nonetheless, they continued to buy not only from shops and market stalls but from a variety of places serving ready-to-eat food. Large towns such as London had cook shops, which, according to J. P. Malcolm in 1810, sold 'baked and boiled meat and flour and pease puddings at a very reasonable rate'. Coffee shops and public houses also sold food as well as beverages, and for dessert one might stop at a pastry shop for ice cream, tarts or gingerbread. Food was also 'cried', or sold, in the streets.

Preparation

Even the most casual reader of literature or history must be aware that food preparation (*P&P* 44, 65; *MP* 383) was done in the absence of most modern devices. However, the actual methods of preparation are often something of a mystery to them. What sorts of things were cooked in an oven and to what extent did it resemble a modern oven? How were dishes cooked over an open fire? What equipment was used? Readers often picture a kitchen fire that is either too early or too late – resembling either the giant open hearths of the Renaissance or the cast-iron stoves of the later nineteenth century.

Regency cooking more closely resembled the former model than the latter, though the huge fireplace with its wood fire had given way to a more compact unit with coal for fuel and a metal grate, consisting of several horizontal bars, to keep the coal from falling out. Cooking at such a hearth could be accomplished in a variety of ways. In many homes, the top bar of the grate could swivel so that it fell into a horizontal plane with the second bar, and on these two bars, pots or pans could be perched. Sometimes they supported a gridiron, a round grating used for broiling steaks and chops. Meat could be roasted on spits or in portable tin-reflector ovens, which contained a drip tray and a three-walled spatter guard to keep grease from soiling the rest of the kitchen. Toasting forks in a variety of shapes were used to toast bread, muffins, sausages and other food, and 'salamanders' – named after a mythical beast that lived in fire – were pieces of metal with one flattened end that could be heated in the fire and passed over food to brown it. Most houses would also have had one or more hooks or swing arms from which kettles could be suspended. These kettles were used not only for making soup and broth but also for boiling meat, vegetables and puddings and for providing hot water for coffee and tea. However, hot water was sometimes made instead in a boiler, an iron or copper container with a lid that stood near the fire and had a tap for drawing off the heated water.

A relatively new enthusiasm for efficiency drove the creation of the boiler, as well as the shallower, smaller fireplace, which saved on fuel. The idea was to capture as much heat as possible from the fire, and to this end, ovens were sometimes built adjacent to the fire. There were at least three ways of heating an oven, none of which allowed for much control over temperature. The first was, as stated, to build the oven right next to the main fireplace so as to radiate heat through the wall that separated them. Small box ovens were often built into the wall next to the fireplace, but they had the obvious disadvantage of being heated only on one side, and they were typically not large enough or hot enough to bake bread. The second method of heating an oven was to pass a large iron bar through both the fireplace and the oven; the fire heated the bar, which

conducted some portion of the heat to the oven. The third method, which
was the standard method for detached ovens (such as the ones in the bake
houses of large homes), as well as for many ovens adjacent to fireplaces,
was to build and light a fire inside the oven and allow it to burn out.
The ashes were swept away, and the food, placed inside, was cooked by
the residual heat in the bricks or stones that lined the oven. The effects
of this cooking technique can be seen in baking recipes of the time, which
sometimes instruct the cook to alternate fire and baking several times
for foods that required long periods of heat.

The typical freestanding oven had its bottom about two-and-a-half feet
above the floor and had a diameter of two to three feet and a rounded roof
about a foot-and-a-half to two feet high. The door was occasionally made
of oak strapped with iron, but a fully iron door was more common. At its
hottest, the oven was usually used for bread, which was inserted using a
'peel', a tool similar to an enormous spatula, made of iron with a wooden
handle. Once the bread was removed, items that required less heat, such
as cakes or pies, might be inserted using a peel made entirely of wood.
When only a small amount of residual heat remained, the oven might be
used for other tasks: allowing dough to rise, drying the icing on a cake
or drying fruit. If none of these tasks needed to be performed, the cook
filled the oven with kindling so that the remaining heat would dry out
the wood, making the next oven fire easier to light.

Baking was subject to certain limitations: ovens could get only so
hot, their temperature was to some extent erratic, their heat could not
be kept constant over long periods of time, and they required great effort
to operate. Indeed, in most houses, baking was done once or twice a
week, if at all; an increasing number of households, particularly among
the working classes, chose not to bother with the oven at all but instead
bought their bread from bakers' shops. (The Austens, when they lived at
Steventon, were not among these families; Mrs Austen made all her own
butter, cheese, bread, beer and wine.)

Economy of effort extended beyond baking to all the cooking done in
the house. There was a tendency to do most of the cooking in preparation
for dinner – the most substantial meal of the day – and to use the leftovers
from dinner to feed the servants and make up cold suppers. This meant
that it was exceedingly difficult to scrape together a dinner at the
last minute or to scrap one in favour of an invitation to dine elsewhere.
Maggie Lane has pointed out that, while last-minute invitations to tea
are common in Austen's writings, her characters know better than to offer
a last-minute invitation to dinner when the prospective guest's servants
are probably already well advanced in their marketing, cutting, chopping,
stewing and broiling. Austen does refer to impromptu or standing dinner
invitations, but these are usually offered to one person at a time – Jane
Fairfax (*E* 283) or Mr Bingley (*P&P* 103), for example – and one person
could easily be accommodated by stinting the servants a little and feeding
them on plainer fare or by substituting a different cold dish at supper for

the dinner leftovers. Once the cooking was finished, there still remained one aspect of preparation to be performed at the table. This was the carving of the meat (*P&P* 163; *MP* 34), an important ceremony, since meat was the centrepiece of every dinner among prosperous people. It was customary for the hostess to sit at the head of the table and for the host to occupy the foot. Meat that came to the table whole was brought to the bottom of the table, where the host would slice it and serve it to his guests. Cookbooks of the time usually include a section on carving, which was a delicate business.

The carving of a turkey, chicken or beef or pork roast is familiar to many home cooks today, but the Regency host had a wider array of animals to divide. He might be called upon to cut up a saddle of mutton, a hare, a pheasant, a goose, a haunch of venison (*P&P* 342; *MP* 52) or a pig's or calf's head. Small wonder that the timid Mr Woodhouse usually relinquishes his place at the bottom of the table (*E* 291); one suspects that the daunting task of carving is taken up either by Mr Knightley or, in his absence, by the servants.

Serving

Many members of the household staff were involved in the preparation and distribution of food. In humble homes, many of the tasks would be performed by a kitchen maid or a maid of all work, with the dishes being passed around with little ceremony. However, in most of the homes that appear in Austen's novels, there are servants not only to cook the food but to present it. In houses that could afford to keep male servants (*P* 129), this job would be performed by one or more footmen (*S&S* 233, 355; *P&P* 162; *MP* 180; *NA* 213; *P* 219), who carried in the platters from the kitchen with a great show of bustle and efficiency. The footmen also stood around the table (*MP* 239), ready to assist diners who needed more of anything.

The dishes were delivered all together, with platters and tureens scattered at the top, bottom, sides, and corners (*E* 218) of the table and extra food, along with wine and glasses, placed on a sideboard (*E* 458). This made for a great show of abundance and wealth, but it was not, perhaps, the most convenient way to serve a variety of dishes. Some dishes occasionally went cold before they could be served (*MP* 239), while others might not reach the diners who wanted them. Nonetheless, the attractive display was too enchanting to be forgone, and there would be no substantial change in the method of service until the second half of the nineteenth century. In the more prosperous households, there would be a 'second course' – not merely a second type of food as we would use this term today, but a removal of most or all of the platters and bowls from the first half of the meal, followed by a completely new set of dishes (*E* 218) – more meat, vegetables, sauces, tarts and so forth. Then, after a decent interval, this food was removed, along with the tablecloth (*S&S* 355), and wine and dessert were served (*Watsons*, *MW* 325; *S&S* 355), the latter being not so much sweets or cakes but as small finger foods such as nuts (*E* 28, 35; *P* 86), olives and dried or fresh fruit.

Other meals were less elaborate. Servants were indeed present to bring the food in (*MP* 344), clear it away and attend to the needs of those who were eating, but there were fewer types of food to serve, and there was less show and ceremony expected. The family took more responsibility for making the tea, the coffee, the sandwiches or whatever else was at hand, leaving less for the servants to do.

French versus English

French cooking, like the French language and French manners, occupied an ambivalent place in English culture. On the one hand, the aristocracy adored all things French and leapt to pay French 'man-cooks' far more than they would pay an Englishwoman. Many people farther down the social ladder then imitated this vogue for France. On the other hand, there was a good deal of patriotic irritation at Francophilia, and this irritation only increased as wars with France dragged on for most of Austen's life.

The battle between French and English only explicitly reaches the dinner table in one of her novels, however. This is *Pride and Prejudice*, in which Darcy's circle is twice identified with French cooking. The first instance brings up the feature of French cooking that was so controversial – sauce. Sauces were integral to French presentation, with the chief meats or vegetables thickly intermingled with their sauce in a ragout. The English style of presentation, on the other hand, was to plop a large piece of meat onto a platter with a comparatively thin sauce spooned around it. To the English, the former method seemed deceptive – *anything* could be hidden in there – and the latter was straightforward and honest. A goose was a goose and looked like a goose. The contrast forms the substance of Elizabeth Bennet's only exchange with Mr Hurst, Mr Bingley's brother-in-law, 'who when he found her prefer a plain dish to a ragout, had nothing to say to her' (*P&P* 35). With that, Austen dismisses Mr Hurst from serious consideration, not only because he thinks too much of food, but also because he has chosen the wrong side of the argument.

Yet French cooks remained fashionable, and those who could afford such a luxury hired them. Few, indeed, could afford it; French chefs charged their employers handsomely for their services. Mrs Bennet refers to this practice in one of her assessments of Mr Darcy's wealth, commenting, 'I suppose he has two or three French cooks at least' (*P&P* 342).

Breakfast

The names and timing of meals differed in some respects from their modern forms. Then as now, breakfast (*LS*, *MW* 284, 285, 286; *NA* 60, 84, 154, 203, 235, 241; *S&S* 63, 83, 96, 164, 172, 201, 202, 369; *P&P* 31, 33, 41, 61, 215, 266; *MP* 156, 445; *E* 10, 50, 237, 258, 259, 293, 472; *P* 58–60, 95, 102, 107, 145, 229) was the first meal of the day, but for the gentry it came late, usually around 9:00 or 10:00 a.m. All meals, as we shall see, were later for the idle and fashionable than for the old-fashioned (*E* 443; *P* 59) and for the working classes. Early breakfasts tend to have a specific reason for being eaten at an uncivilised hour (*NA* 228; *MP* 280, 282–283, 374). The late hour at which breakfast was served among the gentry, however, should not necessarily be taken as evidence that they were late risers or entirely idle before breakfast. Frequently, they rose fairly early and engaged in some activity before breakfast. Jane played piano before the nine o'clock breakfasts at Chawton, for example, and when staying elsewhere, she might write letters to fill the time. Others took walks to work up an appetite (*S&S* 180; *P* 104). The eldest Austen son, James, did so when he was a curate at Deane, walking a mile on some mornings to visit his father at Steventon. A healthy appetite was often necessary, for breakfasts could be quite lavish, even if they paled in comparison to the variety and quantity offered at dinner. Breakfast in a substantial home might include cold meat (*MP* 282), cheese, fish, eggs (*MP* 282), coffee, tea (*L&F*, *MW* 106), chocolate (by which Austen's contemporaries meant the beverage, cocoa, rather than solid chocolate), rolls, toast, bread (*NA* 241) and butter and, on occasion, freshly prepared steaks or chops. Sometimes, the heartier elements of the meal were eschewed, and the meal consisted mostly of some form of bread or cake accompanied by tea or another hot beverage.

Luncheon, Picnics and Dinner
The next meal was dinner (*Visit*, *MW* 52; *Lesley*, *MW* 121; *Cath*, *MW* 229; *LS*, *MW* 299, 303; *Watsons*, *MW* 324–325, 339; *Sand*, *MW* 389; *S&S* 67, 160, 193, 247, 315; *P&P* 45, 54, 342, 344; *NA* 84, 96, 114, 116, 129, 211; *MP* 104, 141, 142, 191, 194, 220–221, 296, 336, 406–407, 412, 469; *E* 6, 14, 50, 108, 209, 213, 226, 290, 303, 344; *P* 39, 54, 95, 98, 137, 140, 219), and it was by far the most significant meal of the day. At one time it had been held around noon, or in the early afternoon, but the association of high status with late mealtimes led to a creeping inflation of the dinner hour. By Austen's day, the upper classes served dinner to their children at about 2:00 or 3:00 p.m., while the adults ate at 5:00 or 6:00 p.m. The result was a long period in the middle of the day when no food was served.

Therefore, as the gap between breakfast and dinner widened, with everyone trying to eat later than their neighbours, it became more common to have a little something between breakfast and dinner. However, this meal, known variously as noonshine, nuncheon or luncheon, did not become standard during Austen's lifetime. Even in families who regularly indulged in sandwiches, cold meat or some other light fare around noon, the food was seen as refreshments or a 'collation' (*H&E*, *MW* 38; *E* 367) rather than as a full meal. It was eaten in the drawing room, or wherever the family happened to be gathered, rather than in the dining room, which further deprived it of full mealtime status. It might also be consumed on the road at an inn, when travellers were at the mercy of schedules and of inn location. In such circumstances, they ate when they had the chance, regardless of time and fashion. *Lunching* was not an English verb until the 1830s and did not become an acceptable term among the educated until still later.

On occasion, people chose to take their afternoon meal outdoors, in which case the meal might be referred to as 'cold meat', a 'cold collation' or a 'picnic'. The practice of eating outside with packed lunches was also known as 'gipsying'. All members of the party were supposed to contribute something to the meal, rather like a potluck dinner today, and the result could either be a good-natured sense of communal purpose or an unpleasant contest of display.

Dinner was not only the largest meal but also an important marker in the passage of time. It officially ended the morning, regardless of when it was scheduled. Morning dress, in which one went walking and paid morning calls, was exchanged for evening dress (*E* 114), which in women's case often meant revealing a little more skin. An invitation to someone's house for dinner (*E* 290) was more intrinsically valuable than an invitation to any other meal, because it was at this meal that the full efforts of the household staff were engaged.

A *Gentleman's Magazine* letter of 1819 about the customs of Herefordshire describes the meal simply enough. Among 'the nobility and the gentry', dinner is served at 5:00 or 6:00 p.m. and consists of 'soup, poultry, butcher's meat, and sweets: the wines, port and sherry'. This, the author insists, is true not only in Herefordshire but everywhere in England. He makes no such claim for the yeomanry, whom he describes as eating 'a profusion of butcher's meat' and drinking cider or beer. Labourers ate more or less meat depending on their circumstances. Live-in servants and farm labourers usually ate the same food as their masters, which generally included a fair amount of meat, while poorer tenant farmers and small craftsmen might be able to afford meat only seldom. According to contemporary accounts, in 1794 in Hampshire, live-in farm labourers mostly ate pork and pudding, while in Middlesex in 1795, labourers ate 'bread and cheese and pork for breakfast, coarse joints of beef boiled with cabbages and other vegetables, or meat pies or puddings for dinner, cold pork, bread and cheese, etc. for supper; and with every meal, small beer'.

8. *A Picnic Excursion*, Rowlandson Etching, 1790, detail.

At its simplest – that is, when no company was present – dinner even among the gentry was not an especially lavish display, especially by the standards of the day. Parson Woodforde, when dining alone at home, lists very simple dinners in his diary: 'Fryed Soals and cold green Goose for Dinner' and 'Giblet Soup and Shoulder Mutton rosted' are two typical entries from July 1791. A dinner of similar simplicity appeared on Henry Austen's London table in 1813 when he welcomed his sister Jane, his brother Edward and three of Edward's daughters – in Jane's words, 'a most comfortable dinner of soup, fish, bouillée, partridges, and an apple tart, which we sat down to soon after five'.

However, dinners for company tended to be as lavish as the host's budget allowed (*MP* 221, 239). Most dinners consisted of one 'course' – that is, one set of dishes, perhaps only three or four or perhaps as many as twelve or fourteen – placed on the table nearly simultaneously. In such cases, the customary formula was for the host to say 'You see your dinner' (*Watsons*, *MW* 354) in order to inform the company that no second course would be forthcoming, and they might eat all they liked of the present dishes without needing to save room for more. In some homes, this first course would be followed by a second course (*P&P* 84, 120, 338). Whether the meal was of one course or two, it was usually followed by dessert (*E* 89, 219).

Dinner, even more than breakfast, was subject to fashionable delay, for postponing this meal advertised one's wealth; a later dinner, and the consequent extension of evening activities into the hours after dark, meant extra expenditure on candles. Only the lowliest workmen still ate dinner at noon, therefore, and among themselves, the gentry, aristocracy, tradesmen and artisans kept tabs on each other to see who reigned supreme at staving off hunger. The difference of an hour or even half an hour was no trivial matter. Comparing the manners of the modest rectory at Steventon to those of her wealthy brother Edward's house in Kent, Jane wrote in 1798, 'We dine now at half after Three, and have done dinner I suppose before you [her sister Cassandra, then visiting Edward] begin. ... I am afraid you will despise us.' Ten years later, she reported, 'We never dine now till five.'

Some of her characters betray the same awareness of dinner hours. The genteelly poor Elizabeth Watson, in Austen's unfinished novel *The Watsons*, has to apologise to the fashionable Lord Osborne when he makes a 'morning' call at 2:55 p.m. (*Watsons*, *MW* 344) and finds the family's housemaid readying the table for dinner. 'I am sorry it happens so,' explains Elizabeth, 'but you know what early hours we keep' (346).* *The Watsons*, perhaps because it examines the life of a family barely

---

*The Watsons had their parallels in the real world. In 1789, novelist Horace Walpole wrote that his unfashionable four o'clock dinners were often interrupted by 'morning' calls from acquaintances. Another fictional example occurs in the Juvenilia, where Lady Greville not only interrupts someone else's dinner but also forces the unfortunate victim to stand at her coach door in the wind and cold (*Col Let*, *MW* 158–159).

holding on to its gentry status, is the most concerned of all Austen's works with the timing of meals and the social consequences of this timing. The self-consciously trendy Tom Musgrave aspires to 'an eight o'clock dinner' (355) and even implies that he might dine as late as nine (356), an absurdly late hour. When he accidentally lingers late enough for supper at the Watsons', he flees, though he has eaten nothing all evening, simply for the pleasure of 'calling his next meal a Dinner' (359).

Musgrave is unusually silly about his mealtimes; most of Austen's characters eat, by early-nineteenth-century standards, at a much more reasonable hour. The Dashwoods at Barton Cottage eat at 4:00 p.m. (S&S 74, 361), as do Catherine Morland, General Tilney and Miss Tilney when they eat at Henry's Woodston parsonage (NA 214). Of course, both Sense and Sensibility and Northanger Abbey are early novels; as the years went by, the dinner hour crept farther and farther into evening. As evidence, Diana Parker, a character in the unfinished late novel Sanditon, eats at 6:00 p.m. (Sand, MW 411), though she is not satirised for any pretence to cutting-edge etiquette. Even within a single novel, however, there may be differences of dinner time based on social stature, London or provincial residence and adherence to London or rural manners when in the country. (London dinner times were generally later.) Henry Tilney, for example, may dine at four, but his richer and more ostentatious father dines at five (NA 162, 165).

Tea

Dinner ended with the withdrawal of the ladies to another room, while the gentlemen remained in the dining room to talk, drink and smoke. Some eighteenth-century sideboards were even equipped with chamber pots so that the gentlemen could relieve themselves without having to exit the room. When they had finished discussing subjects deemed inappropriate or uninteresting to women – politics, financial matters, hunting, bawdy humour and the like – they rejoined the ladies in the parlour or drawing room (MP 334–335), and here tea was served (Col Let, MW 150; Evelyn, MW 187, 189; LS, MW 269; Watsons, MW 354; Sand, MW 390–391, 413; NA 118; S&S 99; P&P 166, 344–345, 346; MP 104, 177; E 8, 124, 347, 382–383, 434).

Tea was, at this point, neither fully a meal nor simply the pouring of a beverage. Its components varied from household to household, but in the homes frequented by the Austens, it included not only tea but coffee as well. The women of the family prepared these beverages, and there was frequently some sort of food offered as well. At its simplest, this was bread and butter, which might take the form of some sort of roll or muffin, toast made in the kitchen or slices of bread to be toasted at the drawing-room fire (MP 383). However, many families chose to provide more than bread. There might be cakes or other sweet offerings.

The time at which tea was served depended on when the family ate dinner. The Austen family, when it dined at 3:30 p.m., served tea at

6:30 p.m., and the fictional Edwardses of Austen's incomplete novel *The Watsons* take their muffin and dish of tea at 7:00 p.m. (*Watsons, MW* 326).

Supper

Supper (*F&E, MW* 8–9; *J&A, MW* 23; *Col Let, MW* 167; *P&P* 84, 348; *MP* 267, 283, 376), too, was dependent on dinner for its schedule and even for its very existence. Supper as a formal meal, with hot dishes, the tablecloth laid, and everyone sitting around the table, was virtually non-existent among the fashionable. Dinner had crept later and later, with teatime following about three hours afterwards, and the result was that there was no time before bedtime to go through the full ritual that a sit-down meal demanded. Therefore, 'supper', when it was eaten at all, became more of a hearty snack – in the words of *The Gentleman's Magazine* letter cited above, it was merely 'a tray of cold meat, or a light thing hot'. Some people who took their dinner and tea especially late eschewed supper altogether (*Watsons, MW* 351). There are several references to suppers in Austen's letters – a supper of tart and jelly with Edward's wealthy benefactress and adoptive mother Mrs Knight; another of widgeon, preserved ginger and black butter served to guests; a third of toasted cheese served to Jane in 1805 by Edward Bridges because it was her favourite supper food. Clearly, in this respect at least, Austen and some of her circle were content to be well fed and unfashionable.

However, at balls, where the participants might stay active until well after midnight, it was not only acceptable but even obligatory to serve a substantial supper (*S&S* 252; *E* 248, 254–256). Public balls, such as those at Bath's assembly rooms, often served tea (*NA* 21, 25, 59), while private balls tended to have more extensive refreshments. The latter might include cold or hot drinks, as the weather dictated, soup, sandwiches or more complex dishes. For the guests who merely played cards, sat by the fire or watched the dancers and gossiped, the supper was a convenience; for those who danced for hours with little intermission, it was a caloric necessity, hence Austen's famous, oft-quoted pronouncement that '[a] private dance, without sitting down to supper, was ... an infamous fraud upon the rights of men and women' (*E* 254). However, this is not Austen's only word on the subject. Another reference, this time from *Sense and Sensibility*, makes clear that while food of some kind was a constant, its presentation was variable and depended on the preferences of the hosts and the requirements of fashion. A 'mere sideboard collation' (*S&S* 171) – that is, a sort of buffet table, at least in its comparative level of informality – will do for the country, but not for London, where a sit-down meal with footmen in attendance is a necessity.

Meat

The constant in all these menus is meat (*Sand, MW* 393; *P&P* 169, 268, 331; *NA* 190, 214; *E* 355, 365; *P* 39), for meat formed the centrepiece of almost every meal. One could get by without it for tea, sometimes for breakfast and on the occasional solemn religious holiday, but for the Georgians, it just was not dinner or supper unless the table held a haunch of something, a small flock of birds or something's steaming head. Meat equalled food so much so that 'to take one's mutton' was an idiomatic way of saying 'to eat' (*NA* 209; *MP* 215, 406). Roast beef (*Lesley*, *MW* 112–113) in particular was wrapped up with the national identity, celebrated in song and pictorial art as the source of British strength and the evidence of British virtue. (A sirloin of beef dances prominently next to John Bull in the illustration *John Bull and His Friends Commemorating the Peace* [Napoleonic Wars].) It was perceived as simple, straightforward, copious and life giving, as opposed to the Frenchman's little bits of things – frogs and snails and pretentious sauces – that, according to the propaganda of the day, left him dangerously lean and jealous of the fat and jolly Englishman. Even those who could not afford to eat meat very often lauded the Roast Beef of Old England.

Cookbooks of Austen's day, as well as contemporary diaries and letters, reveal the variety of meat consumed. Far more mutton and game (*S&S* 30), for example, was eaten then than is eaten today. A modern cook would expect to see headings for chicken (*Lesley*, *MW* 114; *S&S* 33; *P&P* 100; *E* 24), turkey (*Visit*, *MW* 54; *Lesley*, *MW* 119; *Watsons*, *MW* 353–354; *MP* 212, 215–216; *E* 483), duck (*Beaut Desc*, *MW* 72; *Scraps*, *MW* 173; *P&P* 331) and perhaps even goose (*MP* 215–216; *E* 28–29), but a turn-of-the-nineteenth-century housekeeper would also require recipes for partridge (*F&E*, *MW* 8–9; *Scraps*, *MW* 173–174; *Watsons*, *MW* 344; *P&P* 342), pigeon (*F&E*, *MW* 8–9; *Lesley*, *MW* 119, 129; *E* 353), pheasant (*F&E*, *MW* 8–9; *MP* 104, 105, 171), quail, larks, woodcocks, snipe and other game birds. Furthermore, cooks drew distinctions that we are less likely to make today: recipes often differed based on whether a duck was wild or domestic and, if wild, to what species it belonged. Even among domestic birds, there were divisions, such as that between a 'stubble' goose – old enough to have lived through a harvest and fed off the scythe-cut grain fields (and traditionally eaten in late September, around Michaelmas) – and a 'green' goose (*MP* 111), eaten in May, whose name came not from its colour but from its youth. Hens, too, were differentiated by age; a 'chicken' was technically a hen too young to lay eggs, while a 'pullet' (*Lesley*, *MW* 129) laid eggs but had not yet moulted, and a 'fowl' (*Lesley*, *MW* 113–114; *Watsons*, *MW* 346; *S&S* 160) was a fully adult hen that had undergone at least one moult. Then there were hares (*Sand*, *MW* 412), rabbits and leverets (hares under a year old – see *F&E*, *MW* 8–9), as well as venison (*Evelyn*, *MW* 182; *NA* 210; *P&P* 342; *MP* 52). Frequently, several of these types of meat would appear on the table in a single meal.

Nor did variety derive only from the types of animals eaten. It also came from the parts of the animals that made their way onto platters. Few parts of the cow, for instance, went to waste. Diners feasted not only on steaks (*MP* 379), rumps and sirloins (*Lesley*, *MW* 113) but on tongues (*Lesley*, *MW* 119), udders, necks, ribs, feet (*Visit*, *MW* 53), sweetbreads (the thymus glands of calves – see *E* 329), hearts, 'lights' (testicles), tripe (stomach lining – see *Visit MW* 53) and even whole heads. Even the bones were not neglected; their marrow went into soups and sauces.

Methods of preparation included roasting (*Lesley, MW* 112–113; *Watsons, MW* 353–354; *E* 172), boiling (*S&S* 160; *E* 177), baking, stewing (*Lesley, MW* 112–113), braising, frying (*Watsons, MW* 341; *E* 172) and grilling, then referred to as 'broiling' (*Lesley, MW* 113). In many cases, the meat was boiled or roasted, and its drippings – sometimes referred to as its 'gravy' – were combined with mild spices and broth or wine to make a sauce. Common accompaniments to beef (*Lesley, MW* 128; *Scraps, MW* 173) included mustard, horseradish, sauces based on anchovies or oysters, butter and sauces flavoured with onions (*Visit, MW* 53) or a related vegetable such as shallots or leeks. Veal (*Lesley, MW* 121; *S&S* 160; *NA* 68) often appeared in the form of 'collops' – small, thin slices – with some sort of accompanying sauce. Both beef and veal might be 'forced', which meant being stuffed with some sort of seasoning or with forcemeat, a sausagelike mixture. Both might be layered with other types of meat or forcemeat and then rolled, tied and cooked.

Leftover meat did not go to waste. Some of it went immediately to the servants' table for their consumption. The remainder was saved and served up again at supper or breakfast, where it might appear cold (*NA* 214), sliced and used in sandwiches or chopped up and reused in a 'made dish'. Made dishes were more complex than the standard roasted or boiled joint. They used sauces, vegetable ingredients and interesting methods of presentation to overcome the fact that the meat – the real focus of the dish – was not being eaten in its impressive original form. Made dishes included various kinds of minced, hashed (*MP* 413), rolled, spiced and sauced meats, as well as meat incorporated into pies (*P&P* 44; *P* 134) and patties. Some made dishes were served hot; others, at room temperature.

In homes attached to farms, where an entire animal would have to be killed in order to supply meat for the household, it was essential to preserve some of the meat for later use. Some pieces would be prepared for immediate use on the table, while others would be hung or soaked, and still others would be dried, salted, smoked, potted or pickled for use in the far-distant future. Potting meat, for example, involved chopping it up into small bits, mixing it with butter and sealing it into a pot with a cap of clarified butter. Pork (*E* 172, 173, 175, 177), one of the cheapest meats (and thus sometimes less esteemed than beef, venison and other expensive varieties), kept extremely well when cured into ham (*Lesley, MW* 114; *S&S* 33; *P&P* 100) or bacon; Mrs Austen, on one occasion, cured six hams at Southampton to be sent to sea with her son Frank, a naval officer.* On another occasion, in January 1799, she ordered an entire pig to be killed and cured as shipboard provisions for her other sailor son, Charles.

---

*We think of ham today as being exclusively a pork product, but hams were also made from beef, veal and venison.

However, even with multiple methods of preservation, many types of meat remained seasonal. For example, while mutton (*L&F*, *MW* 100; *Lesley*, *MW* 113; *S&S* 197; *MP* 215–216; *E* 109, 119, 168), in a wool-producing nation, remained available year-round, the nature of the sheep's reproductive cycle, with a predictable lambing season, meant that lamb (*E* 353) was a seasonal food. The young, tender lambs who were still nursing rich milk from grass-fed ewes were known as 'grass lambs' and were available from April to September. A few of these lambs were then kept in pens over the winter and were slaughtered as slightly tougher 'house lamb' from November to March.

Two of Austen's references to meat deserve special clarification. The first is a request for 'fried Cowheel & Onion' in her play fragment *The Visit* (*MW* 53). Cow heel turns out to be a nearly impossible dish to find in cookbooks of Austen's era, though dishes that sound somewhat similar are easy to come by. Veal knuckles are fairly common, and many of the recipes for veal knuckles include onions. However, Austen's terminology implies that we are in search of a foot, or part of a foot, rather than a joint of some kind. The *OED* defines *cowheel* as 'The foot of a cow or ox stewed so as to form a jelly' or a dish made from this jelly, but this presents the food historian with a few difficulties. The first, Austen's union of gelatin and onions, is not quite as bizarre as it seems; savoury jellies were an old tradition in English cooking, and though they were being superseded in popularity by sweet jellies, it is not necessarily out of the question to unite jelly and onions in a single dish. However, Austen specifically refers to the cowheel as 'fried', and fried gelatin is indeed hard to imagine. Furthermore, jellies are almost always referred to as being made from calves' feet, not those of cows or oxen. More importantly, the concept of fried gelatin is simply not present in the cookbooks of Austen's day. Therefore, she must have meant something else.

One has to return to much earlier cookbooks to find the dish Austen intends, with the name she gives it. A recipe for 'Cow-Heel' appears in Richard Bradley's *Country Housewife and Lady's Director* (1736), and a somewhat altered recipe, under the name 'Fried Ox Feet', resurfaces in John Farley's *London Art of Cookery* (1783). Both versions meet Austen's requirements. They use the feet of adult cattle, rather than calves; they are fried; and they include onions. By Austen's time, this dish was considered humble fare; in fact, much of the humour in this part of *The Visit* comes from the rustic dishes being served at a genteel dinner.

The second dish requiring clarification is 'Liver and Crow' (*Visit*, *MW* 53), which appears in the same scene. This dish presents us with some difficulties, for none of the major cookbook authors of the later eighteenth century seem to have included a recipe for it. Indeed, since they frequently plagiarise from one another, adding a handful of original recipes to enliven a new cookbook and slightly rewording hundreds of others culled from competitive cookbooks, the researcher encounters the same frustratingly similar description over and over. Hannah Glasse writes of bacon hogs, 'The liver and crow is much admired fried with bacon; the feet and ears are both equally good soused.' Charles Millington and John Farley phrase it in precisely the same words. Clearly, liver and crow was a well-known dish to Austen's contemporaries, so well known that an explanation of its preparation seemed unnecessary.

In order to find a full recipe for the dish, we need to go back to the mid-eighteenth century, to William Ellis' *The Country Housewife's Family Companion* (1750). This volume is only in part a cookbook; in many other respects it is a complete guide to being a farm wife, with extensive sections on keeping the dairy and curing cattle of disease, caring for poultry (*P&P* 222), processing wheat and storing flour and doctoring the family and servants. There is an explicit emphasis on frugality, and many of the recipes are specifically identified as being for 'poor people', while only one is directed at 'the gentry'. French names for styles of preparation, always an indicator of fashion, are absent, but perhaps the strongest evidence that this was a cookbook for the working classes was the almost total reliance on pork as meat. There are plenty of directions for preparing bacon, brawn and pig's innards but only a handful of recipes for beef and mutton, and the references to beef are entirely about using calf guts. The presence of not one but two recipes for liver and crow in this volume confirms that the dishes in *The Visit* were deliberately chosen for their incongruity on a genteel table.

The liver in question was a pig's liver; the 'crow' was its intestines or its mesentery (a piece of tissue adjacent to the stomach and intestines). According to Ellis, both pieces, along with the sweetbread (thymus gland), were 'the first meat we dress of a hog, for this sort is fit for frying as soon as it is cut out'. All three pieces were cut into 2- or 3-inch squares and fried in the fat that melted from the crow, then served with mustard.

Seafood

As an island nation, Britain had plenty of access to good fish (*L&F*, *MW* 79; *P&P* 61; *E* 14). Improving transportation times meant that saltwater fish could maintain their freshness farther and farther inland, much to the delight of the populace. This meant, however, that stew ponds (*S&S* 197; *E* 361), where the gentry had bred freshwater fish, fell somewhat out of favour, as it was believed that freshwater fish had a less pleasant taste than ocean varieties. (However, when Mrs Austen visited Stoneleigh in 1806, she noted that the magnificent estates had, among its other attractions, ponds that produced excellent fish.) Of course, fish could always be salted, in which case perishability was less of a concern, but salt fish were even less desirable than fish from stew ponds.

While the variety of game consumed in the eighteenth century might be surprising to modern home cooks, the variety of fish is a little less so. Hannah Glasse, who tends to be fairly comprehensive on such matters, lists recipes for turbot, carp, tench, cod (*S&S* 160), mackerel, weavers, salmon (*S&S* 160), herring (*Visit*, *MW* 53), water-sokey, eels, lampreys, pike, haddock, sturgeon, skate, sole, crab, lobster, prawns, shrimp, crayfish, oysters, mussels, scallops, smelts, white-bait and miscellaneous small and flat fish. John Farley and Elizabeth Raffald follow her lead, though Farley lists trout among his fish.

Seafood was also used frequently in sauces and stuffings. Oysters (*Watsons*, *MW* 335, 336; *E* 24) often form the basis of 'forcemeat' (meat stuffing), sausages and sauces, while anchovies in small quantities are added to sauces for their intense flavour. Poultry and fish were the dishes most likely to be garnished with seafood-based sauces.

Oysters were beloved in other contexts as well. London cookshops sold cheap oysters to the working classes, just as later in the nineteenth century oysters would be sold by street vendors as a snack. Oddly, during the eighteenth century, it was fashionable to buy green oysters. The oysters of certain Essex Rivers developed coatings of algae around September, and when their odd appearance became appealing to diners, oystermen began 'breeding' green oysters by catching regular oysters and steeping them in salt marshes for a few weeks until they acquired a dark green tint to their shells. Less-reputable dealers saved time and trouble by dyeing the oysters with copperas or other poisonous green dyes.

Dairy and Eggs

In most homes, gentry and working class alike, women had charge of the dairy (*P&P* 163; *MP* 104) and the poultry yard (*P&P* 163; *MP* 104). Here, their tasks included milking, cheese making, butter making, feeding chickens or other fowls and gathering eggs. However, for those women who bought their cheese, eggs and butter at the market, it was important to be a careful shopper. Cheese might be infested with worms, mites or maggots, and housewives were cautioned to make sure that the entire rind of the cheese was intact, 'for, though the hole in the coat may be but small, the perished part within maybe considerable'. The freshness of eggs (*Clifford*, *MW* 43; *MP* 31, 104–105, 106, 282; *E* 24) was to be judged by their temperature, by holding them up to a candle to see if the yolk appeared solid and the white clear, or by placing them in cold water, where John Farley assured his readers that an 'addled or rotten' egg would float. Eggs could be stored for a while in bran, straw, hay, sawdust, ashes or salt, but Farley advised that 'the sooner an egg is used, the better it will be'.

It was always preferable to produce dairy products at home, where their quality could be strictly controlled. Milk (*P* 135), in particular, was valued when it came straight from the cow. However, the milk sold in towns was especially notorious. Watered down, thin and blue (*MP* 439), often contaminated by germs, it was avoided by anyone who had a choice. Mrs Austen, who had had a small herd of dairy cows at Steventon, no doubt missed them after the family moved to Bath, and then on to Southampton and Chawton. At Chawton, Cassandra lamented, 'We have not now so much as a cow.'

Most of the milk consumed in the eighteenth century was cow's milk. Earlier centuries had relied to some extent on the milk of goats and sheep, but this dependence seems to have waned by Austen's day. However, the milk of asses was a delicacy treasured by invalids, who found it easier to digest than cow's milk (*Sand*, *MW* 393, 401). It is worth remembering that pasturage for dairy cows was less consistent than today, and the unfortunate dairymaid might discover, upon milking, that her cows had been eating cabbage, turnips or certain wild plants, which would give the milk a bad odour.

Milk for drinking was taken from the pans after the cream had been skimmed off to make butter. The buttermilk that remained in the churn after the butter was made was also drunk as a beverage. Alternatively, the whole or skim milk could be processed with rennet and made into cheese. The rennet was derived from a calf's stomach bag, pickled in brine or salted, dried and used a piece at a time as needed. A section of the bag would be boiled to yield the rennet.

Cheese (*Col Let*, *MW* 156–157) made in the summer, when cows were pastured on fresh grass, was the richest of all. Full of milk fat, it had a yellow hue, and accordingly, housewives shopping for cheese looked for the golden tinge. It did not take cheese makers long to learn how to simulate the appearance of summer cheese; they simply added saffron, annatto or marigold petals to the mixture. Their deception lives on in the artificial colouring applied to many cheeses, including much cheddar. The same trick was applied to butter sold at markets and in chandlers' shops, using marigold petals or carrot juice as a food colouring.

Domestic cheeses included Stilton (*E* 89), Cheshire, Warwickshire, Gloucester, double Gloucester, north Wiltshire (*E* 89) and Cheddar; imported cheeses, which were more expensive and had to be purchased from grocers and other specialty food dealers, were led in popularity by Parmesan. The cream cheeses mentioned so often by Austen (*Lesley*, *MW* 129; *MP* 104, 105) were then, as now, soft, young cheeses that only took a week or two to cure. Cheese was always well liked at all levels of society, and everyone who could afford to buy it ate it. People of all classes enjoyed toasted cheese (*Beaut Desc*, *MW* 72; *MP* 387), a piece of toast topped with shredded cheese, or a mixture of cheese, wine, mustard and spices, that was browned before the fire or with a tool called a salamander.

Vegetables and Fruit

Vegetables (*Sand*, *MW* 380) in general were far less popular in Austen's day than they are now. To some extent, this was the result of seasonal availability. Not all vegetables could be preserved beyond their natural season, and most were far less palatable in their preserved state than when fresh. To some extent, the blame lay with the tendency of the English, noted by foreign observers, to overcook their vegetables and to smother them in butter sauce. Primarily, the relative absence of vegetables in the diet was due to the primitive understanding of medicine and diet. No one even knew what a vitamin was, let alone where it might be found or what its impact on health might be. Novelist Frances Burney D'Arblay and her husband were unusual in being 'people who make it a rule to owe a third of their substance to the Garden'.

This is not to say that vegetables were not eaten, merely that they were overwhelmed in quantity by the vast piles of meat consumed on the average upper-class or middle-class table. Vegetables – though they were more commonly referred to at the time as 'potherbs' or 'garden stuff' (*Sand*, *MW* 380; *S&S* 30) – appeared on their own as side dishes or as accompaniments to meat or eggs. Almost every country home had a kitchen garden, which in the case of large estates might run to several acres. Jane's mother was an avid gardener well into her old age and grew not only flowers but also herbs, fruit, potatoes, peas and other vegetables. She had a fascination for new plants, judging from the fact that at Steventon she was considered trendy for growing potatoes (*MP* 54), and at Chawton in 1813, she grew tomatoes for eating long before they were considered edible by most of the rest of the nation.

Storage methods varied according to the vegetable in question. Parsnips (*E* 172), for example, could simply be left in the ground over the winter, where their starch would convert to sugar as they froze. Potatoes, carrots (*E* 172) and turnips (*E* 100, 172) could be stored in a cool, dark room such as a cellar. Cookbook author Charles Millington advised keeping beans in jars, alternating layers of beans and salt; peas, he said, should be boiled in salt water and dried. Mushrooms, according to Elizabeth Raffald and others, should be steeped in salt for a while, then drained, baked in an oven at very low temperature, then sealed in jars with the liquid that was yielded by the baking and capped with a layer of suet. Beetroot (*E* 89) was sometimes served fresh; it also lent itself well to pickling; the roots were sliced and often cut into decorative shapes before pickling.

Methods of preparation varied as well; boiling, stewing, broiling, frying and pickling seem to have been the most common. Peas were usually boiled, sometimes in combination with lettuce. Spinach was often served with eggs, while cucumbers (*L&F*, *MW* 100; *P&P* 219), whose shape and firmness lent them to being filled, were often hollowed out and packed with meat or vegetable stuffings. They were also eaten raw or pickled and might, odd as it sounds to modern ears, be given as gifts. In May 1801, Austen writes of the appropriateness of a cucumber as a gift, noting that such a vegetable was worth a shilling, and Parson Woodforde writes of visiting a friend in May 1784 with 'a Cucumber in my Pocket' as a present. Salads (*P&P* 219), like cucumbers, might be served raw or cooked; they might be composed of fresh lettuces or of any boiled and cooled vegetable, served with a light sauce as a dressing.

Some vegetables were prepared in ways that seem especially alien today. Celery (*E* 89), for example, which is today used primarily as a flavouring in stuffings and stocks or as a raw vegetable dipped in dressing or mixed into salad, was then cooked in a variety of ways. It might be stewed, batter fried or served in a thick sauce as a ragout. Cabbage (*Sand, MW* 380; *E* 354) was often boiled as a whole head and served in one gigantic lump, sometimes with interior hollowed out and filled with forcemeat or with forcemeat layered in between the leaves.

Though the English were not wild about vegetables, they were quite enthusiastic about fruit (*Evelyn, MW* 182; *Sand, MW* 380; *S&S* 30). The cultivation of orchards had been a hobby of the well-to-do for centuries, and landowners took pride in locating and nurturing the best varieties.

Parson Woodforde was at least as delighted with his Anson apricot as Mrs Norris was with her husband's Moor Park (*MP* 54).* The ingredients of desserts tended to reflect this pride. Fruit-based confections were quite popular, as was unadorned seasonal fruit and fruit that had been preserved in some way. Fruit found its way into puddings, cakes, jams, marmalades, jellies, dumplings, fritters, wines, pies, tarts, creams and distilled waters. Preserving (*MP* 54–55), drying and pickling kept many fruits available (in some form at least) year-round.

Fruit tended to be eaten after meat and its accompaniments. If there was only one course at dinner, the fruit tarts (*Scraps, MW* 173; *MP* 13, 54–55; *E* 24–25, 239) or other fruit dish would be placed on the table at the same time as the other food, but if there were a second course, the tarts and such would usually make their appearance then. Dessert was composed mostly of 'finger foods' and often had a fruit component, usually something like raisins, other dried fruit (*S&S* 194) or fresh fruit that could be eaten easily without silverware.

Parson Woodforde, once again, provides us with a window into what the gentry actually ate, confirming much of what was printed in contemporary cookbooks. His diaries record fruit as part of pastries and jellies, fruit in sauces to accompany meat and fruit eaten on its own, almost always as part of a dessert course after dinner. On various days between 1780 and 1795, he ate 'Currant Jelly Sauce' as an accompaniment to roast swan; a 'Damson Cheese', a kind of fruit jelly made with damsons and sugar; apple sauce as an accompaniment to pork; apple, currant, gooseberry, raspberry and grape tarts; apple fritters; strawberry and raspberry creams; apple and raspberry puffs; baked apples; brandied cherries; apple, apricot and gooseberry pies and apricot dumplings. Fruit he ate by itself included raisins, pippins, oranges, apricots, strawberries (*E* 354–355, 358–359, 368), black grapes, plums, mulberries, melons, currants (*E* 359), cherries (*E* 359), 'Peaches, Nectarines and Grapes' – the last grouping identical in kind, and almost identical in wording, to the assortment of fruit served at Pemberley (*P&P* 268). Contemporary cookbooks also list recipes for desserts based on pears, peaches, pineapples, lemons, mangoes, cranberries, quinces, citrons, barberries and blackberries.

---

*In fact, according to R. W. Chapman's notes to *Mansfield Park*, these were actually the same variety of tree, which were also called Temple's apricot or Dunmore's Breda.

The more exotic the fruit or the more prized the variety of tree, the more it advertised the wealth and status of its owner. Certain kinds of fruit required special care, and this was especially true of pineapples. A tropical fruit, the pineapple was transplanted to England, where it could grow and produce fruit only in hothouses called *pineries* (*NA* 178). The plants took a long time to mature, and the care and cost that went into nurturing made them a living status symbol. To offer one's guests such a valuable treat was the ultimate gesture of welcome, and the pineapple became a symbol of hospitality. It can still be seen as a motif on everything from cookware to textiles today, where it retains the same meaning, though the symbolism is less widely recognised.

The fruit dish that receives the most attention in Austen's works is the baked apple (*E* 236–238, 240, 328–329), which surfaces repeatedly in *Emma*. Baked apples could be made fairly rapidly in a 'quick oven' or in slow stages in an oven that was cooling after being used for other purposes. The Bateses, who are too poor to own an oven of their own, sent their apples (and, no doubt, their bread as well) to be baked by the local baker, Mrs Wallis, who probably charges them a small fee to use her oven. Since the apples are cooked as the oven is cooling, it takes two to three sessions to get them soft enough; Mr Woodhouse, always careful of his digestion, prefers them cooked three times.

Another apple dessert was the apple dumpling (*E* 237), which was either a very small, cored apple or a segment of a larger apple, wrapped in puff pastry and then wrapped in cloth and boiled. Sometimes, when the cored whole apples were used, the centre was filled with marmalade (*S&S* 121). Apples were also made into puddings, pies and fritters; they were preserved, pickled, roasted and stewed. Part of the reason for the apple's popularity was that, like root vegetables, it kept well. Apples could be harvested in the fall and laid out in some cool, dry place – often a garret or attic – so that they did not touch each other. With luck, they could be stored (*E* 245) this way for several months, and since they were being used in tarts and pies rather than being eaten fresh, their gradual deterioration of texture was less noticeable.

Bread and Porridge

Since potatoes were not yet a principal part of the English diet, and rice was consumed only rarely, most of the starch on the table came from wheat flour in the form of breads (*Col Let, MW* 157; *MP* 7; *E* 165), puddings, pancakes and fritters. That it was wheat flour and, whenever possible, *white* flour was a relatively new development in English history. For centuries, white bread had been a delicacy enjoyed only by the upper class, with humbler levels of society dining on fine whole wheat bread, coarse whole wheat bread, bread made of mixed wheat and rye flours or, at the very bottom of the economic scale, bread made of barley or of barley and peas. However, by Austen's time, the working class had lost its '*rye teeth*', in the words of a description of Nottinghamshire labourers in 1796.

A large loaf of white bread was considered the right of every man, woman and child, and people grew extremely cranky when they were forced by necessity to eat anything else, as they were at times during the shortages caused by the Napoleonic Wars.

They did not always bake it themselves. Not all homes had bread ovens, which used expensive wood as fuel. People without an oven either bought ready-made bread from a baker or else made up their loaves at home and took them to the baker to be baked. Making up one's own loaves was time-consuming, but at least it allowed control over the ingredients. Bakers were frequently accused of whitening their bread with additives, chiefly alum. Some bakers also added potatoes to their dough, as Accum said: 'I have witness that five bushels of flour, three ounces of alum, six pounds of salt, one bushel of potatoes boiled into a stiff paste, and three quarts of yeast, with the requisite quantity of water, produce a white, light, and highly palatable bread.' He acknowledged that there was nothing harmful in this practice, but he was miffed that bakers did not pass their savings along to the customers in the form of lower prices. He was more indignant about bakers who used carbonate of magnesia, gypsum, chalk and even pipe clay in their bread – all without telling the customers what the loaf contained. Accum was ahead of his time; legislation against adulterants in bread would not be passed until 1872.

Those who had an oven of their own, of course, could save money and be sure of the quality of their bread by making it themselves. Baking, because it was so labour intensive, tended to be concentrated into as few days as possible. An entire household's bread for the week, for example, would be baked in just one day.

Whether store bought or home made, however, bread truly was the foundation of the meal. Many people could not afford to eat meat on a daily basis, but a family was considered truly destitute if it could not buy bread. People ate bread and butter (*MP* 383, 439; *E* 168), buttered toast (*L&F*, *MW* 106; *Sand*, *MW* 416, 417; *MP* 383) and rolls for breakfast; for luncheon they often ate sandwiches (*Evelyn*, *MW* 182; *MP* 65; *E* 254), named after John Montagu, fourth earl of Sandwich, who invented that handy snack in about 1760; for dinner there were starchy meat puddings and sweet fruit puddings, both of which had flour as a chief ingredient; for tea there was more bread or toast or possibly muffins (*Watsons*, *MW* 326–327; *P&P* 76; *E* 170; *P* 135), the bread known today in America as 'English muffins' and in England as 'crumpets'; and for supper there might be more bread and butter or bread and cheese or porridge, (*P&P* 24) or gruel (*E* 24, 100, 104–105, 133), a boiled dish made from various types of grain, of varying thickness, and sometimes incorporating spices, fruit or wine. Another type of porridge suitable for supper time was made from arrowroot (*E* 391, 403). Arrowroot is a starch derived from the tubers of *Maranta arundinacea*; similar starches can be extracted from other members of the genus *Maranta*. Along with its close relatives, sago, salop and tapioca, arrowroot was considered an appropriate, nourishing food for invalids, so Emma naturally offers some to the ill and weak Jane Fairfax. It also makes sense that Hartfield would have plenty of arrowroot on hand, since Mr Woodhouse's digestive system is so sensitive.

Pastries and Sweets

Consumption of pastry and confectionery increased substantially during the eighteenth and early nineteenth centuries. It was, after all, the first age in which sugar was abundantly available in Europe, thanks to rapidly multiplying colonies in the West Indies. It was also an age without widespread refrigeration – only the wealthiest people and commercial enterprises such as pastry shops (*NA* 44) could afford to keep ice houses for making chilled desserts. Both these influences had their effect on sweet dishes.

The relative novelty of large quantities of sugar made it the principal flavouring in many dishes. Jellies (*Lesley*, *MW* 119; *Evelyn*, *MW* 182; *MP* 283), for example, which were thickened with isinglass, hartshorn or calves' foot gelatin, often had little flavouring, because the beauty of the apparently frozen liquid was half the fun, and anything sweet was the other half. Cookbooks instructed readers in constructing gelatin models of moons, stars, fishponds, islands and temples using specially designed moulds and filling them with appropriate colours of 'jelly'. The lack of refrigeration meant that puddings, custards (*E* 25), cakes, tarts and biscuits dominated the national sweet tooth. Ices (in other words, ice cream – see *Cass*, *MW* 45; *Evelyn*, *MW* 182; *NA* 116; *E* 290), jellies and other desserts that needed to be cooled were consumed at the homes of the rich, at specialised shops, or during cold weather, when nature could be enlisted as *sous chef*.

Pudding (*MP* 413; *E* 109) was a specific kind of dish that was by no means always a dessert. It might be a floury confection with fruit and suet (*Visit*, *MW* 53), tied in a pudding bag and boiled; a meaty centre surrounded by pastry, tied in the same bag and boiled; or a custardy mass baked in the dripping tray below a joint of roasting meat. There were lemon puddings and almond puddings, chestnut puddings and carrot puddings, spinach puddings and rabbit puddings. The starch in them most often came from flour, but there were also oat, millet and barley puddings. Savoury puddings were often served with the meat in the first course, while sweet puddings followed in the second course.

'Biscuits' (*MP* 413; *E* 329) in Austen's time were also not quite what might be expected. To Austen, they were small baked treats that usually contained flour, sugar and eggs, but rarely butter. They might even be as simple as Hannah Glasse's orange biscuits, composed of dried sheets of orange peel and sugar. The common denominator between all biscuits was that they were baked – the root of 'biscuit' means 'cooked twice' – until they were dry.

Cakes (*P&P* 268; *MP* 344; *E* 156, 213; *P* 45), likewise, differed from their modern counterparts. They might be very small, for eating with tea, or they might be enormous, as they were for special occasions such as weddings and Twelfth Night. These gigantic cakes were not cooked in pans but instead with a large hoop around the dough to keep it roughly in shape. The idea of a specific sort of cake for weddings was just evolving. In general, wedding cakes (*E* 19) were made with a rich batter, into which the cook placed candied citrus peel, nuts, raisins or currants and some sort of alcohol – wine, brandy or rum. The gigantic cake was baked, then covered with an almond icing, baked again to brown the icing, then coated with a very white icing to serve as a contrast to the almond layer beneath.

Rout cakes (*E* 290) were altogether different. These were small cakes dropped onto and baked on a sheet of tin – the eighteenth-century equivalent of a cookie sheet. They were composed of butter, flour, sugar, currants (few cakes seem to have been considered complete unless they included either currants or caraway seeds), eggs, rose- and orange-flower waters, wine and brandy.

Tarts and small pies often had a crust that is similar to what we use today and were not baked all that differently. Savoury pies could be enormous and were baked without pans, in a crust so thick and stiff that it stood alone. Shaped like clay and filled with meat, they were completed in one of two ways. Either the 'gravy' would be added before baking, in which case the top crust would be pinched into place atop the pie, or the top crust (the 'lid') would be baked without attaching it to the bottom, and the liquid would be poured in after baking. Some pies took an intermediate form; mince pies (*P&P* 44), for example, might contain mostly meat, meat and fruit in roughly equal proportions or fruit only.

One treat enjoyed by all levels of society was gingerbread (*E* 233). Gingerbread had long been a special treat among the English, and by Austen's time it had evolved from its medieval roots as a dish made with bread crumbs and wine. It could be made as a breadlike loaf or as bite-size gingerbread 'nuts'. Large cakes of gingerbread were sometimes baked, then pressed into detailed wooden moulds, such as moulds of kings and queens, and occasionally gilded. Other popular treats included sweetmeats (a catch-all category that included marmalade and candied citrus peel – see *S&S* 193) and sugar plums (another general category comprising candies or comfits made with boiled sugar – see *S&S* 191).

Soups, Stew and Curries

Soup (*Lesley, MW* 112–113; *Evelyn, MW* 182; *NA* 116; *P&P* 342; *MP* 52, 180) was the quintessentially cheap meal, the means by which the poor could turn a lump of unappetizing meat, a few handfuls of grain and some vegetables into a tasty and nutritious meal. It was a source of unfailing exasperation to reformer Sir Frederick Eden that the poor insisted upon roasting their meat, or boiling it in a mass, rather than chopping it up for soup, which would have been, to his mind, more economical. Yet soup could be dressed up quite a bit beyond this modest presentation. On the tables of the gentry, it might be the sea in which a French roll, a fowl or a piece of veal rose like an island. It was certainly, if nothing else, an opportunity to display the huge and decorative tureens that formed an essential part of a good china service.

Soups usually started with a broth (*E* 88), to which the cook added herbs, vegetables and usually some sort of meat. Sometimes it was beef, but it might also be fish, oysters or eels. Turtle soup was considered highly desirable, but it was also prohibitively expensive, and most people made do with mock-turtle soup made from gravy, Madeira and calf's head.* To complete the illusion, it was suggested that the cook serve this soup in a turtle's shell.

Generally served as part of the first course, if the meal was grand enough to be divided into courses, the soup was served right away. Once it was finished, its tureen – which usually occupied a place of honour at either the top or the bottom of the table – was removed and replaced with another showy dish. Thus, Jane Austen's uncle James Leigh Perrot wrote of his dinner on 4 July 1806 that he ate 'Mackerell at Top, Soup at Bottom removed for a Neck of Venison'. Soup was also considered appropriate for suppers at balls (*Watsons*, *MW* 315; *E* 330) and for people returning from an outing, such as a trip to the theatre. Austen does not usually specify what type of soup was served, but she does make a reference to 'white soup' (*P&P* 55), which was the most elegant type of soup, based on veal broth, cream and almonds. Its lofty reputation stands in contrast to the humble, everyday 'pease-soup' served at Steventon on 30 November 1798. Pease-soup was ubiquitous and without pretensions, a thinner descendant of the centuries-old 'pease porridge hot, pease porridge cold, pease porridge in the pot, nine days old'.

Stews (*Headache*, *MW* 448) were thicker and more generally full of meat; frequently, they simply consisted of one or more large pieces of meat surrounded by a thick broth. Like soups, they had the advantage of needing little attention from the cook. Once in the pot, they could be left to cook themselves, with only occasional stirring required. Curry (*Lesley*, *MW* 121) was the stew's exotic cousin, which, with 'pillau' or 'pillaw', made its way into cookbooks via Britain's possessions in the East Indies. Curry is not an individual spice but a mixture of several spices, and by the 1780s this mélange, premixed and ready for use, had found its way into English groceries and kitchens.

Sauces and Spices

It has been claimed that the English of Austen's day had only one sauce, or perhaps only two sauces – brown and white. This is a vast oversimplification. While it is true that the most common sauce for meat was its own juices thickened into a seasoned gravy and that the most common sauce for vegetables was 'melted butter' (a combination of butter and flour), there were plenty of other sauces (*Headache*, *MW* 448).

*This is why the Mock Turtle in *Alice in Wonderland* has a turtle's flippers and a calf's head.

There were oyster sauces that were popular with turkey, onion sauces for poultry and rabbit, celery sauces and sauces made with hard-boiled eggs. Most sauces were based on either gravy or cullis, strong broths based on browned beef, veal knuckles, fish or vegetables. Then there were condiments, either home made or store bought, that added to the depth of simple sauces: lemon pickle, mushroom ketchup and mum ketchup (but not tomato ketchup).

The use of spices had declined since the seventeenth century, but Georgian cooks had a wide range of spices available to them, thanks to England's far-flung commercial empire. A well-stocked pantry might have salt, black and white pepper, mustard, nutmeg, mace, cloves, cayenne pepper, Jamaica pepper (allspice), cinnamon, caraway seeds, saffron and even curry powder. Vanilla was prohibitively expensive, but its place was supplied by rose water and orange-flower water, which lent a subtle flavour to fruit dishes and pastries.

See also Beverages; Dishes; Fire; Housework.

French

The English attitude towards France and all things French was strangely paradoxical. On the one hand, France was the home of all things fashionable and desirable; on the other hand, it was a traditional enemy of Britain and in only the most recent war between the two countries, had cost Britain thirteen of its American colonies. The result was a kind of cognitive dissonance; people of good education learned French, spoke French, read French and aped French fashions in clothing and manners yet condemned the French and all they stood for. Attitudes were further complicated by the French Revolution, which some in England condemned immediately but which most greeted with enthusiasm. As the Revolution turned more violent, however, and as Britain went to war with France again for the second and third times in Austen's lifetime, attitudes became noticeably more hostile. While some women studied Parisian fashions and some wealthy men hired French cooks, others bought satirical prints contrasting 'British Slavery' and 'French Liberty'.

As members of the country gentry, the Austen children would certainly have been expected to be acquainted with French (*LS, MW* 252–253; *NA* 14; *MP* 14, 22, 312), just as any well-educated child today would be expected to know algebra. To what extent they were fluent is not precisely known, but Jane, who attended boarding school for a handful of years, whose parents were both extremely literate and who was given a book of French stories, probably read it quite well. Her two sailor brothers, Charles and Frank, were required to learn it at the Portsmouth Naval Academy, even if they had received no instruction in it from their father (which seems unlikely). Charles' academic records, for example, report that he was 'Very diligent' in French in 1791–1792 and 'Pretty diligent' in 1793–1794. In the case of the sailor brothers, knowledge of French would have been useful not only as a mark of gentility but also as an essential skill in times of war. Family tradition holds that knowledge of French was also useful to another Austen connection, Eliza de Feuillide Austen, a cousin who married a French count and then, after his execution during the French Revolution, Jane's brother Henry. She and Henry, according to some accounts, were travelling in France during these troubled times, seeking to recover some of her first husband's property, when the order went out to detain all Englishmen. Henry, who appears *not* to have been fluent, kept his mouth shut, while Eliza, who spoke like a native, got them safely back to England.

Austen's works are peppered with French phrases and references, such as 'the whole *tout ensemble* of his person' (*J&A*, *MW* 14), 'Finis' (*Hist Eng*, *MW* 149), 'Beau Monde' (*Sand*, *MW* 387) and '*au fait*' (*P* 155). 'Adieu' (often misspelled – see *L&F*, *MW* passim; *NA* 67, 229; *P&P* 235, 330) and 'tête-à-tête' (*NA* 243; *S&S* 294, 369; *P&P* 257; *MP* 35, 210, 234, 363; *E* 129, 360, 417, 422) occur frequently throughout Austen's works, so often indeed that they must have been in common use among her acquaintances. Sometimes they are used by silly characters, but not always, and they seem to have lost some of their explicit Frenchness. They are never italicised in order to call attention to their foreign derivation. More noticeably, French terms, such as *gaucherie*, are often associated with unsympathetic characters, such as Robert Ferrars (*S&S* 250) and the pretentious Tom Musgrave (*Watsons*, *MW* 340).

Brian Southam, among others, has noted that Jane, as the years progressed, grew increasingly likely to be the sort of person who would purchase a patriotic print. In *Emma* and *Mansfield Park* particularly, French language and manners are associated with duplicity and immorality. Frank Churchill's devious Frenchness is repeatedly contrasted with Mr Knightley's straightforward manner, to the detriment of the former; the words *espionage* and *finesse*, still very much thought of as French words, are used in reference to his conduct. Austen is even more explicit in the discussion of whether Churchill is amiable (*E* 149) – is he *amiable* (smooth and ingratiating in manner) or amiable (carrying in Austen's day a connotation of, in Southam's words, 'a quality of thoughtfulness and consideration for others')?

Mary Crawford, too, is associated with French language at a critical moment; she calls her brother Henry's elopement with Mrs Rushworth merely 'a moment's *etourderie*' (thoughtlessness – *MP* 437), when clearly, to everyone in the Bertram household, it is much more significant. Not only her manners and language but even her morality has been infected by a supposedly French willingness to overlook infidelity. However, by this time, she and her brother have already been associated with the French by their liberal use of French phrases: *esprit du corps* (*MP* 47), *menus plaisirs* (*MP* 226), *exigeant* (demanding – *MP* 361) and lines passonées

(*MP* 393). The phrase 'à-la-mortal', though used by the narrator, is likewise used in relationship to a Crawford (*MP* 274). Mary thinks highly of the seductive qualities of French women (*MP* 42); Fanny Price, in contrast, 'had never learnt French' (*MP* 14) until she arrived at the Bertrams', and Edmund Bertram asserts that he cannot utter 'a bon-mot' (*MP* 94), using a French term only in order to distance himself from *l'aimable*. The cases of Frank Churchill and the Crawfords perfectly summarise the English attitude towards French language and manners; they behave badly, but they are so handsome and appealing that one cannot help liking them, at least a little.

See also Clothing; Education; Navy.

Furniture

The furniture (*Scraps*, *MW* 176–177; *LS*, *MW* 250; *Sand*, *MW* 393, 427; *NA* 88, 158, 162, 163; *S&S* 12, 13, 26, 69, 119; *P&P* 65, 75, 133, 156, 246, 249; *MP* 41, 48, 152, 182, 202; *E* 184, 355; *P* 10, 22, 32, 37, 137) of the late eighteenth century and early nineteenth century was influenced by classical, Egyptian and Gothic styles. The rococo styles of earlier in the eighteenth century, exemplified by the work of Thomas Chippendale (1718–1779), had been replaced by graceful neoclassical pieces by cabinetmakers like George Hepplewhite (who designed Mr Austen's library bookcase at Steventon) and Thomas Sheraton (1751–1806). From 1810 to 1815, there was a return to interest in French styles of furniture, largely due to the influence of the prince regent. Common design motifs in general included honeysuckle, acanthus leaves, the triple-feather plume of the prince regent, sphinxes, lotuses, chinoiserie, palm leaves, fluting like that found on Greek columns, and winged Victories. The legs of tables, chairs and sofas often were carved to resemble animals or had claw feet.

The woods used in furniture making included native ash, birch and chestnut. Beech was widely used for painted chairs. Mahogany (*NA* 193; *MP* 84) came into use in the second half of the eighteenth century and quickly became popular for its deep reddish-brown colour. Veneers might be of sycamore, bird's-eye maple and various types of heavily figured imported woods. The types of wood that were imported gave a sense of how far-flung Britain's colonial and trading networks already were. Craftsmen used black-and-yellow calamander and pale yellow satinwood from Ceylon; light-brown amboyna from the West Indies; streaky kingwood, rosewood and feather-figured partridge wood from Brazil; ebony from east India; purple wood and zebra wood from Guiana and golden-brown thuya wood from Africa.

Furniture-making techniques included painting, lacquering, veneering, carving (*MP* 84), gilding (*MP* 84, 434) and inlay. The lacquering was referred to as 'japanning' and was often used on pieces that featured

Chinese or Japanese scenes. The technique was used in England from
the late seventeenth century, when the shellac used was tinted red,
green, white, black or other colours. By the late eighteenth century,
the preference was for black on yellow, with the yellow sometimes being
mixed with metal dust to give it sparkle. The best japanning (*NA* 201) had
at least ten coats of lacquer, carefully rubbed between coats to give the
surface a glossy smoothness, while cheaper items had only one or two
coats of lacquer and thus had a slightly bumpy feel.

Chairs and Sofas

One of the design elements characteristic of the period was the curve,
and chairs in particular seemed to be fond of curving. Some, imitating
the curule seats of the ancient Romans, were supported on legs composed
of intersecting semicircles, making a kind of 'X' at the front and back.
Windsor chairs had a top rail that curved around in one continuous line
with the arms and a smoothly rounded hollow in the seat for comfort.
Window seats and sofas had curved, scrolled sides and armrests, and
tables gradually acquired rounded edges.

There were numerous kinds of chairs (*F&E*, *MW* 8; *Visit*, *MW* 51; *Evelyn*,
MW 187; *Cath*, *MW* 215; *Watsons*, *MW* 356; *S&S* 42, 175, 177, 265, 288, 290,
317; *P&P* 162, 341; *MP* 118, 126, 145, 169, 192, 231, 239, 342, 379; *E* 255, 378,
410; *P* 223, 237), some more formal than others. In addition to the Windsor
chair and curule chairs, there were Grecian chairs with sweeping curved
backs and splayed, tapering, rectangular legs. There were chairs with
cane seats and chairs painted to simulate bamboo, complete with carved
'rings'. There were armchairs with swooping, descending, scrolled
armrests and a slight backward tilt to the backrest, making them almost
appear to be frozen for a moment in the midst of swift motion. Trafalgar
chairs had curves everywhere and were often decorated with rope and
cable designs in honour of Nelson's victory at Trafalgar in 1805. Painted
chairs were described in the August 1814 Repository as 'intended for best
bed chambers, for secondary drawing rooms, and occasionally to serve for
routs', and indeed a chair of this type does appear in the late Mrs Tilney's
room at Northanger Abbey (*NA* 193). Parlour chairs, as in the dining
parlour, were used in the dining room and were generally simpler in
design than drawing-room chairs, which were often made of expensive
mahogany or of wood that had been painted and gilded. There were many
more styles of chairs – so many that in 1822, Richard Brown wrote that
they were so various that 'it now baffles the most skilful artist to produce
any new forms'.

One special type of chair was the window seat (*NA* 167). This was a wide
seat, large enough for lounging or for two people to share. It was designed
to be placed in front of the tall windows of grand homes, windows that
in fashionable homes stretched all the way down to floor level to let in
maximum light. Closely related to the window seat was the sofa (*J&A*,
MW 14; *E&E*, *MW* 31; *Mystery*, *MW* 57; *L&F*, *MW* 86, 88; *Lesley*, *MW* 111;

Evelyn, MW 189; *Sand, MW* 413; *S&S* 307; *P&P* 54; *MP* 71, 74, 104, 125, 126, 179, 277; *E* 45, 124, 125; *P* 37, 39, 67–68, 78, 79), a larger piece of furniture, either with a padded back and two arms of equal height or with one tall arm at one end and a short end at the other, with a back panel stretching across only about half the length of the sofa. This latter sofa was designed for stretching out and was an imitation of the Greek and Roman couches used by the diners of ancient times. These pieces often featured classical-style fluting and scrollwork that reflected their origins; the sofa with a full back, after 1812, often had some sort of ornament at the centre along the back; leaves, honeysuckle and shells were common motifs for this sort of carved crest.

Tables
The variety of tables (*L&F, MW* 107; *NA* 158; *S&S* 63, 67, 165, 175, 198, 231, 317; *P&P* 39, 48, 341; *MP* 72, 74, 118, 124, 142–143, 145, 224, 318, 439; *E* 24, 82, 157, 255, 355, 434; *P* 40, 105, 112) was even greater than the variety of chairs, for tables served a great number of purposes. The principal table in a household was the dining-room table (*Watsons, MW* 353; *NA* 165; *P&P* 288, 310; *MP* 220–221, 239; *E* 291), which formerly had been a rigidly rectangular affair with monumental carved legs and feet. Now it became a piece of furniture of lighter weight and more versatility, for its huge legs became pillars, each of which splayed out into four claw-footed supports. The right angles at its ends were rounded, and the middle one developed leaves so that the table could be made larger or smaller as the occasion demanded. The legs were moved away from the corners and towards the centre, with one leg under each leaf. Eventually, the taste for curves led to at least some dining tables being made entirely round (*E* 347, 349), as this did away with hierarchical sitting arrangements and, it was thought, made guests feel more at ease. Circular tables could also be used for breakfast or for playing 'round' card games (games that did not confine themselves to a specified number of players). Early in the period, they had a central pillar that divided into four supporting legs; later, they rested on triangular pedestals. Other circular or octagonal tables were known as drawing-room tables.

Some tables were designed to be used either separately or in conjunction as needed. These included wine tables, which could be pushed together near the fire to hold wine glasses and decanters, and 'sets of dining tables' of the kind purchased by Austen's family in November 1800.

A set of dining tables was a group of three tables, two that stood on four fixed legs and a third, middle table with two fixed legs and two that could swing out to support flaps. To use them together, the middle table would have its flaps raised and the legs extended; then all three tables would be hooked together with brass clips.

The Pembroke table (*Watsons, MW* 355), which this set had replaced, would also have had flaps. Pembroke tables had four legs and a flap at

9. *Messrs. Morgan & Sanders*, 1809.

each short end supported by hinged wooden brackets. At this period, these tables were usually rectangular with rounded corners; earlier examples had often been either oval or more strictly rectangular. After 1812 the four legs were sometimes replaced by a central pillar supported by four legs or feet.

Other kinds of tables included pier tables, which stood against the walls between windows (*MP* 153); console tables, which were supported in some way by the wall; and side tables, which stood against the wall but could be moved if necessary. Some tables that appeared to be side tables were actually card tables (*Watsons*, *MW* 332; *S&S* 144, 145, 151; *P&P* 38, 54, 76, 342; *MP* 119, 203, 239, 249; *E* 290); they resembled a narrow rectangular table and stood against the wall most of the time, but when evening came, they could be pulled away from the wall and the tops unfolded to reveal a square surface covered in baize or leather. Sofa tables (*Sand*, *MW* 413) stood, as their name implies, either in the front or in the back of a sofa and were used for a variety of purposes as people sat in the drawing room. Work tables (*S&S* 144, 181) had a sliding or lifting top beneath which a pleated silk bag or pouch was suspended. When it was time to do sewing, the top could be lifted and sewing supplies inside the bag accessed.

Library tables were massive affairs, with a wide kneehole between two pedestals containing cabinets. When the size of these pedestals was diminished and filled with drawers (*L&F*, *MW* 95) rather than cabinets, the piece became a writing table (*P&P* 305; *P* 237). Writing tables (*MP* 307) could also be supported by four legs and have their drawers in the 'frieze', the level below the tabletop. Some had drawers here as well as in a shallow section atop the table. Also known as a writing desk (*MP* 152; *E* 298, 442), the writing table might have a top that lifted up to provide an angled surface on which to write or draw (*S&S* 104, 105). A dressing table was similar to a writing desk, but it usually had a mirror either sitting on it or incorporated into its structure, and its contents were, of course, different.

Other Furniture

Storage pieces included wardrobes (*NA* 158, 193), chests of drawers (*NA* 158), cabinets (*NA* 160, 168, 201) and bookcases (*MP* 127; *P* 99). Cupboards (*P* 170), unlike the rest of these pieces, were hung on, or otherwise affixed to, the walls. Some pieces served multiple purposes; they might have a few shelves for books, a small space for writing letters and a cabinet at the bottom. Storage could also be accomplished in chests (*NA* 158, 163, 165), though chests and trunks were not as popular as they had been in past years. They tended to be put away in corners rather than prominently displayed.

In the dining room, some items were stored in the sideboard (*P&P* 156; *E* 458), a cabinet longer than it was tall, equipped with drawers and doors. Food and drink were also served from the sideboard, and extra glassware was kept here during the meal. Some sideboards had a top at two levels, with the right and left sides of the top being higher than the middle section. Some sideboards had compartments that could be filled with water for washing dishes or a heated cavity under the stack of dinner plates. Behind the cabinet doors, a chamber pot might be secreted for the use of the gentlemen after the ladies had left.

Beds (*Visit, MW* 50; *Scraps, MW* 172; *Cath, MW* 220; *NA* 49, 158, 159, 168, 172, 193; *S&S* 190, 193, 198, 219, 292, 307; *MP* 13; *P* 113, 154; *E* 378) might be four posters, preferably of mahogany with turned posts.

Canopy beds often had elaborately carved and painted headboards that were quite tall and supported a canopy that extended outward from the wall. Both of these types of beds had valances and curtains (*NA* 171) that could be closed for privacy and warmth at night. Many contemporary prints show people in curtained canopy or four-poster beds, which were the most popular styles. Less popular were sofa beds (in essence, a sofa with a canopy suspended from a dome or rod) and tent beds (the lighter and cheaper form of the four poster, found in servants' rooms and cottages).

Some homes had small pedestals or tables used to support artwork or vases of flowers (*P* 40). They might also have music stands. Footstools (*P&P* 105; *MP* 152) were similar to chairs in design; they were simply chairs without backs or arms. The poor had joint stools, simple wooden stools without upholstery that did duty everywhere from the barn to the kitchen, and genteel artists and walkers had camp stools (*Sand, MW* 383), folding stools that could be taken outdoors. Children had few pieces of furniture that were distinctively theirs; whereas a nursery today might contain a changing table, trash pail, crib, cradle and playpen, children of Austen's time slept in cradles (*Visit, MW* 51; *P&P* 355) until they were old enough to move to beds.

See also Architecture; Gothic; Picturesque.

G

Games

Games tended to fall into one of three categories: mental, social or physical. Physical games were most often played by children, while social games could be enjoyed by all ages, and mental games were especially popular with adults, who took great pleasure in demonstrating their cleverness. The physical games included cricket, trap ball, battledore and shuttlecock, and lawn bowling; of these, only lawn bowling tended to be an overwhelmingly adult pursuit.

Physical Games

Cricket (*NA* 13, 15) had two teams of eleven players each. A few of these players were rotating bowlers, who threw a ball in a strip of ground called the pitch. Sticks called stumps were driven into the ground, in a line, with one batsman next to one stump and another batsman at the other stump directly opposite. The bowler, in between the batsmen, threw the ball overhand towards one of them, who attempted to hit it with a bat. Then the two batsmen attempted to run back and forth, exchanging places as many times as they could before an opponent returned with the ball and tagged one of the stumps with it. The goal was to get safely to a stump before it was hit with the ball. These exchanges of place were called runs, and runs could also be scored by hitting the ball out of bounds or as a penalty when the bowler bowled incorrectly. A batsman could be called out if the ball were caught on the fly, if the bowler hit the batsman's stump while bowling to him, if the stump were hit with the ball while the batsman was running, if the batsman chose to end his turn voluntarily or if the batsman made certain types of errors. The game ended when both teams had bowled a specified number of times or when one team had ten players called out and therefore could no longer field two batsmen.

Trap ball was a similar game, in that it used a bat and a ball, but it was far less complex. A hard wooden ball called a knur was placed in the 'trap', a shoe-shaped box with a lever. The knur was placed on top of one end of the lever, and each player used a long wooden stick to hit the other end, flinging the ball into the air. Then the player used the same stick to hit the ball. Scoring was based either on reaching a base of some kind without being tagged out or on the distance travelled by the ball. Poorer children used a brisket bone as a lever and a hole dug into the ground as a trap, while rich children might have special knurs made of stag's horn and lead. The 'base ball' (*NA* 15) played by the young Catherine Morland might well have been trap ball, or it might have been stool ball, another bat-and-ball game with bases, which dates back to the Middle Ages.

Battledore and shuttlecock was simply an earlier form of badminton, which acquired its present name in the mid-nineteenth century. Austen mentions playing it at Godmersham with a nephew in a letter of 24 August 1805:

> Yesterday was a very quiet day with us; my noisiest efforts were writing to Frank, & playing at Battledore & Shuttlecock with William; he & I have practised together two mornings, & improve a little; we have frequently kept it up *three* times, & once or twice *six*.

Bowls was a more sedate sport, played on a stretch of flat, close-cropped lawn called a bowling green (*MP* 90). Wooden balls, deliberately not quite round to give them a curved trajectory, were rolled at a target ball called the jack. It was a popular game for those who could afford to set aside the requisite piece of land and landscape it appropriately.

Social Games

All games were to some extent social, since they existed to pass time pleasantly with other people, but some games were specifically designed to be played indoors and to facilitate merriment, rather than to demonstrate mental or physical prowess. They might partake mental or physical activity or a little of both, but their main attraction was personal interaction. Among these 'merry evening games' (*E* 28) were hunt the slipper, snapdragon, bullet pudding, blind-man's-buff, hide-and-seek and oranges and lemons. In hunt the slipper, participants sat in a circle and passed a slipper around behind their backs. A guesser in the centre of the circle then had to guess who held the slipper. Snapdragon was a game in which players snatched currants from a bowl of burning liqueur. Bullet pudding, a game often played at Edward Austen's house at Godmersham, used a single bullet hidden in a dish of flour; participants had to find it using their noses and chins only. Edward's daughter Fanny Knight reported that the game turned the players into 'strange figures all covered with flour but the worst is that you must not laugh for fear of the flour getting up your nose & mouth & choking you'. Blind-man's-buff involved blindfolding one person, who was turned around three times and then attempted to locate the other players. When he managed to catch one, he had to guess who it was without looking from beneath his blindfold; if he succeeded, his captive became the next 'blind man'. Hide-and-seek was played very much as it is today; oranges and lemons was a game like 'London Bridge', in which players passed beneath an arch formed by the hands and arms of two other players and tried to avoid capture at the end of a rhyme:

'Oranges and Lemons',
Say the bells of St. Clements,
'You owe me five farthings',
Say the bells of St. Martins,

'When will you pay me?'
Say the bells of Old Bailey,
'I do not know',
Says the great bell of Bow.

For men, one of the principal social games was billiards (*NA* 96; *S&S* 111, 305; *P&P* 180; *MP* 125, 127, 183), a game in which balls were propelled around a green-cloth-covered table using 'maces', the ancestors of today's pool cues. The sides of the table were cushioned with felt; rubber cushions and slate-bedded tables would not be introduced until after Austen's time. There were six pockets on the table, just as there are on a modern pool table – one at each corner and one in the middle of each long side; there were also three balls, one for each of two players and a cue ball.

Mental Games

Mental games were primarily strategic or creative and were not necessarily conducive to conversation or socialising. They included chess, backgammon (*P&P* 69; *E* 9, 329, 377), dominoes, draughts (checkers), nine men's morris, poetry competitions, charades and riddles. The Austen family, well read and inventive, was particularly fond of these sorts of games. Austen's works contain several charades (*E* 76, 77, 82), which were riddles that had to conform to a specific pattern. Each charade took the form of a poem whose answer had to be a two-syllable word. The poem hinted at the meaning of the first syllable, then at the meaning of the second syllable, then at the meaning of both syllables together. An early Austen charade is included in her *History of England*:

My first is what my second was to James 1st, and you tread on my whole. (*MW* 148)

The poetry is lacking here, but the riddle otherwise follows the classic pattern. The first syllable is 'car' (Carr) for Robert Carr, earl of Somerset (*c.*1590–1645), who was for a time the favourite ('pet') of James I. The 'whole', that is, the two syllables together, form 'carpet', which one indeed treads upon. Mr Elton, too, offers a charade, this time in verse:

My first doth affliction denote,
Which my second is destined to feel.
And my whole is the best antidote
That affliction to soften and heal. (*E* 70)

The answers are 'woe', 'man' and 'woman'. Elton's next charade (*E* 71), like his first, is a highly intellectual way of flirting with Emma:

My first displays the wealth and pomp of kings,
Lords of the earth! Their luxury and ease.
Another view of man, my second brings,
Behold him there, the monarch of the seas!
But, ah! United, what reverse we have!

Man's boasted power and freedom, all are flown;
Lord of the earth and sea, he bends a slave,
And woman, lovely woman, reigns alone.
Thy ready wit the word will soon supply.
May its approval beam in that soft eye!

The answers are 'court', 'ship' and 'courtship'. Emma, a clever woman, figures out the charade almost instantly, but Harriet Smith is stumped until Emma explains it to her (*E* 72–73). Three more of Austen's charades are printed in the *Minor Works* (450).

Riddles were similar to charades, but they were not strictly limited to two-syllable answers. Mr Woodhouse's 'Kitty, a fair but frozen maid' (*E* 70, 78–79) puzzle is a riddle rather than a charade, and the answer is 'a candle'. Riddles, charades, anagrams, conundrums, rebuses and the like were collected by a number of people (*E* 69–70), including an Austen connection, Mrs Eliza Chute of the Vyne who amassed about 500 examples. The game with the spelling letters in *Emma* (*E* 348–349) is similar to puzzles involving anagrams, which are words reorganised to spell other words. A conundrum, like a charade, was a specific type of riddle, in which the answer involved some sort of pun. Mr Weston's conundrum is just this sort of play on words; his 'two letters of the alphabet ... that express perfection' are M and A, which, sounded out, are Emm-a (*E* 371). This is a good enough conundrum in itself, but, as David Selwyn has pointed out, Austen, whose family adores these sorts of puzzles, may have included an extra layer of complexity. Mr Knightley's commentary on the conundrum, that '*Perfection* should not have come quite so soon' (*E* 371), may be a reference to a theory of eighteenth-century philosopher Francis Hutcheson's, in which perfection of virtue is expressed as a mathematical formula using the letters M and A as variables. Perfection was achieved when M, representing a moment or occasion of good, equalled A, representing the ability of a person to act for the greater good – in other words, when people did all the good that was in their power. As Selwyn points out, when Mr Knightley makes his observation, Emma is at the Box Hill picnic, acting selfishly and thoughtlessly and therefore not in accordance with moral perfection.

Many types of mental games, other than charades, involved poetry. Mrs Elton refers to an acrostic (*E* 372) – a poem in which the first letters of the lines, read from top to bottom, spell out words, often a person's name; this was one of many ways in which an astute versifier could show off his or her talent.* Other poetic games included bouts-rimés, in which the contestants were given a set of words with which to end their lines; then they had a fixed amount of time, usually half an hour among the Austens, to construct a poem around them. One example, described

*Lewis Carroll's *Alice in Wonderland* begins with an acrostic poem spelling out his inspiration's name: Alice Pleasance Liddell.

by Jane's nephew James Edward Austen-Leigh, had to end its lines with the words 'Sleep—Creep—Chatter—Turn—Burn—Batter'. Sometimes the Austen family would write questions on pieces of paper and nouns on other pieces; then contestants would draw a piece of paper from each pile and have to compose a poem that answered the question while including the specified noun. James Edward Austen-Leigh once composed a quatrain that had to include the word 'fox' and answer the question 'Do you take snuff?' His poem would have been well liked by the family, not only because it met the requirements of the contest but also because it poked gentle fun at himself and another:

> As seldom take I snuff, alack!
> As Robert takes a fox;
> Although for show he hunts a pack,
> And I display a box.

See also Cards.

Gardens and Landscape

Eighteenth-century landowners spent a great deal of time and money remaking the grounds of their estates (*MP* 53, 56–57, 61, 241–243). A series of trends and revolutions altered the formal French-style garden, turning it into a relic and replacing it with the landscape still considered quintessentially English. At first, the formal garden, with its parterres and topiaries, was replaced by an iconic landscape dotted with statues and structures full of symbolic significance. William Kent, a mid-century landscape gardener who invented the sunken fence or 'ha-ha' (a glorified ditch – *MP* 96, 100), created this sort of landscape at Stowe.

He was succeeded by Lancelot 'Capability' Brown (1715–1783), a revolutionary designer who swept away all remaining traces of the rigidly geometric garden, and, making heavy use of ha-has to open up grand vistas, created vast parks or rolling, grassy plains punctuated by clumps of trees (*S&S* 27; *E* 100). His trademarks, aside from the undulating lawns (*F&E*, *MW* 5; *LS*, *MW* 271; *Sand*, *MW* 406; *S&S* 302; *P&P* 267; *MP* 65, 90; *E* 273, 434; *P* 14), were his use of water and trees. He diverted streams (*F&E*, *MW* 5, 9; *P&P* 245, 253; *MP* 56, 242; *E* 358) in order to make them more attractive and built artificial ponds to reflect the mansions of his employers. Trees were arranged in irregular clumps to create a sense of perspective, with a belt of trees enclosing much of the park to screen out views of any land that did not form part of the estate, and a path formed a circuit winding through this belt. Uvedale Price, a leader of the picturesque movement, hated the Brownian belts. Price reacted too late to save many avenues, for the interest in natural landscaping, begun by Brown and Kent, had replaced avenues with lawns, belts and clumps. Price was no fan of the clump either, pointing out dourly that 'if the first letter was taken away' the resulting word 'would most accurately describe its form and effect'. Clumps, he continued, 'from the trees being generally of the same age and growth, planted nearly at the same distance in a circular form, and from each tree being equally pressed by his neighbour, are as like each other as so many puddings turned out of one common mould'.

Brown's revolution, however, amounted to more than trees and water. He also uprooted all superfluous statuary and decreed against flower gardens, reducing the palette of the landscape to shades of green and brown and the silvered blue of the water. Pemberley's rolling hills, simple stream banks, modified stream, rim of 'woody hills' and 10-mile path around the park are characteristic of a Capability Brown landscape (*P&P* 245–246, 253–254). Brown had an enormous impact on the English landscape, not only because he designed about 150 estates at the enormous cost of 10 guineas a day but also because a generation of imitators adopted his ideas and employed them elsewhere.

Brown's successor was Humphry Repton (1752–1818), who believed in the value of land, first and foremost, as it served the needs and comfort of people. He favoured parks over forests and history painting over landscape painting precisely because the former in each pair concerned itself primarily with human activity. Austen stigmatised Repton (*MP* 55) in *Mansfield Park* as a destroyer of the grand avenues (*MP* 56, 82, 103) of old trees (*NA* 177; *MP* 55; *P* 36) that lined paths and roads, and in fact he did recommend doing away with avenues that destroyed the view from the house, but he was actually in favour of preserving most old timber (*Sand, MW* 426; *S&S* 302; *MP* 82, 241). Austen appears to have based her opinion of Repton on the before-and-after views at an estate held by her mother's family, and she may well have seen other examples of his work or heard him discussed in her circle of acquaintances. She knew his practices well enough, at least, to be accurate about his fees: he did, indeed, charge 5 guineas a day (*MP* 53) plus travel expenses. However, she was wrong about many of his theories, for he actually held many of the same ideas about landscape as she did.

Like Austen, Repton approved of building houses in sheltered valleys rather than at the tops of hills (*Sand, MW* 379–380; *S&S* 28–29); like her, he appreciated flowers and restored them to the monochrome Brownian landscape. He also approved of gravel walks and shade near the house for the sake of comfort, though Brown had done away with many such features in favour of bringing the rippling grass right up to the foundation of the house. Despite the fact that Repton invented the term 'landscape gardener' specifically to evoke the connections between scenes on canvas and those in nature, he opposed those gardeners who sought picturesque effects at the expense of utility and comfort. Garden historian John Dixon Hunt has suggested that the description of Donwell Abbey in *Emma* is in fact a Reptonian landscape. Austen describes the farm and its mansion house as snug and practical. She admires

> the respectable size and style of the building, its suitable, becoming, characteristic situation, low and sheltered—its ample gardens stretching down to meadows washed by a stream, of which the Abbey, with all the old neglect of prospect, had scarcely a sight—and its abundance of timber in rows and avenues, which neither fashion nor extravagance had rooted up.—The house was larger than Hartfield, and totally unlike it, covering a good deal of ground, rambling and irregular, with many comfortable and one or two handsome rooms.—It was just what it ought to be, and it looked what it was—and Emma felt an increasing respect for it.

This, Hunt says, is perfectly in keeping with Repton's emphasis on 'the propriety of the buildings, the avoidance of overly calculated picturesque vistas, the retention of old timber, and such formal features as avenues, together with the estate's exact appeal to the mind's judgment'. He points out that the phrase 'It looked like what it was' even unintentionally echoes Repton's own language in his plan for a cottage on the grounds of Blaise Castle: 'it must look like what it is, the habitation of a labourer who has the care of the adjoining woods, but its simplicity should be the effect of Art and not of accident.'

The difference between them is Repton's understandable value for 'Art' in landscape, whereas Austen appears to have wanted to take the inherited landscape, avenues and all, and leave it alone, untouched by 'awkward taste' (*P&P* 245). Virtually all remaking of the landscape meets with her disapproval, and Repton's art merely tinkers with, or tries to restore, what should, in her opinion, have been there all along. The description of Donwell rejects all artifice; there is a river, but it can barely be seen from the house, and there is a pond, but it is not a Brownian mirror of water but a utilitarian fishpond (*E* 361, 362).

Parks, Woods and Shrubberies

Estates with sizable acreage had both a garden and pleasure ground near the house and a vast sweep of grass and woodland (*S&S* 88, 302; *P&P* 245, 267, 301; *MP* 56, 91, 94–95) farther off, known as the park (*Sand, MW* 426; *NA* 178; *S&S* 88, 226, 302; *P&P* 155, 156, 182, 195, 245, 253, 325, 352; *MP* 15, 27, 48, 56, 68, 69, 97, 103; *E* 275). The park, as designed by Brown, Repton and their imitators, was more than pretty or picturesque. It was also practical. Its swaths of meadow* (*Sand, MW* 379; *NA* 214) could be rented out to the owners of livestock, and it actually brought in more money from grazing than it could have from the planting of wheat. In time, the livestock came to seem decorative and pastoral, but they also raised

---

*'Water meadows', mentioned in *MP* 55, were simply meadows that at times were covered by the rising water of rivers or streams.

the park owner's income. Likewise, the fences, hedges (*Watsons, MW* 321; *MP* 208; *E* 83, 189; *P* 86, 87, 90), ha-has and palings (fences – *Sand, MW* 426; *P&P* 155, 195; *E* 89, 275) used to direct the flow of animal traffic came to be seen as essential features of an attractive rural landscape.

The clumps of shrubs and trees that gave variety to the landscape were likewise useful. Like the fences and ha-has, they controlled the movements of animals. They provided habitat for game birds such as pheasants and thus provided pleasure to the men of the family, and they also provided timber (*S&S* 375) that could be culled periodically. Landowners planted fast-growing softwoods among the valuable hardwoods, forcing the hardwoods to grow taller and straighter to compete for sunlight. Coppices* (*NA* 106; *P&P* 253–254), or sections of shrubs and young trees, were planted specifically in order to be cut occasionally. Some landowners, including Jane's brother Edward, created 'plantations' (*Sand, MW* 381; *NA* 250; *S&S* 88, 302, 343; *MP* 54, 191, 218, 432) of trees to be harvested at maturity, and these stores of timber added materially to the value of an estate.

Planting trees had another practical benefit – the shade offered to strollers. Landowners often added a 'wilderness' (*P&P* 352; *MP* 90, 94–95, 103) to the pleasure grounds near the house, a grove of trees that, in its neat gravel paths and conveniently placed seats and benches, bore little resemblance to a real wilderness. These touches of civilisation, however, were not resented by ladies walking in such grounds.

Gardeners planted a wide variety of trees. They planted oak (*NA* 111, 142, 161; *MP* 83, 99, 205) and ash (*S&S* 302) for timber, interspersed with larch (*MP* 91) or pine (*Ode, MW* 75; *Evelyn, MW* 189) to encourage growth. Elms (*L&F, MW* 97, 98) made attractive borders for paths. Firs (*L&F, MW* 100; *Evelyn, MW* 181; *S&S* 302), though they were used in combination with chestnuts as a boundary at Steventon, did not earn a recommendation for this purpose from Uvedale Price. In *An Essay on the Picturesque* (1796), he observed that their lower trunks did not provide enough concealment. Yews (*MP* 241) tended to be found in churchyards.[†]

Some trees and shrubs were grown not for timber or as natural walls but for their shade (*MP* 91) or appearance. These included lime (*E* 360, 362); laurel (*P&P* 155; *MP* 91, 209), which was admired for its full and rapid growth; privet, which grew compactly and thus made good hedges; heath (*MP* 105), in Austen's time any of a number of low, shrubby plants; Lombardy poplar (*Evelyn, MW* 181; *S&S* 302), which grew into a narrow, pointed column; and other species of poplar (*F&E, MW* 5), which were leafier and made a pleasant sound in the wind. Some trees, such as mulberry (*S&S* 197), walnut (*Evelyn, MW* 189), apricot (*MP* 54–55) and

---

*The 'pollard' (*E* 83) also involved cutting, but a pollard was a tree that had been cut down to force multitude of new branches to sprout from the cut trunk.
[†]Though, as the tree may have had pagan religious significance, the sites of the trees may have been co-opted by early churches in order to supplant existing shrines.

10. *The Love Letter*, 1785.

apple (*NA* 214; *E* 186) trees, produced fruit or nuts in addition to shade, and in grounds too small for a separate orchard, these might form part of the shrubbery (*Watsons, MW* 322; *NA* 176, 214; *S&S* 302, 306, 374; *P&P* 86; *MP* 57, 65, 90, 209; *E* 26, 196, 336, 412, 424, 434; *P* 18, 127) – a little area designed for walking (*Evelyn, MW* 184; *LS, MW* 271; *P&P* 52, 301, 351; *MP* 55, 208, 322, 323, 346, 357; *E* 196) and sitting in the shade of shrubs and small trees. In addition to ornamental trees and bushes, a shrubbery might feature flowers, currant bushes and raspberry canes. A paddock (*Sand, MW* 426; *P&P* 301) – a fenced area near the stables – might also be planted with some trees.

Certain trees, imported from warmer climates, were planted to create an exotic atmosphere. Myrtle (*Ode, MW* 74) and citron (*J&A, MW* 18, 20), for example, evoked the Mediterranean. Warren Hastings, governor-general of India and an Austen family acquaintance, bought back his ancestral home at Daylesford and filled its gardens with a dazzling variety of exotics – acacia (*S&S* 302), tamarisk and mango – along with myriad native trees. When the grounds at Steventon were being redone in the fall of 1800, Jane wrote to Cassandra that an earlier plan to plant 'beech, ash and larch' was in danger of being scrapped. The question was 'whether it would be better to make a little orchard of it, by planting apples, pears and cherries, or whether it should be larch, mountain-ash and acacia'.

Gardens

The paths (*NA* 179; *P&P* 53, 327; *E* 360; *P* 90) that ran through gardens, shrubberies and parks were made of gravel (*Evelyn*, *MW* 184; *NA* 161; *S&S* 302, 306, 359; *P&P* 42, 353; *MP* 322; *E* 186), which, unlike dirt, did not turn into mud in bad weather. It was time when too much moisture in either the air or the ground was considered bad for health, and the dryness of gravel spoke in its favour. The paths wound through the shrubbery, if there was one, and into the garden, which was often protected by walls (*S&S* 197; *MP* 54) and an ornamental gate (*Watsons*, *MW* 355; *S&S* 42). In larger gardens, there would be walks intersecting with each other (*P&P* 156); in smaller gardens, one path would make a circuit of the grounds.

A 'garden' (*Sand*, *MW* 379; *Cath*, *MW* 193, 230; *NA* 13, 176, 240; *P&P* 67, 71, 155, 156, 217; *MP* 27, 191, 241–242, 291, 432; *E* 22, 58, 359; *P* 36) could mean all the planted grounds near a house, encompassing shrubbery, hedge mazes, formal topiary gardens if they still survived, flower gardens and the kitchen garden. The term could also apply specifically to an area dedicated to growing flowers (*S&S* 226; *MP* 57; *P* 18) or to the kitchen garden (*Sand*, *MW* 380; *NA* 175–176, 178), which produced food and herbs for household use. In smaller homes, the flower garden and the kitchen garden would be united, and in labourers' cottages the flower garden would be almost entirely sacrificed for the sake of food production (*E* 87). Few people could afford the kind of massive landscaping seen at the fictional Pemberley and the real-world Stowe, so they constricted the park to a little lawn and a few trees and gave the garden most of the available space (*S&S* 28; *MP* 54).

Those who could afford to garden on a grand scale invested not only in a kitchen garden but also in an orchard (*Sand*, *MW* 379; *NA* 178, 240; *E* 238; *P* 23), a walled enclosure for fruit trees. Those who could not grew fruit in kitchen gardens and shrubberies, as, for example, in Mr Knightley's strawberry beds (*E* 354, 358) or in the real-life strawberry beds at Steventon. The Austens managed to grow currants, gooseberries, raspberries and strawberries in their little garden in Southampton, and at Chawton they grew plums, apricots, currants, strawberries and gooseberries.

A garden was hard work. In great homes, the work was done by servants, but in smaller homes such as the Austens', the labour was performed by the family itself.

Gardens and Landscape

Garden Structures

Scattered throughout the park and garden were various structures designed for the comfort of those who used the ground. These included seats (*Cath, MW* 231; *P&P* 327; *MP* 57, 94) and benches (*MP* 95, 208; *E* 273) on which walkers could rest, some of which were backed by stone or brick walls to provide shelter from the wind. Other gardens had statuary, fountains, urns and obelisks that had escaped the clutches of Capability Brown and his followers. These decorative structures sometimes alluded to the history of the family that owned the place and were sometimes intended to look much older than they were. Faux ruins enjoyed a period of popularity in the second half of the eighteenth century, and the only question was how to make a new pile of stone look properly antique, so that it appeared to be the genuine remains of a castle or abbey.

Some landscape designers avoided ruins altogether, favouring brand-new temples (*S&S* 302, 303) and hermitages (*NA* 107; *P&P* 352) in classical or Gothic styles. Despite the austere sound of the word 'hermitage', such houses were modern and habitable. These buildings looked ancient, but they concealed comfortable rooms where guests could drink tea or even take a bath. In one case, a Greek façade hid an old and unsightly building that the landowner in question could not bear to tear down because his mother had been fond of it.

Closer to the house, hothouses (*Visit, MW* 54; *Cath, MW* 230; *NA* 178; *S&S* 226, 303) with glass panels and fireplaces could be built at enormous costs. The cost of glazing such buildings, along with the window tax they involved and the staff required to run them, made them a luxury that only the richest could afford. Inside, exotic flowers bloomed and young plants were cultivated in preparation for transplanting them outdoors when the weather was warm enough. Some hothouses were called 'succession houses' (*NA* 178) because there were a number of them at varying temperatures, and plants could be moved from one to another to fool them into bearing fruit out of season. Another type of specialised hothouse was the pinery (*NA* 178), devoted to the growing of pineapples. This was such an expensive and time-consuming endeavour that the pineapple served as an edible symbol of its owner's wealth, and offering pineapple to guests was the ultimate gesture of hospitality.

See also Public Places.

Gentry

The gentry, the class to which Austen belonged, may be thought of as a kind of upper middle class – not always 'upper' in terms of income, but certainly in terms of social status, and often in terms of income as well. The differentiation between the social and the economic definitions of class is an important one, as money was already tending in Austen's time to blur the distinctions between classes, a phenomenon that troubled many,

People of the late-eighteenth and early-nineteenth centuries had a very clear notion of rank and class. At the top of the hierarchy, of course, was the royal family. Below that lay the nobility, from dukes down to barons. Below that was the gentry, stretching from baronets and knights at the top of the scale down to penurious, but well-educated, clergymen. Members of the professions – law, clergy, medicine and the upper ranks of the military (*MP* 91) – were considered gentlemen, even though they had to work for a living, but the ideal was the gentleman-farmer, who lived off the proceeds of his land and the proceeds of his investments (*E* 136, 358). Below the gentry were tradesmen (*P&P* 15; *E* 183, 481), prosperous tenant farmers (distinguished from the gentry chiefly by education and family lineage) and successful artisans. Most numerous but lowest in status were the common working people – servants, farm labourers, apprentices and so on – who might be called anything from 'the commons', to 'the peasantry', to 'the mob'.

It was at the fringes of each class that difficulties arose. If a man were a wealthy brewer or shipping merchant or industrialist, to what extent was he a gentleman? If he could not qualify as a gentleman, could his idle wife and children be considered gentry? A physician was clearly a gentleman, but what about a surgeon, who held less professional status, or an apothecary, who held less still? Was a writer a gentleman? What about an architect or an academic?

The answer to all these questions was that it depended on a host of circumstances. Being a gentleman or gentlewoman (*P&P* 106; *E* 213) depended largely on birth (*E* 62; *P* 21) and occupation, but what really cemented class membership was behaviour (*E* 278). A good education (*E* 15), good manners and graceful movements when walking, sitting and dancing (*E* 328) mattered a great deal (*E* 33). Emma, the most class-conscious of Austen's heroines, is surprised to find a letter written by a mere yeoman farmer free of 'grammatical errors' (*E* 50–51), just as the letter of a gentleman might be. In *Persuasion*, Charles Hayter, alone of all his family, can be considered a member of the gentry, and Austen explicitly links his upward mobility to education:

> the young Hayters would, from their parents' inferior, retired, and unpolished way of living, and their own defective education, have been hardly in any class at all, but for their connexion with Uppercross; this eldest son of course excepted, who had chosen to be a scholar and a gentleman, and who was very superior in cultivation and manners to all the rest. (*P* 74)

He is further assisted in his rise to the gentry by genteel connections on his mother's side and by his choice of a religious profession. The three factors together combine to make him a more eligible suitor for a Miss Musgrove. If education and polish could raise a man, however, physical awkwardness, bumptious manners, poor grammar and a lack of acquaintance with history, geography or literature carried corresponding social penalties.

Rank within one's profession mattered a great deal. A militia colonel was a gentleman, but a sergeant was definitely not, and a lieutenant might or might not be, depending on his antecedents and deportment. An admiral was a gentleman (*P* 21), and a captain probably was, but the ordinary sailors were not. A physician, who by definition had to have attended one of the universities, was certainly a gentleman, but a surgeon was not. Thus, Mr Edwards, in the incomplete novel *The Watsons*, discourages his daughter from falling in love with Sam, even though he 'is a very good sort of young Man, & I dare say a very clever Surgeon' (*Watsons, MW* 324). Bishops were actually peers for the purposes of membership in Parliament, but by birth they might be members of the gentry. Members of the clergy were treated by almost everyone as gentlemen for the purposes of social ranking, although the snobbish Sir Walter Elliot cannot bring himself to regard a curate, the lowest-ranking type of clergyman, as a gentleman (*P* 23).

Another factor was relationship by marriage; marriage into a genteel family could confer a rosy reflected glow onto other members of one's own family, while marriage down the social scale slightly dimmed the family's social status. Thus, it matters very much that Mrs Bennet is the daughter of an attorney (a less prestigious member of the legal profession), that her sister married a law clerk (lower still) and that her brother is a London tradesman (not genteel at all – *P&P* 28, 37). All of these associations reflect poorly on Elizabeth Bennet's social status and thus her ability to attract a husband from the nobility or even the upper reaches of the gentry.

Personal lineage, too, counted; a writer might be a gentleman if he were born a gentleman and wrote for personal pleasure, as did Horace Walpole, but if he wrote to make a living and had been born the son of a tradesman, he was not a gentleman at all but merely a different sort of artisan. The issue of financial necessity also entered into the class status of tradesmen. A merchant who spent all day, six days a week, engaged in active trade was clearly not a gentleman, while a merchant wealthy enough to delegate most of the day-to-day operations to his inferiors might be fully accepted by genteel society (*E* 33–34).

Money could also be used to buy gentility (*E* 207), at least for the next generation. It could buy a country estate (*E* 16, 310) that reflected some glory on its owner; it could purchase entry by marriage into a genteel or even noble family, by means of a generous dowry; and it could buy expensive education for one's children, resulting in the kinds of social graces and commonly held opinions that were expected among the gentry. Instances of this sort of social mobility occur in Austen's works: the Bingley sisters, for all their snobbery, are only one generation removed from trade, and their family has yet to buy a landed estate to seal its membership in the gentry (*P&P* 15), and Sir William Lucas, for all his pride in his title, began in trade as well and came to the king's attention through his wealth (*P&P* 18). It should be remembered, however, that origins in trade were not easily forgotten by one's associates; Mrs Jennings, in *Sense and Sensibility*, is 'the widow of a man who had got all his money in a low way' (i.e., trade – *S&S* 228), and Maria Williams, in *A Collection of Letters*, is taunted for having been the granddaughter of a wine merchant (*Col Let, MW* 158). Austen, though she was more egalitarian than many of her contemporaries, is not free from all ideas of class, and she scorns those who think that money alone determines gentry status (*S&S* 275).

There was another aspect to the interrelation of money and social class. Since the Middle Ages, it had always been a problem when a person of genteel birth and upbringing was impoverished to a point at which he could no longer maintain the style of living expected of his class. Without luck or external intervention, he was almost certainly doomed to have his children and grandchildren slip to the class below. This is a danger faced by several of Austen's characters, most famously Mrs Bates, Miss Bates and Jane Fairfax, whose relative poverty means they can afford to keep only one servant. In the course of one generation, their family has sunk to a fingernail grip on gentility, with the threat of sending Jane Fairfax into service looming over them all. Less prominently, William Walter Elliot has faced a similar situation; Anne's friend Mrs Smith notes that when he was young, he was poor, 'and it was as much as he could do to support the appearance of a gentleman' (*P* 199). Hospitality was one way of spending money to reinforce status; expenditure on fine clothing was another; hiring multiple servants, especially menservants, was a third (*E* 30).

Finally, gregarious necessity played some role in deciding who was and was not a member of the gentry. There was only so much isolation that a country family could bear; sooner or later, they had to have *someone* over to dinner, and if it were someone a bit below them, simply for lack of any neighbours on an equal footing, so be it. A lonely clergyman might invite a surgeon to his home, and the surgeon thus gained a measure of gentility. Thus, a certain amount of socialising takes place in Highbury among 'the gentlemen and half-gentlemen of the place' (*E* 197); those on the boundaries of gentility are included as a matter of convenience. However, a need for companionship only went so far; Mr Woodhouse may think the world of his apothecary's medical opinion, but he never invites him to dinner.

Many people disapproved of the blurring of class boundaries (*E* 310). A cartoon by Gillray, *c.*1808, displays the pretensions of a tenant farmer, Farmer Giles of Cheese Hall, whose daughter Betty is being trained in the genteel graces, including music. The contrast between the physical

rusticity of the farmer's family and their aspirations to higher rank is
portrayed as a joke on Farmer Giles; he is unaware that by imitating
his social superiors, he emphasises how little he belongs in their world.
With considerably more earnestness and less humour, the anonymous
author of *The Mirror of the Graces* (1811) voiced the concerns of many
who feared to lose their social advantage over ambitious inferiors. She
criticised the 'fashion of educating all ranks of young women alike',
in which 'the brazier's daughter is taught to sing, dance, and play like
the heiress to an earldom.' Girls 'of the plebeian classes', she insisted,
should limit their education to the study of economical housekeeping.
(She would have found a kindred spirit in Mrs Norris, who thought
Fanny Price's reluctance to learn music and drawing contemptible, but
in perfect keeping with what Mrs Norris thinks of as Fanny's class – *MP*
19). At all times, she went on, social class was to be kept in mind. To
inferiors, one should be dignified but not proud, helpful but not overly
intimate. One should praise when appropriate and serve as a good
example. To superiors, deference was the watchword, and how much
deference depended entirely on rank:

> Deportment to superiors must ever carry with it that peculiar degree
> of ceremony which their rank demands. No intimacy of intercourse
> with them, no friendship and affection from them, ought ever to make
> us forget the certain respect which their stations require. Thus, for a
> mere gentlewoman to think of arrogating to herself the same homage
> of courtesy that is paid to a lady of quality, or to deny the just tribute
> of precedence, in every respect, to that lady, would be as absurd as
> presumptuous. Yet we see it; and ridicule from the higher circles is
> all she derives from her vain pretensions.

As a helpful guide to women in their quest to know their place in society,
the anonymous author provides a list of precedence, which reads to a
more egalitarian society as comically complex:

> Queen. Then Princesses. Then follow, in regular order, Duchesses,
> Marchionesses, Countesses. The Wives of the Eldest sons of Marquisses.
> The Wives of the Younger sons of Dukes. Daughters of Dukes.
> Daughters of Marquisses. Viscountesses. Wives of the eldest sons of
> Earls. Daughters of Earls. Wives of the younger sons of Marquisses.
> Baronesses. Wives of the eldest sons of Viscounts. Daughters of
> Viscounts. Wives of the younger sons of Earls. Wives of the eldest
> sons of Barons. Daughters of Baronets. Wives of the younger sons of
> Viscounts. Wives of the younger sons of Barons. Wives of Baronets.
> Wives of Privy Counsellors, Commoners. Wives of Judges. Wives of
> Knights of the Garter. Wives of Knights of the Bath. Wives of Knights
> of the Thistle. Wives of Knights Bachelors. Wives of Generals. Wives
> of Admirals. Wives of the eldest sons of Baronets. Daughters of Knights
> according to their fathers' precedence. Wives of the younger sons of

Baronets. Wives of Esquires and Gentlemen. Daughters of Esquires and Gentlemen. Wives of Citizens and Burgesses. The Wives of Military and Naval Officers of course take precedence of each other in correspondence with the rank of their husbands.

This scale, if every young lady would bear in mind and conform to it, is a sufficient guide to the mere ceremony of precedence; and would effectually prevent those dangerous disputes in ball-rooms about places, and those rude jostlings in going in and out of assemblies, which are not more disagreeable than ill-bred.

A simpler, but equally traditional, view of the social world was proposed by the statesman Edmund Burke, who, in laying out his arguments against the French Revolution, described the English attitude towards class and society. 'We fear God', he wrote; 'we look up with awe to kings; with affection to parliaments; with duty to magistrates; with reverence to priests; and with respect to nobility.' Austen at times echoes these sentiments; the estimable Mr Knightley warns of spoiling Harriet Smith for her sphere in life, which is destined to be somewhere below the gentry (*E* 38). Austen herself pats Mrs Jennings on the back for restricting her circle of friends to people whom a young gentlewoman can 'know' without lowering herself (*S&S* 168). In these sentiments, she was perfectly in line with one of the principal authorities of the age, Mrs Hester Chapone, whose *Letters on the Improvement of the Mind* (1772) were frequently reprinted. Her letter 'On the Regulation of the Affections' reads like advice intended specifically for Emma Woodhouse, advising young women to 'avoid intimacy with those of low birth and education', because their 'servile flattery and submission ... will infallibly corrupt your heart, and make all company insipid from whom you cannot expect the same homage.'*

Yet Austen does not subscribe unquestioningly to the traditional hierarchy. In the same passage that she reassures her readers that Mrs Jennings 'visited no one, to whom an introduction could at all discompose the feelings of her young companions', she expects these readers to approve of Mrs Jennings' loyalty in not dropping 'a few old city friends' – friends from the mercantile districts of London – despite pressure from her more class-conscious daughter (*S&S* 168). Austen's Robert Martin (*E* 65) receives much more sympathetic treatment than Gillray's Farmer Giles, and her titled characters are often pretentious fools – Lady Catherine de Bourgh, 'the Dowager Viscountess Dalrymple, and her daughter, the Honourable Miss Carteret' (*P* 148), Lord Osborne of *The Watsons*, and Sir Walter Elliott come to mind (*P* 166, 248). Invariably in her works, obsession with rank is equated with pettiness; Emma, in

---

*In the preceding paragraph, Chapone offers another piece of advice that echoes Anne Elliot's famous description of 'good company' in *Persuasion* (150): 'When I speak of the best company', Chapone writes, 'I do not mean in the common acceptation of the word,—persons of high rank and fortune,—but rather the most worthy and sensible.'

order to become a laudable woman, must learn to discard her youthful scrupulousness about class (*E* 29, 198, 214). Perhaps the best example of Austen's attitude is Captain Wentworth and all his associates in *Persuasion*; in the naval profession, she shows us, comradeship and merit are more important than birth and elegant posture while sitting. She is far from disdaining genteel education or manners, ridiculing the ignorant at least as much as the snobbish, but she seems to believe in a kind of natural gentility, an elite selected by intellect and decent behaviour rather than by title or occupation.

See also Etiquette; Titles.

Gig

The gig (*Clifford*, *MW* 43; *Sand*, *MW* 425; *NA* 65, 88; *P* 73) was merely one member of a large family of two-wheeled vehicles that included the curricle (*Clifford*, *MW* 43; *NA* 155) and the whisky. Carriages in this group were distinguished from each other not so much by the shape of the carriage body as by the way it was suspended above the wheels or hitched to a horse. In the body, the differences were subtle at best. The curricle seems to have been more likely than the gig or the whisky to have a folding leather hood, while the whisky might be missing part of the lower panel beneath the seat. All three had seats that were chair- or sleigh-like, open in front, with room for one or two occupants, and often with arms that flared outward to protect the passengers from mud flung up by the wheels. Some of these two-wheeled vehicles had a platform in the rear on which a servant could ride (*Sand*, *MW* 425; *NA* 44); on one version, the so-called suicide gig, this seat was especially high and precarious.

The most obvious difference between the gig and the curricle, other than the hood, was in the number of horses used. The curricle was typically pulled by two horses that were separated by a pole, while the gig was typically a one-horse vehicle (*NA* 44). It can be extremely difficult to tell the difference between the two, however, as spring designs changed over time, and the curricle closely resembled the one-horse cabriolet that was introduced into England early in the nineteenth century. John Thorpe adds to the reader's confusion by pointing out that his gig is 'Curriclehung' (*NA* 46) by which he means perhaps that the rear springs are 'C' springs (shaped like the letter), which became common on curricles. Rear springs on gigs might be C springs or might instead be 'whip' springs, which had a gentle overall curve and a small arc at one end.

William Felton, whose *Treatise on Carriages* (1801) is the standard reference to turn-of-the-century vehicles, confirms that the main difference is the number of horses but concedes that, from that point, the variations are nearly endless:

There are two descriptions of two-wheeled carriages; the curricle which is used with two horses, and the chaise that is used with one horse only. The one-horse chaises are of different patterns, and are distinguished by a variety of names, but mostly by the gig and the whiskey, in which there is a material difference; but both the curricle and chaise, like other carriages, are finished in various fanciful ways.

One of these 'fanciful ways' of varying the two-wheeled carriage was the 'changeable curricle, or curricle gig', which was light enough to be drawn by one horse but was 'longer in the carriage than a common gig', and so 'makes the appearance more uniform with that of a curricle, when used as such' – that is, when drawn by two horses. Thorpe's carriage might possibly be of this variety.

Thorpe goes on to brag about the features of his gig: 'seat, trunk, sword-case, splashing-board, lamps, silver moulding, all you see complete; the iron-work as good as new, or better' (46). The seat is self-explanatory. The 'trunk' would have been Thorpe's own travelling-trunk, strapped between the rear wheels above the axle; what he is really asking Catherine Morland to notice is that his carriage has a space for his trunk. The sword case was exactly what it sounds like, though it seems to have been a feature of the post-chaise or chariot, where it formed a horizontal, tubular protuberance on the back of the carriage body. Contemporary engravings do not tend to show a sword case at the back of the gig, so perhaps Thorpe had improvised something. The splashing board could have meant the flared panels at the top of each side of the gig, which minimised the dirt thrown up by the wheels, but since it is singular, it probably refers to a board in front of the driver's feet to block dirt stirred up by the horse's hooves. Illustrations from the early 1790s show extremely small footrests in front of the driver, while later gigs and curricles exhibit tall rectangular splashboards that look rather like large cookie sheets balanced on one long edge. Depending on when this innovation reached Austen's circle of friends, the addition of this detail of Thorpe's equipage may have been one of her later revisions. As for the lamps, these were oil lamps which were not, to judge from contemporary drawings, a standard feature on all gigs at this time. By the 1830s, they were hung below the side splash guards, just above and inside the wheels. Thorpe is perhaps justifiably proud of this extra luxury, though the gig was not a vehicle that was ideal for night driving, so the lamps may also be intended as an example of his general silliness. The 'silver moulding' is, however, consistent with the fancier gigs and curricles of the day, which were often fitted out with silver trim.

Many of these details would have been identical or nearly so on a curricle, making it all the more difficult to tell the two apart. The one-horse whisky, fortunately, can be distinguished from both the gig and the curricle by the manner in which the springs were attached. On the gig and curricle, the carriage body hung from the top ends of the springs, whose bottom ends were in turn connected to shafts or poles. The shafts were then fixed to the axles at one end and ran along the sides of the horse or horses, where they connected to the harness. On the whisky, the process was reversed: the seat was fixed instead to the shafts, and the shafts were then connected to the axles by the springs. In Austen's works, the whisky appears only in *The Memoirs of Mr Clifford*, where she seems to have made an effort to list every type of carriage then in use and very nearly succeeds (*Clifford, MW* 43).

Gigs and curricles, however, make far more than a cameo appearance in her works. The crucial aspect of the gig and curricle, as they relate to Jane Austen, is how they were both used. Gigs – to speak now of the entire family of vehicles – were fast, fashionable and driven not by a professional coachman but by the owner, for pleasure. Because they were carefully balanced and sprung, they provided a pleasant ride on fine days; because they were lightweight and inclined to tip, they required skill to handle. Because the owner himself drove, he got all the credit (or blame) for his handling of the horse or horses (*NA* 44, 157). In other words, curricles and gigs provided drivers with an opportunity to show off, to test their skill, and to experience, in a very direct way, an exhilarating sense of speed. It was this combination of advantages that allowed these vehicles, around the time Jane Austen reached adulthood, to supersede the phaeton as the height of style.

The curricle was more desirable than the gig, for reasons that are not quite clear. It appears to have had something to do with the way it drove; no doubt at least part of its attraction was that it was only slightly heavier than the gig but was driven by two horses and thus could travel somewhat faster (*Watsons, MW* 339; *NA* 156–157). For whatever reason, it became the must-have vehicle for fashionable young men (*NA* 35), and though a gig was nothing to be really ashamed of, a curricle was considered better. This may be why Thorpe hastens to point out that his gig is 'curricle-hung'; if he cannot have the real thing, he can at least have the next best, and he still feels that he must offer some apology for not having a real curricle. He was 'pretty well determined on [buying] a curricle' (*NA* 46), he says, but bought a gig instead because the opportunity arose. In fact, in *Northanger Abbey* carriage ownership serves as a subtle hint about Catherine Morland's proper mate; John Thorpe has the faux curricle, but Henry Tilney owns the real thing. She claims to 'know so little about such things' (46) that she cannot judge whether Thorpe's gig was a bargain, but by the time she joins Henry in his curricle, she has decided 'that a curricle was the prettiest equipage in the world' (156). Her opinion of carriage and man, in both cases, are in sync – indifferent on the one hand, enamoured on the other.

Elsewhere, the ownership of a gig or a curricle is not necessarily as significant. The fawning Tom Musgrave drives a curricle, it is true (*Watsons, MW* 338, 339), as do the false Mr Elliot (*P* 105) and Mr Willoughby (*S&S* 52, 67, 75, 194), but so does William Goulding, a neighbour in *Pride and Prejudice* of whom the reader hears almost nothing (*P&P* 316) and the stupid, but decent, Mr Rushworth (*MP* 84). So, too, does the reasonably sensible Charles Musgrove (*P* 105). The curricle is neither good nor evil, but merely an indicator of a certain degree of youth, virility and wealth. In Willoughby's case, the curricle is an evil, but only because he does not have the income to maintain it, a fact that Mrs Jennings mentions as only one of his many extravagances (*S&S* 194).

Willoughby could, of course, save money by owning a gig instead and getting rid of one of his horses, but he no doubt knows the different impressions the two vehicles would create. Miss Denham, of the incomplete novel *Sanditon*, certainly knows. Status-hungry, she is 'immediately gnawed by the want of a handsomer Equipage than the simple Gig' in which she and her brother travel, and she is embarrassed to see the groom leading it about (to cool down the horse after its exertions) in plain sight (*MW* 394). Likewise, Anne Elliot's sister Mary, prompted perhaps by 'the Elliot pride', refuses a seat in Admiral Croft's gig. She will not 'make a third in a one-horse chaise' (chaise was another term at the time for these open-seated, two-wheeled, roofless carriages), partly it seems because of the indignity of squeezing in and partly because of the nature of the carriage itself, which does not suit her ideas of the grandeur suitable to her station (*P* 90). The gig would, of course, have seated only two (Felton specifies that two-wheeled carriage seats were between 2 feet 10 inches and 3 feet 2 inches wide), but Admiral and Mrs Croft hospitably make room for a third, and Anne gratefully and gracefully accepts their offer (*P* 91). As with so many of Austen's mentions of carriages, this incident elucidates the characters of all involved.

In both the instances just described, it is not the ownership of a gig that is condemned, but the attitudes of others towards the gig. However, there is some evidence that Austen considers a curricle a suitable accessory for a hero. Sir Edward Denham, another male character who seems destined for unsuitability, drives a gig (*Sand, MW* 403), as does the insufferable Mr Collins of *Pride and Prejudice* (*P&P* 168). Mr Darcy, however, drives a curricle (*P&P* 260), setting up the same contrast that Austen draws between Mr Thorpe and Mr Tilney.

There were other vehicles besides curricles and whiskies in the gig family. One of these was the tandem (*Sand, MW* 425), a variant of the dogcart. Dogcarts were two-wheeled carriages that seated four people – two facing forwards, two facing backwards, with the pairs back to back. Beneath their joint seat was a box with louvered sides and a rear door that unlatched at the top. This compartment was for transporting hunting dogs – hence the name of the vehicle – with the louvers allowing the dogs to breathe en route. The name 'tandem' simply meant that the carriage was pulled by two horses, one in front of the other, rather than side by side.

The sulky, not mentioned in Austen, was another two-wheeled, gig-like carriage. It took its name from the fact that there was only one seat, and the driver could thus be alone, presumably sulking for some reason. The buggy was another sort of two-wheeled carriage, sometimes defined as a gig with a hood (*Clifford*, *MW* 43). The Irish car (*E* 374) was very much like a dogcart, but with the box turned 90 degrees, so that the passengers sat sideways with reference to the horse. The driver, too, sat sideways, which could be extremely precarious. It was developed, as its name implies, in Ireland, and Austen uses it with characteristic consistency in *Emma*, the one of all her novels that makes the most dramatic use of Ireland and things Irish.

See also Carriages and Coaches; Phaeton.

Gloves

Gloves (*Watsons*, *MW* 331, 336; *Sand*, *MW* 374; *S&S* 221; *P&P* 316; *E* 237; *P* 236) were an essential part of both men's and women's wear, worn by everyone with any pretence to fashion and even by servants who waited at the table. They became associated with propriety and modesty. For women, they helped to preserve the pallid skin that was so highly prized. Gloves were worn outdoors, while dancing (*Col Let*, *MW* 157) and at evening parties (*Cath*, *MW* 213), but they were removed for dinner. Because they were such common items, and perhaps because they were also so personal – one has only to remember Romeo's speech outside Juliet's balcony to realise *how* personal – they were common 'favours', or gifts, for guests at weddings and funerals.

The funeral gloves were black, often made of 'shammy', the oil-tanned skins of chamois antelopes. Less exalted guests got 'mock shammy', sheep or lambskin tanned in much the same way to imitate the more expensive leather. These funeral gloves were the only ones, for the period in question, that were black. In fact, few gloves were even made in bright colours, as the muted classical palette of the era called for light earth tones, pastels and white.

Women typically wore long gloves, tied above the elbow to keep them from slipping down, though, as the anonymous author of *The Mirror of the Graces* (1811) hinted, women without arms that were 'muscular, coarse, or scraggy' could push their gloves 'down to a little above the wrists'. The gloves were relatively free of ornament. Some white kid gloves had printed and painted designs on the back of the hand, or in imitation of a bracelet around the wrist, with the colours of paint being sometimes chosen to harmonise with other accessories like fans or shoes.

Preferred colours and materials were remarkably consistent through Austen's lifetime. Suede, kid, silk and netting were favourite materials, with buff-coloured suede, white kid and 'York tan' – an undyed suede – consistently leading in popularity. (Linen and worsted gloves were also common, but this was not because they were fashionable but because they were cheap.) Yellow and other pale colours were considered fine for daytime use but were banned as evening wear. One popular and rather unusual material for gloves was 'chickenskin', not the skin of a chicken at all, but the skin of an unborn calf treated with almonds and spermaceti; these gloves were so thin and flexible that they were sometimes sold, to demonstrate their quality, bunched up inside a walnut shell.

Men wore short, wrist-length gloves in the same subdued range of colours as women – primarily tan, buff, yellow and white (*Col Let*, *MW* 157). Like women, they wore York tans (*E* 200), chickenskin, white cotton (occasionally enlivened with a little discreet embroidery or a row of sequins at the wrist), kid and doeskin. Woodstock gloves were especially fine and lightweight and were made of fawn skin. 'Beavers' (*E* 200) were dark brown, like the fur of a beaver, and may have been made of felted cloth. Occasional machine-knitted gloves were seen, and cheap worsted gloves were available for purchase by the poor, but it is unlikely that Austen's fictional gentlemen would have worn these.

Prices varied widely according to the quality of the materials. The bankruptcy valuation of a Norwich milliner in 1785 gave the value of black worsted gloves – for funerals and mourning wear, no doubt – as 10*d*. a pair, but men's kid gloves, even in a damaged state, were worth 11*s*. a pair. Twilled cotton gloves were valued at 1*s*. Parson James Woodforde, without specifying the material, reported paying 2*s*. 2*d*. for a pair of gloves in 1784; later that year, he paid 2*s*. for a pair of riding gloves (presumably of some kind of leather). In London in 1795, while walking through the city, he stopped and bought a pair of gloves for 2*s*. These could hardly have been kid, much less a special material like chickenskin; they must have been made of an inferior leather or of cotton. He does not say what kind of shop (*E* 199–201) sold him his London gloves, but it could have belonged to a perfumer, a breeches maker, a milliner, a dressmaker or a specialist glover, all of whom retailed gloves. Examples of gloves may be seen in the illustrations *Monstrosities of 1799* and *Progress of the Toilet – Dress Completed* (both in the article on Clothing).

See also Clothing.

Gothic

The word 'Gothic' could apply to several different types of art and expression, but it was principally an architectural style and a literary genre. In architecture, it meant a return to medieval or quasi-medieval forms, including pointed windows, pointed arches, asymmetrical design and castle-like towers. At first, genuine Gothic ruins such as abbeys (*NA* 141) were embraced by the picturesque movement, and then the wealthy began to build neo-Gothic structures, beginning with garden follies, faux ruins and guesthouses, and proceeding to sizable mansions. One of the smaller buildings in this style was Blaise Castle, not really a castle at all but an exotic cottage retreat and not ancient as John Thorpe implies but thoroughly eighteenth-century, as Austen's readers would have known. Austen herself was acquainted with several buildings in the Gothic style, including Adlestrop Park, which belonged to her mother's family, and the marquis of Lansdowne's Southampton castle, which stood very near the house she shared with her brother Frank's family in the early-nineteenth century.

Flourishing alongside the interest in Gothic architecture was the interest in Gothic literature. The trend began with Horace Walpole's *Castle of Otranto* (1764), which in its first edition purported to be a translation of an original medieval work; in the second edition Walpole confessed his authorship. It possessed all the hallmarks of the Gothic genre: a medieval setting (often in Italy), a tyrannical parent (or step-parent or guardian), damsels in distress, a noble hero, Catholic clergy and ritual, a supernatural or apparently supernatural occurrences and archaic-sounding language. A typical passage, in which an execution is fortuitously forestalled by the revelation of a birthmark, reads:

'What!' said the youth; 'is it possible that my fate could have occasioned what I heard? Is the princess, then, again in thy power?'

'Thou dost but remember me of my wrath', said Manfred; 'prepare thee, for this moment is thy last.'

The youth, who felt his indignation rise, and who was touched with the sorrow which he saw he had infused into all the spectators, as well as into the friar, suppressed his emotions, and putting off his doublet, and unbuttoning his collar, knelt down to his prayers. As he stooped, his shirt slipped down below his shoulder, and discovered the mark of a bloody arrow.

'Gracious Heaven!' cried the holy man, starting, 'what do I see? It is my child, my Theodore!'

The passions that ensued must be conceived; they cannot be painted. The tears of the assistants were suspended by wonder, rather than stopped by joy. They seemed to inquire into the eyes of their lord what they ought to feel. Surprise, doubt, tenderness, respect, succeeded each other in the countenance of the youth. He received with modest submission the effusion of the old man's tears and embraces; yet, afraid of giving a loose to hope, and suspecting, from what had passed, the inflexibility of Manfred's temper, he cast a glance towards the prince, as if to say, Canst thou be unmoved at such a scene as this?

This passage, with its secret identities, its stilted, faux-antique dialogue and its exotic forays outside Protestantism, has much of what appealed to the readers of the Gothic.

The Gothic genre was further developed and, most would agree, mastered by Ann Radcliffe (1764–1823), whose novels featured all the standard elements. Her works were of epic-length, peppered with her own poetry and full of descriptions of Italian and French countrysides that she had never personally seen. Full of assassins (*NA* 167), banditti, and leering, powerful men, her books offered a taste of the supernatural but always explained the apparitions logically in the end, bringing them back into the realm of the ordinary. Austen refers to several of Radcliffe's works in her own novels, most notably in *Northanger Abbey*, which is a prolonged parody of the Gothic style. R. W. Chapman quotes a particularly relevant passage from Radcliffe's *Romance of the Forest* (1791), in his edition of *Northanger Abbey*, a passage in which a young woman discovers a mysterious document. Austen makes an indirect reference to this passage, or at least to passages of its kind, when Catherine Morland discovers the laundry bill in the cabinet in her room in the abbey. She also parodies the genre in Henry Tilney's mock-Gothic narrative of Catherine's future adventures within the abbey (*NA* 158–160).

A direct reference to Radcliffe's masterwork *The Mysteries of Udolpho* (1794) occurs earlier in *Northanger Abbey*, when Catherine refers to 'such weather … as they had at Udolpho, or at least in Tuscany and the South of France! – the night that poor St. Aubin died! – such beautiful weather!' (*NA* 83). Yet Catherine is wrong on at least two points; the character who dies is St. Aubert, not St. Aubin, and St. Aubert dies at 'about three o'clock in the afternoon', on a day marked by a bright morning sun and pure air. Catherine, lingering miserably inside on a rainy day in Bath, might indeed be thinking of this sunshiny fictional day, but she specifically mentions the weather at night. Perhaps, as Chapman believes, she means the weather on the night of that same day, but Radcliffe offers little description of that night, except to say that it was dark, with an 'effulgent planet' setting in the sky over some woods. Perhaps Catherine instead means the weather on the night *before* 'poor St. Aubin died'. On that night, Radcliffe mentions 'the silver whiteness of the moon-light' and

> the heaven, whose blue unclouded concave was studded thick with stars, the worlds, perhaps, of spirits, unsphered of mortal mould. … The still air seemed scarcely to breathe upon the woods, and, now and then, the distant sound of a solitary sheep-bell, or of a closing casement, was all that broke on silence. Elevated and enwrapt, while her eyes were often wet with tears of sublime devotion and solemn awe, she continued at the casement, till the gloom of mid-night hung over the earth, and the planet, which La Voisin had pointed out, sunk below the woods.

This is a far more descriptive passage than either of the others and more likely to have made an impression on Catherine. However, the interesting thing is that, no matter which of the three passages is intended, Catherine has still read sloppily. She has possibly mistaken the time of day at which the character dies, certainly gotten his name wrong, and chosen a night-time reference for her wish that the daytime weather would improve. It is impossible to believe that in all Jane Austen's reading she could find no more appropriate literary allusion to clear weather. It is equally unlikely, though she sometimes slightly misquotes literary works in her letters, that she could have entirely mistaken the name of a character who inhabits a significant fraction of a well-known novel and who shares his last name with the heroine. The mistakes here are not Austen's, but Catherine's, and they reflect her inability at this point in her development to select and draw proper judgements from her reading. She remembers only a part and misapplies the rest, foreshadowing her obtuseness at the abbey.

The Gothic novel took an entirely different turn in the hands of Matthew Lewis (1775–1818), who wrote *The Monk* in 1796 at the age of nineteen. Where Radcliffe explains away apparently supernatural events, Lewis not only allows them to be magical but positively revels in them, right down to the ending, in which the villain Ambrosio, who has not only threatened the innocent heroine but actually raped and then murdered her, is confronted by the Devil himself:

> As He said this, darting his talons into the Monk's shaven crown, he sprang with him from the rock. The Caves and mountains rang with Ambrosio's shrieks. The Dæmon continued to soar aloft, till reaching a dreadful height, He released the sufferer. Headlong fell the Monk through the airy waste; The sharp point of a rock received him; and He rolled from precipice to precipice, till bruised and mangled He rested on the river's banks. Life still existed in his miserable frame: He attempted in vain to raise himself; His broken and dislocated limbs refused to perform their office, not was He able to quit the spot where He had first fallen. The Sun now rose above the horizon; Its scorching beams darted full upon the head of the expiring Sinner. Myriads of insects were called forth by the warmth; They drank the blood which trickled from Ambrosio's wounds; He had no power to drive them from him, and they fastened upon his sores, darted their stings into his body, covered him with their multitudes, and inflicted on him tortures the most exquisite and insupportable.

Ambrosio's death takes seven full days to accomplish, during which time he is also torn apart by eagles, tortured by thirst as he hears but cannot reach a nearby river, blinded and finally drowned in a flood. This almost self-parodically violent novel, which is fairly shamelessly pornographic in parts, was wildly notorious and earned its author the hated sobriquet of 'Monk' Lewis. It exemplified the darker side of the eighteenth-century Gothic and justified its excesses on the grounds that, because the villain was punished in the end, morality was served.

See also Architecture; Gardens and Landscape; Picturesque; Reading.

H

Hair

Hairstyles in Austen's childhood required enormous maintenance
and were usually extremely uncomfortable. Women in the 1770s and
1780s wore their hair tall and powdered, which required the hair to
be frizzed and built up on pads. In the 1770s, hair was so tall that it
attracted much comment and criticism. The hair, once styled, was
greased with pomatum and then powdered with white or grey hair
powder. This was a messy process, and the woman being powdered
would wear a protective gown while her maid or hairdresser performed
the task. Then she did all she could not to disturb the hairstyle for
days or weeks, sleeping with a bag over the coiffure to protect it. Not
surprisingly, women's heads itched like fury and served as perfect
havens for vermin.

Men shaved their heads or wore their hair (*Harley*, *MW* 40; *L&F*,
MW 93; *P* 142) extremely short in order to facilitate the wearing of wigs,
which were also powdered (*Watsons*, *MW* 353, 357; *P* 20). Wigs (*MP* 189)
came in a dazzling array of styles, some of which gave clues to the wearer's
profession. Clergymen tended to favour one sort of wigs, physicians
another and army officers still another. Naval officers did not wear
wigs; it was too easy to lose them at sea (*P* 20).

The general revolution in fashion in the 1790s, however, altered
hairstyles as well. Young men abandoned their wigs and began growing
their own hair long and wearing it unpowdered. Portraits from this period
of Robert Southey, Samuel Taylor Coleridge and Napoleon all show them
with long, flowing locks. Then, in a vogue for all things classical, men cut
their hair short again. This time, they did not opt for the closely shorn
look adapted to the wearing of wigs but for a layered cut reminiscent of
the hairstyles seen on Greek statues and busts of Roman emperors. This
style, called the 'Titus' or the 'Brutus crop', remained in fashion for the
remainder of Austen's life. Southey, who in the mid-1790s sported long
hair, was painted in 1804 wearing a Titus cut.

Some men still retained the powdered wig. The style was still considered
essential for servants in livery (*Watsons*, *MW* 322; *MP* 189), for example,
perhaps because the wig and powder entailed extra expense and thus
added to the magnificent statement of disposable income represented by
a liveried footman. Older men were generally reluctant to abandon wigs,
and many of them never adopted the new fashion. Barristers were still
required to wear them, and physicians preferred to do so, as it added to
their presence and authority. However, such men were in the minority,
and a tax on hair powder in the late eighteenth century, replaced in the

early nineteenth by a flat fee for a 'powdering license', helped hasten the demise of the powdered wig.

Women, no doubt with great relief, also adopted a simpler and more natural style of hairdressing. Abandoning pads and powder, they cut their hair (*Evelyn, MW* 184; *Cath, MW* 204; *S&S* 60, 98, 135, 329) short at the front, arranging this hair into short curls (*Sand, MW* 390; *NA* 15, 27, 52; *MP* 296–297) to frame the face. The rest, also kept relatively short, was curled and gathered at the back of the head by bandeaus and fillets of ribbon. These thin headbands reminded them of the hairstyles seen in Greek and Roman statuary. A few women, bolder than the rest, adopted a female version of the Titus cut; other extremely fashionable women cut their hair very short and wore various styles of attractively curled wigs. In 1802, for example, Lady Stanley wrote to a friend:

> I have cut off my tail [the hair at the back of her head] for comfort, and as my front hair is always coming out of curl in the damp summer evenings, and as I find everybody sports a false toupee, I don't see why I should not have the comfort of one too. I wish to be as fashionable and as deceiving as possible.

Most women, however, seem to have kept their own hair. The standard coiffure (*S&S* 249; *MP* 360–361) remained short curls or wisps in front and hair of medium length gathered at the back, often covered indoors by a cap and outdoors by a bonnet or hat.

The simpler styles, however, did not do away with the hairdresser (*NA* 20; *E* 323). Women still needed to have their hair cut and, for special occasions, arranged. Men went to barbershops (*E* 205, 212) or had their servants shave them and dress their wigs at home (*P* 32), but in the case of women, hairdressers paid house calls. Writing from London in 1813, Jane told Cassandra that 'Mr. Hall was very punctual yesterday & curled me out at a great rate. I thought it looked hideous, and longed for a snug cap instead, but my companions silenced me by their admiration.' In August 1805, the same Mr Hall had come to Edward's house at Godmersham to dress Elizabeth's and Jane's hair and to give lessons to Elizabeth Austen's lady's maid. He charged 5*s.* for each time he dressed Elizabeth's hair, 5*s.* for each lesson and only 2*s.* 6*d.* for dressing Jane's hair. Apparently he had given Cassandra a similar discount when she visited Godmersham, for Jane remarked drily, 'He certainly respects either our Youth or our poverty.' It was common to join forces in this way and have a hairdresser arrange the hair of all the ladies in a household at once, especially if a ball or other important social event was imminent. In 1782, the local squire's wife asked Parson Woodforde's niece Nancy to her house, and the two ladies had their hair done at the same time:

> Mr. Custance sent after Nancy this morning to spend the Day with Mrs. Custance and to have her Hair dressed by one Brown, the best Ladies Frisseur in Norwich. ... Nancy returned home about ½

past 9 o'clock this Even', with her head finely dressed of [*sit:*] but very becoming her. Mrs. Custance would not let Nancy pay the Barber, but she paid for her and it cost no less than half a guinea. Mrs. Custance gave the Barber for dressing her Hair and Nancy's the enormous sum of one guinea—He came on purpose from Norwich to dress them. Mrs. Custance (God bless her) is the best Lady I every [*sit:*] knew.

The cost of a hairdresser, as Woodforde noted, could be substantial,* and for ordinary occasions, women had their hair done by their maids (*P&P* 344; *E* 134, 324). Good hairdressing skills were, therefore, an important recommendation for a lady's maid.

Hair that did not possess a natural curl was curled artificially (*E* 134) by being twisted or rolled and wrapped in paper (*Watsons*, *MW* 322). The curling papers were cut 4 inches square and then again along the diagonal, then wrapped around the tightly curled hair and twisted so that they would remain in place until removed. When all the thin sections of hair had been rolled and wrapped, wrote London hairdresser James Stewart in 1782, 'they look like regular rows of trees.' Next, the hairdresser took a heated curling iron, known as a toupee iron, which could open rather like a pair of scissors. He pinched the paper between the two sides of the iron, taking care not to touch the hair directly, and held them there until the paper began to smoke. The paper was unwrapped and the curl pinned to the side of the head, and the hairdresser moved on to the next curling paper. Jane had naturally curly hair, at least in front, for she wrote in December 1798,

> I have made myself two or three caps to wear of evenings since I came home, and they save me a world of torment as to hair-dressing, which at present gives me no trouble beyond washing and brushing, for my long hair is always plaited up out of sight, and my short hair curls well enough to want no papering.

She would not, therefore, have needed much help from a servant. Some women wore caps for evening social occasions, but others merely arranged their hair attractively, binding it up with ribbons or pins and adorning it with flowers (*NA* 71), strings of beads (*NA* 56) or twists of satin decorated with spirals of beads or pearls. Sometimes a thin braid (*NA* 118) could be pinned over the front of the head to serve as a bandeau in place of a ribbon, or it could be wrapped around the chignon at the back. Ornaments were held in place by combs or pins (*S&S* 121); the combs themselves were often quite decorative, and the more expensive ones were jewelled.

The 'queer fashion' to which William Price refers (*MP* 235) cannot be determined with any accuracy, as the year in which that part of *Mansfield*

---

*Woodforde, by way of comparison, typically paid his barber only a shilling for a shave, and paid his manservant 2s. 6d. every three months for the dressing of his wigs. Even a shave and the dressing of his wig combined cost him only 1s. 6d. in London.

11. A lady and her maid watch nervously as the professional hairdresser applies a hot iron to her curling papers.

Park takes place is not clear. Critics disagree as to whether the main action of the novel is set in 1808–1809, 1812–1813 or some other year entirely.

It is not even clear, in this instance, whether the fashion in question is for morning or evening. Austen may have left the exact style deliberately vague to avoid dating the novel too much, just as she does not specify the hairstyle worn by Jane Fairfax that Frank Churchill pretends to find 'outré' (*E* 222).

See also Clothing; Hats.

Hats

The typical man's hat (*MW* 445; *NA* 157, 177) when Austen was born was the cocked hat. This was a felt hat, usually black, with a low round crown and a wide brim that was turned up either on three sides to make a triangle (a tricorne) or in the front and back to make a semicircle (a bicorne). As tricorne hats came to seem increasingly old-fashioned, gentlemen at first took to the chapeau bras, a bicorne that could either be worn or folded and carried under the arm. All of these hats might be decorated with a cockade (*Watsons*, *MW* 326), a small decoration made of ribbons or feathers, frequently worn by military men, by revellers at weddings and by crowds at election time (in which case the colours of the ribbons would identify whose supporters they were).

Riders wore a tallish cylindrical hat with a hard crown and a medium-wide brim of the kind. This hat, which over time would lose some of the width on its brim and become the top hat, was widely adopted for use throughout the day. This was consistent with a general trend towards the wearing of sporting attire for all purposes. By 1800, the round hat had triumphed over the tricorne and bicorne everywhere except on military officers and very old-fashioned gentlemen.

Women, especially married women or women of an age to be considered unmarriageable, wore caps (*Cath*, *MW* 207; *Watsons*, *MW* 323; *MP* 204) on all occasions. These were usually mob caps (*MP* 146) or biggins, which were similarly soft and made of cloth such as cambric or muslin (*NA* 28). They both had a rounded shape with a frill of some kind around the edge; mob caps were generally a little smaller than biggins and might have strings to tie under the chin or lappets – panes of cloth, often decorated in some way, which fell down to each side of the cap. Such caps may be seen in various illustrations in this book, including the illustrations 'A Christening' (Clergy) and 'Progress of the Toilet. – The Stays' and 'Progress of the Toilet – Dress Completed' (both in the article on Clothing). Both of these caps were appropriate for 'morning' as it was understood in Austen's time – that is, from rising until dinner at anywhere from 3:00 a.m. to 6:30 p.m.

In the evening, smaller, more decorative caps were generally worn, made of finer materials and sometimes in fanciful shapes. Austen, for example, briefly adopted a 'Mamolouc cap', a fez-like headdress worn in honour of Nelson's victory at the Battle of the Nile, and in December 1798, she was trimming an evening cap with 'silver' (silver ribbon or braid) and a coquelicot feather. (Coquelicot – see *NA* 39 – was a deep shade of red.) There was also a vogue for turbans (*NA* 217), which ranged in size from small to voluminous, and which were either created on the spot by winding fabric around the head or purchased already folded and shaped and ready to wear.

Outdoors, women wore hats (*Cath*, *MW* 202; *Sand*, *MW* 389; *NA* 39, 84, 165; *S&S* 272; *P&P* 6; *MP* 408; *P* 142) or bonnets (*F&E*, *MW* 4; *Cass*, *MW* 45; *Cath*, *MW* 211; *Sand*, *MW* 381; *NA* 71, 104, 161, 165, 177; *S&S* 272; *P&P* 72, 219, 221; *E* 173, 355, 358). The technical difference between them was that hats had a brim all the way around, while bonnets had no brim in the back or only the barest hint of a brim. Hats and bonnets came in many styles and were made of many materials. Hats and bonnets for walking outdoors, for example, could be soft and made of muslin, beaver or velvet; or, quite commonly, stiffer and made of straw (*Sand*, *MW* 389; *NA* 161), decorated with sewn-on or pinned-on ribbons. In a letter of May 1801, Jane mentions both 'Bonnets of Cambric Muslin' and bonnets of 'white chip' (willow fibre).

There were also indoor hats for evening wear that might be made of silk, satin or crepe. For the first decade of the nineteenth century, small veils were common on hats, but afterwards they fell out of fashion. Hats and bonnets were usually worn tilted back a little on the head so that the face was not entirely hidden, but the 'close bonnet' (*MP* 49, 51) mentioned by Mary Crawford had a soft fabric crown and a very deep, almost tubular brim and would have revealed almost nothing of the face unless the wearer was facing one directly. Seen from the side, the wearer's head looked rather like a tilted cupcake. Hats and bonnets were fairly small at the beginning of the nineteenth century, broadening in about 1804 to 1807, flattening for the next few years and then growing tall and narrow towards the end of Austen's life. Some were shaped like truncated cones and worn on a slant, with the hair peeking out through a hole in the back; others were bonnets with brims that sloped away on the sides to reveal the lower half of the face; some were flexible straw hats tied under the chin with wide ribbons; some imitated the round hats worn by men, reinterpreting them in straw, lace and ribbons. A 'witch's hat' from 1809 is little more than a flat circle of white chip; the sides have been pushed towards each other by a band of ribbon, forcing the circle to poke out a little at the front and back and keeping the hat on the woman's head. The front has been decorated with flowers. Perhaps this is the sort of hat that John Thorpe says makes his mother 'look like an old witch' (*NA* 49).

Hats and caps could be made at home, but they were more commonly purchased (*Sand, MW* 381) from milliners (*Cass, MW* 44; *Watsons, MW* 323;

12. *A Bonnet Shop*, Thomas Rowlandson, 1810.

NA 44; *P&P* 219), who sold relatively plain headgear, fully trimmed headgear and materials such as lace and ribbon. The customer could select a cap, for example, and either wear it as it was or take it home and decorate it to suit her own taste (*S&S* 272; *P&P* 6). She could add ribbons in various colours, beads or feathers. In the late 1790s, artificial fruit and flowers were all the rage, and Jane commented on this fashion while she was staying in Bath in June 1799:

> Flowers are very much worn, & Fruit is still more the thing. – Eliz: has a bunch of Strawberries, & I have seen Grapes, Cherries, Plumbs & Apricots – There are likewise Almonds & raisins, French plumbs & Tamarinds at the Grocers, but I have never seen any of them in hats.

Hats could be stored individually in the wide cylindrical bandboxes (*P&P* 221; *MP* 379) provided by the milliner or collectively in some sort of larger trunk or box (*NA* 165). Examples of bandboxes appear in the illustration 'Progress of the Toilet – Dress Completed' (Clothing).

See also Clothing; Gloves; Hair; Shoes; Stockings.

Holidays

Austen mentions three major holidays in her works: Easter, Michaelmas and Christmas. These, as it happens, were three of the four principal seasonal holidays that served as markers for the passage of the year. Easter was associated with spring, Michaelmas with fall and Christmas with winter. The fourth holiday was Whitsuntide, associated with summer. Of all of these, Easter (*P&P* 62; *MP* 69, 359, 430; *E* 79) was the most solemn religious holiday. It therefore seems appropriate that it appears most frequently in Austen's most religious work, *Mansfield Park*. The references to it make little direct reference to the religious significance of the holiday, but Austen's choice is not accidental; the period before Easter that Fanny spends with her birth family in Portsmouth takes the form of asceticism, resistance to temptation and, finally, a symbolic resurrection as Edmund rescues her and carries her off to the comparative heaven of Mansfield (*MP* 423). Henry Crawford and Maria Rushworth, on the other hand, spend it in idle socialising and moral decay (*MP* 434). Mary Crawford sees the holiday merely as the date at which she will trade one fashionable home for another, and she is, at this of all times, relieved that no one can tell by his clothing that Edmund is a clergyman (*MP* 416). The chief reference to Easter as a specifically religious occasion occurs, appropriately enough, in reference to Edmund's clerical duties (*MP* 226). Elsewhere in Austen's works, Easter is principally a time spent quietly with one's family (*S&S* 279; *P&P* 170; *E* 95). The only clergyman who actually delivers an Easter sermon is Mr Collins (*P&P* 172).

Holidays

Several folk traditions centred around Easter. Though these varied from one village to another, coloured eggs were already firmly associated with the holiday. Dyed with cochineal or logwood, they were given in some places to children only and in other places to adults and children alike. The eggs given by wealthy families might be gilded. In some places, children dissolved candy or sugar in water. In Warwickshire, on Easter Monday, the children 'clipped' (embraced) the local churches, standing with their backs against the church's exterior walls, holding hands, until they made a complete chain around the building. In some places, religious plays or comic mummer's plays were performed. Dorsetshire had boys' processions on Easter Eve, while in Twickenham and other places, penny loaves of bread were hurled from the church tower and gathered up by the children. In 1790, a correspondent to the *Gentleman's Magazine* informed its readers that in Harrowgate

> On Easter Sunday, as soon as the service of the church is over, the boys run about the streets, and lay hold of every woman or girl they can, and take the buckles from their shoes. This farce is continued till the next day at noon, when the females begin, and return the compliment upon the men, which does not end till Tuesday evening.

The buckles had to be ransomed from their captors. A similar custom, in which the sexes engaged in mock combat, was 'lifting' or 'heaving'. On Easter Monday, men would lift any woman they could find, holding her parallel to the ground and hoisting her up three times in quick succession. On Easter Tuesday, women reversed the roles and lifted men. Prohibitions of lifting, proclaimed by town bellmen, apparently had not managed to suppress the game.

Michaelmas (*Sand, MW* 377, 378; *S&S* 216; *P&P* 3; *MP* 189; *E* 75; *P* 142), 29 September (*P* 48), was an important date for legal purposes, though not a significant religious festival. Its religious role was largely as an arbitrary date on which many churches offered communion. Contracts often began and ended on Michaelmas, and, in some regions, servants' terms of employment customarily began on that date. Accordingly, Austen uses it in many cases as the date for the beginning or ending of leases (*P&P* 336; *MP* 405; *P* 33). Predictions of people being married by Michaelmas may simply indicate the passage of time, but perhaps the date is chosen for its associations with new enterprises and new legal arrangements (*S&S* 292, 293, 374).

Of all the holidays, Christmas (*Watsons, MW* 350; *NA* 118; *S&S* 112–113; *P&P* 153, 238; *MP* 255, 288, 434; *E* 79, 115; *P* 206) is the one most frequently mentioned. This seems perfectly natural today, when Christmas is the most commercialised and most sentimentalised of all Christian holidays, but it must be recalled that many of our modern associations with Christmas are the legacy of the Victorian era, and especially of the popularisation of Christmas celebrations by Charles Dickens and others. In Austen's time, Christmas was viewed as a holiday in decline, a fairly old-fashioned holiday celebrated for the sake of children rather than adults. Nonetheless, some of the 'gaieties which that season generally brings' (*P&P* 117) were still observed. Family members reunited (*LS, MW* 246; *NA* 33; *P&P* 139, 383; *E* 7, 40; *P* 134), children returned from boarding schools or universities (*MP* 21; *P* 129, 133), friends were invited to dinner parties and dances (*S&S* 44, 152; *MP* 252; *E* 108; *P* 163) and, given that the weather outside was generally unpleasant (*E* 115, 138), people played indoor games like hunt the slipper, blind-man's buff and word games (*E* 372). Indoor theatricals were staged (*MP* 126–127) at Steventon parsonage as well as in more spacious homes. The men and boys might venture out to do a little hunting, if the weather were clear; Jane's oldest brother, James, wrote a poem on the subject to his son, uttering the wish that 'may no frost your sport prevent' and that the weather would prove 'hazy, mild & kind for scent'.

Traditional foods included brawn (a kind of preserved pork – see *P* 134) and plum pudding (made not with plums but with raisins or currants). James Austen's poem on hunting also mentions 'mince pies' at Christmas. Houses were decorated with holly and other green foliage. At church, a special sermon was delivered, and communion was offered. Children and adults alike might sing Christmas carols or watch mummers' plays. People went wassailing, and in some towns, morris dancers performed. Charity was distributed by those who could afford to do so; Parson Woodforde, in 1793 (a particularly hard year with regard to food prices), invited several poor people to dine at his house and sent dinners to others, giving all the recipients a shilling in addition to the food. Christmas gifts were not given on the scale that they would be in later years, but tips were distributed to certain people – Woodforde paid the local church-bell ringers at this time – and upper servants, who had influence over the choice of purveyors for household goods, received ample 'Christmas boxes' by way of thanks from local merchants. All in all, the holiday was a happy, social time.

See also Travel.

Horses

Horses (*L&F, MW* 107; *NA* 53, 66; *S&S* 52, 96; *P* 13, 43) were the engines of the pre-industrial world. They were the sports cars, the exercise machines, the trains, the tractors, the buses, the generators and the race cars all in one package of muscle and hair on four thin legs. They pulled the carts that hauled goods from one town to another and that carried the new-mown hay out of the fields (*MP* 58). They pulled the plough and harrows and hauled barges along England's new canals. They were essential to many types of hunting and, it was thought, preserved health. They certainly also made it faster to get from one place to another.

Horses

England had a number of horse breeds. Just as landowners were beginning to take an interest in improving their stocks of sheep, cattle and pigs, so, too, they began to breed horses with the intention of promoting certain characteristics. They bred 'Great Horses', the ancestor of the Shire horse and heavy black horses descended from horses imported from Flanders and Holland. Oldenburg coach horses were imported from the Continent as well and bred with native stock. Cobs were among the 'road horses' (*NA* 76; *MP* 37) that served the needs of mounted business travellers, while hackneys made such good riding horses that they were widely adopted by cavalrymen. The finest horses, according to many, were the thoroughbreds that populated the racecourses and some of the finest hunting stables in England.

Horseback riding (*Cath*, *MW* 206; *LS*, *MW* 285; *Watsons*, *MW* 331, 345; *NA* 35, 56, 73, 175, 195; *S&S* 65, 86, 359; *P&P* 9, 30–31, 49; *MP* 27, 35–36, 62, 69, 148, 334; *E* 29, 191, 243, 244, 317, 359, 363, 367, 394) was considered to be exceptionally good exercise, especially for ladies.

Women, therefore, as well as men, took riding lessons. These might take place outdoors, as Fanny Price's and Mary Crawford's do (*MP* 66–69), or in a riding ring in a town. A good riding horse needed to be calm, particularly if it was intended to carry a lady (*S&S* 58–59; *MP* 37); when carrying a lady, it also needed to be accustomed to a side-saddle, as women did not ride astride. Riding manuals emphasised that 'a woman's limbs are unsuited to cross-saddle riding, which requires length from hip to knee, flat muscles and a slight inclination to "bow legs!"' The side-saddle made it harder to control a horse. Riding accidents (*Lesley*, *MW* 113) were uncommon, except in the hunt, but they did occur, as in 1804, when Mrs Lefroy, a good friend of Jane's, was killed in a riding accident.

Not all horses were trained as saddle horses. Many were trained to pull carriages and carts (*Watsons*, *MW* 322, 339; *Sand*, *MW* 364; *NA* 45–46, 64; *S&S* 12, 324; *P&P* 67; *P* 13, 35, 106, 114–115; *E* 20, 112, 126, 189, 233, 306, 353, 357, 475). To the upper and, to some extent, the middle classes, they were essential for travel of all kinds. Economic class was an issue, for carriages and carriage horses were taxed by the government on a sliding scale that charged progressively steeper penalties for owning more horses. There was a similar tax on saddle horses, but none on farm horses, which were essential to the work of the nation. The existence of the tax makes all the more humorous the list of horses kept by a character in one of Austen's juvenile works: 'six Greys, 4 Bays, eight Blacks & a poney' (*Clifford*, *MW* 43).*

---

*Horses were typically identified at this time by their colour, rather than by their breed. This was because, after temperament and health, the most important characteristic of a horse was its colour. People liked to match their carriage horses, for carriages that required more than one horse to pull. The marchioness of Lansdowne had a carriage pulled by six or eight ponies in which each pair was a bit darker and larger than the one ahead of it. Therefore, the 'chestnuts' of *NA* 85 are not nuts but chestnut-coloured horses.

To avoid the expense of keeping, feeding and paying the tax on horses, some people refused to keep them altogether (*MP* 62; *E* 213); they kept a simple carriage like a chair, hiring horses from the local inn as needed (*Watsons*, *MW* 323; *MP* 35). Innkeepers were the most common source for hired or 'post'-horses (*Sand*, *MW* 406; *S&S* 311; *P&P* 351; *E* 197), as they had enjoyed a monopoly on the rental of such horses until late in the eighteenth century. Travellers passing through town and needing to continue swiftly on their journeys could opt to hire post-horses rather than waiting to 'bait' (or rest) their own. Pulling a carriage was hard work, especially uphill (*MP* 189–190), and horses needed to stop periodically for rest (*L&F*, *MW* 90; *NA* 116; *P* 95, 117). The day after a long or late journey, they would also need to remain idle (*Watsons*, *MW* 340, 341). John Thorpe's casual dismissal of this necessity (*NA* 47–48), as well as his generally abysmal coachmanship (*NA* 44, 62, 88–89), adds to Austen's characterisation of him as incompetent and insensitive.

Some horses did double duty, serving as both farm horses and as carriage horses. The Bennets in *Pride and Prejudice* employ this strategy, which is why Elizabeth is not permitted to take the family carriage to Netherfield (30–32). This is a case of art imitating life, as the Austens at Steventon were in precisely the same situation. The horses were primarily used for ploughing and similar tasks, and only when this work was done and the horses adequately recovered from their labours could they be used to pull the family carriage. When the Austens moved to Bath in 1801, they tried to reduce expenses and sold the carriage, just as the Dashwoods were forced to do in *Sense and Sensibility* (26).

Keeping saddle or carriage horses entailed a good deal of care and expense. In addition to the taxes on them, horses frequently got sick (*Cath*, *MW* 222; *NA* 172; *MP* 59, 118; *E* 383) and needed medical care. They required a staff of grooms (*MP* 118) to curry and ride them, to clean the stables (*P&P* 251; *MP* 191; *E* 179, 252) and to accompany employers on rides; coachmen to hitch them to the carriage and direct their movements; and farriers (*NA* 172) to shoe them. They had to be given periodic medical checkups, of a sort; in an age that still believed in routine phlebotomy, they were bled once a year to keep them healthy. When they were taken away from home, stables had to be found and rented for them (*MP* 193). Saddlers (*MP* 8) had to be paid to make and repair their tack. They had to be trained (*S&S* 233), if bred at home, or shopped for carefully and purchased.

Some horses were kept not for the sake of transportation or labour but for sport. Hunting fox, deer or hare required the use of horses, and Georgian sportsmen, always serious about their hunting, were intent on finding and breeding the best hunters (*Cath*, *MW* 222; *LS*, *MW* 254, 283; *NA* 76; *S&S* 91, 194, 379; *MP* 37, 229, 237, 241, 342). Women were far less likely than men to engage in this sort of riding, but there were daring souls like Laetitia, Lady Lade, wife of Sir John Lade, a friend of the Prince of Wales. In November 1796, she was declared 'the first horsewoman in the kingdom, being constantly one of the only five or six that are invariably with the hounds'.

Horses were also raced. This was a sport that appealed to the propensity
of Georgian men to gamble recklessly. Some of them raised racehorses,
some bought racehorses and others merely bet their inheritances on the
outcomes of celebrated matches between renowned animals. There were
race meetings at Newbury, Newmarket, Epsom, Salisbury, Doncaster
and Ascot. Newmarket was the most prominent of these sites, with seven
race meetings a year at the end of the Regency. Winchester had a normal
racecourse and one for steeplechase; an announcement of a race to be held
on St. Swithin's Day, 1817, prompted her to write or dictate her last poem
on the amusing conflict of spirit between a saint's day and a loud-talking,
hard-drinking, heavy-gambling race day (*MW* 451–452).

The period from about 1750 until Austen's death in 1817 was one of
the golden ages of horse racing. An act of 1740 to set minimum prizes
of £50 per race and to regulate horses' weights began the regulation
and standardisation of the sport. The Jockey Club was founded in 1752
at Newmarket to set rules for racing colours, pedigrees and the racing
calendar; it eventually gained control over all organised racing in
England. Tattersalls (*P* 8), an auction house specialising in horses,
was founded about twenty years later at Hyde Park Corner in London.
Thereafter, a host of famous races were established: the St. Leger in 1776,
the Oaks in 1779, the Derby in 1780 and the Ascot Gold Cup in 1807.

Different types of races (*Cath, MW* 199, 240; *NA* 66; *MP* 48, 59) were
run, each with its own different style of matching horses and awarding
prizes. Many races were two-horse affairs, with the prize being the
statutory £50, a piece of plate or a hogshead of claret. One unusual
trophy was the Whip, a Newmarket prize said to have belonged to
Charles II that eventually added hairs from the mane and tail of Eclipse,
a phenomenally famous racehorse. The typical race length in all these
cases was 4 miles (6.43 kilometres).

From 1791, there were handicaps with three or more horses entering,
with each horse carrying a different amount of weight. By the 1780s, some
race meetings had adopted the system of weight-for-age, with five-year-old
horses carrying 8 stone 2 pounds (52 kilograms), six-year-olds carrying
8 stone 11 pounds (56 kilograms), mares 3 pounds (1.36 kilograms) and
older horses 9 stone 5 pounds (59 kilograms). Still another method of
handicapping was weight-for-size or give-and-take, in which bigger
horses got more weight to carry.

Clever trainers learned to cheat the system by teaching the horse
to stand with its feet apart to make the measuring rod on its withers
drop a little lower. When race organisers fixed this problem by marking
standard positions for the horses' feet, trainers countered by hitting the
horses repeatedly on the withers. The horses learned to flinch downwards
when touched on the withers and responded in this way when touched
with the measuring rod.

The traditional method of running a race, as stated above, was a
head-to-head 'match' between two horses. Each owner put down a stake,

and the winner took both his stake and the loser's. By the beginning of the nineteenth century, however, successful owners wanted to win more, and this led to the invention of the sweepstake in which a larger field competed. This method of entry increased the winnings and therefore the public interest in each race.

As the period went on, several trends became clear. Horses were getting larger and, more and more, were becoming sprinters. The 4-mile standard race, which had packed most of its excitement into the last quarter-mile, shortened to 2 miles or even 1 in some cases. Another trend was the increasing reliance of owners on professional jockeys; still another was towards the racing of younger and younger horses. The first race for three-year-olds was held at Doncaster in 1776 over a distance of 2 miles. By 1797, 48 racehorses were two years old, 161 three years old, 122 four years old and 262 five years old.

A race day was an exhilarating and sometimes dangerous event. Rowdy crowds of all classes gathered around the tracks, with no barriers between themselves and the horses. They diced, played cards or EO (the ancestor of roulette) and watched cockfights and boxing matches. Sometimes they attended dances. Pickpockets roamed through the throngs looking for easy marks and trying to avoid notice; if spotted, they were usually ducked, beaten or shaved.

The horses, meanwhile, having trained for months in heavy blankets and having been given emetic to purge them, looked, as one spectator put it, 'like toast racks'. They were not only bony; their ears had been cropped, and their tails docked. If they were particularly good runners, they were at risk from dishonest men who might try to poison them. Even if they ran their best, they might not win if it were a 'crimp' match, fixed beforehand by the owners who hoped to cash in on side bets.

See also Carriages and Coaches; Hunting.

Housework

Though women of Austen's class were not solely responsible for housekeeping (*L&F*, *MW* 107), as they almost always had servants to do the dirtiest and most onerous jobs (*NA* 184), they often engaged in household tasks. They had to know something about them, even the chores they did not perform personally, as they had to superintend the work of the servants (*P* 6–7). The quality of a woman's housework – whether it was performed on behalf of her husband, her children, an unmarried brother or uncle or anyone else – was the principal standard by which her worldly usefulness was judged (*P* 43). If she failed as a housekeeper, she failed as a woman.

To succeed, she had to be frugal, efficient, cheerful, creative and competent. She also had to master several different sets of skills, including cooking, cleaning, laundering, gardening, dairying and needlework. Of these, cooking and needlework are discussed in greater depth in other articles within this book. These skills are therefore addressed below principally as they affected the work and rhythm of the household, rather than in terms of the tools they required or the actual techniques used. The specific division of labour between a woman and her servants, moreover, varied from household to household, and the types of tasks typically performed by each sort of servant are discussed fully in the article on servants. Here we look at the work performed and how it was managed, rather than at the specific individual assigned to perform it.

Many of Austen's women, as Maggie Lane points out in *Jane Austen and Food*, are failed housekeepers. Mrs Elton is extravagant, always 'doing too much, and being too careless of expense' (*E* 283). Mrs Norris has the opposite fault; her greed and stinginess are symptoms of frugality run mad. Mrs Price does everything wrong; she is sloppy, a poor manager of servants, lazy and querulous (*MP* 372, 439). There are several concrete examples of her incompetence, but Austen also sums up the case, making it clear exactly where Mrs Price has gone wrong:

> Her days were spent in a kind of slow bustle; always busy without getting on, always behindhand and lamenting it, without altering her ways; wishing to be an economist, without contrivance or regularity; dissatisfied with her servants, without skill to make them better, and whether helping, or reprimanding, or indulging them, without any power of engaging their respect. (*MP* 389–390)

However, not all of Austen's female characters are bad at running a household. One suspects that Elizabeth and Jane Bennet will have no difficulties in that department; nor will Fanny Price, Elinor Dashwood, Anne Elliot or Emma Woodhouse. Emma, indeed, is already an accomplished housekeeper, considerate of her guests, aware of the contents of her storerooms and never, so far as the reader can tell, in conflict with her servants. Of all the heroines, the two most likely to have difficulties after their marriages are the two romantics, Catherine Morland and Marianne Dash-wood. In Marianne's case, she will have the sensible Colonel Brandon's advice, and in Catherine's, though her mother predicts she will 'make a sad heedless young housekeeper to be sure', this warning is followed by 'the consolation of there being nothing like practice' (*NA* 249).

Several of the minor characters, too, appear to be in good control of their households. Mrs Grant does better. The only complaints about the running of her home come from Mrs Norris and from Dr Grant, and Mrs Norris' criticism of Mrs Grant's expenditures can be dismissed as stemming from her stinginess, while Dr Grant is acknowledged by nearly all of *Mansfield Park*'s characters to be unreasonably hard on his wife. Mrs Collins, too, seems to be doing a good job of keeping house for an irritating husband (*P&P* 216–217, 228). The Bateses get by on charity, a tiny income and a good deal of penny-pinching, and they can afford only one servant, but they appear on good terms with this maid-of-all-work, and Miss Bates' flaws are conversational, not domestic.

She is certainly well acquainted with cooking, as she would have to be in a one-servant household. Large homes had at least one cook (*P&P* 44, 65), sometimes more, as well as kitchen boys and scullery maids to do the less complex tasks. The running of a kitchen involved acquiring food, whether from the garden, the farm or shops; the preliminary preparation of food, such as skinning rabbits or plucking and gutting chickens; the careful maintenance of the kitchen fire at the proper temperature for each types of food; and the scouring of dishes, pots and pans after the meal was over. Whoever did the cooking had to be acquainted with basic methods of food preparation, including the making of simple sauces and gravies, the storage of perishable foods such as eggs and butter and the cooking of meat over an open flame (*Lesley*, *MW* 112–113; *Watsons*, *MW* 360). One needed to know how to make butter and cheese (*MP* 104), how to brew beer and how to make wine. In the Austen household at Steventon, Mrs Austen made all the butter, cheese, bread, beer and wine, and as an adult, Jane Austen also made both gooseberry and currant wine. When the Austen women moved to Southampton after Jane's father's death, Mrs Austen cured hams, made preserves and brewed spruce beer and orange wine.

It is noteworthy that Mrs Austen made her own bread. Bread was baked in many homes, but the practice was far from universal, and many people bought their bread from professional bakers. Of course, each home ran according to its own plan.

Cleaning, too, was extremely laborious. Many cookbooks of the day include recipes for cleaning solutions, and *The Toilet of Flora* (1775), a volume devoted mostly to the preparation of cosmetics, also instructs women how to remove rust, urine, ink, pitch, turpentine and oil stains. Directions are given for cleaning gold and silver lace, tapestry, carpets (*NA* 163; *MP* 439, 440) and velvet.

Eliza Haywood's *A New Present for a Servant-Maid* (1771) includes recipes for rust preventatives and cleansers and lists a daunting number of tasks to be undertaken in a single day by a housemaid. According to Haywood, she should rise early, clean out all the hearths and light the fires, clean the locks on the house's doors with an oily rag and then with 'rotten-stone, or white brick' and sweep all the carpets. Then she ought to 'brush and clean the window curtains, and with a broom sweep the windows, and behind the shutters'. She must dust the picture frames, wainscoting, china and stucco work with a bellows or a soft cloth, then rub down the wainscot and windows and dust the chairs. Next, she should sweep the stairs, 'throwing on the upper stairs a little wet sand, which will bring down the dust, without flying about', dust the ceilings and wash the stairs. All this was to happen before her employers woke up.

However, the housemaid's chores were not yet finished. She still had to scour the floorboards with 'a little hard brush', and then with a clean cloth, mop the floors, clean the tea-board, wash the silver, and scrub the china with soft sand and water before soaping and boiling it. Then there was the furniture to be waxed and cleaned and the candlesticks to be polished. Someone, even if it was not Haywood's industrious housemaid, had to perform these tasks, or work very much like them, in most of Austen's fictional households.

Then there was the care of clothing, a very serious business in the days when all clothing was made carefully by hand. No one discarded clothing lightly, and even then it was not tossed into the trash but sold as second-hand clothing to the poor. Stains were therefore given careful treatment, and rips were mended. The washing of clothes was also more arduous, since there were no washing machines, not even the hand-operated ones of the later nineteenth century. In larger households, there was a special room or even a separate building devoted to the washing of clothes. A large cylindrical structure was divided into two parts, with a large lidded tub above and a fireplace below. The laundry maid would build a coal fire in the fireplace base and pump water into the upper portion. Some households pumped the water and allowed it to settle for a few days before using it; others, whose well or other water source yielded hard, mineralised water, might soften it first by using chalk or a mixture of ashes and unslaked lime. Haywood advises dipping the clothes in warm water, soaping them with a 'wash ball' (a lump of often homemade soap, the cousin of the 'breeches ball' of *NA* 172) and agitating them between the hands. 'After that let them lie in hot water till next morning; then wash as usual, and there will be no occasion for more soap till the second lather.' Washing 'as usual' involved boiling the clothes in the big heated tub and stirring them with a paddle. Then the garments were wrung out and spread in the sun to dry (*Sand*, *MW* 384), not only because the sun was warm but also because the sunlight helped to bleach the white linen.

Smaller households could not afford a laundry maid. These homes employed a variety of tactics to get the washing done. Sometimes the washing was sent out (*S&S* 249); sometimes specialised laundresses (*P* 193) came to the house at regular intervals to wash the clothes. Parson Woodforde used the latter strategy, having his laundry done in one great burst every three weeks. He was not unusual in having such a long interval between laundry days; given the fuel, the labour and the soaking, boiling and drying time required to do laundry, it was a mammoth task that required group labour for an entire day. It could not be done casually or frequently.

Clothing required other care as well, and this work, too, was the province of women. Women in working-class families made their own clothes and might also spin flax or wool. Women in the gentry and the aristocracy seldom made their own clothes, but they sewed clothes for the poor and did decorative needlework. Their servants had more onerous tasks: airing, brushing and mending their employers' clothes, as well as removing stains and laying out morning and evening ensembles.

All the preceding work was done principally or entirely indoors, but women had other work that was done outside. In farming families, women might help with the harvest or the sowing. In most homes, gentry and working-class alike, they had charge of the dairy (*P&P* 163; *MP* 104), the poultry-yard (*P&P* 163; *MP* 104) and the kitchen garden. Here, their tasks included weeding, sowing, harvesting, milking, cheese making, butter making, feeding chickens or other fowls, and gathering eggs.

Mrs Austen superintended the dairy at Steventon, though she does not seem to have done the actual work. She also gardened enthusiastically all her life, digging her own potatoes and wearing a labourer's green frock. Jane, too, was an avid gardener, although her tastes seem to have run more to flowers than to potatoes. Even so, she reported at various times, with an accountant's eye for detail, on the produce of the family's fruit trees and garden.

See also Fire; Food; Gardens and Landscape; Sewing.

Hunting

Hunting (*Watsons*, *MW* 360; *S&S* 32, 43, 91–92, 214–215, 379; *P&P* 374; *P* 55, 58, 83, 217) customarily began in the morning (*Watsons*, *MW* 347; *MP* 191; *P* 37), just after or just before breakfast. Earlier in the eighteenth century, it had begun quite early in the morning, beginning well before breakfast, but by the turn of the nineteenth century, gentlemen were willing to sleep in a little, eat a substantial meal and then head out with dogs and guns. James Edward Austen-Leigh, Jane's nephew, remembered that Jane's brothers 'usually took their hasty breakfast in the kitchen' before setting out. The best sort of weather (*LS*, *MW* 254; *Watsons*, *MW* 357; *S&S* 167) for hunting, according to Peter Beckford, author of *Thoughts on Hunting in a Series of Familiar Letters to a Friend* (1781), was 'warm without sun', and the dogs tended to pick up scent best if the air and ground were moist without being wet. Beckford also noted that the English climate did not provide many days with perfect conditions, so avid hunters must have been especially disappointed if forced by circumstances to miss going out with their guns on such a day.

Most hunting took place in the autumn, when certain migratory birds were in season and, most importantly, when the harvest had been brought in. Some types of hunts could range unpredictably over vast swaths of terrain, taking horses and dogs through woods and fields. Cleared fields were easier to ride through and also had nothing left to be damaged by the horses' hooves, as James Austen made clear in a poem written for his son. It was perfectly all right, he wrote, to hunt 'When corn is housed, & fields are clear, / And Autumn's various tints appear'. But, he cautioned,

when the wheat is higher grown
And pease and beans and barley sown,

And fences made up tight,
To gallop all the country over
And cut up saintfoin, grass, & clover,
Is neither fair nor right.

Men spent the spring and summer preparing for the hunting season by breeding and training large packs of dogs and exercising and training their horses. Then, on 1 September (*Mount, MW* 41; *P&P* 318; *MP* 114), the partridge season opened, and men all over England, especially in prime hunting regions like East Anglia and Northamptonshire, surged into the field, hoping to bring home heavy bags.

Not everyone hunted. It was primarily the pastime of the nobility, the gentry, the portion of the merchant class wealthy enough to own some country land and the guests of the above groups. The legal requirement was that the hunter own land worth £100 a year; once this plateau was reached, he could not only shoot on his own land but depute or invite others to do so. After 1784, hunters were also required to take out a certificate and pay an annual fee of 3 guineas, and many of Jane's relatives did so. Blood sports were, later in the nineteenth century, to become disreputable activities for clergymen, but the eighteenth century was rich in 'hunting parsons', as they were called. Austen's life, bridging these two different worlds, brought her into contact with both kinds of clergymen – those who hunted and those who did not. Among those who did were her oldest brother, James, his friend Fulwar Fowle and another of her brothers, Henry, who became a clergyman rather late in life. Among those who did not was her father.

Children began to hunt at a fairly young age. James Edward Austen-Leigh began at fifteen, Henry Austen at fourteen. Francis began to hunt at seven, on a pony named Squirrel that he bought with £1 11s. 6d. of his own money; it seems unlikely that he would have been permitted to ride with the local fox-hunting pack, the Vine Hunt, at such a tender age, but Jane makes the fictional Charles Blake a hunter at the age of ten (*Watsons, MW* 331). Perhaps Francis began with less demanding riding, advancing later to grown-up hunts.

Types and Methods of Hunting

There were two principal types of hunts – hunts that moved and hunts that took place in a relatively fixed location. In the first category were hunts for fox (*MP* 237), rabbit, hares and deer, where the enjoyment of the chase came from speed on horseback (*NA* 66) and from outwitting the native guile of the fleeing quarry. In this type of hunting, it was essential to maintain the goodwill of one's neighbours, for they had to grant permission for the hunt to cross their land, and they had to be repaid in case of damages to crops or livestock. This had not always been the case in Austen's lifetime but was decided in a closely watched legal battle between the Earl of Essex and his half brother.

The 1808 decision gave greater control to landowners, as opposed to hunters and in some cases led to friendly bribery, such as sponsoring a ball or inviting more people into the hunt, simply to keep the neighbourly peace.

Fox-hunting was justified by its proponents on the grounds that it rid the countryside of poultry-destroying vermin, but in areas with especially large and clever populations of foxes, such as Jane Austen's own Hampshire, care was taken not to destroy all these 'vermin', for fear of destroying all the sport as well. Stag hunting, which – like fox-hunting – involved swift, thrilling chases over varied terrain, was rapidly decreasing in popularity, mostly due to the diminishing number of deer. Only the richest landowners could afford to maintain deer parks (*Mount, MW* 41), and newly prosperous men with an interest in taking up hunting could not begin their hobby by pursuing deer. Instead, they turned to hare hunting, which could be accomplished with a relatively small pack of dogs. Hares were also easier to catch than foxes, especially since hunters pursued them not on foot, as in later years, but on horseback. Hares tended to flee in a circle, or to double back over their own paths, which confused the dogs to some extent but also meant that the hares covered less ground than did a fox. Hares also tended to hide or lie still, making it easier for the dogs to catch them too quickly, and the practice of some huntsmen of beating the bushes until a hare popped out meant that the dogs had little trouble in finding the hare. If the huntsman were not careful, the dogs would simply fall upon the hare the moment it appeared, and the sport would be over. The point was to give the hare enough of a head start that the contest was considered reasonably fair to the hare and a worthwhile challenge for the dogs.

Birds (*NA* 66; *P&P* 337) were hunted differently. They were rarely shot from horseback, and they were not pursued. Instead, hunters had either to find them where they nested or to wait for them to land. Birds such as partridges, pheasants (*MP* 181), woodcock and snipe were hunted according to the first method. A party of hunters would go out with a handful of dogs, guns, loaders and so forth and set up at the edge of a likely field or covert (the latter was a thicket of bushes or similar covering in which birds might be hiding – see *S&S* 45). Dogs would be sent to point out or flush out birds, which would then be driven upwards, with all the hunters present taking quick aim and blasting away in an enormous roar of gunfire. The English method of shooting, predicated in part, no doubt, on the weight of the gun, was to raise the gun at the very last moment and take aim in an instant. Keeping continuous aim while waiting for a bird to rise, it was thought, tires the eyes and reduces hand–eye coordination.

While large shooting parties did take place, it was equally common to see one or two men out with a single servant and one or two dogs, moving from field to field in quest of game. The hunters strove for balance, seeking enough birds to justify their day's shooting, but not so many that the overall population of birds diminished over time (*MP* 181). Preservation of game (*P* 43), by destroying predators, controlling the number of birds shot and savagely prosecuting poachers, was a chief concern. The steel trap that breaks Lucy's leg in *Jack & Alice* was probably set out to deter poachers (*J&A, MW* 22).

Ducks, unlike partridges or pheasants, were lured to the hunter rather than tracked to their nests. Some hunters, especially those who hunted and sold wild ducks for a living, used decoys – not the carved wooden decoys of later years, but a cornucopia-shaped tube of pipes, surrounded by netting, with its wide end facing the ducks and its narrow end facing the hunter, who controlled a net at the narrow end. A reddish dog, resembling a fox, was sent into the water and swam into the wide end of the decoy, and the ducks followed, thinking they were driving a fox away from their nests. When the ducks were bunched together at the narrow end of the decoy, they were deliberately startled, whereupon they flew into the hunter's net. Alternatively, tame ducks were released onto the pond and lured up the pipe with whistles and food, and, when the wild ducks followed, they were chased to the narrow end by men or dogs. Shooting ducks by wading through ponds and marshes, with the dirt and damp this entailed, was considered 'by no means gentlemanly' and even dangerous to the health, according to *The Shooter's Guide* (1809).

See also Entertainment; Horses.

I

Inns

Jane Austen travelled a great deal within England and was well acquainted with inns (*H&E, MW* 38; *First Act, MW* 172–174; *Evelyn, MW* 191; *NA* 104; *P&P* 260; *MP* 412, 446; *P* 98, 99, 111, 122). Sometimes, she dined at them only while horses were 'baited' (allowed to rest – see *NA* 156) or exchanged. For example, she dined at Dartford's Bull and George in October 1798 and at a different inn in the same town, the Bull, in 1808. At other times, she stayed in inns, although, like many genteel travellers, she preferred to stay with friends for short visits or to rent lodgings for longer stays. Staying at London's Bath Hotel in June 1808, she found it 'most uncomfortable quarters—very dirty, very noisy, and very ill-provided'.

As an occasional visitor to Bath and a resident of the town from 1801 to 1806, Austen would have been familiar with the Bear Inn, demolished in

1806 to make way for the construction of Union Street, and the White Hart
Inn (*P* 216, 220, 223, 229), which stood in Stall Street across from the Pump
Room. It was generally considered the best inn in Bath. This establishment
did not, however, call itself a 'hotȩl' (*Sand, MW* 378, 384, 401, 406, 413, 422,
425; *P&P* 117, 295; *P* 221), a term just coming into use in the last quarter
of the eighteenth century. A hotel was really just a glorified inn, implying,
by its use of a French-derived name, that it was fashionable and well
equipped. The real-life White Hart appears in two of Austen's novels,
and another White Hart – a fictional one this time – appears in the
incomplete novel *The Watsons* (*MW* 321, 323, 325).

In Lyme (*P* 95), Austen might have been acquainted with the
Golden Lion and the Three Cups, described in an 1810 guide to the city
as 'respectable Inns' renting rooms 'on easy terms'. In Southampton,
where she lived for a few years early in the nineteenth century, she
would certainly have known the Crown (*MP* 400, 406), a respectable inn
on High Street that tended to attract naval officers. Her aunt Mrs Lybbe
Powys stayed there in 1792 and had 'an elegant dinner' but thought the
place a little dirty. As with the White Hart, there is both a real Crown
(Southampton) and a fictional one (Highbury – see *E* 193, 195, 197, 244,
250–254, 319, 382–383) to be found in Austen's work.

Inns provided a variety of services other than the overnight
accommodation and daytime feeding of travellers (*H&E, MW* 38; *S&S* 160;
P&P 222). There was no inn in Steventon, where Austen grew up, but
there was an inn south of town where the main road intersected with one
leading to Winchester. This inn, the Wheatsheaf, was where the Austens
picked up their mail; innkeepers often performed this service for local
residents. Innkeepers also hired out their large rooms for balls (*Watsons,
MW* 327; *E* 197, 250–254, 319) and their smaller rooms for gatherings
of men's clubs (*Watsons, MW* 325; *E* 197) and local officials (*E* 456).
Austen attended balls during the winter months at an inn in Basingstoke,
for example. Working-class wedding parties might also go to an inn for
the post-nuptial festivities. Inns were required at times to billet troops,
a service that innkeepers reluctantly provided; they were more enthusiastic
about their usual service as postmasters, which brought in customers and,
for a number of years, gave them a monopoly on the rental of post-horses
(*Watsons, MW* 323; *E* 197). Regularly scheduled coach services also tended
to pick up passengers and drop them off at inns (*S&S* 354); most inns had
an arched entrance to allow the carriages and horses to be brought into
a courtyard (*H&E, MW* 38; *L&F, MW* 90–91, 108; *P* 105) and led to the
attached stables.

The typical innkeeper (*Watsons, MW* 336; *NA* 45; *E* 255–256, 322)
unloaded his or her guests outside, leading them into a receiving hall
(*Watsons, MW* 326–327) and sending a maid (*P&P* 241) with a candle to
lead them up the main staircase to their rooms. Most inns were more than
one storey tall, with balconies on the upper floors overlooking the central
courtyard. Meals were taken in a dining room (*P&P* 219; *P* 104), which was

usually located downstairs; there might also be a coffee room and some small sitting rooms identified by name, such as the Sun, the Lion or the Paragon (*First Act, MW* 172). Gentlemen almost always took a private sitting room, and ladies always did so, but ordinary stagecoach passengers would not normally have done so. Pedestrians and passengers from the cheap stage wagons were only reluctantly admitted, given the worst food and forced to eat in the kitchen.

A well-run inn would know the scheduled arrival times of coaches that stopped to bait or change horses and would have servants ready to take the passengers' hats and coats, waiters (*NA* 156; *P&P* 220; *P* 105, 193) at hand to serve dinner, and cold meat, cheese and pastries ready for consumption. The price paid for this hospitality (*Sand, MW* 378) varied by location and quality of service, but tips to the staff (*P* 144) always accounted for a large proportion of the bill.

See also Carriages and Coaches; Travel.

Insanity

Mental illness (*Evelyn, MW* 188) was of great concern in the late eighteenth century, not only because madness was supposed to be on the increase (a phenomenon blamed on the cult of sensibility – see *L&F, MW* 99) but also because people were growing uncomfortable with the way the mentally ill were treated. Few positive remedies could be offered to the insane, and care consisted mostly of warehousing the patients, who were little more than prisoners, in frightful conditions. For much of the eighteenth century, London's most famous mental hospital, the Bethlehem Hospital (or 'Bedlam', for short) had been a popular tourist attraction. Visitors could pay a small fee to watch the madmen run through their various caprices, and for a long time, no one saw much harm in this.

By Austen's day, the mood was changing. London had a second mental hospital, St. Luke's, founded at mid-century on more humane principles, and many provincial towns were building similar facilities. There was an increasing feeling that insanity was no one's fault, simply 'the most dreadful of all human calamities', in the words of conduct-book author John Gregory. The mad should be treated gently and with patience.

What occasioned this change of mood is uncertain, but several events and developments might have been responsible. There was, on the whole, a shift away from the Puritan perception that madness was a form of divine vengeance for sin and a shift, in this as in many other fields, towards a rational and scientific explanation. In addition, the same fashionable respect for deep feeling that some critics saw as creating lunatics made excesses of emotion more palatable and less worthy of punishment. A third influence may have been the growing awareness of abuses of the system, particularly as they affected women. It was, for much of the eighteenth century, perfectly legal for a man to lock his wife in a private madhouse with absolutely no medical evaluation or oversight, simply because he was angry with her or wished to take a mistress without interference. A fourth influence may have been the madness of George III, who suffered from a period of serious mental illness in 1788–1789 and recovered, supposedly thanks to the treatment offered by his doctor, Francis Willis.* This may have encouraged people to think of mental illness as treatable and to publicise the issue.

In literature, madness had been a popular topic since at least the time of Shakespeare, whose *King Lear* and *Hamlet* contain long speeches imitating the gibberish spoken by the mentally ill.

Austen's only depictions of madness are comic, and, like most of her *Juvenilia*, they are parodies of the literary efforts of others. Her madwoman's speech in *Love and Freindship* could be read as a parody of Mozeen, Shakespeare or any of the other previous authors who had made an attempt to re-create this sort of monologue:

> 'Talk not to me of Phaetons … – Give me a violin – . I'll play to him & sooth him in his melancholy Hours – Beware ye gentle Nymphs of Cupid's Thunderbolts, avoid the piercing Shafts of Jupiter – Look at that Grove of Firs – I see a Leg of Mutton – They told me Edward was not Dead; but they deceived me – they took him for a Cucumber – ' …
> For two Hours did I rave thus madly and should not then have left off, as I was not in the least fatigued, had not Sophia who was just recovered from her swoon, intreated me to consider that Night was now approaching and that the Damps had begun to fall. (*MW* 100)

Indeed, this passage could hardly be told from Mozeen's, if set typographically as verse and given a few rhymes. What marks it as parody is not the character's subject matter but the end of the episode, in which the supposedly mad character can switch off her ravings at the mention of approaching discomfort.

---

*He relapsed in 1811, prompting Parliament to name the Prince of Wales as his regent; George III never recovered from this second illness and died in 1820.

J

Jewellery

Almost every woman, even poor women, owned some form of jewellery
(*P&P* 378). It came in a wide variety of materials, with most of the items
falling into the categories still worn today: earrings, necklaces, bracelets
and so on. However, some types of jewellery were worn in different ways
than today, and some have become rarities or fallen out of fashion
altogether.

The most popular materials for jewellery, for those who could afford
them, were diamonds and pearls. Diamonds (*Lesley, MW* 137) appeared in
almost every category of jewellery, and, though some were rose-cut, most
were brilliant-cut, with brilliant-cut diamonds increasing in popularity.
(A rose-cut diamond is usually circular in shape, and the facets on its
top come to a shallow point. A brilliant-cut diamond's top is shaped like
a truncated pyramid, with a flat surface, or 'table', at the summit.) Most
diamonds at this time came from India and other parts of Southeast Asia,
as the vast diamond deposits in South Africa and South America had yet
to be discovered. As diamonds were so expensive, substitutes, known as
'paste', were already in existence. Fake diamonds were manufactured from
glass, iron pyrite (marcasite) and rock crystal. The best paste jewels, made
of leaded glass, were much in demand from the early nineteenth century
onwards.

Pearls (*NA* 68–69; *S&S* 221; *E* 292, 324), like diamonds, could be
simulated; false pearls sold for about one-fifth the price of real ones.
However, women could also invest in seed pearls, small pearls that were
strung in decorative arrangements and that were less expensive than
large, round pearls. Matching sets of jewellery, comprising two to four
harmonious pieces, were common. Many women were employed as pearl-
stringers, either in jewellers' workshops or in their own homes as a
cottage industry.

Coloured stones were less popular than diamonds, but they were also
cheaper. A common method of setting them was to surround one large
coloured stone with a rim of small diamonds or pearls. Like diamonds,
they were increasingly set with open 'collets', the metal cups in which
jewels rest. The open-backed collet allowed for more light to pervade the
jewels. (Paste jewels, however, were an exception to the trend; they were
usually set in closed collets with a bright foil backing to increase their
sparkle.)

Coloured stones, including amethyst, garnet, carnelian, agate, sapphire,
emerald, topaz and onyx, increased somewhat in popularity after the 1790s,
but they were never as desirable as pearls and diamonds – not a surprising

preference, perhaps, in the light of the period's love affair with the colour white.

Rich women tended to favour the more-expensive end of this spectrum, such as sapphires and, until the discovery of a large deposit ruined their value, amethysts. Middle-class and working-class women had access to a variety of cheaper substitutes, including Wedgwood jasper ware cameos, tortoiseshell, ivory (*P&P* 221), jet, enamel, mother-of-pearl, brass and stamped metal. Beads of steel faceted like gems and riveted to a back plate were, for a time, fashionable among all classes. The 'cut steel' beads typically had fifteen facets and were found on a remarkable variety of products, from buckles to sword hilts. They remained well regarded throughout Austen's lifetime, but, starting in the 1810s, the Birmingham and Woodstock trade in such items was gradually siphoned off by the French. Gold (*P&P* 221) was always popular, sometimes as a uniform surface, sometimes rendered in various colours or textures for contrast; those who could not afford real gold had to make do with gilt, brass or pinchbeck.

Gilding could be accomplished in at least two different ways. The more reliable of the two was to cover the item in nitrate of mercury, then dip it in a mixture of gold and mercury and heat the surface to fix the gold in place. It took skill to do properly and exposed the unfortunate jeweller to mercury poisoning and an early death. The less reliable method involved simply dipping the object in a gold solution, which yielded a less-durable layer. Women who could not afford even a thinly applied layer of proper gilding had to make do with pinchbeck, a zinc-copper alloy invented in the early eighteenth century.

Jewellery made of hair was surprisingly popular. Sometimes the hair was merely a component; sometimes the entire piece of jewellery was composed of hair. The most common use of hair was as a decorative and sentimental addition to a traditional piece of jewellery. A piece of clipped hair might be placed in a locket, for example, but much of the jewellery that made use of hair did not allow for the removal of the hair. Instead, a special piece of jewellery – a ring, a brooch or a pendant, for example – would be commissioned from a jeweller, who would use the hair as part of a picture or a pattern. The hair might be woven or braided and placed under a lid of crystal, visible through the transparent covering, or it might be used pictorially, as in one piece where the golden hair has become a sheaf of wheat, the seed stalks formed by minute droplets of gold. Hair jewellery was sometimes a love token, as it is in *Sense and Sensibility* (98, 135), but its most common use seems to have been in mourning jewellery, especially mourning rings that were provided for in the deceased's will and distributed to friends and family as a means of remembrance.

More valuable pieces of jewellery were also left as bequests (*Lesley, MW* 120–121, 137; *NA* 68–69; *E* 479), especially from women to their daughters or to favoured servants. Jewellery was a woman's most liquid asset and was thought of very much in those terms. It sometimes had sentimental associations, true; it was pretty, yes; but first and foremost, it was valuable. Princess Caroline, wife of the prince regent, lived off her wedding jewels when her allowance from her husband proved inadequate, and many a woman (and man) sold jewels to pay gambling debts. Because their appeal was aesthetic and financial, women had few qualms about taking the gems out of their settings and rearranging them in fashionable new ways (*S&S* 220; *E* 479). There was little interest in preserving antique settings, particularly as gem cutting had greatly improved in the last century or two, and family heirlooms could look very dull next to new, brilliant-cut specimens.

People could afford to be more sentimental about jewellery that featured portrait miniatures of loved ones, and there was a great interest in all sorts of pieces that featured faces. Cameos showing family members, famous men or classical figures were extremely popular, as were pendants, chatelaines, rings, lockets and other pieces featuring handpainted miniatures. The more expensive examples, following the prevailing taste, might be surrounded by a rim of small diamonds. One curious variation on the theme was the 'eye' portrait, a detailed rendering of one of the lover's eyes, which could be found on a pendant, brooch, clasp or ring. The wearer could see the eye and recognise his beloved, but nosy companions need never know the identity of the woman to whom the eye belonged.

Most types of jewellery popular in Austen's time would be perfectly recognisable today. There were necklaces, brooches (*Sand, MW* 374, 390) and bracelets, the last of these typically sold in pairs. There were rings (*Sand, MW* 390; *NA* 122; *S&S* 135; *P&P* 316, 317) of all kinds, from diamond rings to rings that bore gems engraved with classical designs. Lockets or pendants hung from necklaces or from a ribbon (*MP* 254) tied around the neck. Necklaces (*MP* 257–258, 261, 263, 271, 274) might be in the form of a rivière – a sequence of stones in graduated sizes – or several large stones, cameos, or similar items connected by festoons of pearls, stones, beads or chain links.

Earrings (*S&S* 226) fluctuated in size over time, growing quite long in the late 1790s, contracting again, passing out of favour entirely for a heartbeat in 1807, then returning for both morning and evening wear and gradually increasing in size again in the 1820 and 1830s. The typical earring had a top, backed by the wire hook that passed through the pierced ear, and one or more pendant drops. The girandole, a style that featured three drop pendants, was extremely popular. Others had tassel chains or came in the form of hoops or loops.

While earrings and necklaces still seem quite ordinary, other pieces of jewellery would seem odd if worn today. Men were fond of jewelled shoe buckles and also wore 'stock buckles' to fasten the backs of their cravats. In the evenings, women might wear armlets high on their upper arms, just below their short sleeves. A tremendous amount of jewellery was also worn in the hair (*E* 479), including combs, jewelled fillets for

13. Design for a cut-steel chatelaine.

tying the hair near the back of the head, and aigrettes (feather-shaped brooches for the hair). Some wore tiaras or their close cousins, diadems. Others wore Eastern-inspired turbans decorated with brooches called 'sultanas'.

Men and women alike wore chatelaines. The chatelaine, whose name came from the ring of keys worn from the belt of a medieval great lady, was a ribbon connected to the belt by a hook and weighted at the end by a decorative item of some sort. In many cases, this was a watch, but it might equally be a portrait miniature, a cameo, a seal or a locket. Gentlemen sometimes wore a fob that hung from the waist and held several seals – implying, perhaps, as the chatelaine's keys did, that he had a great deal of responsibility and thus needed multiple ways of sealing his letters. These clusters of seals can often be seen in contemporary prints.

See also Clothing; Hats; Pocketbooks and Reticules.

L

Landau

The landau (*Clifford*, *MW* 43), named after the German town in which it was invented in 1757, was simply a coach with a convertible top. It had four wheels, a box for the driver and seats facing forward and backward. Its leather top divided in the middle and could be folded down, half towards the back of the coach and half towards the front. The window sash was then slid downwards into the door, completing the transformation. When the top was erected, the landau looked almost exactly like a standard coach and provided protection from the elements; when the top was down, the occupants could enjoy pleasant weather and an improved view. It was not a perfect vehicle; the blackened and oiled leather hoods could be greasy and strong smelling, and they never seemed to lie flat enough. However, the versatility of the landau, which could be used day or night, in good weather or bad, made it popular, and variations on the theme soon appeared.

One of these was the landaulette (*Clifford*, *MW* 43; *P* 250), or demilandau, which corresponded to the chariot in the same way that the landau corresponded to the coach. In other words, it had four wheels, a box and one seat that faced forward and held three people, the difference from the chariot being that the hood could be folded. Another variant was the barouche-landau (*E* 274, 343), which purported to have features of both the barouche and the landau. It was not a popular innovation.

See also Carriages and Coaches.

Lodgings

People who travelled in Austen's time stayed in inns if they were merely stopping for a night or two or with friends if they had friends in the area. If they had no friends or family near their destination, however, they took lodgings (*Mount, MW* 41; *Cath, MW* 203; *LS, MW* 294; *Sand, MW* 402, 407; *NA* 19, 91, 102, 138; *P* 122, 149, 154, 170). Lodgings were fully furnished homes (*Evelyn, MW* 180; *NA* 76; *S&S* 26; *MP* 245; *E* 317) of varying size and location and might be found in almost any town in England. They could also sometimes be found in the country, as the private estates of impoverished owners who found themselves forced to move somewhere cheaper (*S&S* 194; *P&P* 3, 310; *P* 18–19, 22, 32) or who simply chose to live elsewhere (*MP* 295).

Price varied greatly by location. London lodgings (*LS, MW* 296; *S&S* 230; *P&P* 295; *MP* 394), especially on the fashionable West End, were by far the most expensive. Bath was a good deal cheaper, thanks to the town's recognition of the importance of tourism. Prices for lodgings there had been regulated before Austen's birth. By 1800, a furnished room rented for 10*s*. 6*d*. a week in season, 7*s*. 6*d*. out of season; a servant's room was 5*s*. 6*d*., three pence less in the off season. Enforcement of the regulations declined somewhat after 1800 and later allowed landlords to charge more for lodgings with especially good furnishings, but the point was that Bath was doing its best to keep prices reasonable. They were more than reasonable at Lyme (*P* 97), which had, according to an 1810 guide, 'several genteel lodging-houses, facing the sea, and each possessing a small plat before it, neatly railed in'. According to the same guide, rates were 'not merely reasonable, they are even cheap'.

The quality of the furniture (*P* 22) and rooms also varied. The better lodging houses in Bath offered attractive tables and chairs, mirrors, fire screens, candlesticks and good-quality beds and mattresses. They had indoor water closets, fashionable wallpaper, parlours, dining rooms, dressing rooms, large bedrooms for the family and small garret apartments for the servants. However, not all lodgings came up to this standard. Austen, who had stayed in many rented lodgings by the time she wrote *Persuasion*, no doubt spoke from experience when she mentioned 'the deficiencies of lodging-house furniture' (*P* 98).

Those who could not afford to rent an entire house and hire a temporary local staff of servants (*Sand, MW* 414) – or those who simply didn't want the bother – stayed instead in boarding houses, in which they rented a room or suite of rooms and took their meals. These were sometimes also referred to at the time, confusingly, as lodging houses, but they were quite different from whole houses rented to one client. The 'Lodgings to let' in *Sanditon* (*MW* 383) are probably actually boarding-house rooms; as boarding houses were less fashionable than lodgings, this less-desirable form of housing would be in keeping with Austen's general description of the town as a substandard resort.

Joseph Farington stayed at a so-called lodging house in Bath in 1800 and recorded the evening schedule: the ladies retired from the general dining room at about 5:30 p.m., and the gentlemen left about an hour later, 'that it may be prepared for Tea at 7'. After tea, the lodgers who wished to do so played cards together, just as they might have done at a private home. They were served supper at 10:00 p.m. and went to bed at about 11:00 p.m.; the rules stated that they were all to vacate the dining room by 11:30 p.m. The provision of public meals makes it clear that this was a boarding house, not private lodgings.

Boarding houses for poor labourers were a good deal less savoury. In these dirty establishments, men and women who were strangers to each other slept in the same crowded rooms, and theft was a frequent problem. Some rented space by the night or by the hour to prostitutes and their clients. Running a boarding house, which in any case brought strangers into one's home, was never considered a perfectly admirable occupation, and in some cases could be downright disreputable (*E* 275–276); it makes perfect sense that Austen should turn Mrs Younge, Miss Darcy's unethical former governess, into a woman who 'maintained herself by letting lodgings' (*P&P* 322). The worst boarding houses, according to John Glyde, were home to 'the dangerous classes', and perhaps because of this unsavoury reputation, they became less popular in certain parts of the country, including Bath, over the course of Austen's lifetime.

Just as today, the quality of rented lodgings varied widely. Staying in Lyme in September 1814, Jane wrote to Cassandra that nothing could 'exceed the inconvenience of the Offices, except the general Dirtiness of the House & furniture, & all it's Inhabitants'. In 1799, she had also found dirt in the Austens' lodgings at 13, Queen Square, Bath. She wrote to Cassandra that they had been in town 'just long enough to go over the house, fix on our rooms, & be very well pleased with the whole of it'. Her description reveals the natural tendency of people in a vacation house to choose rooms with the least possible offence to anyone and to criticise the storage arrangements:

We are exceedingly pleased with the House; the rooms are quite as large as we expected. ... Eliz: has the apartment within the Drawing room; she wanted my Mother to have it, but as there was no bed in the inner one, & the stairs are so much easier of ascent or my Mother so much stronger than in Paragon as not to regard the double flight, it is settled for us to be above; where we have two very nice sized rooms, with dirty Quilts & everything comfortable. I have the outward & larger apartment, as I ought to have; which is quite as large as our bed room at home, & my Mother's is not materially less. – The Beds are

both as large as any at Steventon; & I have a very nice chest of
Drawers & a Closet full of shelves – so full indeed that there is nothing
else in it, & should therefore be called a Cupboard rather than a Closet
I suppose.

Her mention of the quilts is consistent with what is known about lodgings
in Bath. Linen was usually provided by the owner of the building; food and
meals, however, were not. A lodger's first errand was usually to the market
to stock the pantry.

Lodgings could be rented by personal enquiry (*Sand, MW* 411, 414).
A renter might ask around among friends and acquaintances, and
a landlord might advertise in the newspapers (*P* 15). Bath, where renting
lodgings was a major local business, had a register office and circulating
libraries where available lodgings were listed. In Bath, high turnover
meant that something interesting was nearly always available (*NA* 73,
238); one visitor claimed that it was necessary to walk around the town
for only 5 or 10 minutes in order to find suitable lodgings. He exaggerated
somewhat; it took the Austens a great deal longer to find something they
liked and could afford when they moved to Bath in 1801.

See also Inns; Travel.

• London

To those of us growing up in industrialised countries with major urban
areas almost commonplace, the dominance of London (*Clifford, MW* 43;
L&F, MW 89, 90, 92; *Lesley, MW* 112, 122; *LS, MW* 271; *Sand, MW* 373, 378;
NA 113, 220; *S&S* 107, 311, 318; *P&P* 82, 116, 126, 201, 275, 282–283, 293,
295, 298, 299, 319; *MP* 8, 58, 193, 203, 360, 381, 420, 426; *E* 16, 17, 91, 169,
216, 306, 316, 318; *P* 13, 14, 105, 250) during Jane Austen's lifetime is hard
to grasp at an intuitive level. London ruled everything – art, shipping,
shopping, music, society (*S&S* 171), entertainment (*NA* 78; *P&P* 129) and
fashion. Most of the news in provincial newspapers was culled from
London's press. Most publishers were located in London (*NA* 112).
The best girls' schools, it was thought, were there as well (*L&F, MW* 78;
E 164). London's population dwarfed that of any other city. In 1801, the
population of England was about 8,500,000. London accounted for
900,000 of these people, almost twice the total of the next largest six
cities combined.* Nothing encapsulated the position of the metropolis
more than the fact that 'going to town' almost always meant going to
London (*J&A, MW* 17; *Lesley, MW* 131; *Cath, MW* 197, 201, 207; *LS,*

---

*Manchester, Liverpool, Birmingham, Bristol, Portsmouth and Bath, which had a combined
population of about 500,000.

London

MW 249, 251; S&S 110, 114, 325, 359; P&P 67, 141, 147, 211, 238, 293, 378; MP 38, 284, 425; E 79, 116, 308).

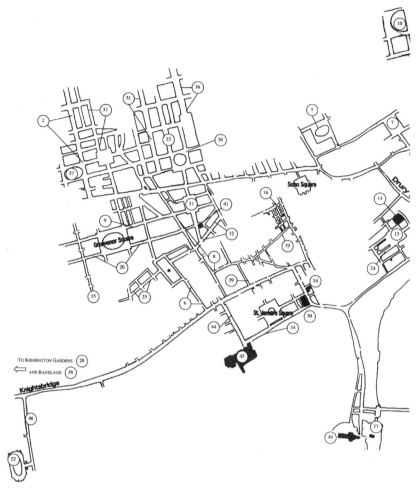

3. Map of London.

This is not to say that everyone approved of London. In fact, it was intellectually fashionable to think otherwise, and it had been so for many years. London offered too much distraction (MP 234) and too many temptations, or so the saying went. It was not as pure and simple as life in the country, and had not life in the country been celebrated by the ancient Romans? London was expensive. It lured women into its bow-windowed shops and men into its dens of iniquity. Mrs Austen, Jane's mother, agreed with those who criticised the city. After a visit, she concluded, 'It is a sad place. I would not live in it on any account; one has no time to do one's duty to God or man.'

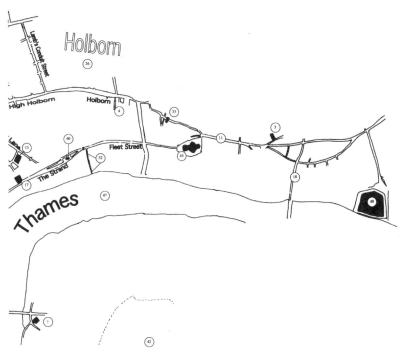

	London Sites	Notes
1	Astley's Royal Amphitheater	*E* 471, 472, 481. *See also* Entertainment.
2	Baker Street	*MP* 49.
3	Bank of England	*NA* 113.
4	Bartlett's Buildings	The Steele sisters lodge here in *S&S;* its easterly location was very unfashionable (*S&S* 217, 230, 277).
5	Bedford Square	*MP* 434.
6	Berkeley Street	Mrs Jennings has her house here (*S&S* 170, 171, 177, 217, 229, 294).
7	Bloomsbury Square	*Cass, MW* 46.
8	Bond Street	*Cass, MW* 44; *S&S* 115, 164, 183, 204, 326; *E* 56.
9	Brook Street	*Cath, MW* 202.
10	Brunswick Square	Home of John and Isabella Knightley (*E* 9, 46, 102–103, 386, 393, 420, 429, 435).

11	Cheapside	*P&P* 37. A street through London's commercial district; *see* Gracechurch Street below.
12	Conduit Street	Site of the Middletons' house (*S&S* 170, 217, 223, 231).
13	Covent Garden	Site of the Bedford Coffee House (*Watsons*, *MW* 356; *NA* 96) and a busy vegetable market.
14	Covent Garden Theater	*L&F*, *MW* 109.
15	Drury Lane Theater	*S&S* 330.
16	Edward Street	*LS*, *MW* 252; *P&P* 322.
17	Exeter Exchange	Like the Tower, Exeter Exchange had a menagerie of wild beasts (*S&S* 221).
18	Gracechurch Street	*P&P* 152, 219, 288, 295.
		The home of Mr and Mrs Gardiner, Elizabeth Bennet's uncle and aunt. The street was located in the City of London – that is, the old central city, now a commercial district – and its association with trade made it decidedly ungenteel.
19	Great Pulteney Street	John Broadwood's pianoforte company was located here.
20	Grosvenor Street	Mr Bingley's brother-in-law Mr Hurst has a house here (*P&P* 116, 147).
21	Hanover Square	*S&S* 110, 301.
22	Hans Place	One of Henry Austen's addresses in London, so far west that Jane spoke of walking 'into town' when she stayed there. Hans Place was a long octagonal plaza with an oval garden in the centre, just a block west of Sloane Street and a few blocks south of Knightsbridge.
23	Harley Street	The house rented by John and Fanny Dashwood is here (*S&S* 230, 231, 248, 254, 257, 273, 282).
24	Henrietta Street	Henry Austen and his wife, Eliza, lived at No. 10 above his bank, and Jane sometimes stayed there.

25	Hill Street	Home of Admiral Crawford (*MP* 300).
26	Holborn	*L&F*, *MW* 89; *S&S* 217, 286. A region of northern London that includes Bartlett's Buildings and the Inns of Court, among other sites.
27	House of Commons	*Cath*, *MW* 197; *P* 8.
28	Kensington Gardens	*S&S* 271, 274–276. *See also* Public Places.
29	King's Theater, Haymarket	London's Italian opera house. *See also* Opera.
30	Little Theater	*P&P* 319. *See also* Theatre.
31	Manchester Street	
32	Middle Temple Street	William Walter Elliot, in his early years, lived in the Temple (*P* 199).
33	Newgate	*L&F*, *MW* 89, 97.
34	Pall Mall	*S&S* 199. Edward Ferrars lodges here for a time (*S&S* 275).
35	Park Street	Site of Mrs Ferrars' home (*S&S* 131).
36	Portland Place	*F&E*, *MW* 8, 9.
37	Portman Square	*Lesley*, *MW* 123, 128, 135; *S&S* 153.
38	Ranelagh	*Cath*, *MW* 204. *See also* Public Places.
39	Sackville Street	*Col Let*, *MW* 162; *S&S* 220.
40	St Clement's Church, Strand	*P&P* 318.
41	St George's Church, Hanover Square	*MP* 416.
42	St George's Fields	*NA* 113.
43	St James's Palace	*P&P* 18.
44	St James's Street	*S&S* 290.
45	St Paul's Cathedral	
46	Sloane Street	Henry Austen lived for a time on Sloane Street.
47	Thames	*P* 32.

48	Tower of London	*NA* 113.
49	Westminster Abbey	
50	Wigmore Street	*LS, MW* 245, 246, 273.
51	Wimpole Street	Site of the Rushworths' London house (*MP* 394, 423, 438, 439).

Jane herself had mixed feelings. On the one hand, she loved country life and appears to have despised women who aspired to nothing more than a large house in London's rapidly expanding, fashionable West End. On the other hand, she often visited her brother Henry in London and soaked up all the pleasures that the city afforded to a woman of her class – principally shopping and the theatre. In her *Juvenilia*, she mocked those who uttered parroted condemnations of London by placing in the mouths of some of her characters the kind of highly literary, conventional attacks on the capital that appeared in sermons and moral tracts (*Lesley, MW* 120). Here, it is a 'hot house of Vice' (*Cath, MW* 239) and a home of 'insipid Vanities and idle Dissipations' (*L&F, MW* 78). Isabella Thorpe echoes the same sentiments in the language of romances rather than the language of sermons (*NA* 120), but we are still meant to hear the threadbareness of her language. Edmund Bertram's assessment is more measured: 'We do not look in great cities for our best morality. It is not there, that respectable people of my denomination can do most good' (*MP* 93). Fanny Price, similarly, is 'disposed to think the influence of London very much at war with all respectable attachments' (*MP* 433). Yet Austen understands perfectly that people like to get into town and have a little fun, and she does not condemn this impulse (*S&S* 155–156; *P&P* 151). Overall, her opinion of London seems to have been summed up by the old saw, 'It's a nice place to visit, but I wouldn't want to live there.'

For shoppers, London was a foretaste of heaven. The newest fashions made their debut in the metropolis (*Cath, MW* 207) and only slowly worked their way outward to the countryside, so a woman who visited London could gain an advantage over her provincial friends. She could also shop in a wider variety of stores (*S&S* 164, 182, 220–221, 326; *P&P* 43), almost all of which had a wider selection than the average shop in a middling-sized town. London had china showrooms, huge bookstores and 'warehouses' (*P&P* 288) – large shops – selling every conceivable kind of ribbon, lace, calico or silk. It had the best hairdressers (*E* 205) and the best makers of musical instruments, including the famous John Broadwood from whom Frank Churchill buys Jane Fairfax's pianoforte (*E* 215, 323). Men and women alike saved up their specialised shopping, sometimes for a whole year, and did it all at once in London. If they could not get to London themselves, they asked friends or relatives who were going to do their shopping for them (*F&E, MW* 4). Jane often bought things for Cassandra when she was in town, writing to inform her of what purchases she had made and to request authorisation for other items.

The prime season for being in London (*MP* 295) was the winter (*J&A, MW* 17; *Cath, MW* 202; *S&S* 110, 150, 214; *P&P* 117, 238) when Parliament was in session (*Cath, MW* 197) and therefore drawing the most illustrious society into town. The principal theatres, Covent Garden and Drury Lane, were open then, and wealthy and titled women gave their best parties. The season extended into spring (*LS, MW* 251; *MP* 20; *E* 259, 308; *P* 7) as far as Easter, but at that point most people went back to their country homes for the holiday.

See also Bath; Travel.

M

Marines

Austen introduces only one marine officer in her works, but he is certainly memorable. He is, of course, Fanny Price's foul-mouthed, hard-drinking, inconsiderate father, 'a Lieutenant of Marines, without education, fortune, or connections' (*MP* 3). Incapable, it seems, of rising through the ranks and 'disabled for active service, but not the less equal to company and good liqueur' (*MP* 4), he is hardly the sort of exemplary character that her naval officers tend to be. This is perhaps because there was a certain degree of inter-service rivalry between sailors and marines, the former priding themselves on their superior knowledge of the ship and the latter comforting themselves with their superior discipline.

The rivalry was at least in part encouraged by naval regulations. Marines had a variety of duties, but they existed in large part to discipline and intimidate sailors. They served in peacetime as guards at dockyards and harbours* and in wartime prevented impressed men from escaping before they could be assigned to ships. In harbours, they guarded against desertion, and aboard ship, they stood by as an emblem of the king's justice when floggings and other punishments were administered. They also served as guards at various points around the ship: at the galley door when food was being prepared, at the captain's door and at the doors

---

*And were replaced in wartime by militia units.

of the rooms where gunpowder and liqueur were stored, to name a few. Afloat or ashore, they discouraged mutiny.

In order to prevent them from developing too strong a sympathy with the men they were supposed to control, the marines were forbidden by regulations to berth or mess with the common sailors. It might be assumed that the marine and naval officers got along somewhat better with each other than the privates and sailors, since at least the officers could dine together and the marines were there in part to help preserve order aboard the ship. This, however, was not necessarily the case. Naval captains were sometimes jealous of the marines' fancier uniforms and the terms of their commissions; naval commissions were somewhat threatening in their wording, hinting at dire consequences for failure. Marines, in turn, chafed at being under the command of naval officers and at ranking lower in the command structure than naval officers of nominally equal rank. A marine lieutenant, for example, ranked not only below a naval lieutenant in the command structure but also below some warrant officers. The danger of disrespect as a result of this situation was so great that the Admiralty had to issue regulations insisting on proper behaviour towards marine officers. Their lesser power, the regulations insisted, was merely a reflection of their lesser involvement with the working of the ship, and they were 'to be considered and treated in all respects as a commissioned officer should be'. The Admiralty's insistence, however, did not guarantee universal goodwill; sailor Samuel Leech reported that the captain of the *Macedonian* 'had a profound hatred of marines'.

Marines were better appreciated in their other capacity, as troops for landing parties and boarding parties. Their original function, to provide musket fire during ship-to-ship combat, had become less important over the centuries as cannon became the chief means of crippling an enemy's crew, but a few marines – perhaps a dozen – could still be found in the rigging as sharpshooters during battle. They also helped to man the great guns, the capstan and the pumps, but their principal role was in amphibious attacks, where they formed the bulk of landing parties.

See also Navy.

Marriage

Marriage (*Watsons, MW* 351; *Sand, MW* 421; *P&P* 316; *MP* 4, 42, 43, 46; *P* 92) began, in most cases, with a willingness to marry (*MP* 42; *P* 61). In the case of women, the motivation might be love, but it was often a more-pragmatic assessment of the fate that awaited an 'old maid' (*Watsons, MW* 317; *S&S* 38; *P&P* 22–23, 221; *E* 65, 84, 85). Unless she had money of her own, a woman considered beyond the marriageable age was thought to be of little use to anyone, besides the relatives for whom she might keep house. She was a burden and, in many eyes, an incomplete woman (*P&P* 122–123). The view of bachelors was more forgiving, but not by very much. Men as well as women were expected to settle down, procreate and be responsible. How was England to conquer the world, if not by breeding more soldiers and sailors and colonial governors? Therefore, bachelors, too, were encouraged to marry. Popular prints portrayed old maids in hell as post-horses ridden by bachelors, but they also portrayed the reverse situation, with the old maids driving the bachelors. There was a tax on bachelors, which Parson James Woodforde, as a life-long bachelor, was compelled to pay; bachelors paid double tax on the servants they employed.

Those disposed to marry put themselves in the way of likely candidates, either by visiting a social resort town such as Bath or Cheltenham or by looking around their own neighbourhood. They went to dinners, balls and evening parties in the hope of finding a suitable candidate. What was 'suitable' depended on the seeker, but in the case of men, Austen's character Charles Adams might speak for the majority: 'his wife, whoever she must be, must possess, Youth, Beauty, Wit, Merit, & Money' (*J&A*, *MW* 21). The 'improbability of … ever meeting with such a Lady' caused many men to settle for the first pretty girl with a decent fortune that caught their eyes.

The decent fortune was of crucial importance. For young people to marry, they had to have a sufficient income not only for their own needs but for the children they would very likely have (*Sand*, *MW* 400; *NA* 135; *P* 66, 217). There were few birth-control options available at the time. Condoms existed, but they were thought of chiefly as guards against contracting venereal disease from prostitutes, and few people even considered using them at home. The menstrual cycle and conception itself were poorly understood, and even cyclical periods of abstinence would have been hard to enforce, as a husband had a legal right to have sex with his wife whenever he wanted it. Most women who tried to control their fertility did so after conception, by swallowing poisonous or nauseating substances, injuring themselves in the abdomen or douching, and these methods appear to have been more common among the desperately poor – chiefly unwed servant girls – than in Jane Austen's social class. Therefore, a woman who married needed to be prepared for numerous pregnancies, and her husband had to be prepared to pay for the upbringing of a horde of children.

In addition, money was necessary to make more money. Cash payments were required to advance in many professions, such as the army, where commissions were purchased outright. Landowners needed cash to acquire additional acres and to improve the ones they already owned. It was frankly in a father's interest, if he wanted his daughter and grandchildren to have the most comfortable life possible, to ensure that comfort by helping the new couple with a sizable cash gift, the dowry (*Amelia*, *MW* 48; *Evelyn*, *MW* 183–184; *Watsons*, *MW* 321, 353; *NA* 68, 251;

Marriage

S&S 3, 194, 224, 266–267, 268, 374; *P&P* 108, 153, 183–184, 302, 304, 308; *MP* 3, 31, 40, 42; *E* 66, 135, 169, 181; *P* 218, 248). This money, once the marriage had taken place, was the property of the new husband, who could do with it as he liked. If he were a sensible young man, he would use it to further his career or invest it and use it to augment the family income; an invested dowry made about 4 or 5 percent interest annually, so Mary Crawford's £20,000 (*MP* 42) would have brought her husband about £900 or £1,000 a year in addition to his own income. If the husband were not sensible, he might use the dowry to pay off gambling debts and incur more or spend it on racehorses or smuggled claret. The wife had little recourse against a man who spent her dowry foolishly.

A woman whose dowry was small had few choices. Working-class women could work in order to augment their dowries, and many did so, saving sums they could proudly hand over to their bridegrooms as proof of their worth, but women of Austen's class were debarred from work, and any job they took – except, in some cases, for intellectual or artistic endeavours, which even then had to be disguised as hobbies – automatically reduced them in caste. Austen had good reason to hide her authorship of her novels from the world. While it would have brought her admiration in some quarters, in others it would have made her seem to be a working woman and no longer a full member of the gentry.

A woman of the upper classes, who had no fortune to speak of, might take a desperate course in order to avoid a marriage that was 'beneath' her or the poverty and loneliness of spinsterhood. She could travel to one of Britain's colonies where Englishmen vastly outnumbered Englishwomen. This entailed a long and sometimes dangerous sea voyage, but women who arrived safely in one of the Caribbean sugar islands or in India found themselves in high demand (*Cath, MW* 194, 205). Jane's aunt Philadelphia, her father's half-sister, had done precisely this. She had travelled to India, married a surgeon named Tysoe Saul Hancock and produced a daughter, Eliza, who was pretty and witty enough to marry a French count and, after his death, Jane's brother Henry. This practice was, however, not universally accepted or admired. Many considered it little better than selling oneself into slavery and decried the shipments of women to the East Indies, but no one did anything to stop the bride boats or to alleviate the need for them.

In exchange for the dowry and the advantages it brought, a man agreed in the 'marriage articles' (*MP* 162; *P* 208), or contract, to a certain amount of his estate in the event of his death. He might specify that his wife was to inherit the property outright, with the right to do with it as she pleased, but he might also set conditions for inheritance, such as a ban on remarriage. A common strategy was to provide a jointure, a regular income derived from a significant percentage of his property (typically one-third), that reverted to the couple's children after the widow's death. This, of course, presumed that he died with income-generating property.

A professional man such as a physician would leave nothing of this kind unless he had saved and invested wisely during his lifetime.

For a woman, the choice of a spouse was the most important decision she would make in her entire life, as she was handing nearly complete legal control over to a man. He would control her earnings, her property and the raising of her children. He could imprison her, beat her and rape her, and the legal system would not lift a finger to help her unless the beatings were considered excessive by the standards of the day. Even then, it was frequently not the legal system but the community that stepped in; staging public protests meant to shame a violent husband into behaving himself. A husband could separate his wife from their children and refuse to allow her to have any contact with them. She could not enter into a contract in her own right. If he chose to sue for a divorce (*MP* 464) on the grounds of her adultery, she was not permitted to testify in her own defence, nor could she sue for a divorce if he committed adultery.

Given the wretched legal position of a wife, it was crucial that a woman choose a man who would not abuse his power over her. He had to be a man whom she could respect, control or at least endure. He ought to be acceptable to her family (*3S*, *MW* 58), older than she was but not ridiculously so (*F&E*, *MW* 6–7; *J&A*, *MW* 26; *3S*, *MW* 58; *NA* 252), and preferably religious but at the very least possessed of good morals. Of course, he needed to have enough money to support their children and to provide his wife with a decent standard of living (*J&A*, *MW* 26; *NA* 249–250). The anonymous author of *Female Tuition* (1784) warned, 'It is generally from disparity of condition that most unhappy matches take place. There is no time of life in which they can with safety be ignorant of this fact, or inattentive to its consequences.' Rich men who took a pretty, but relatively poor, wife (*Evelyn*, *MW* 184–185) were viewed more generously by the society than rich women who 'married down', unless they were relatively poor men with titles, buying a 'my lady' along with a bridegroom (*Watsons*, *MW* 324; *P* 74).

However, while many authors weighed in on the subject of the choice of a husband, the fact was that it was only the prospective husband who chose (*NA* 77). The woman merely got to accept or decline (*F&E*, *MW* 8–9; *J&A*, *MW* 21–22). Nevertheless, there were plenty of opinions on the right criteria for acceptance (*L&F*, *MW* 93; *P&P* 99). Women, however, frequently rejected the sensible, religious type in favour of dashing rakes who talked prettily, flattered, danced well and displayed a fine calf in their stockings. The danger inherent in a bad choice was especially great for heiresses and wealthy widows, who were subject to a higher-than-average degree of flattery and attention from impoverished fortune hunters (*L&F*, *MW* 86; *Watsons*, *MW* 321, 325–326).

For both parties, there was an increasing importance placed on the value of love at the outset of a marriage. Propertied families had long arranged the marriages (*J&A*, *MW* 25) of their children, trusting that affection or at least mutual respect and tolerance would flourish in time, but in the course of the eighteenth century, a higher value came to be placed on individual choice and romantic attachment, even though writers warned young women that, for men at least, sexual conquest usually ended a man's first passion. They warned that a woman should be prepared for her husband's ardour to cool after six weeks and evolve into something else (*MP* 296) – respect and calm affection if she were lucky, contempt and neglect if she were not. Still, novels and plays continued to push romantic love as a prerequisite for marriage. Marriage for purely mercenary reasons (but not for *partially* mercenary reasons – *P&P* 125, 153) came to seem despicable (*LS, MW* 256; *Watsons, MW* 318; *P&P* 376; *MP* 38, 42).

The Wedding

Once a man and woman had agreed to marry each other, they had to get the consent of their parents or guardians (*F&E, MW* 10; *Evelyn, MW* 185; *NA* 119, 135, 249; *MP* 40). Under a law passed in 1753, people could no longer marry clandestinely (*L&F, MW* 87), and those under the age of twenty-one needed parental permission to marry within England. The parental-consent requirement did not apply in Scotland, however. Therefore, couples who knew or suspected that they would meet with parental disapproval hired a coach and eloped (*J&A, MW* 17; *Lesley, MW* 110) with all due speed to the Scottish border (*S&S* 206; *P&P* 273, 274, 282–283; *MP* 442). (Working-class couples who married there tended to live close by and tended to get there by walking.) They usually made for Gretna Green (*P&P* 274), a town on the very southern end of the border, simply because it was easiest to get to, and there they were married.* Under ecclesiastical law, a clergyman was not actually necessary for the proceeding. The couple simply needed witnesses to a verbal contract in which they bound themselves in marriage to each other in the present (not future) tense. Popular prints typically showed Gretna Green couples being married by a blacksmith, because in this case he was forging chains of a different sort.

An elopement was a particularly appealing tactic for impoverished fortune hunters. They could woo a young heiress with talk of love, whisk her away to Scotland and come back to face a father who would never, under normal circumstances, have allowed such an unequal marriage.

Those who did not elope could be married in one of two ways, either by publishing the banns (*S&S* 296) or by license (*H&E, MW* 35; *P&P* 378; *MP* 88). Publishing the banns meant having the local clergyman announce, on three successive Sundays, that the couple in question intended to marry, giving members of the community due notice and a chance to object to the marriage, a typical reason for objection being the prior engagement or secret marriage of one of the parties. Austen, when she lived at Steventon

---

*Austen humorously has one of her fictional couples flee to Gretna Green to be married, even though they are already in Scotland (*L&F, MW* 95).

with her clergyman father, twice jokingly entered banns for herself in the parish record book, each time with a different fictional bridegroom.

Emma Woodhouse makes reference to this formula when she says she will call Mr Knightley 'George' only once: 'I do not say when, but perhaps you may guess where; – in the building in which N. takes M. for better, for worse' (*E* 463). Not all editions of the Book of Common Prayer used 'M' and 'N' to stand for the bride's and groom's names; some used 'N' for both. Yet it is particularly appropriate that Austen uses these initials rather than N for both, for *Emma* is full of word games, including the puzzle about the two letters that equal perfection being M-A (Emm-a). 'M', of course, sounds like the first syllable of Emma's name, and Knightley's name, which begins with a silent K, starts with the sound of the letter N.

Many members of the upper classes found the banns embarrassing and chose instead to be married by license. They took advantage of a loophole in the statutes that kept an incorrect statement of residency from nullifying a marriage and either temporarily resided in a parish other than their own (*P&P* 318), or simply stated their addresses falsely, in order to acquire a license from a different parish and be married there, away from prying eyes. This was an especially common ploy in London (*P&P* 275, 282–283), where the sheer numbers of people made it difficult to check on residency, even if anyone had been motivated to do so, and many couples got married in London who did not actually live there.

The bride's family spent the days before the wedding amassing a new wardrobe for her – the 'wedding clothes' so often mentioned in Austen's works (*F&E, MW* 7, 11; *S&S* 182, 215; *P&P* 119, 288, 306, 310; *E* 271; *P* 217). This was not merely the bridal gown but a whole set of new clothes whose cost was proportional to the family income. The groom often spent his time shopping for a new carriage (*S&S* 215; *P&P* 310; *MP* 202, 203; *E* 267, 308), if his income permitted it. Just as a person planning to start a family today might trade in the two-seater sports car for a family sedan, wealthy men of Austen's time celebrated their new status as husbands by providing a suitable vehicle in which their wives could pay morning visits to friends.

On the day of the wedding, the bride and groom wore their best clothes (*MP* 203). The bride frequently wore a veil (*E* 484), and as white was a fashionable colour, she often wore white, but there was no requirement to wear white as yet (*E* 484). Any stylish dress would do. She also frequently wore flowers. Grooms usually wore full dress, which for the gentry meant knee breeches, silk stockings, white waistcoat and a fine frock coat.

The wedding (*F&E, MW* 10; *L&F, MW* 82; *NA* 123; *S&S* 217; *P&P* 145; *E* 6, 182, 267) typically took place in the morning. The wedding party and a few friends and relatives – more or fewer depending on the size of the neighbourhood and the means of the bride's family – either walked or rode to church. The bride and groom stood at the altar, where the presiding clergyman (*MP* 89, 203; *E* 483) read the service from the Book of Common

THE WEDDING.

14. *The Wedding*, 1794.

Prayer. After some further words about the purpose of marriage and a call to both the congregation and the bride and groom to announce any impediment to the marriage, the bride and groom exchanged vows, and the groom placed a ring (*NA* 122; *P&P* 316) on the bride's ring finger. There was no ring at this time for the groom. After a short prayer, the parson joined the couple's hands (*E* 13) and pronounced, 'Those whom God hath joined together let no man put asunder.' Further prayers – including one for fertility if the woman was still of childbearing age – and a sermon followed. The new husband paid the clergyman for his services; Parson Woodforde reported getting sums of 5*s*., £1 1*s*., £2 2*s*. and so on, according to the ability of the bridegroom to pay. The church bells were rung (*NA* 252; *E* 267), and the bride and groom left the church, where they were pelted with grains of wheat as a symbol of fertility, rice not having been adopted yet for this purpose.

Gifts were distributed to the wedding guests at some point during the morning, either before or after the ceremony. These were often rings, gloves or knots of ribbons but might be more substantial for those closely related to the bride (*E* 322–323). The wedding party then went to someone's house for a wedding breakfast (*Lesley, MW* 112–114) of meat, bread and butter, toast, eggs, chocolate, wine (*MP* 203) and the wedding cake (*E* 19), which was a doughy confection flavoured with dried fruit and covered with two kinds of layered icing. Bits of the cake were passed through the wedding ring by the bride and handed out as good-luck charms to single people who hoped to marry soon. In some places, the bits of cake had to be passed through the ring nine times for the magic to work.

Pieces of cake, other food and liqueur might be distributed to the household servants (*P&P* 307) and to the poor.

The bride's garter was removed by the groom's friends, a procedure for which she usually first partially untied the garter and moved it lower, to lessen this invasion of her skirts. The bedding of the bride, in which the guests acted as witnesses, just outside the door, to the bride's loss of virginity, had been toned down somewhat, and some couples went away after the wedding to get acquainted in relative privacy (*MP* 203).

See also Titles; Visiting; Widow.

Masquerade

Emerging in the early eighteenth century, masquerades evolved out of Elizabethan and Jacobean masques. Masques were quasi-theatrical performances with a theme, often classical and allegorical, in which participants presented themselves in costume, often masked. They might dance, speak or merely process through a banqueting hall, and there was always a point to the performance, such as an elaborate compliment to an honoured guest or host.

Masquerades, in contrast, had no particular point except pleasure, and they had no unifying theme except disguise. It was novel, in a society with rigid social structures and expectations of conduct, to let loose and play another part. Men dressed as women and women as men, or grown ups dressed as children or infants. People dressed as animals, druids, bishops, Punch, the Green Man, foreigners of various nations and allegorical virtues or vices. The essence of the event was secrecy and the license it brought to do and say forbidden things, so the participants not only wore masks (*Lesley, MW* 118) but disguised their voices by speaking in 'squeaking' tones.

By the mid-eighteenth century, masquerades were held in several types of environments: homes, assembly rooms, theatres and public gardens. Masquerades in homes were private parties, while the other venues were open to the public for a fee. Of the public sites, the pleasure gardens of London were perhaps the quickest to cash in on the masquerade fervour. Ranelagh, for example, began holding periodic masquerades in 1742. In the second half of the century, the Venetian opera singer Theresa Cornelys (1723–1796) was the queen of London assembly-room masquerades; she sponsored subscription masquerades from 1760 to 1772 in her rooms at Carlisle House in Soho Square. Events were also held at Almack's club from 1765 and at the Pantheon theatre from 1771. The Pantheon was not the only theatre to participate; the King's Theatre, Haymarket, was holding masquerades into the 1780s, with dazzling numbers of oil lamps being lit for the occasion.*

However, by the 1780s, the masquerade was in decline and had not long to live. The frisson of danger provided by its anonymity was both its chief attraction and the source of its downfall. Warning tales circulated about women who were raped at masquerades by men they thought were their husbands or by assailants whose identity could never be known. Less dramatic, but still disturbing, examples could be cited of women whose masks made them act licentiously. Women talked bawdily; they flirted; they spoke with strangers. The order of society seemed in jeopardy, and the masquerade was laid aside. By 1779, a witness could attest, 'From the thinness of the Company at Monday night's Masked Ball, it is pretty clear that these kinds of exotic amusements are so much on the decline, as to promise a total and speedy extinction.' By 1790, the fashion was dead.

For novelists, this must have been quite a tragedy. Masquerades present all sorts of interesting dramatic possibilities. One of Austen's literary role models, Fanny Burney, made good use of the masquerade in *Cecilia*, for example, and Austen herself uses it to comic effect in her juvenile work *Jack & Alice* (*MW* 12–14). The conclusion of her episode, however, though not intended to be taken seriously, probably reflects fairly accurately the attitude of the majority towards the moral climate of the masquerade:

> The Masks were then all removed & the Company retired to another room, to partake of an elegant & well managed Entertainment, after which the Bottle being pretty briskly pushed about ... the whole party ... were carried home, Dead Drunk.

See also Dance; Entertainment.

Medicine

In the eighteenth century, the medical profession was, for almost the first time since the classical era, attempting to formulate completely new theories of disease and treatment. The old theories of humours were on the way out, and physicians were searching for something new to replace them. A new commitment to scientific method led physicians to test long-standing ideas about the causes and remedies for disease. For example, they investigated, under laboratory conditions, the effects of immersion in cold water on fever. At the same time, new tools such as the thermometer enabled experiments to be performed with greater accuracy.

*The man who provided lighting for the theatre charged by the hundred for oil lamps for operas, but he charged by the thousand for masquerades. A musicians' benefit concert was lit for a cost of £3, while a masquerade cost anywhere from £27 to £84.

Yet the medicine of Jane Austen's time was still pervaded by medieval relics of faith, folk remedy and quasi-magical practices such as the use of substances as medicines because they bore some sort of symbolic resemblance to the ailment they were meant to treat. Physicians (*Clifford, MW* 43; *Sand, MW* 386, 422; *P&P* 40; *E* 454) had relatively few remedies at their disposal – at least, few that actually worked – and, in any case, physicians were the uppermost tier of the medical profession, rare and highly paid. They were seldom consulted by anyone except the very rich and the desperately ill. They were therefore called in late enough in the progress of a disease that there was little hope of a cure, and the consequently high death rate of their patients added to the public perception of doctors as expensive and useless (*Sand, MW* 394). Physicians had no X-rays, no antibiotics and no knowledge of vitamins, and though their focus on a patient's diet might imply that they had a working knowledge of nutrition, their prescriptions in this area were often inimical to health. When Jane's eldest brother, James, experienced ill health, for example, he was put on a diet of bread, water and meat, a regimen that can hardly have hastened recovery. The training of physicians, especially in England, was still weighted more heavily towards classical learning than towards practical medical skills, and even if physicians had been gifted with all the medical knowledge available at the time, they would still have had only the vaguest inkling of the relationship between germs and infection. The most scrupulous might wash surfaces with vinegar to inhibit pests, but few washed their hands routinely.

On the other hand, there was a basic understanding of epidemiology, even if the agents of disease had not been identified. It was clear that some diseases could be spread from person to person and that some places were unhealthy, though it would be 1854 before John Snow would begin to pinpoint *why* certain locales seemed more inclined to disease than others (*E* 22, 103).* Quarantines, usually voluntary and informal, were frequently imposed to halt the spread of some diseases, and smallpox (*Cath, MW* 234) inoculation was already common. The technique had been observed in Turkey by Mary Wortley Montagu, who saw women scratching smallpox lesions and then using the same instrument to scratch the skins of healthy people. Edward Jenner made the same procedure safer by substituting the less-virulent cowpox, a related virus that caused less-serious reactions to inoculation. Members of the royal family volunteered for the procedure, making it widely accepted, and this went a long way towards ending a scourge that had killed many and disfigured more (*Lesley, MW* 136).

Surgery, too, was on the verge of modernisation. Surgeons (*Lesley, MW* 113; *Sand, MW* 365, 366, 372; *P* 111) were among those performing

*In that year, Snow tracked a cholera outbreak to a contaminated well; the organism responsible was discovered later that year and conclusively linked to cholera later in the nineteenth century.

the most promising experiments and developing the most interesting new techniques. Yet surgeons enjoyed less prestige than physicians and inhabited only the fringes of gentility (*Watsons, MW* 321, 324).* This may have been because their work lacked the dignified pace of the physician's sedate enquiries. In the absence of anaesthesia, their skill was reckoned by their speed. They performed a limited number of procedures, such as trepanning, the removal of kidney stones and the excision of cancerous tumours – all operations in which the potential benefit outweighed the significant risk of fatal infection. Surgeons often did not wash their hands – or the surgical table – between patients, and their aprons and floor were awash in blood at the end of a busy day. The lack of gentility was also due to some extent with surgeons' long-standing association with mere barbers. Barbers and surgeons separated their respective professional associations only in 1745, and surgeons did not have a Royal College for training purposes until 1800.

Fanny Burney, during her residence in France in the early nineteenth century, was diagnosed with breast cancer. She was unusually fortunate in having access to a group of the nation's finest doctors, but her surgery was so excruciating that two years later she could barely endure the recollection of it.

Below the surgeon on the social and financial scale was the apothecary (*Sand, MW* 386; *P&P* 33, 40, 41; *E* 19), the type of medical professional most often consulted by ordinary people. Apothecaries dispensed medicines, though they were more than mere druggists, as they often hastened to point out. They were also diagnosticians who referred only the most complicated cases to surgeons or physicians. Jane Austen was treated by apothecaries for most of her life when she was sick, as were most of the people she knew. It is a sign of the rarity of consultation with physicians that even in her final, fatal illness, she was treated not by a physician but by a surgeon, Giles King Lyford of Winchester. Yet her letters express no lack of confidence in apothecaries simply because they were not physicians, anymore than most people today would lack confidence in their family doctors simply because the doctors do not happen to be specialists at leading research hospitals. The apothecary was the standard of care, and anything more was provided only out of necessity or extravagance.

There were also medical practitioners on the fringes of professionalism.

Midwives delivered most babies and were licensed but received no formal training. A host of quack doctors hawked everything from patent medicines to electric current for the relief of pain, while expert bonesetters (*J&A, MW* 22) were called in as specialists when a bone had been broken or fractured. Bonesetting took skill and knowledge

*Austen's paternal grandfather was a surgeon. Even in her later life, Austen would gently point out to a niece with literary ambitions that in reading the niece's manuscript, 'I have also scratched out the Introduction between Lord P. & his Brother, & Mr. Griffin. A Country Surgeon ... would not be introduced to Men of their rank.'

of anatomy as well as enormous physical strength, but it was rarely
a full-time occupation. Dentistry was performed both by full-time
dentists and by farriers with a pairs of pliers and a suitable indifference
to the patient's screams. For most ailments, there was nursing at home.

Women who chose nursing as a profession often did so because they
were unfit to hold a position as servant in a decent private home – or
at least this was the public perception. Professional nurses were accused
from time to time of theft, immorality and drunkenness; even Nurse Rooke,
a far more sympathetic character than many of the nurses portrayed
in Austen's time, is a sly gossip (*P* 154, 155). Nursing for middle-class
and upper-class patients, therefore, was performed by trusted household
servants or, better yet, by the women of the family (*Sand, MW* 370, 371).
Women were considered especially qualified for this task by the combined
motivations of duty, feminine compassion, emotional attachment to the
sufferer and, apparently, a high tolerance for boredom and drudgery. The
importance of home care (*Sand, MW* 367, 386; *MP* 189; *E* 22) is reflected in
the cookbooks of the day, which often list recipes for remedies in a section
after the chapters devoted to food.

However, though mothers and sisters were expected to stay home,
whip up snail soup and hover anxiously by the bedside, it is clear that
not all of them did so. Mary Musgrove's unwillingness to forgo a dinner
out at Uppercross is mirrored in real life by the account of Parson James
Woodforde, who reported in his diary in January 1790 that the local squire
and his wife had joined him for dinner. The couple stayed until 8:00 p.m.
'and would have stayed longer but their eldest Daughter was very bad
in the Scarlet Fever.' Clearly, Mary Musgrove was not the only woman
willing to leave a critically ill child in the care of others for a night.

Disease and Treatment

Diseases (*NA* 186; *E* 6, 163) were not necessarily identified by the same
names as today, which can make it difficult to determine exactly what
disease is being discussed in many cases. A host of illnesses were lumped
together under the heading 'nervous complaints' (*Sand, MW* 407, 411, 415,
416; *S&S* 83, 185; *P&P* 113, 288; *MP* 72–74; *E* 92, 103, 316, 363, 389; *P* 129,
134) and might include everything from chronic headaches (*Sand, MW* 387;
MW 447–449; *S&S* 162; *E* 263, 322, 389; *P* 77) or fatigue to hypothyroid,
seizures (*F&E, MW* 11; *E* 387) or simple hypochondria (*Sand, MW* 412–413).
Ted Bader, in *Persuasions Online*, has suggested that Mr Woodhouse's
complaint is not hypochondria but hypothyroid, a disease consistent with
his sensitivity to cold, nervousness and possible difficulty swallowing due
to an enlargement of the thyroid gland.

Another large category of disease was 'fever' (*E&E, MW* 30; *Clifford,
MW* 43; *NA* 151; *P&P* 33; *E* 95, 332, 351, 379), which encompassed typhoid,
typhus, diphtheria, some kinds of infection, influenza (*E* 102) and almost
any other kind of ailment that included fever among its symptoms.
As the causative agents of such diseases were not known, fevers were

distinguished from each other not by the particular bacterium or virus at work but by how often the fever spiked or dropped ('remitted') and by whether or not it was considered infectious, serious or 'putrid' (*E* 109); putrid fever, for example, was another name for typhoid. Different diseases with similar fever profiles, therefore, might be treated identically, while the same disease with a slightly different presentation might be treated entirely differently. William Buchan's *Domestic Medicine* divided fevers into remitting, intermitting and continual varieties, and Mariane Dashwood's near-fatal fever, as John Wiltshire notes, fits the pattern of a remitting fever.

A common disease of the middle and upper classes was gout (*Evelyn*, *MW* 186; *Cath*, *MW* 204; *LS*, *MW* 296, 298; *Watsons*, *MW* 344; *Sand*, *MW* 374; *E* 383; *P* 163–164), a form of arthritis brought on by, among other things, high alcohol intake (*NA* 63) and obesity. Since the diet of prosperous Britons was high in alcohol, fatty meat, bread and the organ meats and shellfish that can aggravate gout, it was a disease of the wealthy and particularly of men. Jane's brother Edward suffered from gout, as did her uncle James Leigh-Perrot.

Gout tended to attack the lower legs, especially the feet and ankles, and many popular prints of the time show men with gouty feet. Treatment usually consisted of trips to spas (*LS*, *MW* 295–296, 298; *Sand*, *MW* 374; *P* 163–164) to bathe the affected limb in warm or hot water, which probably temporarily relieved discomfort and had the added advantage of forcing people to bathe their whole bodies. When not in the bath, the foot was dressed in special stockings, elevated and wrapped in thick layers of flannel. There was at least a partial understanding of the link between gout and diet, and those who could stand to do so sometimes ate less-rich food and drank less alcohol in order to mitigate the effects of the disease. Other forms of joint pain were lumped together under the heading 'rheumatism' (*Cath*, *MW* 233; *Sand*, *MW* 415; *S&S* 37, 38; *MP* 189; *E* 383; *P* 152), or 'rheumatic complaints'.

Treatments for disease ranged from the non-invasive to the dramatic. Many practitioners, in the absence of better alternatives, opted to keep patients warm, dry, well and blandly nourished and well rested, trusting to time and the patient's strength to effect a cure. Others resorted to the time-honoured practices of purging (using noxious compounds such as calomel – *MW* 448–449), bleeding with leeches (*Sand*, *MW* 387, 424) and 'cupping', a procedure in which small heated cups were placed on the skin to raise blisters. Sarah Harrison's *House-Keeper's Pocket-book* lists medicines (*Sand*, *MW* 413, 416; *E* 317) for colic, jaundice, gout and ague (*MP* 104), most of them simple decoctions or pastes made with ordinary household ingredients. There are similar recipes for dealing with sore throats, eye infections, dropsy, burns and fever. For rheumatism, the housewife is to rub linseed oil on the affected area in the morning and at night. For an intermitting fever, she should make an alcoholic syrup.

Harrison also expected her readers to be able to handle coughs
(*E* 295), wounds, headaches, pains, fits, scurvy, gripes and mad dog bites.
Injuries, according to household texts like Harrison's and according
to more-learned medical texts, were generally treated with 'plasters'
(bandages – *P* 127) or with poultices. The court plaster (*E* 338) was a small
dressing made of isinglass and silk. For faintness, ammonia-based smelling
salts could be applied under the nose; these were derived from shaved deer
antlers and were therefore known as 'hartshorn' (*S&S* 178). Embrocations
(skin lotions – *E* 102) could be applied for a variety of reasons, including
colds, sore throats (*E* 114, 124) and chest congestion.

Colds (*LS*, *MW* 262; *Watsons*, *MW* 345; *S&S* 170; *P&P* 31, 35; *E* 102, 161,
236, 295; *P* 154) were not life threatening, but in the absence of most
of the palliative medications available to us today, they were especially
uncomfortable. They were blamed, as were many other diseases, on cold
or damp conditions; wet ground, wet air and sudden or prolonged exposure
to low temperatures were all considered to be very harmful (*L&F*, *MW* 100,
101; *Cath*, *MW* 210, 233–234; *Sand*, *MW* 415; *NA* 18; *P&P* 31; *MP* 190; *E* 209,
217, 251).

Other supposed causes of disease included overexposure to heat, too
much exercise and too little exercise.

Consumption (*E&E*, *MW* 30; *L&F*, *MW* 102; *Sand*, *MW* 393; *E* 163) was
any disease that tended to have a 'wasting' effect on the body – that is,
that caused the patient to lose weight. Nutrition was therefore of critical
importance to such patients. The most famous of the consumptive illnesses
was tuberculosis, also sometimes called 'galloping consumption'. This
is the 'pulmonary complaint' (*E* 389) that Jane Fairfax is feared to have
contracted, a disease that apparently killed her mother and that was
associated in the public mind with people of Jane Fairfax's obsessively
artistic temperament. A common prescription in such cases was the
alteration of the patient's diet (*Watsons*, *MW* 344; *E* 19). Asses' milk was
considered especially good because it was easily digestible (*Sand*, *MW* 393,
401, 422), and other widely recommended foods included gruel (*E* 104–105),
meat broth and arrowroot (tapioca pudding – *E* 391, 403).

Sea bathing (*Sand*, *MW* 369, 374; *E* 101, 102, 104–106; *P* 97), drinking
spa water (*NA* 71; *P* 146) and bathing in mineral springs (*E* 175; *P* 152, 154)
were all supposed to be of great value for a variety of complaints. Those
with rheumatic disorders could benefit from bathing in the hot mineral
baths, while those with 'bilious' complaints (digestive disorders – see
Sand, *MW* 386, 415) could drink sulphurous-smelling water to cleanse the
system. Sea bathing was recommended for all sorts of illnesses, so many
indeed that Mr Parker's long list is hardly an exaggeration of the claims
made by the proponents of seawater (*Sand*, *MW* 373). A change of 'air'
(*Lesley*, *MW* 116, 118; *E* 94) was also often recommended, and although the
different air in Bristol or Bath or the south of France probably had little
effect on health, a change of scenery and routine might have been of use
to some patients.

Medicine

Some of the home remedies of the time sound so absurd that it is tempting to discount them as the fanciful creations of writers whose advice was seldom followed. Such treatments as eating a fried mouse or wearing a spider sealed in a goose quill to cure whooping cough seem too outlandish to be believed. It is easier to think of people taking patent pills (*Sand*, *MW* 422; *MP* 297), powders and tonics (*S&S* 191) such as Daffy's Elixir, or proven remedies such as quinine, also called Jesuit's Bark. Yet people were willing to try anything in order to feel better, and in the absence of scientific proof of the cause and nature of disease, there was no knowing what might have a positive effect.

See also Death; Teeth.

Money

England's official monetary system was bimetallic – that is, it was based on the actual market values of gold and silver, with coins being issued in both metals in sizes that reflected their actual worth. In practice, gold was more abundant than silver, and very little silver coinage was produced during Jane Austen's life. In fact, most of this 'English' silver was Spanish silver, Spanish dollars countermarked with a bust of George III that began appearing in 1797. Part of the remainder was produced not by the Royal Mint but by the Bank of England, which began striking five-shilling silver pieces in 1804 and two smaller coins, with values of 3s. and 1s. 6d., between 1811 and 1816. These bore a bust of George III on one side, looking very much like coins produced by the mint, and some sort of indication on the reverse that the coin had actually been produced by the bank. In the case of the five-shilling piece, the legend 'five shillings dollar' ran around an oval band, and 'Bank of England', in somewhat larger letters, ran just outside it. In the case of the 1s. 6d. coin (*Scraps*, *MW* 174), the words 'bank token' appeared on the reverse, along with the coin's value and date. Other banks produced silver coins, as did manufacturers and counties; Hampshire and Cornwall, for example, minted silver coins, often labelling them as intended for the furtherance of trade or for the 'accommodation' of the local populace. Silver coins produced by the mint under George III were the crown (worth 5s., or a quarter of a pound), half-crown (2s. 6d.* – see *Watsons*, *MW* 349; *MP* 119, 163), shilling (12d. – see *Lesley*, *MW* 117; *LS*, *MW* 296; *Sand*, *MW* 374, 400; *NA* 28; *S&S* 218; *P&P* 83; *MP* 151; *E* 85, 334) and sixpence (*Watsons*, *MW* 352; *S&S* 11; *P&P* 305; *E* 22). Special four-penny and one-penny silver coins were produced for distribution by the king on Maundy

---

*The abbreviations for old-style English coins were 'g' for guineas, '£' for pounds, 's' for shillings and 'd' for pennies. The £, s and d abbreviations are descended from medieval coinage weights and denominations; £ for libra or livre ('pound' in Latin and French, respectively), 's' for solidus, 'd' for denarius.

Thursday, but these were not in regular circulation. Note that none of the official coins was a 'three-shilling piece'; the one mentioned in *Persuasion* must therefore be a privately issued token (170).

15. Farthing, 1806, actual size.

16. Penny, 1797, actual size.

Gold coins included the guinea (*Scrapsi*, *MW* 174; *Sand*, *MW* 414, 424; *NA* 19, 46, 47, 76; *S&S* 65, 291, 370; *MP* 53), weighing 129 39/89 grains and worth 21 shillings;* the pound, worth 20 shillings (*L&F*, *MW* 107; *Evelyn*, *MW* 182; *Watsons*, *MW* 352; *P&P* 300, 304, 308; *MP* 127, 305, 396); the half-guinea of 10*s*. 6*d*.; the third-guinea of 7*s*. (*S&S* 370) and the half-pound of 10*s*. In 1817, the guinea was eliminated and replaced by a 20-shilling coin, called a 'sovereign'. Most transactions, however, did not take place using gold coins as the currency. A general shortage of silver and eventually gold currency, especially towards the end of the Napoleonic Wars, necessitated other means of making purchases.

17. Sixpence, 1790, actual size.

One way of accomplishing this was by buying goods on credit – often with astonishingly long intervals between the provision of services and the rendering of payment.

*One guinea was the price of a first edition of *Emma*.

18. Shilling, 1817, actual size.

Another expedient to which many businesses and banks resorted was the coining of token coins, worth very little in themselves but redeemable for gold or silver. Usually made of copper, these coins were often stamped with images celebrating local industry or agriculture, the name of the coining agency and the place(s) at which the coin could be redeemed. The theory behind the coins, however, was that they would *not* be redeemed but would circulate much as token currencies do today, representing the *idea* of value rather than possessing intrinsic value. Thus, they would further trade by providing readily available coinage with which to make small purchases. A surprising number of businesses, especially copper miners, produced such coins, usually pennies (*Scraps*, *MW* 174; *NA* 124; *MP* 394) and halfpennies, and these tokens were very well received by the public.

19. Bank token, 1*s*. 6*d*., 1812, actual size.

20. Bank token, three shillings, 1812, actual size.

Eventually, even the government began to warm to the idea of a copper coinage, which had long been resisted in favour of gold and silver. In 1797, Birmingham industrialists Matthew Boulton and James Watt were authorised to produce copper pennies and twopences for the government. Unfortunately, they chose to abandon the idea of a token coinage and

21. Half-crown (2s. 6d.), 1817, actual size.

issued huge coins whose metal content made them actually worth their face value. The 2d. coin weighed two ounces, and the penny weighed an ounce, making a pocketful of 'small' change a weighty burden. They were never popular, but later halfpenny and farthing (a quarter penny – see P 200) denominations caught on, and by the time production was ended in 1807, £679,311 of copper coins had been struck.*

A third way of easing the demand for coin proved to be revolutionary. Travelling merchants had long dreaded the idea of entrusting themselves and a bag full of coins to the toll roads and their burgeoning population of highwaymen. In order to minimise their risk and the weight they carried, a merchant would secure a note from his local bank, which could be redeemed for coin once he reached his destination. Banking was a volatile business, with banks sometimes failing in swarms, to be replaced by similar ventures founded on equal parts of optimism and greed. Still, most of these banks issued notes that were accepted with little question in far-flung parts of the nation.

22. Crown (5s.), 1820, actual size.

23. Half-guinea, 1791, actual size.

*A new copper coinage, this time a token currency, would be issued in the 1820s, after Austen's death.

Money

Paper currency had several distinct advantages other than being lightweight. It could, for example, be cut in half, and the halves sent to a destination via different posts, deterring highwaymen. As a token currency, it could be produced without regard to fluctuating metal values. In theory, banks were supposed to have enough cash on hand to redeem all their notes at once, but not all banks adhered scrupulously to this practice; indeed, in the worst war years, even the government drifted off the gold standard for a time and used paper money as its legal tender. It served as a travelling advertisement for the bank; every time it changed hands, the reputation of the bank was improved. It could be issued in variable denominations – guineas or pounds, from £1 to £500, or whatever amount seemed to be required. Because by its very existence it increased the supply of money available for trade and investment, it had the potential to stimulate the economy, improve consumer confidence and relieve some of the necessity for long extensions of credit.

Banknotes (*H&E*, *MW* 34; *L&F*, *MW* 92, 96; *NA* 19; *MP* 372) were usually larger and more nearly square than British or American paper money today. In fancy print, they announced their value and the name of the banks on which they were drawn. After an act of 1775, they had to be worth at least £1, and all notes were subject to a stamp tax; the latter provision meant that in the 1780s, nine-guinea notes, a rather odd denomination, were suddenly popular, as the stamp tax increased for values of ten guineas and above. The average banknote did not circulate very long, usually only about three or four months, indicating perhaps that the public's faith in them was limited. They were money, true, but not nearly as reassuring as a handful of coins, and they still felt more like a receipt for money than the money itself.

24. Guinea, 1795, actual size.

As they occupied a kind of middle ground between the modern idea of paper money and a more archaic idea of paper money as a small-value letter of credit, banknotes might be used in the modern sense or the archaic one. Sometimes, banknotes were used to make direct payments. Woodforde, however, records instances in which he cashed a banknote received as payment and used the change to make a variety of purchases at different shops. In London in September 1789, he went 'into Lombard Street and changed two of Gurneys Bank Notes of 10 Pd each for Cash'. One feels, from reading diaries, letters and literature of the period, that presenting someone with a banknote was rather like handing them a gift certificate today: 'Here', seems to be the assumption of both giver and receiver, 'here's a little something – go out and get yourself some money with it'. There is still the connotation of paper money as something that is exchanged for the real thing.

There was related uncertainty about the banking industry (*LS*, *MW* 250; *Watsons*, *MW* 322; *S&S* 225), which was almost completely unregulated and thus often unreliable. Austen's brother Henry, for example, was one of the owners of a failed bank, which collapsed partly due to irresponsible loan policies and partly due to a general wave of bank failures that ruined 206 banks between 1815 and 1830. From 1808 onwards, the government tried to enforce the bankers' responsibility to engage in sound business practices and make good on debts. The initial foray into regulation was forcing bankers to sign promissory notes and take out licenses.

However, despite restrictions and risks, England's growing economy stimulated the establishment of new banks. Within London, the Bank of England reigned supreme and unchallenged, but in the provinces an increasing number of small banks emerged, their assets often limited not to gold or silver but to Bank of England notes. The twelve provincial banks of 1750 became 350 by 1790 and 721 by 1810. These banks took deposits, offered loans, issued banknotes and allowed their customers to write cheques in order to move funds from one bank to another. By 1770, the use of cheques was common enough that bank clerks began to meet at a London chophouse in order to settle the transactions in one set of calculations and exchange of coins. This 'clearing house' concept was so successful that it soon moved to its own location nearby and became an established feature of London's banking business.

The Bank of England remained the principal symbol of banking and a major symbol of the nation's financial health. It enjoyed special privileges and was subject to special regulations (such as a cap of 5 percent on the interest it could charge on loans of the money it printed). Unlike the humbler country banks, its premises were deliberately grand, meant to reinforce its solidity and reliability. The bank's unique position made it a target of political protest (*NA* 113), most notably in 1780, during the anti-Catholic Gordon Riots, when the bank was attacked by mobs and had to be garrisoned with troops. Even after the troops were dismissed weeks later, a military night guard was sustained at the bank for almost 200 years, and a neighbouring church was demolished to prevent its tower from being used as a point from which disgruntled citizens could fire on the bank.

People wishing to preserve and increase their money had relatively few options. They could invest in joint-stock companies, but then as now, such ventures were often risky. Contemporary prints satirised both the jobbers and promoters, who sold such stocks, and the greedy would-be magnates who bought them. A more-conservative investment was the 'Navy five per cents', a system of annuities introduced in the 1760s to raise money for 'certain Navy, Victualling and Transport Bills, and

Ordnance Debentures'. Austen herself invested almost all the proceeds of her novels in the navy 5 percents, and she assumes an income of 4 (*P&P* 106) or 5 percent on her characters' invested funds.

See also Debt.

Music

Music (*L&F, MW* 78; *Lesley, MW* 119–120, 129; *NA* 56; *S&S* 17, 47, 48, 83, 155, 343; *P&P* 24, 39, 101, 172, 173–174; *MP* 19, 288; *E* 28, 85, 150, 168, 181, 191, 227, 232, 276–277, 282, 301; *P* 43, 58) was an important part of the lives of the gentry, both for the women (and the occasional man) who played it and for the family members and friends who listened to it. Learning to play some sort of musical instrument (*S&S* 105; *P&P* 24, 248, 345; *E* 170, 456; *P* 71) was considered an important, if not essential, part of a young woman's education (*Cath, MW* 206), and parents paid significant sums to have a music teacher come to the house and give lessons (*Cath, MW* 198; *NA* 14) or to send their daughters to boarding schools where a good musical education could be acquired (*LS, MW* 253). Austen's parents appear to have hired George William Chard, the assistant organist of Winchester Cathedral, to teach her, and she remained musical, to some extent, all her life. Young women who had obtained a suitable musical education were then expected to display their talents (*P&P* 100–101; *E* 229, 276), both in the hopes of attracting favourable male attention and for the purpose of entertaining the family at home (*Lesley, MW* 111; *S&S* 35; *MP* 191; *P* 46, 72). The ideal was that the young woman would practice extensively and become proficient, though then as now, motivating the young student to practice was always the hard part (*LS, MW* 271; *P&P* 173, 175, 176; *E* 231). Austen continued to practice all her life when it was possible; at Chawton Cottage, for example, she practiced every morning, but she does not appear to have enjoyed displaying her talents in public, even in the semi-public forum of an impromptu after-dinner dance.

In order to practice sufficiently, a woman needed access to an instrument and to printed sheet music (*S&S* 342; *E* 242; *P* 38). As published music was often expensive (*S&S* 92, 93), women sometimes borrowed music from friends or relatives and then laboriously copied it out by hand (*S&S* 83), a process that required both skill and time. The Austens' collection of music contained both printed and hand-copied pieces bound into books (*Lesley, MW* 130; *P&P* 51), though what survives is not all of what Jane would have played, as much of her music was sold, along with her first pianoforte, when the family moved to Bath in 1801. Her surviving collection includes two pieces by Mozart, several pieces by Handel (including portions of the *Water Music*, Judas Maccabeus and *Zadok the Priest*), various sonatas by Johann Schobert and fourteen sonatinas by Ignaz Pleyel, an initially celebrated composer who fell out of favour for prolific, but uninspired, pastiches of Handel. She also possessed music by Haydn, Gluck and the popular composers Dibdin, Arne and Shield. The pieces by Dibdin included *The Soldier's Adieu*, which Jane, with 'fine naval fervor' (*P* 167), amended to *The Sailor's Adieu*.

She owned English, French and Italian songs (*P* 186), all of which were popular at the time; songs (*F&E*, *MW* 10; *NA* 122–123) gave a woman a chance to display her voice as well as her playing, while symphonies (then called 'overtures'), sonatas and excerpts from operas (*S&S* 342) focused attention on the music. Keyboard duets (*MP* 14, 20) gave friends a chance to play together, and vocal duets (*NA* 28) offered a man and a woman a chance to unite their voices on the way to uniting their hearts. Country dances (*Lesley*, *MW* 129; *E* 229, 245; *P* 47) need have no words, only a lively and regular tempo to help the dancers along. Glees (*MP* 112, 113) were part-songs for three voices and were sung either in glee clubs or in private homes. One notable glee club, London's Anacreontic Society (founded 1766), opened every meeting with the song 'Anacreon in Heaven', which, with very slight alterations, became the accompaniment to Francis Scott Key's 'Star-Spangled Banner'.

Intriguingly, with all this variety of music available, Austen mentions relatively few specific songs in her works. She makes a humorous reference to 'Malbrook' in Lesley Castle as 'the only song' a notoriously pedestrian character appreciates (*MW* 130). 'Malbrook', a corruption of the title of the duke of Marlborough, was a song popular in France at the end of the eighteenth century. Used widely in satirical French songs, it is an extremely undemanding tune and was slightly adapted in the 1830s as 'For He's a Jolly Good Fellow'.

Consistent with the vogue for all things Gaelic at the time, Austen owned two collections of Scottish songs (*Lesley*, *MW* 124; *P&P* 25, 51–52), though if she owned any Irish music, it has not survived. Nonetheless, she mentions the fashion for Irish tunes as well in her works (*P&P* 25; *E* 242). Always acutely aware of the latest fashions, in music as well as in clothing, she recognised that some of the most interesting and challenging music being produced in her day was by J. B. Cramer and had Frank Churchill send some Cramer compositions to Jane Fairfax (*E* 242), making Cramer the only composer mentioned in any of Austen's novels. The pieces she herself played frequently were usually undemanding, although there were a few that clearly required more talent to play than the rest. She had, for example, a copy of the difficult Grand Concerto by Steibelt, a noisy and complicated work that may have been intended as the 'magnificent concerto' that Marianne plays at Lady Middleton's (*S&S* 149). This was a famous work, well known in 1811 when *Sense and Sensibility* was finally published.

Music was also enjoyed in a public setting. Professional musicians could be found in almost any 'public place' – at assembly balls (*Watsons*, *MW* 327, 328; *NA* 57; *E* 255), when strings like violins (*L&F*, *MW* 100;

Watsons, MW 327; *S&S* 171; *MP* 117, 275) were the rule; at the Pump Room in Bath and in public gardens. Songs and music-accompanied dances filled the intervals between plays at the theatre (*MP* 124), and the upper classes enjoyed opera – Italian operas at the King's Theatre, Haymarket, and English operas at Drury Lane and Covent Garden. Public concerts (*Lesleyi, MW* 133; *NA* 25, 26; *P* 180–193) were held in many cities, often by subscription, meaning that subscribers paid a flat fee to acquire a certain number of tickets to a series of scheduled performances, making the subscription the Georgian equivalent of the season ticket. In the provinces, concerts by top performers were rarer events and individual tickets were sold rather than season passes. Parson James Woodforde reported occasionally on such concerts in his diary. In September 1788, he noted in his diary that 'The Kettle Drums from Westminster Abbey sounded charmingly, beat by a Mr Ash-bridge. Near 100 performers in the Orchestra.' Two years later, he saw Nancy Storace, the leading female comic opera star of London, along with 'Select pieces from the Messiah, Joshua & c.', for a five-shilling ticket price.

Elsewhere, society hostesses arranged 'musical evenings', one-time private concerts with hired music rather than (or in addition to) the normal sequence of amateur after-dinner demonstrations (*S&S* 248; *E* 284). The quality of the professional music depended entirely on the host or hostess' pocketbook, as even the best performers in the nation could be secured for private parties at a price. Austen was in London in 1811 for one such party thrown by her brother Henry and his wife, Eliza, which promised '5 professionals, 3 of them Glee singers, besides Amateurs'. Later, she reported that there had been some good harp music and a singer 'whose voice was said to be very fine indeed'. Note that Austen did not say that she herself found the voice 'fine'. She was notoriously unenthusiastic about singers and was deeply unimpressed with her one recorded visit to the opera.

Musical Instruments

Although women sometimes played unconventional instruments such as the cello or guitar, the two most popular instruments were the keyboard and the harp, both of which were at their heart stringed instruments. The standard keyboard in Austen's childhood was the harpsichord (*Lesley, MW* 130; *Cath, MW* 201, 229, 232) or the spinet (*NA* 14; *E* 216), both of which had quills that plucked the strings. The harpsichord was a slightly more-complicated instrument than the spinet, having one keyboard instead of two.

Both instruments were eclipsed in the late eighteenth century by the pianoforte (*LS, MW* 271; *Plan, MW* 428; *S&S* 26, 30, 35, 62, 281, 342; *P&P* 39, 51, 58, 173; *MP* 127, 288, 395; *E* 216, 240, 241, 242, 244, 384; *P* 50), which instead of having quills had hammers that struck the strings. The first pianofortes in England were German-made grand pianos and were popularised by their use in the theatre. The fact that they used hammers rather than quills made them easier to maintain, as quills needed to be replaced often, while pianofortes needed to be tuned (S&S 144) only occasionally. The problem for pianoforte makers was how to produce a case that held all the strings in the best manner possible, and several solutions were proposed. The most obvious was the grand pianoforte, in which the strings were arranged horizontally from longest to shortest, left to right from the perspective of the performer. The grand pianoforte had the advantage of allowing the performer's face to be seen, but its disadvantage was the amount of floor space it took up, which made it practical only in the large homes of prosperous families (E 215; P 40). Another solution was the square pianoforte (E 214–215), which also had horizontal strings but was less monumental. It compressed the space required for the strings by running the longest strings diagonally across the shorter strings at a different level within the case. A third solution was the vertical alignment of the string case, so that the pianoforte was extremely tall, as tall as a large bookshelf. The space left vacant by the shorter strings could be recaptured as a shelf for sheet music, but the sheer height of the longer strings forced the instrument to be positioned against a wall and meant that the player kept her back to the audience and sang towards the wall rather than towards the room. An improvement was the movement of the string case downwards, so that it rested on the floor, which, combined with the diagonal stringing of the square pianoforte, greatly reduced the height of the instrument. This still resulted in a cabinet that extended much higher than the keyboard, but this 'cabinet' piano was nonetheless superior to the very tall models that had preceded it, because it allowed more of the performer's face and body to be seen.

The posture of the performer was almost as important as skill from the perspective of courtship. A musical performance was one of the occasions on which a woman could legitimately draw attention to herself, and she was supposed to make the most of it.

Improvements in the pianoforte came rapidly. Early mechanisms had lacked power, requiring a firm 'touch' (E 220) to strike a note, and in some cases the hammer would stay against the string and dampen the sound or rebound and strike the string a second time. A series of patents, some of them filed by John Broadwood (E 214–215), addressed these issues. Increasingly complex internal systems kept the hammer exactly where it was supposed to be, resulting in a lighter touch and better sound.

Broadwood, a Scottish carpenter and joiner, had married the daughter of his employer, a prominent harpsichord maker, Burckhardt Tschudi. He filed his first patent in 1773 and by the 1790s was manufacturing 400 square and 100 grand pianofortes a year. He was acknowledged to be one of the best piano manufacturers in England, and English pianos were generally acknowledged at this point to be the best in the world, with a superior tone (S&S 144; E 2220, 34) to most Continental instruments, due in part to the use of felt under the leather cover of the hammers. His pianofortes were played by some of the world's greatest performers and composers, including Beethoven. A square pianoforte of the kind probably given to Jane Fairfax would have cost about £26 in 1815, exclusive of the delivery charges and the price of the sheet music. That the 'other Jane', Jane Austen, took her music seriously is reflected in the fact that in 1808 she proposed spending up to 30 guineas for a pianoforte at Chawton Cottage.

Other improvements to the pianoforte included the expansion of the keyboard. Early models had a very small number of keys by modern standards, but by the turn of the century keyboards with five-and-a-half or six octaves had become the norm. This increase in range, combined with improved reliability, completed the conquest of the harpsichord. Sheet music that had once been for 'harpsichord' and then for 'harpsichord or pianoforte' was now advertised as being for 'pianoforte or harpsichord', with the 'or harpsichord' in much smaller letters or simply for the piano alone. Cabinet, square and, occasionally, grand pianos sprouted in the drawing rooms of lords, squires, tenant farmers and well-to-do artisans.

The harp (*Sand, MW* 383, 421; *Plan, MW* 428; *P&P* 48; *MP* 57, 59, 64–65, 206–207, 227; *E* 301; *P* 40, 47, 50), however, remained an instrument for the rich. It was considered especially graceful and feminine, but it was not as versatile an instrument as the pianoforte. It could not, for instance, be enlisted into the service of a country dance. It therefore remained a means

25. *Harmony before Marriage*, James Gillray, 1805.

by which women could show off their unique charms. Like the pianoforte, the harp experienced revision and renaissance during this period. Its principal improver was Sébastien Erard (1752–1831), originally a piano maker, who in 1808 patented a new method of increasing the range of each string. This double action allowed the string to be functionally shortened by pressing a pedal into one of two notches, which activated a *fourchette* (forked disc) that changed the sound of the string without throwing it out of key as earlier mechanisms had done. Erard's design allowed the flat, natural and sharp notes to be played on each string, vastly widening the harp's range.

See also Dance; Entertainment.

N

Navy

The navy appears repeatedly throughout Austen's works. Its pay, promotions, hazards, reputation and peculiar rhythms feature prominently in the lives of several of her characters. After the clergy, it is the profession she addresses most often, and with good reason. The navy grew dramatically during Austen's lifetime. The officer corps, which numbered about 1,400 in 1794, swelled to nearly 4,700 during 1809–1812, when it was at its highest, and her friends and relatives made up some of this glut. Though the Austens could be said to be first and foremost a clerical family, they were almost equally a naval family, with two of the sons and a good many acquaintances serving at sea. Here, as always, Austen sticks to what she knows.

The gaps in what she relates are as revealing as what she chooses to include. For instance, she does not dwell on the role of the merchant marine, which was almost as important to the nation's security as the regular navy. England's vast trading networks were serviced by these civilian sailors. In 1792, perhaps one-eighth of England's 118,000 civilian and naval sailors were engaged in trade with the West Indies, while another significant block of sailors worked on 'Indiamen' – the ships of the East India Company – bringing tea, cotton and coinage home from India (*MP* 381). These sailors necessarily gained a great deal of experience working in all conditions on long voyages, and they were familiar with the very rich colonial regions likely to be contested in wars between European powers.

Therefore, when war broke out, they were encouraged to volunteer for naval service; the government paid a bounty for volunteers, and London merchants added up to £5 per man for able seamen, setting an example that many seaport towns emulated. Different parts of the country were at times required to supply a certain number of able-bodied men for military service, and local officials often provided handsome bounties to avoid an involuntary draft; one advertisement in the *York Chronicle* from 1792 promises that the churchwardens and parish overseers will pay 30 guineas to a volunteer – an enormous windfall to a labourer in those days. When bounties failed to muster enough volunteers, press-gangs found sailors ashore or even boarded merchant ships and took the men they needed.

Of course, merchants and the sailors themselves – resented this practice. War meant disruption of trade routes anyway, and a drain on manpower was the last thing the importers and exporters needed. However, the defence of the nation came first and was certainly more prestigious. Upon hearing that Fanny Price has a brother at sea, Mary Crawford remarks, 'At sea, has she? – In the King's service of course' (*MP* 60). The 'King's service' was more glamorous than ferrying cargoes of wool and timber – at least for the officers, who might grow very rich indeed in the service of the nation. As for the men, who seldom got rich under any circumstances, they tended to prefer the quieter merchant marine if for no other reason than that they could choose to leave a ship at the end of its voyage if they did not like the captain and his style of discipline. Sailor John Nicol served in the merchant marine in peacetime and did not volunteer when war broke out; the press-gangs came anyway and took virtually every able-bodied man aboard his ship, leaving it to be manned, he said, by 'ticket-porters and old Greenwich men' – the latter a reference to the Greenwich pensioners, aged and infirm sailors fed and housed by the state. Resentment of such press-gang sweeps ran so strong that merchant captains often hid their sailors or even deserters. Young Samuel Stokes was pressed into the king's service in 1806 at the age of fourteen; the following year, he escaped from his ship and was fed and helped by a merchant captain.

Press-Gangs

Merchant officers were not the only ones resisting the press-gangs. In a few places, magistrates refused to sign the necessary orders authorising press-gangs to act. In others, crowds rioted or colluded to protect men from being taken, but, for the most part, the gangs operated with few limitations or even with help from informers, who were paid 20 shillings a man for the apprehension of deserters. Magistrates were often eager to foist their local population of vagabonds and criminals into the waiting arms of the press-gang and, in such cases, probably asked few questions about contested seizures. Best of all, from their perspective, the gangs could simply bypass the authorities onshore by raiding homeward-bound merchant ships.

In theory, the press-gangs could seize only seamen, and then only those who lacked a 'ticket of liberty' from their home ship and only those who were not otherwise exempt by virtue of their trade specialty. Farm labourers and gentlemen, too, were protected from the gangs. So were sailors on ships bound out of England, captains' apprentices who had served less than two years of their term, Thames watermen (who had a special arrangement to provide a quota of volunteers), foreigners, competent ships' pilots, merchantmen's masters and mates, and boatswains and carpenters serving on ships of more than 50 tons. In practice, the system was more fluid. The burden was on the captured sailor to prove that he had a ticket of liberty or that he belonged to a protected ship or trade. The masters, mates, boatswains and carpenters mentioned above had to have an affidavit, sworn before a justice of the peace, and they were safe only aboard ship or on ship's business ashore. If such a man decided to make a visit home, for example, he was just as exposed to the gangs as any other sailor. A gentleman who was not dressed as such also risked being mistaken for a member of the vulnerable class. On the other side of the equation, even a man who was fully subject to the gang's round-ups could buy his way out of trouble with a substantial bribe – up to £20. Foreign citizenship could also be feigned; false American citizenship papers were forged on both sides of the Atlantic with such frequency that the gangs came to ignore them.*

Pressed men, as well as volunteers, were collected in a holding area of some kind. On shore, this would be some sort of building; afloat, it would be a ship called a tender. (Charles Austen's ship, the *Namur*, was used as a tender in the last years of the Napoleonic Wars.) In either case, the area would be heavily guarded by armed marines to prevent premature desertions.

Pressed men had few options left to them at this point, but some opted to make the best of a bad situation. Often, left with no alternative, they would sign on as 'volunteers', which gave them better options for leaving the service later and also offered a signing bounty. Frequently, they gave false names, as many of them had already deserted the service on at least one occasion.

Ranks and Promotion

At the pinnacle of the navy's hierarchy stood the 'first lord' (*MP* 246) of the Admiralty. His immediate underling – but often the more assiduous and important of the two – was the first naval lord; in 1794, the first naval lord was Vice-Admiral Philip Affleck, to whom Austen friends appealed in an attempt to get Francis Austen (*J&A*, *MW* 12; *Harley*, *MW* 40) transferred into a frigate. Other naval 'lords' constituted the Admiralty Board, which served as the top administrative body in the navy.

*The boarding of American vessels and seizure of men with American papers were a principal cause of the War of 1812. Many British sailors preferred to serve on American ships, where they found the discipline lighter and the captains more egalitarian.

However, Jane Austen's interest is less in the bureaucracy of the navy than in its officer ranks – from midshipman up to admiral. At the bottom of this hierarchy were the midshipmen (*J&A*, *MW* 12; *Harley*, *MW* 40; *P* 51), who entered on their service when they were no more than boys; Thomas Cochrane, whose father objected to his joining the navy, finally made it to sea at the extremely advanced age of seventeen-and-a-half. Young as they were, they were officers entitled to give orders to the most experienced able seamen and entitled to expect absolute obedience from the men. They might command a gun crew; handle sails and ropes; calculate the ship's speed; keep logs; take charge of a watch, pacing the quarterdeck and watching for any sign of trouble; and calculate the ship's position using astronomy, sea charts, wind and current speeds, and chronometers that showed the difference between local time and Greenwich Mean Time. Other duties, such as the command of one of the ship's small boats (*MP* 377) or the running up and reading of the signal flags (*P* 234) that transmitted orders and news, might be assigned at the captain's pleasure. The captain was expected to take a special interest in the education of the midshipmen. They were, in a way, his apprentices. Austen's brother Charles appears to have been particularly adept at this fatherly aspect to the captain's duties, if we are to judge from the recollections of Douglas Jerrold, who came aboard Charles' ship, the *Namur*, at age ten in December 1813. Charles let the boy keep pigeons and encouraged his interest in natural history and amateur theatricals. In an earlier instance, Charles had also been kind to the son of the earl of Countess of Leven, who served as a midshipman under him. In 1805, Jane and Mrs Austen paid a call on the aristocratic couple and apparently heard Charles praised in much the same manner that Mrs Musgrove praises Captain Wentworth (*P* 52, 66).

However, the midshipmen (*MP* 381) were not thought of kindly by everyone aboard. Grown men, not surprisingly, resented being ordered about by twelve-year-olds.

Austen's midshipmen seem unconscious of any animosity from below decks, but they do feel keenly their position at the bottom of the officers' ranks. William Price is described as 'only a midshipman' (*MP* 233) and a 'poor scrubby midshipman' (*MP* 245) unworthy of so fashionable a place as Brighton. Of course, he laments that the 'Portsmouth girls turn up their noses at any body who has not a commission. One might as well be nothing as a midshipman' (*MP* 249). Another of Austen's midshipmen, the late Dick Musgrove, really is nothing, partly by virtue of his incompetence (*P* 50–51, 67) and partly by virtue of being dead before the novel begins. She sees midshipmen neither as vile, swaggering officers nor as boys trusted with an extraordinary amount of responsibility but as her brothers must have felt and described themselves – as relative ciphers in the structure of naval command. Thomas Cochrane would probably have echoed their complaints – one of the first things that happened to him aboard ship was that the lieutenant, Jack Larmour, announcing that the new midshipman had brought far too much baggage, sawed open his trunk by way of public punishment.

The way out of the midshipmen's berth and into respectability was by promotion to lieutenant, which in theory was a simple matter of experience and skill. Regulations dictated that a prospective lieutenant had to be twenty years old – an age limit that was lowered to nineteen in 1806 – with at least six years' service at sea, at least three of them as a midshipman. When his captain saw fit, the midshipman would be given certificates testifying to his competence, age, years of service, sobriety and obedience. He would take these documents to a board composed of three captains, who would interrogate him about his logs and his knowledge of seamanship, gunnery, navigation, tides, wind and a host of other topics. Then, at some point afterwards, he would receive a commission to a ship, where he would take a position as the most junior lieutenant (*MP* 368, 384; *Sand, MW* 389) aboard. As a lieutenant, he would have similar duties to a midshipman's, but with generally more responsibility: he might lead gun crews or boarding parties, take watches on the quarterdeck, supervise re-provisioning or the taking on of fresh water, navigate and keep logs, and, if an enemy ship was captured, head a small 'prize crew' to sail the ship to a friendly port.

The first lieutenant (*P* 96) served as the captain's administrator and, when the captain was absent or incapacitated, as his surrogate.

In theory, a man rose in an orderly fashion from midshipman to lieutenant and then up through the ranks of lieutenants until he became a first lieutenant. In practice, promotion to lieutenant could be made easier or more difficult by a dazzling variety of circumstances. One was the number of qualified midshipmen versus the number of ships in commission with open lieutenants' positions. In 'good' years, when battle and disease between them contrived to carry off a number of lieutenants, a midshipman might get lucky. (The hope of ill-fortune to one's superiors was an uncomfortable, but constant, undercurrent in the service, one that William Price alludes to when 'supposing the first lieutenant out of the way' [*MP* 375] in his daydreams of greater glory.) In 'bad' years, such as 1812, there might be as many as 2,000 midshipmen who had passed the lieutenant's exam and were waiting impatiently for a commission (*MP* 362). Service in a particularly splendid naval victory was always helpful in getting extra consideration (*MP* 375). Francis (Frank) Austen got his promotion from commander to captain in this way, after his sixteen-gun *Peterel*, with a diminished crew, wrecked two French ships and captured a third in a daring battle. For those who could not manage such a stunning triumph and even for those who could, it was useful to have the influence of powerful 'friends'.

'Friends', in an eighteenth-century context, were usually not bosom companions but rather people who could be of assistance in one's career (*MP* 109). It was important to have as many of these friends as possible, preferably located in positions of great influence. Naval lords were best;

admirals were very nice indeed; and even captains could make themselves useful, either by offering a position as lieutenant or midshipman aboard their own vessels or by entering a friend's or relative's son on the books prematurely. Many a well-connected youth was actually comfortably at home or at school while nominally serving as a sailor aboard an uncle's or a cousin's ship. His name would appear regularly among the ship's company, and in this way he might acquire most or all of his six service years before he ever set foot on the quarterdeck.

It was, however, necessary to have the *right* connections (*P* 26–27). Francis Austen had an apparently powerful patron in Admiral James Gambier, but Gambier's Evangelical tendencies and his public quarrel with the respected Trafalgar veteran Rear Admiral Eliab Harvey made him unpopular in many parts of the service, and Francis' career appears to have suffered as a result. Another patron of Frank's, Lord Moira, accomplished little because he spread his influence too thinly, asking for too many favours on behalf of too many ambitious officers. Charles Austen's principal patron, Thomas Williams (who had married an Austen cousin, Jane Cooper), had little real power to help him until about 1811.

A midshipman could have all the skill in the world, but his commission might go instead to some boy whose father's vote was needed in Parliament to keep the current ministry (and thus the current first lord) in power. A shifting of the political winds could bring disaster to some and relief to others. One pictures that shifting, fickle wind wafting first to this house, then to that, carrying on its back a steady stream of letters pleading for commissions, ships, better ships and better stations. In the real world, such letters were a constant annoyance to their recipients, but they were effective: Reverend George Austen's correspondence with the right people got Francis his lieutenancy in 1798 and got Charles transferred into a better ship, a thirty-two-gun frigate. In the fictional world, a flurry of letters traces the chain of influence in the promotion of William Price (*MP* 298–299).

The right combination of luck, competence and influence could move a lieutenant to the next rank: commander (*MP* 368). A commander was, as the title implies, in command of a ship, but it was such a small ship that it did not qualify for a real captaincy, known as a 'post-captaincy' or 'post rank'. For Francis, this step up came in 1798, when he was given command of the sloop *Peterel* (16). In her, he captured or destroyed more than forty enemy vessels, and his zeal earned him promotion to captain in 1800. The fictional Frederick Wentworth is similarly energetic in his first command, the sloop *Asp*; Jane Austen includes an authentic detail of protocol in his account that might escape many readers. Since the *Asp* is clearly identified as a sloop (*P* 65), we know that Wentworth is only a commander when he travels to the West Indies in her, yet her refers to himself in the third person in his narration of events as 'Captain Wentworth' (*P* 66). Most readers think nothing of this, since at the time he is telling the story, he is a full captain. Yet the way he mentions himself makes it clear that he is speaking not of the present but of the time when he commanded the *Asp*. The crucial piece of information is that commanders were accorded the courtesy title of 'Captain', although they had not achieved post rank. James Benwick, too, is referred to as 'Captain', though he 'is only a commander, it is true, made last summer' (*P* 171). The reference to his being 'made into the Grappler' means that he has been made a commander and given command of the ship *Grappler* (*P* 108).

Once promoted to post-captain (*F&E*, *MW* 6;* *Coll Let*, *MW* 154;† *MP* 60, 236, 394; *P* 50, 66, 75, 96, 169, 248; *Sand*, *MW* 389), a man had merely to live long enough to rise to admiral; promotion from this point on was a matter of strict seniority; hence the frantic desire of lower-level officers to be made captains: one had to get on the captains' list as soon as possible in one's career (*MP* 60). Both Charles and Francis Austen saw colleagues promoted ahead of them, simply because they happened to have a slight advantage in seniority. This is not to say, however, that favouritism played no further part in advancement. The influence of 'friends' still determined what ship a captain commanded, and it might play some role in whether a captain would receive honours or titles as a reward for particular bravery (*P* 75).

In the Austen brothers' case, their influence was insufficient to get them really good ships. Francis' first command as captain, for example, was the *Neptune* (98), where he served as flag-captain to Rear Admiral Thomas Louis. This would appear to have been an honour; a flag-captain was in charge of the ship on which an admiral sailed and had his floating headquarters. However, as Brian Southam points out, the post was not a desirable one at all. A flag-captain was constantly under an admiral's supervision and never quite the master of his own ship, and any prize money he earned by capturing enemy ships would have to be shared with the admiral. In any case, Admiral Louis's squadron was engaged in blockade duty, which offered little chance of prize money anyway; few ships would leave port and sail directly into the arms of a superior enemy force. A better appointment would have been to a frigate, cruising alone in the hope of catching one or two prizes at a time and trusting to speedy sailing to escape from any sizable French force. Charles, too, served as a flag-captain, this time to his cousin-in-law Admiral Sir Thomas Williams.

Even admirals (*MP* 43, 60, 232, 266, 400; *P* 20, 68, 169) were subject to the vagaries of politics and nepotism. In December 1810, Francis got a plum assignment as flag-captain to Admiral Gambier aboard the *Caledonia* (120), a magnificent three-decker, but by spring of next year the unpopular Gambier was moved from the *Caledonia*, and the new admiral turned it into a 'family ship', bringing his brother and son-in-law aboard and displacing Francis.

*These are references to captains, but whether to an army captain or a navy captain is not specified.
†These are references to captains, but whether to an army captain or a navy captain is not specified.

There was a hierarchy within the ranks of the admirals (*MP* 109, 111). Rear admiral was the most junior rank, followed by vice admiral, and then full admiral.

Within each rank of admirals, there were three levels. A man began as a rear admiral of the blue, then became a rear admiral of the white (*P* 21), then a rear admiral of the red. The next jump took him to vice admiral of the blue, then of the white, then of the red and in the same way through the divisions of full admirals. The most senior (full) admiral of the red graduated to the top rank: admiral of the fleet, a rank Francis Austen reached in 1863. When an admiral was sailing aboard a ship, it carried special flags (*MP* 60) to indicate his presence and exact rank. Admirals of the red had a solid red flag flown from the top of one of the masts, admirals of the white a white flag with a red cross, and admirals of the blue a solid blue flag. Rear admirals flew this flag from the mizzen or rear mast, vice admirals from the foremast, and full admirals from the mainmast (*MP* 152). The admiral of the fleet, in place of these, flew a Union Jack from the mainmast. Each admiral also flew a flag from the stern of the ship – solid red, solid blue, or white with a red cross – with one of its upper quadrants filled by the Union Jack.

Set as it were to the side of this hierarchy were two sets of officers who did not rise through the ranks in the same manner. Ships usually had a surgeon (*MP* 380, 384), who might be a man of relatively little medical experience. One of his duties was to revive men who were being flogged, but his job was principally to tend to wounds during battle, a grisly business performed without anaesthetic and in highly unsanitary conditions. Men were brought to him not in order of the seriousness of their injuries but in the order they had been wounded, with exceptions often made for officers, who tended to bypass the queue.

The other quasi officer was the chaplain (*Harley*, *MW* 40; *Plan*, *MW* 429; *MP* 111). His presence was not as much a necessity as the surgeon's, as the captain was authorised to act as a chaplain and to read a passage from the Bible to the crew on Sundays. The chaplain was a warrant officer, ranking lower therefore than the commissioned officers such as lieutenants and captains and being approximate in rank to a master gunner, though he might vastly exceed the gunner in education.

Given the experience of Austen's brothers, it is hardly surprising that she confines herself to the officers of ships. However, her readers would have known that a typical large naval ship carried a variety of specialists, such as a master gunner (whose wife was often entrusted with the care and feeding of the cabin boys), a cooper (traditionally known as 'Bungs'), a carpenter (dubbed 'Chips'), the captain's clerk and the boatswain (*MP* 383) and his mates (who harried, shouted at and sometimes struck the men to wake them and to keep them at their tasks). Below these were the seamen, divided by skill level and pay into able seamen, ordinary seamen and landsmen. A fair number of women and boys might also be present.

The women were usually wives of warrant officers, but they were not present merely for companionship. They might cook, nurse the wounded or, in battle, fetch powder and bring it to the gunners.

Officer Training

There were two principal routes to becoming an officer: the formal training offered by the Royal Naval Academy at Portsmouth (*Curate*, *MW* 73), and the hands-on training combined with some academic education offered by captains at sea (*P* 52). Both of Austen's brothers chose the former route, or had it chosen for them, but in this they were not typical. Enrolment at the academy was never high during Jane's lifetime; Francis, who entered the academy in April 1786 a few days shy of twelve years old, was one of a class of twelve; Charles, who matriculated in July 1791, was one of a class of only four. In fact, during the time that Jane would have had an interest in the academy, it was never more than half full. During 1792–1794, for example, there were only twenty-eight scholars in all. A typical incoming class numbered only six boys, despite the fact that scholarships were offered to a certain number of officers' sons. In part, this was due to a negative impression of the moral climate at the school – not that shipboard life was a much better instructor in that area – and in part, it was due to the fact that officers' sons could often find patronage without having to go to a special school.

The typical student at the academy entered at age twelve to fifteen, studied two or three years and then went to sea. The Austens would have paid £25 per year in fees plus the cost of a uniform; no doubt they gave their boys a little pocket money as well. The curriculum, according to articles drawn up in 1773, was 'Writing, Arithmetick, Drawing, Navigation, Gunnery, Fortification, and other useful Parts of the Mathematicks; and also in the French Language, Dancing, Fencing, and the Exercise of the Fire-lock [musket]'. The 'other useful Parts of the Mathematicks' included logarithms, geometry, trigonometry, navigational calculation, surveying, mechanics, chronology (the study of the measurement of time, useful for using precise clocks to calculate longitude at sea) and astronomy (which enabled position at sea to be confirmed). French and dancing were useful for diplomatic purposes, while drawing, surveying and writing were essential for making maps, sketches, and records during one's voyages. It appears that classes were also held in ship construction; Charles Austen, according to the academy's shipwright, learned the manner of bringing to and fastening the main wales, lower, upper, quarterdeck and forecastle clamps, scarphing the beams and so on of the swift sloop – also the use of the draught, laying off and taking the bevellings of the square and cant timbers, crossing and levelling the floors, getting up and securing the frame bends and the use of the bollard timbers and nause pieces.

This was not the full extent of his studies, for the shipwright mentioned several other facets of ship construction that Charles' class had learned, using captured French ships and British ships under construction as models.

Once his training was complete, an academy student could go aboard a ship as a 'volunteer'. This meant he served without official rank but was treated as an honorary midshipman; some captains resented this system, which was seen as an infringement on their traditional method of educating officers. This was to take several 'servants' aboard, four for each 100 men assigned to the ship, each of whom was in training to be an officer. Some of these so-called servants would have been taken on as favours to other officers or patrons; others would buy their way in, thus increasing the captain's salary. These young officers in training, typically twelve or thirteen years old (*S&S* 103), had to bring a uniform (*MP* 390), a sea chest filled with a few belongings (*MP* 305) and an allowance for their food and supplies of perhaps £30 to £40 per year.

Captains' servants learned exactly what the academy graduates did, once they were finally at sea (*MP* 21, 377; *P* 50). They handled ropes and sails, engaged in gunnery drills, navigated, kept logs and learned how to manage sailors. Perhaps most important of all, they learned how to cultivate the goodwill of their fellow shipmates.

Pay

The base rate of pay in the navy was not especially bad by the standards of the time, but neither was it lavish. An officer's pay was based not on seniority but on the type of ship he commanded; for example, when Francis Austen moved from the fourth-rate *Leopard* (fifty guns) to the third-rate *Canopus* (eighty guns), his salary increased from £182 10s. 0d. to £237 a year plus miscellaneous payments that approximately doubled his income. Lieutenants, too, were paid on a sliding scale, those on first- or second-rate ships receiving £7 per lunar month, while all others made £5 12s. Captains were 'paid off' (*P* 50) at the end of a voyage, when all relevant paperwork, including the ship's log, had been submitted to the Admiralty; this caused Francis some trouble on one occasion when a fierce storm damaged many of his papers. He had to have all of his logs reconstructed, delaying his payment until nearly two years after his command in the ship had ended. Another difficulty that captains faced was their responsibility for entertaining fellow officers and distinguished guests, which added significantly to expenses, and the larger the ship, the more onerous these expenses became. He had to buy his own provisions, plate and glassware, uniforms, navigational instruments, telescopes and charts. He also had to pay up to £80 for his own chronometer, a clock that kept to London time and thus, by showing the difference between local noon and London noon, enabled him to establish his longitude.

Captains could, however, supplement their income in various ways. They could, for example, carry freight for the government or for private interests, which was good for the captains but not altogether advantageous for the navy, as hopeful captains might hover near friendly ports in hope of cargo rather than patrolling the waters for the enemy. An extremely profitable type of cargo was 'Company Treasure' or 'Treasure Money', the proceeds of the East India Company's ventures. In exchange for carrying this currency, a captain would receive a 1–2 percent commission; the ultimate authority in distributing such largesse was the governor general of India, Warren Hastings, who, as it happened, was an Austen family friend. Merchants might also reward diligent captains for protecting their shipping convoys; Francis Austen was, at various times from 1808 to 1809, awarded sums of 200 guineas, 400 guineas and 500 guineas for convoying East India Company ships. In 1810, he delivered ninety-three chests of company treasure, receiving £1,500 in compensation for his efforts. Cash awards were also sometimes made in cases of valour in battle, as after Trafalgar (*P* 21–22), when Lloyd's Patriotic Fund gave prizes of £25 to £100 to lieutenants and the wounded of the victorious ships. Rewards of this kind were not always directly paid in money. At times, merchants or city governments awarded heroic or conscientious officers with ceremonial swords or gifts of plate. The Trafalgar captains got swords from Lloyd's, and Francis Austen received a gold medal and a vase for his part in the Battle of St Domingo.

Prize Money

Officers and common sailors alike dreamed of the ultimate financial bonus, prize money (*MP* 375; *P* 17, 96). This was awarded by the Admiralty for various types of victorious naval encounters. When an enemy ship was captured, the value of its cargo was assessed, and sometimes the ship itself was 'purchased into the service', that is, turned into a British naval vessel

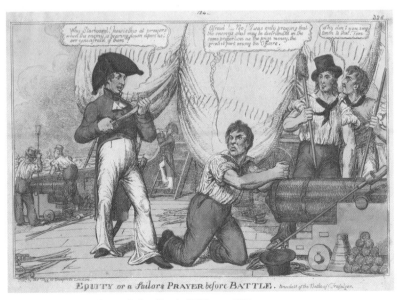

26. *Equity or a Sailors Prayer before Battle*, Williams, 1805.

and rechristened. About 450 ships were so purchased during the French Wars, and a well-equipped thirty-two-gun frigate could be valued at £16,000, a sizable sum.

Prize money varied widely. Luck was certainly a factor, but it helped to be clever, to have a fast and powerful ship such as a frigate and to be stationed close to enemy shipping lanes. Francis Austen, for all his good fortune in convoying valuable cargo, was often stuck on blockade duty, where he paced back and forth waiting for enemy ships to steal out of harbour while having few chances to capture anything. Those manning captured ships were the unluckiest of all, for their ships were not officially commissioned by the navy. If a 'prize crew' captured another enemy ship on the way back to a friendly port, the new prize and all its goods became the property of the Admiralty.

Not all prizes, however, were ships. Captured cities could also be a gold mine to a fortunate captain or admiral. All arms, ammunition and military supplies in captured fortifications belonged to the victor, as did ships captured in port and the goods of conquered (but not voluntarily surrendered) towns.

Daily Life in the Navy

Life in the navy could be difficult, demanding and unpredictable. Mail delivery was erratic at best, as a ship could be suddenly ordered away to another station with very little notice (*MP* 377–378, 388). The Austen family letters often reflect this reality. Letters (*P* 51) to and from Charles and Frank might arrive very late or out of order, so the family adopted the practice of many naval families, numbering their letters so that they could be put in order again upon arrival. As she was unsure where her letters might find him, Jane wrote to Francis twice to announce the death of their father in 1805; one letter went to Dungeness, while the other pursued him to Portsmouth. Frank numbered his letters, too. On 18 October 1805, he wrote to his fiancée Mary Gibson that your No. 3 has come to hand; it was brought by Brigadier-General Tilson and was enclosed under cover from Henry. It has been months on the journey. There are still three of yours missing, Nos. 5, 6 and 7, some of which I suppose are gone to seek me in the West Indies.

Naval officers and sailors often missed their families at home (*MP* 232). Parents and spouses died, children were born, finances improved or collapsed, all at a distance and without any knowledge of when a reunion might come. This state of affairs was made even worse during wartime when the family at home worried constantly about death in battle. At all times, death from disease or accident was a distinct possibility, and the Austens liked to hear frequently from their sailor sons, to be assured of their continuing health.

Worries about health and welfare extended to any dependents who sailed as well. Jane fretted over the condition of her niece Cassy, Charles' daughter, whom she thought looked thin and unwell due to her life aboard

Charles' ship. Cassy had been experiencing another of the discomforts
of life at sea: motion sickness.

The pseudonymous sailor Jack Nastyface included, in his memoirs,
a vivid description of life aboard for as man-of-war. At 4:00 a.m., he wrote,
a new watch came on deck and began holystoning the deck:

> Here the men suffer from being obliged to kneel down on the wetted
> deck and a gravelly sort of sand strewed over it. To perform this work
> is very injurious. In this manner the watch continues till about four
> bells or 6 o'clock; they then begin to wash and scrub the decks till seven
> bells, and at eight bells the boatswain's mate pipes to breakfast. This
> meal usually consists of burgoo made of coarse oatmeal and water;
> others will have scotch coffee which is burnt bread boiled in some water
> and sweetened with sugar. This is generally cooked in a hook-pot in
> the galley where there is a range. Nearly all the crew have one of these
> pots, a spoon and a knife; for these are things indispensable. There are
> also basons, plates, etc. which are kept in each mess, which generally
> consists of eight persons who berth in between two of the guns on the
> lower deck, where there is a board placed which swings with the rolling
> of the ship and dash all the crockery to pieces; they are then obliged
> to eat out of wooden or tin utensils, until they come into harbour.

Punishments at 11:00 a.m. were followed by dinner at 12 noon, and this
is the pleasantest part of the day, as at one bell the fifer is called to play
'Nancy Dawson' or some other lively tune, a well-known signal that the
grog is ready to be served out. It is the duty of the cook from each mess
to fetch and serve it out to his messmates, of which every man and boy
is allowed a pint, that is one gill of rum and three of water, to which is
added lemon acid sweetened with sugar. Here I must remark that the
cook comes in for the perquisites of office by reserving to himself an extra
portion of grog, which is called the over-plus and generally comes to the
double of a man's allowance. Thus the cook can take upon himself to be
the man of consequence, for he has the opportunity of inviting a friend
to partake of a glass or of paying any little debt he may have contracted.

Cooks who neglected their duties, he reported, were judged by a jury
of cooks from different messes; each man took a turn serving as cook for
his own group of messmates. Supper, he said, consisted of 'half a pint of
wine or a pint of grog to each man with biscuit, and cheese, or butter'.

Food was always of great concern to the navy, for sailors needed an
immense number of calories in order to perform their strenuous duties,
and the problem of providing the quantity of food needed for huge numbers
of men over long periods of time in limited space was always vexing.
Officers filled their own larders. Some brought live animals aboard to
be slaughtered as needed, while others brought preserved food of various
kinds; Frank Austen once took six hams cured by his mother.

There was a limited understanding of scurvy and the role played
by fresh provisions in its prevention, though vitamin C, the preventive

compound, was a long way from being discovered. Salt-preserved food was blamed for everything from general weakness to dysentery, and various types of food were tried as supplements, from sauerkraut to potatoes.

Likewise, there was a good deal of fiddling with the alcoholic beverages consumed by the crew. Grog was the standard drink aboard ship. This was a lightly alcoholic mixture of rum, fruit juice and water, which was given various names depending on the proportion of rum to water. 'Three-water grog', the default recipe, had a ratio of one part rum to three parts water, while 'five-water grog' – a mutinously weak drink – had a ratio of 1:5. Experimenters replaced the grog, from time to time, with wine or spruce beer, but these innovations were not popular. Grog and beer were considered the only decent beverages for a sailor, and substitutions were rarely tolerated for long.

The average sailor's diet, however, despite efforts at reform, remained monotonous, copious and heavily salted. Salt fish, beef and pork were supplemented with cheese, beer, bread and 'biscuit'. The last of these was a hard, round or hexagonal piece of bread, stamped with an iron press to insert holes and to stamp upon it the 'broad arrow' – a simple crow's-foot pattern indicating that the biscuit was the property of the navy. Biscuits were to be no more than a fifth of a pound in weight and were stored in barrels.

The officers ate their meals off pewter or silver plates, while the men ate off square wooden plates – hence, 'three square meals a day' – with a lip to prevent food from falling off the plates in rough seas. It is possibly a pewter mess kit that William Price seeks from William Turner, a merchant who was recorded as arranging supplies for sailors in Portsmouth in 1811.*

In their leisure hours, the men sewed new clothes for themselves, combed lice and fleas from their long hair and plaited their pigtails and sealed them with tar. Some sang, told stories or played music. Gambling was rife. Officers might read, keep logs and journals or lead the men in amateur theatrical presentations.

One activity that was seldom allowed was shore leave. Officers were frequently terrified that their men would desert a very sensible fear with regard to pressed men – and rarely permitted this greatest of all pleasures. Instead, they let prostitutes come aboard the ship, while peddlers pulled alongside in small boats to offer food, drink and trinkets for sale. Accommodations were better for the officers, but not by much. They had shared or private cabins, while the men had only 14–16 inches in which to sling a hammock, but the cabins were usually minuscule, and only the captain enjoyed the remotest approximation of privacy.

Still, though life aboard ship was cramped and often uncomfortable, it was not without its conveniences, especially for officers who had personal servants to pour their wine, serve their food and tend to their uniforms

*The Austens were acquainted with Turner, who was proposed as an agent for sending a letter to Francis in 1805 and who supplied a rug and corks to Charles in 1808 and 1815, respectively.

(*P* 64). Mrs Croft found the life quite acceptable, but she was not necessarily typical. Other officers' wives found life aboard ship intolerable, what with seasickness, the fear of death in battle and the lack of privacy. Betsey Fremantle, who accompanied her husband, Thomas, on a voyage, was disturbed by storms, the noise of the guns, the groans of the wounded and the brutality of flogging. Partly for the sake of the wives but mostly to avoid distraction, officers' wives were discouraged from accompanying their husbands on their voyages (*P* 31).

Sailors' Behaviour

Sailors were certainly not renowned for their pious or mannerly behaviour. Jack Nastyface noted that the more-experienced sailors loved to play tricks on new colleagues, heaping ridicule on them and playing pranks such as mutilating their clothing and stealing their shoes and blankets while their victims slept by using fishhooks and fishing line. Sailors whored, swore and drank heavily.

Drunkenness, above all, was rampant, especially in the West Indies, where men believed it would protect them from tropical diseases. Another sailor, Samuel Stokes, wrote that when he had prize money, 'I think I was not sober one hour while I was awake, while the money lasted.'

In part, this decadent behaviour was no doubt due to the rare opportunities to relieve a life of hard work and tedium interrupted only by brief periods of mortal danger. In part, it was a symptom of the eighteenth-century way of life, which at times revealed in cruelty, but to a large extent, it was also due to the nature of the shipboard population. The men, especially the pressed men, might be convicts or men who *ought* to have been convicts.

Behaviour among the officer ranks was sometimes only slightly better. Lord Nelson, almost universally lauded as a hero, was widely known to be an adulterer, and he was not the only one; more than one titled officer tried to bring a mistress aboard. Jane Austen's Admiral Crawford may have been intended, says Brian Southam, to represent such a debauched character.

Hazards at Sea: Punishment

The dangers (*MP* 235, 236) and discomforts of life at sea included far more than a tendency to sunburn (*P* 19–20). Sailors might suffer from shortages of food or water, storms, boredom, homesickness (*P* 235) and 'ruptures' (hernias).

For the men, as opposed to the officers, there was always the fear of corporal punishment. This usually meant flogging (*MP* 440), a punishment attended with much ceremony and observed by the whole crew in the hope of deterring future bad behaviour. Flogging could be imposed at the captain's discretion without a court-martial, and three dozen lashes was a typical sentence, although in one instance in 1795, when Francis Austen was a lieutenant, a man aboard his ship was given forty-nine lashes for theft. Flogging could be administered for a wide variety of crimes, including inattention to duty, improper performance of duties, drunkenness, mutinous talk, attempting to strike an officer or failing to report promptly for one's watch.

Some captains were far more willing than others to order floggings, and these became known throughout the fleet as 'flogging captains' or 'tartars'. They included Charles Paget (one of Charles Austen's superior officers), John Gore, Alexander Frazer (one of Francis' superiors) and, apparently, Francis Austen.

Even worse than an ordinary flogging was 'flogging through the fleet'. Reserved for serious offences where an example to all ships present was deemed necessary, such as attempted desertion, this was a circuit of floggings, one at each ship. Unlike a standard flogging, it could be administered only after a court-martial. The prisoner had stockings placed over his wrists to prevent the ropes from cutting into them as he writhed; he was lashed to a capstan bar and, attended by the master of arms and the ship's surgeon, was rowed from ship to ship. At each ship, boatswain's mates lashed him a specified number of times – about two dozen, according to Jack Nastyface – and then rolled him in a blanket for his journey to the next ship. If the man fainted, he would be held in the sick bay until he felt better, and then his punishment would resume. Nastyface wrote, 'When there are many ships in the fleet at the time of the court martial, this ceremony, if the prisoner can sustain it, will last nearly half the day ... his back resembles so much petrified liver.' John Nicol recounted the story of a man flogged through the fleet for stealing some treasure from a captured ship. This unfortunate sailor drank a large quantity of rum beforehand to dull his pain, but the stratagem was discovered, and the remainder of his punishment was 'delayed until he was sober'. His back, according to Nicol, was swollen 'like a pillow, black and blue'. Vinegar-soaked paper was laid on his wounds, and 'his shrieks rent the air'.

A common punishment for theft was running the gauntlet. The offender was seated in a tub, which was then lashed to a grating and drawn between two rows of men. The boatswain began by giving the offender a dozen lashes, and then the men standing in rows were obliged to strike the prisoner as he passed with a 'three yarn nettle', which Jack Nastyface describes as 'three rope yarns tightly laid together and knotted'. Periodically, the punishment administered by the ship's company was interrupted so that the boatswain's mates could lash him again with the cat o'nine tails. Running the gauntlet could be ordered by the captain without a court-martial.

There is also a reference in Austen's works to being 'run up the yardarm' (P 108). This could be a reference to the practice of keelhauling, obsolete in Austen's time but well known enough to have become archetypal for severity. In this type of punishment, a rope was slung from one yardarm to another, and the prisoner was raised to one yardarm, dunked in the ocean and hauled up on the other side, half drowned and much battered by the sharp barnacles on the ship's hull. Austen's reference could equally refer to hangings for mutiny, which were traditionally conducted at the yardarm.

For officers, punishments were very different. A court-martial might issue a reprimand, cashier (dishonourably discharge) the officer involved or reduce him in rank or seniority. An example of the process can be seen in the March 1807 court-martial of Sir Home Popham, who was accused of disobeying orders by leaving the Cape of Good Hope undefended while he took his squadron on an unauthorised and personally profitable mission to wrest Buenos Aires from the Spanish. Popham was a complex character who had, in 1805, been charged with skimming profits from the repair of his ship; although acquitted, the rumours alone were enough to taint his career. Deeply concerned with the health and safety of his men, he was an expert in combined sea and land manoeuvres, the inventor of the sea fencibles, an experimenter with mines and torpedoes and the creator of an efficient system of signalling that was used at Trafalgar. He was widely distrusted within the navy, however, considered a charlatan, and tarnished by reports of shady business dealings. Austen wrote a poem in his defence (*Popham*, *MW* 446), perhaps because of her Tory sympathies Popham was a Tory – and perhaps because of some sort of indirect personal acquaintance, unproven but possible, as Francis Austen and Popham were in the East Indies at the same time, and Henry Austen may have been involved in Popham's attempts to profit from his South American adventure. The evidence in either case is entirely circumstantial. Popham, incidentally, experienced the fate of many reprimanded officers; with a change in government, he was back in favour again.

Hazards at Sea: Battle

A sailor's greatest fear, especially in the heat of the moment, was being killed in battle. Naval battles had once been gentlemanly affairs, in which frigates not taking direct part in a fleet-to-fleet combat were exempt from attack, but in the 1790s this attitude changed, and by the Battle of the Nile in 1798 all ships present were considered fair game. For the officers in particular, who stood to gain substantially both in prize money and in reputation, battle was a thing to be sought; Francis Austen regretted bitterly being temporarily absent from the fleet at the time of Trafalgar. Particularly valuable was 'an action with some superior force' (*MP* 375), in which the skill of the officers was made evident, bringing them to the favourable attention of the Admiralty.

For the men, it was a different story. Their share of prize money was small, and their risk was enormous. Battle was confusing and terrifying, as the accounts of ordinary sailors attest. Samuel Leech's job was to run powder cartridges back and forth to his gun. He would dash to the magazine, where boys passed the powder through a hole in a wooden screen, cover a cartridge with his jacket 'to prevent the powder taking fire before it reaches the gun' and hurry to the gun so that the crew could fire. He acknowledged being frightened the entire time, but he kept up a brave front because he had no choice, praying all the while to be spared. Though he was fortunate enough to survive the war, he saw his share of death in battle and vividly describes the tearful farewell of one messmate to another, carrying the dead friend's body in the wake of a battle and with his own hands consigning it to the sea. During the battle, gun crews had little information about its progress. They could see only their gun, their little patch of deck and the view through the gun port; most of their information about the battle came from women and boys carrying gunpowder.

Francis Austen, writing to his wife after the Battle of St Domingo (P 26), noted, 'Our people behaved admirably well, and displayed astonishing coolness during the whole time.'

After the battle, the bodies of the dead were heaved overboard, and men went around the decks, enquiring after their messmates everywhere they went. Dead sailors were sewn up in their sailcloth hammocks before being buried at sea; the bodies were usually weighted with a cannonball, and the last stitch through the hammock also went through the dead sailor's nose, in case he was faking or merely unconscious.

Small wonder, then, that the average sailor anticipated battle with feelings of dread. He had no way to escape his fate and would be subjected to extraordinary punishment if he tried. He would be oblivious of most of the action and would not know whether his side had won or lost until it was almost too late to do anything about it. He could only hope. For relatives at home, too, there was fear of battle (P 252), for actual combat was the condensed version of all their concern for their loved ones.

The goal of a naval engagement was to cripple the enemy without actually sinking her, for a sunken ship meant far less prize money. Accordingly, fire was directed ideally either at the masts, thus taking down the sails by force and rendering the enemy incapable of manoeuvring, or at the men on the decks. The latter tactic was particularly important if there was any expectation of having to board the enemy ship. For destroying the masts, cannonballs were used. Rigging and sails could be damaged with chain shot (shaped like two hockey pucks joined by a short, heavy chain) or bar shot (shaped like a dumbbell), while grapeshot and canister shot were effective at killing men. Grapeshot was, according to Leech, a bundle of 'seven or eight balls confined to an iron and tied in cloth'. Canister shot was 'made by filling a powder canister with balls, each as large as two or three musket balls'. Both tended to scatter with 'direful effect' among the men on deck.

Hazards at Sea: Disease and Injury

For all the terrors of battle, however, the biggest killers at sea were disease and accidental injury. Accounts of the numbers involved vary widely, but it is certain that death from disease and accident were many times more common than deaths in action. Accidents could include falls from masts and rigging, injuries or deaths in fires that spread rapidly aboard wooden ships loaded with gunpowder, and hernias. It is possible that Mr Price, in Mansfield Park, was injured in battle, but it seems far more likely, according to statistics, that he suffered some sort of accidental injury (*MP* 4).

Illnesses (*P* 66) that afflicted many sailors included scurvy, 'yellow jack' (yellow fever) and various sexually transmitted diseases.*

Disease flourished in ships, partly because of the lack of fresh food, partly because of the crowded living conditions, and partly because, for all the attention to the ship's cleanliness, there was little understanding of the connection between personal hygiene and health. A great many sailors could not swim and had little occasion to take baths, and the 'head' – the ship's toilet – was sometimes smeared with faeces as a joke at the expense of the next person to sit down. The ship's surgeon was unlikely to wash his hands between patients, and vermin of all sorts inhabited the ship, from rats to lice to weevils. The lice were particularly dangerous, as they carried typhus. Casualty rates from disease were especially high in the Caribbean, where the standard complement of military diseases was augmented by a variety of tropical ailments.

Desertion and Mutiny

Under the combined weight of press-gangs, crowded living conditions, monotonous food, the fear of death in battle and the constant threat of disease, it is hardly surprising that some sailors should wish to escape the naval establishment or at least improve their working conditions. Desertions, especially of pressed men, were common. Francis Austen had thirteen men desert his ship at St Christopher in 1806, shortly before the Battle of St Domingo. Desertion was especially high in the Caribbean, where the men had a real fear of disease magnified by legend and superstition, and highest of all in Jamaica, which had numerous trade routes and thus more opportunities to sign on to a ship out of the region. From 1793 to 1801 alone, there were 3,000 desertions in the Caribbean.

Mutinies, unlike desertions, were aimed less at getting away from the service than at improving conditions within it. Men mutinied over the discipline imposed by officers, reductions in grog rations, low pay and bad food. A significant mutiny erupted at Spithead in 1797, primarily over pay and food; at that time, wages had not been raised since the mid-seventeenth century. Acknowledging the justice of the complaints, the Admiralty granted the men's requests and imposed no punishment on the mutineers. However, a second revolt at the Nore over much the same issues was perceived by the Admiralty as superfluous and disruptive and was harshly suppressed, with several executions of lead mutineers.

*The presence of contagious disease aboard was signalled to other ships by the use of a yellow quarantine flag.

Ships

Ships were chiefly categorised by size, rigging and armament. Austen, as the sister of two naval men, would have been keenly aware of the differences between ships. As her brothers moved from ship to ship, their pay, status and duties altered, as did their opportunity to take valuable prizes. The number of guns on a ship and the consequent size necessary to sustain that number of guns determined its 'rate'. First-rate ships were thus the largest, with three gun decks (*MP* 403) and a crew of 900. They carried more than 100 guns until 1810, more than 110 guns after 1810; 120 guns would have been a typical number. Second rates had 84 to 100 guns (90 to 110 after 1810); third rates carried 70 to 84 (80 to 90); fourth rates carried 50 to 70 (60 to 80).

Fifth- and sixth-rate vessels were frigates with only one gun deck. They were less useful for pounding the enemy with monumental broadsides during fleet actions, but they were splendid for sailing quickly across the seas, scooping up prizes. (Francis Austen, like most ambitious captains, longed to command a frigate.) Fifth-rate frigates carried thirty-two to fifty guns (thirty-two to sixty after 1810), and sixth rates, both before and after 1810, had anything up to thirty-two guns, though few of these ships had fewer than twenty guns. A sixth rate, in contrast to a first rate, might have a crew of only 135. A technicality of rank made the same ship either a sixth-rate or unrated, depending on the rank of its captain. A ship of this size with a post-captain was a sixth rate, but the same ship with a commander in charge was merely a sloop (*MP* 299, 372, 384; *P* 65–66). A sloop might also be an even smaller ship of as few as ten guns, seldom able to capture a prize of any value.

Guns were placed symmetrically on both sides of the ship, so that the number of guns was always even; Jane Austen makes a joke about this in a juvenile work, in which she sails her heroes from France to England 'in a man of War of 55 Guns' (*H&E*, *MW* 36). Accounts of ships in the newspapers (*MP* 232; *P* 30, 66), Navy List (*MP* 389; *P* 30, 64) and naval records often indicate the number of guns after the ship's name, for example, *Speedy* (14) or *Neptune* (98). Mr Price, in praising his son William's new sloop, the *Thrush*, expresses his praise in terms of the number of guns: 'anybody in England would take her for an eight-and-twenty' (*MP* 380).

A ship's defence and offence, however, depended only in part on the strength of its armament. Another factor was speed and manoeuvrability, which was largely determined by its sails and rigging. The sails were made of 2-foot-wide panels of heavy flax-and-hemp canvas, stitched by a master sailmaker whose skilled labour earned him much respect, a warrant officer's rank and freedom from impressment. The outer edge of each sail was sewn to a rope with special twine that was often spun by sailors' widows and was sealed with a compound of beeswax and turpentine. The finished sails were either mounted on the proper yards (horizontal poles attached to the masts) or stored in the hold, marked with a tally, a small flat piece of wood that bore the ship's name, the type of sail and the amount and weight of canvas in that particular sail.

Other important ship's equipment included rope, tar, additional canvas for making such items as hammocks and clothing, anchors, a lightning rod to minimise the danger of fire and ballast. Rope was made in special buildings called 'ropewalks' that might be as much as a quarter of a mile long. Dried hemp was combed into yarn, which was made into thread and then twisted into strands. The rope maker walked backwards in the ropewalk with an approximately sixty-five-pound bundle of hemp wrapped around his waist. As he walked, he spun or twisted the rope into various thicknesses. A three-strand rope was 'hawser laid'; a pair of two-strand ropes twisted together made a 'shroud laid' rope; and three hawser-laid ropes spun together were 'cable laid'. Most ropes were 120 fathoms (720 feet) long, but the ropewalk had to be longer than this, as the strands before they were twisted were longer than 720 feet (just as a braid is shorter than the same hair falling freely).

The rope, tarred for water resistance, was used to hold sails in place and sometimes to keep the ship in place, either by attachment to an anchor or, when in harbour, to a mooring buoy. Jane Austen made a slight mistake in the first edition of *Mansfield Park* when she described the Thrush as under weigh. 'Under weigh' implies the weighing of an anchor, which would not have been the case for a ship in harbour, and Austen, perhaps upon advice from one of her brothers, changed it to 'slipped her moorings' for the 1816 edition (*MP* 380). When the anchor was dropped, one spoke not of being in harbour but of being at anchorage (*P* 234).

Tar, which was so common on a ship that it gave its name to the slang word for a British sailor, could be made of pitch, pine resin, coal tar or bitumen. It was used for sealing and waterproofing on sails, hats, coats, planks and ropes. Sailors used it in their pigtails as a preventive against vermin, and surgeons used it to seal stumps after amputations.

Ballast could be made either of iron or of 'shingle', an assortment of seaside stones that was cheap and widely available but more likely to shift and to pummel the inside of the hull. There was plenty of shingle ballast lying on the beaches near Portsmouth, which was fortunate, as the larger warships might have an 8-foot layer of it in their holds, serving to lower the centre of gravity and make the ships more stable in the water. Cargo, anchor, cannonballs and other items could also be embedded in the ballast to keep them from rolling around the hold.

Supplying ships with all this material could take a long time and was one of the principal bottlenecks in getting ships to sea. The process was also, as Cochrane noted, full of corruption and false economy. Bolts were improperly driven to save time. Unsatisfactory clothing was supplied to the sailors at inflated prices. Supplies were damaged, stolen or resold before their arrival and consequently never even made it to their ships. Fraudulent billing, 'hampering' (gifts of wine, ale, etc. to inspectors and clerks) and outright bribery were rampant.

The ships themselves were built of oak in dockyards like the one at Portsmouth or in old ships called 'sheer hulks' (*MP* 380), too old for active service and turned instead into floating dockyards. The Portsmouth dockyard was surrounded by a red brick wall and, like most dockyards, housed an enormous supply of timber and other materials; this was an absolute necessity, for a large ship like HMS *Victory* could require 2,500 large trees – the produce of 60 acres of woodland – to construct. A ship of *Victory*'s size also needed four acres of sails and 30 miles of rope.

Dockyards, because of their scale and activity, were popular tourist attractions. Artists, writers and ordinary travellers came to marvel at the piles of timber (*MP* 403) and the scurrying shipwrights. At Portsmouth, the dockyard (*MP* 372, 388, 389, 400, 402) covered 82 acres, had forty-five machines (in 1810) producing 130,000 pulley blocks a year and already had Nelson's *Victory* on display as an added attraction.

Periodic maintenance was required to keep ships in good condition, and this was sometimes performed at the dockyards and sometimes at sea. The upper portions of the ship were painted, while the portions below the waterline had to be either tarred to prevent infestations of sea worms or brought in occasionally to have the worm-ridden planks replaced. Gaps that developed between planks had to be filled with tar or oakum; the oakum was pounded in, while tar was heated and then ladled into the seams. Drips were sanded away with holystones.

Reputation

Except for a few bleak periods, when consecutive naval defeats accumulated to an embarrassing degree, the navy was highly regarded by the general public (*S&S* 103; *MP* 109; *P* 99, 167). Its officer ranks were considered a perfectly acceptable destination for sons of the gentry and aristocracy (*MP* 91), and the 'jolly tars' who made up the crew were fondly regarded by the British citizenry (*P* 18–19). In his derision for the service, Sir Walter Elliot was in a distinct minority, and his prejudice against sailors would automatically have disposed Austen's readers to dislike him (*P* 19–20). The navy was widely referred to as 'the wooden walls of England' and considered the best defence against invasion and the protector of British overseas trade. The army and militia fared poorly by comparison, chiefly because the English were deeply suspicious of standing armies as potential instruments of tyranny.

Austen does more than fall in line with the general idea of naval excellence. She specifically notes their 'alertness' (*P* 48), 'domestic virtues' (*P* 252) and 'national importance' (*P* 252). This is a tribute to her sailor brothers and their colleagues, as is her treatment of sailors in general in her works. Her principal naval characters – William Price, Admiral Croft and Captains Wentworth, Harville and Benwick – are all virtuous and admirable men, a statement that cannot be made about her clergymen or her soldiers. Even the overly emotional and poetically enthusiastic Benwick, the most likely of all of them to be ridiculous, is handled with gentleness. Dick Musgrove (*P* 67), who appears only indirectly, and some of Admiral Croft's acquaintances, who also never speak, are the only ones referred to in a negative manner. Admiral Crawford is certainly a negative character, but he, too, never appears on centre stage and merely influences events from afar.

Austen may have felt a special need to defend the navy, however, at the time she wrote *Persuasion*. Defeats in the War of 1812 had tarnished the reputation of the service. The prince regent was, in Byron's words, 'all for the land-service, / Forgetting Duncan, Nelson, Howe, and Jervis', and many Britons agreed with him. In the latter parts of the Napoleonic Wars, attention had shifted away from the early sea victories at the Nile and Trafalgar to the land campaigns in Spain and the final victory at Waterloo.

See also Marines; Time.

Newspaper

The newspaper (*Lesley, MW* 135; *Cath, MW* 215; *NA* 197–198, 203; *S&S* 106, 107, 108; *MP* 110, 118, 389, 439; *E* 206; *P* 43) was born in the early years of the eighteenth century and soon became an essential aspect of urban life. By 1783, London had nine daily papers (*MP* 438) and ten that appeared two or three times a week. In 1790, the numbers had risen to fourteen dailies and nine bi- or tri-weeklies, and by 1811 the total number of papers had risen again to fifty-two, including several Sunday papers that were technically illegal (due to sabbatarian restrictions) but extremely popular nonetheless. The circulation of these papers differed, but historians of the newspaper industry have theorised that a circulation of about 1,500 to 2,000 was necessary to keep a paper solvent and successful. London's *Daily Gazetteer* had a circulation of about 1,650 in 1790; the *Leeds Mercury* claimed in April 1795 that its circulation was 1,500. The *Morning Post* claimed sales of 5,000 copies per day in 1778, and the *Daily Advertiser* claimed equal circulation in 1779, but both these figures may be inflated. For short periods of time, a newspaper with a popular political perspective might see a jump in its circulation; William Cobbett's *Political Register*, for example, was selling 40,000 to 50,000 copies a week during the political turmoil that followed the Napoleonic Wars, but this dropped to 400 when he was forced to raise prices in the 1820s.

The number of provincial papers also rose dramatically. There had been only ten newspapers outside London in 1710, but this had grown to somewhere between sixty-five and seventy in the 1790s. Sixteen towns had more than one paper. They needed slightly smaller circulation than

London papers to survive, but many did much more than survive, and some, in the 1780s and 1790s, were selling as many as 2,500 to 4,000 copies per day. Most borrowed the bulk of their news from London papers, adding items of local interest as necessary and tailoring their choice of copied articles to the reading interests of the local populace. By 1801, provincial papers were selling more total copies than London papers; of the 16 million tax stamps sold that year, 7 million applied to London papers and 9 million to papers in the provinces.

Estimating total circulation is somewhat easier because newspapers were subject to a stamp tax. This had been introduced in 1712 and occasionally raised, reaching a peak at the end of the Napoleonic Wars. (Publishers then added a penny or two to cover their costs and generate profit.) Calculating the total number of newspapers produced would seem to be fairly simple: look at the tax records and find the number of papers and readers, but the reality was far more complicated.

In 1775, 12.6 million newspaper stamps were issued, meaning that an average of 34,521 papers were printed each day. Other contemporary estimates put the number higher, with perhaps 41,000 to 45,000 papers being printed each day in London alone. In 1801, 16 million stamps were issued, and in 1816, this had risen to 22 million, but we must assume that the actual number of newspapers was even higher. This was because not all papers paid the tax. Some, like the *Political Register* before the 1820s, operated illegally instead. The tax also, despite being based on the paper's size, does not necessarily show the actual size of a newspaper. Printers evaded the tax by issuing a standard paper and then adding a free supplement that was exempt.

The question of readership is further complicated by the fact that not all newspapers had a single reader or even a single owner. Some newspapers were bought by inns and alehouses and used to entice customers inside. Some were bought by newspaper reading rooms that took in up to eighty different papers and charged readers a fee for access to all of them. Others were bought by one man and read aloud to a crowd at an alehouse or on a street corner or lent, when the original owner was finished, to friends (*S&S* 30; *MP* 382, 384). On occasion, although the publishers of newspapers hated this practice and tried unsuccessfully to stamp it out, the vendors (*P* 135) of papers would 'rent' a paper for a penny, allowing passers-by to read the paper and then return it. Those who bought a paper in the traditional manner would usually take it home, where it would be read by various members of the family. Estimates vary, but each paper produced may actually have been read by as many as ten or twenty people.

The upper classes may have been the biggest consumers of newspapers, as they could afford to pay the high prices necessitated by the increasing stamp tax, but working-class people could share a paper, and some even formed clubs for this purpose. A reported 5,000 such clubs existed between 1746 and 1821, each formed of perhaps half a dozen to a dozen families who shared newspapers. Foreign observers, radicals and conservatives alike agreed that working-class readership was very high and that the English people as a whole seemed to be remarkably well informed.

Surviving copies show that the standard newspaper for most of the eighteenth century was four pages – one large sheet of paper printed on both sides and then folded crosswise to make four four-column pages. The newspaper of Austen's day, however, was a good deal denser than that of Addison's or Swift's, because smaller type was being used, and articles and advertisements were increasingly warring with each other for space. There were still no illustrations, however. By the end of the Napoleonic Wars, some newspapers, including the *London Times*, had gone to an eight-page format. They were assisted in this expansion by the invention in 1803 of a paper-making machine and the resulting drop in the price of paper. The typical newspaper might be owned jointly by several people, run by a hired editor and produced by a small staff. The printing was often done by a 'jobbing' printer who produced several different newspapers at once.

Newspapers could be picked up at the printer's office or bought from street vendors. They could also be sent through the mail, and from 1792 the post office delivered newspapers in this way for free. Some papers were also delivered by newspaper employees to individual houses. In the provinces, successful papers had a widely distributed network of newsmen and agents who sold papers and collected advertisements; the *Sheffield Advertiser*, for example, had agents in nineteen towns in 1790. The printer would deliver copies to the agents and to the newsmen who delivered on foot; in one study of a Derby newspaper, most subscribers got their papers the same day they were printed, and the rest of the customers received theirs by the following morning.

Newspaper Content

Newspapers got their information from all kinds of sources: soldiers serving overseas, diplomats, members of Parliament who wanted to be sure that their speeches were reported accurately, private citizens writing letters, and outright plagiarism from other newspapers. The items were selected and slanted according to the political preferences of the editor, for while many papers claimed to be politically unbiased, many others made no pretence of neutrality. These supported either the government or the opposition by choosing to print articles that favoured one side and by printing letters to the editor that espoused only their own viewpoint.

Until late in the eighteenth century, printing speeches made in the House of Commons was illegal, but most papers ignored this stricture. Their reporters sat in the gallery and, forbidden to take notes until the 1780s, remembered as much as they could of what was said and then hurried out to jot it all down. Some reporters had truly prodigious memories and could retain entire speeches, word for word, in their heads. Their job, however, was hampered by the fact that any member could call for the gallery to be cleared at any time and by the fact that the gallery was routinely cleared before a vote, but they were assisted by MPs who wanted their glorious speeches to be printed verbatim. These MPs would slip a reporter a copy of the speech in advance, a tactic that could sometimes prove potentially embarrassing if the speech, for one reason or another, was never made. John Wilkes, for example, once begged for permission to make a particular speech because, he explained, 'I have sent a copy to the "Public Advertiser", and how ridiculous should I appear if it were published without having been delivered.'

The government, though it never explicitly limited the freedom of speech of opposition papers, went to some lengths to control the political content. They paid editors to include certain pieces and exclude others and paid 'subsidies' to favourite papers. The post office, in providing its free delivery, also managed to misdirect opposition papers from time to time. Readers were not oblivious to the slant in coverage and sought the most accurate reporting. The *Morning Chronicle* and the *Gazetteer* were considered among London's most politically balanced papers.

Politics in one form or another was the staple subject of most newspapers (*NA* 71), but it was far from being the only subject. Spectacular trials and marital scandals (*MP* 439–440) were always popular, as were stories about escaped madwomen and near-death adventures. Newspapers covered crimes such as robberies by notorious highwaymen, and quite early they began printing shipping news. Arrivals of merchant vessels and navy ships were noted (*MP* 232), as were the outcomes of naval and land battles (*P* 30). Births (*S&S* 246), deaths (*Evelyn, MW* 190), bankruptcies and marriages (*S&S* 217; *P&P* 336), too, received brief mention, when the parties involved were socially prominent enough to be of interest. Other topics included US and European affairs, fashion, literary and theatrical reviews, economic news such as stock and commodities prices, provincial news and sports – chiefly horse racing, cockfighting and cricket.

Dailies tended to be heavier on politics, while weeklies were more like magazines and had a broader and more balanced set of topics.

Newspapers also published advertisements, which took up more room than anything else except political news. There were advertisements for real estate (*Scraps, MW* 177; *MP* 342; *P* 15) and employment (*Sand, MW* 366). Clergymen seeking livings or curacies advertised their availability, and those who had the power to bestow clerical livings advertised the value of the living, the likely life span of the current occupant and the amount for which the living could be bought. Similarly, servants advertised for posts, and employers advertised for servants. Horses (*MP* 342), patent medicines, cream of violet soap, coffee, tea, wine and cosmetics were all touted in advertisements. Private groups used advertisements to notify each other of joint-stock company meetings or to lobby for new projects or for the benefit of a particular occupational group. The lottery issued its notices through advertisements, and people who had lost items advertised for their return. There were political advertisements and announcements of upcoming horse races, pleas to use such-and-such a commercial staple or such-and-such a dentist. Advertisements, like the newspapers themselves, were taxed, with the person or company placing the advertisement paying a few pennies to the government along with the newspaper's fee.

See also Reading.

P

Parish

The parish (*Evelyn, MT4T* 180; *Cath, MT4T* 193; *Sand, MT4T* 365–366, 368; *P&P* 101; *MP* 30, 93; *E* 20, 456; *P* 39, 125) was both a religious and a governmental unit, serving both as a division within the Church of England and as an important centre of local administration. It was a legal entity and required an act of Parliament to divide, which was sometimes necessary because certain parishes, especially in the industrialising north, grew so rapidly in population that traditional services were overwhelmed. The number of parishes therefore varied slightly, but for most of the eighteenth century there were about 10,000. There was little consistency as to physical size or population (*E* 456). The parish of Childerley in East Anglia, for example, had a population of only 47 in 1801 and 54 in 1841, while another East Anglian parish, Doddington, had a population of 7,500 in 1830. In theory, one parson was supposed to serve each of these parishes with identical efficiency.

As a religious unit, the parish had a parson (*MP* 248–249), who might or might not have a curate (*S&S* 61) to assist him in his duties. A few of the physically larger parishes had 'chapels of ease' so that not everyone had to travel to the main parish church for services. There would also be a parish clerk (*E* 383) who recorded all Anglican baptisms, marriages (*P&P* 318) and funerals and participated in the church services by leading the congregation during responsive readings. Other staff took charge of the graveyard, and a group of leading citizens called churchwardens (*E* 455) made sure that the church was kept in good repair. Each parish was part of a deanery, which was part of a larger archdeaconry, which in turn was part of a diocese run by one of England's twenty-six bishops. Again, the number of parishes in each diocese was variable. Rochester had 150 parishes, while Lincoln had ten times that number, and the other dioceses fell somewhere in between.

In its secular capacity, the parish served as the local unit for the collection and distribution of the 'poor rates' – local charity dispensed to the poor of that particular parish. Overseers of the poor (*E* 455), who set the rates and dispensed the aid, could be nitpicky about who had the right to charity. Pregnant, itinerant women were sometimes driven away so that their unborn children would not become 'chargeable' to the parish, and even unmarried women who were natives of a particular parish were often subjected to pressure from officials to name the fathers of their illegitimate children; if the father could not be made to pay support, at least he might reside in another parish, and the impoverished children would become another region's responsibility.

Overseers of the poor were selected once a year at a meeting of the vestry (*NA* 209), usually at Easter. At this time, the previous year's books were examined and the rates for the new year set. Other parish officers were also installed, such as surveyors of the highways, who were responsible for maintaining the major roads that ran through the parish. Complaints were often made about this system, which tended to fall unfairly on parishes with long stretches of busy roads. Austen does not specify what 'parish business' (*E* 221, 425) her characters engage in, but one suspects that some of her gentlemen served the vestry, at one time or another, as churchwardens and possibly as overseers of the poor.

See also Clergy.

Pen

The pen (*Hist Eng, MW* 149; *Cath, MW* 192; *LS, MW* 283; *NA* 216; *S&S* 180, 203, 287; *MP* 59, 265, 424, 426, 461; *P* 233, 249), towards the end of Austen's life, was on the verge of its first major transformation in centuries, but the pens she used were still more like those used by Shakespeare than those used by Mark Twain or Henry James. Pens were still crafted out of quills, wing feathers collected from a variety of birds, but mainly from geese. Lincolnshire, with its great goose flocks, was a prime producer of quills. Four or five feathers from each wing were gathered during the moulting season; according to author Isaac Taylor, writing in 1823, this was near the end of March. The feathers were then 'dutched', or baked in hot sand, to remove the outer layer of skin that surrounded the shaft of the feather. Finally, they were cleaned in a solution of alum and tied in bunches to be sold.

The bird's natural wing curvature influenced the shape of the pens; left-wing feathers were said to be more comfortable for right-handed writers, while right-wing quills were better for left-handers. The pen's nib, or writing tip, would be formed by using a sharp penknife (*E* 338) to cut an angled slice from the end of the feather; then the remaining thin tip would be slit parallel to the shaft. A new pen, once crafted, had to be tested on a piece of scrap paper to be sure the point would work properly. If it did not, or if it were damaged later and began to spatter, it would have to be mended by having its point cut anew (*P&P* 47). Repeated mending might eventually whittle a pen away to almost nothing, making it hard to hold. In between uses, it was essential to keep the tip clean and moist, so most inkstands had quill-sized holes around the inkwell in which pens could be safely propped.

Efforts were made to extend the length of pens. In 1809, Joseph Bramah patented a method of cutting one quill into several disposable nibs that could be mounted on a durable holder, but this was a transitional technology. Steel pens, which would come to dominate the nineteenth century, were already on the way. The first known example in England was made in 1780 by a Birmingham manufacturer, Samuel Harrison, for chemist Dr Joseph Priestley. Such pens were first patented in 1808 and began to be produced by machine in 1822, but the early specimens were awkward to use. Reservoir pens were patented in 1809 but likewise took some time to become widely adopted.

See also Pencil; Writing.

Pencil

Graphite was a well-known material long before Jane Austen was born; a huge deposit of unusually pure graphite had been discovered in Borrowdale, Cumberland, in 1564. At first thought to be a type of lead (and named 'plumbeus' as a result), graphite was discovered in 1779 to be a carbon compound, and it acquired its modern name, derived from the Greek word 'to write', in 1789. As this new name implies, people had rapidly discovered its utility for making marks. Mistakes, it was found, could be scratched out by rubbing bread crumbs on the paper – a laborious process, but much easier than trying to fix an inkblot. Writing with a pencil was also easier than writing with a pen, for a pen required a precise angle, the constant trimming and mending of the nib, dipping in an inkwell and blotting. Austen, it was noted after her death, abandoned writing in pen when she became too ill to perform all these tasks: 'She wrote whilst she could hold a pen, and with a pencil when a pen was become too laborious.' Ease of use and ease of correction both contributed to the pencil's success.

Graphite soon became a popular substance for drawing (though not yet for composing letters or other documents). However, when the Borrowdale deposit was depleted in the seventeenth century, some way had to be found of using less-pure chunks of the material. The most common solution was to grind the graphite into dust and add some sort of adhesive, then roll the resulting mass into a thin stick and place it in a holder. This graphite insert, in a nod to the original name of 'plumbeus', was still called a 'lead' (*E* 339).

At first the holders were made of metal, later of wood. By Austen's day, therefore, the pencil (*S&S* 41; *MP* 227; *E* 47, 187, 339) was about halfway to its modern form. It was typically a thin, baked, round lead encased in

Pencil

a wooden stick, just as it is today. However, the wooden holders were not equipped with an eraser; though Joseph Priestley, in 1770, had espoused a South American vegetable gum and named it 'rubber' for its ability to correct pencil marks, the vulcanisation of rubber would not be achieved until 1839, and the affixed pencil eraser would have to wait until the 1850s. Mechanical pencils, also, post-date Austen's life. They would be invented in 1822.

See also Pen; Writing.

Phaeton

One of the most fashionable vehicles of its day, the phaeton (*Clifford*, *MW* 43; *NA* 85, 87, 93; *P&P* 158, 168) was a four-wheeled carriage that had many variants. In general, it had four wheels, the back wheels being larger than the front ones. It was most commonly pulled by a pair of horses or ponies (*P&P* 67, 325), harnessed side by side, but one print shows a lady driving a phaeton with four ponies, and one type of phaeton was designed for use with only one horse. Austen's nephew recalled in his *Memoir* that the marchioness of Lansdowne, who lived in Southampton at the same time as Jane Austen, owned a phaeton that she drove out with six or eight ponies, 'each pair decreasing in size, and becoming lighter in colour, through all the grades of dark brown, bay and chestnut, as it was placed farther away from the carriage'.

A small sleighlike body with room for only two people sat atop very high springs. The body of the carriage might sit very far forward, centred between the pairs of wheels, or even over the back wheels; the 'Perch-High' phaeton, for example, had its body directly over the 4-foot-high front wheels, with 5-foot-8-inch rear wheels located far behind, under a platform for servants or baggage. Wherever the body was located, there was generally space underneath it and over the axles for trunks that carried belongings on longer journeys and also lowered the carriage's centre of gravity. Some phaetons, but not all, had a folding leather roof that could be lifted in case of rain, but this roof only partially covered the driver and passenger; the phaeton was a fair-weather conveyance.

The tall springs of the phaeton made it unlike any other vehicle on the road and opened it up to ridicule. A 1776 print, *Phaetona or Modern Female Taste*, exaggerates the female phaeton driver's hairstyle and shrinks her horses for comic effect; a 1780 effort, *The Delight of Ply[mouth]*, shows a bulky man climbing a tall ladder to get into his phaeton's seat. However, even realistic depictions show the base of the seat as being above the level of the taller wheels, as indeed it had to be to leave room below for luggage. This height, combined with the overall lightness of the carriage, made the phaeton liable to tipping. Austen therefore uses a phaeton for a fortuitous carriage accident in *Love and Freindship*:

From this Dilemma I was most fortunately relieved by an accident truly apropos; it was the lucky overturning of a Gentleman's Phaeton, on the' road which ran murmuring behind us. ... We instantly quitted our seats & ran to the rescue of those who but a few moments before had been in so elevated a situation as a fashionably high Phaeton, but who were now laid low and sprawling in the Dust. (*MW* 98–99)

The phaeton's dangers, however, only increased its attractiveness to those who were, or wished to appear, daring. It remained popular among fashionable people (*NA* 232) and, along with the curricle, was the sports car of its day.

See also Carriages and Coaches.

Picturesque

In the 1790s, as Austen began her first mature works of literature, two budding fashions that had been raging for centuries intersected and produced the fashion known as the 'picturesque' (*NA* 111, 177; *S&S* 47). One of the new interests was in art. While the ruling class had always had its portraits painted for the sake of posterity (*Sand*, *MW* 427; *NA* 180–181, 191; *S&S* 215; *P&P* 52–53, 247, 249, 250; *MP* 84–85; *P* 40), the eighteenth century saw a rising interest in the acquisition of 'accomplishments' by ladies of leisure (*Cath*, *MW* 198; *P&P* 39). In theory, accomplishments were supposed to equip them to make their homes decorative, pleasant places for their husbands and children. Art became one of these essential skills, and a well-educated young woman who aspired to gentility was expected to try her hand at sketching or painting in order to see if she had a gift for it (*MP* 18, 19). Artistic performance was less essential to a man's education, but an educated man was expected to be knowledgeable about art (*S&S* 19), and many men drew (*E* 364). Jane's brother Frank, a naval officer, made very competent sketches and maps during his career, for example. Jane's sister Cassandra, too, dabbled in art – it is to her pencil that we owe the only sketch of Jane Austen's face made during her lifetime – and so did many of Austen's characters (*Sand*, *MW* 421; *S&S* 17, 30, 104, 105, 108, 234–235, 281; *E* 43, 44, 46–47, 85, 150, 455–456). Jane herself, though she received some education in drawing and painting as a child, was never an enthusiastic artist, although she did enjoy visiting galleries of paintings in London.

The other passion that had seized England was the desire to travel, not for business or necessity or religion but merely to see new things. It was the birth of tourism, and much of what we now associate with tourism – standardised expectations of lodgings, professional tour guides, even souvenirs – became widespread during the late eighteenth and early nineteenth centuries. Travel for pleasure was not entirely new; wealthy young men had for decades been taking the Grand Tour, a journey abroad of months or even years as a formal completion of their education, but tourism by the middle and labouring classes was a new phenomenon, and tourism within England rather than on the continent was, likewise, quite novel. For the first time, the English were racing around England to *look at things*, and, as anyone would when learning to do something new, they were curious to know how to do it properly.

The third influence in the development of the picturesque was one that had been a continuing interest for generations: landscape gardening. Owners of country estates had long been fiddling with the best way to present their grounds to the eye. During the sixteenth and seventeenth centuries, this had been accomplished by ornate, geometric patterns of paths and plantings, dotted with topiaries and classical statues. Over the eighteenth century, however, an increasing vogue for the natural emerged. Avenues of trees were uprooted, and rigidly regular beds of flowers were razed. In their place, landowners installed lawns and meadows, artificial lakes and streams and irregular clumps of trees.

These three influences – a shift in the production of art from professionals only to professionals and a large body of amateurs, an itch to travel and look at new things and a pervasive interest in the shape of individual landscapes – united to produce the fashion for the picturesque. How these different movements shaped each other has been the subject of a great deal of discussion and has produced any number of graduate theses. For our purposes, it is sufficient to say that each phenomenon fed off the others. The popularisation of the picturesque, however, can be traced largely to the writings of one man, the Reverend William Gilpin (1724–1807), vicar of Boldre in the New Forest.

Gilpin (*Hist Eng*, *MW* 143), like many gentlemen of his time, had been impressed by paintings of the Italian landscape. The masters of this genre, Claude Lorrain, Gaspar Poussin and Salvator Rosa, created rugged, moody scenes that had captured the imagination of young men who had seen their works while on the Grand Tour. Gilpin, however, did more than admire. He took a series of tours around Britain in the 1770s in which he applied the principles of landscape composition to the scenery he saw. His notes and paintings, circulated privately for a few years and then published, were quite popular and encouraged others to look at the terrain before them as if it were part of a picture – hence the term 'picturesque'.

Readers ate it up. After all, what more lofty purpose could there be in travelling to new places than to record the landscape in works of art? They gathered their sketchbooks and their watercolours and followed Gilpin's itineraries, standing in the same spots and seeking the same insights about artistic composition. In some cases, they used perspective glasses, devices held up to the eye, in order to limit their view of an expansive scene to what could be contained on a canvas. Following Gilpin's advice, they 'improved' the actual landscape by sketching in features that did not occur in nature. Those who chose not to sketch but merely observe the landscape had to imagine the improved scenery even as they gazed at the real thing.

After Gilpin, the most influential proponent of the picturesque was probably Uvedale Price, who brought the circle around completely from landscape to art to travel to landscape again, advising that the lessons gleaned from observation of the land, either directly or in works of art, should be translated into improvements in landscape gardening. In *An Essay on the Picturesque* (1796), he found the vogue for artificial lakes and lawns boring and urged greater 'intricacy in landscape', which he defined as 'that disposition of objects which, by a partial and uncertain concealment, excites and nourishes curiosity'. He advocated irregularity in both architecture and landscape design, championing the Gothic style with its 'variety of forms, of turrets and pinnacles' and its 'appearance of splendid confusion'.

The picturesque soon had its own vocabulary of foregrounds (*NA* 111), backgrounds and middle distances. The ideal view also had to have some sort of boundary at the side – trees, ruins or mountain slopes – to frame the picture and force the gaze into the middle distance; these objects are the 'side-screens' of Henry Tilney's discourse (*NA* 111). From Edmund Burke's 1757 essay *A Philosophical Enquiry into the Origin of Our Ideas of the Sublime and the Beautiful*, the picturesque vocabulary adopted the terms 'sublime' and 'beautiful' to mean specific kinds of visual appeal. Sublime settings were grand, overpowering and masculine; beautiful landscapes were soft, sinuous, delicate and feminine. Gilpin's picturesque was a medium between the two, with a variety of textures, an atmosphere of wildness and a visual balance of all the elements, even if it meant introducing objects into his pictures that were not present in the original scenery. Later, the term 'romantic' came to be applied to similar landscapes, though this term was, like 'picturesque', rather vague and greatly overused.

In fact, most elements of the picturesque came to be overused. Its terminology seemed to leach the spontaneity out of tourism, and the paintings that were created under its influence often had laughable inconsistencies, such as Welsh valleys suffused with Mediterranean light or English lakes threatened by Italian banditti. Crumbling ruins and spectrally dark forests became far more commonplace on canvas than they were in real life. The doyens of the picturesque dictated what was appropriate and attractive, down to the very trees and animals that could be safely depicted; Uvedale Price favoured old oaks and elms over beech and ash, Pomeranians and water dogs over sleeker varieties, sheep with ragged fleece over those with even coats, and lions and raptors over domestic animals.

Austen was definitely familiar with this intellectual approach to landscape. Gilpin is mentioned by Henry Austen in the Biographical Notice that accompanied the publication of *Northanger Abbey* and *Persuasion*, and Austen herself makes reference to his 'Tour to the

Highlands' (*L&F*, *MW* 105) in which he is so critical of Arthur's Seat. Two of her brothers, James and Henry, followed some of Gilpin's itineraries. In both her letters and her novels, she uses the terminology of the picturesque. Writing from lodgings in Queen's Square, Bath, in 1799, for example, she explains that 'the prospect from the drawing-room window, at which I now write, is rather picturesque, as it commands a perspective view of the left side of Brock Street, broken by three Lombardy poplars in the garden of the last house in Queen's Parade'. (Three was a pleasant quantity in picturesque theory, whereas four was irritatingly symmetrical, a concept also reflected in Elizabeth Bennet's refusal to walk with Mr Darcy, Miss Bingley and Mrs Hurst, thus making a fourth in their group – *P&P* 53.) Her description of Lyme, furthermore, reads like a section of Gilpin's works or of the travel writers who imitated him (*P* 95–96).

However, familiarity with the picturesque does not necessarily mean that she agreed with this way of looking at the outdoor world. She seems to have been in the camp of those who thought that the picturesque had been taken too far. Austen was certainly not one to dismiss a tidy farm because it appeared too domesticated, and she repeatedly introduces the theory of the picturesque only to reject it. In *Northanger Abbey* she uses the Tilneys' knowledge of the picturesque to establish them as people of education and taste, but she makes it clear that Catherine Morland's less-tutored perspective is more genuine and appreciative than theirs (*NA* 110–111).* Marianne Dashwood's appreciation of twisted old trees (*S&S* 92), like the rest of her cultivation of picturesque taste, is extremely well informed, but it is inferior, in Austen's eyes, to Edward Ferrars' broader appreciation of scenery and his unfashionable defence of the prosperous agricultural landscape (*S&S* 88, 97–98).

See also Architecture; Gardens and Landscape; Gothic; Reading.

Places

Austen mentions a large number of specific places in her works, some of them real and some of them fictional. The real ones are listed below; where appropriate, notes about the locations of important fictional places are included in the notes on English counties. Tables indicate on which map(s) locations may be found: England, West Indies, Hampshire or London area (map abbreviations used in the keys are noted in the map captions). Streets maps of Bath and London may be found accompanying the articles about those cities. Several places have been listed below, which do not appear in Austen's works but have relevance to her life. For the purposes of map clarity, I have chosen to believe that my readers

---

*The rejection of the view of Bath is a deliberate poke at Uvedale Price, who similarly dismissed this panorama in *On Buildings and Architecture* (1798).

can locate the few regions of the world not contained in maps of Europe, the Mediterranean and the West Indies. Omitted locations are noted.

Europe, the Mediterranean and the West Indies
Boundaries between countries are the modern lines, not the Georgian ones.

See also Bath; London.

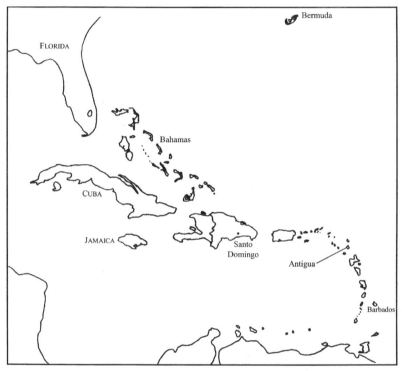

4. Map of the West Indies (WI).

Location	Map Location	Notes
Aberdeen	Not shown	*Lesley, MW* 110, 118.
Alps	Not shown	*NA* 200.
America	Not shown	*H&E, MW* 38; *MP* 119. Might refer to any part of North or South America, but in the example from *Mansfield Park*, Tom Bertram is probably referring to the United States.
Antigua	WI	*MP* 30, 107, 177, 251.
Asia Minor	Not shown	*MP* 18.

Places

Location	Map Location	Notes
Bahamas	WI	*P* 70.

Mrs Croft insists that Bermuda and the Bahamas are not part of the West Indies, although the Bahamas at least would be considered so today. Mrs Croft may be including in her definition of the West Indies only the Greater Antilles (the island group that includes Cuba and Jamaica) and the Lesser Antilles (containing the Windward and Leeward Islands such as Antigua, Martinique and St Martin).

| Barbados | WI | *Cath*, *MW* 205. |
| Bermuda | WI | *P* 70. |

See note to Bahamas. Charles Austen's first and second wives were daughters of a governor-general of Bermuda.

| Cape of Good Hope | Not shown | *P* 232. |

'The Cape' is the Cape of Good Hope at the southern tip of Africa. One of the duties performed by Jane's brother Francis, a naval captain, was convoying merchant ships back and forth to the Cape.

| Dresden | Not shown | *NA* 175. |
| East Indies | Not shown | *Cath*, *MW* 194, 205; *S&S* 51, 206; *MP* 5, 305; *P* 22, 70. |

'East Indies' was a term used to refer to an extraordinarily wide swath of territory, encompassing everything from parts of Afghanistan to the southeastern-most parts of Indonesia. Sometimes China was included in the term, sometimes not. Bengal (*Cath*, *MW* 205), a region that contains the mouths of the Ganges river and includes Bangladesh and part of northwest India, is the only section of the East Indies named specifically by Austen in her works, though she would have been indirectly familiar with the geography of this part of the world. Both of her naval brothers, Francis and Charles, served in the East Indies and would have reported at length on the sights they had seen, including 'nabobs, gold mohrs, and palanquins' (*S&S* 51). Jane also had an aunt who went to the East Indies to find a husband and gave birth to Jane's dashing cousin Eliza de Feuillide. Overall, the region remained for most English people an exotic source of wealth, tea and textiles, without too much more detail as yet.

France	Not shown	*NA* 83, 200. *See also* French; French Revolution; Napoleonic Wars.
Avignon	Not shown	*S&S* 63.
Lyon	Not shown	*Cath*, *MW* 218, 222.
Paris	Not shown	*Lesley*, *MW* 116.
Sèvres	Not shown	*NA* 175.

Location	Map Location	Notes
Gibraltar	Not shown	*MP* 235; *P* 66, 70.

Jane's brother Frank's first command, the *Peterel*, was stationed at Gibraltar. Gibraltar was one of the principal ports at which British ships resupplied when cruising in the Mediterranean.

Location	Map Location	Notes
Ireland	Not shown	
Cork	Not shown	*P* 70. Cork was the home station of the navy's Irish Squadron.
Dublin	Not shown	
Italy	Not shown	*Lesley, MW* 116, 138; *NA* 200.
Naples	Not shown	*Lesley, MW* 137–138.
Sicily	Not shown	*MP* 254.
Tuscany	Not shown	*NA* 83.
Venice	Not shown	*E* 363.
Lisbon	Not shown	*P* 68, 70.
The Mediterranean	Not shown	*MP* 152, 232, 236; *P* 67.
New South Wales	Not shown	

State in southeast Australia that includes many major cities, including Sydney. It was the first region of the country to receive transported prisoners from England.

Location	Map Location	Notes
Niagara Falls	Not shown	

Huge waterfall on the border between Ontario (Canada) and New York (United States).

Location	Map Location	Notes
Ontario	Not shown	*MW* 443. Province in eastern Canada.
Pyrenees	Not shown	*NA* 200.
Russia	Not shown	*MP* 18; 'Kamschatka' is mentioned in *Plan, MW* 430.
Santo Domingo	WI	*P* 26.
Straits of Gibraltar	Not shown	*P* 70.
Switzerland	Not shown	*NA* 200; *E* 362, 364, 365.
Texel	Not shown	Island off the coast of the Netherlands.
Timbuktu	Not shown	*Sand, MW* 405–406.

Places

Location	Map Location	Notes
		Can be found well inland along the Niger River in the Western African nation of Mali.
Trafalgar	Not shown	
		The French and British fleets met off this cape in 1805 at the Battle of Trafalgar. *See also* Napoleonic Wars.
'Western Islands'	Not shown	*P* 67. The Azores, located in the north Atlantic Ocean, about 1,300 miles southwest of England.

British Isles

County lines are the old county lines, based primarily on John Cary's 1814 *Cary's Traveller's Companion.*

Before county lines were redrawn, small bits of counties were actually contained entirely within the borders of adjoining counties. These separate areas are omitted on this map for the sake of clarity.

Location	Map Location	Notes
Ireland	ENG	*L&F*, *MW* 90; *Watsons*, *MW* 326; *E* 159, 161, 168, 285, 298, 343; *P* 149, 188. *L&F*, *MW* 90, 92; *Lesley*, *MW* 111; *Hist Eng*, *MW* 148–149; *S&S* 206; *P&P* 273; *MP* 442.
Scotland	ENG	
		Scotland had, ever since its union with England, been providing its southern neighbour with middle-class and professional men of all sorts. Part of the reason for the Scots' success in such fields as estate management, architecture, medicine and civil engineering was the Scottish educational system. Scotland had four universities to England's two, and the Scottish curriculum tended to have more relevance to the real world. As the author of *A Compendious Geographical and Historical Grammar* (1795) noted, 'Scotland has been for many ages famous for learning. It has produced poets, philosophers, and historians, all excellent in their kind; and its literary reputation continues to be much on the increase.'
Aberdeen	Not shown	*Lesley*, *MW* 110, 118.
Edinburgh	ENG	*L&F*, *MW* 102, 105; *Lesley*, *MW* 122.
Gretna Green	ENG	*L&F*, *MW* 95; *P&P* 274, 282–283.
		Gretna Green was located right on the English–Scottish border and so was a popular destination for couples eloping to take advantage of Scotland's more liberal marriage laws. *See* Marriage.

Location	Map Location	Notes
Perth	ENG	*Lesley, MW* 111, 112.
Stirling	ENG	*L&F, MW* 105.
Wales	ENG	*J&A, MW* 20; *L&F, MW* 77, 78, 81; *Scraps, MW* 176; *Cath, MW* 203.
Holyhead	ENG	*E* 161.
Pembrokeshire	ENG	*Scraps, MW* 176–177.
Vale of Uske	ENG	*L&F, MW* 77, 81.
		The Uske River flows north to south through Monmouthshire.

England County/City	Map Abbreviation	Map Location	Notes
Bedfordshire	BEDS	ENG	
Berkshire	BERKS	ENG	*J&A, MW* 16.
Jane's uncle, Leigh-Perrot, had an estate here.			
Newbury	BERKS	ENG	*MP* 376.
Reading	BERKS	ENG	*S&S* 304.
From 1785 to 1787, Jane and Cassandra attended the Abbey School in Reading. The school was housed in a twelfth-century building that once been home to the third-richest abbey in England.			
Windsor	BERKS	ENG	*E* 388, 394, 442, 454, 459.
Eton College (*MP* 21) is located near Windsor.			
Buckinghamshire	BUCKS	ENG	*F&E, MW* 10.
Cambridgeshire	CAMBS	ENG	
Cambridge	CAMBS	ENG	*P&P* 200; *MP* 61.
Cheshire	CHES	ENG	*P* 4.
Cornwall	CORN	ENG	
Cumberland	CUMB	ENG	*Lesley, MW* 117; *MP* 152.
Cumberland, Westmorland and the upper part of Lancashire contained the Lake District (*LS, MW* 298; *Cath, MW* 199; *P&P* 154, 239, 382), famous for its dramatic scenery.			
Carlisle	CUMB	ENG	*Evelyn, MW* 184–185.

5. Map of the British Isles (ENG).

England County/City	Map Abbreviation	Map Location	Notes
Derbyshire	DERBY	ENG	*Col Let, MW* 160–161; *Cath, MW* 200; *P&P* 38, 240, 265, 385.

Home of Elizabeth Bennet's aunt Mrs Gardiner (*P&P* 239) and of Mr Darcy (*P&P* 10, 239, 240).

Featured in William Gilpin's picturesque tour of the Lake District; Derbyshire was the centre of the equally picturesque Peak District (*P&P* 240).

Bakewell	DERBY	ENG	*P&P* 256.
Chatsworth	DERBY	ENG	*P&P* 239.
Dovedale	DERBY	ENG	*P&P* 239.

The 'dale' or valley of the River Dove runs primarily along the border of Staffordshire and Derbyshire. The sections described by William Gilpin had gray cliffs dotted with trees and a river with small waterfalls.

Matlock	DERBY	ENG	*Cath, MW* 199, 200; *P&P* 239.

Matlock was a warm, sunny, sheltered spa in the Derwent Gorge, very small and rustic. What drew visitors was not the spa but the scenery. It lost some of its charm in the 1790s, when textile mills went up in the surrounding area, and John Byng complained, 'Every rural sound is sunk in the clamours of cotton.' A boat, with a band to play music on summer nights, took tourists onto the river for 6*d*.

DEVONSHIRE	DEVON	ENG	*Cath, MW* 215; *S&S* 251.

Home of the Dashwoods for most of *S&S* and of Sir John and Lady Middleton (23, 25, 26, 87). Barton is a long day's journey from the fictional Cleveland (*S&S* 280) and 4 miles north of Exeter (*S&S* 25).

Location of Allenham, the estate Willoughby is expected to inherit (*S&S* 40).

Devon was noted for its seaside resorts, especially Exmouth and Teignmouth; from the 1790s, Sidmouth, Dawlish, and Torquay were successfully developed as bathing places. A low cost of living made it a popular place of residence for retired East India Company personnel and half-pay officers.

Dawlish	DEVON	ENG	*S&S* 251, 360, 376.

Dawlish was one of Devonshire's principal seaside resorts in the early years of the nineteenth century. The Austens considered taking a holiday there in 1801 but went elsewhere. They finally visited Dawlish the following year.

Places

England County/City	Map Abbreviation	Map Location	Notes
Exeter	DEVON	ENG	*Cath, MW* 240; *S&S* 25, 118, 119, 134, 143, 353, 354, 370.
Honiton	DEVON	ENG	*S&S* 65, 325.
Plymouth	DEVON	ENG	*S&S* 87, 130, 134, 355, 370; *P* 69, 103, 108, 133, 171.
Sidmouth	DEVON	ENG	*P* 105.
DORSETSHIRE	DOR	ENG	*S&S* 208; *P* 217.

Colonel Brandon's estate, Delaford, is located here (*S&S* 223, 375).

Lyme (Regis)	DOR	ENG	*P* 94–110, 121, 122, 125, 126, 130, 132, 171, 183.

Lyme was a relatively inexpensive haven (*P* 97) for middle-class people. It had a pebbly beach, an assembly room, a card room and a billiard room in 1810. Austen presumably approved of the town as she puts a very favourable assessment of it into *Persuasion* (94–95); she had ample opportunity to become acquainted with it as she and her parents vacationed there in 1803 and 1804.

The Cobb (*P* 95, 108–109) was a jetty in the harbour, originally constructed in the fourteenth century and rebuilt as needed. It had a platform for walking along the top and steep steps to the beach along its side. The steps from which Louisa Musgrove falls are known as 'Granny's Teeth'. Some of these steps have risers, but many are simply lumps of stone projecting from the wall like blunt fingertips.

Up Lyme and Pinny, both mentioned in *P* 95, were nearby communities. Up Lyme is about a mile inland of Lyme Regis, while Pinhay – which Austen spells 'Pinny' – lies west of Lyme along the coast, between Lyme Regis and Seaton. Charmouth (*P* 130) is about a mile and a half east of Lyme.

Weymouth	DOR	ENG	*S&S* 114; *MP* 114, 121; *E* 96, 160, 169, 194, 227, 241, 322, 437.

One of the most popular of the seaside resorts, Weymouth was visited by George III in 1789. This increased its popularity, and a wave of expansion followed, making it distasteful to Jane, who disliked overbuilt resorts. In 1804, on a holiday in Lyme, she remained at Lyme while Cassandra, her brother Henry and Henry's wife, Eliza, went on to Weymouth. The town was then in a ferment over the visit of the Duke of Gloucester, but Cassandra was apparently more concerned by there being no pastry shop in town where one could buy ice cream. 'Weymouth is al together a shocking place, I perceive', replied Jane, 'without recommendation of any kind, and worthy only of being frequented by the inhabitants of Gloucester'.

England County/City	Map Abbreviation	Map Location	Notes
DURHAM	DUR	ENG	
ENGLISH CHANNEL	–	ENG	*MP* 232.
ESSEX	ESX	ENG	*Col Let, MW* 160–161.
Southend	ESX	ENG	*E* 101, 105–106.

Charles Austen took his family to Southend for a holiday in 1813.

GLOUCESTERSHIRE	GLOCS	ENG	*NA* 68, 149; *P* 3.

Northanger Abbey is located in Gloucestershire (*NA* 139, 140), 30 miles from Bath (*NA* 155).

Adlestrop Park, a magnificent Gothic mansion owned by Mrs Austen's relatives, was located here. The Austen women visited there in 1806 after leaving Bath but before moving to Southampton, staying not at Adlestrop itself but at the rectory, home of Mrs Austen's cousin, the Reverend Thomas Leigh.

Cheltenham	HAMP	ENG	*Cath, MW* 203; *MP* 199.

Cheltenham was a fashionable resort town, with a pump room, assembly rooms, famously pretty gravel paths sheltered by shady trees, and a theatre that attracted London talent. Two of its masters of ceremonies, James King and Richard Tyson, had also served as MCs at Bath. The town attracted a fashionable clientele from the 1780s, though visitor John Byng found it dull, with poor inns and stables, poor lodgings and high prices. Improvements were made, and by 1796 the streets had been newly paved and the houses numbered. Its lodging houses were principally brick faced with stucco, and their number gradually increased. A crescent was built in the first decade of the nineteenth century, and one of its units had nine bedrooms. A new theatre was built in 1805 at a cost of £8,000, and by the second decade of the nineteenth century, more mineral wells had been dug and more pump rooms built. A period of rapid expansion during the French wars led to improved transportation to and from the town, the founding of a newspaper, and the building of 'hotels', a type of dwelling considered more fashionable than a mere inn. Two coffee rooms, one for men and one for women, lent newspapers to their customers, and other shops lent out books and musical instruments. Visitors included King George III in 1788, novelist Fanny Burney in the same year as part of the court, Austen's cousin Eliza de Feuillide in 1797, actress Dorothea Jordan in 1810 and Jane and Cassandra Austen in 1816.

Clifton	*See* Bristol (SOMERSET-SHIRE)		
Petty France	GLOCS	ENG	*NA* 156.
Tetbury	GLOCS	ENG	*NA* 45.
Tintern Abbey	GLOCS	ENG	*MP* 152.

Places

England County/City	Map Abbreviation	Map Location	Notes
HAMPSHIRE	HAMP	ENG	*MW* 420.

Home of the Misses Parker in Sanditon.

Hampshire was Jane's home for most of her life. She was born in Steventon and lived there until 1801, when her family moved to Bath. In 1806, she returned to the county to live at Southampton with her brother Frank and his wife; she then moved, in 1809, to Chawton Cottage, owned by her brother Edward. Some of her other brothers occasionally occupied Chawton House, a larger home that Edward also owned in the same neighbourhood.

Ashe	HAMP	HAMP	

Home of the Lefroy family from 1783. The Lefroy were friends of the Austens, and the two families visited back and forth.

Basingstoke	HAMP	HAMP	*Clifford, MW* 44.

When the Austens lived at Steventon, they often attended winter balls in Basingstoke, 7 miles away. Their closest doctor was here as well, along with a shop that sold drawing supplies.

Beaulieu Abbey	HAMP	HAMP	*Hist Eng, MW* 141–142.
Chawton	HAMP	HAMP	

The Austen women and Martha Lloyd lived at Chawton Cottage from 1809. Francis Austen lived at Chawton Great House and in the neighbourhood of Alton from 1814 until the end of Jane's life. The cottage was a short walk from the parish church and close enough to Steventon, Ashe and Deane for occasional visits by old friends and family. It was about a mile from Alton, a market town with a bank, an apothecary and a few shops. More specialised goods had to be bought from Winchester, Farnham or Guildford. Chawton was a small town, with a population of only 347 in 1811.

Clarkengreen	HAMP	HAMP	*Clifford, MW* 44.
Deane	HAMP	HAMP	*Clifford, MW* 43.

Mr Austen possessed the living of Deane as well as that of Steventon. He rented the parsonage there to the Lloyd family, but when his eldest son James married, Mr Austen made him his curate at Deane, and the Lloyds had to move. The Lloyds then moved to Ibthorpe, about 15 miles away. Deane was a very small village; when James began his term as a curate there in 1792, there were only twenty-four families. Nonetheless, two London coaches stopped there daily. When the Lloyds were living there, the Austens often walked the mile and a half to Deane to visit with Mrs Lloyd and her three daughters, Eliza, Mary and Martha.

Ibthorpe	HAMP	HAMP	

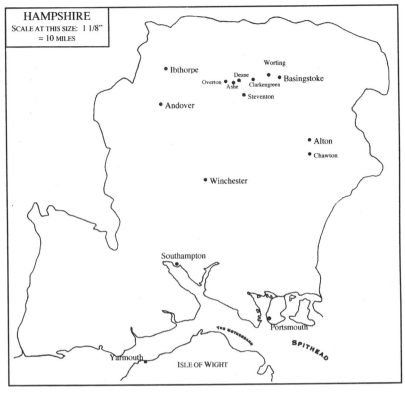

6. Map of Hampshire (HAMP).

England County/City	Map Abbreviation	Map Location	Notes
In 1792, the Lloyd family, good friends of the Austens, moved to Ibthorpe, over 15 miles from Steventon. It was a pretty village, considered by William Cobbett 'a sight worth going many miles to see'.			
Isle of Wight	ENG		*Evelyn, MW* 184–185; *Sand, MW* 387; *MP* 18, 409; *P* 96.
The Isle of Wight was a common destination for excursions from Southampton.			
Overton	Not shown		*Clifford, MW* 43. James Austen's first curacy was at Overton.
Portsmouth	Not shown		*MP* 249, 368, 371, 373, 392, 401, 416, 443.

England County/City	Map Abbreviation	Map Location	Notes

Site of the Royal Naval Academy (*Gen Cur*, *MW* 73), which Austen's brothers Frank and Charles attended.

Home of the impecunious Price family, Portsmouth was also a major naval port (*MP* 232, 245, 254, 266, 400; *P* 69, 108), and between the natural harbour and the Isle of Wight was a channel called Spithead (*MP* 232, 378, 380, 384, 389, 409). Ships preparing to set sail would head into this channel and await favourable winds (*MP* 388). The far side of Spithead, adjacent to the northeast coast of the Isle of Wight, was known as the Motherbank (*MP* 389).

The town was located on an island and was approached by a road that ran from the north side of the island. The town was, however, in the southwest quadrant of the island, and new construction therefore tended to spread north and east. As an important military base, Portsmouth had a legacy of fortifications – hence the ramparts (*MP* 388, 409) near the water's edge, which by Austen's time had been turned to peaceful uses as a promenade.

On the landward side, the town was guarded by a moat, drawbridge and additional fortifications (*MP* 376). A gate called the Landport led into the main part of the town whose principal thoroughfare was the High Street (*MP* 376, 401), home of several good shops (*MP* 403), including Turner's at 85 High Street, where William Price shops for supplies before going to sea. The Austens knew Turner's and had had dealings with them on at least two occasions, in 1809 and 1815, and possibly on a third occasion in 1805.

The southern end of the town had a small northward-facing peninsula called the Point; from the end of Broad Street one could stand at this Point and watch ships go in and out of harbour, but once ships passed the Point heading southwards out of the large natural harbour, the buildings along Broad Street blocked one's view. A better vantage point was the cannon platform at the base of High Street, which had a less superb view of the initial move out of the harbour but a much longer view as the ships passed from the harbour out into the Spithead channel. Austen initially had Mr Price watching the *Thrush* depart from the Point but changed it in the second edition to the platform instead, perhaps on advice from one of her brothers. A little south and inland of the platform stood the Garrison Chapel, where Fanny Price and her family worship on Sundays (*MP* 408).

Portsmouth had several notable sights, chief among them the dockyard (*MP* 372, 388, 400, 402–403), which was impressive both in its size and in the pace and variety of its activities. The dockyard lay north of the main portion of the town and covered 82 acres. It had a massive bakery, a salting house for the preservation of meat, a rope-making shed a quarter of a mile long, and, just offshore, the huge ships that to William Gilpin resembled 'floating castles, and towns'.* The dockyard's steam engines and saw mills were

*One of the ships he saw in the harbour was the *Namur*, which would be commanded by Charles Austen beginning in 1811.

England County/City	Map Abbreviation	Map Location	Notes

regular stops for tourists, who gaped at the forty-five block mills that made 130,000 blocks a year for holding the pulleys that kept ship ropes taut. Designed in the first decade of the nineteenth century by the great engineer Isambard Brunel and built with convict labour, the block mills were an early industrial marvel. Gilpin visited the dockyards in 1774, long before the construction of the block mills, but he still found them impressive. 'Every where as we approached Portsmouth', he wrote, 'we saw quantities of timber lying near the road, ready to be conveyed to the King's magazines. – This is both a *picturesque* and a *proper* decoration of the avenues to a dockyard'.

Southampton	HAMP	ENG	*L&F, MW* 78–79.

The first boarding school that Jane and Cassandra attended in Oxford later relocated to Southampton, taking the girls and their cousin Jane Cooper along. While in Southampton, the small population of the school was struck by an epidemic, possibly of diphtheria or typhoid, and both Janes became ill. Jane Austen recovered at school, but Jane Cooper's mother came to claim her and take her home. The little girl regained her health but not before her mother fell ill, too, and died of the disease.

Jane was not fond of the theatre at Southampton. However, other diversions were available. Southampton was a resort town in a small and fading way, and it had the usual assortment of assembly rooms and other amenities associated with 'public places'. A popular activity was taking boating trips to the Isle of Wight or to the ruined Netley Abbey. Trips on land could be taken to Chiswell and Beaulieu Abbey.

Jane, Cassandra, Mrs Austen and Martha Lloyd moved in with Francis Austen and his wife, Mary, partly to save on expenses and partly to keep Mary company in the long months while Frank was away at sea. They moved into cramped lodgings in 1806 and were happier when they removed to a larger house at No. 2 Castle Square in March 1807. This house had a sizable garden and access to a walkway that had been constructed on the old city walls. The Austen women moved from Southampton to Chawton Cottage in 1809.

Steventon		Not shown	

The Austens' home for many years, Steventon was a small village with a small, plain church and an unpaved main street. The local manor house was owned by Thomas Knight but rented to the Digweeds, a respectable but not a cultured or scholarly family. When George Austen first became rector there in 1764, there were perhaps only thirty families living in the village; there were no doctor and no shops. The church is much as it was in Austen's day, with the addition of a steeple and a stained-glass window in her honour, but the rectory was torn down in the 1820s.

Winchester	HAMP	ENG	*MW* 451–452.

Austen moved here in May 1817 to No. 8, College Street. Desperately ill, she was placed under the care of a surgeon named Giles King Lyford, but though she appears to have

England County/City	Map Abbreviation	Map Location	Notes
experienced a temporary improvement in her condition, she died on 18 July and was buried in Winchester Cathedral.			
Worting		Not shown	*Clifford, MW* 44.
Yarmouth	ENG		*P* 92, 170.
Yarmouth, a minor naval base, had docks, a small theatre and a modest sea-bathing business aimed mostly at people from nearby villages.			
Herefordshire	HERE	ENG	
Hereford	HERE	ENG	*Scraps, MW* 176; *NA* 224, 239.
Hertfordshire	HERTS	ENG	*P&P* 146, 172, 178–179, 219, 275.
Site of Longbourn, the home of the Bennets, and Meryton, their nearest town (*P&P* 10, 117, 333).			
Hatfield	HERTS	ENG	*P&P* 275.
Huntingdonshire	HUNTG	ENG	
Huntingdon	HUNTG	ENG	*MP* 3.
Kent	KENT	ENG	*LS, MW* 254; *P&P* 172, 178–179.

Rosings Park and Mr Collins' parsonage are located here (*P&P* 146).

Jane was familiar with Kent, as her brother Edward's home, Godmersham, was in this county. She and Cassandra often visited Edward, who had been adopted by a wealthy childless couple. His adoptive mother had moved out of Godmersham and given it to Edward, retiring to Goodnestone Farm, where Jane also visited. Jane's wealthy great-uncle, Francis Austen, also lived in Kent, and her first known trip to the county was a visit to his house at Seven Oaks. The Austen women considered taking a house in Kent when they left Southampton in 1809 but opted instead for Chawton Cottage in Hampshire.

Kent, as R. W. Chapman points out, is one of the counties frequently referred to as 'the garden of England' (*E* 273). Kent had two principal seaside resorts: Ramsgate and Margate.

Bromley	LON	LON	*P&P* 212.
Dartford	LON	LON	*S&S* 252.

Jane often travelled through Dartford on her way to visit relatives in Kent. She dined at the Bull and George inn there in October 1798 and at the Bull inn (a different

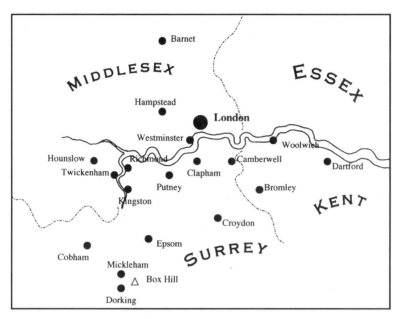

7. Map of the London area (LON).

England County/City	Map Abbreviation	Map Location	Notes

establishment) in 1808. Apparently she also ate at the Bull in 1792, for in a letter about the 1808 visit, she recalled a similar trip 'fourteen years ago' and reported, 'At Dartford, we went to the Bull, the same inn in which we breakfasted in that said journey, and on the present occasion we had about the same bad butter.'

England County/City	Map Abbreviation	Map Location	Notes
Deal	KENT	ENG	*P* 71, 170.
Dover	KENT	ENG	*H&E*, *MW* 36; *Mount*, *MW* 41.

Dover was the principal port for travel to and from the continent.

Godmersham	KENT	ENG	

Home of Jane's wealthy brother Edward Austen, who later took the surname Knight in honour of his adoptive parents. Jane and Cassandra were frequent visitors there.

Margate	KENT	ENG	

A notable seaside resort; Eliza de Feuillide took her chronically ill son Hastings there to bathe for his health in 1791.

Ramsgate	KENT	ENG	*P&P* 201; *MP* 51.

A seaside resort where Jane's brother Francis met his future first wife, Mary Gibson.

Places

England County/City	Map Abbreviation	Map Location	Notes
Tunbridge wells	KENT	ENG	*Lesley, MW* 112; *Sand, MW* 363; *NA* 33; *MP* 199.

A popular spa, though one that had lost its ability to lure an aristocratic clientele, Tunbridge was only a day's journey from London. It had assembly rooms, a circulating library, a theatre and a large number of inns, lodging houses and stables. Its development stagnated towards the end of the eighteenth century but recovered with the outbreak of war with France in 1793.

Westerham	KENT	ENG	*P&P* 62.
Woolwich	LON	LON	*MP* 5

Since 1741, Woolwich had been the site of the Royal Military College, which trained future officers of the artillery and engineer corps. The entrance requirements tended to favour the well off, sons of gentlemen and sons of military officers.

Lancashire	LANCS	ENG	
Liverpool	LANCS	ENG	*P&P* 220; *MP* 178.

A major port for the shipment of sugar, slaves, and cotton; its population rose to 78,000 by 1801, making it the second-most populous city in the nation.

Leicestershire	LEICS	ENG	*NA* 76.
Bosworth field	LEICS	ENG	*Hist Eng, MW* 141.

Site of the final battle between the armies of Richard III and the future Henry VII, in which Richard was killed.

Leicester	LEICS	ENG	Site of Leicester Abbey (*Hist Eng, MW* 142).
Lincolnshire	LINC	ENG	
Middlesex	MDX	ENG	*L&F, MW* 82.
Barnet	LON	LON	*P&P* 275, 282.
Hampstead	LON	LON	*Cass, MW* 45.
Hounslow	LON	LON	*Scraps, MW* 173
London	LON	LON	*See* London.
Twickenham	LON	LON	*MP* 57, 434, 455.
Westminster	LON	LON	*S&S* 251; *MP* 61, 212, 469.

England County/City	Map Abbreviation	Map Location	Notes
Norfolk	NFLK	ENG	Henry Crawford's estate, Everingham, is located in Norfolk (*MP* 40, 114, 193, 393, 411).
Cromer	NFLK	ENG	*E* 105–106.
Northamptonshire	NHANTS	ENG	Site of Mansfield Park (*MP* 21, 295, 360, 368, 416).
Northamptonshire was renowned for the quality of its hunting.			
Fotheringhay castle	NHANTS	ENG	*Hist Eng, MW* 145.
Northampton	NHANTS	ENG	*MP* 12, 57, 130, 250, 266.
Peterborough	NHANTS	ENG	*MP* 255, 282, 288, 354.
Northumberland	NTHUMB	ENG	
Newcastle on tyne	NTHUMB	ENG	*P&P* 317, 330.
Nottinghamshire	NOTTS	ENG	
Oxfordshire	OXF	ENG	
Banbury	OXF	ENG	*MP* 193.
Blenheim palace	OXF	ENG	*P&P* 240.
Oxford	OXF	ENG	*NA* 46, 64, 201, 216; *S&S* 275, 288, 353, 362; *P&P* 240; *MP* 21, 376, 446; *E* 188, 189.
One of England's two universities was in Oxford; Jane's father and her brothers James and Henry were all educated there, and Jane went for a short time to a boarding school in the town.			
Rutland	RUT	ENG	
Shropshire	SHROP	ENG	*Watsons, MW* 321, 350; *P* 134.
Somersetshire	SOM	ENG	*P* 21, 26.
Home of Kellynch Hall and Uppercross (*P* 3, 188).			
Home of Willoughby (*S&S* 44, 58, 114, 279, 302); site of Cleveland, the home of Mr and Mrs Palmer (*S&S* 114, 116, 279, 302).			
Bath	SOM	ENG	*See* Bath.

England County/City	Map Abbreviation	Map Location	Notes
Bristol	SOM	ENG	*Lesley, MW* 114, 118, 119; *NA* 85; *S&S* 280; *E* 183, 272, 359.

Bristol lies on the border of Somerset and Gloucestershire and is actually its own county. In Austen's time, it was no longer the leading slave-trading port, but it was a busy commercial centre with a large shipping industry and a porcelain manufactory.

One of its suburbs was the spa village of Clifton (*NA* 85, 87, 89, 97, 105; *E* 307), located on a cliff. Just inside the boundary of Gloucestershire, Clifton had a warm sulphurous spring, assembly rooms, a pump room and fashionable shops that sold such diverse wares as confectionery and mineral crystals from the Avon Gorge (the 'spars' of *NA* 116). The Austens visited Clifton in June 1806. Bath, though near Clifton, was not in direct competition with it, as the towns' seasons did not overlap (*NA* 115).

Blaise Castle (*NA* 84–85, 86, 101), a Gothic garden structure built in 1766, is located just to the northwest, near Kingsweston Down (*NA* 84; *E* 274). A beautiful mansion called Kingsweston stood 2 miles from the Severn and commanded extensive views of the surrounding countryside.

Crewkherne	SOM	ENG	*P* 121.
Keynsham	SOM	ENG	*NA* 88.
Minehead	SOM	ENG	*P* 171.
Taunton	SOM	ENG	*P* 21, 24, 76.
Staffordshire	STAFFS	ENG	*LS, MW* 247, 251.

The county was noted for its excellent ceramics (*NA* 175).

In 1806, the Austen women paid a visit to Stoneleigh Abbey, which Mrs Austen's cousin Thomas Leigh had just inherited. The abbey bears a marked resemblance to Jane's description of Northanger Abbey. On the same visit to Staffordshire, the women visited Hamstall Ridware, home of Jane's cousin Edward Cooper, an Evangelical parson whose fervour Jane found off-putting.

Burton-on-trent	STAFFS	ENG	*Sand, MW* 424.
Stoke	STAFFS	ENG	*MP* 148, 189.
Suffolk	SFLK	ENG	*Col Let, MW* 160–161.
Newmarket	SFLK	ENG	*MP* 426.

Famed for its horse racing.

Surrey	SRY	ENG	*H&E, MW* 35; *Mount, MW* 41; *Sand, MW* 387; *E* 273, 274.

England County/City	Map Abbreviation	Map Location	Notes

The Watson family in *The Watsons* live in the fictional village of Stanton, supposedly located in Surrey, four hours from London (*MW* 321, 356). The 'D' and 'R' listed as towns nearby are probably Dorking and Reigate (*MW* 317).

The fictional estates of Hartfield and Donwell Abbey are located in Surrey (*E* 91), as is the town of Highbury, possibly modelled on Cobham or Great Bookham. The latter was the home of the Reverend Samuel Cooke, Jane's godfather.

England County/City	Map Abbreviation	Map Location	Notes
Box hill	LON	LON	*E* 352, 367.
Camberwell	LON	LON	*Sand*, *MW* 387.
Clapham	LON	LON	*P&P* 274, 293, 295.
Cobham	LON	LON	*E* 95.
Croydon	LON	LON	*Watsons*, *MW* 319, 348, 350, 353.
Dorking	LON	LON	*E* 369.
Epsom	SRY	LON, ENG	*P&P* 293, 295.
Guildford	SRY	ENG	*Watsons*, *MW* 321, 341.
Kingston	LON	LON	*E* 32, 244.
Mickleham	LON	LON	*E* 369.
Putney	LON	LON	*NA* 122, 205.
Richmond	LON	LON	
Sussex	SSX	ENG	*Lesley*, *MW* 112, 119, 180; *E&E*, *MW* 30; *Scraps*, *MW* 170–171; *Evelyn*, *MW* 185; *LS*, *MW* 254, 271; *Sand*, *MW* 363, 368.

The Dashwoods' original home, Norland, is in Sussex (*S&S* 3, 87).

Sussex had several notable seaside resorts and gained many more from 1810 to 1820. Hastings had a head start on development, but the prince regent's patronage of Brighton made it the most fashionable of all the seaside resorts of the period. The fictional village of Sanditon is located in Sussex.

England County/City	Map Abbreviation	Map Location	Notes
Beachy head	SSX	ENG	*MP* 245.

Places

England County/City	Map Abbreviation	Map Location	Notes
Brighton	SSX	ENG	*Lesley*, *MW* 120, 138; *Sand*, *MW* 368; *P&P* 219, 229, 232, 274, 288, 300; *MP* 203, 245.

Austen did not think much of Brighton originally named 'Brighthelmstone', partly because she disapproved in general of resorts that had become too fashionable and formal and probably also because it was associated with the debaucheries of the prince regent. In January 1799, she wrote in a letter, 'I assure you that I dread the idea of going to Brighton as much as you do, but I am not without hopes that something may happen to prevent it.'

Chichester	SSX	ENG	*Watsons*, *MW* 317, 351; *Sand*, *MW* 407, 409.

William Gilpin, visiting in 1774, noted, 'An old cross is one of the most beautiful objects we observed in the town. The cathedral is an ordinary, heavy Saxon pile, – though the cloisters and their appendages are of a more pleasing mode of architecture.'

Eastbourne	SSX	ENG	*Sand*, *MW* 364, 368, 382, 425; *MW* 444.

A resort for sea bathing.

Hailsham	SSX	ENG	*Sand*, *MW* 367.
Hastings	SSX	ENG	*Sand*, *MW* 363, 382.

The second-most popular Sussex seaside resort after Brighton.

Worthing	SSX	ENG	*Sand*, *MW* 368.

A smaller and less-formal alternative to Brighton, Worthing expanded rapidly from the 1790s on. It had two circulating libraries and a bathhouse in 1798 and erected a theatre in 1806 at a cost of £6,992.

Warwickshire	WARWK	ENG	*Gen Cur*, *MW* 73.
Birmingham	WARWK	ENG	*P&P* 240; *E* 310.

James Bisset's 1800 poem, *Ramble of the Gods through Birmingham*, described the well-known industrial character of the city. He admired wharves piled with a 'thousand tons of coal', the pin factories that could 'point and cut twelve thousand pins an hour', the crowds of boats afloat and wagon on shore, the gun works, the buckle works and the shops where metal buttons were made and gilded and 'paper trays japanned'.

Kenilworth castle	WARWK	ENG	*P&P* 240.
Warwick	WARWK	ENG	*P&P* 240.
Westmorland	WESTM	ENG	

England County/City	Map Abbreviation	Map Location	Notes
Wiltshire	WILTS	ENG	

Site of the fictional Fullerton, near Salisbury (*NA* 232), where Catherine Morland lives (*NA* 120, 122, 124, 233).

Tom Fowle, Cassandra Austen's ill-fated fiancé, had a living at Allington in Wiltshire.

Devizes	WILTS	ENG	*Clifford*, *MW* 43; *NA* 122.
Marlborough	WILTS	ENG	*S&S* 318.
Salisbury	WILTS	ENG	*NA* 224, 232.
Worcestershire	WORCS	ENG	*Sand*, *MW* 424.

One of the counties typically referred to as 'the garden of England' (*E* 273).

Yorkshire	YORKS	ENG	*Lesley*, *MW* 117; *Cath*, *MW* 200; *E* 388.

Site of Enscombe, Frank Churchill's home, 190 miles from London (*E* 15, 120, 121, 306, 426).

Harrogate	YORKS	ENG	*MW* 445.
Pontefract castle	YORKS	ENG	The 'Pomfret' of Shakespeare and of *Hist Eng*, *MW* 139.
Scarborough	YORKS	ENG	*Cath*, *MW* 199, 200; *P&P* 342.

Scarborough was northern England's largest resort, with a population of 6,000, forty bathing machines and thriving fishing and shipbuilding industries.

York	YORKS	ENG	*Sand*, *MW* 424; *MP* 193.

List of English Towns or Physical Features and Their Counties

City	County Abbreviation	City	County Abbreviation
Barnet	MDX	Charmouth	DOR (Lyme)
Basingstoke	HAMP	Chawton	HAMP
Beachy Head	SSX	Cheltenham	GLOCS
Beaulieu Abbey	HAMP	Chichester	SSX
Birmingham	WARWK	Clapham	SRY

Places

City	County Abbreviation	City	County Abbreviation
Blaise Castle	SOM (Bristol)	Clarkengreen	HAMP
Blenheim	OXF	Clifton (GLOCS)	SOM (Bristol)
Bosworth Field	LEICS	Cobham	SRY
Box Hill	SRY	Crewkherne	SOM
Brighton	SSX	Cromer	NFLK
Bristol	SOM	Croydon	SRY
Burton-on-Trent	STAFFS	Dartford	KENT
Camberwell	SRY	Dawlish	DEVON
Carlisle	CUMB	Dean Gate	HAMP
Deane	HAMP	Newmarket	SFLK
Devizes	WILTS	Northampton	NHANTS
Dovedale	DERBY	Overton	HAMP
Dover	KENT	Oxford	OXF
Eastbourne	SSX	Peak District	DERBY
Epsom	SRY	Peterborough	NHANTS
Eton	BERKS (Windsor)	Petty France	GLOCS
Exeter	DEVON	Plymouth	DEVON
Fotheringhay Castle	NHANTS	Pontefract Castle	YORKS
Godmersham	KENT	Portsmouth	HAMP
Guildford	SRY	Putney	SRY
Hailsham	SSX	Ramsgate	KENT
Hampstead	MDX	Reading	BERKS
Harrogate	YORKS	Richmond	SRY
Hastings	SSX	Salisbury	WILTS
Hatfield	HERTS	Scarborough	YORKS
Hereford	HERE	Southampton	HANTS
Honiton	DEVON	Southend	ESX

City	County Abbreviation	City	County Abbreviation
Hounslow	MDX	Taunton	SOM
Ibthorpe	HAMP	Tetbury	GLOCS
Kenilworth Castle	WARWK	Tintern Abbey	GLOCS
Kingston	SRY	Tunbridge Wells	KENT
Kingsweston	SOM (Bristol)	Twickenham	MDX
Lake District	CUMB	Weymouth	DOR
Leicester Abbey	LEICS	Winchester	HAMP
Liverpool	LANCS	Windsor	BERKS
Lyme Regis	DOR	Woolwich	KENT
Margate	KENT	Worting	HAMP
Marlborough	WILTS	Worthing	SSX
Matlock	DERBY	Yarmouth	HAMP
Newcastle	NTHUMB		

Pocketbooks and Reticules

A pocket case or letter case was a folding enclosure that usually folded twice (like a business letter today) and had a clasp or ties of some kind to keep it closed. There were several types; some were made of leather, while others were made of linen or silk and ornately embroidered. Carried by men and women alike, they could hold money, small scissors, letters (*S&S* 329), receipts, newspaper clippings (*Sand*, *MW* 366) and other small, relatively flat items (*S&S* 60, 329). Some could also be used as covers for pocketbooks.

The pocketbook was precisely what its name implies – a small book (*Sand*, *MW* 306; *NA* 18–19; *E* 339) that could fit in a pocket, often taking the form of a diary, or datebook, specific to a certain year. Some contained riddles, a calendar, pages for keeping track of expenses of keeping a diary, recipes, puzzles or song lyrics. Parson Woodforde writes of a woman receiving from a suitor the gift of 'a very handsome red Morocco Almanack and Pocket Book, gilt with a silver clasp to the same – quite new fashioned' in 1788. This red leather pocketbook would have had the datebook,

then, and possibly a compartment to hold papers and money also.
Many pocketbooks, as this one probably did, had a place to keep paper
and pencil.

Purses (*Sand*, *MW* 392; *NA* 116, 229) generally held money and were
small bags, usually closed by means of a drawstring, and decorated in
some way. The best purses came from France and featured designs made
of tiny glass beads, up to 1,000 of them per square inch. Other purses and
reticules were embroidered or beaded at home. Some were knitted, with
a bead added at every stitch; others were sewn. Some were closed with
drawstrings, while others had elaborate metal clasps. Netting was
a popular way of making purses; many of these netted purses resembled
stockings and were carried loosely in the hand, in the case of women, or
in the pockets, in the case of men. They opened in the middle, with a pouch
for coins on either side, and often featured stripes of different-coloured
thread and tassels around the edges. They were a common gift from ladies
to gentlemen.

From the 1790s, women began carrying all their different belongings
in a larger bag called a reticule. Initially called a ridicule (*E* 453) (the
name by which it went in France), then an 'indispensable', and finally
a reticule, this handbag solved a common problem of the late eighteenth
century, when more streamlined women's dresses came into vogue. The
old way of carrying money, letters, bottles of scent, handkerchiefs, purses,
fans and similar items had been to strap a cloth pocket (*Cass*, *MW* 46; *NA*
203; *E* 339) around one's waist. Items went into the pocket and were
accessed through a slit in the skirt. When the voluminous skirts and
projecting bustles that concealed the pockets were discarded, women
had to have a way of carrying their belongings, and reticules supplied
this need. Because, unlike the pockets, they were designed to be visible,
their decoration was a large part of their appeal. They might be round,
hexagonal or lozenge-shaped; decorated with beading, embroidery
or even painting; and either soft or hard.

See also Clothing; Money.

Public Places

A public place was, in Austen's time, a setting in which one's behaviour
could be observed by strangers, but it was also a place of amusement –
a place in which relative strangers could become acquaintances through
shared activities. It was a place in which those who could afford a little
idleness, whether for a month or for an afternoon, engaged in a wide
variety of diversions specifically planned for their pleasure.

The term 'public place' thus carried connotations with which we
are not familiar today. The careful person was expected to be not only
properly behaved in a 'public place' but extremely cautious. For women

in particular, a public place, with all its perilous intimacy, could lead
to moral lapses and to public disgrace (*Lesley, MW* 120).

Critics of public places are fond of this theme: that young women
brought into social gatherings in which the company cannot be selected
are inherently in danger.

Public places (*Lesley, MW* 128, 133; *NA* 104) fell into several broad
categories. Among these were 'watering places', which could include both
sea-bathing resorts and spas where invalids went to drink and bathe in the
water of mineral springs. These sorts of places attracted long-term visitors,
who made a special journey to relax, recuperate and enjoy various forms
of entertainment over a period of weeks or even months. Then there were
pleasure gardens, which attracted visitors for only a few hours. Other
places could be considered 'public places', but Austen mentions primarily
watering places and gardens.

Of the watering places (*Sand, MW* 389; *P&P* 237; *E* 146), the spas were
longer established than the seaside resorts. The latter were just becoming
popular, and they tended to imitate the amenities of the spas. Both types
of towns typically had one or more assembly halls (*H&E, MW* 35) where
balls could be held; visitors to a well-organised town would pay a fee* that
entitled them to admittance to these balls and would be greeted soon after
their arrival by a master of ceremonies, who would ascertain that they
were not irreparably vulgar in origins or demeanour. In practice, few
visitors who could pay the steep fees were barred from doing so; the
proprietors of the assembly rooms were perfectly happy to take almost
everybody's money. However, the master of ceremonies was entitled
to issue hints or commands regarding dress code and behaviour, and
this went a long way towards enforcing a code of conduct.

Watering places also usually had at least one circulating library (*Sand,
MW* 389), which charged its own fees for book borrowing. There might
also be a tea room, a card room, concerts, lotteries and raffles, as well
as private parties among acquaintances. A theatre was always desirable;
some towns, such as Brighton and Weymouth, invested heavily in new,
lavishly decorated theatres in the late eighteenth and early nineteenth
centuries and worked hard to lure London talent to their stages. Each of
these venues might have its own set of fees, and then, of course, there were
fees for the ostensible purpose in visiting such a place – taking the waters,
whether by drinking or immersion.

Shops of all kinds catered to the wealthy clientele in watering places,
selling everything from hats to rock crystals to inlaid wooden boxes.
Public works legislation in the more prominent towns improved the
lighting, paving and sanitation; Bath and Clifton, for example, raised
their pavements to protect pedestrians from the filthy drainage in the
streets. Many towns imitated the example of Bath, building townhouses
in imposingly huge rows, terraces and crescents, the entire swathe of

---

*In 1799, these could be up to 10*s*. 6*d*. for the assembly room and 5*s*. for the circulating library.

houses unified into a single façade, appearing from the street to be
one gigantic neoclassical mansion. New construction presented this
impressive face to the wide street front, while smaller, less-monumental
buildings on side streets housed servants, horses and less-prosperous
renters.

In these settings, people made acquaintances and hoped to guard
against impostors and hypocrites. As they might be rubbing shoulders
with almost anyone, precautions had to be taken to ensure that any new
acquaintances were trustworthy; in part, this function was performed by
the master of ceremonies, who vetted candidates for admission to public
gatherings and who could therefore introduce suitable strangers to each
other. In part, new friendships were formed when people were introduced
by mutual acquaintances, but to approach a stranger and strike up
a conversation without some sort of formal introduction was unforgivably
rude, and if a young woman were one of the parties to such a conversation,
the sin was graver still. Even in the best of circumstances it was possible
to end up, unwillingly or unintentionally, being acquainted with
a person of annoying habits or dubious reputation. Catherine Morland's
association with John Thorpe reflects the common fear of having to
'know' someone distasteful because of mutual acquaintances, and
Emma returns repeatedly to the theme of the superficiality of 'an
acquaintance formed only in a public place' (372), without the benefit
of seeing one's companions in their own environment or of hearing about
their faults and virtues from those who have known them all their lives
(*E* 169, 428).

At the public gardens, less care could be taken to weed out those
deemed undesirable. This was primarily because the fees for entrance into
the public gardens were much lower than the subscription fees at spas.
London's principal public gardens were Vauxhall (*Lesley, MW* 128),
Ranelagh, Marylebone and Kensington Gardens; Bath, where Austen lived
from 1801 to 1806, had Sydney Gardens; and some of the other large towns
had similar establishments. Each offered somewhat different terrain and
services, but there was a great deal of overlap. The standard public
pleasure garden had 'serpentine' (winding) paths for strolling, elaborate
landscaping designed in fashionable style, refreshments and both regularly
scheduled and special entertainments such as concerts, water shows and
fireworks. Most of the gardens suffered periodically from the public
perception that they encouraged vice – all those shady, unchaperoned
pathways! – and allowed the rabble such as servants and minor tradesmen
to sup, walk and gaze at statuary uncomfortably close to peers and
gentlemen.

Vauxhall was the most popular of the great pleasure gardens and the
longest lived; it had its origins in Elizabethan times and survived until
1859. In the mid-eighteenth century, it acquired Chinese pavilions, faux
ruins, a waterfall, a fifty-piece orchestra and a 300 guinea statue of Handel.

By Austen's lifetime, opinions about it varied; at least one visitor in 1780 found it 'a most disagreeable place', while others found it a perfectly acceptable place for young women. The food served included cold meat, sliced thinly in order to extract maximum profit (*Lesley*, *MW* 128); patrons, irritated at spending a shilling for a parsimonious helping of cold ham, joked that a single ham thus sliced could cover the entire acreage of the gardens.

Ranelagh (*Cath*, *MW* 204), located on the north side of the Thames, was famed for its huge rotunda: 150 feet across inside, it had supper boxes and room for grand balls. Founded in 1742, it had an organ in the rotunda that was played by Mozart in 1764, a lake, a Chinese pavilion and extremely high entrance fees – 2*s*. 6*d*. and 5*s*. on nights with fireworks. Vauxhall was less than half as expensive, and Marylebone cost only sixpence, or a fifth as much as Ranelagh. Evelina, in Fanny Burney's novel of the same name, found it 'a charming place', brilliantly lit and almost magical in its effect. However, it was to succumb to the eventual fate of most of the great pleasure gardens; it went out of business in 1805.

Marylebone, founded in 1650 and expanded in the first half of the eighteenth century, was lauded for the quality of its food, music and fireworks. It does not feature at all in Austen's works, however, despite these virtues, for it closed in 1778, when she was not yet three years old. Neither does she mention Sydney Gardens in her published works, though it features in her letters. Established in 1795, Sydney Gardens was, in 1801, a 16-acre plot across the river from the core of Bath. It hosted concerts, lavish public breakfasts and four or five gala nights, complete with thousands of lamps and extensive fireworks, every season. Austen attended one of these, a postponed celebration of the king's birthday, and thought that the fireworks 'were really beautiful, & surpassing my expectation'. A typical gala cost two shillings. The Austens' first lodgings in Bath were near Sydney Gardens, and we may assume that Jane often availed herself of its walks, though she was seldom impressed with more formal entertainments such as concerts.

She does make some use of Kensington Gardens, sending Elinor Dashwood there to encounter Anne Steele (*S&S* 271, 274, 276). This public garden began as the 17 acres of landscaping around William III and Mary II's palace at Kensington. Expanded by Queen Anne in the early eighteenth century and often renovated thereafter, it contained, at various times, wide paths, ponds, a paddock for exotic animals and a ha-ha. Initially, the gardens were opened to the public only on weekends when the royal family was not in residence, but by George III's time, the gardens were opening daily to members of the public who appeared well dressed and well behaved. Though the gardens had been a popular gathering place for the aristocracy at one time, by Austen's time they were more of a middle-class promenade.

See also Bath; Bathing; London; Places.

R

Reading

Reading (*Lesley, MW* 111; *Cath, MW* 197, 198, 220; *LS, MW* 273; *Watsons, MW* 361; *NA* 60; *S&S* 343; *P&P* 37, 60, 71; *MP* 22, 71; *E* 37, 85, 312; *P* 132, 219) was a common form of entertainment in Austen's time and growing increasingly common as literacy rates steadily rose, facts that should have afforded great satisfaction to intellectuals but did not. Despite the existence of numerous volumes of perfectly acceptable non-fiction, people – especially women – seemed to resist reading these works. Critics claimed that women avoided the nutritious fare of histories (*Lesley, MW* 129; *Cath, MW* 198; *NA* 37), sermons, travel journals (*NA* 108) and religious and moral tracts (*P* 101) in favour of lighter, literary junk food. They left 'all the Essays, Letters, Tours & Criticisms of the day' (*Sand, MW* 404) on the shelves of the local circulating library but swept the shelves bare of mindless claptrap.

This claim could not have been made about Austen herself, who raided her father's 500-volume library and that of the Austens' neighbour Mrs Lefroy, and who, throughout her life, read a wide variety of material. She was not, for example, among those who, like Catherine Morland, found all histories tedious (*NA* 108–109). The fictional Catherine enjoys books 'provided that nothing like useful knowledge' can be derived from them (*NA* 15), but Austen read many histories and accounts of current events, including Oliver Goldsmith's *History of England* (*MP* 419), of which her own *History of England* is a parody; Charles William Pasley's *Essay on the Military Policy and Institutions of the British Empire* (1810), a book whose excellence made her, she joked, 'much in love with the Author'; Thomas Clarkson's *History of the Abolition of the Slave Trade* (1808); Robert Henry's *History of England*, unusual in being divided by topic rather than by historical period; and another *History of England* by philosopher David Hume (*NA* 109).

She also read travels, essays and religious works. She refers to accounts of George, Lord Macartney's embassy to China (*MP* 156), a trip that captured the popular imagination and spawned works in various media. She also read Sir John's Carr's *Descriptive Travels in the Southern and Eastern Parts of Spain* (1811), a work that was particularly relevant given Britain's ongoing military forays in Spain against Napoleon and that caused her to revise a detail in *Mansfield Park*.* Austen's reading probably included at least some works on art, architecture or landscape design, as the picturesque and its connection to landscape were topics much discussed in her day. As a child, she was exposed to didactic

---

*She changed 'Government House' to 'Commissioner's' when referring to an event in Gibraltar (*MP* 235).

collections of stories, dialogues and plays designed to develop her sense of morality. Although these sorts of anthologies were not nearly as entertaining or engaging as later children's literature would be, the very concept of special literature for children was relatively novel.

Her interest in religion and moral philosophy continued, however, throughout adulthood. Though she was not fond of the strident tone of some evangelicals, including the popular author Hannah More, she consumed some of their works if only to stay apprised of the state of the theological debate. Her sister Cassandra urged her to read More's *Coelebs in Search of a Wife* (1809 – *Cath, MW* 232),* a suggestion that Jane resisted and met with ridicule at the awkward name of the hero. She was kinder to Thomas Gisborne's *Enquiry into the Duties of the Female Sex*, another evangelically authored work that she was initially reluctant to open. This is an extended essay whose description of the female sphere of influence would come to seem all too familiar by the end of the Victorian period, as it was echoed and expanded by hundreds of authors and clergymen, but in 1805 it no doubt seemed fresh and sensible. Several collections of sermons came her way, not only because she came from a family well stocked with clergymen but also because such books were commonly read by ordinary people for edification and meditation. Her works demonstrate that she was familiar with the *Sermons* of Hugh Blair (*Cath, MW* 232; *MP* 92), as well as his *Lectures on Rhetoric and Belles Lettres* (*NA* 108). She also refers to James Fordyce's *Sermons to Young Women* (1766 – *P&P* 68), another in the long line of works instructing women about their religious and moral duties. Her letters reveal that she was fond of Thomas Sherlock's sermons as well, and this tells us something about her theology, as he was a middle-of-the-road thinker, balancing carefully between deism and evangelism, offering reason with one hand and faith with the other. Religious texts are mentioned or quoted in her novels – hardly a surprise given that she was a regular churchgoer and that the words of the Bible and Prayer Book (*MP* 340, 387) must have been, like those of Shakespeare, in the very air she breathed. Miss Bates, for example, quotes (or, rather, misquotes) Psalm 16 when she says 'that "our lot is cast in a goodly heritage"' (*E* 174).[†]

Austen's other non-fiction reading included the picturesque tours of William Gilpin, who made several journeys around England and Scotland (*L&F, MW* 105) in the 1770s and later published his reflections on the suitability of various sites as the possible subjects of paintings. Elizabeth Bennet's northern tour, which ends at Pemberley, follows the route of Gilpin's *Lakes* tour. We are told that she particularly liked the works of Samuel Johnson, and his words crop up now and again in allusions within her own works. There is a reference to Boswell's *Life*

---

*A later substitution for her original choice, Archbishop Thomas Secker's (1693–1768) *Lectures on the Catechism of the Church of England* (1769).
[†]The actual passage is, 'The lot is fallen unto me in a fair ground: yea, I have a goodly heritage.'

of Johnson, for example, in one of her poems (*MW* 442), and Fanny
Price's musings echo a famous sentence from *Rasselas:* 'Marriage has
many pains, but celibacy has no pleasures' (*MP* 392). His dictionary
is alluded to in *Northanger Abbey* (108), and his periodical, *The Idler*
(1758–1760 – *MP* 156), also shows up on the table of Fanny Price, whose
reading habits are clearly meant to be exemplary. R. W. Chapman also
argues that the passage in *Love and Freindship* (*MW* 97) that begins, 'we
left Macdonald Hall' is reminiscent of Johnson's *Journey to the Western
Islands* (1775).

Austen mentions other assorted works that would have been found
in a literate household, such as pamphlets (*NA* 187) about political
affairs (*P* 215) or agricultural improvements, collections of letters (*P* 101),
memoirs (*P* 101) and biographies, and accounts of titles and heraldry such
as Debrett's *Baronetage of England* (*P* 3–4, 249) and Sir William Dugdale's
*Antient Usage in Bearing of Such Ensigns of Honour as Are Commonly
Call'd Arms* (*P* 4). Occasionally, we see references to works associated
with certain professions, such as the 'Agricultural Reports' (*E* 29, which
R. W. Chapman suggests may be the *General Review of the Agriculture of
the County of Surrey)* and the Navy List (*MP* 389; *P* 64). There is a reference
to Madame de Genlis' sentimental volume on education, *Adelaide and
Theodore* (1783), which embraces the trend towards finding a more natural
and holistic method of education (*E* 461); works on education, whether
fictionalised or not, were widely read in intellectual circles.

Periodicals mentioned include newspapers and that increasingly popular
format, the magazine. Magazines had begun in the early eighteenth century
as collections of essays and satires such as the *Spectator* (*NA* 37, 38) and
the *Tatler*. Samuel Johnson, one of Austen's favourite authors, contributed
to this format with his *Rambler* (*NA* 30) and *Idler*. By the turn of the
nineteenth century, there were fashion magazines such as *Ackermann's
Repository*, literary magazines such as Henry Mackenzie's *The Mirror*
(whose issue of 6 March 1779, contains the story 'Consequence to Little
Folks of Intimacy with Great Ones, in a Letter from John Home-spun' –
see *NA* 241) and magazines with general content such as news, fashion,
articles on hunting, society tidbits and puzzles and games. Some took
a political stance, as did the *Quarterly Review* (*MP* 104) and the *Edinburgh
Review*. The *Edinburgh Review* supported Whigs and reform, while the
Quarterly Review, founded in 1809 by publisher John Murray, supported
Tory policies and the maintenance of the status quo.

Poetry

Yet, though Austen read such a wide variety of what her contemporaries
would have called 'serious' books, she was no Mr Collins, lecturing
young women on the importance of reading 'books of a serious stamp, ...
written solely for their benefit' (*P&P* 69). As with so many things, including
hunting, music, fashion and food, she urges moderation. The overly studious
Mary Bennet (*P&P* 7, 60) is treated no more kindly than the hypocritically

superficial reader Caroline Bingley; nor is she given any particular credit for reading and copying passages from serious texts, for Austen, like most people of her time, thoroughly enjoyed reading poetry, plays and novels and endorsed the same enjoyment in others – in *moderation*.

Moderation is, again, the watchword. Austen was an enthusiastic consumer of poetry (*NA* 16; *P&P* 44–45; *P* 215), especially that of William Cowper (*S&S* 18, 47, 92) and Sir Walter Scott (*S&S* 47, 92; *P* 107, 167). Cowper was supposedly her favourite poet, and indeed his name and words appear frequently in her works.

Fanny Price also reads Cowper and thinks of his *Tirocinium* when she feels homesick (*MP* 431); the passage she contemplates can be found in the 'Education' entry earlier in this book.

The Task is quoted again in *Emma* (344), and Austen famously alluded to it yet again in one of her letters, when she announced that she intended to plant laburnum and syringa in her Southampton garden because they had been mentioned by Cowper.

Austen refers obliquely to Robert Burns (*Sand, MW* 397) and his imitators in the 'Scotch poems' of *Lesley Castle* (*MW* 124), though her sensible character Charlotte Heywood found that Burns's notorious drinking and womanising spoiled some of her enjoyment of his poems (*Sand, MW* 398). Another of the famous Scottish poets of the time was Sir Walter Scott (1771–1832), whom Jane enjoyed without any such reservations about his private character. She mentions *Marmion* and *The Lady of the Lake* in her works (*Sand, MW* 397; *P* 100) and quotes from *The Lay of the Last Minstrel* in *Mansfield Park* (86). Once again, it is Fanny Price who recalls from memory, 'Full many a scutcheon and banner riven / Shook to the cold night-wind of heaven', and the Scottish king buried below a marble stone, though she fails to recall the exact wording (*MP* 86).

Other poets mentioned include James Montgomery (1771–1854), whose works included abolitionist and religious poems (*Sand, MW* 397); William Wordsworth (1770–1850), one of the principal Romantic poets whose verse often described the scenery of his native Lake District (*Sand, MW* 397); and Thomas Campbell (1777–1844), who addressed various subjects in his works, from the beauties of nature to the deeds of famous men. Sir Edward Denham mentions his *Pleasures of Hope* (1799 – *Sand, MW* 397) and quotes a line from it. Oliver Goldsmith, whose *History* Austen also read, earns a nod for his poetry as well when Austen summarises his two-verse poem, *When Lovely Woman Stoops to Folly* (*E* 387) – the 'folly', in Goldsmith's poem, being sexual looseness and presumably nothing to do with Mrs Churchill's character or cause of death.

Matthew Prior (1664–1721) is mentioned (*NA* 37) but not quoted, though his poem *Henry and Emma* is alluded to in the context of Anne Elliot's desire to serve as Louisa Musgrove's nurse.

The Beggar's Petition, a work by a much less well-remembered poet, Thomas Moss, is one of the pieces that the young Catherine Morland is required to memorise (*NA* 14). It was a conventional and uninspired poem about the pangs of starvation amid wealth:

> My faithful wife, with ever-straining eyes,
> Hangs on my bosom her dejected head;
> My helpless infants raise their feeble cries,
> And from their father claim their daily bread.

Its tired language may be one of the reasons that Catherine has such difficulty committing it to memory.

There is a possible reference to Alexander Pope's *Rape of the Lock* in the phrase 'eleven with its silver sounds' in *Persuasion* (144); a watch in that poem makes a 'silver sound'. A more explicit reference to Pope (*NA* 37; *S&S* 47) can be found in *Northanger Abbey* (15), where Catherine Morland reads his *Elegy to the Memory of an Unfortunate Lady*, with its dead heroine whose friends will not even

> Grieve for an hour, perhaps, then mourn a year,
> And bear about the mockery of woe
> To midnight dances, and the public show.

Mrs Elton also quotes Pope's *L'Allegro* (*E* 308), and Mr Elliot alludes to his *Essay on Criticism* (1711) with its famous line, 'A little learning is a dang'rous thing' (*P* 150).

George Crabbe's *Tales* (1812), a series of stories told in rhyming couplets, are briefly mentioned as being among Fanny Price's books (*MP* 156). This is a typical Austenian aside. Many of her readers would have been familiar with Crabbe's other works, including the *Parish Register*, which features a young woman named Fanny Price who resists marrying a wealthy man.

John Gay's *Fables* are mentioned in two novels; Catherine Morland learns the fable of *The Hare and Many Friends* (*NA* 14), and Mrs Elton quotes from the same fable in speaking to Jane Fairfax (*E* 454). The choice of fable is interesting, as the short poem depicts the plight of a hare pursued by hounds. Desperate for assistance, she asks one animal after another to carry her on their backs so that she may fool the dogs, but all of her supposed 'friends' refuse for one reason or another to come to her aid. Jane Fairfax has been, for most of the novel, in a similar situation. She, too, is in urgent need of help, but all those who should be of assistance to her – her aunt, Frank Churchill, Mrs Elton and Emma – do her harm instead through, respectively, incompetence, deception, officiousness and jealousy.

This poetic contribution of Mrs Elton is an example of the fact that it is not only Austen's admirable characters that read and recall poetry. Henry Crawford quotes Milton (*NA* 37) in his reference to 'a wife' as 'Heaven's *last* best gift' (*MP* 43); the relevant lines are from *Paradise Lost*, Chapter 5, where Adam discovers the newly created, sleeping Eve:

Her hand soft touching, whispered thus,
'Awake! My fairest, my espoused, my latest found,
Heaven's last, best gift, my ever-new delight ... '

Of course, he subverts Milton's intent by implying that taking a wife is
the last thing he personally would wish to do. His sister likewise tampers
with a poet's lines. She parodies Isaac Hawkins Browne (1705–1760), who
wrote poems on the subject of tobacco in the style of other authors – not
only Pope, as in the sample quoted by Mary Crawford (*MP* 161), but also
Jonathan Swift and James Thomson (1700–1748 – *NA* 15; *S&S* 92), best
remembered for *A Poem Sacred to the Memory of Sir Isaac Newton* and the
lyrics to *Rule, Britannia*. Mrs Elton, too, is well read, for she only slightly
misquotes two lines from Thomas Gray's *Elegy Written in a Country
Churchyard* (1751 – *E* 282) – the last two lines of the following stanza:

Full many a gem of purest ray serene
The dark unfathom'd caves of ocean bear:
Full many a flower is born to blush unseen,
And waste its sweetness on the desert air.

It is unclear whether the reader is meant to interpret her misquotation of
the passage as a jab at the character's literary pretensions. In *Northanger
Abbey*, Austen quotes the same two lines in exactly the same way, using
'fragrance' instead of 'sweetness' (*NA* 15).

George Gordon, Lord Byron (1788–1824 – see *P* 107, 109, 167), is referred
to occasionally.

Austen no doubt read all the poems she cites and many more, for she
owned several anthologies of poetry. William Whitehead's *The Je Ne Sais
Quoi* (quoted in *MP* 292) appears in an anthology of poems collected by
Robert Dodsley, a copy of which Jane Austen owned. A similar anthology,
the *Elegant Extracts* (*E* 29), compiled by Vicesimus Knox in 1789, is
mentioned incorrectly in *Emma* as the source of the riddle 'Kitty, a fair
but frozen maid' (*E* 70, 79); R. W. Chapman points out that it first appeared
in *The New Foundling Hospital for Wit* (1771) and was thereafter reprinted
in numerous subsequent anthologies. Austen owned a copy of *Elegant
Extracts*, which she gave to her niece Anna upon moving to Bath in 1801,
so perhaps by the time of the composition of *Emma*, she had forgotten
where she originally read 'Kitty'.

Plays

Austen was fond of theatre and went to plays (*NA* 108; *E* 74) whenever
she got the chance, but she also read plays at home. Shakespeare (*S&S* 85;
MP 338) appears to have been a perennial favourite. There are references
to *Henry VIII* (*MP* 336–337), *A Midsummer Night's Dream* (*E* 75), *Henry IV
Part II* (*Hist Eng*, *MW* 139), *Hamlet* (*S&S* 85; *MP* 131), *Julius Caesar* (*MP* 126),
Macbeth (*MP* 131), *Measure for Measure* (*NA* 16), *The Merchant of Venice*
(*MP* 123), *Othello* (*NA* 16; *MP* 131), *Richard III* (*MP* 126), *Romeo and Juliet*

(*E* 400) and *Twelfth Night* (*NA* 16). She mentions more contemporary plays as well, which are discussed at more length in the 'Theatre' article. Her novels and Juvenilia contain references to John Home's *Douglas* (*MP* 126, 131), Edward Moore's *The Gamester* (*MP* 131), Hannah Cowley's *Which Is the Man?* (*3S*, *MW* 65), Nicholas Rowe's *Jane Shore* (*Hist Eng*, *MW* 141) and, famously, *Lovers Vows* (*MP* 122, 168, 191) by Kotzebue, adapted by Elizabeth Inchbald. Three of Richard Brinsley Sheridan's plays are mentioned – *The Rivals* (*MP* 131), *School for Scandal* (*MP* 131) and *The Critic* (*Hist Eng*, *MW* 147), making him her most mentioned playwright after Shakespeare.

Novels

Her greatest enthusiasm and her most devastating parodies, however, are reserved for the novel, a genre with which she was intimately familiar even before she began to write. Her family did not harbour the prejudice against novel-reading that was a fashionable intellectual stance at the time (*Sand*, *MW* 403; *NA* 48; *S&S* 43; *P&P* 68). Novels (*Cath*, *MW* 198–199; *Sand*, *MW* 389, 391; *NA* 37–38) were widely regarded as being a cause of moral decay among the young and a source of foolish ideas about romantic love that ruined people, especially women, for the realities of marriage. The most criticised novels fell into two classes: romances, which taught readers to expect obstacles to true love such as parental opposition (*L&F*, *MW* 81) or mismatched wealth, and which, it was thought, encouraged elopements and seductions; and Gothics, which were filled with superstition, exotic scenery, ominous villains (*NA* 181), perjured priests, ghosts and dark family secrets. Austen gently parodied both forms. *Sense and Sensibility* pokes fun at novels of sentiment and romance, such as Johann Wolfgang von Goethe's *The Sorrows of Young Werther* (1774 – see *L&F*, *MW* 93), which actually led some young men to commit suicide for love, holding copies of Goethe's book as they died. Such books encouraged readers to fancy themselves supremely sensitive, emotional people brimming with potential suffering and ready to sacrifice all for the sake of love. They celebrated impulse and feeling and often derided conventional mores. Austen demonstrates, through the character of Marianne Dashwood, how difficult and dangerous it can be to live one's life according to such ideals. *Northanger Abbey* subverts the Gothic novel by demonstrating how far removed its dark plots were from everyday Regency life. In the course of demonstrating the shortcomings of the Gothic, Austen names many of the most popular examples of the genre, including Eliza Parsons' *Castle of Wolfenbach* (1793 – *NA* 40) and *The Mysterious Warning* (1796 – *NA* 40), Francis Latham's *The Midnight Bell* (1798 – *NA* 40), Regina Maria Roche's *The Children of the Abbey* (1798 – *E* 29) and *Clermont* (1798), Peter Teuthold's *The Necromancer; or the Tale of the Black Forest* (1794 – *NA* 40), Eleanor Sleath's *Orphan of the Rhine* (1798 – *NA* 40), Peter Will's *Horrid Mysteries* (1796 – *NA* 40) and Matthew Lewis' notorious *The Monk* (1796 – *NA* 48). Charlotte Smith's *Emmeline or the Orphan of the Castle* (1788 – *Cath*, *MW*

199) concerns, in part, the unsuccessful attempts of the hero Frederick Delamere to win Emmeline's love (*Hist Eng, MW* 146). Smith (1749–1806) also wrote *Ethelinde* (1789 – *Cath, MW* 199), a novel that, like *Emmeline*, features copious description of picturesque landscapes.

Ann Radcliffe (*NA* 49, 106, 110), queen of the Gothic, receives the most attention from Austen. There are direct references to her works *The Mysteries of Udolpho* (1794 – *NA* 39, 41–42, 49, 83, 86, 106–108, 187) and *The Italian* (1797 – *NA* 40) and indirect references to plot points from her novels that readers of Austen's time would have recognised immediately, such as the black veil and 'Laurentina's skeleton' from *Udolpho* (*NA* 39, 40) and the roll of paper from *The Romance of the Forest* (1791 – *E* 29, 32). At other times, she merely imitates the tone of the Gothic in order to contrast it with the reality of a simple visit to an English country house (*NA* 88, 167, 190–191). Austen also wrings a little humour out of Eleanor Tilney's misunderstanding of Catherine's description of a forthcoming Gothic novel, with 'murder and every thing of the kind' (*NA* 112), as a prediction of a London riot.

Austen's minor works took potshots at additional literary conventions, from the epistolary form (*L&F*) to the extended narrative-within-a-narrative (*Plan*) that so often intruded into the clumsier examples of the genre. Both the *Plan of a Novel* and *Northanger Abbey* subvert the tradition of making the heroine an exemplary creature, though the latter work accomplishes the task by making the heroine deliberately ordinary, while the former does it by making her absolutely without a flaw, or even a hint of a flaw.

Austen herself preferred more realistic fiction. She enjoyed Henry Fielding's *Tom Jones* (*NA* 48), a rollicking tale that parodies the vogue for the classical at the same time that it tells the story of an amorous young bastard and his quest for love and fortune. She was also fond of the novels of Samuel Richardson, though she acknowledged that his constant return to the theme of sexual and romantic conquest bordered on the prurient (*Sand, MW* 404). (The 'Lovelace' on which Sir Edward Denham patterns himself is the heartless seducer of Richardson's *Clarissa Harlowe*.) Her favourite among his works was *Sir Charles Grandison* (*J&A, MW* 15; *Evelyn, MW* 186; *NA* 41–42), which she tried at one point to turn into a play. Fanny Burney D'Arblay's novels *Evelina*, *Cecilia* (1782 – *NA* 38; *P* 189) and *Camilla* (1796 – *Sand, MW* 390; *NA* 38, 49, 111) were also works she admired. (Her father, knowing she appreciated Burney, gave her a subscription to the first edition of *Camilla* as a present, and her name can be found on the list of subscribers.) Burney's plots generally turned on the introduction of a young woman into society and her consequent education in its ways, ending with her marriage to a decent and handsome young man, a series of events that bears a striking resemblance to the pattern of Austen's mature works.

Other novels mentioned include Maria Edgeworth's *Belinda* (1801 – *NA* 38), Oliver Goldsmith's *The Vicar of Wakefield* (*E* 29) and Richard Graves' *Columella* (1779 – *S&S* 103), in which the hero apprentices his son 'to a very celebrated man … who had united in his own person the several professions of apothecary, surgeon, man-midwife, bone-setter, tooth-drawer, hop-dealer, and brandy-merchant'. There is an allusion to Laurence Sterne's *Sentimental Journey* (1768 – *NA* 37) in *Mansfield Park* (99) and to Samuel Johnson's *Rasselas* later in the same book (392).

Naturally, she read a great many novels that are not alluded to in her published works. Maria Edgeworth was a particular favourite, and Austen read many of her works, including *Castle Rackrent* and *Patronage*. She also read novels that are forgotten today, such as Robert Bage's *Hermsprong* (1796) and Sarah Burney's *Clarentine* (1798). She found the latter novel 'foolish … [F]ull of unnatural conduct & forced difficulties, without striking merit of any kind'. If there was anything that Austen found annoying in literature, it was 'unnatural conduct & forced difficulties'. She did, however, enjoy the parodies of other authors who, like herself, could not resist calling attention to literary clichés. Among these other authors were Charlotte Lennox, who wrote the romance parody *The Female Quixote* (1752), and James and Horatio Smith, who wrote verse parodies.

Collections of short stories would not become popular until the Victorian age and the dominance of the magazines that printed such stories. However, Austen makes two references to the *Arabian Nights*, a collection of Middle Eastern tales first translated into English in the early eighteenth century. She mentions Scheherazade, the purported narrator of the exciting tales, who told them in order to enchant the sultan and keep him from executing her, in *Persuasion* (229). The tale of Aladdin is mentioned in *Emma* (322) and in a deleted passage in *The Three Sisters* (*MW* 65), in which Mary Stanhope requests as many jewels from her new husband as were possessed by Princess Badroulbadour, Aladdin's beloved.

Buying and Reading Books

A typical novel consisted of a dedication to some illustrious person, who had either given specific permission for this particular work to be dedicated or blanket permission for the dedication of some future work by the author. The dedication served two purposes: for the author, it was a kind of brand name or seal of approval – if the duchess of Whateverington likes my work, so will you – and for the recipient of the dedication, it was an irresistible form of public flattery. Most dedications were fawning affairs of one or two paragraphs, attesting to the patron's unfailing commitment to the author's work, the author's unworthiness to receive such tributes and the author's hope of the patron's satisfaction with this latest humble offering. Austen, who even in childhood studied all forms of writing and grasped what made them recognisable, even in condensed form, could not resist parodying the bloated dedication. Her youthful works are dedicated to all sorts of supposedly illustrious citizens, including her cousin Jane Cooper (*H&E*, *MW* 33; *Col Let*, *MW* 149); her brothers Francis (*J&A*, *MW* 12), Edward (*3S*, *MW* 57), Henry (*Lesley*, *MW* 109), James (*Visit*, *MW* 49) and Charles (*Mount*, *MW* 40; *Clifford*,

MW 42); her mother (*Amelia*, *MW* 47); her father (*Mystery*, *MW* 55); her niece Fanny, Edward's daughter (*Scraps*, *MW* 170); her sister-in-law Mary, James' wife (*Evelyn*, *MW* 179) and her sister Cassandra who was fortunate enough to have four works dedicated to her: *The Beautifull Cassandra*, *Ode to Pity* (*MW* 74), the *History of England* (*MW* 138) and *Catharine or the Bower*. The dedication to *The Beautifull Cassandra* (*MW* 44) is a dead-on imitation of the tone, if not the wording, of most dedications:

Dedicated by permission to Miss Austen.
Dedication.
Madam

You are a Phoenix. Your taste is refined, your Sentiments are noble, & your Virtues innumerable. Your Person is lovely, your Figure, elegant, & your Form, majestic. Your Manners are polished, your Conversation is rational & your appearance singular. If therefore the following Tale will afford one moment's amusement to you, every wish will be gratified of

Your most obedient humble servant
The Author

One of the dedications is actually to a noblewoman, but the noblewoman in question, 'Madame La Comtesse De Feuillide' (*L&F*, *MW* 76), was in fact Jane's first cousin Eliza, who had married a French count. The only dedication of one of Austen's novels to an illustrious personage in the traditional sense was the dedication of *Emma*, by royal hint (which essentially equalled a royal command), to the prince regent.

Non-fiction works were also often dedicated to a patron or friend whose name had some degree of public recognition. These works would also often have an index, though items in the index might be simply grouped by first letter rather than fully alphabetised. Books of all sorts might have a frontispiece (an engraved illustration facing the title page) and a table of contents that could offer rather more detail about chapter contents than we are accustomed to today. A guide word (the first word or partial word from the following page) appeared at the bottom right-hand corner of each page, both as a help to the bookbinder in assembling the pages in the right order and as a link from one page to the next for those reading aloud (*NA* 107; *S&S* 48; *P&P* 68; *MP* 336–337, 338, 340; *E* 46–47). The paper was made of shredded cotton rags and was far more durable than most paper used in books today. The size of the paper was determined by how many times the large printed sheet was folded. One fold yielded four pages, a folio; two folds yielded eight pages, making a quarto; three folds produced the sixteen pages of an octavo and four folds the thirty-two pages of a duodecimo (*NA* 113). The pages were printed, folded and sewn together, and then the folded edges that faced the outer edges of the book were cut with a sharp knife.

Reading

Books (*LS, MW* 273; *Sand, MW* 383; *NA* 204; *S&S* 20, 26, 30, 41, 47, 83, 93, 155, 304, 307; *P&P* 12, 54–55, 93, 172, 180, 223, 289; *MP* 151, 200; *E* 34; *P* 38, 82, 97, 100, 131, 234), once printed and collated, were bound (*NA* 107; *MP* 191) either by the printer or by the customer, who could take them to a specialist bookbinder (*Col Let, MW* 158). Binding in 'boards' – essentially a thick cardboard front and back with a flexible connection to the spine – was cheaper than binding in leather, and some types of leather were more expensive than others. Books were also sold at shops, by peddlers and by immense bookshops (*S&S* 92) such as Lackington's in London, which would seem small by today's standards but at the time offered an enormous selection. Booksellers, who often combined their business with printers' shops and circulating libraries, proliferated during Austen's lifetime. By the 1790s, there were almost 1,000 booksellers in the provinces, plus many more in London.

Publishers might agree to pay a royalty of sorts, but more commonly they tried to purchase the copyright to a work. This strategy was risky, but if the book were successful, the publisher stood to make an enormous profit. In some cases, wary authors sold only the copyright for one edition and held out in the hope of a second or third edition and further income. Other books were printed by subscription, meaning that people agreed to purchase the book in advance, trusting in the author's reputation. They paid a sum and received a copy of the book when it appeared.

Circulating Libraries

Book prices ranged from perhaps nine shillings for a cheap three-volume novel to a guinea per volume for a large, handsomely bound book. Even the cheap novel represented about half a month's wages for an ordinary servant, so it was only the well-off who could afford to amass large personal libraries (*S&S* 343; *P&P* 37, 38, 55, 71, 349; *MP* 27; *P* 99) like the 500 volumes owned by Austen's father. People who did not wish to invest heavily in books, or who simply wanted to read a wider variety than was available to them at home, borrowed books from friends, joined book clubs and societies that jointly acquired volumes or subscribed to circulating libraries.

Circulating libraries (*Sand, MW* 374, 384, 391, 398–399, 403; *P&P* 30, 68; *MP* 389; *P* 130) were a feature of most sizable towns. Often run by people who ran a side-business such as bookbinding or trinket-selling (*Sand, MW* 389; *P&P* 238), they served not only as libraries but also as social centres. Advertisements for lodgings to rent or servants for hire were sometimes placed there, and the list of subscribers (*Sand, MW* 389) offered, at a glance, a sense of the sort of middle- and upper-class society present in town.

Subscription libraries had been established in Scotland in the seventeenth century, gradually spreading south throughout the eighteenth century. Around the turn of the century, working-class libraries began to be founded on the same lines but with lower subscription rates. A share in a more genteel library might cost anywhere from 1 to 5 guineas,

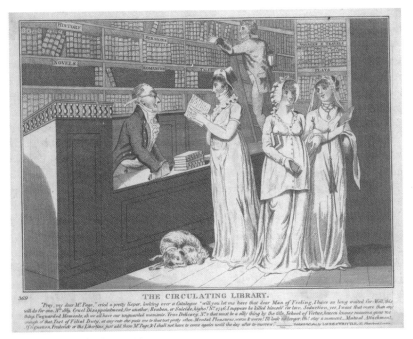

27. *The Circulating Library*, 1804.

with an annual subscription costing perhaps 6 to 10 shillings. The stock of books might be anywhere from a few hundred to a few thousand; one of the largest was a library in Liverpool with 8,000 books in 1801. Book selection was by ballot among the subscribers, and the librarian had little control over the inventory, being merely a paid functionary in many cases. Some librarians owned their libraries, having started them as entrepreneurial ventures, and these were almost certainly people who owned a second business such as a print shop. Bookselling was a natural combination with library lending, as booksellers could lend extra stock to customers for a small fee.

Library hours were quite limited at first. In the 1780s, for example, the Birmingham library was open six days a week, but only from 2:00 p.m. to 5:00 p.m. By the turn of the century this library was open for more hours, from 11:00 a.m. to 1:00 p.m., from 3:00 p.m. to 6:00 p.m. and from 7:00 p.m. to 8:00 p.m., and the librarian's salary was raised to 40 guineas a year to reflect the additional workload. Fines for late return of books often depended on the size of the book – for example, 1*d.* per day for pamphlets, 2*d.* for octavos and duodecimos, 3*d.* for quartos and 4*d.* for folios, as in Leeds in the 1760s. The borrowing period was usually two or three weeks.

When a new library was founded, its proprietor did whatever she could to acquire new business. This might mean advertising in the local paper; it might also mean making contact with the local gentry and their families as well as the more-prosperous tradesmen. Austen reported in 1798 that

she had been approached by a Mrs Martin, 'requesting my name as
a Subscriber to her Library which opens the 14th of January, & my name,
or rather Yours, is accordingly given'. I suppose to the self-consequence
of half her subscribers.

Circulating libraries could be found in increasing numbers in resort
towns such as Bath, where a subscription cost 15s. a year or 5s. a quarter
from 1789.

See also Gothic; Newspaper; Picturesque; Theatre.

S

Servants

In the early years of the industrial age, when electricity had yet to be
harnessed; when laundry was done by hand over a tub heated by fire;
when the fire was lit not with matches but with flint, steel and tinder; and
when the water had to be pumped laboriously or carried, still more
laboriously, bucket by bucket from a well, the labour of servants (*Clifford*,
MW 43; *L&F*, *MW* 107; *Lesley*, *MW* 119; *Col Let*, *MW* 159; *Evelyn*, *MW* 181,
189; *Cath*, *MW* 194; *Watsons*, *MW* 327; *Sand*, *MW* 391, 393, 416, 425, 427;
NA 61, 167, 173, 194, 200; *S&S* 28, 75, 91, 194, 286, 293, 312, 317, 318; *P&P* 44,
162, 215, 249, 250, 258, 268, 292, 310, 333, 335; *MP* 28, 188, 205, 233, 302, 385,
389–390, 391, 392, 426, 447, 455; *E* 184, 303, 355, 458, 469; *P* 13, 64) was
essential to the running of any household that aspired to at least the
middle class. The greater the number of servants in a home (*NA* 166, 184;
S&S 233; *P&P* 160; *E* 207; *P* 219), and the more of life's disagreeable tasks
they performed, the greater the display to the world that this was the
abode of prosperous and comfortable people. In the largest homes,
servants did everything that required real work. They plucked the
chickens, cooked the food, cleaned the plates, swept the floors and the
cobwebs built in corners, cared for the children and washed the clothes,
the carpets, the dresses, the dirty linen and the stairs. They carried
messages and packages, held the reins of horses, kept the accounts, did the
shopping and lugged chamber pots full of night-time human waste out to
'Jericho', the garden outhouse. In return, they received housing, food and
sometimes clothing and other perquisites.

This system was viewed with suspicion and discomfort from both sides.
Employers carped about the poor quality of available servants, the high
wages they demanded and the difficulty of getting them to stay at one
house for more than a year or two. In addition, though they did not like

to dwell on this disquieting fact, they lost almost all privacy in a house full of servants (*MP* 451). Servants stood behind the chairs at dinner in order to bring food and clear plates and thus heard all the dinner conversation. They dressed their masters and mistresses in the morning and just before dinner, hearing gossip of all kinds as they did so. They also chatted with servants in other households, especially when those servants travelled from one household to another in attendance on dinner guests. Many an employer must have wondered what was being said about him in the kitchen as he played whist in the drawing room.

Jonathan Swift's *Directions to Servants* (1731) considerably predates the period under consideration, but the work performed by servants did not change radically between 1731 and, say, 1811; nor did the expectations of employers change. Swift's satirical 'advice' to servants on how to cheat their masters and subvert the morals of the household may not have been meant literally, but it does offer a window into the causes of employer dissatisfaction. He mockingly urges servants not to come except when called specifically by name, to hide the bad behaviour of their fellows (except when they have some grudge against the offender), to make excuses for taking too long on an errand and to ask often for raises in pay. Those who have authority to spend money, he says, should spend money freely without bargaining for the best price. 'When you have done a fault', Swift suggests, 'be always pert and insolent, and behave yourself as if you were the injured person'.

From Swift's indirect complaints, we can see that servants wrote their names in candle smoke on their ceilings, used the employers' knives at the servants' table, gossiped, left the front door open, drank too much, forgot the names of callers and used the same pot to 'boil milk, heat porridge, hold small beer, or in case of necessity serve for a jordan [chamber pot]' but never washed it 'for fear of taking off the tin'.

Servants, in turn, felt constantly short-changed. They had to work long hours, beginning work in some cases before dawn and ending, on nights when the employers attended late parties, well after midnight. They, too, had little privacy and little free time, and employers always seemed to be fussing about how that free time was spent. Seldom were they allowed to have romantic relationships, and even friendships could be difficult to maintain. The work, in many cases, was physically demanding and apparently endless, with only low wages to show for the drudgery. Books purporting to help them in their work were written from the employers' perspective and advised meek obedience and resignation. The keys to succeeding in one's post were cleanliness, a positive attitude, industry and an unwillingness to dawdle when sent on errands.

Yet there was no alternative. The servants needed the work, and the employers needed their servants. Besides, not every servant–employer relationship was contentious. Austen deeply appreciated the services of James, a servant her family employed while vacationing in Lyme. In September 1804, she wrote,

> James is the delight of our lives; he is quite an Uncle Toby's annuity
> to us. – My Mother's shoes were never so well blacked before, and
> our plate never looked so clean. He waits extremely well, is attentive,
> handy, quick, & quiet, and in short has a great many more than all the
> cardinal virtues.

Nor was the approval all on the employer's side. When Jane's Aunt
Mrs Leigh-Perrot was falsely accused of shoplifting and held in jail for
months, a former servant wrote to her husband offering his support and
recalling the couple's kindness to him:

> I shall never forget yours and my mistresses great goodness to me when
> I was taken with the small pox in your sarvice. You sent me very careful
> to mothers, and paid a nurse and my doctor, and my board for a long
> time as I was bad, and when I was too bad with biles all over my head
> so as I could not go to sarvice for a many weeks you maintained me.
> The famaly as I lives with be a going thro' Bath into Devonshire and
> we stops two days at the Inn and there I heard of the bad trick as those
> bad shopkeepers has sarved my mistress and I took the libarty of going
> to your house to enquire how you both do and the housekeeper said she
> sent a pasel to you every week and if I had anything to say she could
> send a letter. I hope Honored Sir you will forgive my taking such
> a libarty to write but I wish anybody could tell me how to do you and
> mistress any good. I would travel night and day to serve you both.

This may have been self-serving loyalty, as John Trusler would assert,
but it must have touched the Leigh-Perrots anyway.

Servants were simultaneously a necessity and a luxury. At least one
servant was necessary for any measure of comfort (*P* 152–153, 154, 197),
and only the poor would avoid hiring a maid of all work (*S&S* 277) –
a girl who scrubbed, lit the kitchen fire and did whatever else the lady of
the house needed. The best example of this hardworking creature is the
Bateses' Patty, who tends to the fireplace (*E* 326), cooks (*E* 173), answers
the door and announces visitors (*E* 452) and can be sent on errands as
necessary (*E* 296). Such a servant was so essential that in some boarding
houses in Bath, tenants would not be accepted unless they brought
at least one servant to lighten the burden on the landlord's staff.

Magistrate Patrick Colquhoun estimated in 1796 that there were 240,000
families in London, with 100,000 of those employing an average of two
servants. Most of the 200,000 servants in his calculations would have been
women, for although large households tended to employ roughly equal
numbers of men and women, the families that could afford to keep only
one or two servants hired women. This was because women would work for
lower wages and because women, on the whole, expected to do more work.
Also, menservants were principally for show and for taking care of luxury
goods such as wine cellars, hunting dogs and carriages, exactly the sorts
of possessions that one-servant households could not afford. Estimates

between 1777 and 1806 put the number of menservants in England and Wales at about 100,000 to 110,000 and the number of maidservants at about 800,000, meaning that approximately one of every ten people was in service and that perhaps seven of every eight servants was a woman.

The fact that women did most of the essential domestic labour affected the structure of taxes. A tax on employing servants was first introduced in 1777 by Lord North, who set the rate at one guinea per male servant, with female servants exempt from taxation. Bachelors paid double, while families with children paid less. In 1785, Prime Minister Pitt raised the tax, creating a sliding scale based on the number of male servants employed and charging a base rate of between £1 5s. and £3 for each male servant, with the tax still doubled for bachelors. Female servants were now taxed as well, but at a lower rate, ranging from 2s. 6d. to 10s., depending on the number of women employed.

Male Servants

If we assume the existence of a large household, such as, perhaps, the one at Mansfield Park or at Pemberley, we can safely assume that there would be a substantial number of both upper and lower menservants (*Evelyn*, *MW* 183; *Watsons*, *MW* 319; *NA* 44, 46; *S&S* 26, 353; *P&P* 212; *MP* 223; *E* 20). In 1771, the Duke of Bedford had forty-two male servants at his London home.

Upper menservants* wore ordinary clothes rather than livery and were generally paid higher wages. At the top of the hierarchy – and there was a hierarchy, both within and between households, based not only on job title and pay but also on family background and the status of one's employer (*Cass*, *MW* 44; *P* 4) – was the steward. He could be a land steward (*Cath*, *MW* 195; *NA* 139; *S&S* 259; *P&P* 81, 199; *MP* 34, 36, 82, 191, 411–412), who served as the manager of his employer's estate, settling disputes, dealing with tenants, keeping accounts and managing the acres that were not rented out but farmed directly by the employer. Or, he could be a house steward, the supreme authority within the household and the chief purchaser and budgeter. Stewards were found only on large estates and might have underlings called bailiffs (*MP* 58, 191; *E* 104), who purchased seed and livestock, supervised ploughmen and might wait at the table (but without donning livery). On smaller estates, the functions of the steward were performed by the employer himself, by a combined land steward–house steward or by a bailiff. A land or house steward might make from 30 to 50 guineas a year, while a bailiff would make somewhat less. The Austens had a bailiff, John Bond, who may have been the model for Mr Knightley's steward William Larkins.

---

*Upper servants of both sexes were usually referred to by their surnames, and occasionally an honorific such as 'Mrs.' would be added (*LS*, *MW* 284; *Sand*, *MW* 389; *P&P* 306, 317; *MP* 251, 277, 344; *E* 458). Lower servants were referred to by first name (*LS*, *MW* 283; *NA* 103; *S&S* 153; *P&P* 344; *E* 228, 236, 237), although one encounters the occasional hybrid form, such as a real-life maid of all work who was called 'Mrs. Becky'.

In especially large households, there might be a clerk of the stables, who advised his employer on travel routes, supervised the feeding and doctoring of horses and oversaw the care of carriages and stables. There might also be a clerk of the kitchen, who disbursed funds to tradesmen after the expenses were authorised by the steward, but these were increasingly rare offices. So, too, was that of the 'man cook', a male chef, preferably from France. This servant could well be the highest-paid member of the household. He could make anywhere from 30 to 90 guineas depending on the level of his skill, a sum that put his services out of the range of all but the richest employers.* The employment of a man cook conferred a great deal of status on the employer, and contemporaries who could not afford such magnificence took every chance they got to satirise such needless extravagance.

Large estates might also have a confectioner, who specialised in pastries, and a baker, who specialised in bread. At Stoneleigh, a mansion owned by a relative of Mrs Austen's, there was, according to Mrs Austen, a 'man servant ... called the Baker, he does nothing but brew and bake'. Most wealthy men had a valet (*P* 4), who helped them to dress and took care of their clothes; such a man might make anywhere from 18 to 30 guineas a year.

The butler (*Cass*, *MW* 44; *P&P* 301; *E* 204, 211; *P* 142; and *MP*'s 'Baddeley' – 273, 324–325) took care of the estate's wine, beer, glassware and plate. When new wine was purchased in large casks, it was his job to bottle it and then to serve it with dinner. He took on the duties of the valet in households where there was none and, in any case, supervised the setting out of the breakfast things. According to the Adamses, a footman would carry the tea urn, and the butler would carry the 'eatables' and possibly wait at the table during the meal. After seeing that all the breakfast dishes were removed and cleaned, the butler would take his own breakfast with the housekeeper, returning to the public part of the house to answer the door, 'receive cards, deliver messages, & c.' He carried in the luncheon tray and served wine if called for, kept the cellar keys and paid the bills for wine, beer and spirits if there was no steward to do this. At dinner he released the requisite articles of plate from their locked chest, carried in the first dish and served wine throughout the meal. Afterwards, he took his own dinner, then carried in the tea tray (*MP* 180), though he did not actually make the tea; he was also in charge of serving supper if it was wanted. He was in charge of 'Slippers, dressing gown, [and] night candles' (*NA* 187), again according to the Adamses. His wages ranged, in 1825, from £50 to £80 in large households or from £30 to £50 in smaller ones. Swift's remarks concerning butlers reveal that the fears or complaints of employers regarding butlers concerned cleanliness, promptitude and probity. He accused butlers of poor hygiene

---

*The Adamses noted that the Duke of York was reputed to pay his "French Cook" £500 a year.

('Take special care that your bottles be not musty before you fill them, in order to which, blow strongly into the mouth of every bottle, and then if you smell nothing but your own breath, immediately fill it'), laziness ('Give no person any liqueur till he has called for it thrice at least') and peculation – an easy charge given that butlers had a number of perquisites in addition to their wages. They were traditionally entitled to unused candle ends, used playing cards and, if they served as valet as well, their master's cast-off clothes. All these bits and pieces could be sold and used to pay for the butler's own clothes and laundering, which came out of his pocket.

The gardener (*Sand, MW* 380; *S&S* 303; *P&P* 251; *MP* 91, 104, 105; *E* 359) had responsibility for the grounds of the estate. He supervised the growing of flowers and vegetables, the maintenance of the orchard and hothouses, the construction of paths and the mowing and rolling of lawns. He was often Scottish and usually occupied a cottage somewhere on the estate, separate from the main house. This extraordinary degree of privacy must have been prized and compensated somewhat for his lower salary than the butler's – anywhere from £10 to 20 guineas. Parson Woodforde's gardener, Will Coleman, earned 'a shilling a Day and his Board for 2 Days in a Week', but he had to find his own lodgings.

Below the gardener were a host of lower servants, distinguished from the upper servants by their livery. This livery (*Cath, MW* 214; *Watsons, MW* 322; *P&P* 260, 351; *P* 22, 106) was a uniform, constructed along the lines of fashionable men's clothing but executed in special colours, often colours that were chosen from the employer's coat of arms, and heavily trimmed with 'lace', that is, metallic braid. Though servants often aspired to reach the ranks of the upper servants, who did not have to wear livery, they prized good livery and prided themselves on the cost of the trimmings. Servants contemplating taking a new post would often include the magnificence of the livery in their calculations.

Liveried servants included the coachman (*Sand, MW* 364, 386; *MP* 69, 189, 222, 251, 375; *E* 126, 128, 195), who cleaned the carriage, harnessed the horses and drove the carriage; undercoachmen, who assisted the coachman and drove additional carriages; the gamekeeper (*MP* 114), who looked after the wild game on the estate, helped with bird shooting and guarded against poachers; and the porter (*S&S* 165), who lived in a lodge at the gate of a country estate or sat at the door of a town house and controlled access to the front door. Coachmen made about 15 guineas a year, porters about the same.

Grooms (*Sand, MW* 394; *S&S* 58, 67; *MP* 99, 118, 237; *P* 104) and footmen (*NA* 184; *MP* 87, 180, 202) bore somewhat the same relationship to each other that gardeners did to butlers. One was an outdoor helper, the other primarily an indoor helper. Both were liveried servants. The groom helped with the horses and accompanied his employers when they rode out on horseback (*S&S* 86). The footman answered the door (*Sand, MW* 406; *NA* 89, 102; *S&S* 161), announced visitors (*E&E, MW* 31) and led them into the public rooms (*Cath, MW* 218, 220; *NA* 102–103; *P&P* 335), ran errands

(*S&S* 353; *P&P* 276; *MP* 57; *E* 295), carried packages and messages (*S&S* 165; *P&P* 30) and waited at the table (*Visit*, *MW* 52; *S&S* 355). In smaller households, the positions of groom, footman and butler might be collected in one post, with the same servant bottling wine, waiting at table, opening the door and accompanying riders and carriage passengers (*P&P* 211–212). Postilions (*L&F*, *MW* 85; *NA* 156), similar to grooms in their connection with horses, rode one or more horses harnessed to a carriage and helped to steer; they also assisted their employers when it was time to stop for a meal or an overnight stay. Grooms made about 12 to 15 guineas a year, footmen perhaps a little more, postilions a little less.

Large estates might also have a host of craftsmen. They might devote their services exclusively to the estate or divide their time between private and public commissions. They included carpenters (*MP* 127, 130, 141–142, 184, 191) and blacksmiths. Huntsmen and whippers-in helped with the care of dogs and the conduct of foxhunts and hare hunts.

Such servants tended to be fairly well paid, unlike the footboys, who were the most junior of the male servants. These footboys were essentially servants in training and might actually receive no wages at all, or at most 4 or 5 guineas a year. They ran errands for the other servants or, in a few cases, waited on ladies dressed in gorgeous livery. They might be as young as eight or nine years old.

Female Servants

Female servants, unlike lower male servants, did not wear livery. They instead wore a simpler and often darker-coloured version of fashionable women's wear, so indistinguishable from the clothes of their employers that critics complained that they could not tell maid and mistress apart by their clothing. The chief female servant in a large household was the housekeeper (*NA* 158, 211; *S&S* 64, 292; *P&P* 40, 246, 248, 249, 251, 301, 317, 331; *MP* 85, 91, 104, 105–106, 180, 254, 267; *E* 84, 89, 204, 391, 469), who was immediately subordinate to the house steward, if there were one, and who served as his replacement if there were not. She bought and distributed provisions for the household, kept accounts and sometimes hired other servants on her employer's behalf. Her equivalent in rank, and sometimes even her superior, was the lady's maid (*Watsons*, *MW* 350, 360; *Sand*, *MW* 421; *NA* 164; *S&S* 206; *P&P* 353; *MP* 202, 254, 283, 377, 450; *E* 211) to the lady of the house, who dressed the mistress (*MP* 277), took care of her clothes (*MP* 254), styled her hair (*E* 134) and waited on her throughout the day. (Ladies' maids may be seen in the illustrations *Progress of the Toilet – The Stays* and *Progress of the Toilet – Dress Completed* [both in the article on Clothing] and Hairdressing [Hair].) The housekeeper's immediate subordinate was the cook (*Sand*, *MW* 382, 414; *NA* 183; *P&P* 65; *MP* 31, 111, 215–216; *E* 105), who had the same duties (but not the same prestige) as a man cook. It was to her advantage if she had 'lived under a man cook', that is, if she had served in a household as the assistant to a male chef. She could also earn higher pay if she were a 'professed cook', in other words a cook who knew how to make complex dishes and sauces. A woman who could not do such things was generally described as a 'good plain cook'.

In smaller households, two or even three of these offices might be combined, with a single servant acting as housekeeper and lady's maid or as housekeeper and cook. Longbourn's 'Hill' appears to occupy such a post, serving, it seems (though Austen is frustratingly vague about the specific duties of her upper servants) as both housekeeper and lady's maid to Mrs Bennet (*P&P* 301, 306), while another maid helps the Bennet daughters to dress and do their hair. Netherfield's 'Nicholls', likewise, may be a cook or a cook-housekeeper (*P&P* 55). Hartfield's 'Serle' and Donwell Abbey's 'Hodges' may fill this combined post as well (*E* 172, 211, 355). Mrs Elton's 'Wright' appears, like Hill, to fill the post of housekeeper lady's maid or cook-lady's maid, as she does Mrs Elton's hair and also trades recipes with other housekeepers (*E* 324, 458).

A lady's maid or housekeeper might earn about 10 to 20 guineas a year in the late eighteenth century, while a cook's salary varied widely based on her skills, ranging from as little as £7 to as much as £20. A cook who doubled as housekeeper could earn £25. In addition, cooks and ladies' maids had perquisites that added substantially to their income. Cooks, for example, got to keep all the used fat from the kitchen and sell it – a benefit that often led employers to accuse their cooks of using too much butter when cooking, simply to augment the amount of drippings left in the pan. Ladies' maids often got their mistresses' cast-off clothing, which they could either wear or sell to second-hand clothes dealers.

Below these upper female servants were various other maids (*Lesley*, *MW* 113; *Col Let*, *MW* 159; *Cath*, *MW* 213, 217, 236; *Watsons*, *MW* 315; *Sand*, *MW* 370; *NA* 20, 172, 232; *S&S* 26, 260, 353; *MP* 14, 379, 383, 385, 387, 444; *P* 129). The larger the household, the more their duties were divided. The smaller the household, the more likely they were to combine two or more job descriptions, until, in the very smallest establishments, all duties were united in the maid of all work. A chambermaid (*NA* 172; *P&P* 241) made the beds, swept the bedroom floors, dusted, lit the bedroom fireplaces and cleaned them and used a bed warmer – a large brass pan with a hinged lid and a long handle, into which hot coals could be placed – to warm the chilly bedclothes before her employer retired for the night. A housemaid (*Sand*, *MW* 401, 414; *NA* 194, 203; *S&S* 180; *P&P* 41, 317; *MP* 87, 105–106, 270, 322; *E* 9) performed similar tasks for the entire house, cleaning stairs, fire grates and irons, hearths, carpets, furniture, locks and door knockers, mirrors and knick-knacks. She might also do some sewing (*MP* 130, 141). The duties and titles of housemaids and chambermaids were often interchangeable, and both earned in the neighbourhood of £9 or £10 a year.

In a home without male servants, or where the male servants were otherwise occupied, the housemaid would also tackle some of the tasks normally assigned to footmen, such as answering the door (*L&F*, *MW* 79, 80; *Evelyn*, *MW* 181; *MP* 399), announcing visitors' names and showing them into the proper rooms (*L&F*, *MW* 80, 84; *Cath*, *MW* 213–214; *S&S* 173,

232; *MP* 298; *E* 452), accompanying female travellers (*NA* 224; *MP* 8, 9, 410; *E* 285, 362), serving dinner (*Visit*, *MW* 52, 53; *Watsons*, *MW* 344, 346, 347, 359; *Sand*, *MW* 389; *MP* 407; *E* 218, 290) and carrying messages (*Col Let*, *MW* 159; *S&S* 222, 311; *P&P* 31, 34; *E* 374; *P* 176). In many households, housemaids and chambermaids were expected to sew and mend as well (*P&P* 292; *MP* 141).

Ranking below the housemaids and chambermaids were kitchen maids, who assisted the cook, cleaned the kitchen (*E* 173) and scrubbed the dishes (*MP* 413, 439); the laundry maids, who sweated in the laundry shed over washtubs heated by brick ovens; and dairy maids, who milked the cows and made cheese and butter. Nursery maids took care of small children. A laundry maid earned about £7 to 10 guineas in the late eighteenth century, and a dairy maid about 5 to 6 guineas. A maid of all work, who did many of the tasks assigned to the other types of maids, usually earned somewhere between 7 and 8 guineas a year, though sometimes the amount fell outside this range.

Servants specialising exclusively in dairying or laundry or cleaning bedchambers were found only in larger homes. Smaller establishments, such as the Austens' home at Steventon, Parson Woodforde's, William Gilpin's and those of the other minor gentry, were likely to have about three to five servants (*S&S* 12, 26, 260, 277) – two to five women (*Cath*, *MW* 218; *Watsons*, *MW* 341) and the rest men, with the possible exception of a boy kept at little expense to run messages and do light chores. In such households, there might be a designated cook, housekeeper or lady's maid, but the likely division was simply between 'upper' (*Watsons*, *MW* 336; *E* 27; *P* 45) and 'lower' servants, with the lower servants receiving lower wages and doing the majority of the less-pleasant and less-skilled work. One of the menservants might be an 'outdoor' man – that is, a farm helper rather than a domestic servant, though he might wait at the table or run errands when necessary.

Hiring

Servants could be hired (*P&P* 68) either through an agent or through personal recommendation. The professional sources of hired help included statute fairs, where servants out of work lined up for inspection and interrogation by prospective employers and employment agencies (*E* 300–301) that ranged in scope from side businesses run by publicans or chandlers to large-scale, highly professional London organisations. The large agencies, which might send one candidate a day to the employer's home for inspection, thrived mostly in large towns and cities. Servants and employers also advertised in the newspapers. Servants listed any special qualifications they might have, while employers listed salary and benefits. In the countryside, one tended to find servants through the recommendations of family and friends (*S&S* 260; *E* 284), who might know that a relative of one of their own servants wanted work or that a servant of their own wanted to change households for some reason.

In the case of a servant who was personally unknown to the employer, it was important to ask for references, known as a 'character', from the previous employer or employers. One could also seek out additional sources of information; when Emma tries to think of an excuse for going to Mr Elton's house, she raises and dismisses the possibility of using enquiring about the reputation of a specific servant as a pretext to talk to the housekeeper (*E* 84). One of the perpetual scourges of the employer was the manufacture of counterfeit characters by London forgers who specialised in this branch of the trade. The risk taken by the servant was that the household would turn out to be something other than what she expected. She might be asked suddenly to do work that she was unfamiliar with or that she considered unnecessarily onerous, and if she broke her contract, she could be jailed. Or she might become the sexual prey of her employer or his sons.

Another option was to hire a relative, as Parson Woodforde and many others did. He hired his unmarried niece Nancy as his housekeeper at £10 a year, expecting her to do a good deal of household work but treating her more as a relative than a servant and often buying her presents. The term of service for domestics was traditionally a year (*MP* 385), renewable when the term was up and breakable with sufficient notice by either master or servant, but this limitation would not apply in the case of relatives who were also servants.

Sometimes, servants looking for work would hear of an opening or take a chance on there being one and simply show up at the employer's door and ask for a job.

The best servants were supposedly the children of one's own tenants, who had a long history of deference towards the employer and strong motives for doing a good job. One could also acquire a servant from a workhouse or charity school, and this was always an inexpensive option, but such servants were not necessarily very skilled. The worst servants, according to popular opinion, were those from London. Against these servants, the prejudice was so strong that some of them would leave London just long enough to hop a wagon back into town so that they could appear to have recently arrived from the country.

Conditions of Service

Wages were generally higher in London than in the countryside, but a servant's wages were only a part of his total income. Until the latter half of the eighteenth century, the giving of vails had been a universal practice. Vails were tips distributed to the staff upon departing a household after a visit. The amount of the vails depended on how long the stay had been, the degree to which one wanted to ingratiate oneself with the servants, and the quality of the service experienced and, to a much lesser extent, the financial resources of the tipper. Inadequate vails were punished by the servants on return visits by slow and surly service. At the time of a guest's departure, the relevant members of the staff would line up and wait to be paid, a practice that many guests and employers found humiliating. As a result of their embarrassment, they overcame serious opposition from their servants and gradually abolished the practice, raising their servants' wages to compensate for the lost tips.

The practice of vails had not completely disappeared by Austen's time, however. Even when vails had vanished, servants expected or at least appreciated tips in other circumstances – for example, when delivering a package or a message. The kinds of services rewarded with tips made it especially common for footmen to be the servants receiving them, a perk that added to the prestige of the job. Livery servants such as footmen also received a portion of their clothes for free. They were generally issued a frock coat, breeches, boots and sometimes stockings and were usually responsible for buying their own shirts, cravats, wigs and dress shoes. Employers were very specific about whether the livery was a gift or a loan.

Maids, too, received augmentations to their salaries. They were often entitled to tea and sugar as part of their wages, and ads for maids often specified how many times a day they would receive free tea (*Evelyn, MW* 189). Some employers gave an additional sum of money in lieu of tea and let the servants buy their own.

Servants might also receive board wages, a sum of money in lieu of meals, usually provided when the family was travelling with the servant in tow or when the family was living elsewhere and large dinners were therefore not routinely provided. In the last quarter of the eighteenth century, board wages ranged from about 5s. to 10s. 6d. a week. Employers liked the system because it supposedly reduced waste and theft of provisions but suspected that their servants were then idling too much in the public houses where they got their meals.

Upper servants got used goods as perquisites of their posts, and they could use or sell as they saw fit. The butler was usually entitled to the stubs of candles and old bottles. The cook got bones and chunks of fat in addition to the buttery drippings. The coachman got the old carriage parts after they were replaced, and the gamekeeper got to keep the guns and dogs of the poachers he arrested. Valets and ladies' maids got cast-off clothes, and at card parties, the footman or butler who supplied the cards was paid 'card money' for each deck. Huntsmen were paid by all the gentlemen in the hunting party every time a quarry was killed. Porters got bribes to let visitors in to see important people, and housekeepers and gardeners got tips for showing tourists around their employer's house and grounds. Stewards, who kept the books, made large purchases and superintended leases, were in the best position to fatten their own purses. All upper servants who did any of the household purchases expected kickbacks and/or 'Christmas boxes' of goodies from the shops they patronised. Some savvy shop owners even threw parties for upper servants to attract and keep their business.

Events of importance within the employer's family could also have benefits for the servants. When a death occurred in the employer's family (but not in the servant's own family), mourning clothes were distributed, and this sort of gift reduced wear and tear on the servant's own wardrobe. Bequests to faithful servants might also have been made by the deceased. When the employer celebrated, whether at a wedding or for some patriotic occasion, the servants were likely to come in for special treats such as food, drink or the right to throw a little party of their own at a discreet distance. Some employers let their servants invite other servants over for social occasions, and when people travelled to each other's houses for dinner or long visits, they brought servants with them who then had a chance to gossip, play cards and make new friends.

These were among the reasons that many people considered service a comfortable occupation. Another of its advantages was the amount and quality of the food that tended to be superior to that consumed by soldiers, sailors and many artisans and labourers. At a time of steeply rising food costs, servants ate plenty of bread, reasonable quantities of meat (*Sand, MW* 393) and generous amounts of beer or ale, with other kinds of liqueur on special occasions (*P&P* 307). Servants in smaller households ate, in most cases, exactly what their owners ate. In very small establishments, such as the alehouse owned by Francis Place's father, they might even eat with the family. In larger households, the servants ate at a separate table in the kitchen, sometimes seated hierarchically according to their job titles. In still larger households, there was the 'first table' for the employers and their guests, a 'second table' for the upper servants (this table being usually laid in the housekeeper's room – *E* 204) and a 'third table' for the lower servants. In such cases, the second table ate exactly the same food as the employers, while the third table got simpler food prepared especially for them, supplemented with leftovers from the first table. This system led to complaints from some employers that the footmen serving in the dining room cleared away the platters too quickly in the hope of securing more dainties for themselves.

Another advantage of service was that, in households with kind masters, there was often a great deal of care taken to provide a reasonable standard of living for the servants. Upper servants often got rooms to themselves, and valets and ladies' maids might have very good rooms adjacent to the employers' bedrooms. Medical professionals were often brought in to diagnose sick servants, who were sometimes worried over as much as a family member would have been. Some employers paid to have their servants taught to read and write, and while this was almost certainly for their own convenience, it obviously benefited the servants as well. Footmen and grooms got to do a good deal of travelling and might go on hunts; though they were not permitted to do any actual hunting themselves, it was an exciting change of pace. Aged servants were sometimes given pensions (*S&S* 11) or allowed to live rent-free or at reduced rent in cottages on the estate.

28. *Nobody's Song*, 1807.

The disadvantages of service, however, were many. There was the loss of caste, a serious issue for people who had been raised 'above' service but were driven to it by financial necessity. Middle-class employers often felt obligated to emphasise the small social difference between themselves and their servants by being especially rude. The beating of servants was common, and a maidservant unfortunate to become pregnant was certain to be fired for bringing moral corruption into the household, even if the source of the moral corruption was the employer who molested her. Servants also had to wait a long time to get married, as their wages were so small that it was hard to save enough money to start a business or amass a dowry.

Terminating Employment
When things went wrong, either the master or the servant could choose to end the contract (*P&P* 68), though it was legally a bit harder for servants to do so. Common reasons for leaving a post voluntarily were taking another post in a more-desirable household or at better wages, personal conflict with a member of the family or staff, desire to open a business of one's own such as an alehouse or, in the case of female

servants, marriage. Employers fired servants for a host of reasons, including pregnancy, drunkenness and insolence.

See also Carriages and Coaches; Housework; Hunting.

Sewing

Needlework (*NA* 240; *P&P* 47, 104–105; *MP* 19, 296; *E* 9) was one of the essential skills for a woman and, unlike the knowledge of French or the ability to play the harp, it was considered equally essential for women of the working class, the gentry and the nobility. The specific set of skills varied somewhat by class, with wealthier women spending a greater percentage of their time on strictly ornamental sewing, such as embroidery, than on the construction of their own garments. However, even these women would have known how to do what was called 'plain sewing', for all but the richest would have done some alterations (*MP* 381; *E* 237) for themselves and sewn simple clothing for the poor (*MP* 71). Nor were advanced skills solely confined to the gentry and nobility, for many of the fine, delicate embroidered or beaded gowns worn by rich women were actually sewn by professional working-class seamstresses. Jane and Cassandra Austen, for example, are known to have made alterations to their clothing, but the original manufacture was in the hands of others. However, Edward Austen's wife, Elizabeth, made shirts (*MP* 236, 385) for her husband, and Mrs Austen was a source of embarrassment to Jane and Cassandra for her willingness to do plain sewing (*NA* 240; *MP* 390) before company, when only tiny, ladylike, decorative projects would have been preferable.

Jane was perfectly capable of both types of 'work' (*Cath, MW* 197; *NA* 204, 241; *S&S* 181; *P&P* 104, 335; *MP* 18, 71, 125, 126, 147, 168, 220, 336–337, 360, 390; *P* 83). Like most little girls, she probably began by making samplers (*NA* 107), mottoes and alphabets embroidered onto plain fabric as a way of practicing different types of stitches and, later, as a way of demonstrating precision and prowess. Items that she sewed or embroidered still survive and show her to have been adept at the small, even stitches for which seamstresses strove. Plain sewing – seams (*MP* 166), hems (*E* 388), mending and so on – was done in the mornings, before and sometimes during morning visits. This sort of sewing required few tools: a small, sharp pair of scissors (*S&S* 120, 360); pins (*P* 99), pincushions (*P* 155) and 'pin-poppets' (lidded containers that concealed a small pincushion); and tape measures, often marked in increments called 'nails', each unit equal to 2¼". A spool for thread (*NA* 60; *MP* 236; *P* 155) might be in the barbell shape common today, or it might be a spindle concealed inside a carved miniature barrel, from which the thread was extracted through a tiny hole in the side. Needles were sometimes kept in small hinged boxes with angled tops, the front lower than the back. Inside the box were compartments for keeping paper packets of needles. Needles

(*NA* 60, 241; *MP* 236) might alternatively be kept in a needle book (*S&S* 254), a tiny 'book' with fabric 'pages' through which the needles could be inserted. Some of these were very simple, while others were bound in expensive materials such as silver filigree. Still other needle cases were tubes of ivory or filigree, often quite elaborately carved.

Sewing tools could be kept in any of a number of containers. One popular type was the etui, a tiny, decorative holder for small implements such as scissors, miniature knives (*S&S* 120), bodkins and 'ear spoons' – the Georgian equivalent of the Q-Tip. Etuis could be hung from a chatelaine, a jewelled pendant that hung from the waist. One example from about 1780 is cone-shaped, with diminutive enamelled pictures of a woman gathering flowers, an urn filled with more flowers, birds and a playful dog. Another from about the same time is shaped like a fish and is jointed so that the tail and body can curve in different directions. The case opens at the fish's neck, exposing a tiny knife, scissors and ear spoon.* For more extensive collections of sewing supplies, it was necessary to have a sewing bag (*MW* 444–445; *S&S* 120; *E* 168), basket (*E* 471) or box (*MP* 153). A common type was the 'housewife' or 'huswife' (*S&S* 275; *E* 157), a piece of fabric with pockets for sewing tools that could be rolled up or folded and, sometimes, placed in a separate cloth bag. Beautiful sewing boxes were made of wood, decorated at times with rolled gilt-edged paper,

29. *Miss Goodchild's first Sampler*, 1793.

*Etuis, incidentally, were also used at times by men.

with painted or inked designs or with inlay. They could of course contain a hodgepodge of tools from different sources, but many women owned matching sets of wooden, ivory, tortoiseshell or metal tools.

Midway between useful and decorative sewing was patchwork quilting, which used up fabric scraps and was thus a frugal as well as an aesthetic activity. A quilt made by Jane, Cassandra, Mrs Austen and perhaps Martha Lloyd in spring 1811 still exists at Chawton Cottage. Sometimes less practical, but no doubt equally enjoyable, were the making and decoration of small, elegant presents for friends and family. An Austen niece made slippers for a male relative, for example, and Jane herself made a bag and housewife at age sixteen for her future sister-in-law Mary Lloyd.

These little projects took far less time than large-scale embroidery, which might be white-on-white or coloured (S&S 160) and serve either as a border decoration on clothing or table linen or as a piece of art in its own right, looking from a distance like a painting (S&S 160). Embroidery used many of the same tools as plain sewing, but it had some special tools of its own. While the material being embroidered was sometimes held loosely in the hand, many women preferred to stretch it in a round or rectangular frame (MP 65) or hoop. Embroiderers might use a silk holder that kept spare silk thread handy in a decorative ball dangling from a bracelet. Alternatively, they might use a silk winder, a cross- or star-shaped object. The embroidery thread was wrapped around the winder between the points of the star. In some cases, the winder was roughly rectangular in shape, with undulations or points along the long sides to hold the thread. Winders were made from a variety of materials, including cardboard, lacily carved ivory, mother-of-pearl, straw-work, steel, cut glass, ceramic and wood.

Other needle crafts included carpet work, rug making, tatting and netting, all of which – except for tatting (lace-making) – are mentioned in Austen's works. Carpet work (S&S 258, 303; MP 179; E 85) was simply embroidery with either silk or wool on a sturdy backing of canvas rather than the lightweight linens and cottons used for other work. It had its origins in Renaissance attempts to imitate the rich colours and dense ornamentation of Turkish carpets and was used primarily for upholstery rather than as floor carpeting. Rugs (S&S 181), like carpet work, are not necessarily the floor coverings they sound like. They can instead be blankets or coverlets, knitted of wool or worsted. Mrs Austen was fond of knitting (P 155; E 86, 156, 454) rugs and gloves; it was useful work that must have appealed to a pragmatic mother of eight children.

Tatting makes no appearance in Austen's works, though its end product – lace – is frequently mentioned (MW 389; P&P 13; E 292, 329; P 156), leading one to believe that few women of Austen's acquaintance bothered to make their own lace. This impression is borne out by the number of shops that sold lace panels and trims and by contemporary diaries, which often record the purchase, rather than the manufacture, of lace. Austen is not generally specific about the kind or pattern of lace, or even where

Sewing

it is located on the clothing, although she does make one reference
to 'Mechlin' (*NA* 238), a high-quality lace made in Mechlin, Belgium.

Unlike tatting, the activity of netting (*NA* 201; *P&P* 39) is mentioned
often. This craft was exactly what it sounds like – the making of nets –
and, unlike most other needle crafts, it was often pursued by men. Jane's
brother Frank and her nephews Edward and George Knight were all
fond of it. Though it was not unknown for men to knit or embroider for
pleasure, netting had an atmosphere of utility that made it especially
acceptable to men (*P* 99). After all, the same process used to make the
fine meshes that adorn purses (*P&P* 39), pincushions and dresses was
used to make fishing and fowling nets and the nets that protected fruit
trees from the depredations of hungry birds. Still, like most needle crafts,
it was primarily performed by women. Parson Woodforde's niece and
housekeeper Nancy Woodforde was apparently quite good at it, for in 1787
he had recorded in his diary that Mrs Custance, the squire's wife, 'stayed
with us till 3 o'clock, learning of Nancy to make diamond-edge-netting'.

Netting (*NA* 40) required several specialised tools, the most important
of which were the needles, the meshes and the clamp, box (*NA* 176;
MP 153), or stirrup. The needles (*P* 99), unlike sewing embroidery needles,
were very slightly open at the end of the eye and had an eye at each end.
They came in various sizes depending on the fineness of the net to be
woven. This 'needle' was really more like a shuttle, as the thread, cord
or rope being used to make the net was wound around it lengthwise
and gradually unwound as the net took shape. The meshes (or 'gauges')
were thin sticks with rounded ends, rather like overly narrow tongue
depressors. They were used to hold loops of thread in place. The last tool
held the original loop of the net firmly anchored to a table or the floor.
This could be accomplished with a clamp, which attached itself to some
heavy object and caught the end of the net on a hook; with a stirrup,
in ,which the net-maker placed his foot, using his or her own body to
keep the thread taut; or with a special netting-box, distinguished from
an ordinary sewing box by lead weighting to keep it stable and an interior
roller with a ratchet to anchor the foundation loop.

See also Housework.

Shoes

From the 1780s to the 1810s, the general trend in footwear was towards
simplicity. Men's shoes (*E* 10), which had for decades been decorated
with often elaborate and expensive buckles, were increasingly given long
tongues and ribbon ties (*NA* 172). In 1784, Parson James Woodforde was
impressed that an acquaintance, Mr Micklethwaite, 'had in his Shoes a
Pair of Silver Buckles which cost between 7 and 8 Pounds' and that 'Miles
Branthwaite had a pair that cost 5 guineas'. Twenty years later, such

expenditure on shoe buckles would be very rare. The heels on men's shoes, which had risen quite high in the mid-eighteenth century, dropped lower, and colours grew more uniformly sedate, restricted in almost all cases to black or dark brown. When a man was in mourning, he always wore black shoes, but this was hardly different from his normal daily practice.

Boots (*Watsons*, *MW* 327) of all kinds became popular for men, partly in imitation of military uniforms and partly as an outgrowth of sporting activities in the countryside. The former influence spawned Hessian boots, which had angled tops and reached to just below the knee, and boots with metal fittings. The latter influence made top boots one of the most common footwear styles for men, so common, in fact, that cartoons of John Bull usually showed him wearing them. Top boots were tall boots, sometimes ridiculously tight, with tall tops that folded over and made a wide flap all the way around the top of the boot. They were pulled on with U-shaped straps, and these straps were such a characteristic feature of the boots that some were made with two pairs of straps – one for actual use and the other to hang outside the boot for show. Men also occasionally wore half boots, boots that rose a little above the ankle.

Women's shoes, like men's, grew generally flatter as time went on. Earlier in the eighteenth century, most women's shoes were high heeled and made of fabric (*Scraps*, *MW* 176), but by the 1790s, leather was increasingly common, and heels were lower. From the 1790s through the 1810s, a variety of heel styles enjoyed popularity, often at the same time. There were wide wedge heels, narrow Italian heels and slippers (*Scraps*, *MW* 176) with the faintest hint of a heel or no heels at all. Toe shapes, like heel sizes, were not uniform. Toes might be pointed or rounded, though rarely square.

Buckled shoes, as in the case of men, lost ground rapidly. The ornate buckles of former decades had come to seem out of place in an era devoted to classical simplicity. Accordingly, women adopted slippers without fasteners, faux-Greek sandals with ribbon straps and shoes with tongues and ribbon laces. Colours (*S&S* 249) varied, with far more choice than was available to men. While black shoes (*NA* 26) were standard, women showed a willingness to wear shoes in pale colours (*Scraps*, *MW* 176), often chosen to match a fan, pelisse, gloves or gown border. Coloured shoes, however, were not worn all the time and were considered something of a luxury. Mr Parker is astounded to see coloured shoes in a store in *Sanditon* (*Sand*, *MW* 383), and Mrs Austen was dismayed when her daughter-in-law Mary, James Austen's wife, bought a pair of coloured shoes in 1811.

Women did not adopt the tall boots worn by men, but at some point in the first years of the new century, perhaps around 1804, they began adopting ankle-high lace-up half boots (*Watsons*, *MW* 347) made of leather or heavy-duty cotton. These are the shoes suggested by Lord Osborne to Emma Watson, whose family is so poor it can just barely muster an appearance of gentility:

> 'Have you been walking this morning?' 'No, my Lord. We thought it too dirty.' 'You should wear half-boots. ... Nothing sets off a neat ankle

more than a half-boot; nankin galoshed with black looks very well. – Do not you like Half-boots? 'Yes – but unless they are so stout as to injure their beauty, they are not fit for Country walking.' – 'Ladies should ride in dirty weather. ... A woman never looks better than on horseback. – '
(*Watsons*, *MW* 345)

R. W. Chapman, basing his estimate on information from one of Jane's great-nieces, dates the composition of *The Watsons* to 1804 – in other words, just as half boots were coming into style. Lord Osborne, who reveals his social clumsiness and obliviousness to any lifestyle but his own on several occasions, does so again here. His main gaffe is in recommending any new shoe to a woman who undoubtedly cannot afford to buy a pair whenever she likes, let alone the latest fashion, which would place her in the middle of a sartorial arms race she could not hope to win; he then compounds that by suggesting that she ride, when she is equally unable to buy a horse. He concludes the error two pages later by offering to give Emma the name of his sister's shoemaker (*Watsons*, *MW* 347), which is equally ludicrous. Women of limited means bought their shoes ready-made from shoe 'warehouses'. Some women, for fun, embroidered and made their own or added ribbon straps to the ankles and rosettes of ribbon or silk at the toes (*P&P* 88). Only a woman of comfortable means would still have had her shoes custom-made by a shoemaker (*MP* 361).

Half boots were designed for morning wear and especially for walking outdoors. Their increasing adoption by women as walking shoes is reflected in their recurrence in three of the later novels, *Emma* (88–89), *Persuasion* (174–175) and *Sanditon* (383). In the example from *Sanditon*, they are again made of 'nankin', or nankeen, which was a sturdy yellow-brown or buff cotton fabric named after Nanking, China. Lord Osborne, in his recommendation of nankin boots, suggests not unreasonably that they be 'galoshed with black', that is, partially covered with black leather.

Not all footwear was appropriate for all purposes. Even women who adopted half boots for walking or morning wear would have set these aside and put on slippers or heeled shoes for evening (*E* 127). Men preferred boots for almost every purpose, especially for hunting, travelling and riding (*NA* 210), but they had to wear buckled shoes at court. Similarly, they adopted shoes and stockings for evening wear (*Cath*, *MW* 218). At Bath, boots were actually forbidden at assemblies.

Yet a woman would have been mad to wear a fine pair of slippers on a country walk or in wet weather (*S&S* 306; *P&P* 156; *E* 156, 322). Women employed various devices to protect their shoes when they had to brave the dirt, as, for example, when they were going to a ball and had to get from the house to the carriage and from the carriage to the ballroom. They might wear matching toe pieces that covered the pointed toe of a shoe and looked very much like the shoe itself, fastening these decorative coverings with a strap in the back. Alternatively, they might wear overshoes called clogs (*MW* 452; *NA* 19), removing these in a cloakroom when they arrived at the ball.

Women walking around a muddy town on errands or walking along country roads might adopt pattens (*MW* 452; *NA* 184). The patten was a shoe sole with a strap over the arch of the foot that tied it on and with a metal ring on the bottom that raised the wearer's shoe an inch or two off the ground. Pattens were considered rustic and awkward, but in some cases they were necessary. Bath (*P* 135), for example, could be particularly dirty during its winter season, and Betsy Sheridan, writing in 1789, proclaimed, 'We ladies here trot about in pattens, a privilege granted nowhere else to genteel women.' Outside Bath, pattens were generally associated with women who were relatively poor, unfashionable and countrified.

When attempts to preserve shoes from damage failed, the shoes were more likely to be repaired than discarded. Austen refers to having some pairs of worn-out shoes 'capped & heelpeiced' (*Scraps, MW* 176). This probably means that both the uppers and the lowers were replaced, which would be in keeping with the humorous tone of the piece in which the reference occurs.

Two important innovations were made in this period, although one was more of a reintroduction than a new invention. The true innovation was patent leather, also known at this time as 'japanned' leather (after the black lacquer items of Japan). It was introduced in the early 1790s and soon came into widespread use. The not-so-original innovation was the reintroduction, after a lapse of nearly 200 years, of right and left shoes; since about 1600, shoes had been made as 'straights', with no distinction between left and right.

See also Clothing; Stockings.

Shops

Customers shopped (*P&P* 152; *E* 234) at establishments ranging from tiny village shops to London 'warehouses' (*P&P* 288) that seemed enormous by the standards of the time but would be dwarfed by modern department stores and bulk grocery warehouses. The smallest and humblest of all shops was the village chandler's shop, which took its name from the fact that the proprietor sold wax or tallow candles, but most chandler's shops offered an assortment of staples such as soap, butter, bacon and tea as well. Small towns might have chandler's shops (*NA* 212; *MP* 58) and a handful of specialty shops (*S&S* 199; *P&P* 72; *MP* 403; *P* 221) such as a stationer's (*S&S* 199), which sold writing paper, ink, sealing wax and the like, or an all-inclusive clothing shop that sold fabric for dresses, gloves, ribbons, lace and hats. Ford's in Highbury (*E* 199–201, 235–237) is such a store. Larger towns would divide clothing sales (*NA* 20) among shops devoted to a particular article.

Shops

Linen drapers (*E* 178) sold linen and cotton fabrics by the yard, while
woollen drapers (*E* 178) sold wool cloth, haberdashers (*E* 178) sold small
articles like ribbons and tapes and milliners (*Cath*, *MW* 201; *Watsons*, *MW*
322; *P&P* 28, 219) sold women's hats, caps and bonnets. Mercers sold silk.

The large towns would, in addition to these shopkeepers in the clothing
trades, have dealers in china, wine, tobacco, furniture (*Scraps*, *MW* 176–177),
books (*S&S* 92), prints (*S&S* 92; *P* 169) and sheet music (*S&S* 92). Then
there were the food sellers: grocers (*Col Let*, *MW* 158), who sold sauces,
spices, dried fruit and imported ingredients; butchers (*S&S* 197; *MP* 379)
selling meat and sometimes specialist poulterers (*MP* 212–213) selling
poultry; bakers selling bread and pastry cooks selling pies, jellies, ices and
the 'biscuits and buns' (*MP* 413) that Fanny Price sends her brothers out to
buy. Parson Woodforde, on his trips to Norwich, recorded purchases at
'Bakers', where he bought smelling salts, a comb, netting cord for his niece
Nancy, a whip, 'a Habit brush for Nancy with a looking Glass at the back
of it' and a pair of riding gloves. At Mr Priest's shop, at various times,
he bought medicine, rum and wine. From 'one Studwell China Man in the
Market Place', he bought basins, tumblers, beer glasses and a teapot. At
Beale's, a fishmonger, he had a running account that he paid periodically.
He also made purchases from a bookseller, a silk mercer, an ironmonger,
a timber merchant, a hatter, a brazier (who sold brass goods), a tailor,
a tobacconist and an upholsterer (who sold wallpaper as well as fabric for
furniture). 'Graham's Shop' supplied him with stockings, and his barber
supplied him with wigs. A 'Cabinet Maker on Hog Hill Norwich' sold him
furniture, and Cook's Glass Shop sold him some cut-glass saltcellars.
Clearly, Norwich had a wide variety of shops, and these were not without
competition, for on at least one occasion he mentions switching from one
supplier to another in the same town.

30. *Wedgwood & Byerly*, 1809.

Cities noted for the excellence of their shops, such as Bath (*NA* 25, 29, 217; *P* 141) and London (*S&S* 164, 182; *P&P* 152; *E* 435), had the largest shops with the widest selection of goods. Wherever the rich congregated, one could find the best luxury goods – carriages, musical instruments (*E* 214–215, 241), porcelain dishes, hunting rifles (*P* 239) and expensive jewellery (*S&S* 220–222, 226). Where the rich merely visited temporarily, there were innumerable 'toy' shops that sold not children's playthings but souvenirs and small objects such as penknives, pincushions, china knickknacks, 'spars' (crystalline fragments – *NA* 116), pocketbooks, purses (*NA* 116), buckles, combs and needle cases.

Many stores extended credit to their customers, and this flexibility helped to sustain the chandlers' shops, which thus earned the business of small farmers whose earnings were largely seasonal. They might also take goods in trade; the farmer's wife might bring in eggs, for example, and take a little bacon, sugar or tea with the credit she earned. (Sometimes the chandler *was* the farmer's wife, running a small shop part-time in order to increase her income.) The more-fashionable shops also extended credit to prominent clients, with sometimes disastrous results for those who racked up huge debts with tailors, wine merchants, butchers and such (*P&P* 294; *P* 9). Parson Woodforde, who was good about paying his debts, was only billed once a year by his butcher and paid his other suppliers either on the spot or after buying on credit for a few months.

Spectacles

Eyeglasses in one form or another had been around for centuries, but it was only in the eighteenth century that significant advances were made in keeping the eyeglasses in place. Until the early eighteenth century, spectacles (*E* 158) consisted of two round lenses attached by a springy nosepiece, and the tension in the nosepiece was supposed to keep the spectacles precariously perched on the bridge of the nose. The innovation was the addition of temple- or side-pieces to shift the burden from the nose to the ears. The idea of involving the ears was not new; more primitive spectacles had made use of cords that wrapped around the ears, but rigid side-pieces were altogether novel.

However, the side-pieces did not usually look like the ones with which we are now familiar. Instead, on some pairs the bar ended in a round loop that sat behind the ear and was visible above it. Other examples had 'turnpin' temples – side-pieces with one section hinged to the lens frame and another section nearer the ear that could swivel to facilitate folding the glasses when they were not in use. The back sections did not drop behind the ear as we might expect but extended straight back and sometimes even met behind the head.

Spectacles

Variety could be found not only in the method of suspending the eyeglasses but in their lenses and the materials of which the frames were made. Lenses, which had historically been designed for farsighted readers only, were increasingly available for the nearsighted. Bifocals, too, were sold, as were glasses with tinted lenses, which were believed by some to be easier on the eyes. The shape of the lenses was also changing. At the turn of the nineteenth century, the traditional large, round lenses were being challenged by smaller lenses and by oval and rectangular forms, patented by Dudley Adams in 1797. Oval lenses certainly pre-dated Adams' patent, but rectangular lenses would not become popular until just after Austen's death.

Other types of eyeglasses were also in use. The old pince-nez, which perched on the nose without the aid of temple-pieces, remained popular. The fashionable might instead sport a 'prospect glass' – rather like an upside-down pair of pince-nez with a handle. The Y-shaped contrivance could be held up to the eyes as needed. Alternatively, a dandy might use a ,quizzing glass, a single lens on a handle that was to be the ancestor of the monocle. (The monocle itself, a single lens without a handle, which was held in place between the cheekbone and the eyebrow ridge, was developed around 1806.) Quizzing glasses and their cousins were popular accessories and not just for those who had trouble with their vision.

Some of these aids to vision were elaborately decorated and made of expensive materials. Silver spectacles tended to be of good quality, while cheaper pairs were made from steel or iron. Parson James Woodforde, in his diary entry of 19 September 1786, speaks of 'a Pair of Spectacles with a very handsome Tortoise-shell Case and Silver mounted – they were formerly the Treasurers I believe'. Tortoiseshell and leather were also used for the lens frames. A cheap pair of pince-nez could be bought for one shilling in 1773; a pair of fairly average temple spectacles cost 3s. 6d. in 1804. Whether the spectacles were cheap or expensive, however, the onus was on the customer to make sure that they functioned properly. There were no elaborate eye exams, no studying charts of letters through carefully calibrated sets of lenses. Instead, the customer simply picked up one pair of glasses after another, trying them on until he found one that seemed to improve his vision to the correct degree.

The real questions for the reader of Austen: What kind of spectacles is Frank Churchill fixing in *Emma*, and what is wrong with them in the first place? I was able to determine the answers, at least in part, with the invaluable assistance of Neil Handley, curator of the museum collection of the College of Opticians. The two most important clues lie in Mrs Weston's mock criticism of Frank's progress on Mrs Bates' spectacles and in the part of the spectacles that is blamed for the trouble.

When she enters the Bateses' drawing room, Mrs Weston chides Frank, saying, 'What! … have you not finished it yet? you would not earn a very good livelihood as a working-silversmith at this rate' (*E* 240). The implication, then, is that we are dealing with a pair of silver spectacles – in other words, a pair on the higher end of the spectrum of quality. This in itself is rather surprising, as we are familiar by this point in the novel with the Bateses' poverty. However, it is a genteel sort of poverty. Mrs Bates has come down in the world, but she is still a gentlewoman, and she therefore wears a gentlewoman's spectacles.

As for the part that has gone wrong, this is said to be a 'rivet' (*E* 236, 238, 242). The fullest description of the problem is given by Miss Bates, who says that Frank is

> fastening the rivet of my mother's old spectacles. ... For my mother had no use of her spectacles – could not put them on. And, by the bye, every body ought to have two pair of spectacles. ... At one time Patty came to say she thought the kitchen chimney wanted sweeping. Oh! said I, Patty do not come with your bad news to me. Here is the rivet of your mistress's spectacles out. (*E* 236)

This identifies Mrs Bates' spectacles, with a good deal of probability, as temple spectacles, and furthermore as temple spectacles of the turnpin variety. Rivets were found on various types of temple spectacles at the points where the temple-pieces join the lens frame. According to Mr Handley, these rivets might be left exposed on iron-framed spectacles but were unlikely to have protruded enough on a fine silver pair to have come loose. However, on turnpin temples, there was also a rivet attaching each temple-piece to its folding extension. These rivets quite frequently came loose; as evidence, Mr Handley cites the large number of surviving examples of these spectacles that are missing one or both extensions. It is therefore not certain, but quite likely, that Mrs Bates' spectacles are silver with turnpin temples and that the turnpin rivet is the one that has fallen out. The absence of one of the extensions would indeed make it impossible to wear the spectacles comfortably, as they would rest on only one ear.

See also Clothing.

Stockings

Stockings (*S&S* 306; *P&P* 32; *E* 294; *P* 122) were worn by both men and women throughout Austen's lifetime. Increasingly machine-knitted on stocking frames, they could be made of cotton, silk or worsted; Jane reported buying 'ten pair of worsted stockings' in October 1800, but these were almost certainly intended as gifts for the poor, as worsted stockings were generally cheaper and coarser than silk and cotton. Personally, she preferred silk stockings (*S&S* 274) and bought three pairs in London in April 1811 'for a little less than 12.*s*. a p^r'. This appears to have been a relatively good price; Lord and Lady Middleton paid 18*s*. 6*d*. a pair in Nottingham in 1799. Cotton stockings were generally of quite good quality;

Stockings

Jane's niece Fanny Knight, who was rich enough to buy any stockings she wanted, bought both silk and cotton stockings in 1813 at prices of 12s. and 4s. 3d. a pair, respectively.

Men tended to wear extremely plain stockings (*NA* 169). They favoured white, sometimes with vertical ribs or the appearance of ribs. Vertically or horizontally striped or zigzagged stockings were not unknown, especially in the 1790s, but the flamboyant styles of the earlier eighteenth century were being replaced by simpler styles and more muted colours, and men's stockings reflected this trend. In general, thicker stockings were worn for riding or hunting and fine ones for evening parties and dinners.

Women's stockings also tended to be simple, if for no other reason than that so little of the stocking was ever seen. Long skirts kept all concealed except the ankle, and it was therefore the ankle that received some form of decoration. This was usually a 'clock', a triangular patch of embroidery or lace covering the ankle. It was widest at the base of the foot, tapering as it rose along the outside of the leg; the height of the decoration varied from pair to pair. Most women confined themselves to white or black stockings, more commonly white, with discreet clocks of white, pink, blue or green, or no clocks at all. Clocks on black stockings were always black. At the turn of the century, there was a brief vogue for pink stockings, which made women look even more naked under the thin, almost transparent muslin dresses then in fashion. A writer in 1803 sneered, 'The only sign of modesty in the present dress of the ladies is the pink dye in their stockings, which makes their legs appear to blush for the total absence of petticoats.'

Stockings were held up by garters (*E* 86), thin strips of ribbon or embroidered cloth, that tied above the knee. Men also wore gaiters (*E* 287), an entirely different garment, which were designed to protect stockings from damage when walking or riding. These gaiters were cylindrical pieces that were wrapped around the lower leg and buttoned from knee to ankle. Some boots had short gaiters built into them; the boot went on up to the knee, and then the gaiter buttoned up over the knee to keep the boot from slipping down and wrinkling.

See also Clothing; Shoes.

T

Tea

It's no accident that Austen mentions tea (*Watsons*, *MW* 326; *Sand*, *MW* 416; *S&S* 198; *P&P* 217, 299, 344, 346; *MP* 108, 324, 381; *E* 21, 22, 124,

255, 310, 323, 329, 344, 347, 434) more than any other beverage. The only drink to rival it in popularity during the eighteenth century was beer, and beer was drunk in contexts that were at least one degree removed from Austen's genteel female world. Tea, however, was at the heart of the gentry's social life, providing occupation for the hands, a subject for discussion, and a means, even in the way it was bought and prepared, of maintaining class distinctions. It became a part of the ritual and pace of the day and reached from the royal family all the way down to the humblest labourers.

Sources vary as to the exact amount that was consumed. Peter Clark claims that in 1800 Britons consumed 23 million pounds of tea and that consumption rose slowly but steadily thereafter; Hoh-cheung Mui and Lorna Mui state that the annual retained imports averaged 16 million pounds from 1799 to 1801. In any case, it would be hard to calculate the exact amounts involved, because so much of the tea that came into the country was smuggled and thus avoided tabulation. Richard Twining, of the famous tea-selling family, commented in his *Observations on the Tea & Window Act and on the Tea Trade* (1785) that 'the smuggler has become so formidable a rival [to the East India Company], that, upon the most moderate computation, they shared the Tea-trade equally between them; and according to some calculations, the smuggler had two thirds of it'. Smugglers, who were paid in tea, were depicted as carrying the leaves into the country strapped around their midriffs and thighs, packed into the panniers of ladies' skirts and stuffed in bundles under hats. Even quite respectable people bought smuggled tea; the comfort-loving diarist Parson Woodforde certainly did so. The reduction of the tea tax from 119 percent to 12.5 percent in 1784 may have diminished the trade somewhat – official consumption jumped from 5 million pounds in 1784 to 11 million in 1785 – but Richard Twining was still disturbed by the problem a year after the tax cut, and tea remained one of the two most smuggled items in the 1820s (the other was foreign liqueur). Another aspect of tea consumption that the official statistics do not reflect is the way tea made its way down the social scale. One fairly obvious measure of income, as reflected in tea drinking, is that the rich drank the better quality and thus more-expensive teas, while the less affluent purchased cheaper varieties. This comes as no surprise to modern readers, who understand perfectly well the difference between Lipton's, purchased pre-bagged in cartons at the grocery store, and a fancy, exotic variety of tea purchased by the pound in a coffee shop. Each caters to a different audience. Nor is it surprising that the rich drank more tea than the poor. The comfortably wealthy Edward Austen's household at Godmersham consumed 48 pounds of tea a year, according to Jane's estimate, but their tea bill was dwarfed by the Earl of Stamford's, who in the 1790s ordered 85 to 95 pounds a year from Twining's. This, too, makes perfect sense to us: if you have more money, you can buy more tea. What does come as a surprise to modern readers is the *reuse* of tea. Yet, in Austen's time, tea was a valuable enough commodity to be brewed as many as three times. In well-off households, the members of the family would drink the first brew. Then the leaves would pass to the servants, to be enjoyed a second time. Finally, a servant entitled to this perquisite (usually the cook or housekeeper) would sell the twice-used leaves to the poor and pocket the money. Even within a single social episode, the tea might be steeped several times.

Opinions varied as to whether the poor should be drinking tea at all. Even third-hand tea caused some reformers to recoil in horror at beggars' insistence on drinking it. Wholesome, traditional beer, they chided, was being forsaken for mere fashionable tea. The poor were aping their betters and wasting money on a frivolous luxury. As early as the mid-eighteenth century, a witness claimed that in Nottingham 'almost every Seamer, Sizer and Winder will have her Tea in a morning ... and even a common Washer woman thinks she has not had a proper Breakfast without Tea and hot buttered White Bread!' Jamaican sugar planter Edward Long, delighted by this turn of events, exulted that sugar was 'so generally in use, and chiefly by the assistance of tea, that even the poor wretches living in almshouses will not be without it'. By 1773, Richard Price was asserting that the 'lower ranks of the people are altered in every respect for the worse, while tea, wheaten bread and other delicacies are necessaries which were formerly unknown to them'. Frederick Eden, in the 1790s, bemoaned the change as bad for labourers' health, but by that time tea had been accepted as one of the necessities of life; in some parishes, the very definition of poverty was the inability to buy tea and sugar.

Ironically, tea was wholesome in its own way: it forced workers to boil their often-contaminated water, thus sparing them many parasitic and bacterial illnesses.

Dust, twigs, sloe leaves, blackberry leaves and 'smouch' were all mixed into genuine tea by unscrupulous shopkeepers. Smouch was made by drying and baking ash tree leaves, then crushing them, steeping them in copperas and sheep's dung; Richard Twining estimated that the production of smouch in one small 9-mile area amounted to 20 tons annually. Nor were shopkeepers alone to blame. The Chinese, from whom all the tea of Austen's time was purchased, knew that people expected the best green teas to have a bluish cast, and they sometimes added Prussian blue and gypsum to their teas before shipping. There was a general perception among the tea-buying public that green teas were easier to adulterate, and over time, perhaps because of this perception, preference shifted to black teas.

Several types of both green and black teas were available in the late eighteenth and early nineteenth centuries. The black teas (which were distinguished from the green teas by being dried longer) included bohea, souchong, congo (or congou) and pekoe. Of these, bohea was the cheapest, and when duties were reduced and prices fell, it was scorned. Even the unfashionable word 'bohea' was avoided by tradesmen, who began mixing it with low-quality congou and selling it as 'congou kind'. Pekoe was the best of the black teas, but it was not popular on its own. Rather, it was mixed with other black teas to produce tasty blends. The cheapest green tea was singlo, and other green teas (*Sand, MW* 418) included hyson, caper, Twankey, gunpowder and bloom. Like the black teas, these were often combined in special blends. Gunpowder, for example, a high-quality tea with a rolled leaf, had too intense a flavour for many, and it was often mixed with hyson. The singlo variety bloom green, conversely, was thought to be too weak on its own and was typically mixed with other varieties of singlo. There were also some intermediate teas, dried for longer than the green teas but less than the black; these included Bing and Imperial.

Within each kind of tea – bohea, gunpowder and so on – there were nine different grades of quality recognised by the tea trade. A well-supplied tea dealer, then, might have as many choices as a fancy coffee house today. While a small village shop would have few choices on hand, a large city grocer might carry six, seven or even nine different types of hyson, plus other varieties and a whole host of blends. In 1791, London's Brewster and Gillman carried nine grades of congou, ranging in price from 3s. 3d. to 5s. per pound; nine grades of singlo from 3s. 3d. to 9s. 6d.; and twelve types of hyson, costing from 5s. 3d. to 9s. 6d. This was a fairly typical price range. Other examples from the 1790s show prices per pound falling mostly between three and ten shillings.

Unlike many commodities, tea was never sold in the outdoor public markets. By law, it had to be sold in 'entered places' such as grocers' shops or the Twinings tea shop in the Strand. China, glass, wine and brandy merchants also sometimes sold tea. In the smaller towns and villages, a chandler's shop – which dealt in a variety of wares, including bacon and candles – might be the place where locals purchased their tea and sugar. (However, when they lived at Steventon, the Austens sent to Twinings in London for their tea.) Shops that dealt in tea needed to pay an annual fee of 5s. 6d. to be licensed by the government, so there is some record of the kinds and numbers of places that retailed tea. In the tax year 1783–1784, for example, London had about 3,000 licensed tea dealers, the larger towns of England and Wales about 7,000 more, and the small towns and villages an additional 24,000. The total number of tea dealers in 1783 was 32,754, a figure that rose to 48,263 by 1787 and to 56,248 by 1801. Of course, there may have been many more individuals selling smuggled tea without paying the license fee.

Once purchased, tea was kept in a locked chest or closet, partly to prevent pilfering and partly to monitor the supply for fear of running out. It was drunk both at breakfast (*NA* 175) and at the close of the afternoon; the idea of 'tea' as a distinct meal was yet to evolve, but already the ceremony of drinking tea and perhaps eating a little something was fully entrenched as a way of ending the afternoon and beginning the evening (*Watsons, MW* 354; *NA* 118; *S&S* 99, 106, 166; *P&P* 68, 160, 166;

Tea

MP 104, 177, 180, 227; *E* 8, 209, 210, 311, 382–383). Tea was 'brought in' or 'handed round' at a specified interval after the beginning of dinner, typically about three hours, which allowed plenty of time for a leisurely meal and either a walk or some after-dinner conversation (*Sand, MW* 390–391). The Edwardses, in *The Watsons*, drink their tea at 7:00 p.m. (*MW* 326); the Watsons appear to drink it at about the same time, as they are sitting at tea when a guest calls on his way 'home to an 8 o'clock dinner' (*MW* 355). Tea might also be enjoyed at evening social events (*Watsons, MW* 332; *NA* 21, 23, 25; *P* 189) such as parties, dances and concerts; at a 'fete' at Kingston Hall in 1791, the hostess, Frances Bankes, served orgeat (a barley or almond-based drink), lemonade, two types of negus and tea. Though tea was usually drunk indoors, the great public gardens at Ranelagh and Vauxhall had given people a taste for taking their tea outside as well. Accordingly, people who could afford to indulge in landscaping often added little buildings to their gardens in which they could serve tea and partake of the surrounding scenery (*E* 27). By the 1810s, tea rooms had sprung up in resort towns to free travellers from the necessity of preparing the beverage in their lodgings; like a good circulating library and a sizable ballroom, the tea room became an indispensable attraction for a tourist town.

When tea was made at home, servants (*MP* 180) would bring in the 'tea things' so often mentioned by Austen (*Watsons, MW* 326, 355; *MP* 335, 379, 383). These included cups (*MP* 439), which for much of the eighteenth century had no handles – hence the expression 'a dish of tea', which became a vulgarism by the end of Austen's life (*Watsons, MW* 326; *MP* 379). Saucers (*MP* 439) and spoons were also provided; when a drinker had finished, he or she was supposed to place the spoon in or across the cup to signal that no more tea was desired. On occasion, the spoons themselves were numbered, so that the hostess could return the appropriate cup to each guest after refilling it. Lumps of sugar were retrieved from a bowl with a small set of tongs, and, in any household that could afford it, milk or cream would be offered as well. The hostess brewed the tea herself (*Watsons, MW* 319; *S&S* 98, 163; *P&P* 341; *MP* 219, 335, 344) either in a teapot or in an urn (*MP* 344), a large metal container shaped rather like a Greek vase. The water inside the urn was kept hot either by a charcoal fire in the base or by inserting a red-hot cylindrical piece of metal. While lovely ceramic teapots figure in many engravings and oil paintings of the era, the urn was for many people of Austen's time the definitive symbol of tea.

See also Beverages; Dishes; Food.

Teeth

It was understood that care of the teeth was important, and people aspired to have good teeth (*Lesley, MW* 119; *MP* 44) and good breath.

How to accomplish this goal was somewhat trickier, for there was no suitable way yet of straightening teeth (*P* 34), and the proper method of cleaning them was a matter of much discussion. Various sorts of tooth powders were sold in apothecaries' shops, each apothecary mixing his own particular variety. Greenough's, near St Sepulchre's in London, sold one-shilling Greenough's Tinctures, one of which supposedly cured toothache and the other of which promised that it 'perfectly cures the scurvy in the gums, fastens and preserves the teeth, renders them white and beautiful, prevents their decaying and keeps such as are decayed from becoming worse'. Some bought these premixed powders, but others chose to make their own at home. Books such as *The Toilet of Flora* (1775) explained how to make various kinds of dentifrices, including tooth powders, tooth liquids, toothbrushes made of liquorice roots and marshmallow roots, and 'A Coral Stick for the Teeth' in which tooth powder was mixed with gum tragacanth to make sticks that were then rubbed against the teeth. Some of the preparations in this book would have done far more harm than good:

> *A Receipt to clean the Teeth and Gums, and make the Flesh grow close to the Root of the Enamel.*
>
> Take an ounce of Myrrh in fine powder, two spoonfuls of the best white Honey, and a little green Sage in fine powder; mix them well together, and rub the teeth and gums with a little of this balsam every night and morning.
>
> *Ditto, to strengthen the Gums and fasten loose Teeth.*
>
> Dissolve an ounce of Myrrh as much as possible in half a pint of Red Wine and the same quantity of Oil of Almonds: Wash the mouth with this fluid every morning.

This is also an excellent remedy against worms in the teeth.

Other tools used to clean the teeth included a piece of wood bitten and softened to separate the fibres and egg-sized sponges dyed red and infused with 'Essential Oil of Cinnamon, Cloves, Lavender, & c.' (The poor, lacking adequate access to oil of cinnamon, simply rubbed their teeth with soot.)

This was part of the problem with eighteenth- and early-nineteenth-century dentistry. Practitioners and patients had a tendency to do far too much or far too little to the teeth, often with truly disgusting results. Thomas Berdmore, the first man to be appointed dentist to the royal family and author of an important 1768 treatise on dental and periodontal disease, recorded the case of a twenty-three-year-old bank employee whose teeth 'gave him constant pain':

> I found them perfectly buried in Tartar, by which each set was united in one continuous piece, without any distinction, to show the interstices of the teeth, or their figure or size. The stony crust projected a great way over the gums on the inner side, as well as on the outer, and pressed

I upon them so hard as to have given rise to the pain he complained of. Its thickness at the upper surface was not less than half an inch.

At the other extreme, Berdmore discovered that some tooth powders could wear away the enamel of the teeth in as little as an hour. He applied the scientific spirit of the age to dentistry, using a microscope to study the parts of the teeth, researching the action of different acids on the teeth and advocating the sensible use of tooth powders.

He also understood that sugar played a role in tooth decay, something that not all of his contemporaries knew. The causes of tooth decay were still extremely mysterious. Some still thought that caries was caused by tiny worms within the teeth.

Dentistry was still emerging as a serious medical practice. No specialised training was required to set up shop, and the treatment afforded by most dentists tended to be limited to pulling offending teeth. A few notable practitioners performed more-advanced surgical techniques, performed re-implantations and transplantations or made fillings of gold or metal alloys. These people tended to refer to themselves as 'dentists', a term derived in the 1750s from French that sounded more sophisticated than 'tooth-drawer'. The tooth-drawer was the more common practitioner, and all he required was a pair of forceps or, if he were especially well equipped, a dental key, a tool that looked rather like a large house key with a claw at one end. The tooth-drawer used this key to grab the tooth, twist and wrench it out with one enormous pull (*Sand, MW* 388). Parson James Woodforde described the process in October 1785:

> The Tooth-Ach so very bad all night and the same this Morn' that
> I sent for John Reeves the Farrier who lives at the Hart and often draws
> Teeth for People, to draw one for me. He returned with my Man about
> 11 o'clock this Morning and he pulled it out for me the first Pull, but
> it was a monstrous Crash and more so, it being one of the Eye Teeth,
> it had but one Fang but that was very long. I gave Johnny Reeves for
> drawing it 0.2.6. A great pain in the Jaw Bone continued all Day and
> Night but nothing so bad as the Tooth Ach.

As Woodforde's diary entry points out, the local tooth-drawer was as likely as not to be a farrier or blacksmith; he rarely knew anything more advanced about dentistry than how to grab and pull. Dentists, who provided a range of other treatments, were not required to study their craft, but many signed up for short training courses or even apprenticeships of several years. They needed to be able to scrape off tartar, lance abscesses, kill infections in teeth and fill cavities. The fact that Harriet Smith goes to London to visit a dentist (*E* 451, 463), rather than resorting to a local tooth-drawer, means that she is probably interested in preserving the tooth or perhaps in diagnosing the cause of her pain. She might have visited someone like James Spence, a protégé of Hunter's who eventually became dentist to George III. The actor Samuel

Foote visited his shop in hopes of ending a toothache and found it to be neat and clean, with a painted hand in the window, lace-cuffed, holding a tooth, and with pulled teeth exhibited around the room 'as white and polished as ivory, the only wonder was how they came to lose their destined homes and how they were found where I saw them'. The difference between the tidy, professional Spence and Woodforde's farrier is no doubt why Harriet Smith chose to go to London. Many people, terrified of having a tooth drawn (*Sand, MW* 387), dreaded going to the dentist at all (*Cath, MW* 208–209). Jane wrote pityingly of her nieces in 1813; they, too, had gone to London to see a dentist, and Lizzy had had hers 'filed & lamented over', while Marianne had two of hers extracted to the accompaniment of 'two sharp hasty Screams'.

See also Medicine.

Theatre

Theatregoing (*NA* 25, 26, 34, 70, 92–93; *P&P* 152; *P* 180) was a popular pastime for the rich and poor alike. Prices at the Drury Lane theatre ranged from 6s. for a box to 1s. for the highest gallery, half that for patrons who came in after the end of the third act of the five-act main presentation. The typical theatre (*MP* 169) had a pit (*MP* 124) section with long undivided benches on the floor and rows upon rows of private boxes (*NA* 35, 92–93, 95; *MP* 124; *P* 223) built up along the walls. Until the 1760s, patrons could pay a fee of 10s. to sit on the stage itself at both Drury Lane and Covent Garden, but the practice was abolished and customers sent to their proper places. Cheaper tickets could be had in a balcony or 'gallery' section (*MP* 124), and this was where the common people, the footmen and the prostitutes sat. Some prostitutes also ensconced themselves in the minute upper boxes, but the more spacious lower boxes were reserved for the well bred and prosperous members of society.

Footmen had attended for free during most of the eighteenth century. They had been sent by their masters to hold seats for them in the pit, for seats (except for boxes, hence the term 'box office') could not be reserved in advance. Their masters could arrive fashionably late and displace their servants, who migrated up to the upper gallery or balcony area. In the second half of the eighteenth century, however, this practice was abolished, and footmen had to pay for their seats or convince their employers to do so. Periodic attempts to raise prices usually failed; one such attempt at Covent Garden in 1809 resulted in riots.

The principal London theatres, the only ones that possessed royal patents for producing spoken-English plays, were Drury Lane (*S&S* 330) and Covent Garden (*L&F, MW* 109). These were the largest theatres in the kingdom, seating 3,600 and 3,000, respectively, by the 1790s and even more after being rebuilt in the wake of fires in 1809 and 1808. Large stages allowed for monumental scenery but caused a loss of intimacy that was regretted by patrons who could recall the smaller, older incarnations of these theatres. Austen attended performances at Covent Garden in April 1811, September 1813 and March 1814 and, though she was sometimes critical of the actors' performances, appears to have had no quarrel with the design of the theatre itself.

These two theatres were usually open from September to June for their principal season. During the summer months, London's stars often toured the provinces in their most heralded roles, hoping to make a little extra money. Operas were performed at the King's Theatre, Haymarket and at George Colman's Little Theatre (*P&P* 319); the latter of these was permitted to perform spoken dramas during the summer months when Drury Lane and Covent Garden were closed, and in the winter it staged operas.

In season, plays were performed every night except Sundays. The theatres also closed for a few religious holidays, such as Ash Wednesday and the week leading up to Easter. During Lent, the Wednesday and Friday plays were replaced by oratorios. All theatres closed in the event of a royal death.

Plays were advertised in advance in the newspapers, announcing the titles of the principal play and afterpiece, the names of the starring actors, ticket prices, times of performance and (where relevant) the composer of the music. Performances typically began at 6:00 p.m., and the doors opened an hour earlier. People planning to sit in the pit or galleries lined up well in advance of 5:00 p.m., however, in order to get the best possible seats. On occasion, when interest was high at the opening of a new play, for example, doors might open especially early – as much as two or three hours beforehand.

Once safely inside, people could buy oranges to eat and programs to read from the 'book women' who walked about with their paper-lined fruit baskets. About half an hour before the curtain rose, the orchestra would play for half an hour or so, and a warning bell would sound to advise people to take their seats. Theatre orchestras were quite substantial in size, consisting of as many as thirty musicians and various functionaries such as music copyists, keyboard tuners and a chorus master. The orchestra was conducted either by the music director from the harpsichord or pianoforte or, if he were not present, by the lead violinist.

When the music concluded, the curtain (*MP* 123, 141, 195) would be gathered along ropes that ran vertically at various points along its length. The gathering pulled it into festoons that remained visible at the top of the stage (*MP* 167). An actor came out and recited a verse prologue to the mainpiece – the principal play of the evening. A typical night at the theatre, with the exception of oratorio nights, contained the main play or opera and a lighter, shorter afterpiece (*MP* 124), sometimes called the farce; less commonly, three afterpieces would be performed instead of a mainpiece and an afterpiece. Interspersed between these pieces were dances and songs (*MP* 124).

The behaviour of the audiences was generally fairly rowdy. The low gallery prices ensured that a broad cross-section of society was admitted, and not even the gentry were entirely silent during the play. They talked among themselves or looked in the other boxes for friends or celebrities rather than paying strict attention to the play. The actors sometimes broke character to chastise particularly annoying members of the audience, and this disruption onstage does not seem to have been upsetting or unexpected to the audience at large. They were perfectly capable of restoring their suspension of disbelief as soon as the play resumed, though they respected actors who could continue to concentrate in the midst of distractions.

Scenery (*MP* 141, 164, 191) was expensive and often reused from play to play. Some of the scenery was painted on backcloths that could be raised or lowered quickly. Other pieces were painted on flats and wings that were set in grooves and slid back and forth by ropes. Costumes were not always historically accurate; in fact, before the turn of the century, they were almost never so. There was an increasing interest in making the costumes fit the play, however, largely as a result of the activism of the actor John Philip Kemble (1757–1823), who managed Covent Garden from 1803 to 1817. Lighting was by means of candles, some of which were set in front of the stage and could be lowered below it to darken the scene, and some of which were placed on side-pieces or in chandeliers; these, too, could be moved in order to dim or raise the level of light, but the stage could not be made entirely dark.

London's minor theatres had to restrict themselves to forms other than traditional drama and comedy. Instead, they staged puppet shows, equestrian performances, exhibitions of wild animals, pantomimes, burlettas and musical performances, none of which came under the terms of the 1737 Licensing Act limiting the patented theatres to two. One of these theatres was the Lyceum, which Austen attended in 1811; normally the Lyceum was restricted to quasi-theatrical entertainments such as hot-air balloon displays and animal acts, but during this period it housed the Drury Lane company while Drury Lane was being rebuilt after the fire. She went to the Lyceum again in 1813.

In the provinces, travelling troupes of actors (*L&F*, *MW* 107; *Cath*, *MW* 240) staged performances for a few days or weeks, moving on to a different town when the audiences thinned. Some provincial towns, dissatisfied with this peripatetic entertainment, built their own theatres. The theatres went up first in resort towns, where the families of invalids come to drink the spa waters hungered for a way to spend their extra time and money. Eventually, there were theatres in York, Canterbury, Bristol, Bath, Cheltenham, Tunbridge Wells and Norwich. Austen is known to have visited the Theatre Royal in Southampton in 1807 and the Orchard Street theatre in Bath in 1799. It is not known whether she ever attended the new Bath theatre in Beaufort Square, which had better traffic access, but it was typical of many provincial theatres. Decked out at a cost of £20,000 and opened in 1805, it had crimson and gold décor, cast-iron pillars, expensive chandeliers and three exits – this last, an important factor when one was part of an impatient crowd eager to depart after the show.

Provincial theatre tickets tended to be cheaper than those in London. At the Norwich theatre, Parson James Woodforde paid 12s. for four box seats in 1784, and much less, only a shilling, for two box seats in 1794; perhaps he saw the latter show at half price. At Drury Lane in 1795, however, he paid 7s. for only two tickets, and he does not specify that these were box seats. In fact, they would have been seats in the pit, which went for 3s. 6d. each at the time.

Plays

There is evidence, both within her writings and in her letters, that Austen was exposed to a large number of plays (*NA* 79, 92, 217; *P&P* 154; *MP* 130, 167, 338; *E* 276; *P* 223). She read them, she saw them performed and at times she even acted in them at home. It is not always possible, however, to tell in which way she familiarised herself with individual plays.

Most of her references are to the works of Shakespeare. In her writings, she refers to *Macbeth* (*L&F*, *MW* 108; *MP* 131), *Henry IV* (*Hist Eng*, *MW* 139), *Henry VIII* (*MP* 336–338), *Julius Caesar* (*MP* 126–127), *Hamlet* (*MP* 130) and *Othello* (*MP* 131). The *History of England* contains a reference to Shakespeare's portrayal of Catherine of Valois in *Henry V* (*Hist Eng*, *MW* 139). Henry Crawford's interest in playing either Shylock or Richard III (both cruel characters, as David Selwyn has noted) alludes to both *The Merchant of Venice* and *Richard III* (*MP* 123). Austen had a special interest in *The Merchant of Venice*, for in 1814 Edmund Kean made his debut as Shylock, electrifying theatre audiences with his revolutionary acting style. Austen saw him in this role only a month after his debut, and while she was unimpressed with most of the cast, she found his individual performance outstanding. She does not name *Midsummer Night's Dream*, but Emma quotes from it, noting that a Hartfield edition of Shakespeare would have a long annotation to the line, 'The course of true love never did run smooth' (*E* 75). David Selwyn observes a number of nods to Shakespeare, or at least thematic similarities to his work, in Austen's novels. He likens the wilderness at Sotherton to the wood in *Midsummer Night's Dream*, Marianne Dashwood to Ophelia and the overall plot of *Mansfield Park* to the theme of filial fidelity in *King Lear*.

Playwrights other than Shakespeare whose works are alluded to include Nicholas Rowe, who wrote *Jane Shore* (*Hist Eng*, *MW* 140); George Colman the Younger, who wrote *The Heir at Law* (*MP* 131); Susanna Centlivre, author of *The Gamester* (*MP* 131); Richard Cumberland, whose Wheel of Fortune (*MP* 131) features a misanthropist named Penruddock, a son who (like Tom Bertram) is jeopardized by his gambling, and a lawyer named Timothy Weasel; John Home, author of Douglas, the play in which the phrase, 'My name was Norval' (*MP* 126–127) appears; and Richard

Brinsley Sheridan, manager of Drury Lane and author of *The Critic* (*Hist Eng*, *MW* 147), *The Rivals* (*MP* 131) and *School for Scandal* (*MP* 131). At a private theatrical performance at Godmersham in 1808, in fact, Austen played Mrs Candour in *School for Scandal*. Her juvenile fragment *The Visit* alludes to the line, 'The more free, the more welcome' (*MW* 50), from James Townley's *High Life Below Stairs,* a play that was performed in amateur theatricals at Steventon.

Finally, she gives Tom Bertram a singularly tactless joke that turns on the title of the afterpiece *My Grandmother* by Prince Hoare. When the death of Lord Ravenshaw's grandmother ends the amateur theatricals at Ecclesford, he says, 'Lovers Vows were at an end, and Lord and Lady Ravenshaw were left to act My Grandmother by themselves' (*MP* 123). One wonders if Austen had in mind, as well as the title of the play, its previous association with death; it was one of three Hoare works being performed at a royal command performance at the Little Theatre in the Haymarket on the night of 1 February 1794. Michael Kelly, whose memoirs record many details of theatrical performances at the time, recalled what happened:

> The crowd was so great that at the opening of the doors, in going down the steps which led to the pit, three or four persons slipped and fell and several others were hurried over them; sixteen persons were trampled to death and upwards of twenty were taken up with broken limbs.

The news of this fatal accident was, very judiciously, kept from their Majesties until after the performance was over, when they evinced the deepest sorrow and regret at the event.

Austen's most sustained theatrical reference, however, is to *Lovers Vows*, Elizabeth Inchbald's adaptation of *Das Kind der Liebe* (*The Love Child*) by the German playwright August von Kotzebue. The play is about Agatha Friburg (*MP* 132, 135, 137), who has been seduced, impregnated and abandoned by Baron Wildenhaim (*MP* 132), and their illegitimate son Frederick. Frederick, after robbing his father and revealing his identity, convinces the Baron to marry Agatha. Meanwhile, the clergyman Anhalt (*MP* 132, 144, 358) is wooed in an inversion of gender roles by the Baron's daughter Amelia (*MP* 133, 135, 137), who does not wish to marry the idiotic Count Cassel (*MP* 122, 132, 138–139, 144), her father's choice for her husband. Paula Byrnehas studied the play and its casting in *Mansfield Park* and finds satisfying correspondences between the parts and the players: Tom Bertram, who can take nothing seriously, snaps up all the minor comic roles (*MP* 132, 164); the empty-headed Mr Rushworth plays the equally brainless Count; the clergyman Anhalt is played by the future clergyman Edmund and his aggressive lover by the brazen Mary Crawford. Fanny Price is drafted for the role of Cottager's wife (*MP* 134, 135, 146), a role considered appropriate at Ecclesford only for the governess, and which Fanny, ever shy, feels unable and unwilling to play. Henry

31. *Lovers Vows.*

Crawford takes the hero's part, and Maria Bertram gets to play his mother, a role that involves, according to the stage directions, repeated embraces of her 'son'. At one point, they embrace (*MP, LV* 483); on the next page she leans her head on his chest (484); a few pages later, there is another embrace (488), and then she 'presses him to her breast' (489). At the play's end, he 'throws himself on his knees by the other side of his mother – She clasps him in her arms' (536). The play, like *Mansfield Park*, is concerned with the plight of a woman who loves but is denied the right to speak her feelings by convention and the right of parents to arrange their children's marriages despite lack of love.

Inchbald toned down the play a good deal from the original German, and her play was extremely popular. However, not all people found it tasteful. German drama was often described as encouraging young people to indulge in fits of emotion and hasty elopements. Furthermore, the themes of illegitimate birth, seduction and assertive female courtship were offensive to some, making them perfect to test the morals and character of the Mansfield group. Despite the fact that they know its subject matter to be questionable, and despite the fact that they all know, to a greater or lesser extent, that Sir Thomas would disapprove of their actions, they all, except for Fanny, become seduced by the idea of performing it just as surely as Agatha is seduced by the Baron. Austen sticks closely to the text of the play, referring to its stage sets of 'cottages and ale-houses' (*MP* 143; *MP, LV* 481), to the love scene between Anhalt and Amelia (*MP* 168, 358; *MP, LV* 504–505) and to Frederick's imprisonment (*MP* 135; *MP, LV* 513–514).

In all, Austen refers to more than forty plays, and it must be assumed that she saw and read far more than this number. We know with certainty that she saw Hannah Cowley's *The Belle's Stratagem*, a play that resembles *Pride and Prejudice* in its use of false impressions and the search of five country sisters for husbands. She also saw Isaac Bickerstaffe's *The Hypocrite*, an adaptation of Molière's *Tartuffe*; Garrick and Colman's *The Clandestine Marriage;* Charles Dibdin's *The Farmer's Wife*; and Thomas Arne's opera *Artaxerxes*. Notably, the first theatre performance on record as having been attended by her was *The Birthday*, Thomas Dibdin's adaptation of a play by Kotzebue, whose heroine, Emma Bertram, has an invalid father and feels unable to marry as a result. Musical pieces and farces that she saw included *Bluebeard*, *The Beehive*, *Don Juan*, Charles Coffey's *The Devil to Pay*, Thomas Dibdin's and Michael Kelly's *Of Age Tomorrow* and Samuel Beazley's *The Boarding House: or Five Hours at Brighton*.

Actors and Acting

Actors of Austen's time operated with a stock catalogue of theatrical gestures and postures that conveyed, more iconically than realistically, the emotions they were supposed to be portraying. They declaimed in tones that would sound stilted today, and many adopted a 'ranting' (*MP* 123, 164, 394) style of delivery, shouting in a manner that was supposed to sound grand but bore little resemblance to actual human speech. Comic characters were delineated less by their mannerism than by their outlandish dress (*MP* 179–180), which signalled to the audience that they were to be laughed at.

A revolution began in the late eighteenth century with the somewhat more-natural style of Charles Macklin and David Garrick. It continued at the end of the period with Edmund Kean's portrayal of Shylock. Nonetheless, Austen, who had been an enthusiastic patron of the theatre in her younger years, gradually became disenchanted with the performances she saw. Too many male actors relied on old tricks she had seen before; too many celebrated young women were nothing more than pretty faces and, occasionally, pretty voices. While she often refers to specific actors in her letters, she mentions only two in her works: the '*Lewis & Quick*' of *Love & Freindship* (*MW* 109). William Thomas Lewis

(1748–1811), known as 'Gentleman' Lewis for his refined voice and style, acted for thirty-five years at Covent Garden in a wide variety of comedies. John Quick, who often acted with him, was another comedian best known for playing bumpkins.

Nonetheless, there were many famous thespians on the stage in her day, and she saw most of them at one time or another. She lived during the dawn of modern theatre criticism, and in an age without movies, the escapades of stage actors were discussed with great interest. Players like Sarah Siddons, John Philip Kemble and Dorothea Jordan, all of whom she saw onstage, were the first great show-business celebrities. Other popular actors included Richard Yates, the comedian who originated the role of Oliver Surface in *School for Scandal*, and his wife, Mary Ann Yates, a leading tragic actress in Garrick's company. Their last name is shared by the enthusiastic amateur actor Mr Yates in *Mansfield Park*, and Henry and Mary Crawford share their last name with Ann and Thomas (Billy) Crawford, a married pair of actors. Theatre managers (*L&F*, *MW* 107–108; *MP* 123), too, enjoyed fame, as their control over the great London play houses controlled what thousands of theatregoers saw.

At the same time, actors (*L&F*, *MW* 107–108) enjoyed a poor personal reputation. Actresses were considered little better than prostitutes, and it did not help matters that some, like Dorothea Jordan, carried on highly publicised sexual relationships with peers of the realm. The actress Elizabeth Farren was accused of having a lesbian affair with Anne Seymour Damer, and the great Mrs Siddons herself had her name romantically linked with that of her fencing teacher. Though many women participated in amateur theatricals with their reputations untarnished, one can imagine why Sir Thomas Bertram might object to having his daughters pretend to be actresses, especially in a play considered indecorous in itself.

See also Entertainment; Public Places; Reading.

Time

The schedule of the gentry differed greatly from the schedule followed by working people. Farmers and fishermen, for example, were dominated by the natural world; tides and unmilked cows wait for no man. Workers also had little money to spare for expensive candles (*Col Let*, *MW* 156), so they regulated their day by the course of the sun. Once it set, little was done, and bedtime soon followed. However, some people could and did stay up late: the gentry, nobility and prosperous workers such as merchants and substantial tenant farmers. Instead of rising at or before dawn, they stayed in bed a little longer and extended their day into the evening, when the glow of several, or even dozens of, candles set a distinctive mood.

Austen ignores the workers' schedule and pays great attention to the nuances of the hours kept among the gentry. In a society that valued consumption and display, late hours meant more candles and therefore more wealth, which was definitely a good thing (*Col Let*, *MW* 157; *Watsons*, *MW* 346). During Austen's lifetime, there was a slow, but deliberate, movement towards later and later hours (*MP* 266), for meals particularly, with the somewhat comical result that supper was gradually being eliminated as dinner came later and later, while lunch was slowly emerging to fill the place vacated by dinner, resulting in much the same meals under different names.

Since there was this gradual inflation of hours, and since the hours kept in one household often differed markedly from those down the street or across town, it can be hard to state with certainty that people got up or ate or went to bed at such-and-such an hour. A rough picture, however, can be drawn. People of Austen's class might rise at 8:00 a.m. or so, then walk, play music or write letters until breakfast at nine or ten (*P&P* 319; *E* 443). Departures from this pattern were typically made only for the sake of travel (*NA* 228; *P* 95) or from extreme asceticism (*S&S* 343). Men might go hunting before breakfast (*Watsons*, *MW* 347; *P* 37). In fashionable London, however, breakfast was served later.

From the end of breakfast until the beginning of dinner, people took care of their daily business. Women sewed, supervised the servants' dinner preparations and engaged in charitable work. Men wrote business letters (*S&S* 304) or supervised the care of their land, crops, horses and dogs. Both sexes paid so-called morning visits (*Watsons*, *MW* 338; *MP* 298), which might take place until as late as 3:00 p.m. or 4:00 p.m., depending on when dinner was served. They might also read (*NA* 60), walk for exercise and amusement (*NA* 80, 177) or go out riding on horseback or in carriages (*NA* 45, 67).

Dinner officially ended the morning and began the afternoon. The unfashionable ate it at 3:00 p.m. (*Watsons*, *MW* 344), the fashionable at 6:30 p.m. (*Watsons*, *MW* 355; *P&P* 35), with many people setting the time somewhere in between (*Sand*, *MW* 411; *NA* 193, 195, 199, 214; *S&S* 74; *MP* 89, 221; *E* 188–189). (The Austens, for example, ate at 3:00 p.m. in 1798 at Steventon, but their dinner hour had crept back to 5:00 p.m. by 1808.) An 1819 letter to the *Gentleman's Magazine* gave the dinner hour as 5:00 p.m. (*Col Let*, *MW* 159) or 6:00 p.m. and asserted that this was, by then, a standard time for the meal among the gentry and nobility. Everyone ate together for a time, and then the ladies withdrew to talk among themselves in another room, while the gentlemen lingered over port and conversation in the dining room. When the gentlemen joined the ladies, tea and coffee were served (*E* 8), usually about three hours after the commencement of dinner, that is, somewhere between 6:00 and 10:00 p.m. (*Watsons*, *MW* 326, 355; *S&S* 315); this light meal officially began the 'evening', though the people enjoying it had been in their evening dress since dinner. Cards (*Watsons*, *MW* 359) and conversation, possibly music or dancing as well, filled the hours after tea until people either ate supper (*Watsons*, *MW* 359) or went to bed. On nights when there was company in the house, people tended to stay up a little later.

Parson Woodforde tended to dine between 3:00 p.m. and 5:00 p.m.; he considered 5:00 p.m. as late enough to be worthy of note in 1785. When he dined out, he usually returned at about 9:00 p.m. He and his niece-housekeeper Nancy rose at seven, but this appears to have been something of a struggle; they had to fine themselves sixpence for failure to rise early. For the most part, he appears to have gone to bed relatively early, around 10:00 p.m. or so, but on special occasions he stayed out very late indeed. In July 1784, he stayed at a friend's until 4:00 a.m. and did not get back home until 5:00 a.m. More typically, he went to bed at about midnight after social gatherings.

Jane Austen seems to have kept similar hours. In August 1805, she wrote to Cassandra that she had stayed out late and gotten home 'considerably past eleven'. Sometimes, dinner parties kept her up late; at other times, it was the theatre. At least we know for certain when she finished dancing in Bath; there, the assemblies shut down at 11:00 p.m., even in the middle of a dance. Not so at Tunbridge Wells, where a correspondent of the Austens' danced till 2:00 a.m. in 1787. Bedtime for most of the gentry was between 10:00 p.m. and midnight (*NA* 222; *P&P* 273; *E* 126), with exceptions made for special parties and other forms of entertainment (*S&S* 44); Fanny Price's late night at her debut ball is a good example of such an exception (*MP* 279). The ball in *The Watsons* ends earlier; it has already been going on for some time when a young guest notices that it is eleven o'clock (*Watsons*, *MW* 332).

There was one other way of measuring out the day besides the timing of meals, but it does not appear in any of Austen's novels. However, since she does make frequent reference to the navy, it is perhaps appropriate to make some mention of how time was kept aboard ship. A half-hour 'hourglass' was kept on deck and turned as it ran out. Each time the glass was turned, a bell was struck – once the first time it was struck, twice the second time and so on, up to eight bells. At eight bells, a new watch took over, and the next time the bell was struck it would be struck only once. Most watches lasted four hours and therefore had eight bells, but the first and second dog watches lasted only two hours each and thus had only four bells before the pattern began again.

Watch	Hours*	Bells
First	20–24 hours	8
Middle	0–4 hours	8
Morning	4–8 hours	8
Forenoon	8–12 hours	8
Afternoon	12–16 hours	8
First Dog	16–18 hours	4
Second Dog	18–20 hours	4

*Using twenty-four-hour rather than twelve-hour notation, so that '20', for example, means 8:00 p.m.

Most days of the week were similar in their pattern, but Sunday
(*MP* 401) was different. Ideally, people of all classes were supposed to
throng to their parish churches for morning service, then eat and take
a walk, or engage in some other innocent diversion, and return in the
afternoon for evening service (*NA* 190). In practice, this was not always
the case. Servants tried to absent themselves from church in order to
socialise with each other; Dissenters went to their own chapels after,
or instead of, the parish church; some of the gentry and aristocracy
skipped divine service altogether, for which they were often chided by
reformers who insisted that they set a good example for the lower orders.
To the dismay of clerics and reformers alike, many labourers also skipped
services and went instead to the local alehouse. For many people, Sunday
had a holiday feel to it, and even those who went dutifully to church
services felt themselves entitled to a little fun.

In many towns, this meant that after church, throngs of people
took walks simultaneously in some public place (*NA* 232). This had the
advantage of being conveniently close to home and also afforded people
a chance to stop and chat informally with acquaintances. Austen shows
her readers this traditional promenade twice: once in Bath, where the
principal strolling was done in the area around the Royal Crescent
(*NA* 35), and once in Portsmouth, where the gathering place is the
ramparts (*MP* 408–409).

There were cycles not only to the days and weeks but also to the
months and seasons of the year. Among farmers, it was the relevance
of the seasons to agricultural labour that mattered. They ploughed,
planted and harvested according to the time of year and sometimes,
superstitiously, according to the phases of the moon. Austen's world,
however, is aware of the cycles of farming but not intimately involved
in it; in her novels, the seasonal change that matters is the one between
London (or watering places) and the country. Though she demonstrates
in *Mansfield Park* that she understands the demands of the harvest season
(58), which was so critical to financial success that responsible farmers
reserved the best labourers months ahead of time, and though *Emma* is
a book subtly propelled by agricultural rhythms, Austen's characters
are mostly moved by the fashions and customs of the winter and summer
social seasons.

Winter and summer were ruled to some extent by competing migrations,
but the oldest pattern and the one most people yearned to follow was the
winter migration to London (*P&P* 238). Parliament opened in October or
November (*MP* 199) and conducted business until the spring (*MP* 20, 202;
E 259, 308), usually May; the members (*MP* 20) then returned to their
country homes (*MP* 422) to supervise their estates, preside over the harvest
and enjoy the fall hunting season, which began 1 September (*P&P* 318;
MP 114, 181). The families of the members of Parliament naturally trotted
along in their wake, setting up London households for the winter season
(*S&S* 153, 214). Since the members of Parliament included some of the

most notable men in the kingdom, as well as all the peers and bishops, their arrival in the capital naturally drew acquaintances and would-be acquaintances who longed to mingle with the rich and powerful. As lodgings in the West End – the fashionable part of London – were not to be had cheaply, a London season was a luxury that women in particular craved. A house in London (*S&S* 153; *MP* 20), to which one could return year after year, was a still greater prize; Austen does not seem to have thought much of women who yearned for one, but her works are a testament to London's attraction.

Some people spent a part of the year in a watering place, either instead of, or in addition to, London. These sites featured some sort of mineral spring with supposedly healthful properties, which invalids would drink in hope of a cure. Their families, like the families of MPs, came along with them and amused themselves at balls, plays and concerts. Each spa town had its own season; Southampton's was from July to October, Clifton's from late March to late September. Bath had two principal seasons, one from February to June, and the other from September to Christmas (*MP* 202–203). It was practically deserted in the summer. Towards the end of Austen's life, seaside towns were also developing seasons of their own, often during the summer months (*Sand, MW* 389).

See also Entertainment; Food.

Titles

The English system of titles (*Sand, MW* 395; *MP* 47–48), if the royal family is excepted, had seven levels, not all of which conferred membership in the peerage (*L&F, MW* 77). Each level had its own rules for addressing the title-bearer himself, his wife and his children. At the top of the hierarchy were dukes, and at the bottom were knights. For the purposes of clarity in the following discussion, assume that 'Smith' is the last name of our fictional titled family and that 'Whateverington' is the title name. (A well-known example of the difference between the two would be George Gordon, Lord Byron; Gordon is his family name and Byron the title name.) It was not unknown for the title name and the surname to be identical, but again for clarity we will assume that the two names are different.

A duke and his wife, a duchess (*H&E, MW* 35), were addressed as His (or Her) Grace (*H&E, MW* 35, 36; *Cass, MW* 44). Their eldest son held the next highest family title, example, earl or marquess. Other sons were lords (e.g. Lord John Smith), and were referred to in conversation as Lord John or Lord James. John's and James' wives bore the title 'Lady' along with their husbands' first names, that is, 'Lady John' and 'Lady James'. The duke's daughter, on the other hand, would use her own first name, example, Lady Anne (*H&E, MW* 35) or Lady Anne Smith. As will be seen,

Lord and Lady were titles that appeared at several ranks, and it can thus be difficult to tell the exact rank of many of Austen's characters.

The next highest rank was that of marquess (*NA* 139). The marquess could be referred to variously as the marquess of Whateverington, the Most Honourable the marquess of Whateverington or simply Lord Whateverington. His wife was likewise the marchioness of Whateverington, the Most Honourable the Marchioness of Whateverington or Lady Whateverington. The titles and forms of address were exactly the same for the sons and daughters of marquesses as for the sons and daughters of dukes.

Earls occupied the next level. An earl was referred to as the earl of Whateverington, the Right Honourable the earl of Whateverington or Lord Whateverington. His wife was a countess (*Cass*, *MW* 45; *NA* 232), referred to as the countess of Whateverington, the Right Honourable the Countess of Whateverington or Lady Whateverington. An earl's daughter had the same titles as a duke's or a marquess's – Lady Anne Smith – but the sons' titles were somewhat different. The eldest, like the eldest son of a duke or a marquess, bore the next highest title held by the family, but a younger son would be known as the Honourable John Smith or Mr Smith, and his wife as the Honourable Mrs John Smith or Mrs Smith.

The next rank was the Viscount (*Cass*, *MW* 45; *NA* 251). The Viscount was known as the Viscount Whateverington, the Right Honourable the Viscount Whateverington or Lord Whateverington. His wife was the Viscountess Whateverington, the Right Honourable the Viscountess Whateverington or Lady Whateverington (*NA* 251; *P* 148). All sons, including the eldest, bore the title 'Honourable' and the family surname, as in the Honourable John Smith; in conversation, like the earl's younger son, he might be called Mr Smith. John's wife would be the Honourable Mrs John Smith or simply Mrs Smith. A Viscount's daughter was either the Honourable Anne Smith or Miss Smith (*P* 148).

Barons followed a similar pattern. The Baron himself was the Right Honourable Lord Whateverington – never Baron Whateverington – or Lord Whateverington. His wife, if she held her title by virtue of her marriage, was the Right Honourable Lady Whateverington or Lady Whateverington. If she held the title in her own right, she could also be addressed as Baroness Whateverington. Sons and daughters of Barons followed the same pattern as the sons and daughters of Viscounts.

As readers have no doubt noticed, there are a great number of ranks at which someone may be referred to as 'Lord' or 'Lady', which can make it very difficult to determine the exact rank of the various lords (*NA* 18; *S&S* 251; *MP* 361; *P* 19–20) and ladies (*MP* 359) who appear in Austen's novels. The 'Lady Dorothea' of *Love and Freindship* (*MW* 81) could with equal likelihood be the daughter of a duke, a marquess or an earl. Mr Dudley, 'the Younger Son of a very noble Family' (*Cath*, *MW* 195), could be the younger son of an earl, Viscount or Baron, all of whom would have been referred to in ordinary conversation as 'Mr'. 'The Honourable John Yates' (*MP* 121), who marries Julia Bertram, belongs somewhere in the same three ranks. Lord Osborne, of *The Watsons*, could hold almost any rank.

Lady Catherine de Bourgh presents an especially interesting case. Mr Collins describes her as 'the Right Honourable Lady Catherine de Bourgh, widow of Sir Lewis de Bourgh' (*P&P* 62), and she is repeatedly referred to by others as Lady Catherine, not as Lady De Bourgh. Her rank, therefore, comes not from her husband but from her birth into a noble family, a fact confirmed by the fact that her sister is called 'Lady Anne' (83, 212) rather than Lady Darcy. A peer's daughter who married a knight, baronet or commoner was permitted to keep her rank and precedence, which appears to have happened in both these cases, but exactly what rank the two ladies retained is unclear. 'Honourable' was a common addition to titles of the daughters of peers (*S&S* 224), but 'Right Honourable' was reserved for earls, Viscounts, Barons and their wives. Daughters were not entitled to this magnification of the honorific. It seems likely, then, that the addition of 'Right' is Mr Collins' error and merely one more example of his tendency to exaggerate Lady Catherine's importance.

Frequently, however, it simply is not important. The lords (*P* 4) and ladies, by their very titles, are identified as significantly superior in social status to Austen's heroines, and this is usually all that matters. One important detail to remember, however, is that a Lord John or Lord James, in other words any pairing of 'lord' followed by the first name, will always refer to the son of a peer, not a holder of a title by inheritance. Lord Whateverington or John, Lord Whateverington, is the actual title, not a son's courtesy title.

Baron was the lowest rank of the peerage, and it is worth noting at this point that the actual modes of address could vary widely depending upon the length of acquaintance between the parties and their relative social rank. An inferior, for example, would always address a duke as 'Your Grace' or 'Sir', while a social equal could call him 'Duke', and a close friend might be able to get away with 'Whateverington' (*S&S* 252). The formality with which one addressed a peer also depended greatly on the circumstances. Addresses on letters and announcements of the peer's arrival by servants were intended to be more formal than the terms and titles used in conversation. In conversation, even though an acknowledgment of the peer's title was expected at first, for the rest of the conversation, 'my lord' (*Watsons*, *MW* 345) or 'my lady' was usually sufficient ('sir' or 'ma'am' for dukes and duchesses). Among equals who were friends, particularly if they were both men, the use of the title name only was perfectly acceptable, just as among the gentry, men commonly referred to each other by surname only (*Lesley*, *MW* 117). Austen accepted that this was common practice among men, but she found it vulgar in women; only her more-distasteful young women use men's surnames without an honorific (*NA* 120, 144; *E* 278, 353, 456). She also found it unpleasant when, instead of an honorific, a more-casual appellation was added; thus, Mr Price's reference to a comrade as 'Old Scholey' (*MP* 380) reveals his lack of good manners.

Several rules regarding titles applied specifically to women. Women could inherit peerages and retain these titles even after marriage to a man of inferior rank, but their husbands did not acquire the corresponding male title by their marriage to a peeress. Women who held titles in their own right could not sit in the House of Lords, nor could they undertake any hereditary government posts associated with the title; these duties would be performed by their husbands. A woman who acquired a title through marriage, such as Austen's cousin Eliza, the comtesse de Feuillide, lost it if she married again. The comtesse de Feuillide, for example, when she married Austen's brother after being widowed, became simply Mrs Henry Austen. If a woman were married to a peer who died, her eldest son inherited the title, and she became the dowager marchioness/countess/so on of Whateverington (*P* 148).

Titles below the Peerage

There were two ranks among the upper gentry that merited special titles, and they were very similar in their usage. Both baronets (*Col Let, MW* 163; *LS, MW* 296; *NA* 16, 18, 206; *MP* 3, 42, 395; *P* 4, 11, 75) and knights (*P* 11) were referred to as Sir Robert Smith (*P&P* 18; *P* 158) or Sir Robert (*E&E, MW* 30; *Visit, MW* 51; *P* 20), but never Sir Smith. One difference between them was that a baronet could add an abbreviation after his name in writing: Sir John Smith, Bart. or Sir John Smith, Bt. A more-important difference between the two titles was that a baronetcy could be inherited, while a knighthood could not. The wives in both cases were referred to as Lady Smith, as the use of a first name would have made it seem as if the woman in question was a peer's daughter rather than a knight's wife. Thus, we encounter Lady Russell (*P* 11), Lady Lesley (*Lesley, MW* 116) and so on (*J&A, MW* 15; *E&E, MW* 30; *Visit, MW* 51; *Col Let, MW* 152; *P&P* 222; *P* 75). Daughters of baronets and knights bore no special titles, but their sons (*L&F, MW* 80) might add the title 'Esquire' (*MP* 434) to their names, for example, John Smith, Esq. (*J&A, MW* 12; *Mount, MW* 40; *Amelia, MW* 47; *Cass, MW* 49; *S&S* 246; *P&P* 336; *P* 3, 4). Esquire was a term of uncertain boundaries; in theory, it was applicable only to the sons of upper gentry, judges, military officers and people of similar standing (such as the chief local landowner or 'squire' – see *NA* 16), but in practice it could safely be adopted by almost any gentleman.

Members of the gentry, yeoman farmers and most merchants and artisans would be known by the honorific titles still in use today in the United States, such as Mr, Mrs (*P&P* 317) and Miss. Husbands and wives addressed each other with far more formality than is now customary, calling each other 'Mr. Smith' and 'Mrs. Smith' in front of others (*Lesley, MW* 133), including servants and children. It was considered disrespectful to do otherwise (*E* 272, 278). Some families were no doubt a little less formal (*E* 172), calling the patriarch 'your Papa' instead of 'your father', but the Austens appear to have fallen into the more formal camp. Even when we know that letters were often read aloud to friends, it sounds strange to modern ears to hear Jane writing to Cassandra of 'my mother', when of course she was mother to both of them. Use of a person's first name required both long acquaintance and an invitation to advance to this level of familiarity or a family relationship, whether by blood relation, marriage or betrothal (*S&S* 59–60; *MP* 303; *E* 324).

Unmarried sisters were distinguished by the use of first names for any younger sisters and the title and surname alone for the eldest. Thus, in a family with three unmarried girls, the eldest would be Miss Smith, the second Miss Jane Smith and the youngest Miss Catherine Smith (*Cass*, *MW* 49). When the eldest married, Jane would now be referred to in public as 'Miss Smith', while Catherine would have to wait until Jane married to inherit that title. Grown-up sons of the gentry were referred to as 'Mr.', but young sons were called 'Master' instead (*Watsons*, *MW* 332).

Some titles were occupational. 'Doctor', which today is most usually associated with the practice of medicine or with advanced academic degrees, in Austen's time was predominantly applied to doctors of divinity, that is, to certain clergymen. Austen never uses the title 'Dr.' for a physician, reserving it instead for the clergy (*S&S* 218; *MP* 119). Servants were usually called either by their first names alone or by their last names alone, depending on their status within the household and on the custom of the family for whom they worked. The use of the first name alone was probably more typical, especially in households with only a handful of servants, but in large establishments, the upper servants were called by their last names. On occasion, one sees a hybrid form of address, such as the case of one eighteenth-century maid of all work, who was referred to by her employer as 'Mrs. Becky'. A companion or a governess would possess a status on the fringes of gentility and would be called by her last name, along with Mrs or Miss (*P&P* 158).

See also Education; Etiquette.

Travel

Travel (*NA* 155–156; *MP* 375; *E* 104–106, 285; *P* 13) was improving in Austen's day. Earlier in the eighteenth century, roads (*L&F*, *MW* 85; *Sand*, *MW* 426; *MW* 445; *NA* 198; *P&P* 275, 281, 282; *MP* 39, 82; *E* 83, 127) had been hazardous in the extreme, full of fatally deep potholes and bone-jarring ruts (*MP* 189), and often impassable (*Sand*, *MW* 363–364; 373) in the winter (*MP* 189). This was, in part, because each parish was responsible for the upkeep of the roads within its boundaries, and the task was simply too huge for many localities to manage well. Labour was hard to come by, and in parishes through which heavy London traffic passed, the road surveyors (*Watsons, MW* 349–350) could not keep up with the continual damage. The answer was the formation of turnpike trusts, whose creation peaked during the third quarter of the eighteenth century. The trusts, formed by means of a private act of Parliament (private because the drafting and passage were privately funded), built and maintained the turnpikes (*Ode, MW* 75; *L&F, MW* 97; *Watsons, MW* 321; *Sand, MW* 367; *S&S* 197; *P&P* 275) and erected toll gates (*Watsons, MW* 322). Most people, livestock, carts, wagons and carriages were subject to a toll every time they passed a gate, though mail coaches and troops were exempt.

As soon as it was clear that turnpikes could be profitable, they snaked across the map of England like the roots of some fast-growing plant. Hundreds were built, cooperating with improvements in horse breeding and carriage design to increase the rate at which people could travel. Furthermore, turnpikes, which were naturally placed along the busiest city-to-city routes, eased the pressure on local road surveyors. Increased interest in the state of the roads also developed during the wars with France, when rapid troop movement could be of great importance. From the mid-eighteenth century, cartographers had been making road maps specifically designed for travellers, sometimes showing only one town-to-town route with distances, villages and likely places to stop along the way (*NA* 45).

This is not to say that travel became free from all inconvenience. On the contrary, filthy inns (*E* 193, 306), stinking or snoring fellow passengers and poor weather (*NA* 19) remained as irritating as always. Travellers packed their trunks and boxes (*L&F, MW* 89; *NA* 227; *P&P* 213–214; *MP* 444; *E* 186) and loaded them on a stagecoach, post-chaise or stage wagon, tying the luggage to the vehicle's top with rope or shoving it into the huge basket that hung off the back of the coach (*Sand, MW* 406, 407; *P&P* 216).* A few items could be kept under the coach seat (*NA* 163), in laps (*P&P* 221), in side pockets sewn into the coach lining (*NA* 235) or in a woman's reticule or a man's coat pocket. Everything else remained out of reach. The roads, even the turnpike roads, were still bumpy and rutted in places, although this situation was gradually improving. Travellers hoped that the coach would not lose a wheel or, still worse, be overturned (*Sand, MW* 364; *NA* 19; *E* 126), as both kinds of accidents were fairly common. Mr Woodhouse's fear about 'the corner into Vicarage-lane' (*E* 280) is a fear of being overturned. Highwaymen haunted the turnpike roads, and their numbers were multiplied in the minds of fearful passengers (*NA* 19). On dark nights (*E* 128), travel was especially dangerous, for the coachman could not always see every obstacle in time to avoid it. Night-time journeys, therefore, tended to be performed when the moon was full, and people scheduled balls and other events accordingly (*Col Let, MW* 159; *Evelyn, MW* 189; *S&S* 33).

Stops, in most coaches, were frequent. The coachman would rein in his horses at a decent-looking inn and either rest or change the horses,

---

*Heavy baggage was sent by either water or over land by wagon (*P* 38–39).

perhaps allowing the passengers time to get something to eat (*L&F*, *MW* 106). If the stop were near the intersection of two major roads, he might need to allow some passengers to disembark (a process that entailed finding and unloading their luggage) so that they could wait for a coach that ran along the intersecting route (*NA* 232, 235). When the hour grew late, a halt would be called for the night, and the passengers would stumble wearily into an inn, where they would be shown to their possibly vermin-infested beds. Once they reached their destination, they might find that they had left belongings behind in one of these inns or else in the coach itself (*NA* 235), and there would be little or no hope of retrieving their lost property.

Slower conveyances travelled at about 4 to 6 miles per hour, though higher speeds were possible in light carriages (*NA* 88). Darcy, with good carriages and excellent horses at his command, can call 'fifty miles of good road' just over 'half a day's journey', implying that his top speed is somewhere in the neighbourhood of 8 miles per hour (*P&P* 179). General Tilney, likewise, estimates that a 20-mile trip (*NA* 212) will take him about 2 hours and 45 minutes (*NA* 210), giving him an average speed of a little over 7 miles per hour. Normally, in a post-chaise or similar vehicle of ordinary capabilities, a journey of about 100 miles would take two days of travel. The journey from Sotherton to Mansfield Park, then, a distance of about 10 miles (*MP* 73, 104), and not all of it good road, would take about 2 hours. A multiple-day journey might well take longer if it included a Sunday. Many travellers still followed the old habit of not travelling on Sunday (*P* 161), though this rule was often broken by the end of the eighteenth century.

Most of Austen's travel times are accurate. Journeys of any length take two to three days (*E&E*, *MW* 30; *Sand*, *MW* 409; *S&S* 160, 301–302, 304, 341; *P&P* 285–286; *MP* 446), which is about right for the distances involved. Some travel times, however, are intentionally wrong. For the sake of humour, for example, she has a character travel from Scotland to London in minutes or hours (*L&F*, *MW* 92), when in fact the journey took several days. On the opposite end of the spectrum, she sends Mr Clifford from Devizes to Bath, 'which is no less that nineteen miles', in a full day of travel. She then has him travel from Devizes to Overton, a distance of about 35 miles, in three days of 'hard labour', where he collapses and has to spend five months recuperating. He then takes four days to travel from Overton to Basingstoke, a journey of about 6 miles (*Clifford*, *MW* 43–44).

All of the journeys above were assumed to take place in some sort of vehicle. A man on foot obviously travelled more slowly, and a man on horseback (*Evelyn*, *MW* 187; *S&S* 86; *P&P* 49) could travel a bit more quickly, though he would still have to stop periodically to allow his horse to rest. Gentlemen travelling on horseback, as well as ladies and mixed parties out for day rides, would take along a mounted groom or two (*S&S* 86–87) to hold the horses, see that they were fed and watered when feasible, and help anyone who needed assistance to mount or dismount. Working-class women might ride in a coach alone, and men of all ranks did so, but genteel young women were supposed to have an escort (*NA* 225, 226; *S&S* 280; *P&P* 211–212; *MP* 12, 410, 425). This might be a male relative, an older woman or a servant.

Travel by water could be faster than travel over land, but it had its own set of woes (*Cath, MW* 205; *MP* 108, 125, 178, 235). England's new system of canals had generated an entrepreneurial boom that foreshadowed the turnpike craze. Each canal linked two rivers together and, like a turnpike, had to be authorised by a private act of Parliament (*MW* 449). Canals were useful for transporting cargo, but they were not fast enough to attract passenger business. Sea travel was occasionally used to get from one far-flung part of the British Isles to another or to send cargo between coastal towns (*S&S* 26), but its main passenger business was in carrying people abroad (*Amelia, MW* 47; *Evelyn, MW* 185; *E* 221, 364–365) – to the continent for sightseeing trips, to fields of battle across the world, to tea plantations in India and to sugar plantations in the West Indies. To reach these places, passengers faced the possibility of seasickness, enemy privateers (*MP* 180), storms (*Evelyn, MW* 185) and delays due to uncooperative winds (*MP* 225). A passage to America (*H&E, MW* 38) or the Caribbean or back could take several weeks (*MP* 32, 34, 107). Travellers to the Caribbean also confronted the peril of tropical diseases, which were so feared that soldiers posted there often deserted or injured themselves to avoid the trip.

Within England, however, travel was so much easier than it had been in the past that a new industry, the tourism industry, arose. People visited inland spas and seaside resorts (*Sand, MW* 374), which competed with each other to provide the best amenities and touted the health benefits of their waters and air. Nor were such trips only for the wealthy. Middle-class people also visited such places, and one or two were close enough to London to be frequented by a broad cross-section of society, omitting only the very upper and very lower ends. People visiting a new town such as Bath or Tunbridge Wells laid out a few shillings for souvenirs, such as a pincushion painted with the legend, 'A Gift from Bath'. The gift-shop trinkets of today thus have a very long pedigree indeed.

People also took day trips to visit sites of interest nearby. Old churches (*P* 131), the graves of famous people and heights from which a good stretch of countryside could be seen were all popular destinations, as were public gardens and that marvellous novelty, the factory. Parson James Woodforde, entertaining guests in June 1790, took them to 'Bunns Rural Gardens and the Iron-Foundery' to see the wonders of nature and technology in a single day.

A growing belief in the uplifting powers of nature also drew people to sites of scenic beauty within Britain, such as mountains and the northern Lake District (*P&P* 154, 238–240). They packed into sightseeing boats, listened to tour operators' firing a cannon to demonstrate the mountain echoes, and frequently, like many modern tourists, stayed only long enough to be able to say that they had seen the lakes. Educated visitors searched the landscape for resemblance to the works of Claude, Poussin and Rosa. Windermere was thought to evoke the works of Claude, in the words of novelist Ann Radcliffe, because of its 'Diffusiveness, stately beauty, and, at the upper end, magnificence'. Tourists considered Ullswater more appropriate to be depicted by Poussin, though some reversed their judgement, awarding Ullswater to Claude and Windermere to Poussin. Almost everyone agreed that only Rosa could have done justice to Derwentwater. Guides for travellers written from a picturesque point of view advised visitors where to stand and what to look for so that they could make the most of their journey.

Another popular tourist activity was visiting stately homes (*MP* 95–96). These were not old mansions preserved as museums but homes, old or new, that were still inhabited by their owners. No one knows who first strode up to the door of some great family, knocked and asked to be shown around or how he convinced the servant to take him around the house. No doubt it involved a monetary bribe, preserved in the habit of giving tips to the servants who conducted the tours, but, whatever the origin, the pastime grew extremely popular. People were admitted to a house, provided they looked genteel, and led from room to room by a servant, usually the housekeeper, who illuminated the history of each object and painting. Sometimes, the visit to a house would be combined with a look at the gardens, although in many cases it was the gardens that were the main attraction. Wealthy landowners spent small fortunes remaking their grounds in the latest style, and a passion for gardening, for nature and for fashionable improvement drew many visitors into wildernesses and walks, parks and paths. Some gardens, in fact, were so popular that their owners were forced to ban all tourist traffic (*S&S* 62).

Within cities and towns, travel presented a different set of problems. Here the streets (*NA* 91; *P&P* 72; *E* 162; *P* 107, 115, 179) could be narrow and dirty, and wash water or even the contents of chamber pots could be flung out of upper windows by servants. Many of the bigger towns invested in better drains, street lighting and wide pavements (*NA* 87) to ameliorate the condition of the streets, hiring street sweepers (often children) to brush the filth from the crossings, but in bad weather, even the sidewalks could be dirty (*NA* 82; *E* 179, 195). A thick pall of coal smoke hung over many towns, particularly early in the morning when servants in almost every home were busy lighting the day's first fires. In London, the fog could be so thick that people ran into each other in the streets, pin-balling their way to their destinations.

Those who could afford to do so took sedan chairs or carriages through London's streets, but travelling this way could create its own set of problems. London's layout, except in the newly constructed, spacious streets of the West End, was still based on fairly narrow streets, and traffic jams formed frequently. Other cities sometimes had similar problems. The crowds on foot (*NA* 44) were so thick that a servant sometimes had to walk ahead to clear the way, and in some parts of town, carriages met and passed in such numbers that the passengers might be stuck in one place for a long while or make such slow progress that it would have been faster to walk.

See also Carriages and Coaches; Chair; Inns.

U

Umbrellas and Parasols

In Austen's lifetime, umbrellas and parasols were not entirely new, but they were very nearly so. Both came into fashion for the first time in the latter half of the eighteenth century, overcoming sceptics who thought them silly, effeminate or awkward. Both were initially imported from overseas; for most of the eighteenth century, France and Italy made the best ones, and those made in England were rather shoddy, but once the English embraced the concept, they began to innovate, and soon there were patents for folding umbrellas, collapsible pocket umbrellas and umbrellas that opened automatically.

The terms 'parasol' and 'umbrella' were sometimes used interchangeably, but Austen uses them in the modern sense. The parasol, for her, is a shade against the sun, while the umbrella offers protection from the rain. In an 1801 letter, she describes a walk up Sion Hill, near Bath, with a Mrs Chamberlayne: 'we posted along under a fine hot sun, *she* without any parasol or shade to her hat, stopping for nothing.' Here the parasol is clearly meant to be a sunshade; in the novels and fragments, the term is either indeterminate (*Sand*, *MW* 374, 381; *P&P* 238) or used in the context of protection from the sun (*P&P* 352). Her umbrellas, in contrast, are usually explicitly introduced in the context of rain or the chance of rain (*Col Let*, *MW* 159; *NA* 82–83; *MP* 205; *P* 177).

The parasols of Austen's youth, in the 1770s to 1790s, were often 'staff' parasols (a later term). The typical staff parasol was mounted near the top of a long stick, almost as tall as the woman herself. The staff might be topped with a knob or a token hook and may have been meant to echo the pastorally inspired 'shepherdess' fashions with their hitched-up back skirts. By 1799, many parasols had become smaller, with shorter sticks and shades mounted on 'marquise' hinges so that they could fold parallel to the sticks (see the illustration *Monstrosities of 1799* [Clothing]). These round, rather shallow parasols often had sticks of turned wood – that is, they were shaped on a lathe, like a fancy chair leg – and shades of green silk. Around 1807, the turned sticks were replaced by plain ones, and the marquise hinges and plain, shallow shades went out of fashion around 1810. At about this time, a new shape became fashionable – the 'pagoda' shape – in which the parasol had a wide bottom that rose steeply, swept in horizontally and then pointed up again in the centre with the help of an internal spring. From 1800 to 1810, it was common to find parasols that were fringed at the edge, and colours other than green eventually became popular. Around 1816, turned sticks again came into favour, and some of the more-elaborate examples from this period had turned ivory sticks intricately carved with Chinese motifs.

Men did not carry parasols, but both men and women eventually made use of umbrellas (*E* 12, 178, 321; *P* 127). They were introduced to the country by philanthropist Jonas Hanway, who carried a pocket-sized, folding, foreign-made model with a carved ebony handle, a green silk outside and a grey satin lining. His enthusiasm for the new device led it to be nicknamed a 'Hanway', but the moniker did not stick, and by Austen's lifetime, the name 'umbrella' – from the Latin word for 'shade' – had become standard.

32. *The Battle of Umbrellas,* Collings and Thomas, 1784.

At first, people felt awkward about using umbrellas. After all, carrying one meant that the user was at the mercy of the weather. In other words, he was walking rather than riding in a coach. Genteel men were also somewhat unaccustomed to having their hands occupied as they walked.

Furthermore, the early umbrellas were difficult to use, hard to open and subject to damage by strong winds. However, the usefulness of an umbrella in the wet English climate was too obvious to be resisted for long. London footman John Macdonald, who had been mocked in the 1770s for his Frenchified habit of carrying an umbrella, reported in 1790 that umbrella-making 'is become a great trade in London and a very useful branch of business'. In 1810, the *Universal Magazine* noted that people of all classes carried umbrellas. Even children and servants were equipped for wet weather. Fashionable men, who still refused to carry parasols, could sometimes be observed using an umbrella as a sunshade.

In the last decade of Austen's life, umbrellas might be found with wood or metal sticks and decorative wooden, ivory or antler handles. The ribs, which ran along the inside of the cover, were usually of whalebone or cane, with brass tips that stuck out beyond the cover; the cover itself was of waxed cloth – silk in the better models and cotton in the others, with green, blue, red and brown the dominant colours. The stretchers, which spread the cover outwards away from the stick, were usually of steel.

See also Clothing; Pocketbooks and Reticules.

V

Visiting

There were two principal kinds of visits: the long visit and the morning call. Long visits were paid to friends or family who lived far away (*Evelyn*, *MW* 190; *Cath*, *MW* 197; *NA* 224; *S&S* 231; *P&P* 63, 146, 317; *MP* 28; *E* 435; *P* 128). They entailed a certain amount of expense for coach fare and a great deal of trouble in packing and preparing. Therefore, these visits tended to last several days or even several weeks. As a child, Austen saw her parents host guests in this way – usually at the Christmas holidays, when Mr Austen's pupils had gone home to see their own parents. As an adult, Jane paid such visits herself, travelling to London to stay with her brother Henry, to Kent to visit her brother Edward and to Ibthorpe to visit the Lloyd family. The length of such visits tended to be linked to the closeness of the relationship between guest and host and also to the host's ability to cater to the needs of another person for an extended period of time; in her Juvenilia, Austen includes an instance of a deliberately exaggerated stay of 'five or six months' (*Scraps*, *MW* 171–172); a stay of such duration would not even have been suggested by Austen's wealthy brother Edward, let alone the characters whom Austen describes.

Visiting

The other kind of visit (*F&E, MW* 6; *Watsons, MW* 337; *S&S* 168; *P&P* 5, 147; *MP* 62; *E* 53, 184; *P* 39–40, 47, 149, 162, 165) was the polite social call, paid in the 'morning' (*S&S* 74; *MP* 39; *E* 17–18, 46, 455; *P* 87, 212, 215). Morning was understood in the contemporary sense of 'everything between breakfast and dinner', a span of time that could last from 9:00 or 10:00 a.m. until 6:00 or 6:30 p.m. (*LS, MW* 303; *MP* 298), depending on how late the visited family ate dinner. Out-of-sync dinner hours sometimes caused confusion and hurt feelings, as one person who tended to eat late might accidentally call in the middle of dinner at a house that took its meal earlier in the day. Most visitors, however, could safely call between 12:00 p.m. and 3:00 p.m. (*Watsons, MW* 338), which they usually did, as it was generally considered incumbent on the visitor to choose a reasonable time, especially if the visitor's superior rank made it impossible to refuse an untimely visit (*Col Let, MW* 158–159).

A visitor rang the bell or used the knocker at the front door and waited for someone – usually a servant (*MP* 399) – to open it. She would identify herself to the servant and be asked to wait while the servant determined whether or not the visited party was 'at home' (*LS, MW* 303; *E* 452). The servant, of course, already knew whether the visited party was in the house, but being *at home* was different from being in the house. Being at home meant being willing and ready to receive visitors of any kind, specifically the visitor who waited at the door. The servant could deny that his master or mistress was at home (*J&A, MW* 15; *NA* 91; *S&S* 294) for a host of reasons, including genuine absence (*NA* 89), illness, disinclination to receive guests and personal animus against the visitor in question. If told that the visited party was not at home, the visitor left her card (*NA* 89, 91; *S&S* 169, 177, 230, 287; *P* 138, 149) as evidence that she had stopped by; she could then expect to receive a return visit, assuming she and the resident of the house were on good terms. Sometimes people left their cards not only to show that they had visited but to announce their presence in town, for example, upon arriving in Bath, London or another place where people took lodgings for extended stays (*S&S* 168, 170). A call where only a card was left (*S&S* 216; *P* 215) could, with due politeness, be repaid with only a card in exchange. A card, however, that was left by a complete stranger required no acknowledgement (*P* 138).

The visiting card was a piece of cardstock, often the approximate size of a business card, but sometimes larger or more nearly square. The Lewis Walpole Library has a collection of visiting cards from the period. The back of each card is plain or has a simple repeated design. On the front, often surrounded by a decorative border, is the name of the visitor in ink that may be black, green or blue. Many of the cards of different ladies have identical borders, implying that printers had a selection of standard borders from which customers could choose. The borders are mostly neoclassical in design; one for 'Lady Archer' has an acanthus-leaf border, while one for 'Lady Catherine Stanhope' has a classical swag.

If the visitor were admitted, she was shown by the servant (*P* 142) into a parlour (*Col Let, MW* 151; *Cath, MW* 214; *E* 190) or drawing room (*Sand, MW* 394), and the servant, in many households, announced her name (*Watsons, MW* 338). In this room, the lady or ladies of the house would already be sitting, perhaps 'working' (i.e. sewing) or taking some sort of refreshment. If it was the latter, they would offer food and drink to the guest. Sometimes, even if they were not eating, they would invite the guest to stay and take some sort of refreshment with them (*Sand, MW* 390–391); this might be accepted or declined, as the visitor might have other visits to pay before heading home for her own dinner. Fifteen minutes was the absolute minimum duration for politeness (*Scraps, MW* 172; *S&S* 229; *P&P* 147; *E* 185–187, 199). To leave more quickly would be tantamount to a snub unless all parties were very good friends and the visit was for a very specific purpose.

Often a visit was mandatory or nearly so. Those who expected to be absent for a long time would usually pay farewell visits before departing (*P&P* 145). People returning home after a long absence could likewise expect to be visited by their friends (*E&E, MW* 31; *P&P* 332–333; *MP* 192). Similarly, when a woman married, it was incumbent upon her nearby friends and relatives to pay a call on her at her new home as soon as she had returned from her honeymoon (*S&S* 213, 216; *E* 9, 17–18; *P* 251). If she were moving into a new neighbourhood, her husband's friends and acquaintances would also be expected to call upon her (*E* 271, 280, 290). She would then have to return these visits; virtually all visits required a reciprocal visit (*P&P* 9, 21, 147, 266; *E* 185, 305; *P* 48, 53, 168) so that once one started visiting at a particular house, it was hard to stop. Unlike the paper exchanges in which cards were left back and forth, a visit in which the parties met face-to-face required a similarly personal visit in response.

Sometimes, in order to avoid all the formalities associated with paying a visit, or perhaps merely to display that one had plenty of servants on staff, a servant was sent instead. This was never done in place of a required social call but only in cases where there was a specific purpose in mind. For example, a person of genteel rank would not bother to walk to his neighbour's house to deliver a gift of produce from his garden. He would send a servant with a basket instead. A host giving a large party might deliver printed invitations personally (*P&P* 86; *P* 226–227, 236), if it were convenient to do so, and might combine this delivery with a social visit, but he might equally choose to send a servant on this errand.

Servants expected to be tipped for their efforts in delivering goods and invitations to prosperous households. On occasion, they would also be invited in for something to eat or drink – but in the kitchen, with the other servants, rather than in the parlour or drawing room.

Men could pay visits to women (*S&S* 99; *MP* 298; *E* 455), but the reverse was not true. The majority of visiting consisted of visits paid by women to women, although men made some morning calls, and children might be brought along, as they matured, in order to teach them the rudiments of the ritual (*Col Let*, *MW* 150). Some people objected to the whole idea of visits. The anonymous author of *Female Tuition; or, an Address to Mothers, on the Education of Daughters* (1784) concluded '*Visiting*, especially as practised among the great, seldom terminates in any thing but vanity, scandal, or intrigue'.

See also Etiquette; Marriage; Titles.

W

Walking

Walking (*Lesley*, *MW* 111; *Evelyn*, *MW* 190; *NA* 35, 80, 85, 103; *S&S* 41; *P&P* 157; *MP* 334; *E* 8, 18, 26, 58, 191, 195, 196, 294, 333, 344, 356, 362; *P* 39–40, 41, 60, 84, 132, 168–169, 227) was a necessity for the working class (*E* 29, 31), who had few transportation options and walked on many occasions to get to market and to visit friends. Even among the gentry, who might not own a coach or might not have it at their disposal because the horses were being used for other purposes, walking was likewise necessary for making morning visits (*Sand*, *MW* 406; *S&S* 40, 343; *P&P* 28, 293; *E* 456, 457). Mr Weston walks to Hartfield, for example, because his wife has already gone over in their carriage, and the distance is short (*E* 302). Those who lived in town, gentry or not, might walk for the purposes of running errands (*NA* 114; *P&P* 28; *MP* 205; *E* 293–295), whether for the pleasure of walking, for lack of a carriage or because calling for the carriage was too time-consuming.

For many, walking was an avocation, a way of spending time between breakfast and dinner (*Sand*, *MW* 384; *E* 209), of seeing interesting landscape (*S&S* 40–41, 88, 343) and of keeping one's figure in a time when beef and butter constituted a large part of the evening meal. Physical exercise of some sort was also considered necessary for good health (*MP* 322, 409; *E* 296), and walking had the advantage of being as inexpensive as possible. The anonymous author of *The Mirror of the Graces* wrote in 1811 that, to be beautiful, a woman must exercise outdoors and recommended the 'morning, about two or three hours after sun-rise', as 'the most salubrious time for a vigorous walk'. A number of Austen's characters take her advice and walk in the morning, either just before or just after breakfast (*S&S* 83; *P&P* 32–36; *E* 293; *P* 102, 104).

Jane Austen herself was an avid walker and had great respect for anyone who could keep up with her. In 1801, she was impressed with the stout walking pace of her companion, a Mrs Chamberlayne:

> in climbing a hill Mrs Chamberlayne is very capital; I could with difficulty keep pace with her – yet would not flinch for the World. – on plain ground I was quite her equal – and so we posted away under a fine hot sun, She without any parasol or any shade to her hat, stopping for nothing, & crossing the Church Yard at Weston with as much expedition as if we were afraid of being buried alive. – After seeing what she is equal to, I cannot help feeling a regard for her.

Many of Austen's most admirable characters, such as Elizabeth Bennet (*P&P* 36) and Anne Elliot (*P* 174, 176), are likewise enthusiastic walkers (*Sand*, *MW* 416; *NA* 174; *P&P* 257); many of her less-admirable characters, such as Mary Musgrove (*P* 83), are not (*Col Let*, *MW* 159; *P&P* 365).*

Walking was also customary after morning church services on Sundays (*MP* 401), when whole families would stroll around the streets together. In Bath, the Royal Crescent was a favourite spot for this activity (*NA* 35, 68, 97, 100–102), while Portsmouth had its ramparts (*MP* 408) and Lyme its Cobb (*P* 108). Some towns, such as Dawlish, had a specially built promenade for afternoon walks, such as the fictional 'Terrace' at Sanditon (*Sand*, *MW* 395). In seaside resorts and spas, walking was a way of getting outside the limits of the town and finding attractive views (*P* 183). Sidmouth, in 1810, was said to have 'very pleasant' walks. Southampton, too, had some lovely routes nearby; when Jane Austen lived there in the first decade of the nineteenth century, she often walked to Chiswell, a little less than 2 miles from town.

At country estates that had their own gardens, walks could be taken along level gravel paths. In parks (*P&P* 253–254; *MP* 15), which were more extensive, the ground was often more rolling, and the landscapes, if one walked far enough, were usually more varied. Walks in gardens (*F&E*, *MW* 5; *J&A*, *MW* 18; *Cath*, *MW* 230; *NA* 179, 240; *P&P* 156, 182, 195, 301, 351, 352–353; *MP* 322; *E* 196) afforded a certain measure of privacy that was not available in a house full of servants, and it is not surprising that Austen uses the intimacy and privacy of garden strolls for dramatic purposes. Many of her characters become engaged while walking in gardens or in the countryside; Elizabeth and Darcy come to an understanding while walking, as do Anne and Captain Wentworth, Henry Tilney and Catherine Morland, and Emma and Mr Knightley. Charlotte Lucas contrives to be walking in order to be proposed to by

---

*The system is not infallible; however, Mr Collins (*P&P* 71) and Lady Denham (*Sand*, *MW* 390) are also good walkers. While formidable characters, they cannot really be said to be admirable.

Walking

Mr Collins, an awkward, false arrangement that perfectly mirrors their marriage (*P&P* 121). Paintings, porcelain figurines and popular prints, too, showed garden walks as occasions for conversation, flirtation and informal socialising.

On long walks outdoors, young women were expected to take a companion (*NA* 114–115; *P&P* 36), male or female, to guard against a host of real and imagined dangers. Any outdoor walk also required the adoption of special clothing. Men were expected to wear hats out of doors (*NA* 177), while women wore bonnets (*NA* 177) that protected them to some extent from the sun. Walks in dirty town streets or on wet rural roads required the use of pattens, overshoes with a wide metal ring on each sole that slightly raised the walker's feet above the ground. On cooler days, a woman might wear a pelisse (a long coat – see *LS*, *MW* 276) or a spencer (a short, high-waisted coat). When Elizabeth Bennet goes 'up stairs to get ready' for a long walk (*P&P* 375), she is probably finding her bonnet and perhaps one of these two types of outer garments.

However, not every day was suitable for an outdoor walk. When it was raining, or when recent rain had left the ground especially wet and muddy, walking was simply out of the question for those who wished to preserve their expensive clothing (*Watsons*, *MW* 345; *NA* 84, 85; *S&S* 40–41, 88; *P&P* 36, 88). It was also impossible to take long walks at night. Therefore, those who wished for exercise at such times walked indoors, walking up and down long galleries or round and round in drawing rooms after dinner (*Lesley*, *MW* 127; *NA* 33, 71, 134, 147; *P&P* 56).

Men had special duties when they walked with women. In town, it was their responsibility to keep the women from walking in puddles and filth (*E* 195) and to steer them towards the clearest and driest parts of the pavement. On long walks, men were expected to lend an arm to anyone who became tired (*NA* 87; *MP* 94; *P* 90, 169). (Good friends of either sex might also walk arm in arm – see *NA* 37; *P* 142.) Men were also expected to help women over stiles (*P&P* 32; *P* 86, 89, 109) – steps that allowed walkers to cross over fences without having to open and close a gate. They certainly were not expected to march on ahead without bothering to see whether they were leaving their female companions behind, as does the boorish Mr Price (*MP* 403).

See also Dance; Entertainment; Travel.

Widow

The widow (*H&E*, *MW* 36; *Mount*, *MW* 41; *Cass*, *MW* 46; *LS*, *MW* 247; *E* 163; *P* 11) was often an object of charity in Austen's time, for women could make far less money than men and, in the case of gentry widows, were not permitted to work at all without loss of caste (*E* 275–276). Even the impoverished invalid Mrs Smith (*P* 152–153) works not for her own keep but in order to offer charity to others. Widowhood almost always meant a loss of income, as the oldest son inherited the bulk of a family's estate. The widow received a jointure (*J&A, MW* 13; *Sand, MW* 401; *S&S* 36, 226; *MP* 123) – customarily, but not always, a third of the estate – which was agreed upon at the time of the marriage. This might be ample for some women, but for others, a fraction of their previous income was simply not sufficient for their needs. The case of widows of the clergy, such as *Emma's* Mrs Bates (*E* 21) and Austen's own mother, was even more perilous. If the husband had not managed to save a substantial sum, or if he had no independent property of his own, his widow could be left virtually penniless. Once the husband was gone, so, too, was his 'living' – the income he derived from tithes and church land – and the widow could be left with little or nothing. In Mrs Austen's case, it took voluntary contributions from most of her sons to give her enough to live on, as her own property was quite small.

Wealthy widows (*H&E, MW* 35; *Watsons, MW* 352; *Sand, MW* 375, 400; *S&S* 36, 228; *MP* 202–203), however, were in a unique position that many of them quite relished. For the first time, they were free from the oversight of a man, be he father or husband, and they could make their own legal and financial decisions. These basic rights were denied to married women, whose legal identity was subsumed in their husbands', but widows had control over their own lives and property. No doubt many declined to remarry because they had truly loved their first husbands, but others, one suspects, knew that remarriage would deprive them of their legal freedom. Others hastened to remarry, out of love, financial necessity or fear of conducting their own business; such motives were understood, but a certain degree of disapproval attached to a widow who remarried (*LS, MW* 299; *S&S* 47; *P* 5). Remarriage by widowers (*E* 96) was viewed far less harshly.

See also Death.

Writing

Elegant handwriting (*S&S* 328; *P&P* 47, 116; *E* 297–298, 305) was prized in Austen's day, not only by the gentry and nobility but also by the mercantile class as well. It was taught (*NA* 14) by tutors or specialised writing masters (*E* 297), by books that provided model styles of penmanship to copy and at boarding schools; Charles Austen, the youngest of Jane's siblings, studied it at the Portsmouth Naval Academy, where he showed 'industry' and 'improvement' in his writing from 1792 to 1794. In earlier ages, he might have been learning how to ornament every line of his writing with elaborate, fanciful flourishes; in the late years of the eighteenth century, however, he would have learned a more practical, streamlined handwriting, so as to become, in the words of one handwriting book's title, a 'Useful Penman'. For the most part, English handwriting was clear and legible, with few Baroque flourishes, though some handwriting models emphasise the difference between thin and thick strokes so much that the writing becomes hard to read. The 'coarse and modern characters' (*NA* 172) read by Catherine Morland are probably discernible as modern because they lack complex flourishes of an antique 'hand'.

In order to write (*NA* 105; *P&P* 238, 304; *MP* 59, 64, 73, 296–297, 362) a letter, a bill of lading, a letter of credit or any other document, the writer needed several supplies (*MP* 16, 307; *P* 229): pen, ink, paper, a tool for blotting, a penknife and wax or wafers. Pens were usually made of goose quills, and they were shaped and mended with small penknives. The penknife could also be used in some instances to scrape mistakes off the paper. The ink was typically an iron-gall ink, composed of ground and steeped gall nuts (also called 'oak apples') and copperas (hydrated ferrous sulphate, also known as 'green vitriol'). Gum arabic was added to make the ink smoother, and water to make it thinner. Additional ingredients might be added to intensify the blackness of the ink.

Some people made their own ink at home, but it could also be bought from itinerant ink sellers or from apothecaries. Once purchased, the ink needed to be stored carefully to prevent it from drying out or growing mould. It could be kept in its original bottle or transferred to an inkwell or inkstand. Inkwells might be made of stone, lead or ceramic and were typically squat and heavy bottomed to minimise the chance of spills. Inkstands had an inkwell plus other features, such as holes in which to prop quills.

Once a document was written, it frequently needed to be blotted (*P&P* 48) to remove excess ink. There were two ways to do this. One was by placing a sheet of absorbent paper, called blotting paper, over the inked page; this method grew increasingly popular after 1800. Another method was to use a sander, a container looking much like a salt shaker but with a convex lid, filled sometimes with chalk but more commonly with sand. The sand was shaken onto the page, where it wicked excess ink upwards, increasing the surface area and speeding drying. The sand was then poured back from the page into the sander to be used again. Some writing sets also had a pounce container; pounce was a gum resin that decreased the absorbency of writing paper.

Paper (*P&P* 382; *E* 76) was made primarily from cotton or linen rags, frequently by hand. The rags were dusted, sorted by quality to be made into either good or coarse brown paper, washed, chopped up and laid in piles to rot. The mass of fermented cotton was then washed and pounded, sometimes by large hammers driven by a waterwheel, sometimes by a machine called a 'Hollander' that had a huge bladed roller. Mixed in tubs with warm water, the fibrous mass, called stock or stuff, waited for a papermaker to dip his mould, a rectangular screen in a wooden frame with an insert called a deckle. In a 'laid' mould, fine wires ran perpendicular to a few heavier wires, and there might also be a piece of wire twisted into a design identifying the type or size of paper and the manufacturer. In a 'wove' mould, fine wires were woven together to create a fabric-like network of perpendicular lines; here, too, there might be a wire design identifying the paper. As the stock settled in the mould, the wire created thinner areas that show up in handmade paper as fine lines and as a watermark that is easily visible when the paper is held up to the light. The papermaker shook the fibres in the mould to interlock them and then handed it to an assistant, who turned the wet sheet of paper onto felt. Felt and paper were alternated until a large stack – usually 144 sheets – had been assembled, and then the entire stack was placed into a press and squeezed until it was merely damp. This job took about six men to accomplish; then the sheets of paper were removed from the felt by another assistant and pressed again. Small groups of pages were then draped over ropes to dry further, after which paper intended for writing (*S&S* 287, 328, 372; *P&P* 309; *MP* 16, 415; *P* 241) would be dipped in a material called 'size'* to keep it from absorbing too much ink. Sized paper would be dried again and then polished. Really fine writing paper would also be 'hot pressed' (*P&P* 116), pressed between glazed boards and hot sheets of metal to smooth the surface. Finally, the paper was stacked in quires (24 sheets) and reams (240), folded in half like a greeting card and wrapped for sale, in grey paper with the mill's label on it.

Paper was sometimes treated in other ways. Chlorine, discovered in 1774, was being used for whitening paper by the early 1790s. China clay was added in some cases to whiten paper or to increase its weight. From the 1770s, lined paper was produced, and manufacturers began making embossed paper in 1796.

Demand for all types of paper was steadily increasing, as literacy improved and newspapers became more popular. By 1800, Britain's 400 paper mills could no longer find enough cotton and linen rags at home and were importing about £200,000 worth of rags every year from other countries. Consumers were urged to save their rags to conserve this valuable resource. Desperate attempts were made to find another source of paper pulp, and experiments were made with various plants, straw and wood. However, though wood had been suggested by the French as a possible source of paper pulp as early as 1719, it was not in wide use during Austen's lifetime.

Inventors also tried to find improved ways of turning the pulp or stuff into paper. The invention of the steam engine had inspired many creative thinkers to devise ways of applying its power, and it was only a matter of time before steam was harnessed for making paper. A steam engine was first employed at a paper mill in about 1786, and in 1803, a paper-making machine was invented. Vast improvements in productivity followed. A papermaker and his staff could create about 50 to 60 pounds of paper a day; a machine could make as much as 1,000 pounds, although the paper still needed to be hung up to dry in the old-fashioned way, on ropes.[†]

---

*Typically made of starch or gelatin.
[†]This problem would not be solved until 1820, when Thomas Bonsor Crompton patented a heat-drying machine.

Writing

John Dickinson of Hertfordshire invented a woven-wire cylinder that continuously rotated through a vat of stuff, but the most significant development in the industry during Austen's lifetime was the invention, in 1810, of the Fourdrinier machine.

Developed by two brothers, Henry and Sealy Fourdrinier, who owned a stationery firm in London, the machine used a wove-patterned belt, rather than a cylinder, to distribute the stuff. It created long rolls of unwatermarked paper and quickly became a standard equipment in any mill large enough to afford its steep price. Commercial use of the Fourdrinier machine began in 1812, and its appearance, like that of many new machines designed to replace human labour, was greeted by riots.

Because paper was sold already folded in half, it became customary to write letters (*H&E*, *MW* 34; *L&F*, *MW* 76–109; *Col Let*, *MW* 164; *Sand*, *MW* 385, 394; *NA* 27, 139, 201, 203, 235, 250; *S&S* 63, 173, 202, 259; *P&P* 47–48, 51, 61, 177, 281, 292, 295, 296, 346, 361–363; *MP* 50, 107, 108, 114, 232, 425, 437; *E* 51, 96, 119, 379; *P* 50, 148–149, 162) as if the folded paper were a little, four-page book (*P&P* 383). The writer began on the first page, then opened the sheet and continued to write on pages 2 and 3

33. 'Crossed' letter.

and might possibly write a little on page 4 as well, though an important blank space was left on this page. If the writer had more to say and wished to save the cost of posting a second sheet of paper (*MP* 429), she might turn her paper 90 degrees and 'cross' her writing, making a new series of lines at right angles to the first, and intersecting her original lines to make a kind of woven or checkerboard pattern (*E* 157). Once all of the space had been used twice, the lack of additional room ended the letter, whether the writer wanted to conclude or not (*S&S* 278). The letter was finished with a formulaic compliment or statement of humility, such as, 'I am, very sincerely, your must humble servant, Kirstin Olsen'. Since almost all letters ended in a similar fashion (*P&P* 325), Austen frequently omits the compliments and writes '& c.' (*F&E*, *MW* 28), but real correspondents in her time did not sign their letters, 'Your's, & c.' or 'I am, & c.' (*S&S* 278; *P&P* 149). They wrote out the whole phrase.

When the letter was finished, it was folded with the blank space on the fourth page on the outside (*NA* 14; *P&P* 63, 205; *MP* 435; *E* 266, 453). The address, or 'direction' (*NA* 216, 228; *S&S* 134; *P&P* 273), was written here, and, if the letter was being sent through the post, it was stamped or franked in the same area. On the other side, the letter was sealed (*P* 236) either with wax or with a wafer. Wax was melted on the outside of the letter, over the fold, and might be stamped as it cooled with a signet ring or stamp to identify the sender and inhibit tampering; it is this sort of 'seal' that John Dashwood seeks to buy for his wife in *Sense and Sensibility* (222). Sealing wax was usually red, although black wax was customary in mourning. It was melted either in a spoonlike melter that was held over a lamp or by directly melting the end of the wax stick and dripping the wax onto the paper. The latter method was messier and less thorough; it could take several rounds of melting to get enough wax in the right place.

Wafers, on the other hand, went underneath the fold. They were made of flour, water, gum, possibly gelatin and some type of colouring – red for everyday and black for mourning, though some were made in light blue, and Austen herself, in 1799, mentions receiving a letter sealed with a yellow one. Wafers were moistened and applied to the underside of one flap and the top of the other; they were sold in boxes that each had a sample wafer glued to the outside. Inkstands sometimes contained a special compartment to hold wafers.

Austen sometimes refers to envelopes (*P&P* 116), though these are not the pre-manufactured, pre-gummed envelopes of today. The envelope was merely another sheet of paper, wrapped and folded around the letter and sealed, as an ordinary letter would be, with either wax or a wafer. Few people would pay the extra postage to receive a blank sheet of paper, so an envelope in this sense was generally reserved for messages carried by servants from one house to another. When a letter was sent through the post, the 'envelope' was simply the name given to the outer portion of the letter when folded, the portion that was addressed and sealed.

Writing

With all the equipment that writing required, it was easiest to do it sitting down at a comfortable desk or table (*P&P* 305). However, there were writing sets for travellers, with small quantities of the requisite supplies packed in a compact box or an angled tabletop writing 'desk' (*NA* 155). Portable writing desks provided both a writing surface and a storage for supplies.

Rules of etiquette governed the sending and receiving of letters. Anxious parents, for example, forbade their daughters to engage in correspondence with men other than relatives, husbands or fiancés (*NA* 250; *S&S* 80, 134, 172). The sending of letters might also be governed by class; novelist Fanny Burney, who had served in the royal household, had to get permission from Queen Charlotte before embarking on a correspondence with one of the princesses. The reading of letters, too, was subject to the rules of politeness; if one received a letter while in company, it could not be read silently before the others unless the recipient was invited to do so (*Watsons*, *MW* 338). Finally, letters might or might not be intended to be read aloud, and it was usually the recipient who had the final say over what might be shown to others (*Sand*, *MW* 386; *P* 204).

See also Education; Pen; Pencil.

List of Illustrations

Maps

1. Map of Bath, 1804. By Kirstin Olsen. (1) Abbey churchyard (pump yard); (2) Argyle Buildings; (3) Avon; (4) Baths; (5) Beaufort Square theatre; (6) Beechen Cliff; (7) Belmont; (8) Bond Street; (9) Broad Street; (10) rock Street; (11) Camden Place; (12) Cheap Street; (13) Circus; (14) Claverton Down; (15) Edgar's Buildings; (16) Gay Street.

2. Map of the Lower Town, 1804. By Kirstin Olsen. (17) Gravel Walk; (18) Green Park Buildings; (19) Lansdown Hill; (20) Laura Place; (21) Lower Rooms; (22) Marlborough Buildings; (23) Milsom Street; (24) Octagon Chapel; (25) Old Bridge; (26) Orchard Street theatre; (27) The Paragon; (28) Pulteney Bridge; (29) [Great] Pulteney Street; (30) Pump Room; (31) Queen Square; (32) Rivers Street; (33) Royal Crescent; (34) Sydney Gardens; (35) Sydney Place (Sydney Place ran to both the north; and south sides of Sydney Gardens); (36) Trim Street; (37) Union Passage (Replaced, along with the Bear Inn; Yard to the west, by Union Street); (38) Upper Rooms; (39) Walcot Church; (40) Westgate Buildings; (41) White Hart Inn; (42) Wick Rocks.

3. Map of London. A city the size of London, even as it stood in the early nineteenth century, is hard to reproduce on a page this size. Either a sense of the city's true size is lost, or the reader becomes unable to locate the relevant sites mentioned by Austen. I have chosen to emphasize Austen's details rather than to attempt to show the overall size and shape of the metropolitan area. This is therefore an extremely simplified map, intended to show relative location only. Readers interested in detailed contemporary maps without the size constraints of this volume may wish to examine my bibliography, under the headings 'Time and Space' and 'Web sites', for useful resources. A few sites are included as landmarks because they are sites mentioned in other articles within this book.

4. Map of the West Indies.

5. Map of the British Isles.

6. Map of Hampshire.

7. Map of the London area.

Figures

1. *The Union Coach*, Isaac Cruikshank, 1799. The political satire in this print may be ignored for the present purpose. However, the basic features of a stagecoach are well represented: the large basket in the back, in this case carrying passengers rather than luggage; a rider on the top of the carriage; the coachman on his box, sitting on a green hammer-cloth fringed with gold; and the inside passengers crowded together. In the original print, the box and upper parts of the coach are painted black, the door and lower panels purple and the trim yellow; the wheels are orange but may have been intended by the artist to be the traditional red. The springs from which the compartment was suspended are visible at front and back as the tall, arched pieces curving in towards the coach. Courtesy of the Lewis Walpole Library, Yale University. 799.6.4.6.

2. *A Trip to Brighton*, Dent, 1786. This satirical print, which shows the Prince of Wales and his wife on their way to Brighton, deliberately portrays them as strapped for cash and thus travelling in less than the highest style. Accordingly, baggage is stowed on top of the coach, while the coachman keeps eggs, meat and carrots under his seat. Humbler people than the prince, however, no doubt carried belongings in this way when they travelled in their coaches. The print also shows how coaches were decorated with the owner's heraldic symbols. Side glasses, or mirrors, appear above the door and in each upper panel; the one nearest the coachman has the blind drawn. Courtesy of the Lewis Walpole Library, Yale University. 786.7.15.1.

3. *Progress of the Toilet – The Stays*, James Gillray, 1810. A lady, assisted by her maid, gets dressed for the evening. She has already washed at least her face and hands, as is hinted by the presence of a basin and pitcher in the left foreground. She inserts a busk, a stiff front piece, into her stays while her maid laces the stays at the back. The petticoats of former days have been replaced by drawers, and her stockings have discreet white-on-white clocks. The maid's costume is a simple blue dress, white apron, modesty piece and white cap with lappets that are presumably tied under the chin, although Gillray does not show a knot or a bow. Courtesy of the Lewis Walpole Library, Yale University. 810.2.2.6.1.

4. *Progress of the Toilet – Dress Completed*, James Gillray, 1810. The lady, having put on her dress and chosen her jewellery, is ready for dinner in a low-necked, short-sleeved gown. Courtesy of the Lewis Walpole Library, Yale University. 810.2.2.6.3.

5. *A Master of the Ceremonies Introducing a Partner*, Thomas Rowlandson, 1795. Dancers at assembly rooms had to be introduced to each either by mutual acquaintances or by the master of ceremonies, who knew all the subscribers to the assembly rooms and had a fair idea of their level of gentility. Courtesy of the Lewis Walpole Library, Yale University. 795.11.24.1.

6. *A Rout*, 1790. Cards, crowds and conversation are the essence of this form of entertainment. Courtesy of the Lewis Walpole Library, Yale University. 790.1.2.6.1.

7. *The Honor of Precedence*, 1804. In a parody of the quest of ladies for precedence, the artist depicts the wives of a cheese-monger, a tobacconist and a grocer taking precedence: 'when they were taking leave', the caption reads, 'the cheesemonger's wife was going out of the room first, upon which the grocer's lady pulling her back by the tail of her gown, and stepping before her. "No, madam, (says she) nothing comes after Cheese." – "I beg your pardon, madam," replies the cheesemonger's wife, putting the tobacconist's lady back, who was also stepping before her, "after cheese comes tobacco"'. Courtesy of the Lewis Walpole Library, Yale University. 804.10.22.1.

8. *A Picnic Excursion*, Rowlandson Etching, 1790, detail. Courtesy of the Lewis Walpole Library, Yale University. 790.6.27.1.

9. *Messrs. Morgan & Sanders*, 1809. A well-equipped London furniture showroom. Courtesy of the Lewis Walpole Library, Yale University. 809.8.1.4.

10. *The Love Letter*, 1785. This view of a country estate's garden shows shady trees, a bench and a gardener smoothing the gravel paths with a roller. Courtesy of the Lewis Walpole Library, Yale University. 785.10.11.1.

11. A lady and her maid watch nervously as the professional hairdresser applies a hot iron to her curling papers. Courtesy of the Lewis Walpole Library, Yale University. 787.2.3.1.

12. *A Bonnet Shop*, Thomas Rowlandson, 1810. At 'Mrs. Flimsy's Fashionable Warehouse', a variety of straw hats and bonnets hang from the ceiling while a sales lady flatters a customer and a group of milliners trim more hats. Courtesy of the Lewis Walpole Library, Yale University. 810.5.15.1.

13. Design for a cut-steel chatelaine. From a sketch in Matthew Boulton's pattern books, Volume B.

14. *The Wedding*, 1794. The wedding, like most of those in Austen's works, is a simple affair. The bride does not wear white, and only the parson, his clerk, the bridal couple and a few witnesses are on hand. Courtesy of the Lewis Walpole Library, Yale University. 794.5.12.45.

15. Farthing, 1806, actual size. Obverse: Bust of George III, date, his name in Latin, and 'd : g • rex', an abbreviation of 'Dei Gratia Rex', meaning 'by the grace of God.' Many British coins used this formula, following it with a list of names of places ruled by the monarch. On a farthing, there simply was no room to list George III's full title. Reverse: a seated Britannia. Courtesy of HeritageCoin.com.

16. Penny, 1797, actual size. Pennies were unusually large because they contained their face value's worth of copper. Obverse: Georgius III Dei Gratia Rex (By the Grace of God, King). Reverse: seated Britannia and date. Courtesy of HeritageCoin.com.

17. Sixpence, 1790, actual size. Obverse: crowned cipher of GR for 'Georgius Rex.' Reverse: seated Britannia and date. Courtesy of HeritageCoin.com.

18. Shilling, 1817, actual size. A shilling was worth twelve pence. Obverse: Bust of the king, date and GEoR[Gius] : iii D : G: BRirr[ANiA]: REX F : D:. The 'F.D.' stood for 'Fidei Defensor', Defender of the Faith, a title granted to Henry VIII in his pre-Reformation days

by the Pope and retained by British monarchs ever since. Reverse: Royal arms surrounded by a buckled garter and the motto 'HoNi soiT Q[ui] lsIAl y pENsE', the motto of the Knights of the Garter, which translates roughly as, 'Evil be to he who thinks evil.' Courtesy of HeritageCoin.com.

19. Bank token, 1*s*. 6*d*., 1812, actual size. This coin was issued by the Bank of England, not by the government. Obverse: Royal bust and GEORGIUS III DEI GRATIA REX. Reverse: Wreathed legend, 'BANK TOKEN 15. 6D.' and date. Courtesy of HeritageCoin.com.

20. Bank token, three shillings, 1812, actual size. Obverse: Royal bust and GEORGIUS III DEI GRATIA REX (By the Grace of God, King). Reverse: BANK TOKEN 3 SHILL[INGS] and date. Courtesy of HeritageCoin.com.

21. Half-crown (2*s*. 6*d*.), 1817, actual size. Obverse: Royal bust, date, and GEORGIUS III DEI GRATIA. Reverse: Gartered royal arms with HONI • SOIT˙ QUI • MAL˙ Y˙ PENSE on the garter and BRITANNIARUM REX FID[EI]: DEF[ENSOR]: around the border. Courtesy of HeritageCoin.com.

22. Crown (5*s*.), 1820, actual size. Obverse: Royal bust, date, and Georgius III, By the Grace of God, King of Britain, Defender of the Faith. Reverse: St George slaying the dragon, with a faint buckled garter and the motto of the Knights of the Garter. Courtesy of HeritageCoin.com.

23. Half-guinea, 1791, actual size. Obverse: Royal bust with long hair and laurel wreath; GEORGIUS III Dei Gratia. Reverse: royal arms, date, and m • b • f • et˙ h • rex˙ f • d • b • et˙ l˙ d • s˙ r˙ i˙ a˙ t˙ et e (Latin abbreviations for 'By the Grace of God, King of Great Britain, France, and Ireland, Defender of the Faith, Duke of Brunswick and Luneburg, High Treasurer and Elector of the Holy Roman Empire). Courtesy of HeritageCoin.com.

24. Guinea, 1795, actual size. Obverse: Royal bust and GEORGIUS III DEI GRATIA. Reverse: royal arms, date, and the same heavily abbreviated Latin inscription as the half-guinea. Courtesy of HeritageCoin.com.

25. *Harmony before Marriage*, James Gillray, 1805. The harp was considered an especially feminine instrument. *The Mirror of the Graces* (1811) gushed, 'The shape of the instrument is calculated, in every respect, to show a fine figure to advantage. The contour of the whole form, the turn and polish of a beautiful hand and arm, the richly slippered and well-made foot on the pedal stops, the gentle motion of a lovely neck, and, above all, the sweetly-tempered expression of an intelligent countenance; these are shown at one glance, when the fair performer is seated unaffectedly, yet gracefully, at the harp.' Courtesy of the Lewis Walpole Library, Yale University. 805.10.25.2.

26. *Equity or a Sailors Prayer before Battle*, Williams, 1805. The sailor is praying to be spared in the coming battle but 'that the enemys shot may be distributed in the same proportion as the prize money, the greatest part among the Officers'. Courtesy of the Lewis Walpole Library, Yale University. 805.0.9.

27. *The Circulating Library*, 1804. The shelves marked 'Novels', 'Romances' and 'Tales' are nearly empty, as these books were in high demand.

28. *Nobody's Song*, 1807. Sexual harassment was often a problem for female servants, who had little privacy and little means of resisting advances by their employers. Courtesy of the Lewis Walpole Library, Yale University. 807.3.28.1.

29. *Miss Goodchilds first Sampler*, 1793. Littlegirls began embroidering at a very young age. This child has sewing tools in her lap and a workbag on the floor. Courtesy of the Lewis Walpole Library, Yale University. 793.11.12.1.

30. *Wedgwood & Byerly*, 1809. Wedgwood's showroom in St James' Square. Courtesy of the Lewis Walpole Library, Yale University. 809.2.0.1.

31. *Lovers Vows*. Left to right: Amelia, Anhalt, the Baron, Agatha, Frederick.

32. *The Battle of Umbrellas*, Collings and Thomas, 1784. The newly fashionable umbrella as a source of pain, confusion and embarrassment. Courtesy of the Lewis Walpole Library, Yale University. 784.9.1.2.

33. 'Crossed' letter. Courtesy of Eunice and Ron Shanahan.

Bibliography and Topic Guide

BEHAVIOUR

By a Lady of Distinction. 1811. *The Mirror of the Graces*. Reprint. 1997. Mendocino, CA: R. L. Shep.

Doddridge, P. 1807. *The Friendly Instructor; or, A Companion for Young Ladies and Gentlemen*. London: W. Baynes.

Gomme, George Laurence, ed. 1883. *The Gentleman's Magazine Library – Vol. 1: Manners and Customs*. Reprint. 1968. Detroit: Singing Tree Press.

Gregory, John. 1773. *A Father's Legacy to His Daughters*. Reprint. 1804. Boston: Joseph Bumstead.

Holmes, Richard. 2001. *Redcoat: The British Soldier in the Age of Horse and Musket*. New York: W. W. Norton & Company.

Montagu, Ashley. 1967. *The Anatomy of Swearing*. New York: Macmillan.

Southam, Brian. 2000. *Jane Austen and the Navy*. London: Hambledon and London.

BUSINESS, WORK AND FINANCE

Adams, Samuel, and Sarah Adams. 1825. *The Complete Servant*. Reprint. 1989. Lewes, East Sussex: Southover Press.

Clark, Peter. 1983. *The English Alehouse: A Social History 1200–1830*. London: Longman.

Ellis, William. 1750. *The Country Housewife's Family Companion*. Reprint. 2000. Totnes, Devon: Prospect Books.

Fitzmaurice, Ronald Myles. 1975. *British Banks and Banking: A Pictorial History*. Truro, Cornwall: D. Bradford Barton.

Fussell, G. E., and K. R. Fussell. 1955. *The English Countryman: His Life and Work from Tudor Times to the Victorian Age*. Reprint. 1981. London: Orbis.

Haywood, Eliza. 1771. *A New Present for a Servant-Maid*. London: G. Pearch.

Hecht, J. Jean. 1956. *The Domestic Servant in Eighteenth-Century England*. Reprint. 1980. London: Routledge & Kegan Paul.

Hembry, Phyllis. 1990. *The English Spa 1560–1815: A Social History*. London: Athlone Press.

Hixson, William F. 1993. *Triumph of the Bankers: Money and Banking in the Eighteenth and Nineteenth Centuries*. Westport, CT: Praeger.

Kowaleski-Wallace, Elizabeth. 1997. *Consuming Subjects: Women, Shopping, and Business in the Eighteenth Century*. New York: Columbia University Press.

Langford, Paul. 1989. *A Polite and Commercial People: England 1727–1783*. Reprint. 1992. Oxford: Oxford University Press.

Langton, John, and R. J. Morris, eds. 1986. *Atlas of Industrializing Britain 1780–1914*. London: Methuen.

Monckton, H.A. 1969. *A History of the English Public House*. London: The Bodley Head.

Mui, Hoh-Cheung, and Lorna H. Mui. 1989. *Shops and Shopkeeping in Eighteenth Century England*. Montreal: McGill-Queen's University Press.

Plumb, J. H. 1950. *England in the Eighteenth Century*. 1950. Reprint. 1990. London: Penguin Books.

Porter, Roy. 1982. *English Society in the Eighteenth Century*. Reprint. 1990. New York: Penguin Books.

Richardson, A. E., and H. Donaldson Eberlein. 1925. *The English Inn, Past and Present: A Review of Its History and Social Life*. London: B. T. Batsford.

Seebohm, M. E. 1927. *The Evolution of the English Farm*. Reprint. 1952. London: George Allen & Unwin.

Sutherland, C. H. V. 1973. *English Coinage 600–1900*. London: B. T. Batsford.

Swift, Jonathan. 1731. *Directions to Servants*. Reprint. 1964. New York: Pantheon.

Virgin, Peter. 1989. *The Church in an Age of Negligence: Ecclesiastical Structure and Problems of Church Reform 1700–1840*. Cambridge: James Clarke & Co.

Woodforde, James. 1935. *Passages from the Five Volumes of the Diary of a Country Parson 1758–1802*. Selected and edited by John Beresford. New York: Oxford University Press.

CLOTHING AND ACCESSORIES

Armstrong, Nancy. 1974. *A Collector's History of Fans*. New York: Clarkson N. Potter.

Black, J. Anderson. 1981. *A History of Jewelry*. New York: Park Lane.

Bruton, Eric. 1967. *Clocks and Watches 1400–1900*. London: Arthur Barker.

Buc'hoz, Pierre J. 1775. *The Toilet of Flora; or, a Collection of the Most Simple and Approved Methods of Preparing Baths. ...* London: J. Murray.

Buck, Anne. 1979. *Dress in Eighteenth-Century England*. New York: Holmes & Meier.

Bury, Shirley. 1991. *Jewellery 1789–1910: The International Era. Volume 1, 1789–1861*. Woodbridge, Suffolk: Antique Collectors' Club.

By a Lady of Distinction. 1811. *The Mirror of the Graces*. Reprint. 1997. Mendocino, CA: R. L. Shep.

Byrde, Penelope. 1999. *Jane Austen Fashion: Fashion and Needlework in the Works of Jane Austen*. Ludlow: Excellent Press.

Corson, Richard. 1980. *Fashions in Eyeglasses*. London: Peter Owen.

———. *Fashions in Hair: The First Five Thousand Years*. 1965. Reprint with revised supplement. 1984. London: Peter Owen.

Crawford, Morris DeCamp. 1924. *The Heritage of Cotton, the Fibre of Two Worlds and Many Ages*. New York: G. P. Fairchild.

Crawford, T. S. 1970. *A History of the Umbrella*. Newton Abbot, Devon: David & Charles.

Cumming, Valerie. 1982. *Gloves*. New York: Drama Book Publishers.

Cunnington, C. Willett. 1937. *English Women's Clothing in the Nineteenth Century*. Reprint. 1990. New York: Dover.

Cunnington, C. Willett, and Phillis Cunnington. 1951. *The History of Underclothes*. Reprint. 1992. New York: Dover.

Cunnington, Phillis, and Catherine Lucas. 1972. *Costume for Births, Marriages and Deaths*. London: Adam and Charles Black.

Davidson, D. C., and R. J. S. MacGregor. 2002. *Spectacles, Lorgnettes and Monocles*. Princes Risborough, England: Shire.

De Marly, Diana. 1985. *Fashion for Men: An Illustrated History*. Reprint. 1989. London: B. T. Batsford.

Farrell, Jeremy. 1992. *Socks and Stockings*. London: B. T. Batsford.

———. 1985. *Umbrellas and Parasols*. London: B.T. Batsford.

Foster, Vanda. 1982. *Bags and Purses*. New York: Drama Book Publishers.

———. 1984. *A Visual History of Costume: The Nineteenth Century*. Reprint. 1986. London: B. T. Batsford.

Hart, Avril. 1998. *Ties*. New York: Costume and Fashion Press.

Hart, Avril, and Emma Taylor. 1998. *Fans*. New York: Costume and Fashion Press.

Mackrell, Alice. 1986. *Shawls, Stoles and Scarves*. London: B. T. Batsford.

Pratt, Lucy, and Linda Woolley. 1999. *Shoes*. London: V&A Publications.

Ribeiro, Aileen. 1986. *A Visual History of Costume: The Eighteenth Century*. 1983. Reprint. London: B. T. Batsford.

Ribeiro, Aileen. 1995. *The Art of Dress: Fashion in England and France 1750 to 1820*. New Haven, CT: Yale University Press.

Swann, June. 1982. *Shoes*. New York: Drama Book Publishers.

Taylor, Lou. 1983. *Mourning Dress: A Costume and Social History*. London: George Allen & Unwin.

Wilcox, Claire. 1999. *Bags*. London: V&A Publications.

Williams, Neville. 1957. *Powder and Paint: A History of the Englishwoman's Toilet*. London: Longmans, Green and Co.

EDUCATION AND INTELLECTUAL LIFE

Andrews, Malcolm. 1989. *The Search for the Picturesque: Landscape Aesthetics and Tourism in Britain, 1760–1800*. Stanford, CA: Stanford University Press.

Barker, Hannah. 2000. *Newspapers, Politics and English Society 1695–1855*. Harlow, Essex: Pearson.

———. 1998. *Newspapers, Politics, and Public Opinion in Late Eighteenth-Century England*. Oxford: Clarendon Press.

Black, Jeremy. 1987. *The English Press in the Eighteenth Century*. London: Croom Helm.

A Compendious Geographical and Historical Grammar: Exhibiting a Brief Survey of the Terraqueous Globe. 1795. London: W. Peacock.

Crone, G. R. 1968. *Maps and Their Makers*. 4th edition. London: Hutchinson University Library.

Gilpin, William. 1804. *Observations on the Coasts of Hampshire, Sussex, and Kent, Relative Chiefly to Picturesque Beauty: Made in the Summer of the Year 1774*. London: T. Cadell and W. Davies.

————. 1789. *Observations, Relative Chiefly to Picturesque Beauty, Made in the Year 1776, on Several Parts of Great Britain; Particularly the High-Lands of Scotland*. London: R. Blamire.

————. 1973. *Observations on the Western Parts of England*. Richmond, Surrey: Richmond Publishing Co.

Jordan, Elaine. 2000. 'Jane Austen Goes to the Seaside: Sanditon, English Identity and the 'West Indian' Schoolgirl'. In *The Postcolonial Jane Austen*. Edited by Youme Park and Rajeswari Sunder Rajan. London: Routledge.

Lister, Raymond. 1965. *How to Identify Old Maps and Globes*. Hamden, CT: Archon, 1965.

Mayhew, Robert J. 2000. *Enlightenment Geography: The Political Language of British Geography, 1650–1850*. New York: St. Martin's.

Price, Uvedale. 1796. *An Essay on the Picturesque, as Compared with the Sublime and the Beautiful; and, on the Use of Studying Pictures, for the Purpose of Improving Real Landscape*. London: J. Robson.

Thrower, Norman J. W. 1972. *Maps and Man*. Englewood Cliffs, NJ: Prentice-Hall.

Tooley, R. V. 1949. *Maps and Map-Makers*. Reprint. 1990. New York: Dorset Press.

ENTERTAINMENT

Altick, Richard D. 1978. *The Shows of London*. Cambridge, MA: Belknap.

Bayne-Powell, Rosamond. 1939. *The English Child in the Eighteenth Century*. New York: E. P. Dutton.

Beaufort, James. 1775. *Hoyle's Games Improved*. London: S. Bladon.

Beckford, Peter. 1951, 8th edition. (1st edition. 1899; orig. pub. 1781). *Thoughts on Hunting in a Series of Familiar Letters to a Friend*. London: Methuen & Co.

Brander, Michael. 1971. *Hunting and Shooting from Earliest Times to the Present Day*. London: Weidenfeld and Nelson.

Brinsmead, Edgar. 1879. *The History of the Pianoforte*. Reprint. 1969. Detroit: Singing Tree Press.

Byrde, Penelope. 1999. *Jane Austen Fashion: Fashion and Needlework in the Works of Jane Austen*. Ludlow: Excellent Press.

Byrne, Paula. 2002. *Jane Austen and the Theatre*. London: Hambledon and London.

Castle, Terry. 1986. *Masquerade and Civilization: The Carnivalesque in Eighteenth-Century English Culture and Fiction*. Stanford, CA: Stanford University Press.

Chalmers, Patrick R. 1936. *The History of Hunting*. Philadelphia: J. B. Lippincott.

Colley, Linda. 1994. *Britons: Forging the Nation 1707–1837*. New Haven, CT: Yale University Press.

Dawson, Lawrence H., ed. 1950. *The Complete Hoyle's Games*. Reprint 1994. Ware, Hertfordshire: Wordsworth.

Fiske, Roger. 1973. *English Theatre Music in the Eighteenth Century*. London: Oxford University Press.

Girdham, Jane. 1997. *English Opera in Late Eighteenth-Century London: Stephen Storace at Drury Lane*. Oxford: Clarendon Press.

Harding, Rosamond E. M. 1978. *The Piano-Forte*. 2nd edition. Old Woking, Surrey: Gresham Books.

Hare, Arnold, ed. 1977. *Theatre Royal Bath: A Calendar of Performances at the Orchard Street Theatre 1750–1805*. Bath: Kingsmead Press.

Hembry, Phyllis. 1990. *The English Spa 1560–1815: A Social History*. London: Athlone Press.

Hoyle, Edmond. 1859. *Hoyle's Games: Containing the Rules for Playing Fashionable Games*. Philadelphia: Henry F. Anners.

————. 1782. *Hoyle's Games Improved: Being Practical Treatises on the Following Fashionable Games …* London: W. Wood.

Keller, Kate Van Winkle, and Genevieve Shimer. 1990. *The Playford Ball: 103 Early Country Dances 1651–1820*. Chicago: A Cappella Books.

Langford, Paul. 1989. *A Polite and Commercial People: England 1727–1783*. Reprint. 1994. Oxford: Oxford University Press.

Le Beau Monde, September 1807, p. 94.

Longrigg, Roger. 1977. *The English Squire and His Sport*. London: Michael Joseph.

————. 1972. *The History of Horse Racing*. New York: Steven and Day.

Manning-Sanders, Ruth. 1952. *The English Circus*. London: Werner Laurie.

Moir, John. 1784. *Female Tuition; or, an Address to Mothers, on the Education of Daughters*. London: J. Murray.

The Netting Book. 1981. Seabrook, NH: Tower Press.

Parlett, David. 1990. *The Oxford Guide to Card Games.* Oxford: Oxford University Press.

Piggott, Patrick. 1979. *The Innocent Diversion: A Study of Music in the Life and Writings of Jane Austen.* London: Douglas Cleverdon.

Playford, John. 1651. *The English Dancing Master.* Reprint. 1984. London: Dance Books.

Porter, Roy. 1982. *English Society in the Eighteenth Century.* Reprint. 1990. New York: Penguin Books.

Price, Curtis, Judith Milhous, and Robert D. Hume. 1995. *Italian Opera in Late Eighteenth-Century London, Vol I: The King's Theatre, Haymarket 1778–1791.* Oxford: Clarendon Press.

Rensch, Roslyn. 1969. *The Harp: Its History, Technique, and Repertoire.* New York: Praeger.

———. 1989. *Harps and Harpists.* London: Duckworth.

Richardson, Philip J. S. 1960. *The Social Dances of the Nineteenth Century in England.* London: Herbert Jenkins.

Selwyn, David. 1999. *Jane Austen and Leisure.* London: Hambledon Press.

Sharp, Cecil J. 1927. *The Country Dance Book, Part II.* 3rd edition. London: Novello and Company.

Sharp, Cecil J., and George Butterworth. 1927. *The Country Dance Book, Part III.* 2nd edition. London: Novello and Company.

———. 1927. *The Country Dance Book, Part IV.* 3rd edition. London: Novello and Company.

Sharp, Cecil J., and Maud Karpeles. 1918. *The Country Dance Book, Part V.* London: Novello and Company.

Taunton, Nerylla. 1997. *Antique Needlework Tools and Embroideries.* Woodbridge, Suffolk: Antique Collectors' Club.

Thompson, Allison. 2000. 'The Felicities of Rapid Motion: Jane Austen in the Ballroom', *Persuasions Online* 21, no. 1.

Vamplew, Wray. 1976. *The Turf.* London: Allen Lane.

Walton, John K. 1983. *The English Seaside Resort: A Social History 1750–1914.* New York: St. Martin's.

Woodfield, Ian. 2001. *Opera and Drama in Eighteenth-Century London: The King's Theatre, Garrick and the Business of Performance.* Cambridge: Cambridge University Press.

Woodforde, James. 1935. *Passages from the Five Volumes of the Diary of a Country Parson 1758–1802,* selected and edited by John Beresford. New York: Oxford University Press.

FOOD AND DRINK

Accum, Frederick. 1820. *A Treatise on Adulterations of Food.* Reprint. 1966. N.p.: Mallinckrodt Collection of Food Classics.

Ashley, William. 1928. *The Bread of Our Forefathers: An Inquiry in Economic History.* Oxford: Clarendon Press.

Black, Maggie, and Deirdre Le Faye. 1995. *The Jane Austen Cookbook.* Chicago: Chicago Review Press.

Bradley, Richard. 1736. *The Country Housewife and Lady's Director in the Management of a House, and the Delights and Profits of a Farm.* Reprint. 1980. London: Prospect Books.

Briggs, Richard. 1798. *The English Art of Cookery.* Dublin: P. Byrne.

Burnett, John. 1979. *Plenty and Want: A Social History of Diet in England from 1815 to the Present Day.* Revised edition. London: Scolar Press.

Carter, Susannah. 1795. *The Frugal Housewife, or Complete Woman Cook.* London: E. Newbery.

Charsley, Simon R. 1992. *Wedding Cakes and Cultural History.* London: Routledge.

Cheke, Val. 1959. *The Story of Cheese-Making in Britain.* London: Routledge & Kegan Paul.

Clark, Peter. 1983. *The English Alehouse: A Social History 1200–1830.* London: Longman.

Collingwood, Francis. 1801. *The Universal Cook, and City and Country Housekeeper.* 3rd edition. London: C. Whittingham.

Ellis, William. 1750. *The Country Housewife's Family Companion.* Reprint. 2000. Totnes, Devon: Prospect Books.

Farley, John. 1783. *The London Art of Cookery.* Reprint. 1988. Lewes, East Sussex: Southover Press.

Glasse, Hannah. 1796. Revised edition. *The Art of Cookery Made Plain and Easy.* Reprint. 1994. Schenectady, NY: U.S. Historical Research Service.

Grossman, Anne Chotzinoff, and Lisa Grossman Thomas. 1997. *Lobscouse and*

Spotted Dog. New York: W. W. Norton & Company.

Hackwood, Frederick W. 1909. *Inns, Ales, and Drinking Customs of Old England.* Reprint. 1985. London: Bracken Books.

Harrison, Sarah. 1748. *The House-keeper's Pocket-book; And Compleat Family Cook.* London: R. Ware.

Hartley, Dorothy. 1954. *Food in England.* Reprint. 1999. London: Little, Brown and Company.

Hazlitt, William Carew. 1793. *The French Family Cook: Being a Complete System of French Cookery.* London: J. Bell.

Hunter, Alexander (using pseudonym Ignotus). 1805. *Culina Famulatrix Medicinae.* York: T. Wilson.

Lane, Maggie. 1995. *Jane Austen and Food.* London: Hambledon Press.

Latham, Jean. 1975. *A Taste of the Past.* London: Adam and Charles Black.

Mennell, Stephen. 1985. *All Manners of Food: Eating and Taste in England and France from the Middle Ages to the Present.* Reprint. 1996. Urbana: University of Illinois Press.

Millington, Charles. 1805. *The Housekeeper's Domestic Library; or, New Universal Family Instructor.* London: M. Jones.

Monckton, H. A. 1969. *A History of the English Public House.* London: Bodley Head.

Pendergrast, Mark. 1999. *Uncommon Grounds: The History of Coffee and How It Transformed the World.* New York: Basic Books.

Pettigrew, Jane. 2001. *A Social History of Tea.* London: National Trust.

Raffald, Elizabeth. 1769. *The Experienced English Housekeeper.* Reprint. 1997. Lewes, East Sussex: Southover Press.

Roberts, Jonathan. 2001. *The Origins of Fruit and Vegetables.* New York: Universe Publishing.

Rundell, Maria. 1816. *A New System of Domestic Cookery.* Reprint. 1977. New York: Vantage Press.

Simpson, Helen. 1986. *The London Ritz Book of Afternoon Tea: The Art and Pleasures of Taking Tea.* New York: Arbor House.

Wilson, C. Anne. 1973. *Food and Drink in Britain from the Stone Age to the 19th Century.* Reprint. 1991. London: Constable.

Woodforde, James. 1935. *Passages from the Five Volumes of the Diary of a Country Parson 1758–1802.* Selected and edited by John Beresford. New York: Oxford University Press.

THE HOUSEHOLD

Adams, Samuel, and Sarah Adams. 1825. *The Complete Servant.* Reprint. 1989. Lewes, East Sussex, England: Southover Press.

Banfield, Edwin. 1977. *Antique Barometers: An Illustrated Survey.* Long Ashton, Bristol: Wayland Publications.

———. 1993. *The Italian Influence on English Barometers from 1780.* Trowbridge, Wiltshire: Baros Books.

Bell, Geoffrey Howard, and E. F. Bell. 1952. *Old English Barometers.* Winchester: Warren & Son.

Bruton, Eric. 1967. *Clocks and Watches 1400–1900.* London: Arthur Barker.

Buehr, Walter. 1953. *The Story of Locks.* New York: Charles Scribner's Sons.

Byrde, Penelope. 1999. *Jane Austen Fashion: Fashion and Needlework in the Works of Jane Austen.* Ludlow: Excellent Press.

Clark, Garth, and Tony Cunha. 1996. *The Book of Cups.* New York: Abbeville Press.

Clark, Peter. 1983. *The English Alehouse: A Social History 1200–1830.* London: Longman.

Copeland, Robert. 1999. *Spode's Willow Pattern and Other Designs after the Chinese.* 3rd edition. Bath: Studio Vista.

Crone, G. R. 1968. *Maps and Their Makers.* 4th edition. London: Hutchinson University Library.

Crowley, John E. 2001. *The Invention of Comfort: Sensibilities and Design in Early Modern Britain and Early America.* Baltimore, MD: Johns Hopkins University Press.

Dawson, Aileen. 1984. *Masterpieces of Wedgwood in the British Museum.* London: British Museum Publications.

Eras, Vincent J. M. 1957. *Locks and Keys Throughout the Ages.* Amsterdam: H. H. Fronczek.

Girouard, Mark. 1978. *Life in the English Country House: A Social and Architectural History.* New Haven, CT: Yale University Press.

Goldberg, Benjamin. 1985. *The Mirror and Man.* Charlottesville: University Press of Virginia.

Goodison, Nicholas. 1969. *English Barometers 1680–1860.* London: Cassell.

Greysmith, Brenda. 1976. *Wallpaper*. London: Studio Vista.

Hadfield, Miles. 1969. (Originally published as Gardening in Britain, 1960, Hutchinson & Co.) *A History of British Gardening*. London: Spring Books.

Haywood, Eliza. 1771. *A New Present for a Servant-Maid*. London: G. Pearch.

Hecht, J. Jean. 1956. *The Domestic Servant in Eighteenth-Century England*. 1956. Reprint. 1980. London: Routledge & Kegan Paul.

Hembry, Phyllis. 1990. *The English Spa 1560–1815: A Social History*. London: Athlone Press.

Hill, Bridget. 1996. *Servants: English Domestics in the Eighteenth Century*. Oxford: Clarendon Press.

Hoskins, Lesley, ed. 1994. *The Papered Wall: History, Pattern, Technique*. New York: Harry N. Abrams.

Hunt, John Dixon. 1992. *Gardens and the Picturesque: Studies in the History of Landscape Architecture*. Cambridge, MA: MIT Press.

Hunt, John Dixon, and Peter Willis, eds. 1975. *The Genius of the Place: The English Landscape Garden 1620–1820*. New York: Harper and Row.

Kowaleski-Wallace, Elizabeth. 1997. *Consuming Subjects: Women, Shopping, and Business in the Eighteenth Century*. New York: Columbia University Press.

Latham, Jean. 1975. *A Taste of the Past*. London: Adam and Charles Black.

Lister, Raymond. 1965 *How to Identify Old Maps and Globes*. Hamden, CT: Archon.

Meikleham, Robert (using pseudonym Walter Bernan). 1845. *On the History and Art of Warming and Ventilating Rooms and Buildings*. London: George Bell.

Meister, Peter Wilhelm, and Horst Reber. 1983. *European Porcelain of the 18th Century,* translated by Ewald Osers. Ithaca, NY: Cornell University Press.

Musgrave, Clifford. 1961. *Regency Furniture 1800 to 1830*. Reprint. 1970. London: Faber and Faber.

Pettigrew, Jane. 2001. *A Social History of Tea*. London: National Trust.

Price, Percival. 1983. *Bells and Man*. Oxford: Oxford University Press.

Quest-Ritson, Charles. 2001. *The English Garden: A Social History*. London: Viking.

Roberts, Hugh D. 1981. *Downhearth to Bar Grate*. Bath: Dawson & Goodall.

Swift, Jonathan. 1745. *Directions to Servants*. Reprint. 1964. New York: Pantheon.

Taunton, Nerylla. 1997. *Antique Needlework Tools and Embroideries*. Woodbridge, Suffolk: Antique Collectors' Club.

Thoday, A. G. 1978. *Barometers*. London: Her Majesty's Stationery Office.

Thrower, Norman J. W. 1972. *Maps and Man*. Englewood Cliffs, NJ: Prentice-Hall.

Tooley, R.V. 1949. *Maps and Map-Makers*. Reprint. 1990. New York: Dorset Press.

Watkin, David. 1982. *The English Vision: The Picturesque in Architecture, Landscape and Garden Design*. London: John Murray.

Wilkinson, Vega. 2002. *Spode-Copeland-Spode: The Works and Its People 1770–1970*. Woodbridge, Suffolk: Antique Collectors' Club.

Woodforde, James. 1935. *Passages from the Five Volumes of the Diary of a Country Parson 1758–1802,* selected and edited by John Beresford. New York: Oxford University Press.

Wright, Lawrence. 1964. *Home Fires Burning: The History of Domestic Heating and Cooking*. London: Routledge & Kegan Paul.

Young, Hilary, ed. 1995. *The Genius of Wedgwood*. London: Victoria and Albert Museum.

Younghusband, Ethel. 1949. *Mansions, Men and Tunbridge Ware*. Slough: Windsor Press.

JANE AUSTEN

Austen-Leigh, William, and Richard Arthur Austen-Leigh. 1965. *Jane Austen: Her Life and Letters*. New York: Russell & Russell.

Cecil, David. 1978. *A Portrait of Jane Austen*. London: Constable.

Halperin, John. 1984. *The Life of Jane Austen*. Baltimore, MD: Johns Hopkins University Press.

Hodge, Jane Aiken. 1972. *The Double Life of Jane Austen*. London: Hodder and Stoughton.

Le Faye, Deirdre, ed. 1997. *Jane Austen's Letters*. 3rd edition. Oxford: Oxford University Press.

MILITARY LIFE

Baynham, Henry. 1969. *From the Lower Deck: The Old Navy 1780–1840*. London: Hutchinson and Co.

Blake, Nicholas, and Richard Lawrence. 2000. *The Illustrated Companion to Nelson's Navy*. Mechanicsburg, PA: Stackpole Books.

Chandler, David, ed. 1994. *The Oxford Illustrated History of the British Army*. Oxford: Oxford University Press.

Cochrane, Thomas, Earl of Dundonald. 1861. *The Autobiography of a Seaman*. 2nd edition. London: Richard Bentley.

Duffy, Michael. 1987. *Soldiers, Sugar, and Seapower: The British Expeditions to the West Indies and the War against Revolutionary France*. Oxford: Clarendon Press.

Haythornthwaite, Philip, and Charles Hamilton Smith. 2002. *Wellington's Army: The Uniforms of the British Soldier, 1812–1815*. London: Greenhill Books.

Haythornthwaite, Philip, and William Younghusband. 1993. *Nelson's Navy*. London: Osprey.

Holmes, Richard. 2001. *Redcoat: The British Soldier in the Age of Horse and Musket*. New York: W.W. Norton & Company.

Houlding, J. A. 2000. *Fit for Service: The Training of the British Army, 1715–1795*. 1981. Reprint. Oxford: Clarendon Press.

Hubback, J. H., and Edith C. Hubback. 1906. *Jane Austen's Sailor Brothers*. Reprint. 1986. Westport, CT: Meckler Publishing.

Kemp, Peter, ed. 1976. *The Oxford Companion to Ships and the Sea*. Reprint. 1994. Oxford: Oxford University Press.

Lavery, Brian. 1989. *Nelson's Navy: The Ships, Men and Organisation 1793–1815*. London: Conway Maritime Press.

McGuane, James P. 2002. *Heart of Oak: A Sailor's Life in Nelson's Navy*. New York: W.W. Norton & Company.

Roberts, Warren. 1979. *Jane Austen and the French Revolution*. New York: St. Martin's Press.

Rogers, H. C. B. 1977. *The British Army of the Eighteenth Century*. London: George Allen & Unwin.

Southam, Brian. 2003. *Jane Austen and the Navy*. London: Hambledon and London.

Tuchman, Barbara. 1988. *The First Salute: A View of the American Revolution*. New York: Alfred A. Knopf.

PEOPLE

Bayne-Powell, Rosamond. 1939. *The English Child in the Eighteenth Century*. New York: E.P. Dutton.

Bernier, François. 1968. *Travels in the Mogul Empire A.D. 1656–1668*, translated by Irving Brock and Archibald Constable. Delhi: S. Chand & Co.

Charsley, Simon R. 1992. *Wedding Cakes and Cultural History*. London: Routledge.

Endelman, Todd M. 2002. *The Jews of Britain, 1656 to 2000*. Berkeley: University of California Press.

———. 1979. *The Jews of Georgian England 1714–1830: Tradition and Change in a Liberal Society*. Philadelphia: Jewish Publication Society of America.

Eraly, Abraham. 2003. *The Mughal Throne: The Saga of India's Great Emperors*. London: Weidenfeld & Nicolson.

Gisborne, Thomas. 1806. *An Enquiry into the Duties of the Female Sex*. 7th edition. London: Cadell.

Gregory, John. 1773. *A Father's Legacy to His Daughters*. Reprint. 1804. Boston: Joseph Bumstead.

Johnson, Samuel. 1992. *The Letters of Samuel Johnson*. Edited by Bruce Redford. Princeton, NJ: Princeton University Press.

Kittredge, George Lyman. 1929. *Witchcraft in Old and New England*. Reprint. 1956. New York: Russell & Russell.

Notestein, Wallace. 1911. *A History of Witchcraft in England from 1558 to 1718*. Reprint. 1965. New York: Russell & Russell.

Olsen, Kirstin. 1994. *Chronology of Women's History*. Westport, CT: Greenwood Press.

Opie, Iona, and Peter Opie. 1951. *The Oxford Dictionary of Nursery Rhymes*. Reprint. 1995. Oxford: Oxford University Press.

Sales, Roger. 1994. *Jane Austen and Representations of Regency England*. London: Routledge.

Sidky, H. 1997. *Witchcraft. Lycanthropy, Drugs, and Disease: An Anthropological Study of the European Witch-Hunts*. New York: Peter Lang.

Srivastava, Ashirbadi Lal. 1959. *The Mughal Empire (1526–1803 A.D.)*. 3rd revised edition. Agra: Shiva Lal Agarwala & Co.

Stone, Lawrence. 1990. *Road to Divorce: England, 1530–1987*. Reprint. 1995. Oxford: Oxford University Press.

Taylor, Lou. 1983. *Mourning Dress: A Costume and Social History*. London: George Allen & Unwin.

Vesey-Fitzgerald, Brian. 1944. *Gypsies of Britain: An Introduction to Their History*. Reprint. 1973. Newton Abbot, Devon: David & Charles.

Woodcock, Thomas, and John Martin Robinson. 1988. *The Oxford Guide to Heraldry*. Oxford: Oxford University Press.

READING AND WRITING

Barker, Hannah. 2000. *Newspapers, Politics and English Society 1695–1855*. Harlow, Essex: Pearson.

———. 1998. *Newspapers, Politics, and Public Opinion in Late Eighteenth-Century England*. Oxford: Clarendon Press.

Black, Jeremy. 1987. *The English Press in the Eighteenth Century*. London: Croom Helm.

Browne, Christopher. 1993. *Getting the Message: The Story of the British Post Office*. Stroud, Gloucestershire: Alan Sutton.

Crocker, Alan. 1988. *Paper Mills of the Tillingbourne: A History of Papermaking in a Surrey Valley 1704 to 1875*. Oxshott, Surrey: Tabard Private Press, 1988.

Ellis, Kenneth. 1958. *The Post Office in the Eighteenth Century: A Study in Administrative History*. London: Oxford University Press.

Hemmeon, J. C. 1912. *The History of the British Post Office*. Cambridge: Harvard University Press.

James, Alan. 1970. *The Post*. London: B. T. Batsford.

Joyce, Herbert. 1893. *The History of the Post Office from Its Establishment down to 1836*. London: Richard Bentley & Son.

Kelly, Thomas. 1966. *Early Public Libraries*. London: Library Association.

Lewis, Matthew. 1796. *The Monk*. Reprint. 1998. Oxford: Oxford University Press.

Nickell, Joe. 1990. *Pen, Ink, & Evidence*. Lexington: University Press of Kentucky.

Radcliffe, Ann. 1794. *The Mysteries of Udolpho*. Reprint. 1983. Oxford: Oxford University Press.

Shorter, A. H. 1971. *Paper Making in the British Isles*. Newton Abbot, Devon: David & Charles.

Tomkins, Thomas. 1808. *The Beauties of Writing Exemplified*. London: Published for the Author, Foster Lane.

Whalley, Joyce Irene. *English Handwriting 1540–1853*. London: Her Majesty's Stationery Office, 1969.

———. 1975. *Writing Implements and Accessories*. Newton Abbot, Devon: David & Charles.

RELIGION

Albers, Jan. 1993. '"Papist Traitors" and "Presbyterian Rogues": Religious Identities in Eighteenth-Century Lancashire'. In *The Church of England, c. 1689–c. 1833*. Edited by John Walson, Colin Haydon, and Stephen Taylor. Cambridge: Cambridge University Press.

Barrie-Curien, Viviane. 1993. 'The Clergy in the Diocese of London in the Eighteenth Century'. In *The Church of England, c. 1689–c. 1833*. Edited by John Walsh, Colin Haydon, and Stephen Taylor. Cambridge: Cambridge University Press.

Burns, R. Arthur. 1993. 'Diocesan Reform in the Church of England'. In *The Church of England, c. 1689–c. 1833*. Edited by John Walsh, Colin Haydon, and Stephen Taylor. Cambridge: Cambridge University Press.

Carpenter, S. C. 1937. *Church and People, 1789–1889: A History of the Church of England from William Wilberforce to 'Lux Mundi'*. London: Society for Promoting Christian Knowledge. 1933. Reprint. London: SPCK.

Collins, Irene. 1993. *Jane Austen and the Clergy*. London: Hambledon Press.

Ditchfield, G.M. 1993. 'Ecclesiastical Policy under Lord North'. *The Church of England, c. 1689–c. 1833*. Edited by John Walsh, Colin Haydon, and Stephen Taylor. Cambridge: Cambridge University Press.

Elbourne, Elizabeth. 1993. 'The Foundation of the Church Missionary Society: the Anglican Missionary Impulse'. *The Church of England, c. 1689–c. 1833*. Edited by John Walsh, Colin Haydon, and Stephen Taylor. Cambridge: Cambridge University Press.

Fitzpatrick, Martin. 1993. 'Latitudinarianism at the Parting of the Ways: A Suggestion'. *The Church of England c.1689–c.1833*. Edited by John Walsh, Colin Haydon, and Stephen Taylor. Cambridge: Cambridge University Press.

Gibson, William. 2001. *The Church of England 1688–1832: Unity and Accord*. London: Routledge.

Gregory, Jeremy. 1993. 'The Eighteenth-Century Reformation: The Pastoral Task of Anglican Clergy after 1689'. *The Church of England, c.1689–c.1833*. Edited by John Walsh, Colin Haydon, and Stephen Taylor. Cambridge: Cambridge University Press.

Gregory, John. 1773. *A Father's Legacy to His Daughters*. Reprint. 1804. Boston: Joseph Bumstead.

Nockles, Peter. 1993. 'Church Parties in the Pre-Tractarian Church of England 1750–1833: The "Orthodox" – Some Problems of Definition and Identity.' *The Church of England, c.1689–c.1833*. Edited by John Walsh, Colin Haydon, and Stephen Taylor. Cambridge: Cambridge University Press.

Price, Percival. 1983. *Bells and Man*. Oxford: Oxford University Press.

Reed, Michael. 1986. *The Age of Exuberance: 1550–1700*. London: Routledge & Kegan Paul.

Smith, Mark. 1993. 'The Reception of Richard Podmore: Anglicanism in Saddleworth 1700–1830'. *The Church of England, c.1689–c.1833*. Edited by John Walsh, Colin Haydon, and Stephen Taylor. Cambridge: Cambridge University Press.

Virgin, Peter. 1989. *The Church in an Age of Negligence: Ecclesiastical Structure and Problems of Church Reform 1700–1840*. Cambridge: James Clarke & Co.

Vonier, Anscar. 1928. *The Angels*. New York: Macmillan.

Walsh, John, and Stephen Taylor. 1993. 'The Church and Anglicanism in the "Long" 18th Century'. *The Church of England, c.1689–c.1833*. Edited by John Walsh, Colin Haydon, and Stephen Taylor. Cambridge: Cambridge University Press.

Woodforde, James. 1935. *Passages from the Five Volumes of the Diary of a Country Parson 1758–1802*. Selected and edited by John Beresford. New York: Oxford University Press.

RIDING AND HUNTING

Beckford, Peter. 1951. *Thoughts on Hunting in a Series of Familiar Letters to a Friend*. 8th edition. (1st edition 1899; orig. pub. 1781). London: Methuen & Co.

Brander, Michael. 1971. *Hunting and Shooting from Earliest Times to the Present Day*. London: Weidenfeld and Nelson.

Chalmers, Patrick. 1936. *The History of Hunting*. Philadelphia: J. B. Lippincott.

Landry, Donna. 2000. 'Learning to Ride at Mansfield Park'. *The Postcolonial Jane Austen*. Edited by Youme Park and Rajeswari Sunder Rajan. London: Routledge.

Longrigg, Roger. 1977. *The English Squire and His Sport*. London: Michael Joseph.

———. 1972. *The History of Horse Racing*. New York: Stein and Day.

Plumb, J. H. 1950. *England in the Eighteenth Century*. Reprint. 1990. London: Penguin Books.

Porter, Roy. 1982. *English Society in the Eighteenth Century*. Reprint. 1990. New York: Penguin Books.

Vamplew, Wray. 1976. *The Turf*. London: Allen Lane.

Woodforde, James. 1935. *Passages from the Five Volumes of the Diary of a Country Parson 1758–1802*. Selected and edited by John Beresford. New York: Oxford University Press.

SCIENCE, MEDICINE AND TECHNOLOGY

Accum, Frederick. 1820. *A Treatise on Adulterations of Food*. Reprint. 1966. N.p.: Mallinckrodt Collection of Food Classics.

Bader, Ted. Summer, 2000. 'Mr. Woodhouse Is Not a Hypochondriac'. *Persuasions Online* 21, no. 2. http://www.jasna.org/persuasions/on-line/vol21no2/bader.html

Banfield, Edwin. 1977. *Antique Barometers: An Illustrated Survey*. Long Ashton, Bristol: Wayland Publications.

———. 1993. *The Italian Influence on English Barometers from 1780*. Trowbridge, Wiltshire: Baros Books.

Bell, Geoffrey Howard, and E. F. Bell. 1952. *Old English Barometers*. Winchester: Warren & Son.

Brock, William H. 1993. *The Norton History of Chemistry*. New York: W. W. Norton.

Corson, Richard. 1980. *Fashions in Eyeglasses*. London: Peter Owen.

Davidson, D. C., and R.J.S. MacGregor. 2002. *Spectacles, Lorgnettes and Monocles*. Princes Risborough, England: Shire.

Duffy, Michael. 1987. *Soldiers, Sugar, and Seapower: The British Expeditions to the West Indies and the War Against Revolutionary France*. Oxford: Clarendon Press.

Goodison, Nicholas. *English Barometers 1680–1860*. London: Cassell, 1969.

Guerini, Vincenzo. 1967. *A History of Dentistry from the Most Ancient Times until the End of the Eighteenth Century*. 1909. Reprint. Amsterdam: Liberac.

Langford, Paul. 1992. *A Polite and Commercial People: England 1727–1783*. 1989. Reprint. Oxford: Oxford University Press.

Lindsay, Lilian. 1933. *A Short History of Dentistry*. London: John Bale, Sons and Danielsson.

North, John. 1994. *The Norton History of Astronomy and Cosmology*. New York: W. W. Norton & Company.

Porter, Roy. 1990. *English Society in the Eighteenth Century*. 1982. Reprint. New York: Penguin Books.

Prinz, Hermann. 1945. *Dental Chronology*. Philadelphia: Lea & Febiger.

Ring, Malvin E. 1986. *Dentistry: An Illustrated History*. New York: Harry N. Abrams.

Thoday, A. G. 1978. *Barometers*. London: Her Majesty's Stationery Office.

Walton, John K. 1983. *The English Seaside Resort: A Social History 1750–1914*. New York: St. Martin's Press.

Williams, Guy. 1996. *The Age of Agony: The Art of Healing, 1700–1800*. 1975. Reprint. Chicago: Academy Chicago Publishers.

Wiltshire, John. 1992. *Jane Austen and the Body*. Cambridge: Cambridge University Press.

Wynbrandt, James. 1998. *The Excruciating History of Dentistry*. New York: St. Martin's Press.

TIME AND PLACES

Augier, F. R., and Shirley C. Gordon. 1970. *Sources of West Indian History*. 1962. Reprint. Trinidad: Longman Caribbean.

Barker, Felix, and Peter Jackson. 1992. *The History of London in Maps*. New York: Cross River Press.

Duffy, Michael. 1987. *Soldiers, Sugar, and Seapower: The British Expeditions to the West Indies and the War against Revolutionary France*. Oxford: Clarendon Press.

Edwards, Anne-Marie. 1985. *In the Steps of Jane Austen*. 2nd edition. Ashurst, Southamp and Rajeswari Sunder ton: Arcady Books.

Egan, Patrick. 1818. *Walks through Bath*. Bath: Meyler and Son.

Fawcett, Trevor, comp. 1995. *Voices of Eighteenth-Century Bath*. Bath: Ruton.

Gerzina, Gretchen. 1995. *Black London: Life before Emancipation*. New Brunswick, NJ: Rutgers University Press.

Gomme, George Laurence, ed. 1883. *The Gentleman's Magazine Library – Vol. 1: Manners and Customs*. Reprint. 1968. Detroit: Singing Tree Press.

Halperin, John. 1984. *The Life of Jane Austen*. Baltimore, MD: Johns Hopkins University Press.

Hembry, Phyllis. 1990. *The English Spa 1560–1815: A Social History*. London: Athlone Press.

Hodge, Jane Aiken. 1972. *The Double Life of Jane Austen*. London: Hodder and Stoughton.

Hyde, Ralph. 1981. *The A to Z of Georgian London*. Lympne Castle, Kent: Harry Margary.

Jordan, Elaine. 2000. 'Jane Austen Goes to the Seaside: Sanditon, English Identity and the 'West Indian' Schoolgirl'. *The Postcolonial Jane Austen*. Edited by Youme Park and Rajeswari Sunder Rajan. London: Routledge.

Lane, Maggie. 1986. *Jane Austen's England*. New York: St. Martin's Press.

Lasdun, Susan. 1992. *The English Park: Royal, Private and Public*. New York: Vendome.

Porter, Roy. 1990. *English Society in the Eighteenth Century*. 1982. Reprint. New York: Penguin Books.

———. 1995. *London: A Social History*. Cambridge, MA: Harvard University Press.

Rogozinski, Jan. 1992. *A Brief History of the Caribbean: From the Arawak and the Carib to the Present*. New York: Facts on File.

Sales, Roger. 1994. *Jane Austen and Representations of Regency England*. London: Routledge.

Selwyn, David. 1999. *Jane Austen and Leisure*. London: Hambledon Press, 1999.

Walton, John K. 1983. *The English Seaside Resort: A Social History 1750–1914.* New York: St. Martin's Press.

Watson, Jack. 1982. *The West Indian Heritage: A History of the West Indies.* 2nd edition. London: John Murray.

TRANSPORTATION AND TRAVEL

Adams, Samuel, and Sarah Adams. 1825. *The Complete Servant.* Reprint. 1989. Lewes, East Sussex, England: Southover Press.

Aldcroft, Derek H., and Michael J. Freeman. 1983. *Transport in the Industrial Revolution.* Manchester: Manchester University Press.

Andrews, Malcolm. 1989. *The Search for the Picturesque: Landscape Aesthetics and Tourism in Britain, 1760–1800.* Stanford, CA: Stanford University Press.

Bayne-Powell, Rosamond. 1951. *Travellers in Eighteenth-Century England.* London: John Murray.

Borer, Mary Cathcart. 1972. *The British Hotel through the Ages.* Guildford: Lutterworth Press.

Brown, R. A. 1973. *One Hundred Horse Drawn Carriages.* Welwyn Garden City, Hertfordshire: Quartilles International Limited.

A Compendious Geographical and Historical Grammar: Exhibiting a Brief Survey of the Terraqueous Globe. 1795. London: W. Peacock.

De Quincey, Thomas. 1907. *Joan of Arc and the English Mail-Coach.* Boston: D.C. Heath & Co.

Felton, William. 1796. *Treatise on Carriages.* London.

Gilpin, William. 1804. *Observations on the Coasts of Hampshire, Sussex, and Kent, Relative Chiefly to Picturesque Beauty: Made in the Summer of the Year 1774.* London: T. Cadell and W. Davies.

———. 1973. *Observations on the Western Parts of England.* Richmond, Surrey: Richmond Publishing Co.

———. 1789. *Observations, Relative Chiefly to Picturesque Beauty, Made in the Year 1776, on Several Parts of Great Britain; Particularly the High-Lands of Scotland.* London: R. Blamire.

Hecht, J. Jean. 1956. *The Domestic Servant in Eighteenth-Century England.* Reprint. 1980. London: Routledge & Kegan Paul.

Ingram, Arthur. 1977. *Horse-Drawn Vehicles since 1760.* Poole: Blandford Press, 1977.

Reid, James. 1933. *The Evolution of Horse-Drawn Vehicles.* N.p.: Institute of British Carriage and Automobile Manufacturers.

Richardson, A. E., and H. Donaldson Eberlein. 1925. *The English Inn, Past and Present: A Review of Its History and Social Life.* London: B. T. Batsford.

Rowlandson, Thomas. 1963. *Rowlandson's Drawings for a Tour in a Post Chaise.* San Marino, CA: The Huntington Library.

Straus, Ralph. 1912. *Carriages & Coaches: Their History & Their Evolution.* London: Martin Secker.

Sumner, Philip. 1970. *Carriages to the End of the Nineteenth Century.* London: Her Majesty's Stationery Office.

Swift, Jonathan. 1964. *Directions to Servants.* 1745. Reprint. New York: Pantheon.

Thompson, John. 1980. *Horse-Drawn Carriages: A Source Book.* Fleet, Hampshire: John Thompson.

Thrupp, G. A. 1877. *The History of Coaches.* Reprint. 1969. Amsterdam: Meridian.

Vale, Edmund. 1967. *The Mail-Coach Men of the Late Eighteenth Century.* 1960. Reprint. Newton Abbot, Devon: David & Charles.

Walrond, Sallie. 1980. *Looking at Carriages.* Reprint. 1992. London: J. A. Allen, 1992.

Walton, John K. 1983. *The English Seaside Resort: A Social History 1750–1914.* New York: St. Martin's Press.

Woodforde, James. 1935. *Passages from the Five Volumes of the Diary of a Country Parson 1758–1802.* Selected and edited by John Beresford. New York: Oxford University Press.

WEBSITES

These were helpful in my research and contain reliable-enough information to be of use to other researchers. Listing them here does not mean that I endorse any specific product or for-profit service supplied by the hosting company or organization, nor have I received financial consideration for their inclusion.

www.botanical.com and
www.habitas.org.uk

Useful information about English flora and ingredients in food and medicines of the period.

http://lwlimages.library.yale.edu/walpoleweb/
Search page for images at the Lewis Walpole Library. To search by year, enter the last three digits of the year under 'Call Number Query'. Items without day or month information will be indicated by a zero and an item number, for example, 799.0.14. If month and day of publication are known, these will be indicated in American rather than European order; for example, 799.3.12 would indicate a print issued on 12 March 1799.

Keyword searches return results only if the keyword is in the title of the print. This can cause difficulties, since the titles are not necessarily obvious. For example, enter 'Symptoms' in this box to see how a particular format was applied to a variety of topics.

Images can be enlarged on this website and examined closely. They can also be seen in colour and printed out. Highly recommended. Many of the illustrations in this book can be seen there in colour and in greater detail.

Excellent charts of the differences between naval uniforms by rank and period; depictions of admirals' flags.

www.gamesacrosstheboard.com Game rules.

http://freepages.genealogy.rootsweb.com/~genmaps/index.html
Photographs and scans of old maps of the British Isles by country, by county and sometimes by city. The quality of the images varies according to the methods used to create them, and each search generates pop-up advertisements, but the maps can be very helpful in getting a feel for distances, roads and physical features.

www.geog.port.ac.uk/webmap/hantsmap/hantsmap/milne1/milne1.htm
Excellent high-resolution clickable map of Hampshire in 1791, clearly showing the towns Austen visited and resided in.

www.davidparlett.co.uk/histocs/
Rules for several historical card games.

www.pemberley.com
Good information about details from Austen's novels with extensive and reliable footnotes.

www.printsgeorge.com
A delightfully tongue-in-cheek website, full of reproductions of maps and prints that can be ordered for reasonable prices. A CD-ROM with maps of and facsimiles of contemporary books about Jane Austen's Bath.

http://users.bathspa.ac.uk/greenwood/imagemap.html
Excellent high-resolution clickable map of London in 1827.

www.motco.com/Map/
Excellent high-resolution clickable maps of London and the London area, including maps from 1799, 1802 and 1830.

www.jasna.org
Home page of the Jane Austen Society of North America, with a good deal of information, links to the organization's online journal and links to other information on the web about Jane Austen.

Sites showing franked letters.

Index

Page numbers in **bold** indicate the location of the main entry.

Colds, 245
Colleges, 124
Coloured stone jewels, 218
Colours: in rooms, 27; of walls, 26
Columns, 19
Combs, 220
Commander, of ship, 262–63
Commerce game, 56–57
Communion, 83
Commutation, 75–76
Complexion, **96–97**
Concerts, 128, 254
Condoms, 233
Conduct manuals, 130
Confectioners, 35
Conservatories, 20–21, 24
Constantia, 44
Containers, 118
Continental wines, 44
Contredanse, 107
Conundrum, 173
Conversation, 132, 134
Cookbooks, of Austen's day, 150,
    153, 157
Cooke, Samuel, 81
Cooking methods, 141–42, 151
Cooper, Edward, 81
Copper coins, 248–49
Copper-plate engraving, 116
Corinthian columns, 33
Corkscrews, 118
Cornish stone, 115
Cornwall kaolin, 113
Coronets, 64
Cosmetics, **97–99**; recipe books, 98
Costume, 96–97
Cotillion balls, 106
Cottages: of Barton, 21, 25; Chawton, 25;
    ideal model, 20; Lady Elliott, 21; of
    Musgroves at Uppercross, 21; non-
    fictional, 21
Cotton fabric, 94–95
Country dance, 105–6
Country dances, 253
*The Country Housewife's Family
    Companion*, 152
Court dress, 92
Court plaster, 245
Covent Garden, 231
Cow heel recipe, 152
Cowper, William, 79
Cows, 43
Crab, 154
Crabbe, George, 322
Cravat, 86–87
Crawford, Henry, 27, 322
Crawford, Mary, 164–65
Crayfish, 154

Cream cheeses, 155
Creamers, 113
Creamware, 114
Creditors, 111–12
Crenellated parapets, 19
Cribbage, 49
Cricket, 170
Crumpets, 159
Cucumber, 156
Culinary sitting-room, 22
Cupboards, 169
Curates, 76–77, 80
Curfew, 136
Curling, of hair, 197
Currant Jelly Sauce, 157
Currant wine, 44
Curricle, 186–88
Curriculum, 125–26
Curriers, 66
Curries, 161–62
Curry powder, 163
Curtain fabric, 95
Curtains, 27
Cut, 132–33
Cut-steel jewellery, 219, 221
Cyprus wine, 44

Daffy's Elixir, 246
Daily Advertiser, 279
Daily Gazetteer, 279
Dairying, 208
Dairy products, 154–55
Damer, Anne Seymour, 368
Dame schools, 120
Damson Cheese, 157
Dance, **99–107**
Death, **108–11**
Debt, **111–12**; and jewellery, 220
Debtors, 111–12
Decanter, 119
Decent fortune, 233
Decks of cards, 48
Dedication, 326–27
Deference, 184
De Feuillide Austen, Eliza, 164
Demilandau, 222
Denham, Sir Edward, 321
Dentistry, 243, 360
De Quincey, Thomas, 63
The Derby, 207
Desertions, 275
Dessert, 157
Devole, 52
Dials, of clocks, 84
Diamonds, 218
Dibdin, Charles, 29
Dimity, 95
Dining rooms, 20, 23

About the Author

KIRSTIN OLSEN is an independent scholar and the author of several reference books, including *All Things Shakespeare: An Encyclopedia of Shakespeare's World* (2002) and the two-volume *All Things Austen: An Encyclopedia of Austen's World* (2005).